Mermaid Scales
and the
Town of Sand

Story & Art by
Yoko Komori

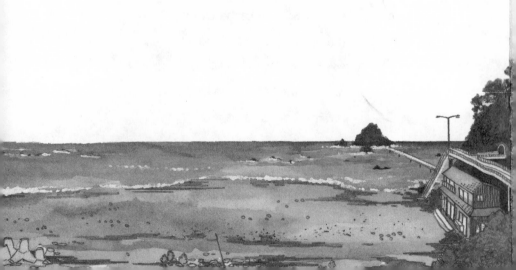

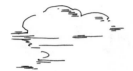

TIDES

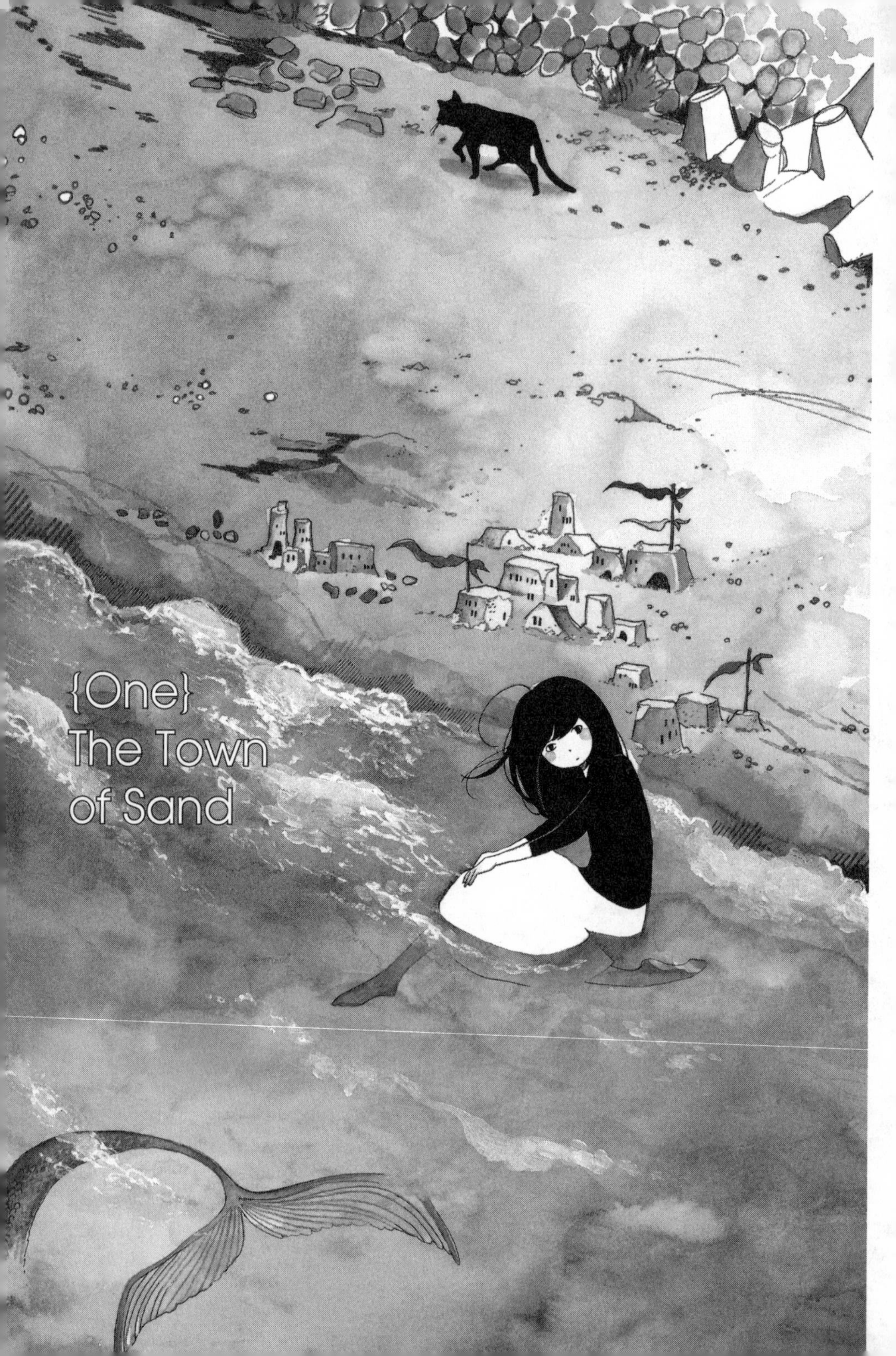
{One}
The Town
of Sand

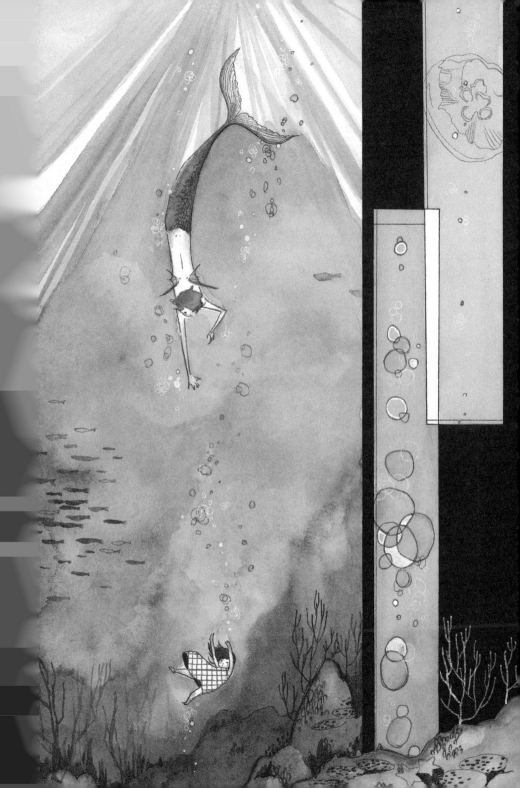

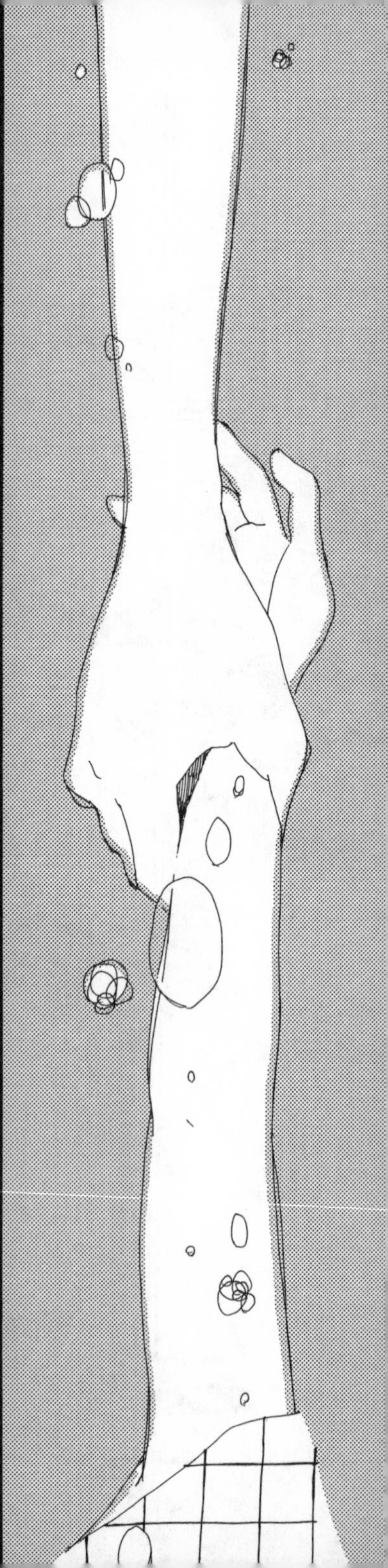

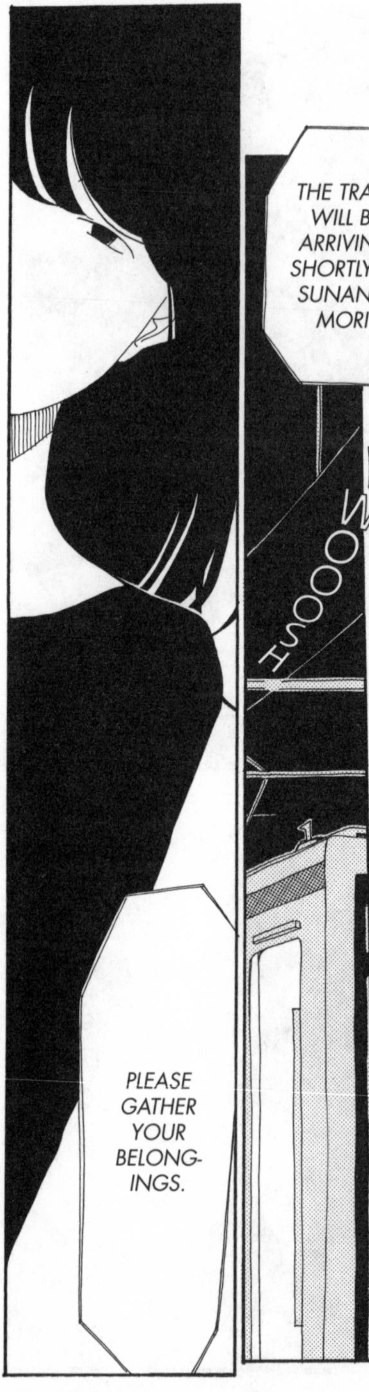
THE TRAIN WILL BE ARRIVING SHORTLY IN SUNANO-MORI.
VWOOOSH
PLEASE GATHER YOUR BELONGINGS.

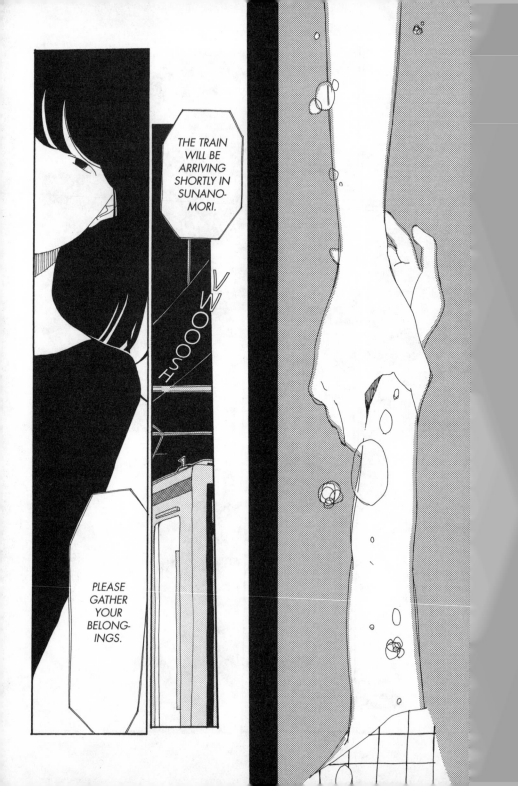

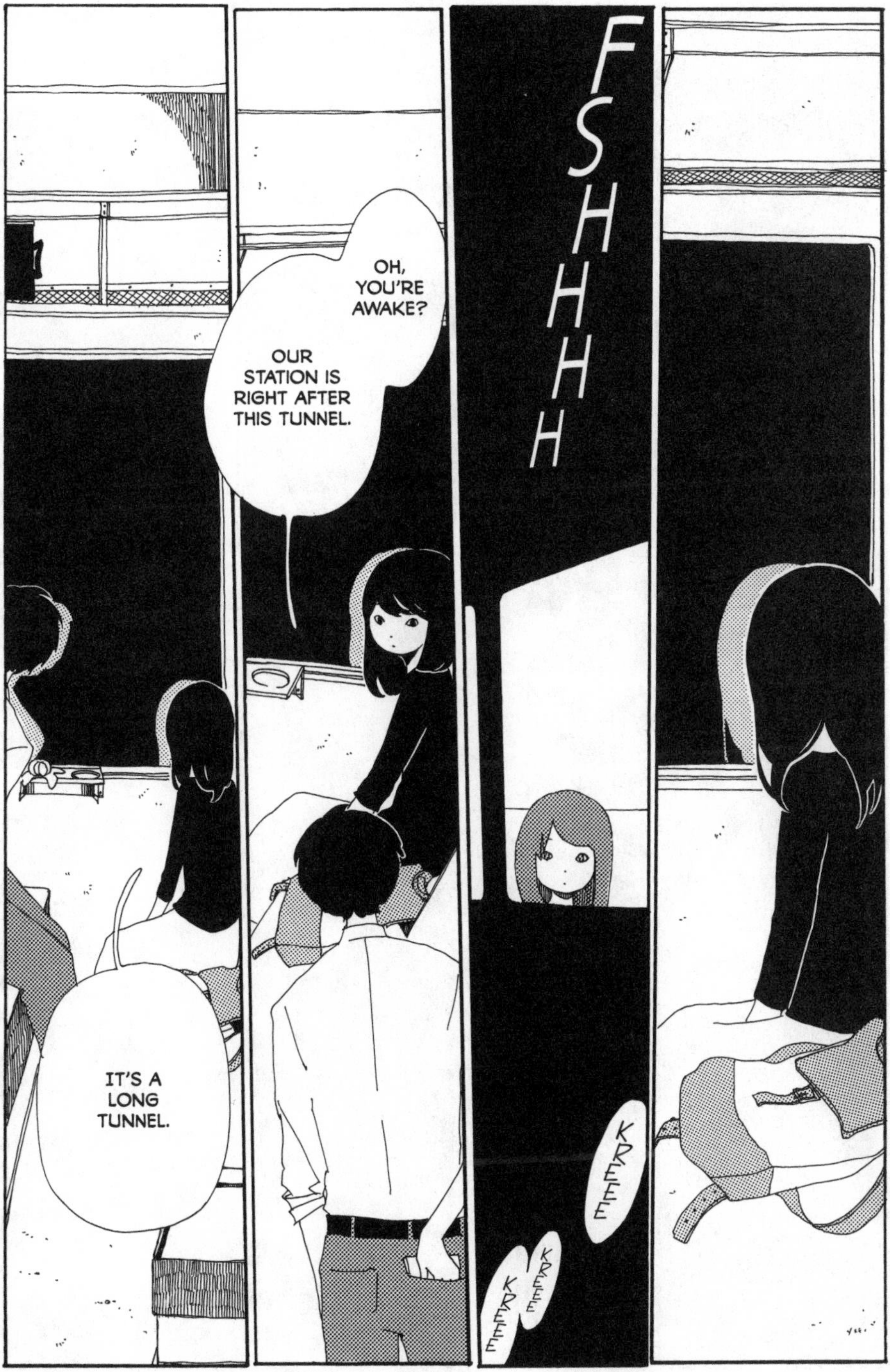
FSHHHH
KREEE
KREEE
KREEE
OH, YOU'RE AWAKE?
OUR STATION IS RIGHT AFTER THIS TUNNEL.
IT'S A LONG TUNNEL.

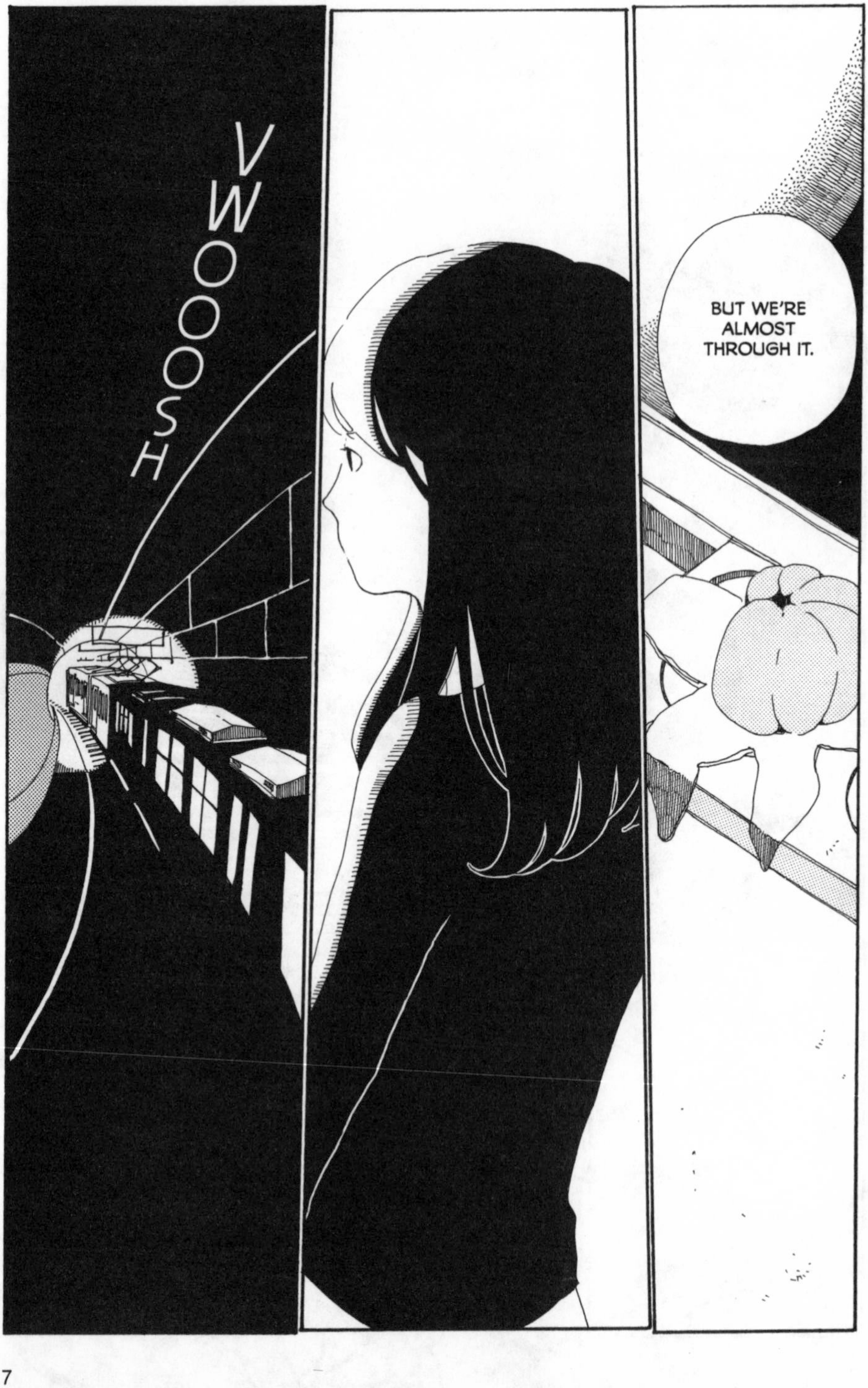
BUT WE'RE ALMOST THROUGH IT.
VWOOOOSH

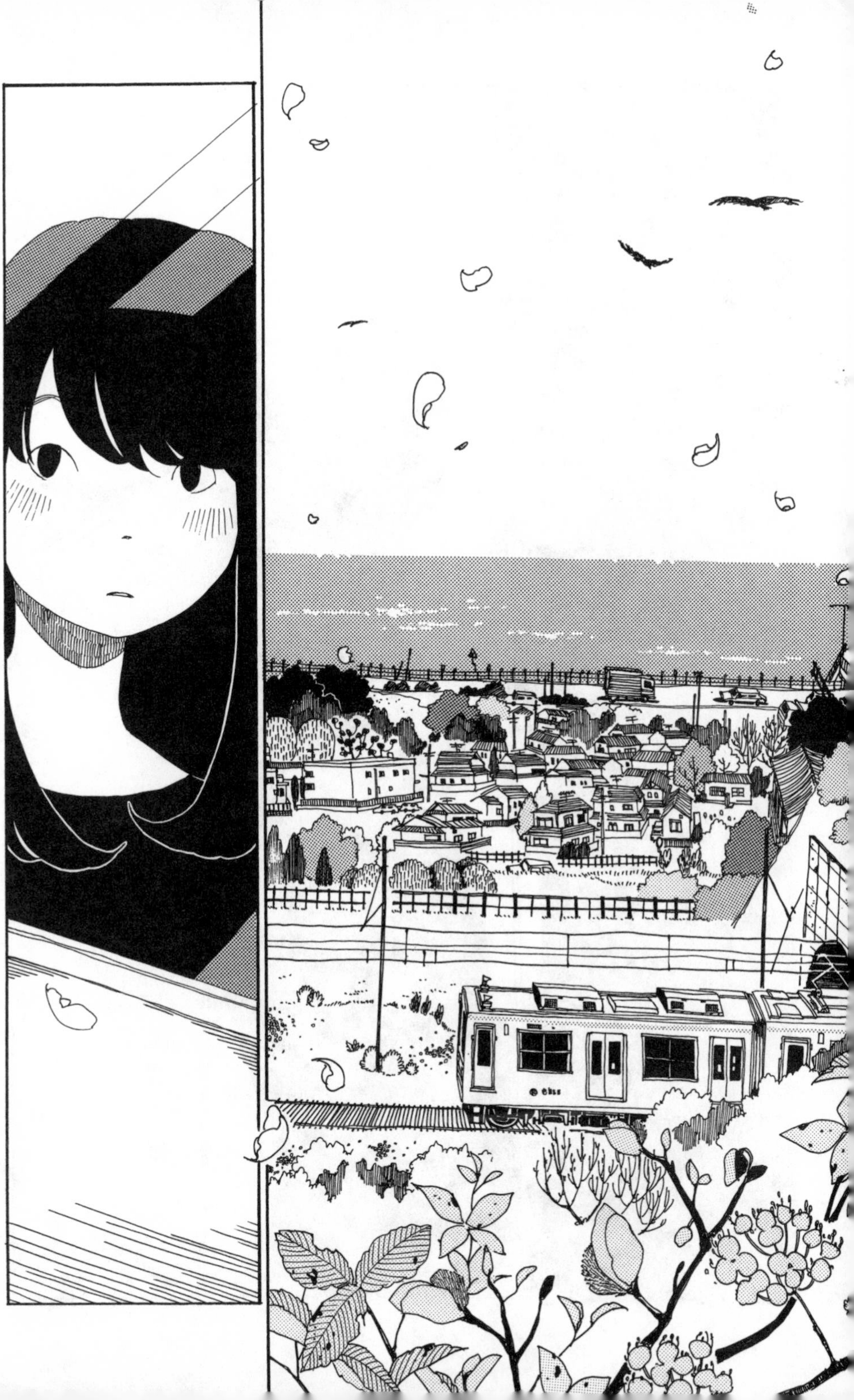

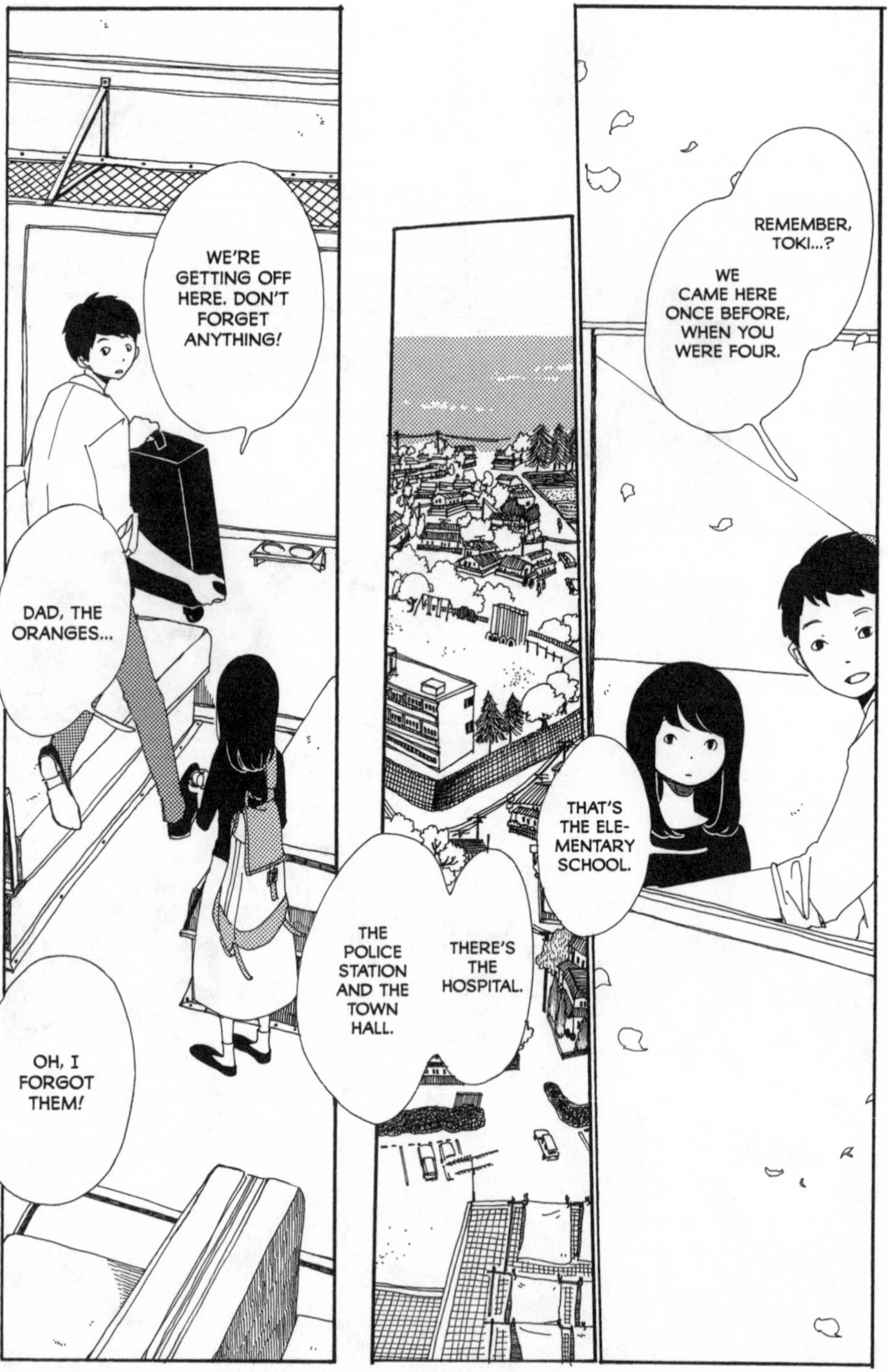
REMEMBER, TOKI...?
WE CAME HERE ONCE BEFORE, WHEN YOU WERE FOUR.
THAT'S THE ELEMENTARY SCHOOL.
THERE'S THE HOSPITAL.
THE POLICE STATION AND THE TOWN HALL.
WE'RE GETTING OFF HERE. DON'T FORGET ANYTHING!
DAD, THE ORANGES...
OH, I FORGOT THEM!

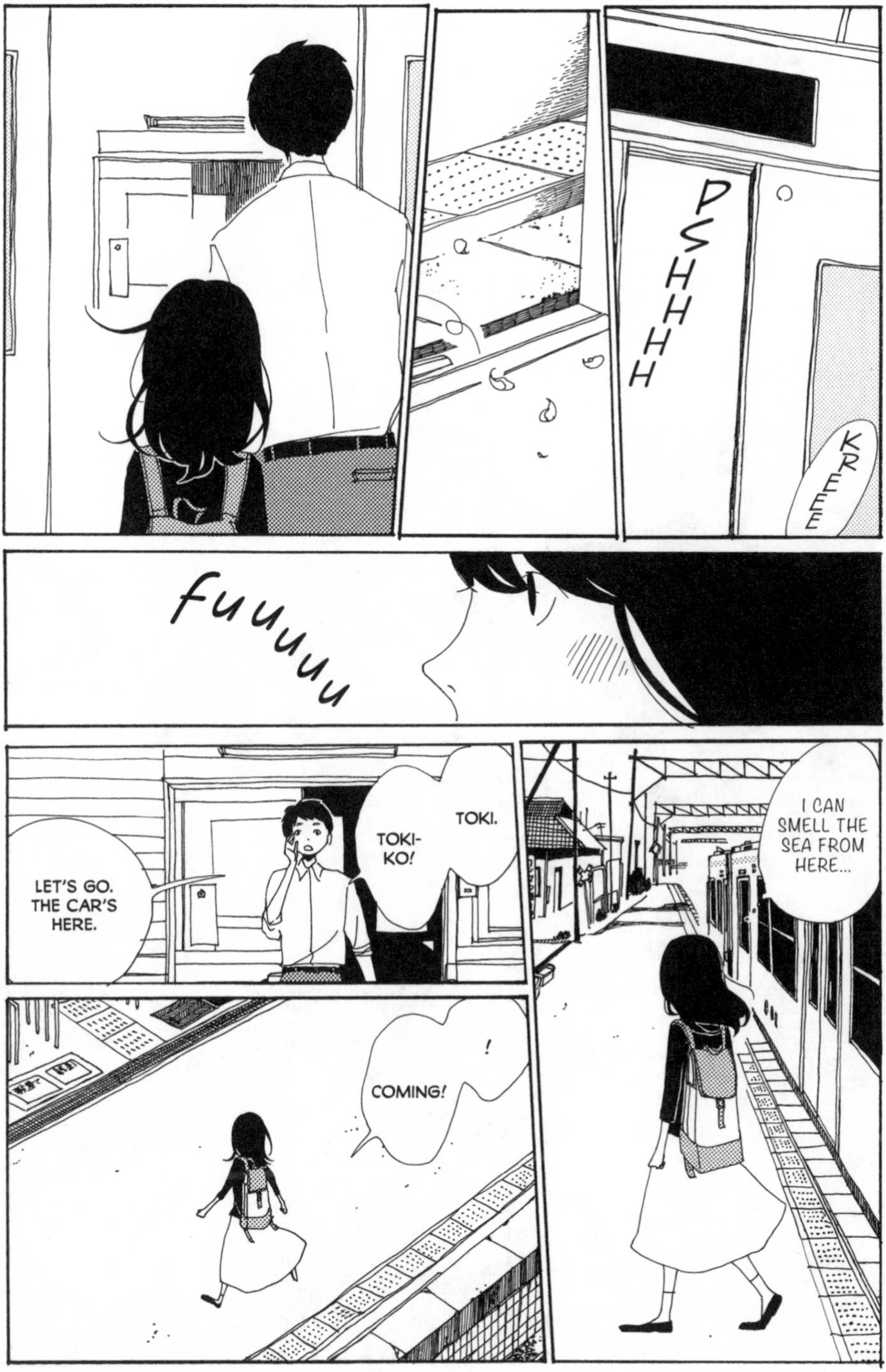

PSHHHH
KREEE
fuuuuu
I CAN SMELL THE SEA FROM HERE...
TOKI.
TOKI-KO!
LET'S GO. THE CAR'S HERE.
!
COMING!

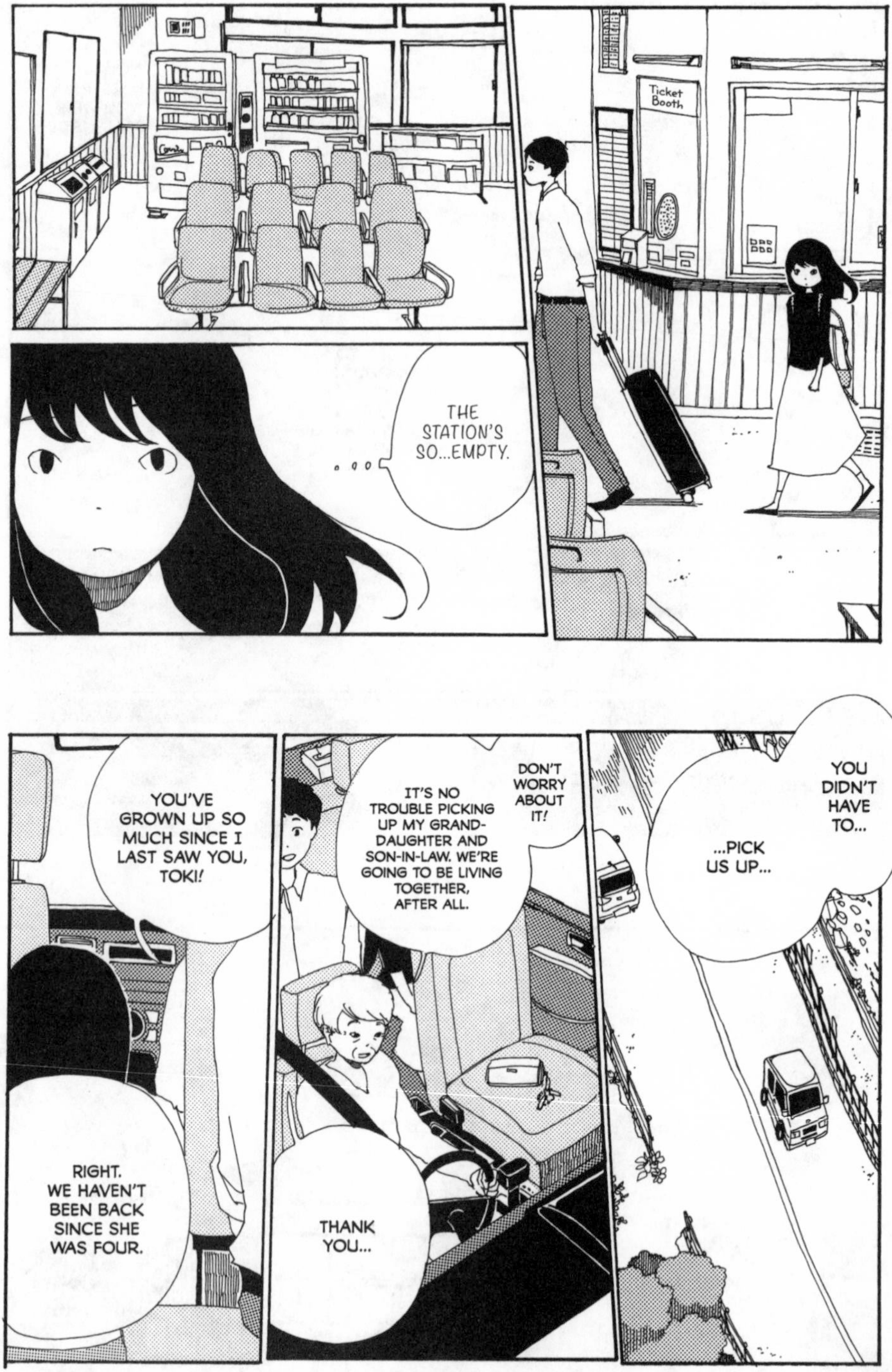
Ticket Booth
...
THE STATION'S SO...EMPTY.
YOU DIDN'T HAVE TO...
...PICK US UP...
DON'T WORRY ABOUT IT!
IT'S NO TROUBLE PICKING UP MY GRAND-DAUGHTER AND SON-IN-LAW. WE'RE GOING TO BE LIVING TOGETHER, AFTER ALL.
THANK YOU...
YOU'VE GROWN UP SO MUCH SINCE I LAST SAW YOU, TOKI!
RIGHT. WE HAVEN'T BEEN BACK SINCE SHE WAS FOUR.

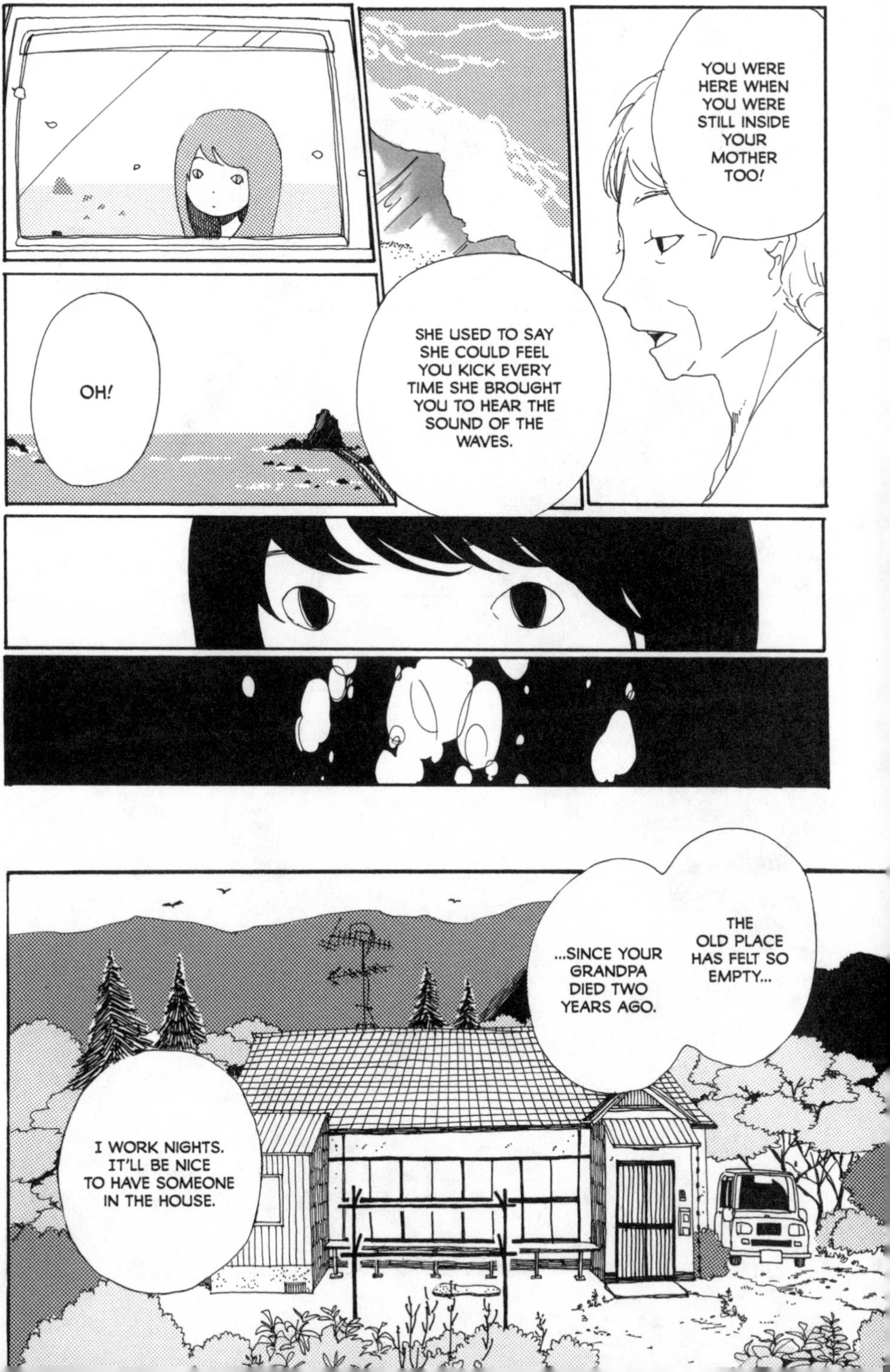
YOU WERE HERE WHEN YOU WERE STILL INSIDE YOUR MOTHER TOO!
SHE USED TO SAY SHE COULD FEEL YOU KICK EVERY TIME SHE BROUGHT YOU TO HEAR THE SOUND OF THE WAVES.
OH!
THE OLD PLACE HAS FELT SO EMPTY...
...SINCE YOUR GRANDPA DIED TWO YEARS AGO.
I WORK NIGHTS. IT'LL BE NICE TO HAVE SOMEONE IN THE HOUSE.

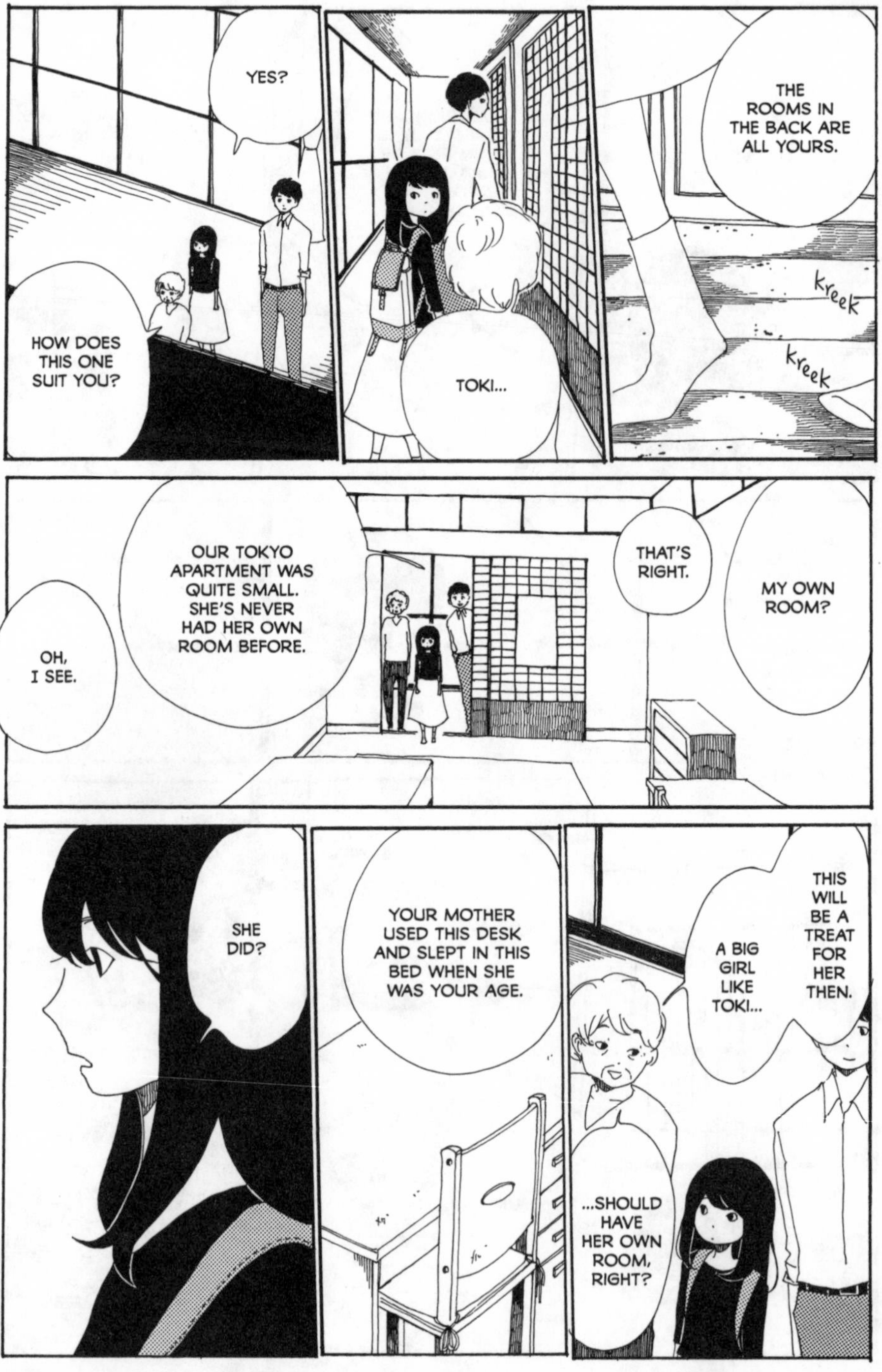
THE ROOMS IN THE BACK ARE ALL YOURS.
kreek
kreek
TOKI...
YES?
HOW DOES THIS ONE SUIT YOU?
MY OWN ROOM?
THAT'S RIGHT.
OUR TOKYO APARTMENT WAS QUITE SMALL. SHE'S NEVER HAD HER OWN ROOM BEFORE.
OH, I SEE.
THIS WILL BE A TREAT FOR HER THEN.
A BIG GIRL LIKE TOKI...
...SHOULD HAVE HER OWN ROOM, RIGHT?
YOUR MOTHER USED THIS DESK AND SLEPT IN THIS BED WHEN SHE WAS YOUR AGE.
SHE DID?

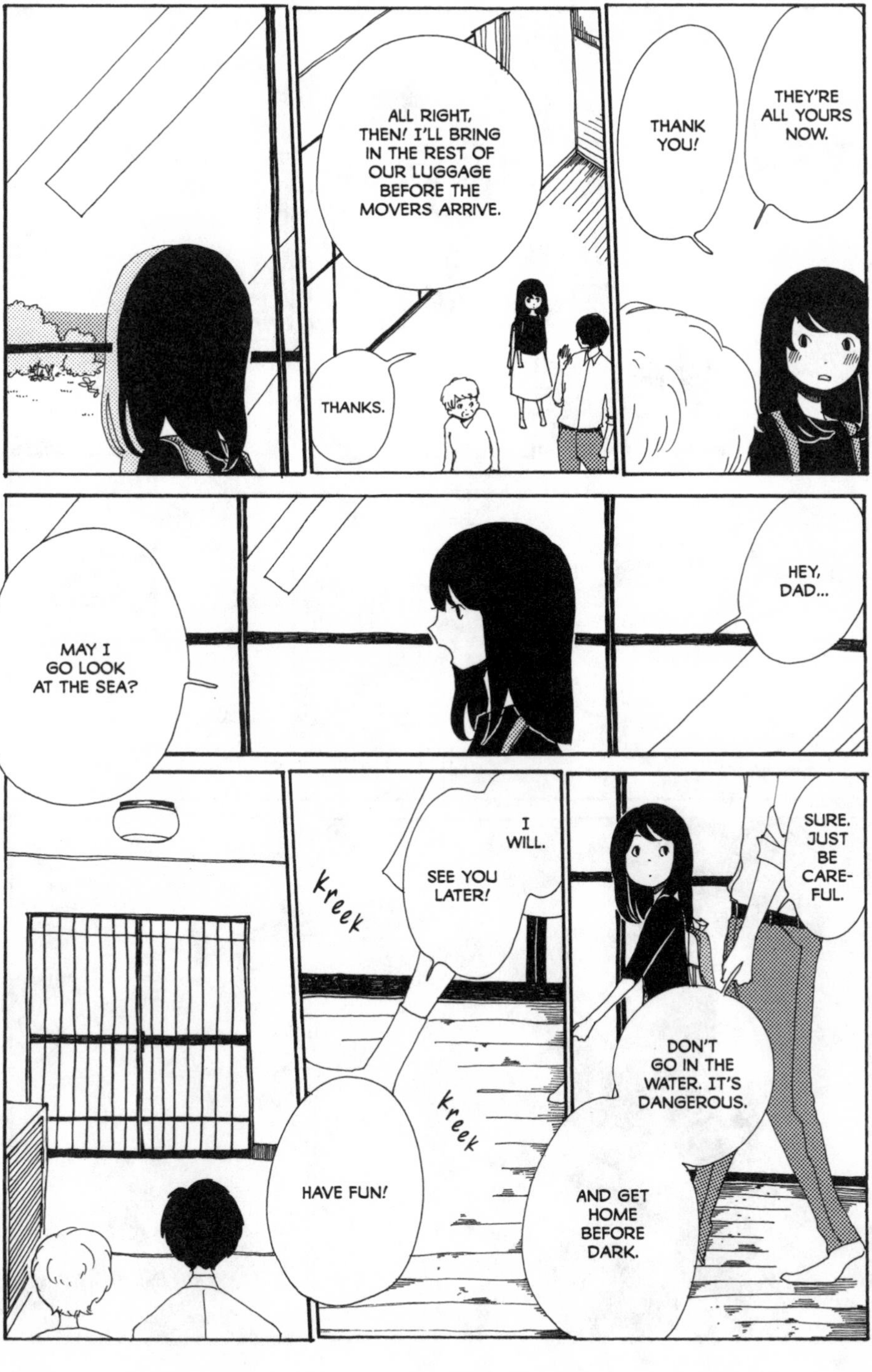
THEY'RE ALL YOURS NOW.
THANK YOU!
ALL RIGHT, THEN! I'LL BRING IN THE REST OF OUR LUGGAGE BEFORE THE MOVERS ARRIVE.
THANKS.
HEY, DAD...
MAY I GO LOOK AT THE SEA?
SURE. JUST BE CARE-FUL.
DON'T GO IN THE WATER. IT'S DANGEROUS.
AND GET HOME BEFORE DARK.
I WILL.
SEE YOU LATER!
kreek
kreek
HAVE FUN!

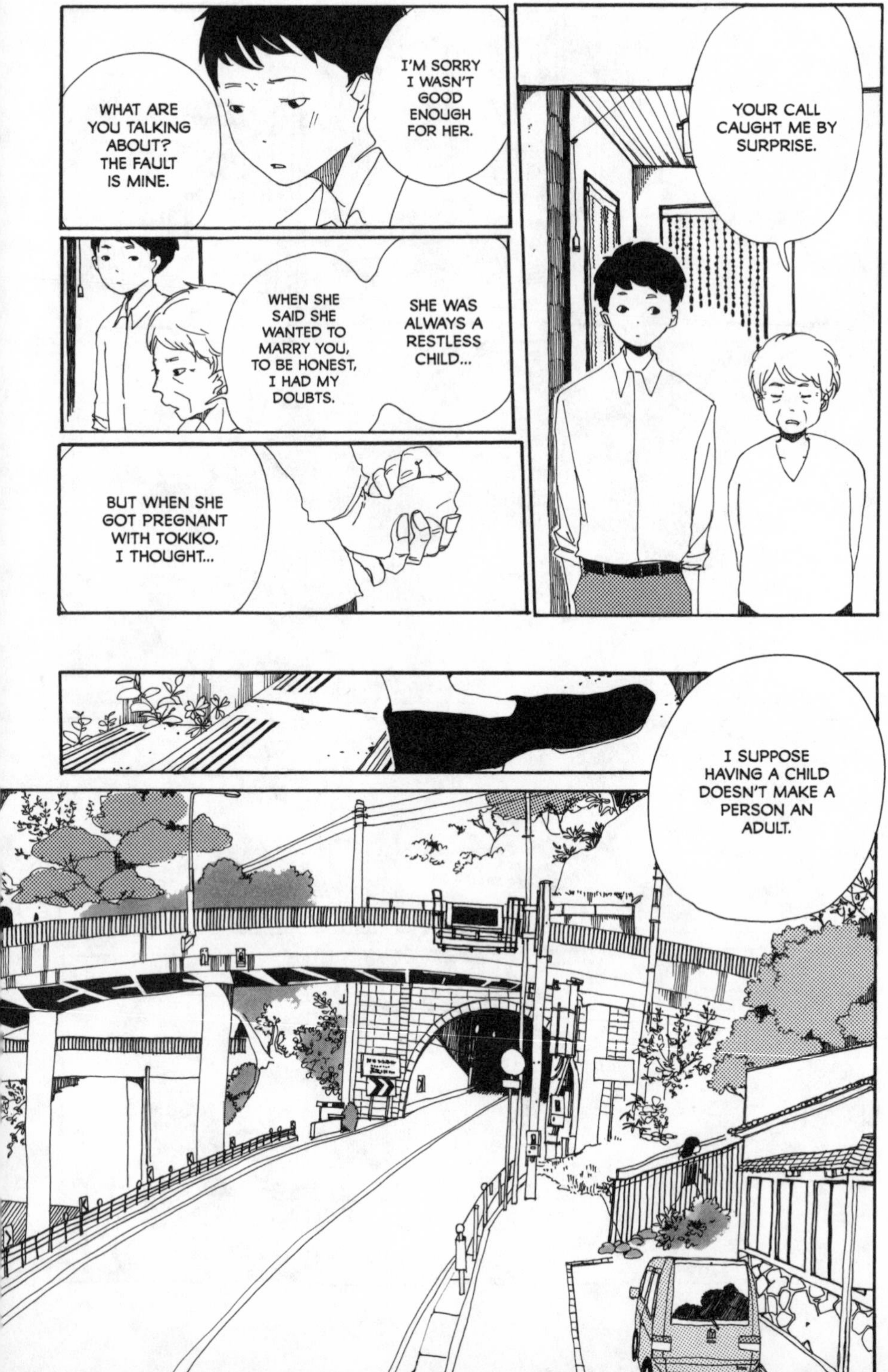
YOUR CALL CAUGHT ME BY SURPRISE.
I'M SORRY I WASN'T GOOD ENOUGH FOR HER.
WHAT ARE YOU TALKING ABOUT? THE FAULT IS MINE.
SHE WAS ALWAYS A RESTLESS CHILD...
WHEN SHE SAID SHE WANTED TO MARRY YOU, TO BE HONEST, I HAD MY DOUBTS.
BUT WHEN SHE GOT PREGNANT WITH TOKIKO, I THOUGHT...
I SUPPOSE HAVING A CHILD DOESN'T MAKE A PERSON AN ADULT.

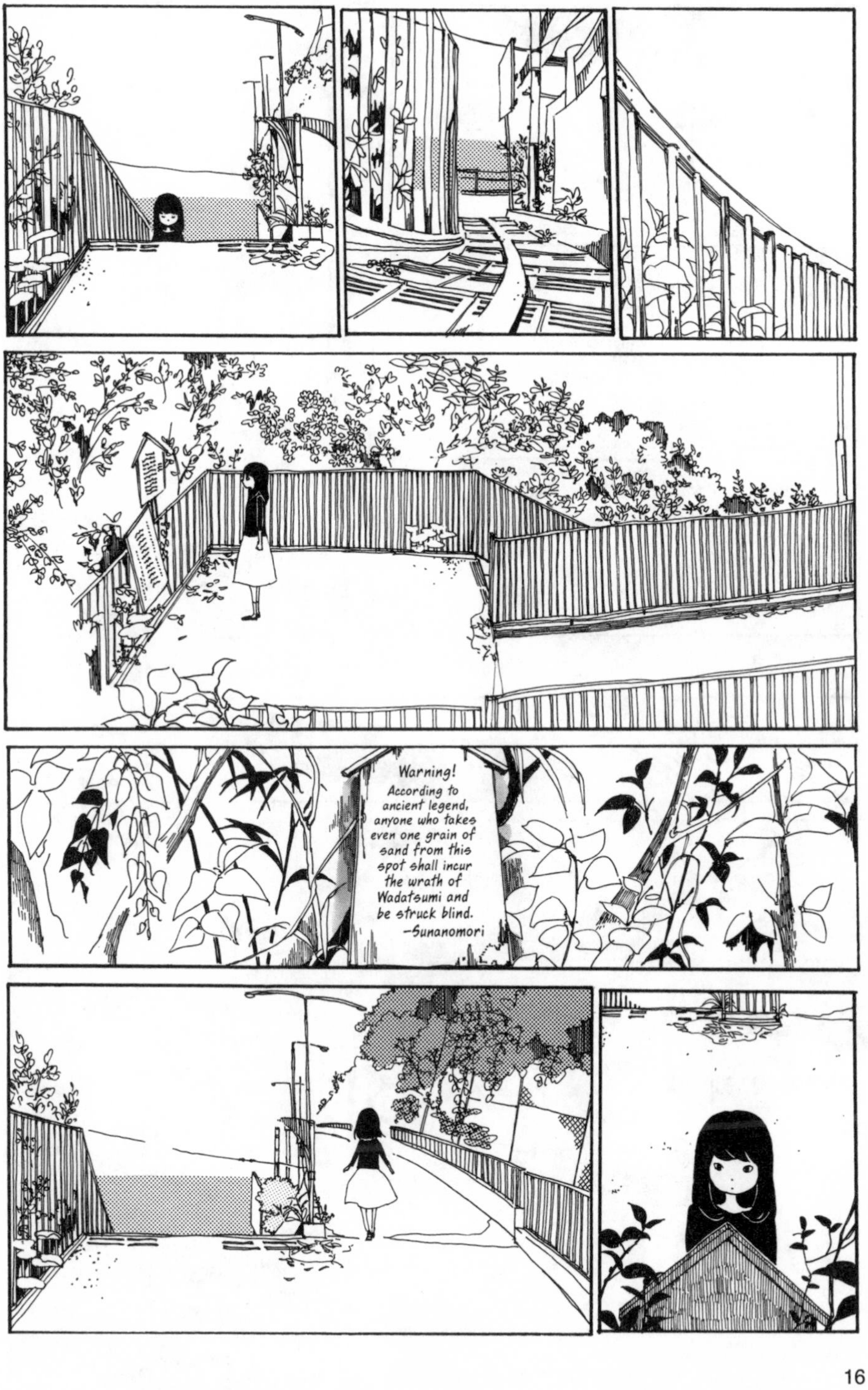
Warning!
According to ancient legend, anyone who takes even one grain of sand from this spot shall incur the wrath of Wadatsumi and be struck blind.
—Sunanomori

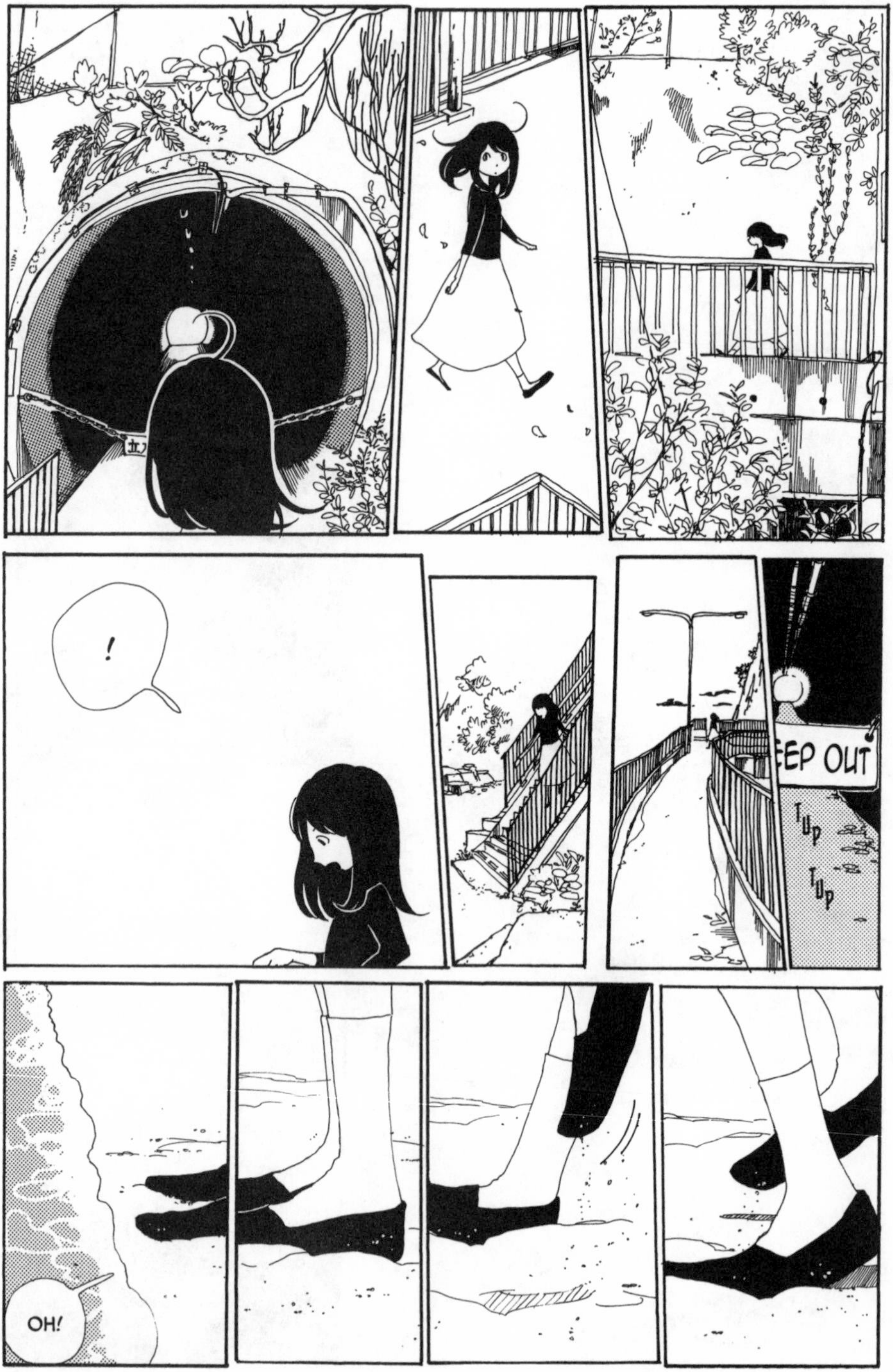
EEP OUT
TUP
TUP
!
OH!

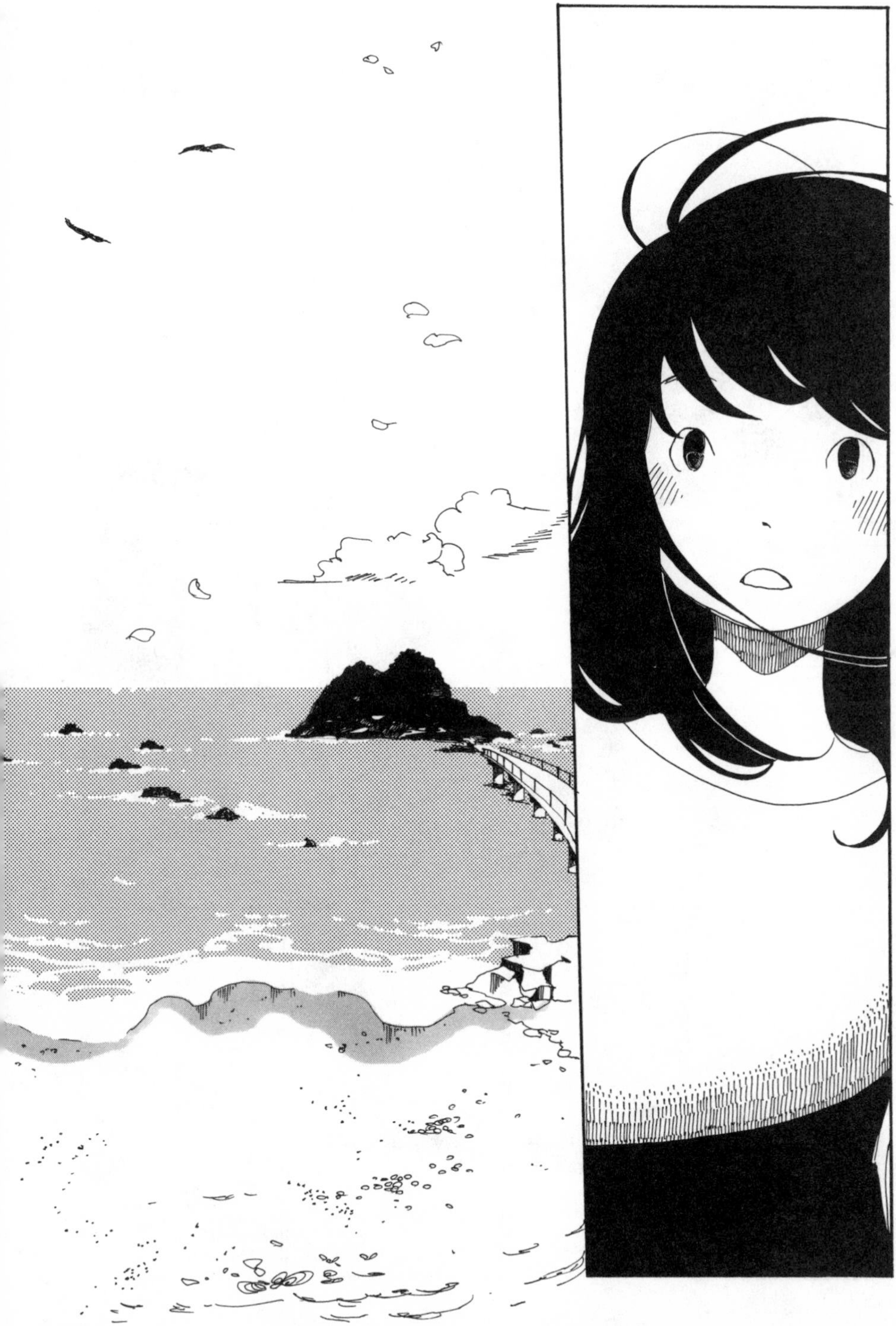

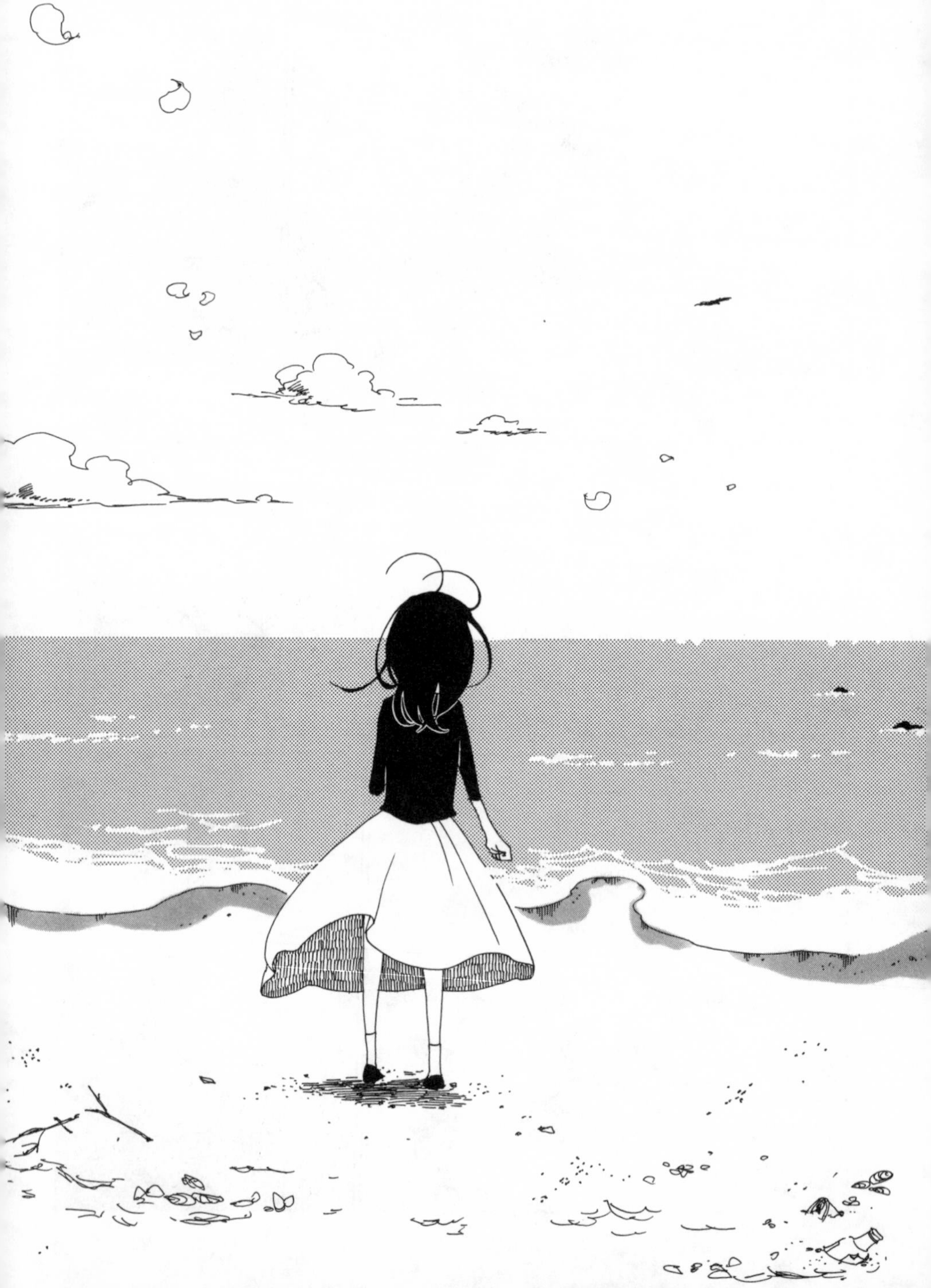

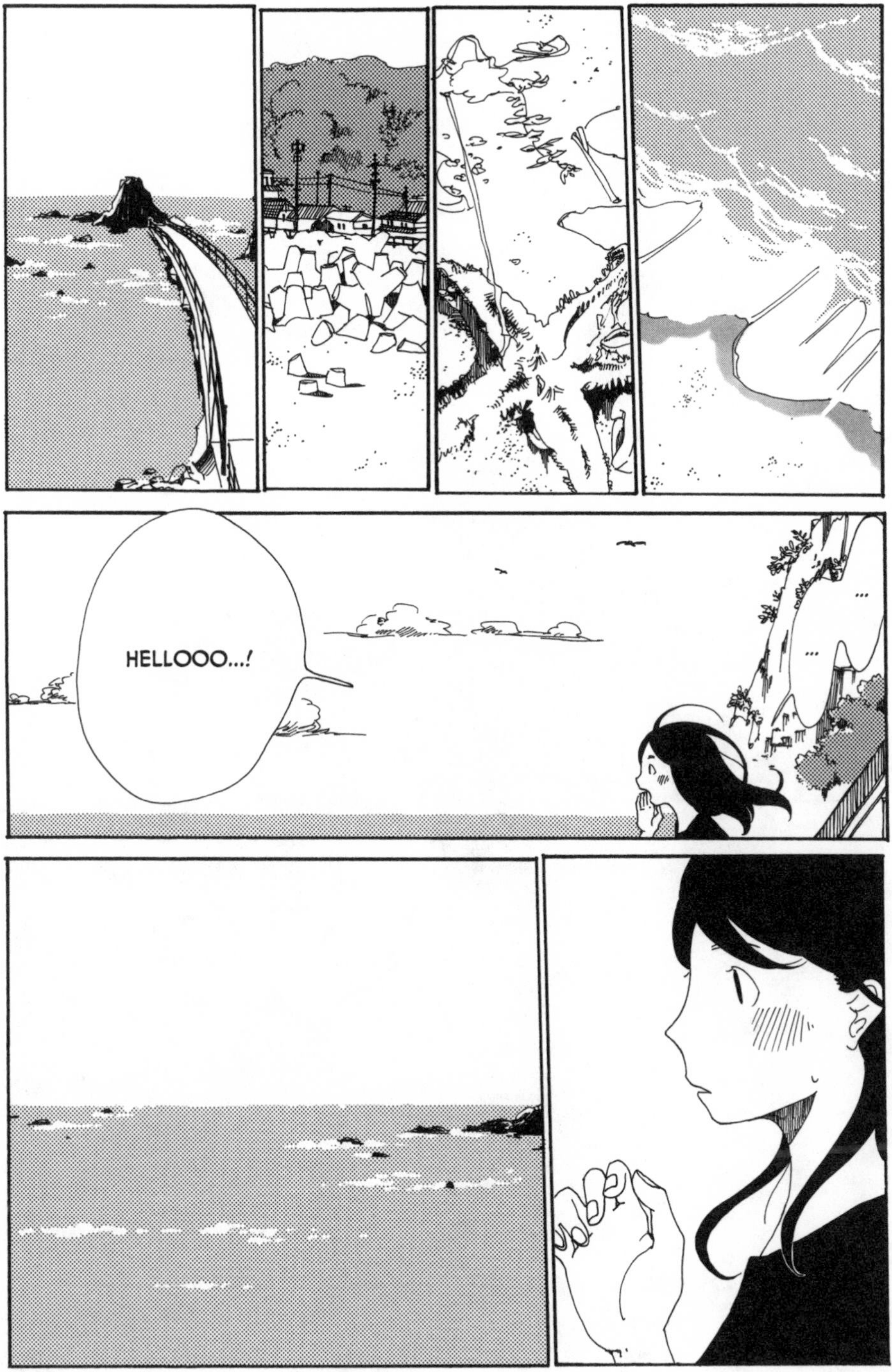
...
...
HELLOOO...!

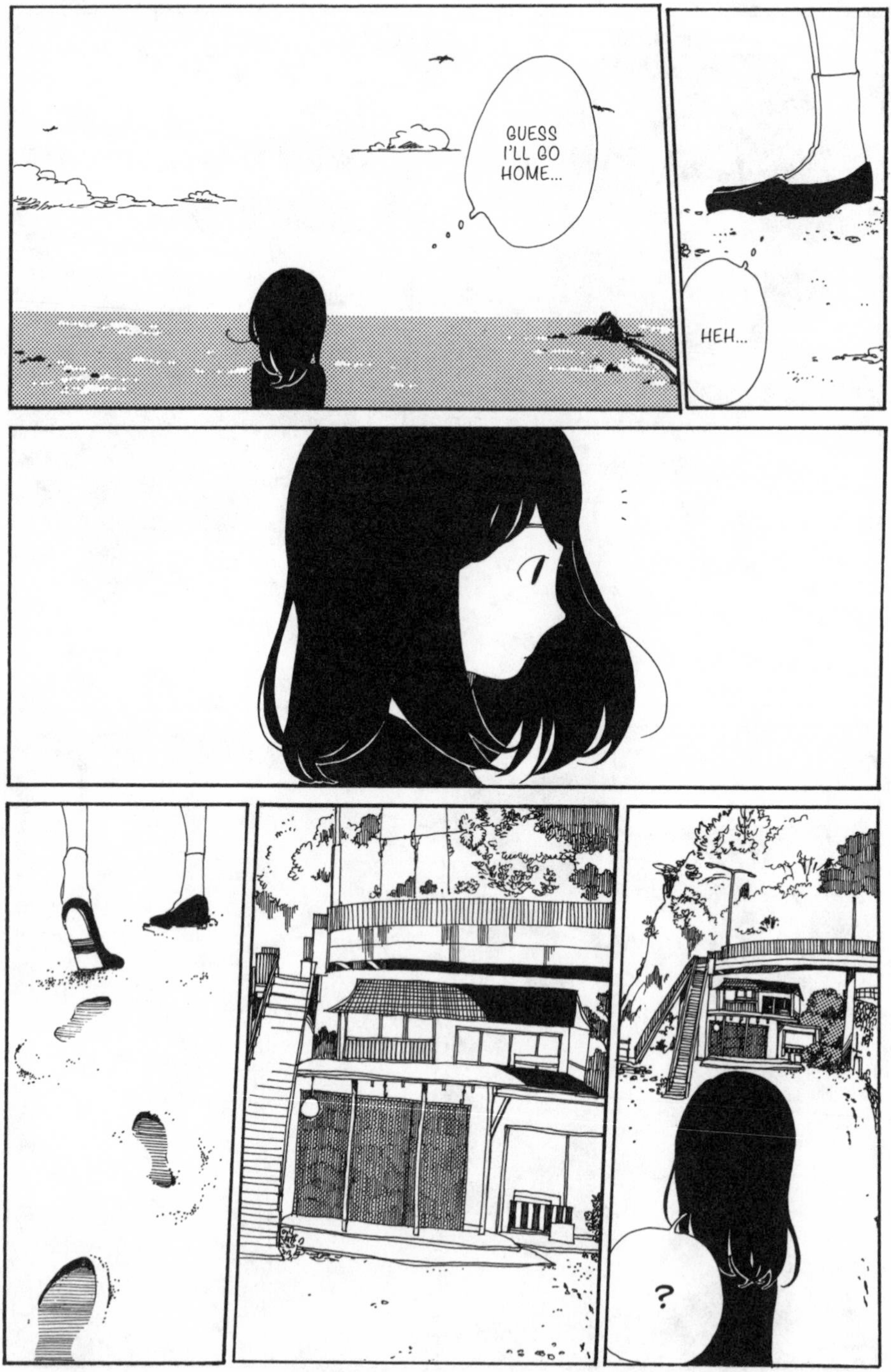
HEH...
GUESS I'LL GO HOME...
?

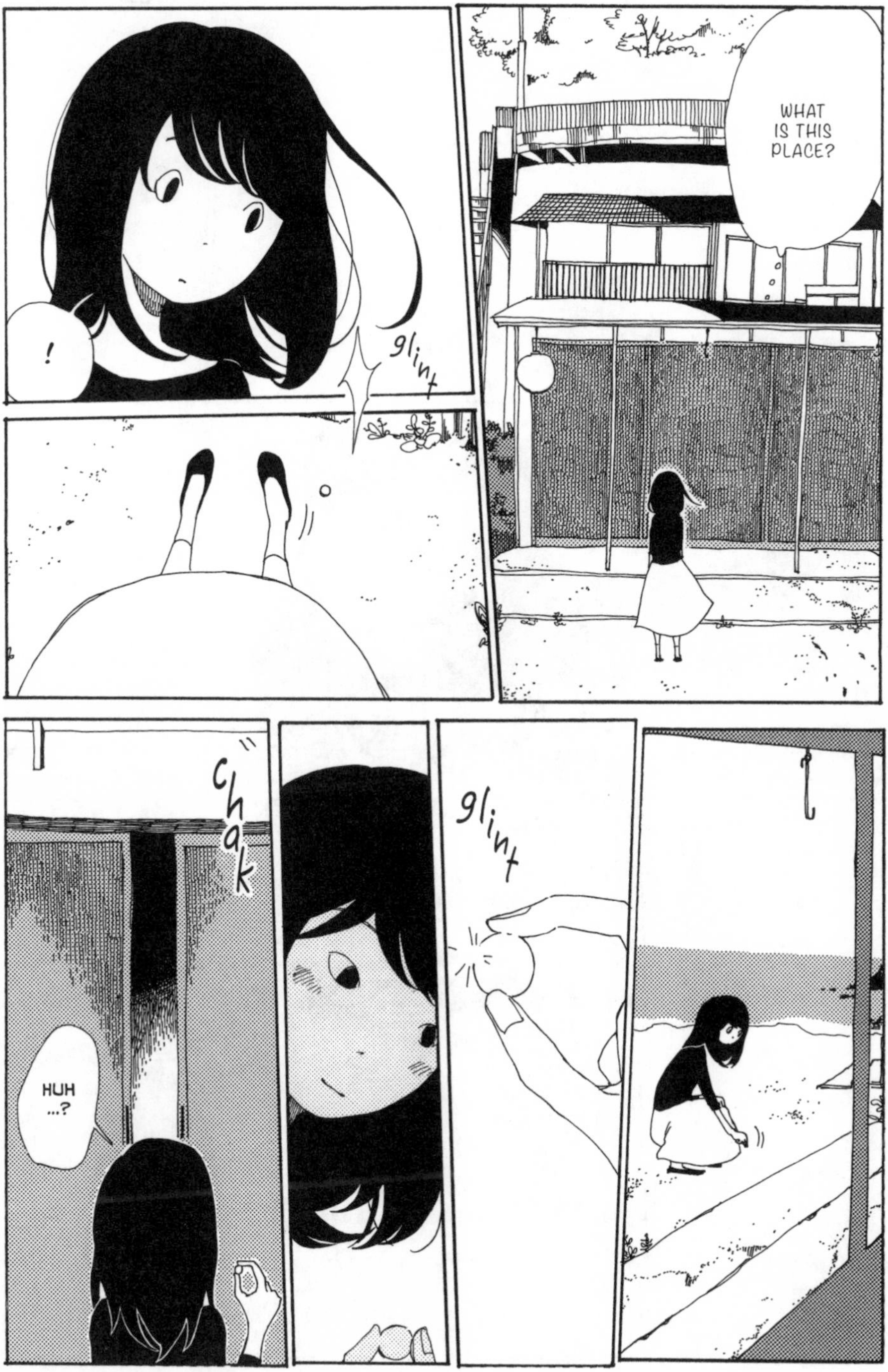

WHAT IS THIS PLACE?
!
glint
glint
chak
HUH ...?

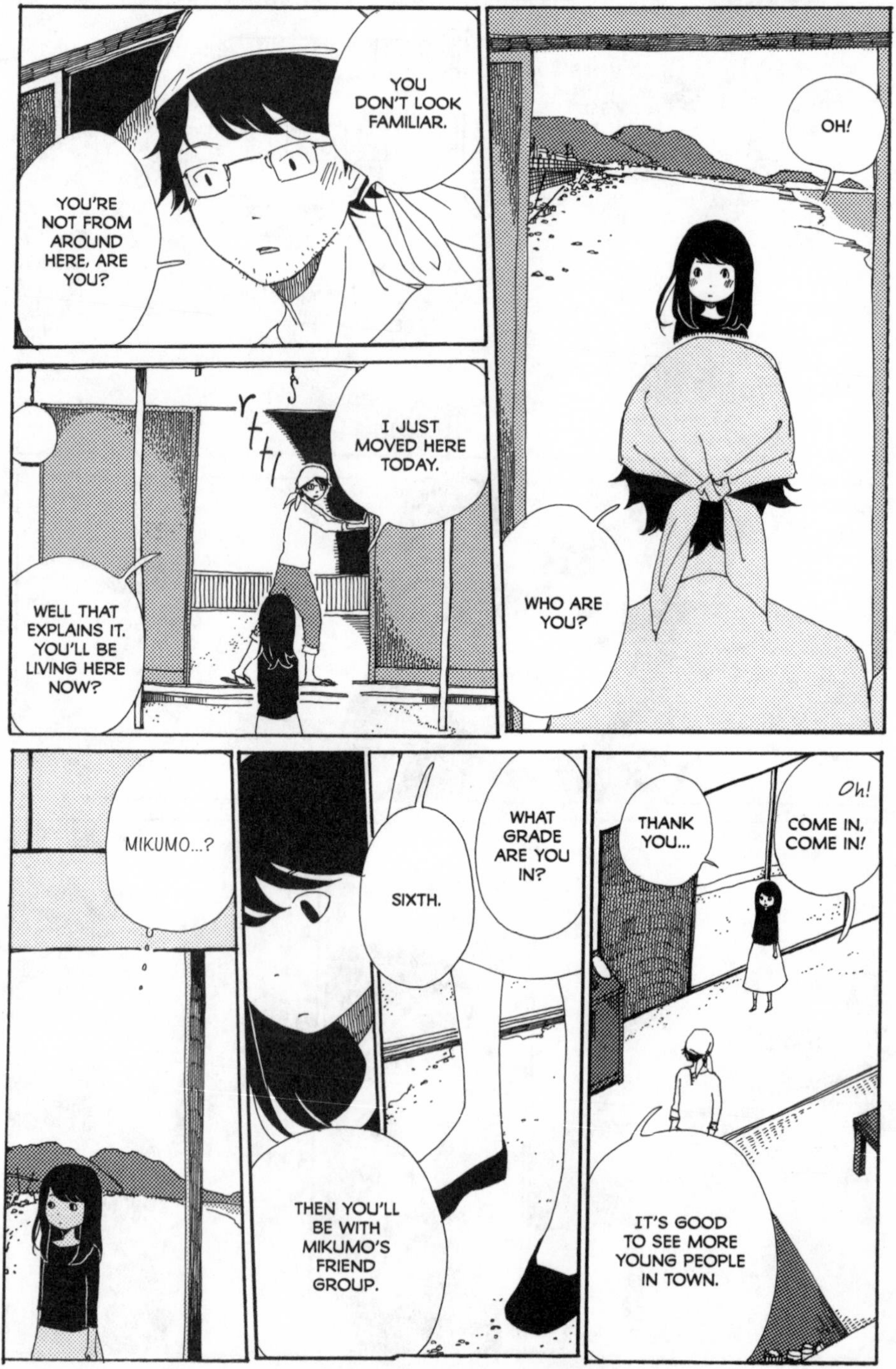
OH!
WHO ARE YOU?
YOU DON'T LOOK FAMILIAR.
YOU'RE NOT FROM AROUND HERE, ARE YOU?
I JUST MOVED HERE TODAY.
WELL THAT EXPLAINS IT. YOU'LL BE LIVING HERE NOW?
Oh!
COME IN, COME IN!
THANK YOU...
IT'S GOOD TO SEE MORE YOUNG PEOPLE IN TOWN.
WHAT GRADE ARE YOU IN?
SIXTH.
THEN YOU'LL BE WITH MIKUMO'S FRIEND GROUP.
MIKUMO...?

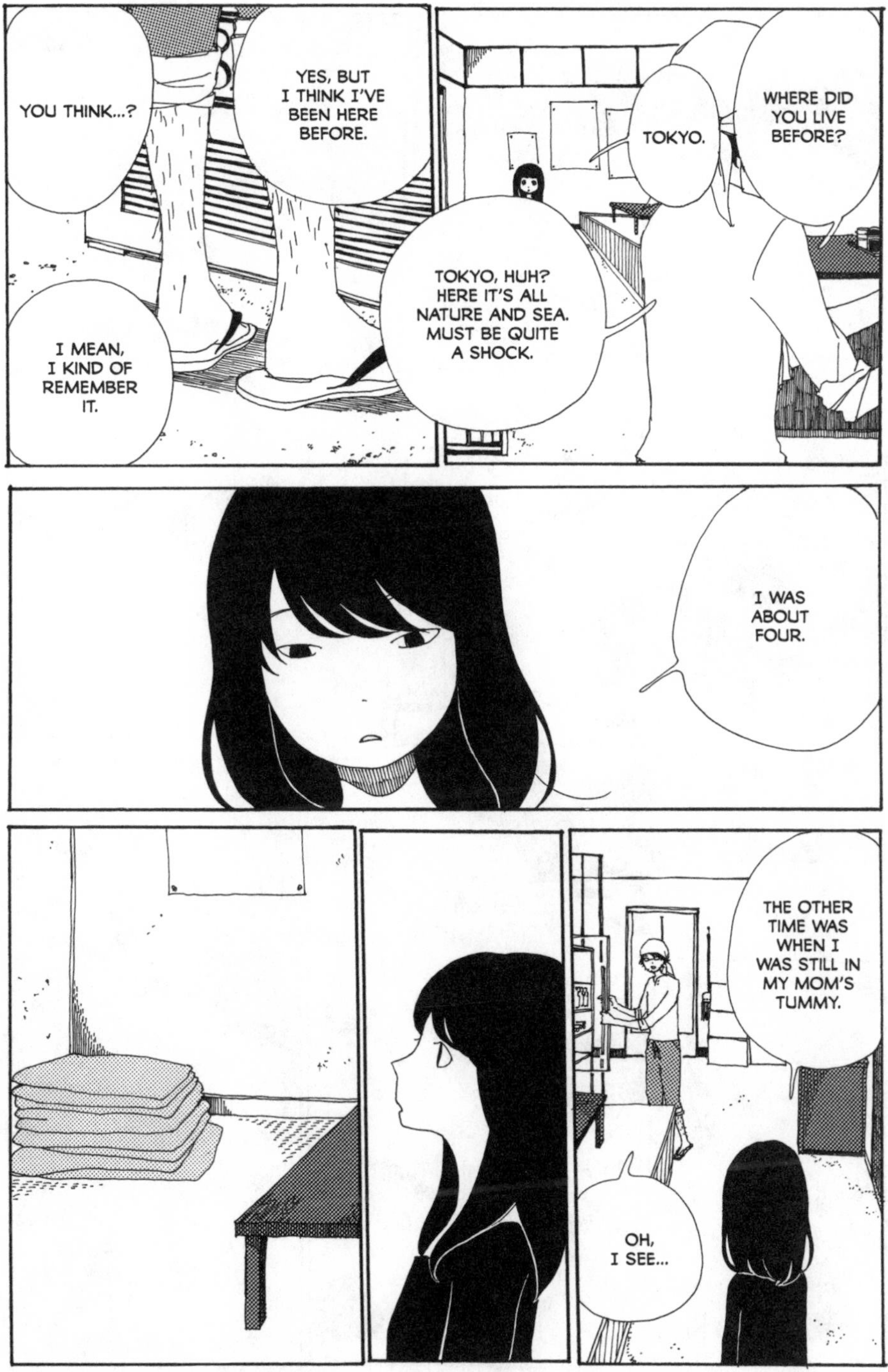
WHERE DID YOU LIVE BEFORE?
TOKYO.
TOKYO, HUH? HERE IT'S ALL NATURE AND SEA. MUST BE QUITE A SHOCK.
YES, BUT I THINK I'VE BEEN HERE BEFORE.
YOU THINK...?
I MEAN, I KIND OF REMEMBER IT.
I WAS ABOUT FOUR.
THE OTHER TIME WAS WHEN I WAS STILL IN MY MOM'S TUMMY.
OH, I SEE...

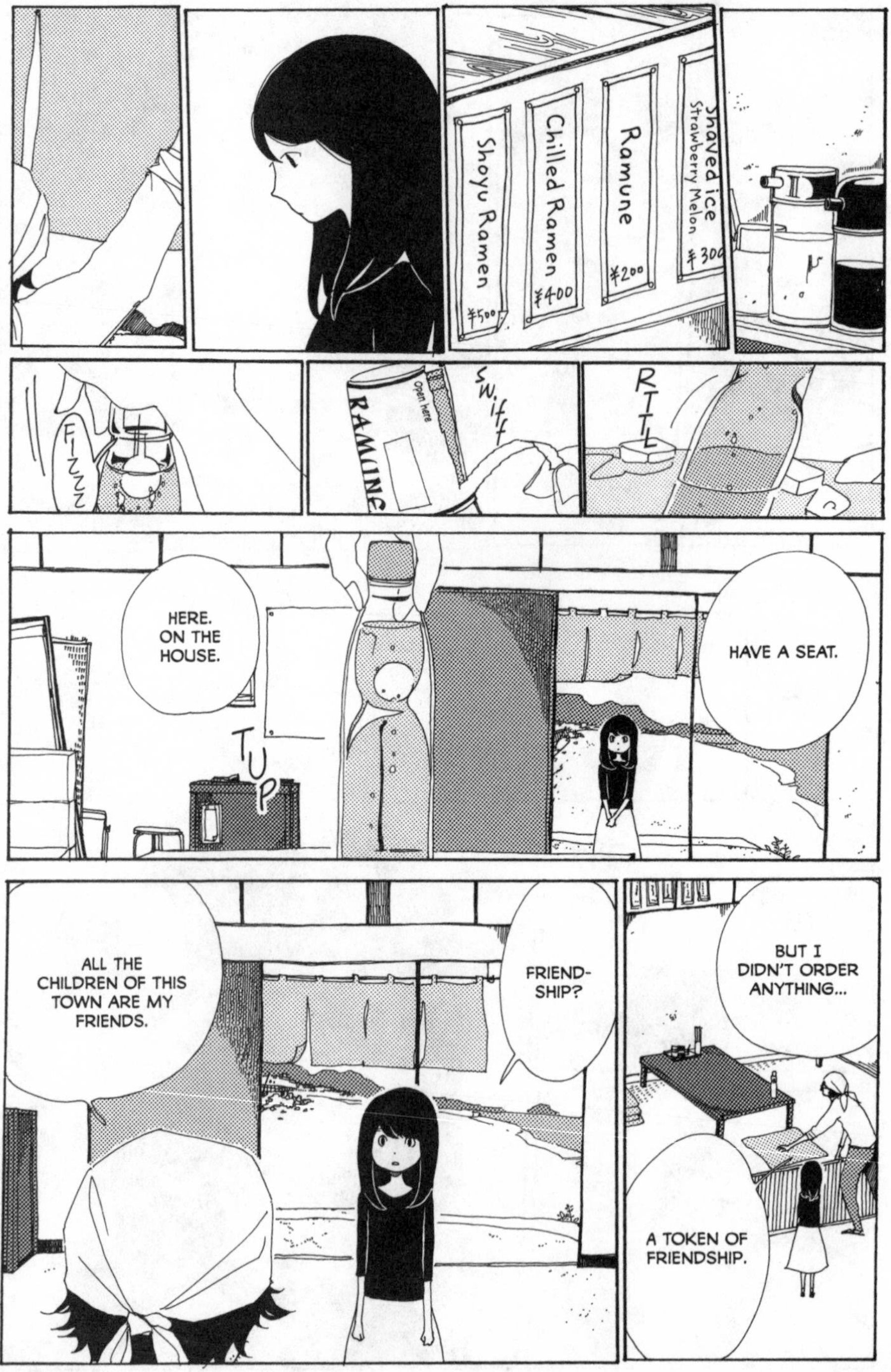
Shaved ice
Strawberry Melon
¥300
Ramune
¥200
Chilled Ramen
¥400
Shoyu Ramen
¥500
RTTL
swiff
Open here
RAMUNE
FIZZZ
HAVE A SEAT.
HERE. ON THE HOUSE.
TUP
BUT I DIDN'T ORDER ANYTHING...
A TOKEN OF FRIENDSHIP.
FRIEND-SHIP?
ALL THE CHILDREN OF THIS TOWN ARE MY FRIENDS.

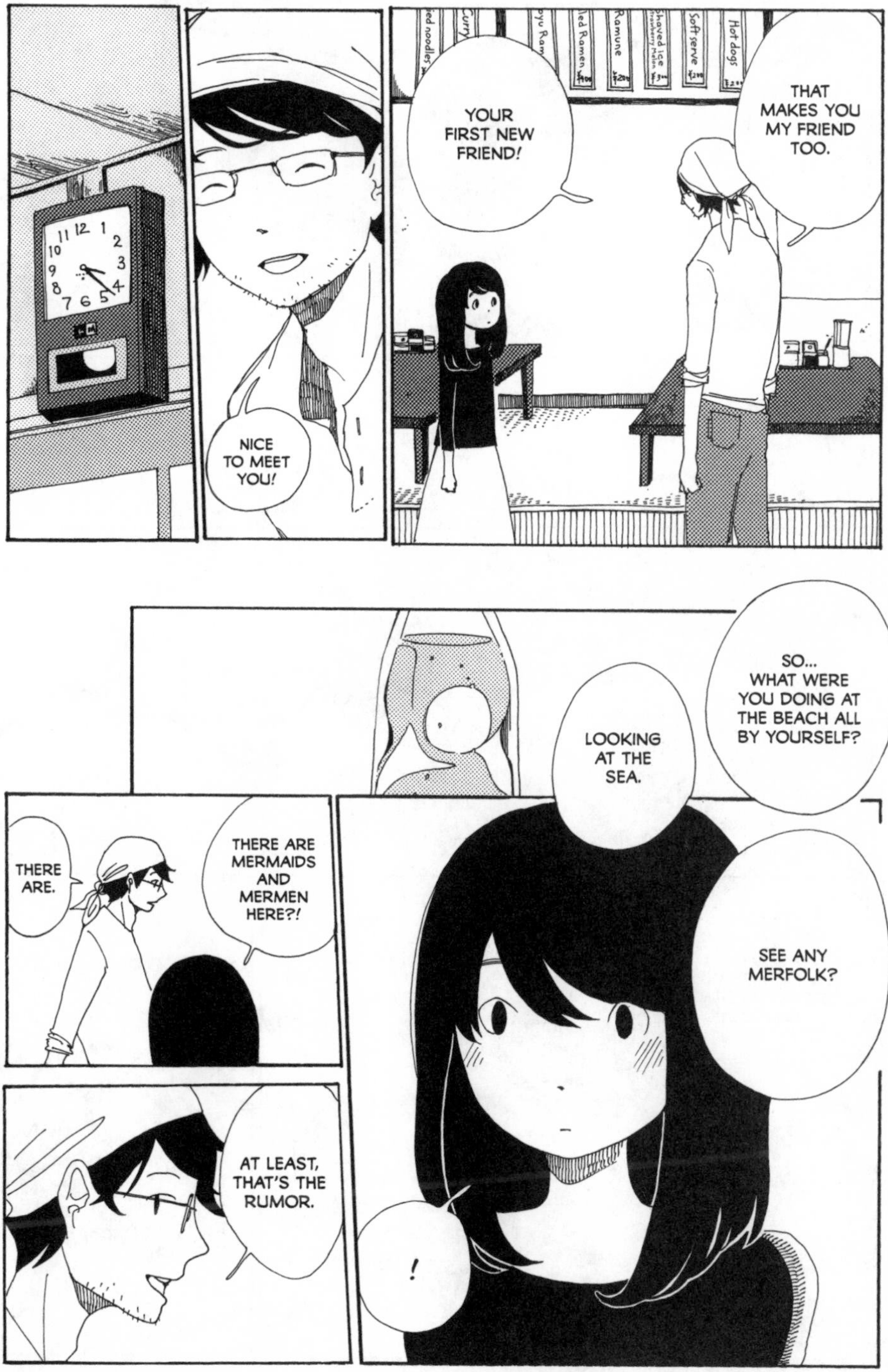
Hot dogs
Soft-serve
Shaved ice
Strawberry Melon
Ramune
Curry
THAT MAKES YOU MY FRIEND TOO.
YOUR FIRST NEW FRIEND!
NICE TO MEET YOU!
SO... WHAT WERE YOU DOING AT THE BEACH ALL BY YOURSELF?
LOOKING AT THE SEA.
SEE ANY MERFOLK?
!
THERE ARE MERMAIDS AND MERMEN HERE?!
THERE ARE.
AT LEAST, THAT'S THE RUMOR.

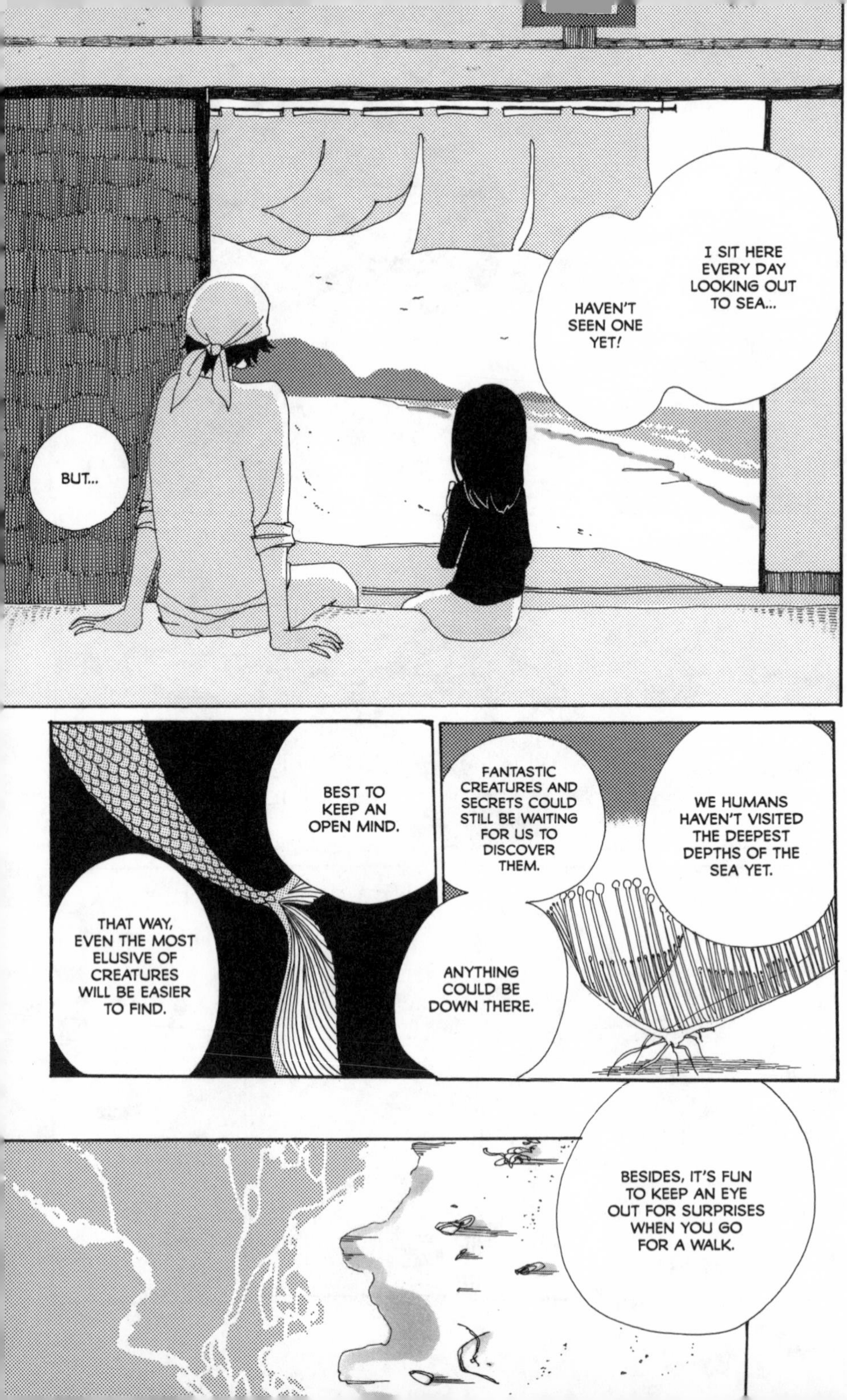
I SIT HERE EVERY DAY LOOKING OUT TO SEA...
HAVEN'T SEEN ONE YET!
BUT...
WE HUMANS HAVEN'T VISITED THE DEEPEST DEPTHS OF THE SEA YET.
FANTASTIC CREATURES AND SECRETS COULD STILL BE WAITING FOR US TO DISCOVER THEM.
ANYTHING COULD BE DOWN THERE.
BEST TO KEEP AN OPEN MIND.
THAT WAY, EVEN THE MOST ELUSIVE OF CREATURES WILL BE EASIER TO FIND.
BESIDES, IT'S FUN TO KEEP AN EYE OUT FOR SURPRISES WHEN YOU GO FOR A WALK.

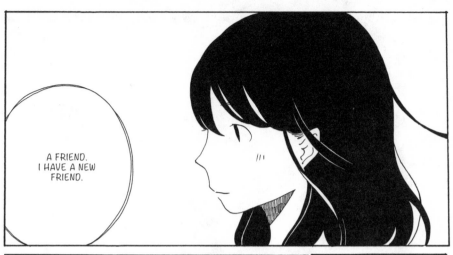

A FRIEND.
I HAVE A NEW
FRIEND.

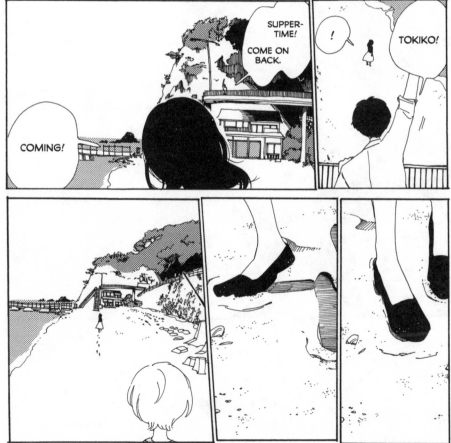

SUPPER-
TIME!

COME ON
BACK.

!

TOKIKO!

COMING!

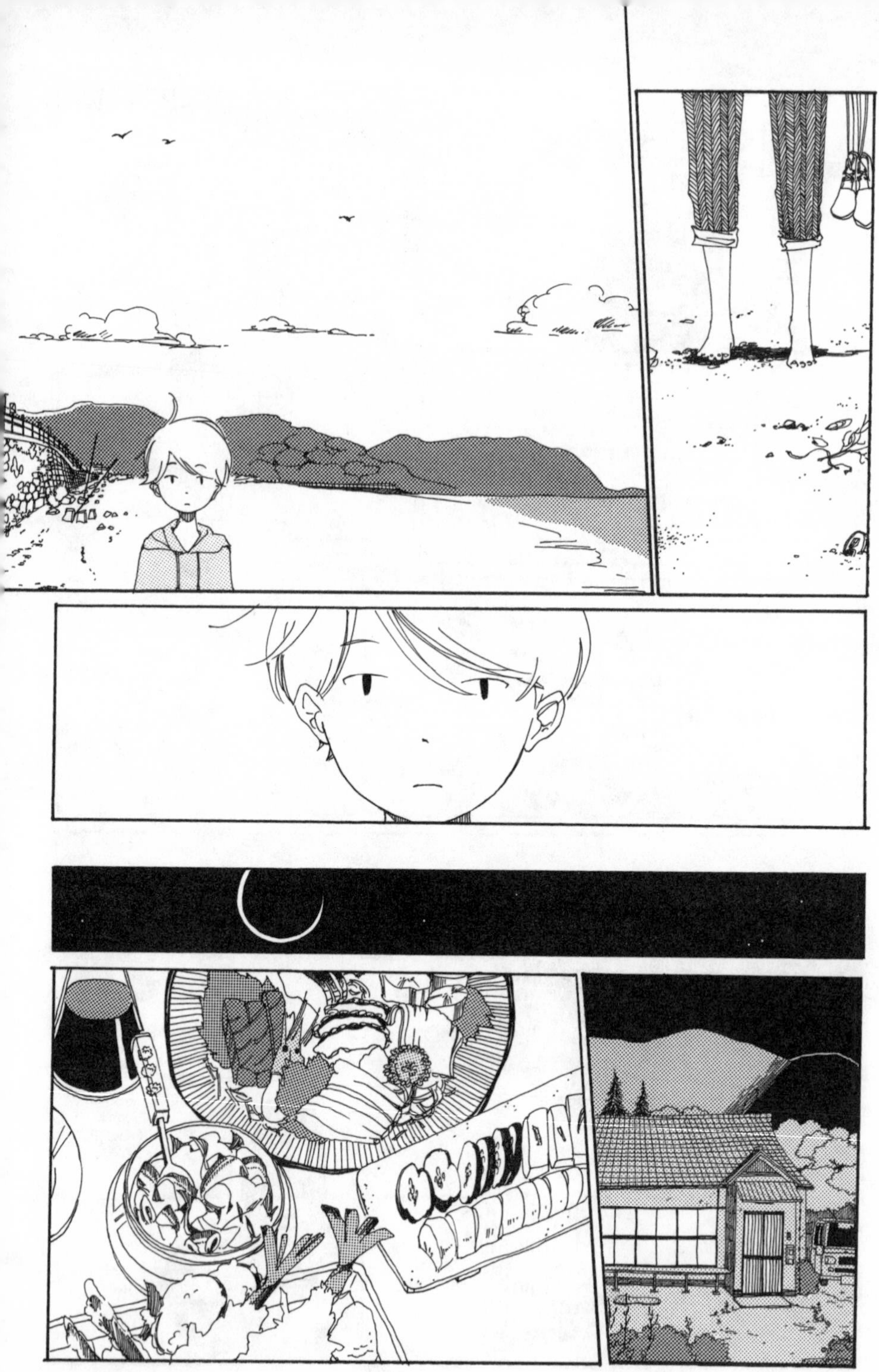

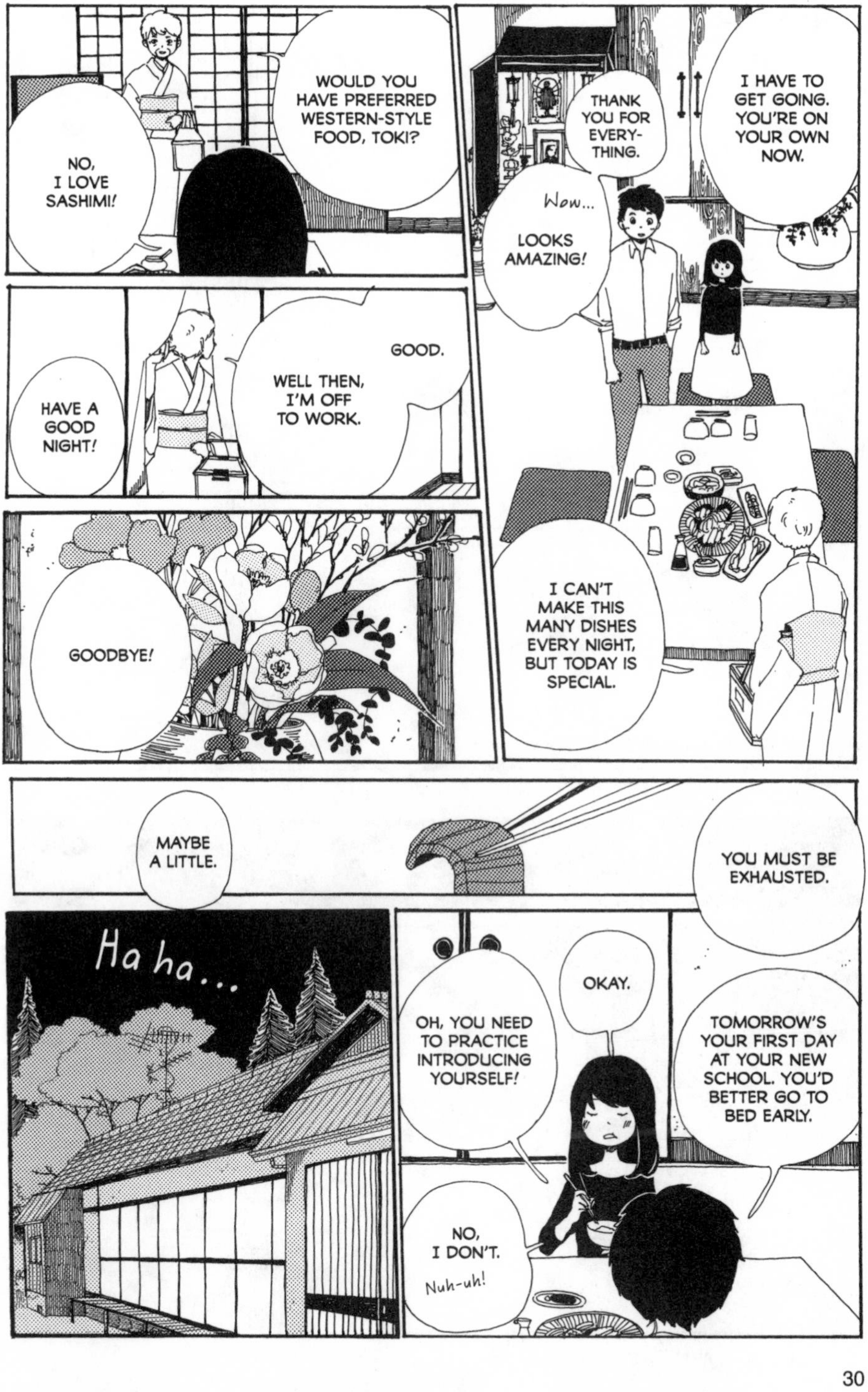
I HAVE TO GET GOING. YOU'RE ON YOUR OWN NOW.
THANK YOU FOR EVERY-THING.
Wow...
LOOKS AMAZING!
I CAN'T MAKE THIS MANY DISHES EVERY NIGHT, BUT TODAY IS SPECIAL.
WOULD YOU HAVE PREFERRED WESTERN-STYLE FOOD, TOKI?
NO, I LOVE SASHIMI!
GOOD.
WELL THEN, I'M OFF TO WORK.
HAVE A GOOD NIGHT!
GOODBYE!
YOU MUST BE EXHAUSTED.
MAYBE A LITTLE.
TOMORROW'S YOUR FIRST DAY AT YOUR NEW SCHOOL. YOU'D BETTER GO TO BED EARLY.
OKAY.
OH, YOU NEED TO PRACTICE INTRODUCING YOURSELF!
NO, I DON'T.
Nuh-uh!
Ha ha...

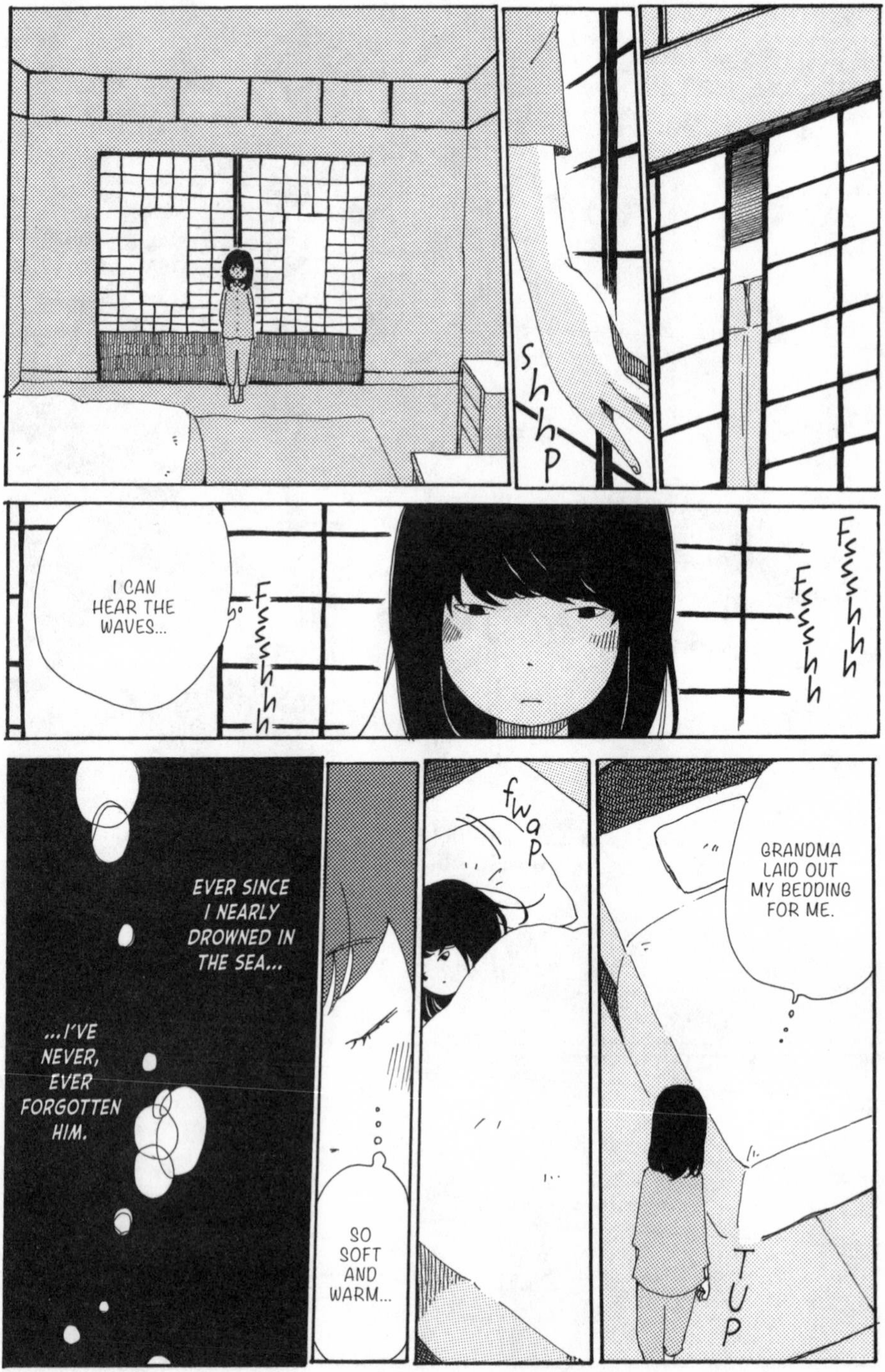
shhp
Fsshhh
Fsshhh
I CAN HEAR THE WAVES...
Fsshhh
GRANDMA LAID OUT MY BEDDING FOR ME.
TUP
fwap
SO SOFT AND WARM...
EVER SINCE I NEARLY DROWNED IN THE SEA...
...I'VE NEVER, EVER FORGOTTEN HIM.

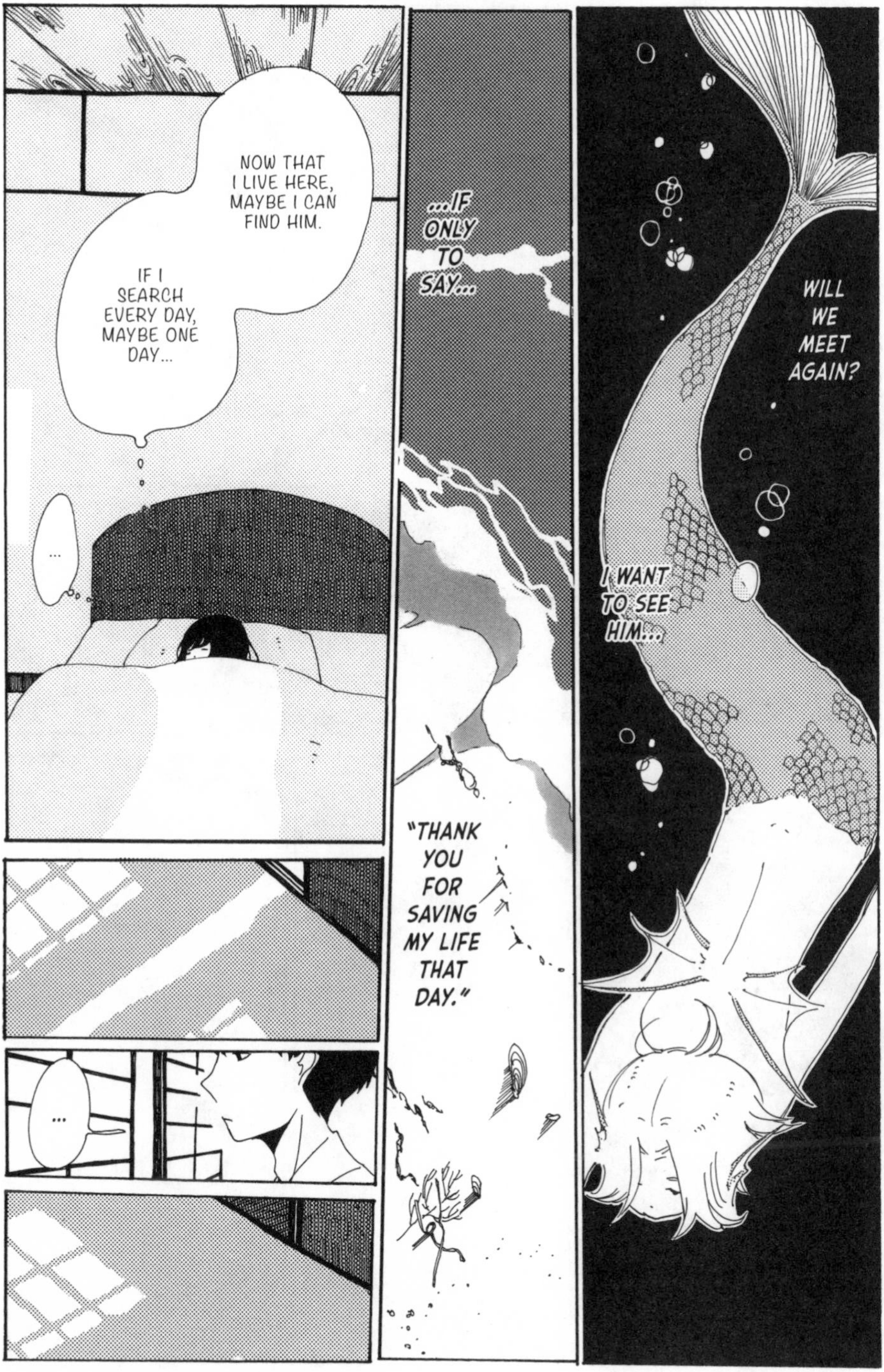
WILL WE MEET AGAIN?
I WANT TO SEE HIM...
...IF ONLY TO SAY...
"THANK YOU FOR SAVING MY LIFE THAT DAY."
NOW THAT I LIVE HERE, MAYBE I CAN FIND HIM.
IF I SEARCH EVERY DAY, MAYBE ONE DAY...
...
...

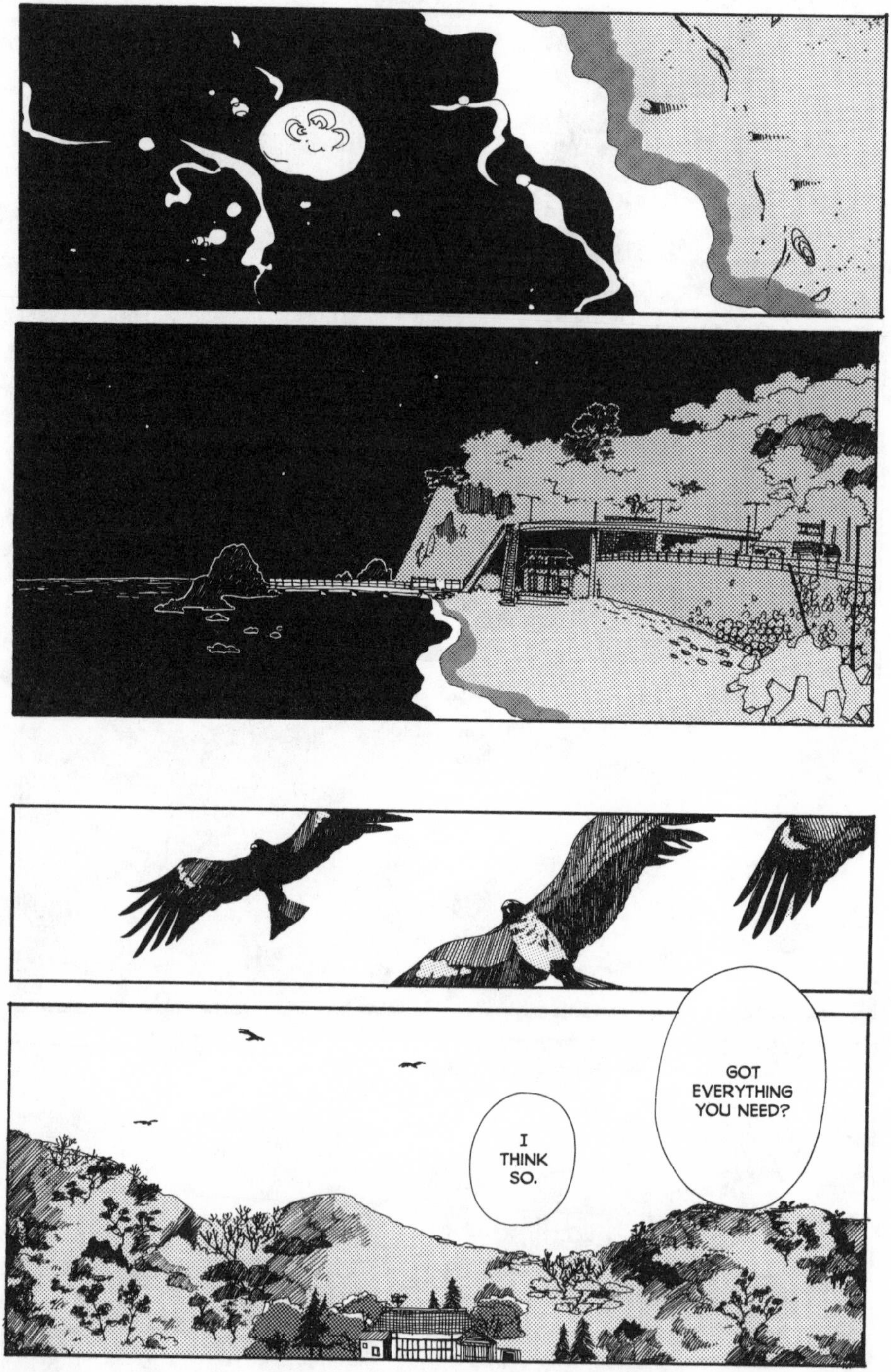
GOT EVERYTHING YOU NEED?
I THINK SO.

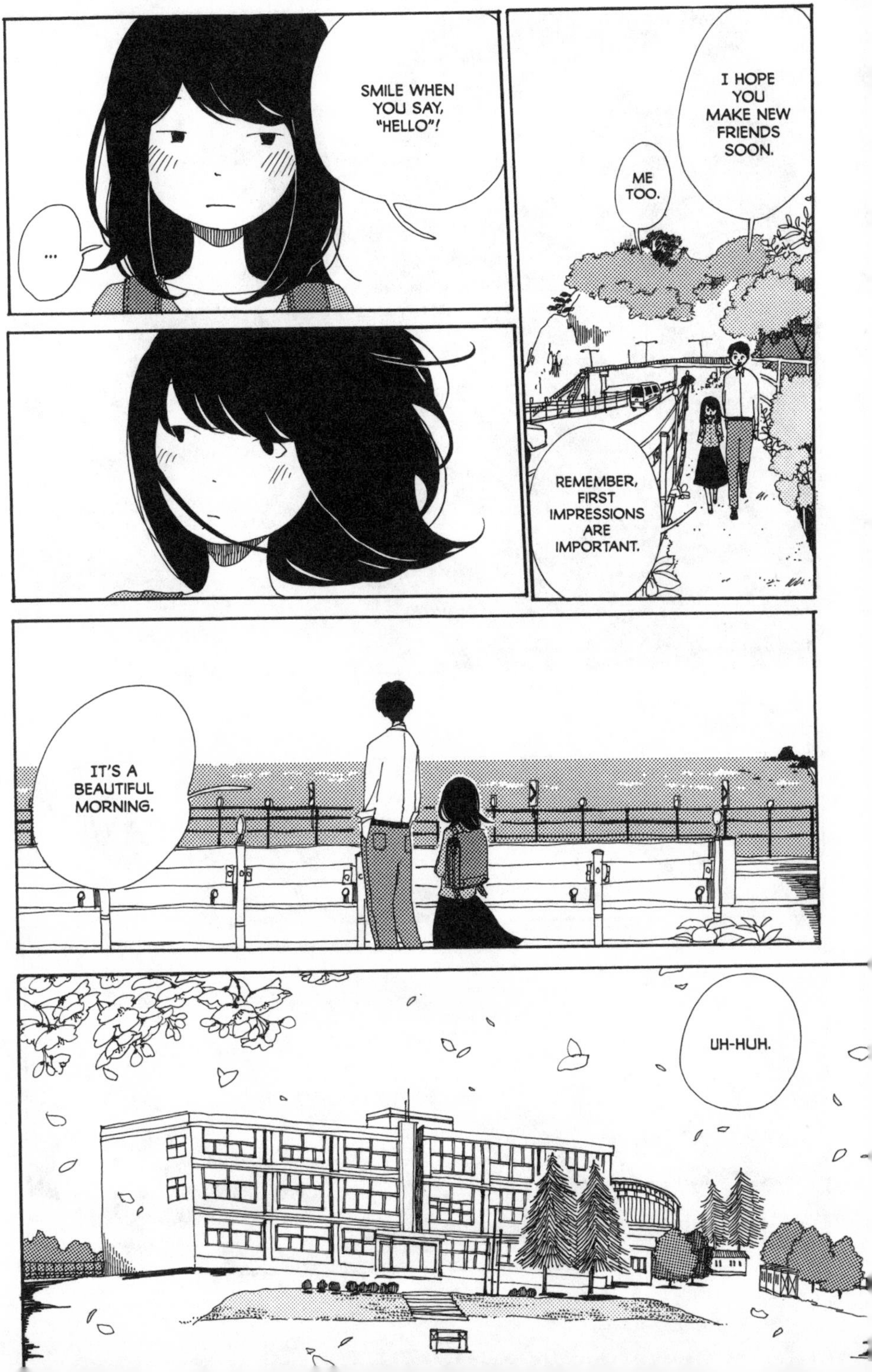
I HOPE YOU MAKE NEW FRIENDS SOON.
ME TOO.
REMEMBER, FIRST IMPRESSIONS ARE IMPORTANT.
SMILE WHEN YOU SAY, "HELLO"!
...
IT'S A BEAUTIFUL MORNING.
UH-HUH.

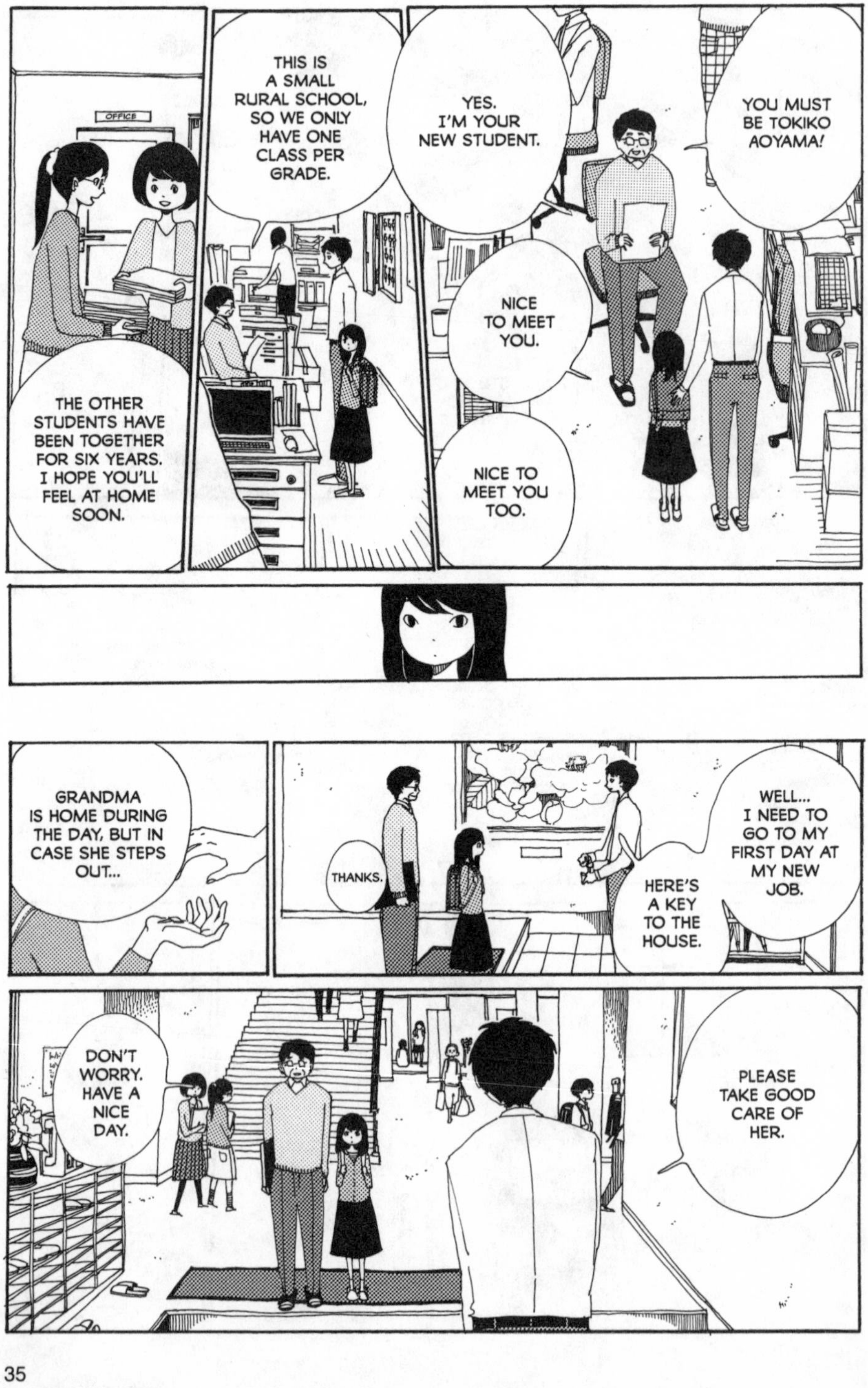
YOU MUST BE TOKIKO AOYAMA!
YES. I'M YOUR NEW STUDENT.
NICE TO MEET YOU.
NICE TO MEET YOU TOO.
THIS IS A SMALL RURAL SCHOOL, SO WE ONLY HAVE ONE CLASS PER GRADE.
OFFICE
THE OTHER STUDENTS HAVE BEEN TOGETHER FOR SIX YEARS. I HOPE YOU'LL FEEL AT HOME SOON.
WELL... I NEED TO GO TO MY FIRST DAY AT MY NEW JOB.
HERE'S A KEY TO THE HOUSE.
THANKS.
GRANDMA IS HOME DURING THE DAY, BUT IN CASE SHE STEPS OUT...
PLEASE TAKE GOOD CARE OF HER.
DON'T WORRY. HAVE A NICE DAY.

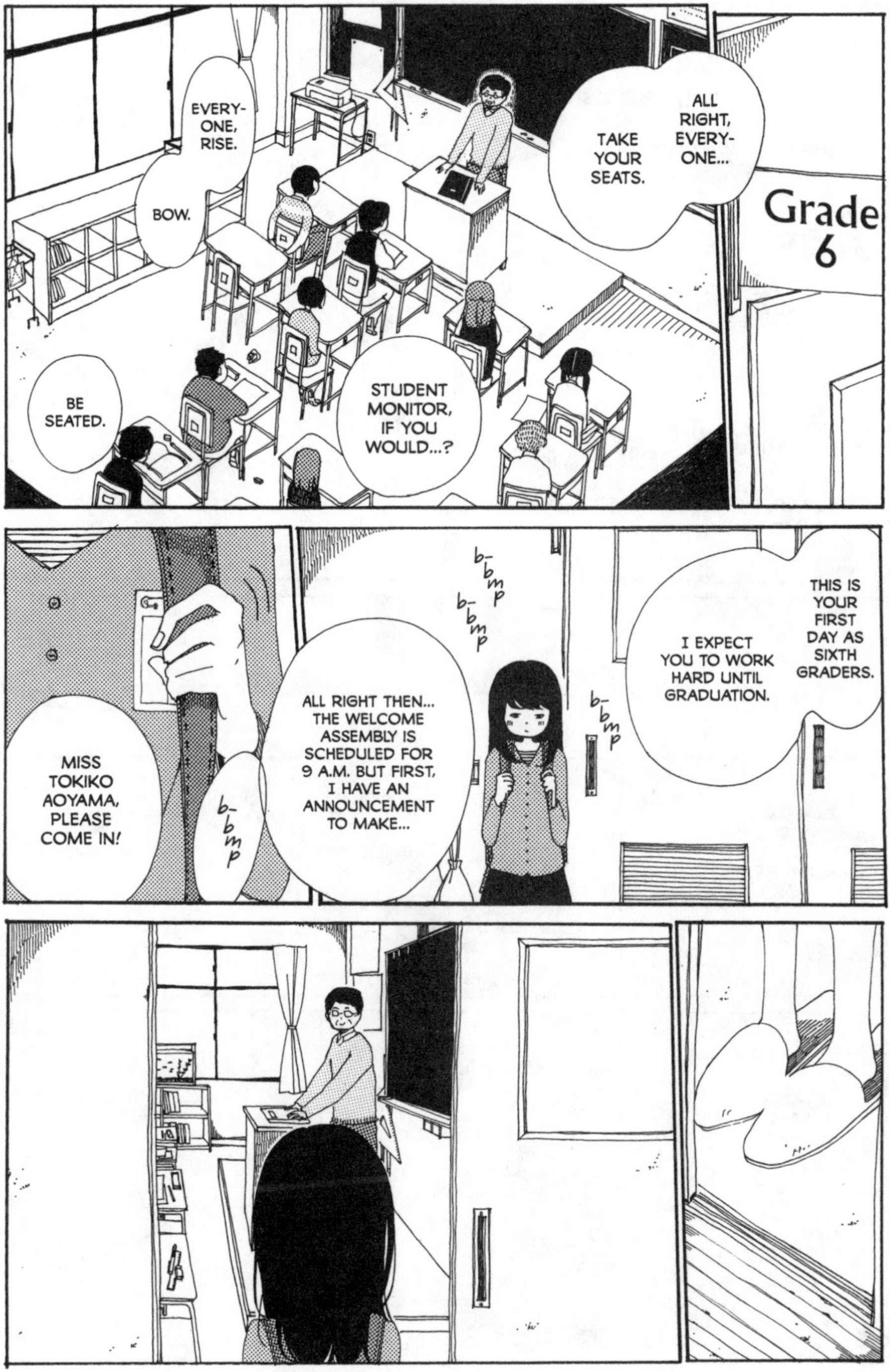
Grade 6
ALL RIGHT, EVERYONE...
TAKE YOUR SEATS.
STUDENT MONITOR, IF YOU WOULD...?
EVERYONE, RISE.
BOW.
BE SEATED.
THIS IS YOUR FIRST DAY AS SIXTH GRADERS.
I EXPECT YOU TO WORK HARD UNTIL GRADUATION.
b-bmp
b-bmp
b-bmp
ALL RIGHT THEN... THE WELCOME ASSEMBLY IS SCHEDULED FOR 9 A.M. BUT FIRST, I HAVE AN ANNOUNCEMENT TO MAKE...
b-bmp
MISS TOKIKO AOYAMA, PLEASE COME IN!

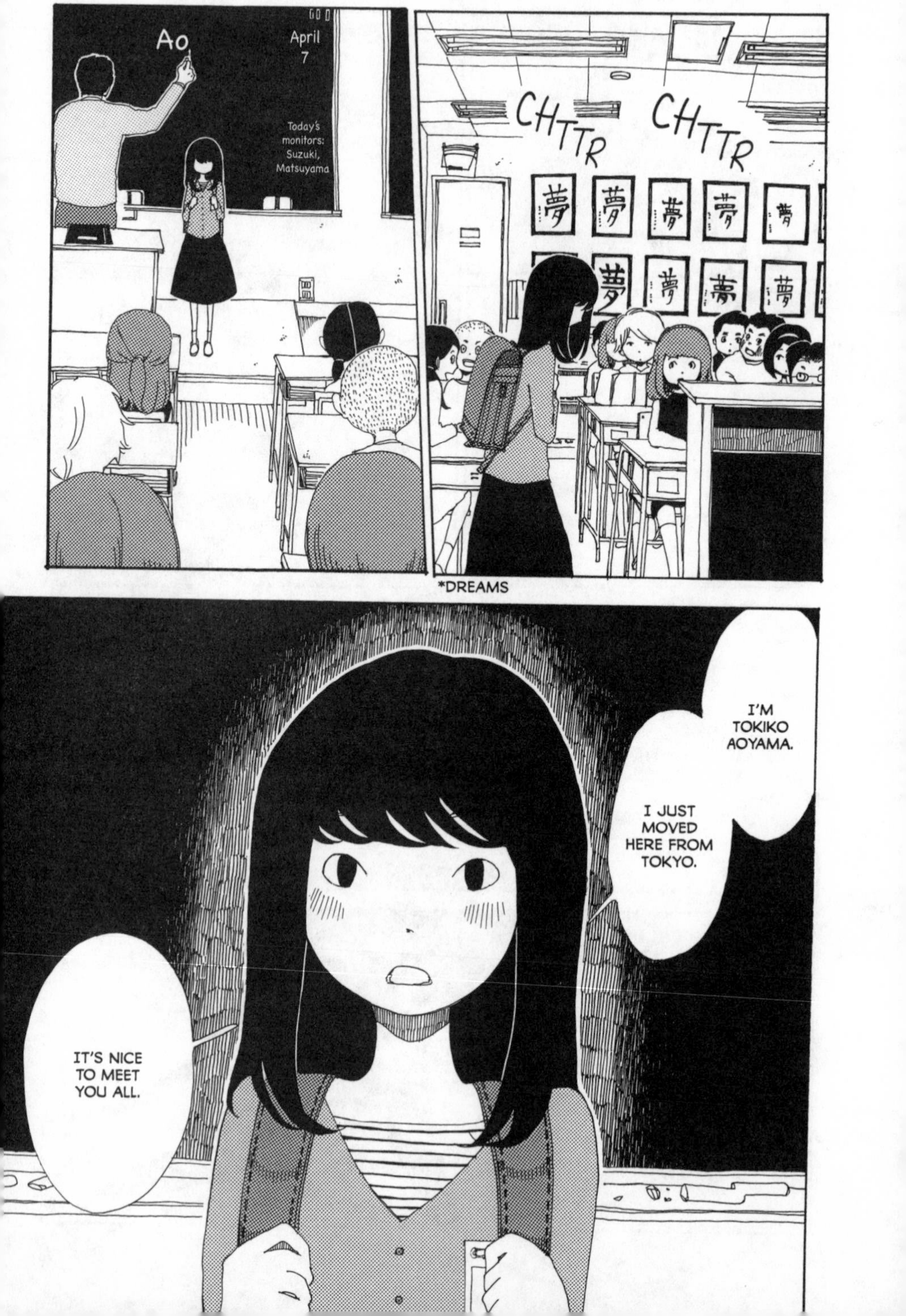
CHTTR CHTTR
*DREAMS
Ao
April 7
Today's monitors: Suzuki, Matsuyama
I'M TOKIKO AOYAMA.
I JUST MOVED HERE FROM TOKYO.
IT'S NICE TO MEET YOU ALL.

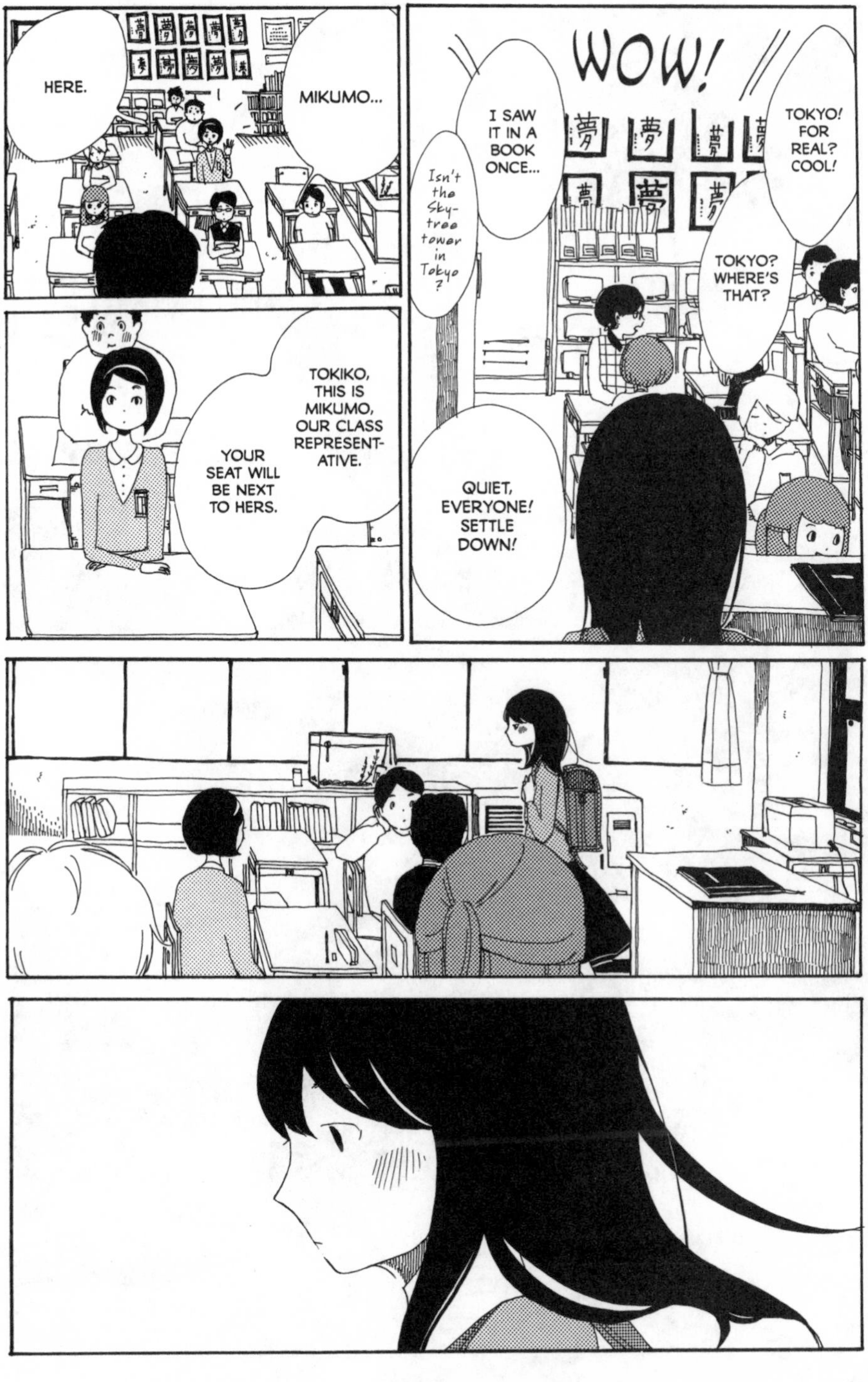
TOKYO! FOR REAL? COOL!
WOW!
TOKYO? WHERE'S THAT?
I SAW IT IN A BOOK ONCE...
Isn't the Sky-tree tower in Tokyo?
QUIET, EVERYONE! SETTLE DOWN!
MIKUMO...
HERE.
TOKIKO, THIS IS MIKUMO, OUR CLASS REPRESENT-ATIVE.
YOUR SEAT WILL BE NEXT TO HERS.

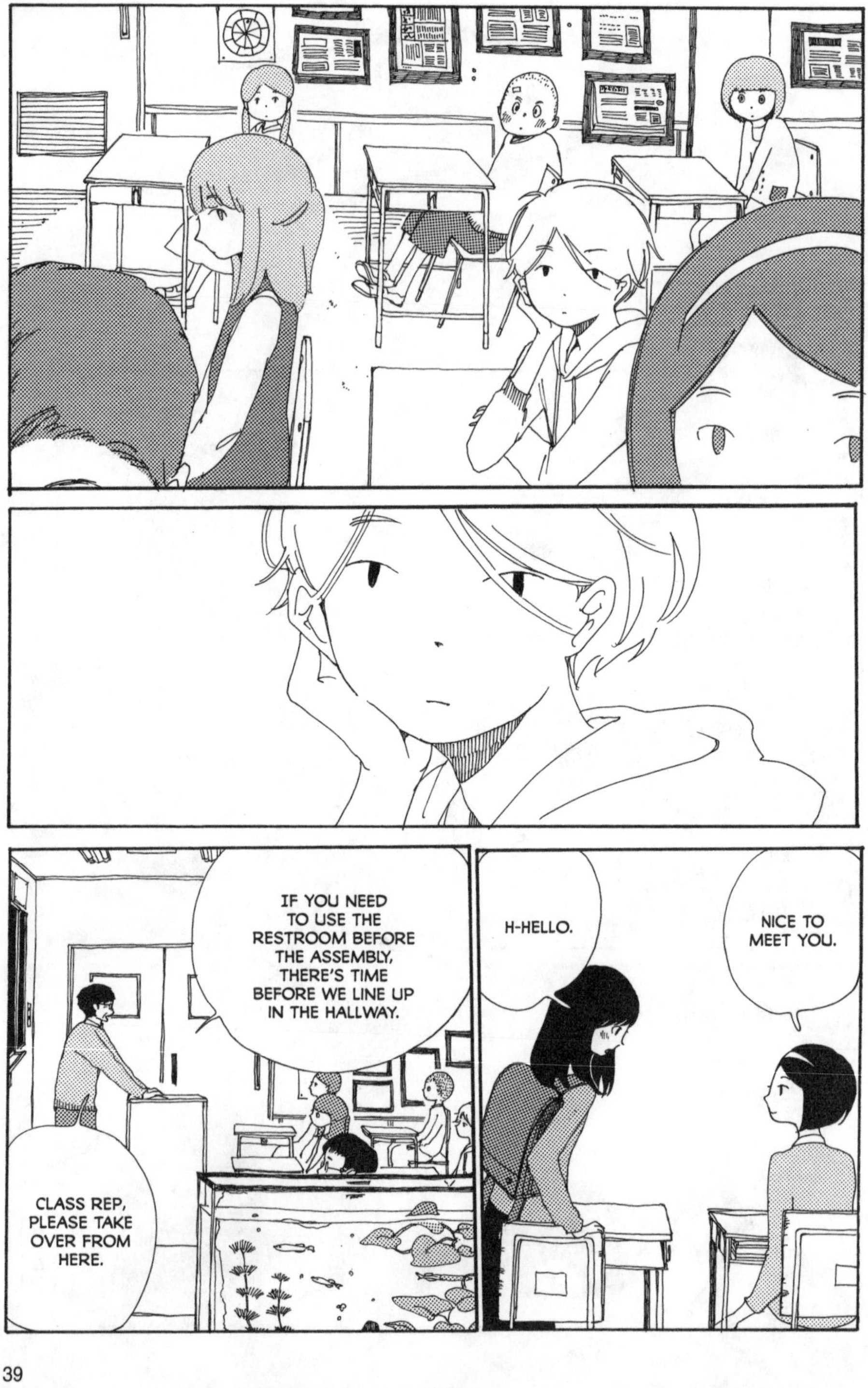
NICE TO MEET YOU.
H-HELLO.
IF YOU NEED TO USE THE RESTROOM BEFORE THE ASSEMBLY, THERE'S TIME BEFORE WE LINE UP IN THE HALLWAY.
CLASS REP, PLEASE TAKE OVER FROM HERE.

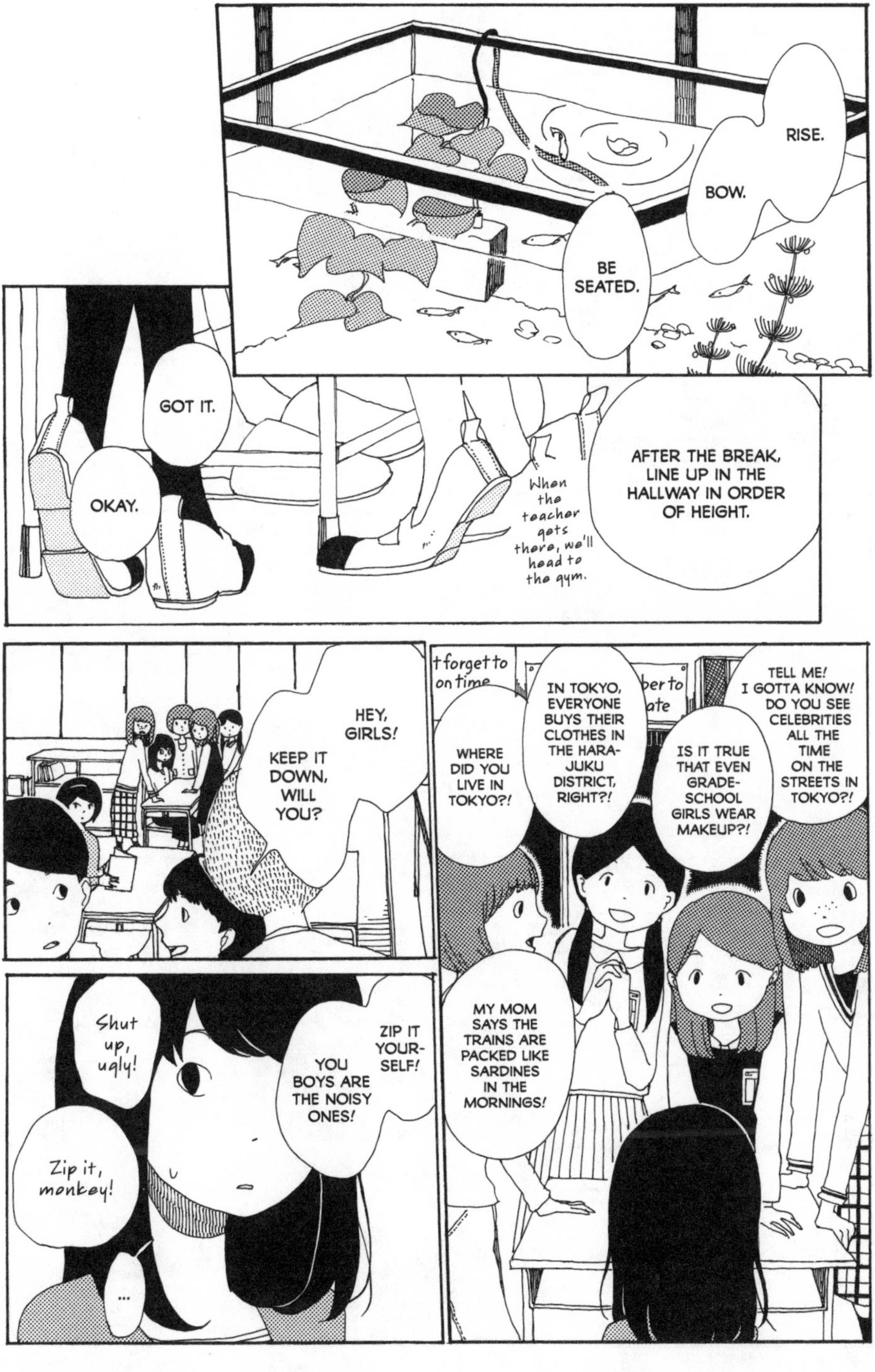
RISE.
BOW.
BE SEATED.
AFTER THE BREAK, LINE UP IN THE HALLWAY IN ORDER OF HEIGHT.
When the teacher gets there, we'll head to the gym.
GOT IT.
OKAY.
TELL ME! I GOTTA KNOW! DO YOU SEE CELEBRITIES ALL THE TIME ON THE STREETS IN TOKYO?!
IS IT TRUE THAT EVEN GRADE-SCHOOL GIRLS WEAR MAKEUP?!
IN TOKYO, EVERYONE BUYS THEIR CLOTHES IN THE HARA-JUKU DISTRICT, RIGHT?!
WHERE DID YOU LIVE IN TOKYO?!
MY MOM SAYS THE TRAINS ARE PACKED LIKE SARDINES IN THE MORNINGS!
HEY, GIRLS!
KEEP IT DOWN, WILL YOU?
ZIP IT YOUR-SELF!
YOU BOYS ARE THE NOISY ONES!
Shut up, ugly!
Zip it, monkey!
...

UM... WHERE'S THE REST-ROOM?
THE NEAREST ONE IS OUT IN THE HALLWAY TO THE LEFT, NEXT TO THE STAIRWELL.
WANT ME TO TAKE YOU?
UM...NO. I CAN FIND IT MYSELF.
I'M, UH... GOING TO USE IT BEFORE THE ASSEMBLY.
OKAY.
SEE YOU IN LINE.
TOKYO GIRLS ARE DIFFERENT...
INDE-PENDENT, JUST LIKE THEY SAY.
So cool!
Ha ha ha ha
So last night, on that singing competition—
Oh, I forgot to watch it!
Cleaning supplies
Bathroom monitor duties
Sigh
CHAK

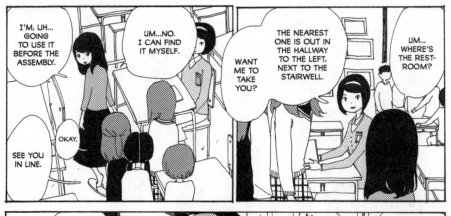

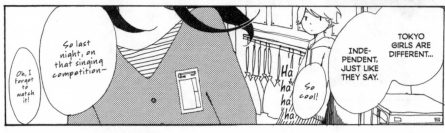

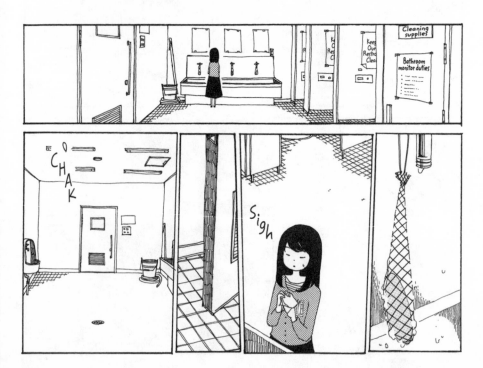

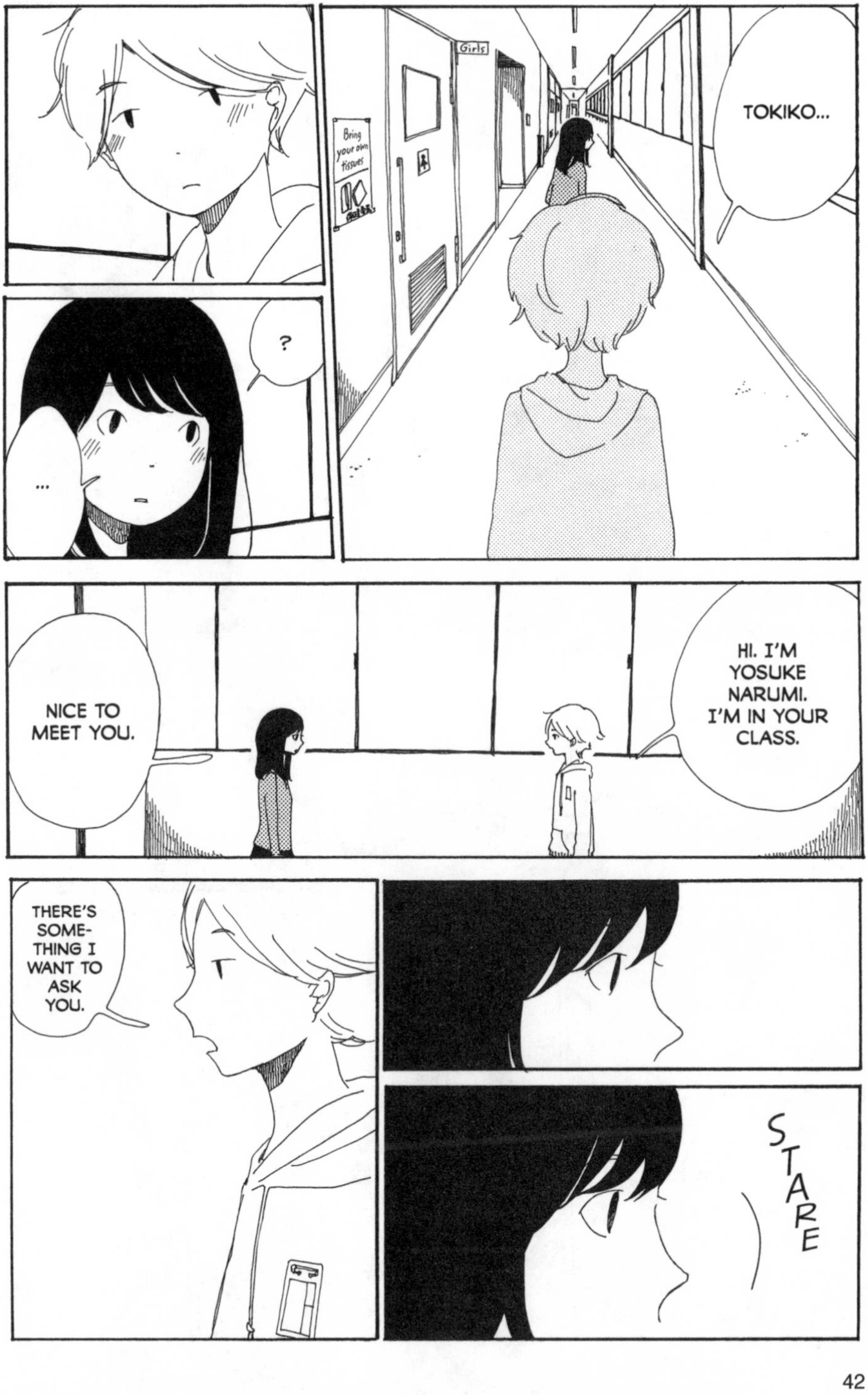
Girls
Bring your own tissues
TOKIKO...
?
...
HI. I'M YOSUKE NARUMI. I'M IN YOUR CLASS.
NICE TO MEET YOU.
STARE
THERE'S SOME-THING I WANT TO ASK YOU.

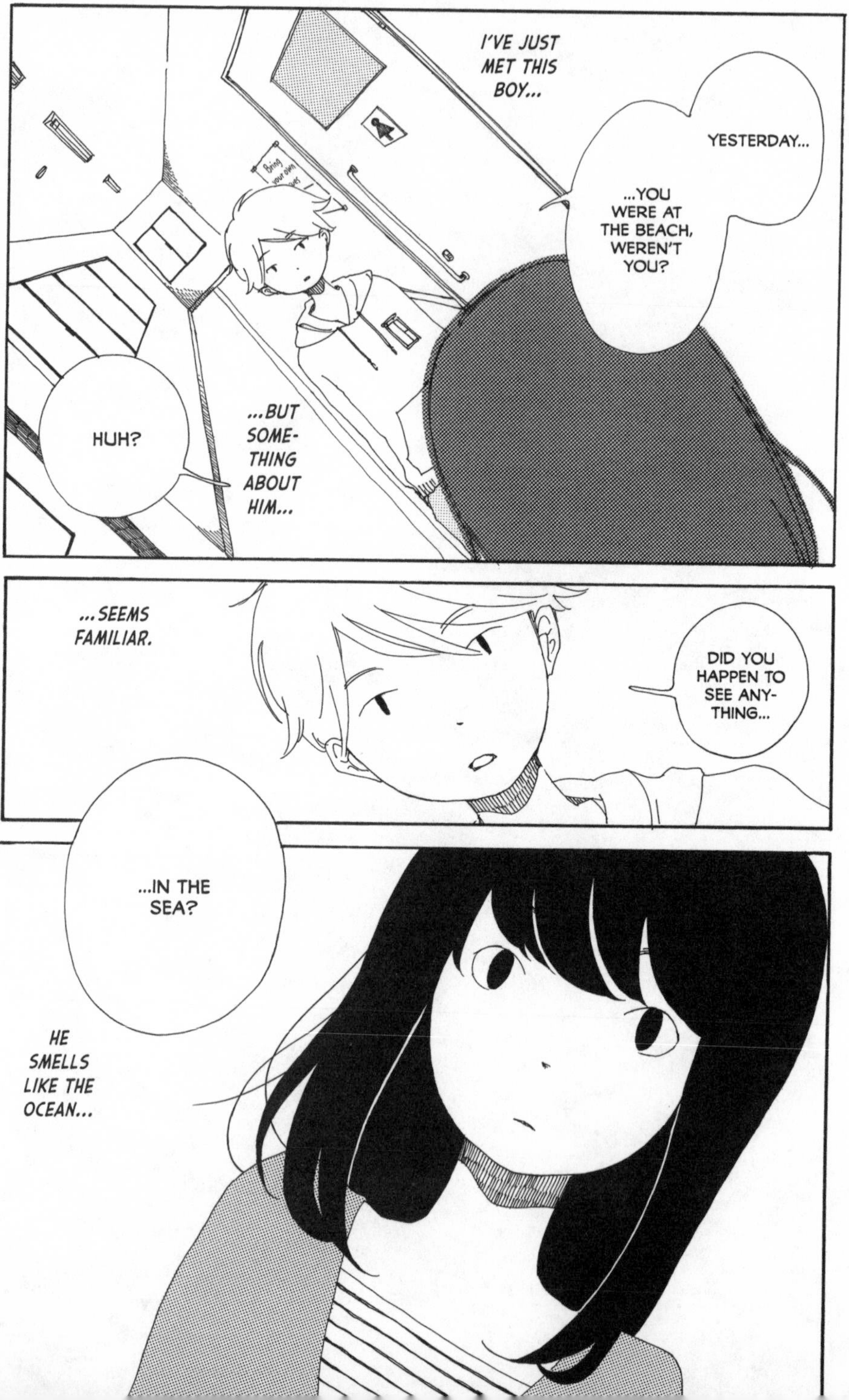
YESTERDAY...
...YOU WERE AT THE BEACH, WEREN'T YOU?
I'VE JUST MET THIS BOY...
...BUT SOMETHING ABOUT HIM...
HUH?
DID YOU HAPPEN TO SEE ANY-THING...
...SEEMS FAMILIAR.
...IN THE SEA?
HE SMELLS LIKE THE OCEAN...

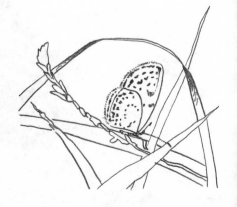

{Two} Depths

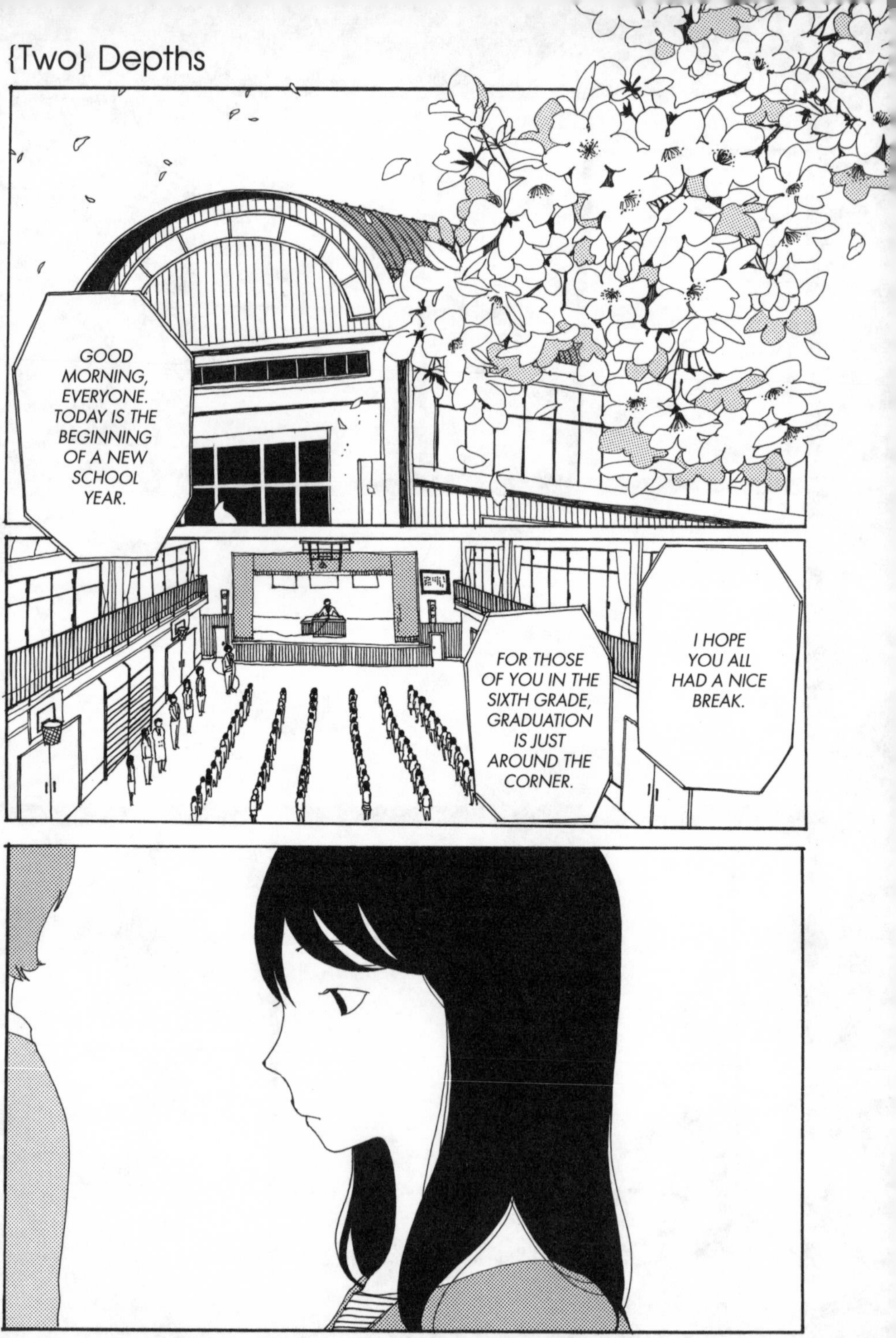
GOOD MORNING, EVERYONE. TODAY IS THE BEGINNING OF A NEW SCHOOL YEAR.
I HOPE YOU ALL HAD A NICE BREAK.
FOR THOSE OF YOU IN THE SIXTH GRADE, GRADUATION IS JUST AROUND THE CORNER.

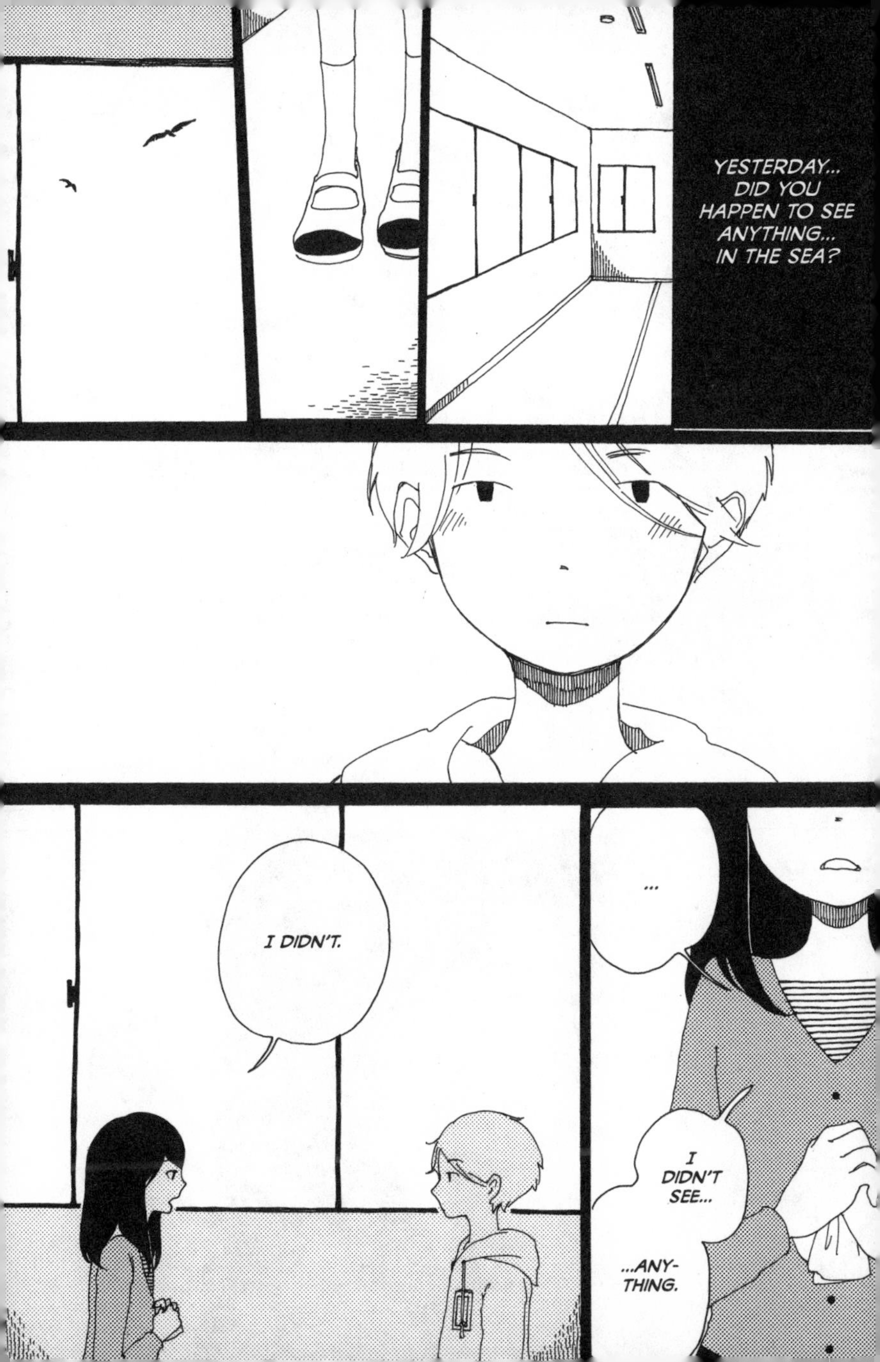
YESTERDAY... DID YOU HAPPEN TO SEE ANYTHING... IN THE SEA?
...
I DIDN'T SEE...
...ANY-THING.
I DIDN'T.

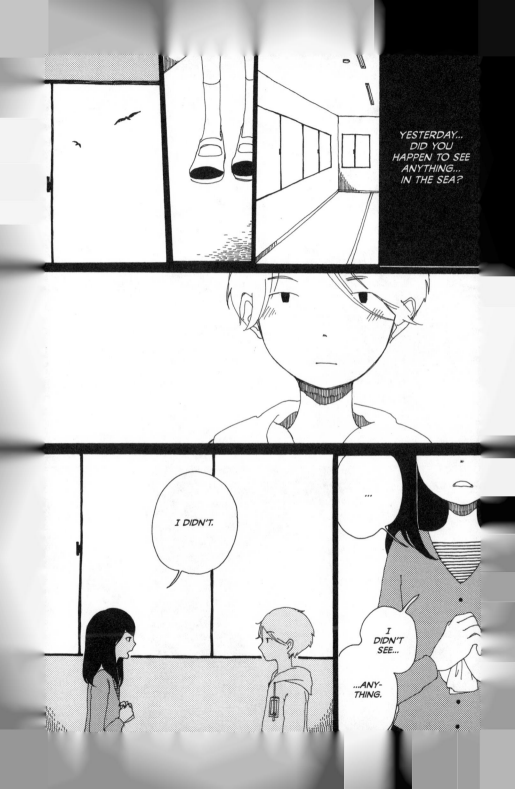

{Two} Depths

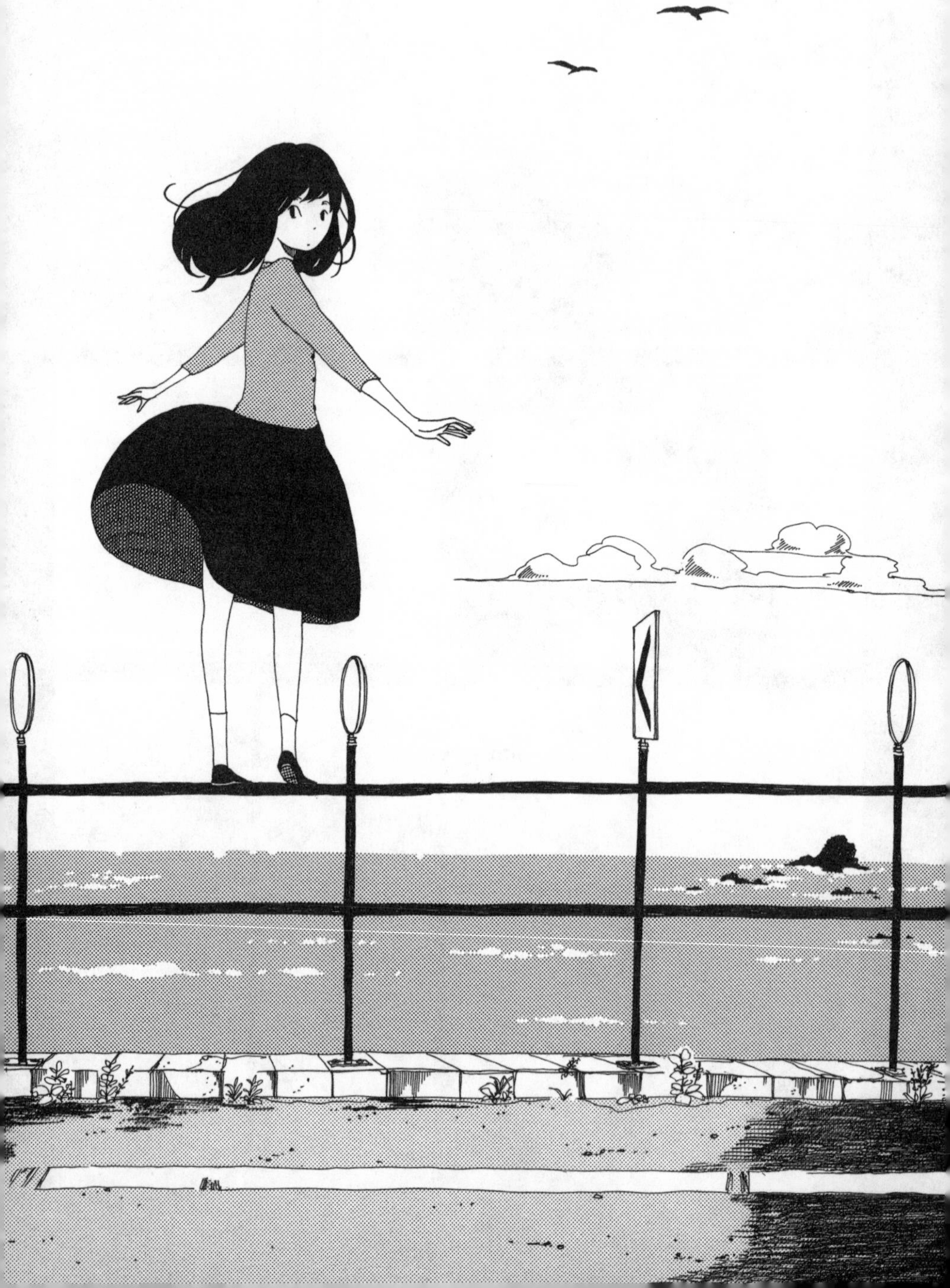

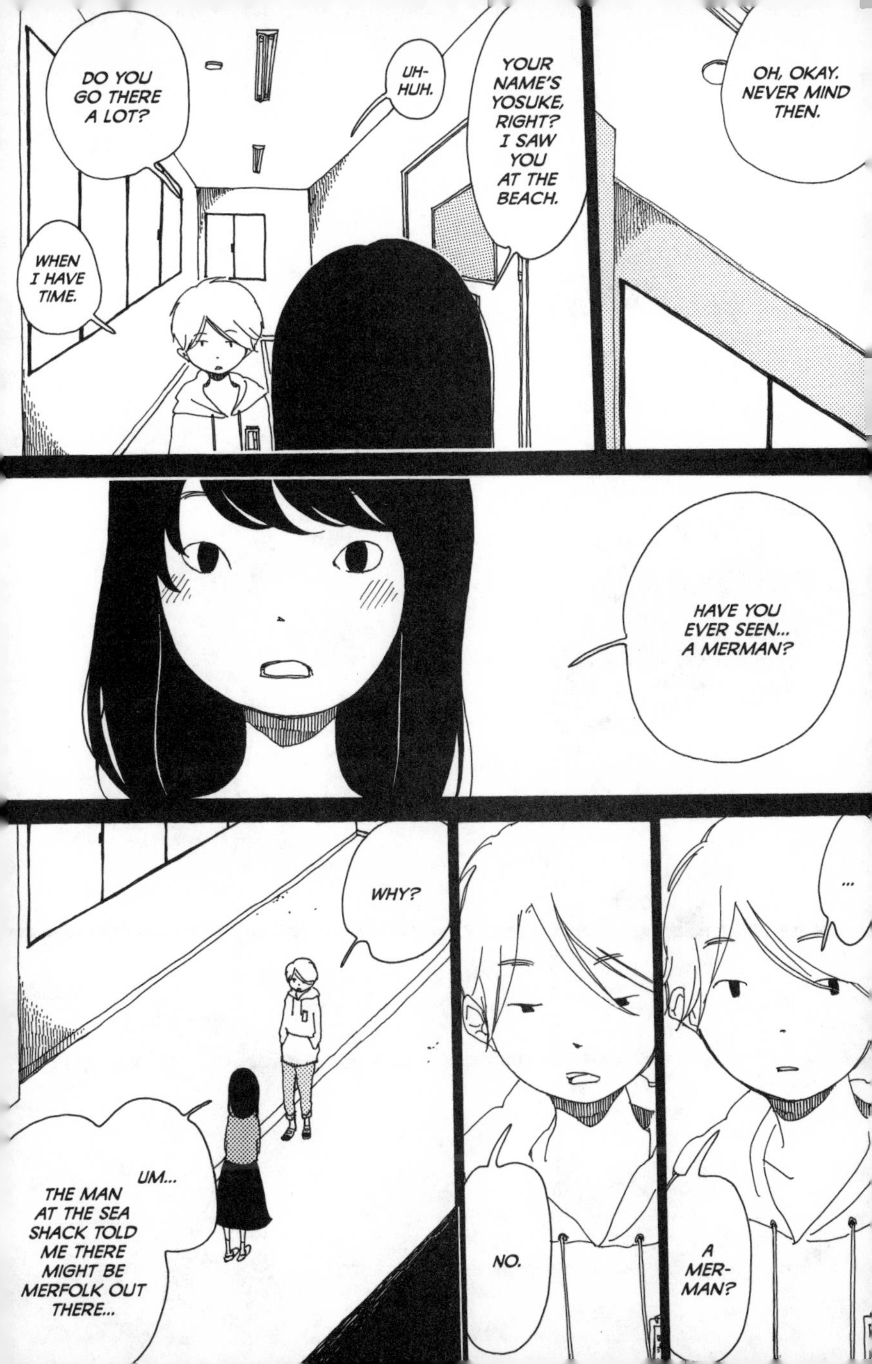
OH, OKAY. NEVER MIND THEN.
YOUR NAME'S YOSUKE, RIGHT? I SAW YOU AT THE BEACH.
UH-HUH.
DO YOU GO THERE A LOT?
WHEN I HAVE TIME.
HAVE YOU EVER SEEN... A MERMAN?
...
A MER-MAN?
NO.
WHY?
UM...
THE MAN AT THE SEA SHACK TOLD ME THERE MIGHT BE MERFOLK OUT THERE...

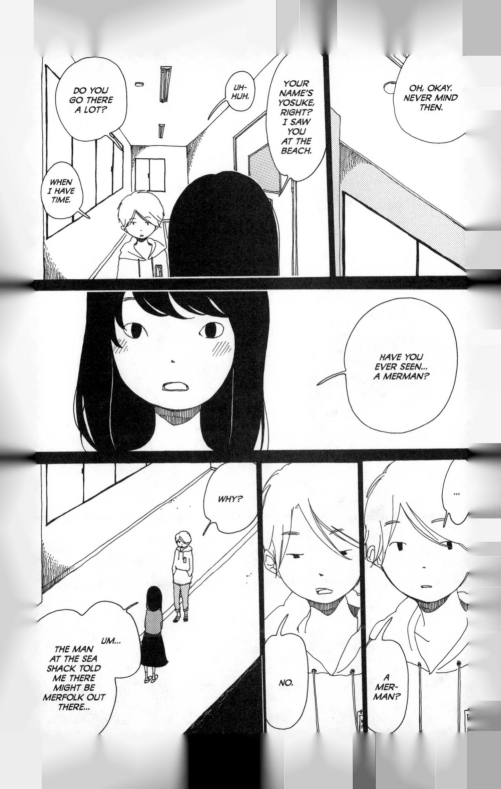

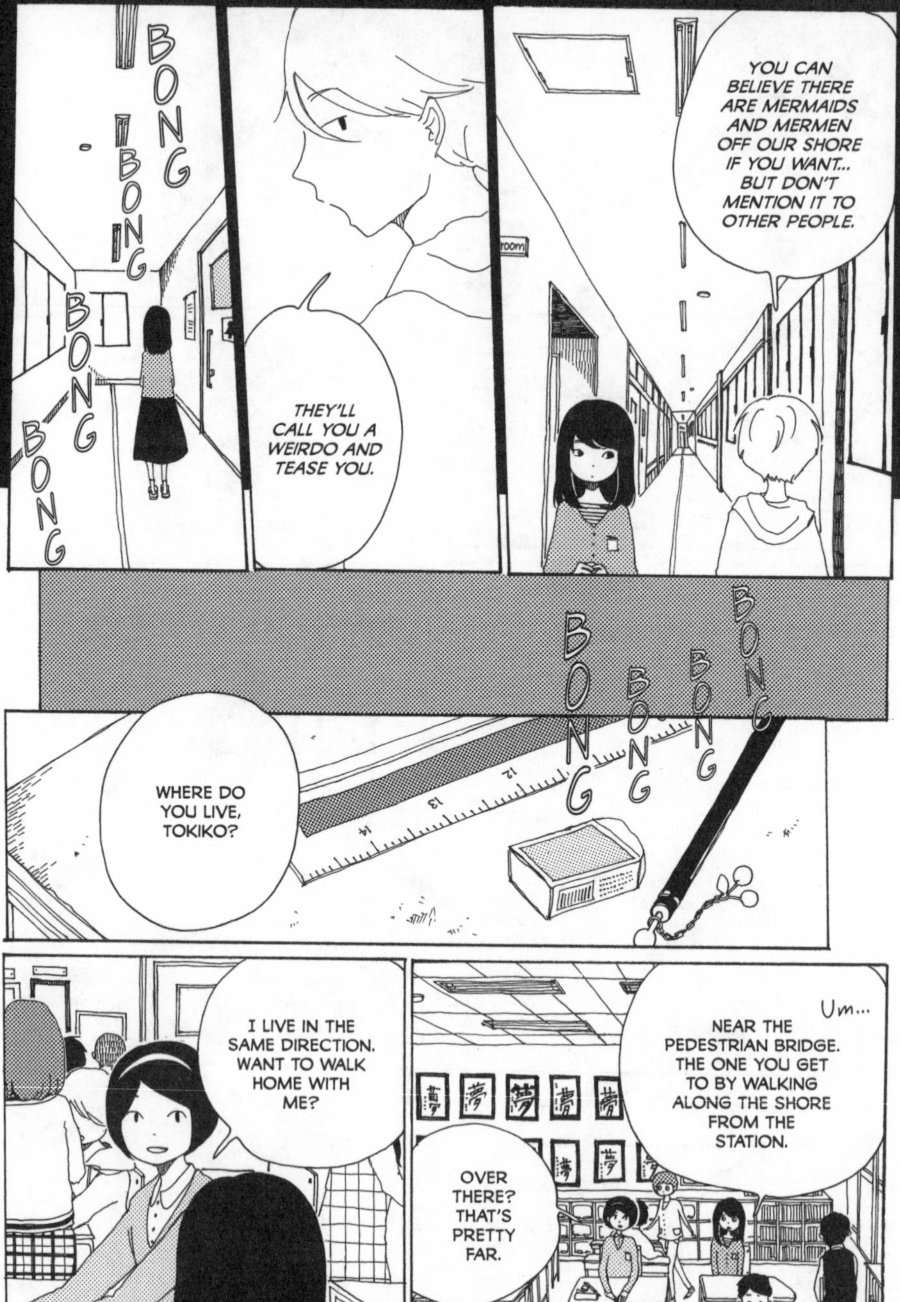
YOU CAN BELIEVE THERE ARE MERMAIDS AND MERMEN OFF OUR SHORE IF YOU WANT... BUT DON'T MENTION IT TO OTHER PEOPLE.
room
THEY'LL CALL YOU A WEIRDO AND TEASE YOU.
BONG
BONG
BONG
BONG
BONG
BONG
BONG
BONG
WHERE DO YOU LIVE, TOKIKO?
Um...
NEAR THE PEDESTRIAN BRIDGE. THE ONE YOU GET TO BY WALKING ALONG THE SHORE FROM THE STATION.
OVER THERE? THAT'S PRETTY FAR.
I LIVE IN THE SAME DIRECTION. WANT TO WALK HOME WITH ME?

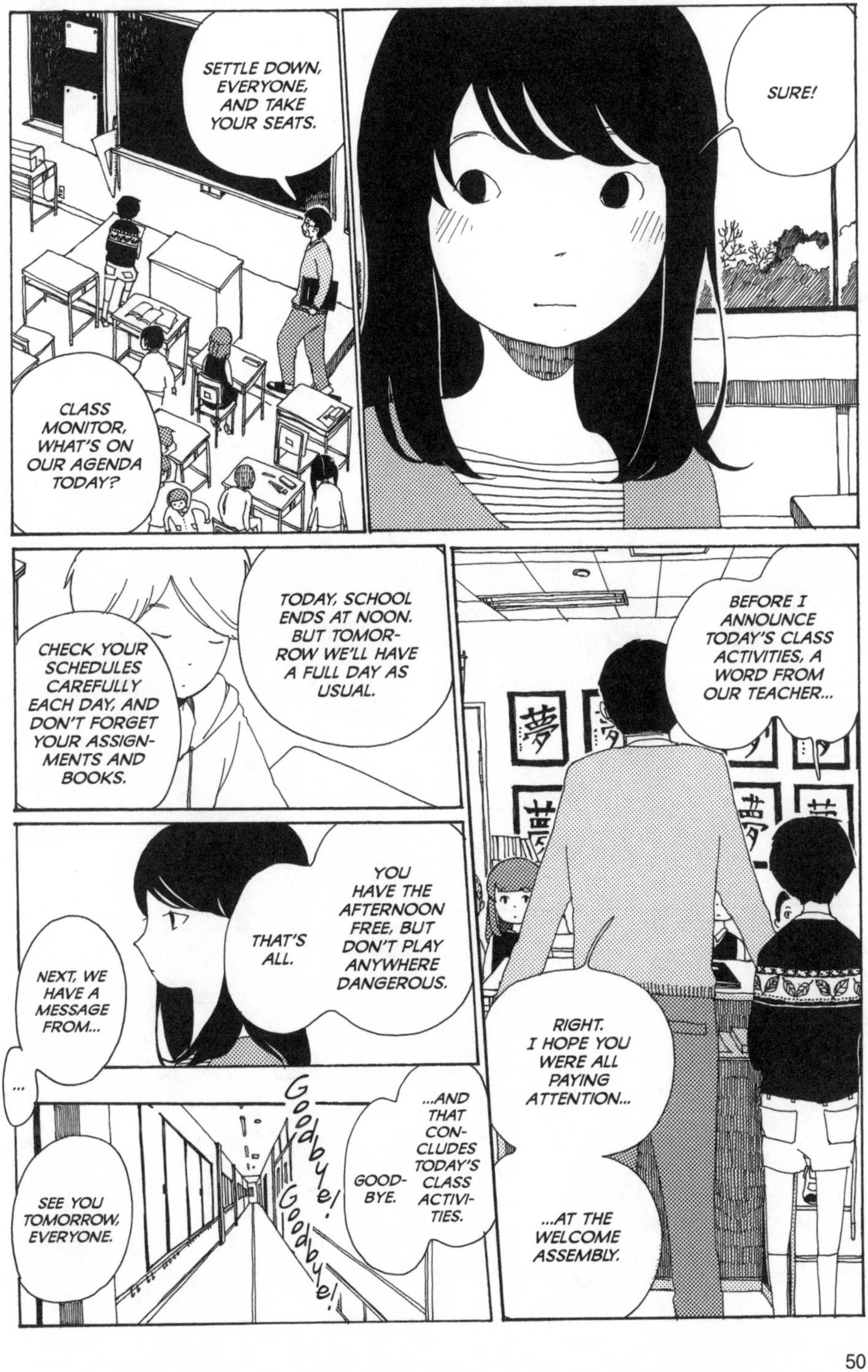
SURE!
SETTLE DOWN, EVERYONE, AND TAKE YOUR SEATS.
CLASS MONITOR, WHAT'S ON OUR AGENDA TODAY?
BEFORE I ANNOUNCE TODAY'S CLASS ACTIVITIES, A WORD FROM OUR TEACHER...
RIGHT. I HOPE YOU WERE ALL PAYING ATTENTION...
...AT THE WELCOME ASSEMBLY.
TODAY, SCHOOL ENDS AT NOON. BUT TOMORROW WE'LL HAVE A FULL DAY AS USUAL.
CHECK YOUR SCHEDULES CAREFULLY EACH DAY, AND DON'T FORGET YOUR ASSIGNMENTS AND BOOKS.
YOU HAVE THE AFTERNOON FREE, BUT DON'T PLAY ANYWHERE DANGEROUS.
THAT'S ALL.
NEXT, WE HAVE A MESSAGE FROM...
...
...AND THAT CONCLUDES TODAY'S CLASS ACTIVITIES.
GOODBYE.
Goodbye!
Goodbye!
SEE YOU TOMORROW, EVERYONE.

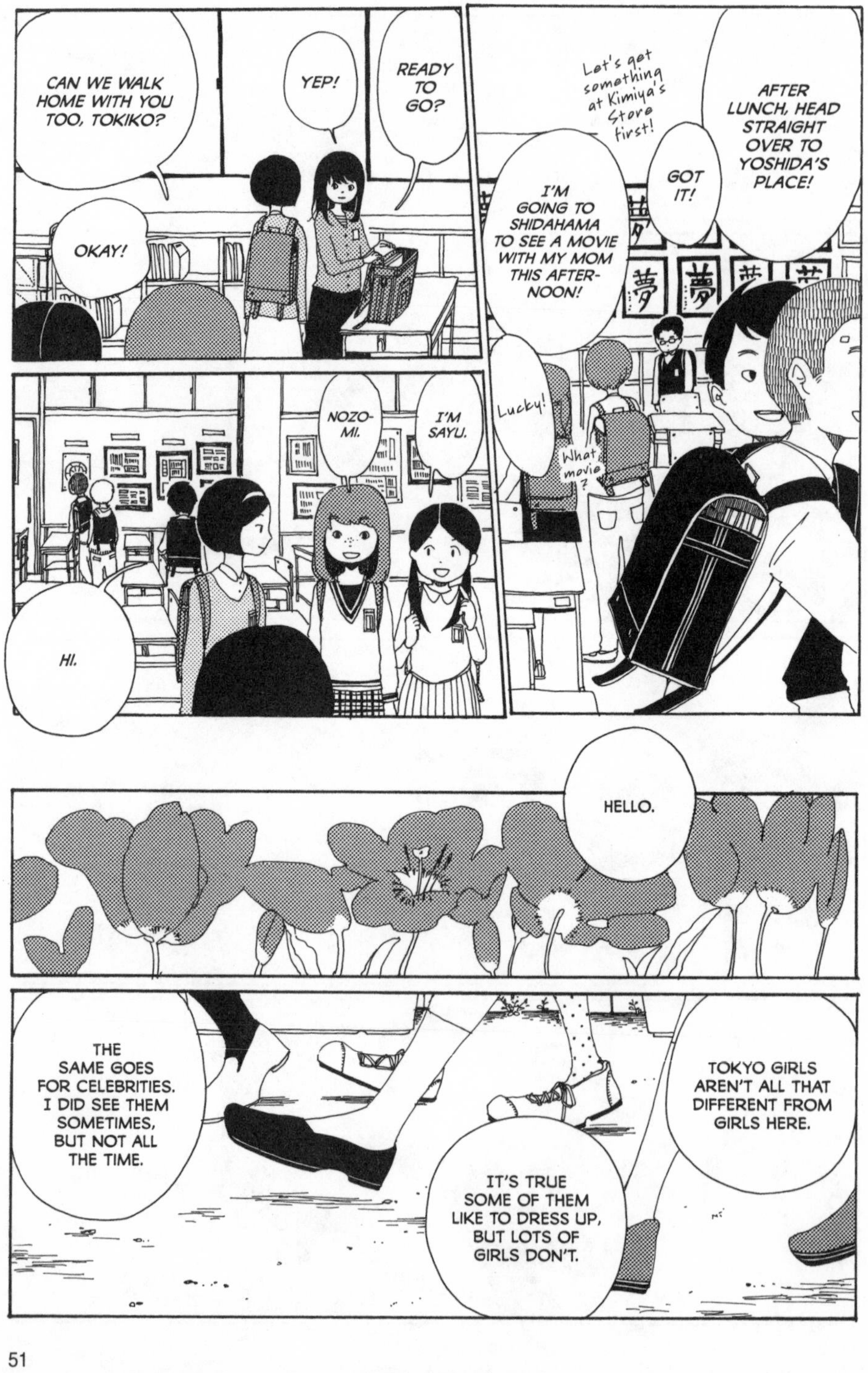
AFTER LUNCH, HEAD STRAIGHT OVER TO YOSHIDA'S PLACE!
GOT IT!
Let's get something at Kimiya's Store first!
I'M GOING TO SHIDAHAMA TO SEE A MOVIE WITH MY MOM THIS AFTER-NOON!
Lucky!
What movie?
READY TO GO?
YEP!
CAN WE WALK HOME WITH YOU TOO, TOKIKO?
OKAY!
I'M SAYU.
NOZO-MI.
HI.
HELLO.
TOKYO GIRLS AREN'T ALL THAT DIFFERENT FROM GIRLS HERE.
IT'S TRUE SOME OF THEM LIKE TO DRESS UP, BUT LOTS OF GIRLS DON'T.
THE SAME GOES FOR CELEBRITIES. I DID SEE THEM SOMETIMES, BUT NOT ALL THE TIME.

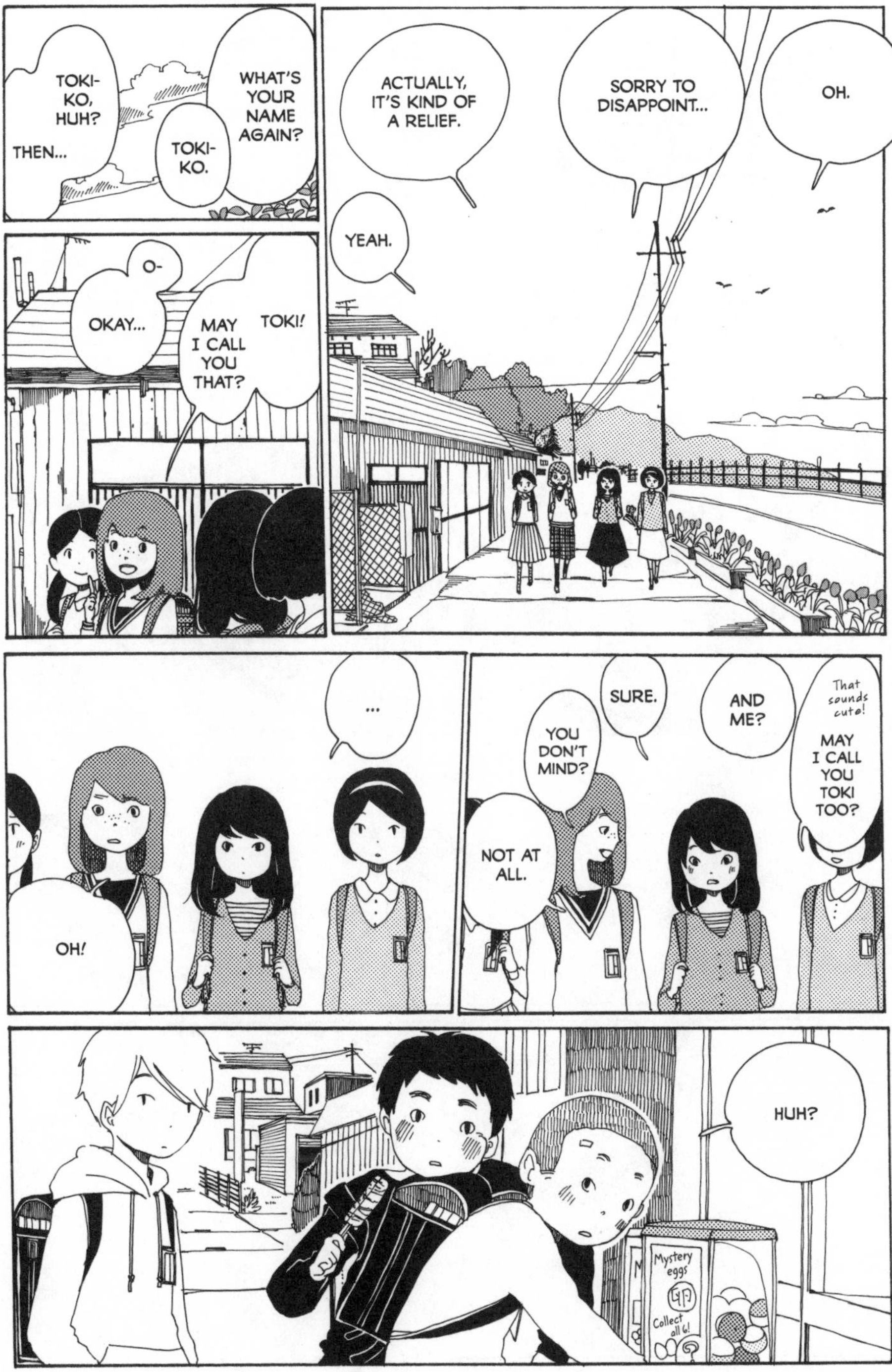
OH.
SORRY TO DISAPPOINT...
ACTUALLY, IT'S KIND OF A RELIEF.
YEAH.
WHAT'S YOUR NAME AGAIN?
TOKI-KO.
TOKI-KO, HUH?
THEN...
TOKI!
MAY I CALL YOU THAT?
O-
OKAY...
That sounds cute!
MAY I CALL YOU TOKI TOO?
AND ME?
SURE.
YOU DON'T MIND?
NOT AT ALL.
...
OH!
HUH?
Mystery eggs
Collect all 6!

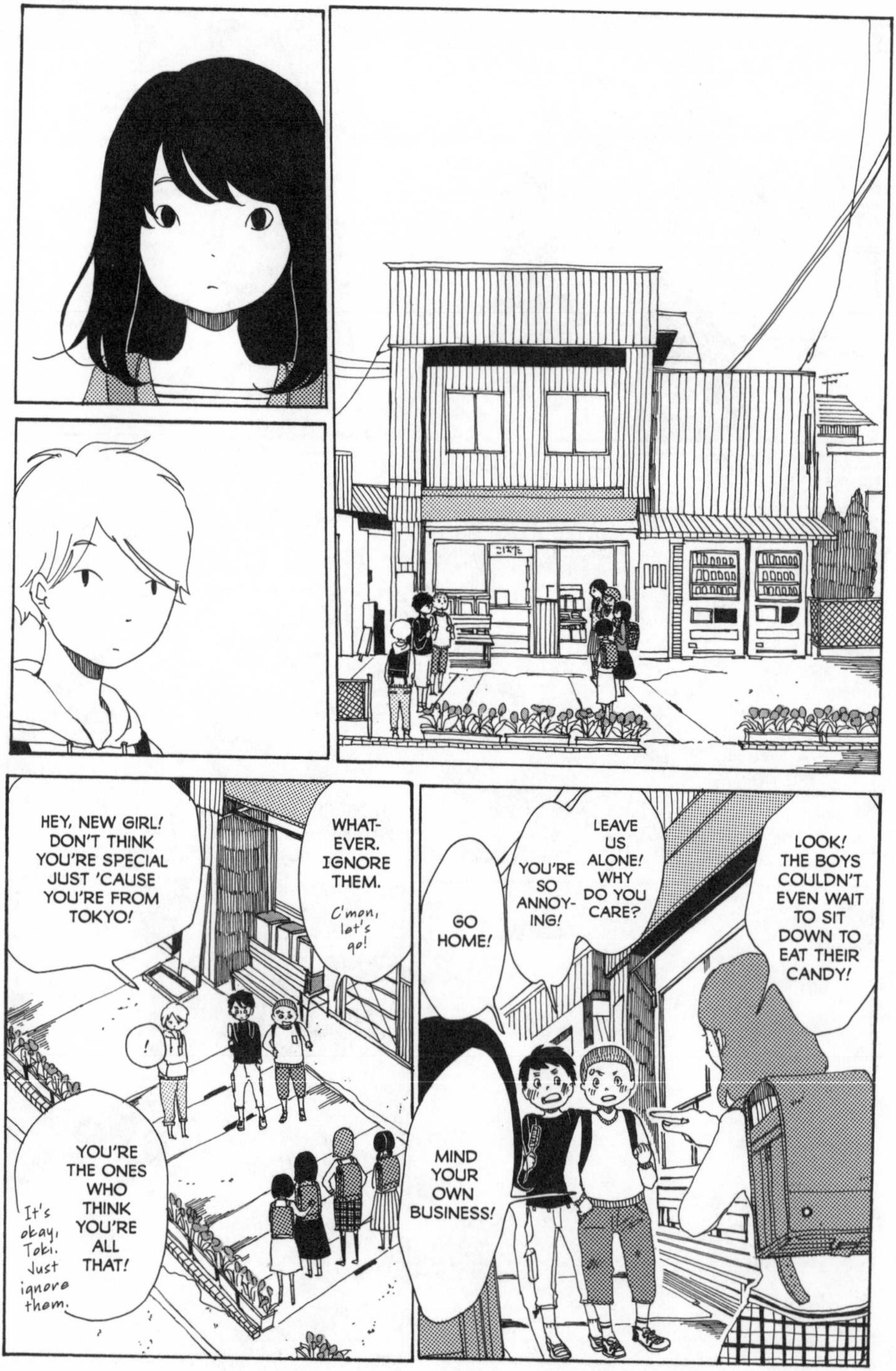
LOOK! THE BOYS COULDN'T EVEN WAIT TO SIT DOWN TO EAT THEIR CANDY!
LEAVE US ALONE! WHY DO YOU CARE?
YOU'RE SO ANNOY-ING!
GO HOME!
MIND YOUR OWN BUSINESS!
WHAT-EVER. IGNORE THEM.
C'mon, let's go!
HEY, NEW GIRL! DON'T THINK YOU'RE SPECIAL JUST 'CAUSE YOU'RE FROM TOKYO!
!
YOU'RE THE ONES WHO THINK YOU'RE ALL THAT!
It's okay, Toki. Just ignore them.

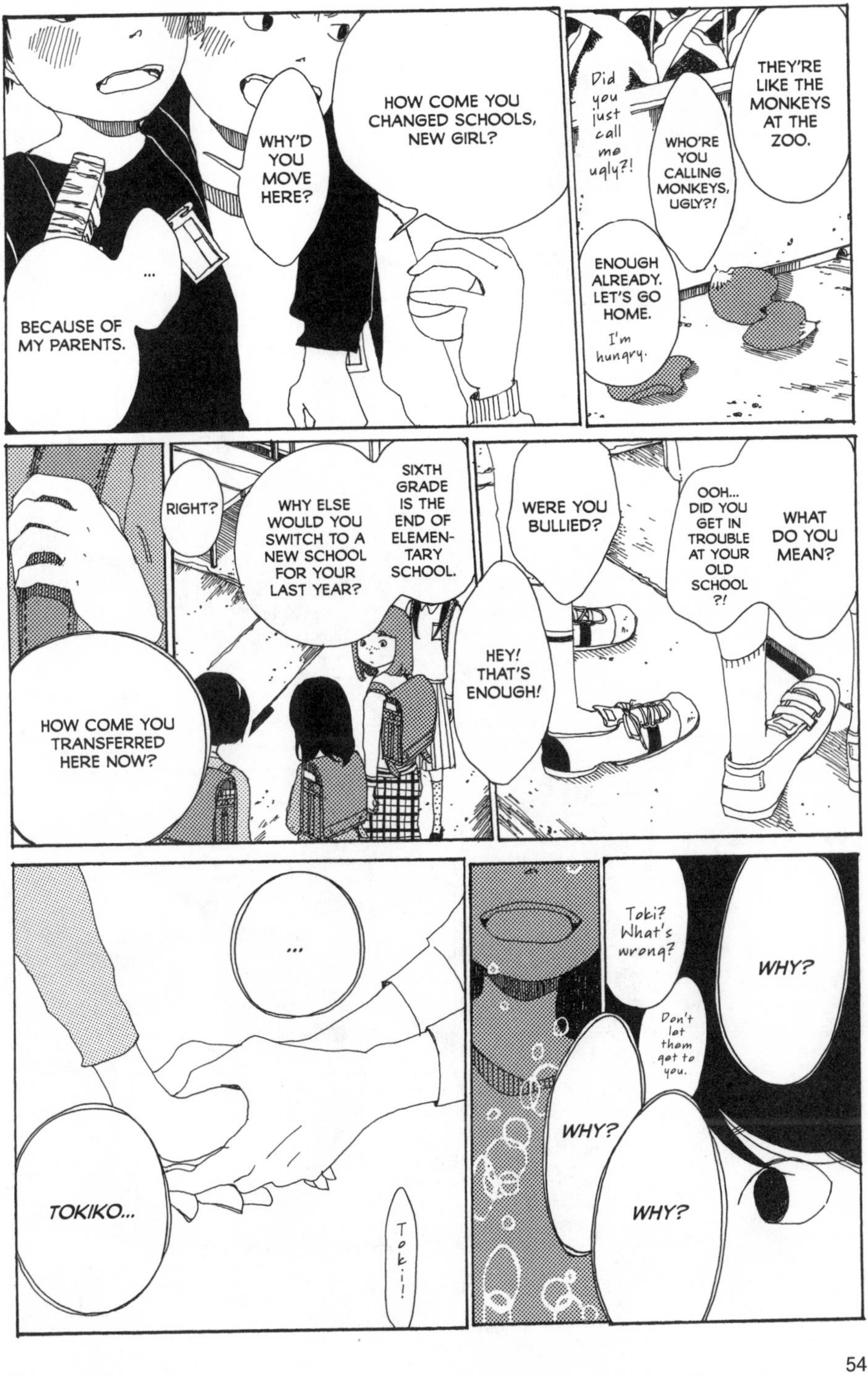
THEY'RE LIKE THE MONKEYS AT THE ZOO.
WHO'RE YOU CALLING MONKEYS, UGLY?!
Did you just call me ugly?!
ENOUGH ALREADY. LET'S GO HOME.
I'm hungry.
HOW COME YOU CHANGED SCHOOLS, NEW GIRL?
WHY'D YOU MOVE HERE?
...
BECAUSE OF MY PARENTS.
WHAT DO YOU MEAN?
OOH... DID YOU GET IN TROUBLE AT YOUR OLD SCHOOL?!
WERE YOU BULLIED?
HEY! THAT'S ENOUGH!
SIXTH GRADE IS THE END OF ELEMENTARY SCHOOL.
WHY ELSE WOULD YOU SWITCH TO A NEW SCHOOL FOR YOUR LAST YEAR?
RIGHT?
HOW COME YOU TRANSFERRED HERE NOW?
WHY?
Toki? What's wrong?
Don't let them get to you.
WHY?
WHY?
...
Toki...!
TOKIKO...

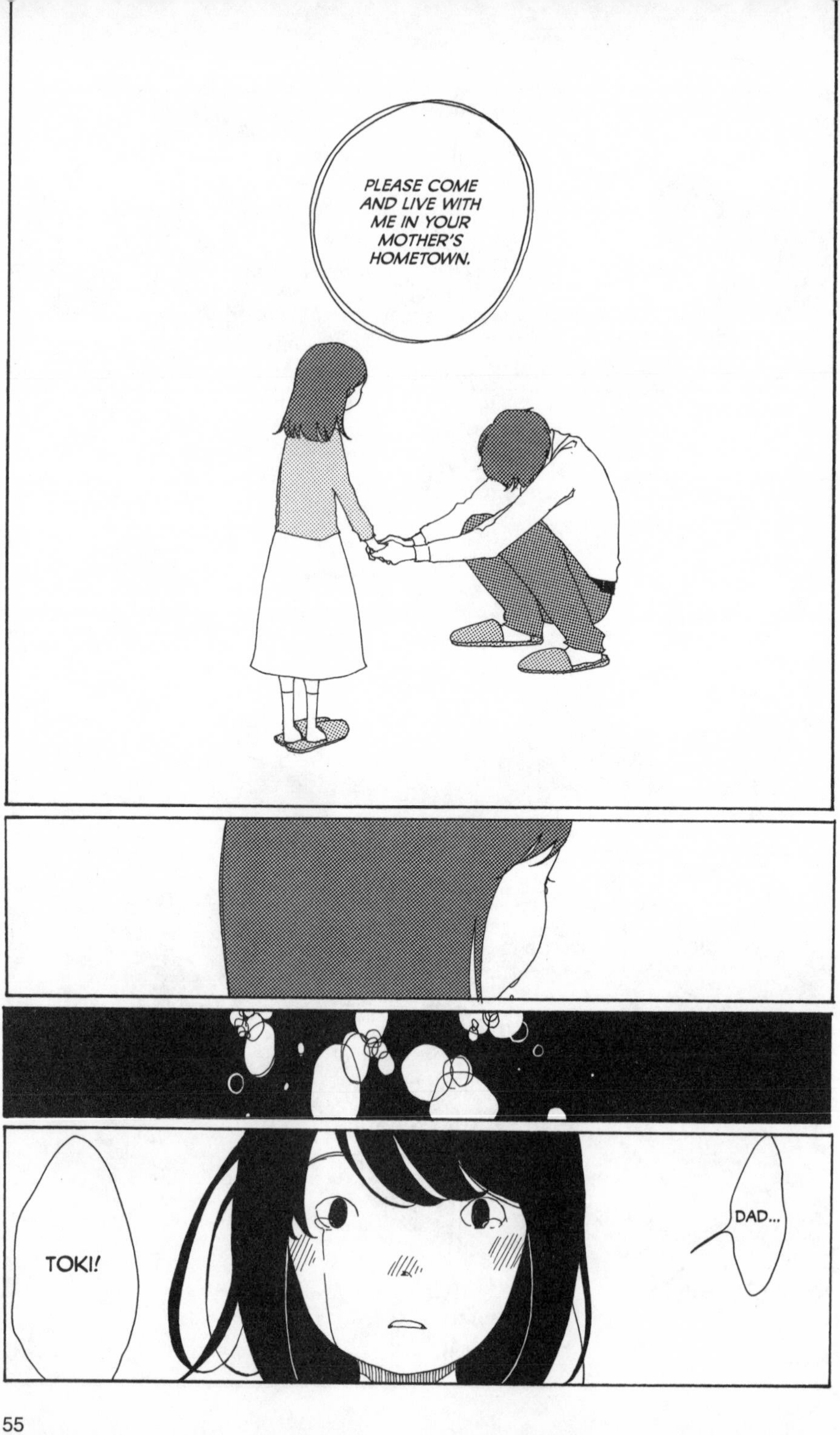
PLEASE COME AND LIVE WITH ME IN YOUR MOTHER'S HOMETOWN.
DAD...
TOKI!

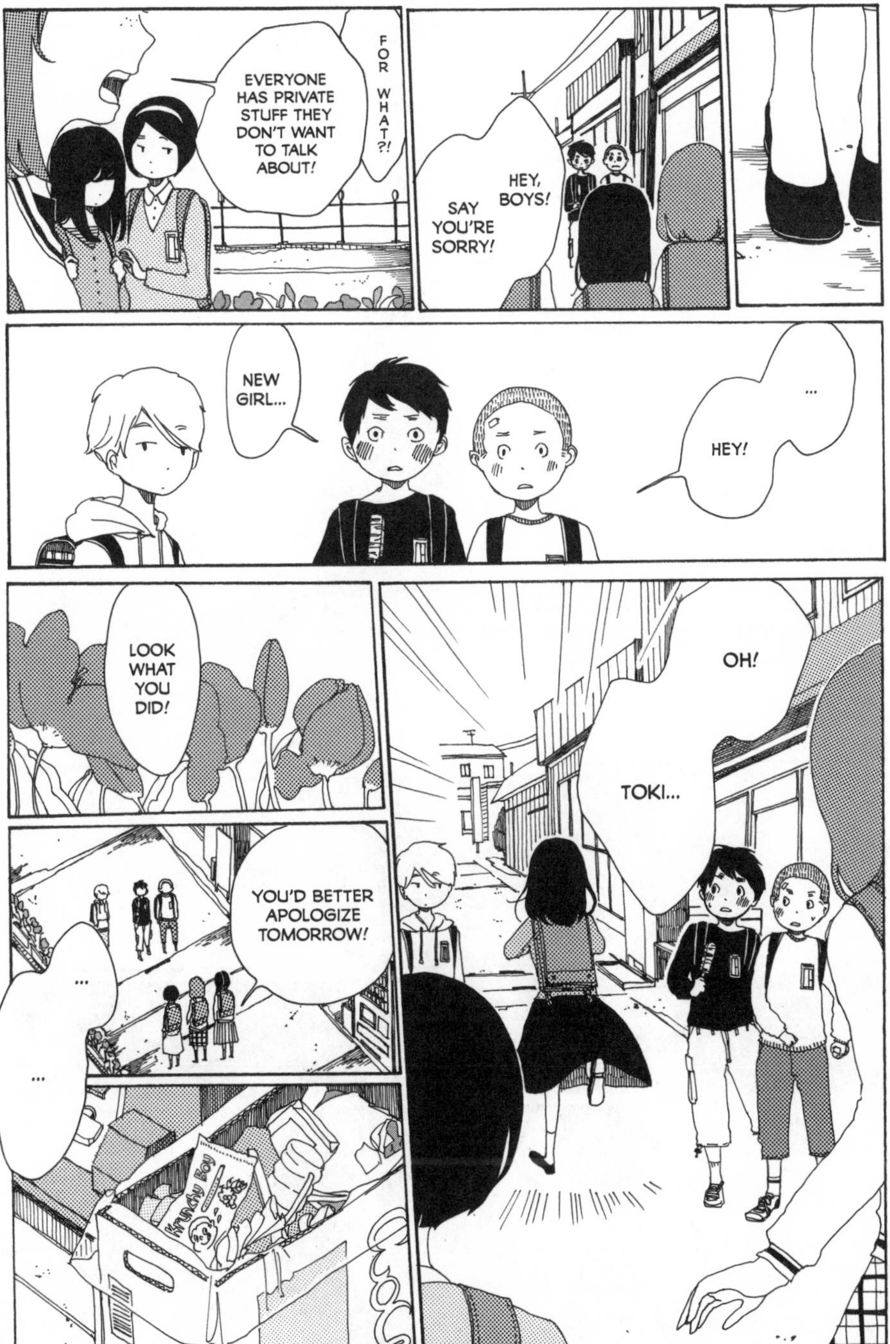
HEY, BOYS!
SAY YOU'RE SORRY!
FOR WHAT?!
EVERYONE HAS PRIVATE STUFF THEY DON'T WANT TO TALK ABOUT!
...
HEY!
NEW GIRL...
OH!
TOKI...
LOOK WHAT YOU DID!
YOU'D BETTER APOLOGIZE TOMORROW!
...
...
Krunchy Boy

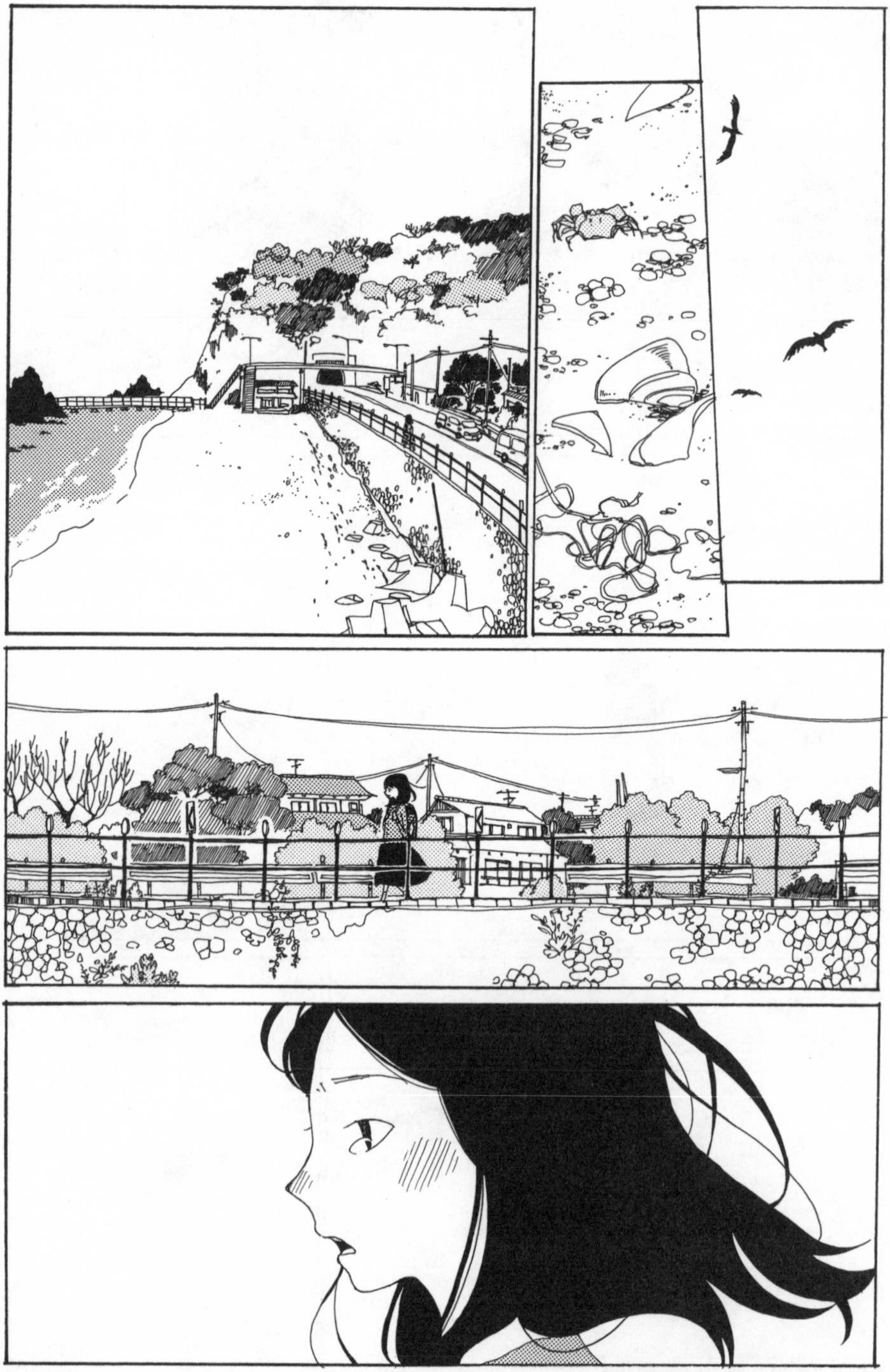

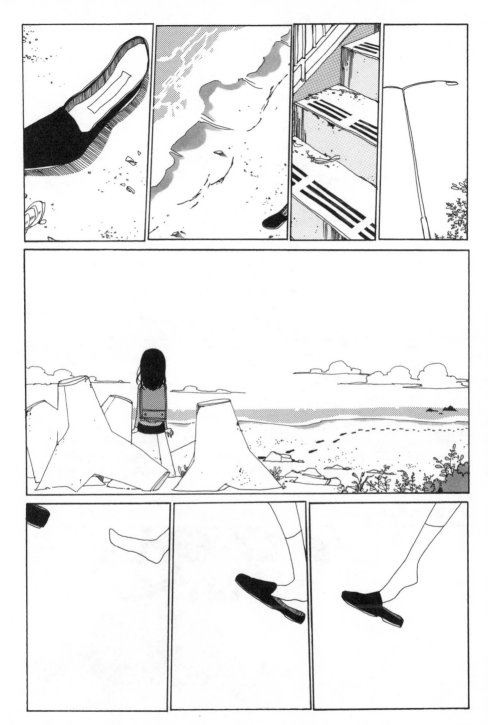

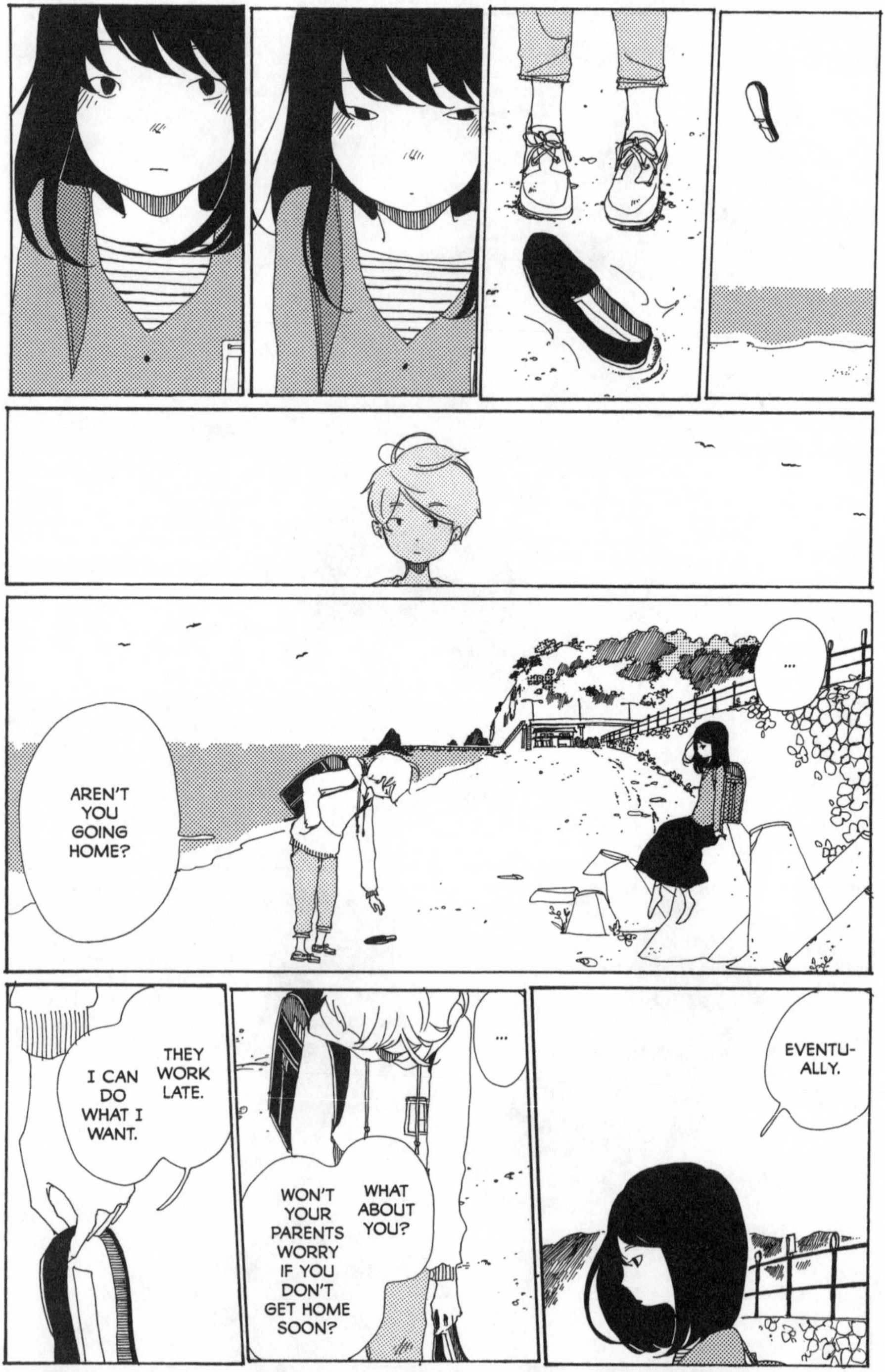
...
AREN'T YOU GOING HOME?
EVENTU-ALLY.
...
WHAT ABOUT YOU?
WON'T YOUR PARENTS WORRY IF YOU DON'T GET HOME SOON?
THEY WORK LATE.
I CAN DO WHAT I WANT.

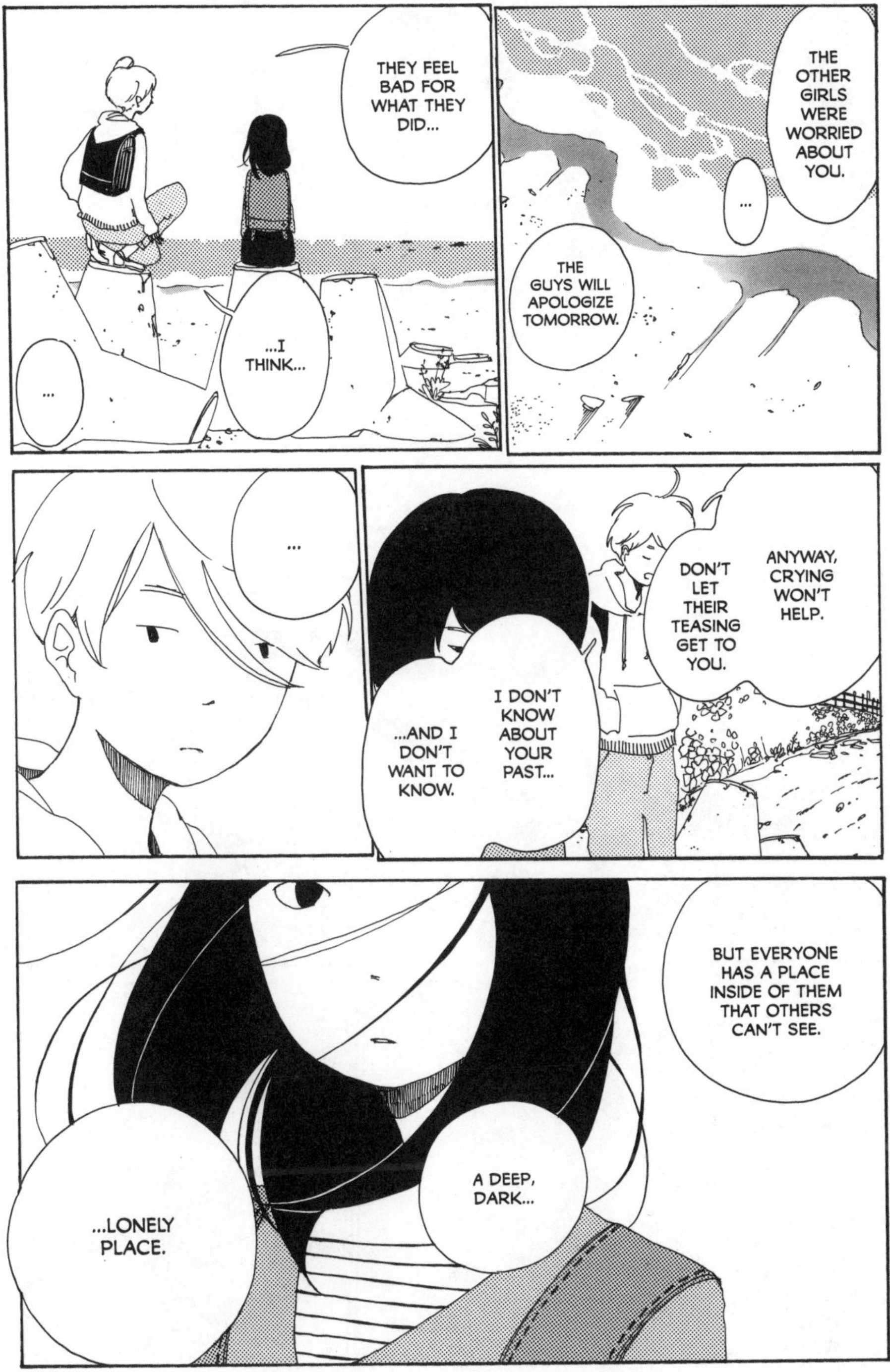
THE OTHER GIRLS WERE WORRIED ABOUT YOU.
...
THE GUYS WILL APOLOGIZE TOMORROW.
THEY FEEL BAD FOR WHAT THEY DID...
...I THINK...
...
ANYWAY, CRYING WON'T HELP.
DON'T LET THEIR TEASING GET TO YOU.
I DON'T KNOW ABOUT YOUR PAST...
...AND I DON'T WANT TO KNOW.
...
BUT EVERYONE HAS A PLACE INSIDE OF THEM THAT OTHERS CAN'T SEE.
A DEEP, DARK...
...LONELY PLACE.

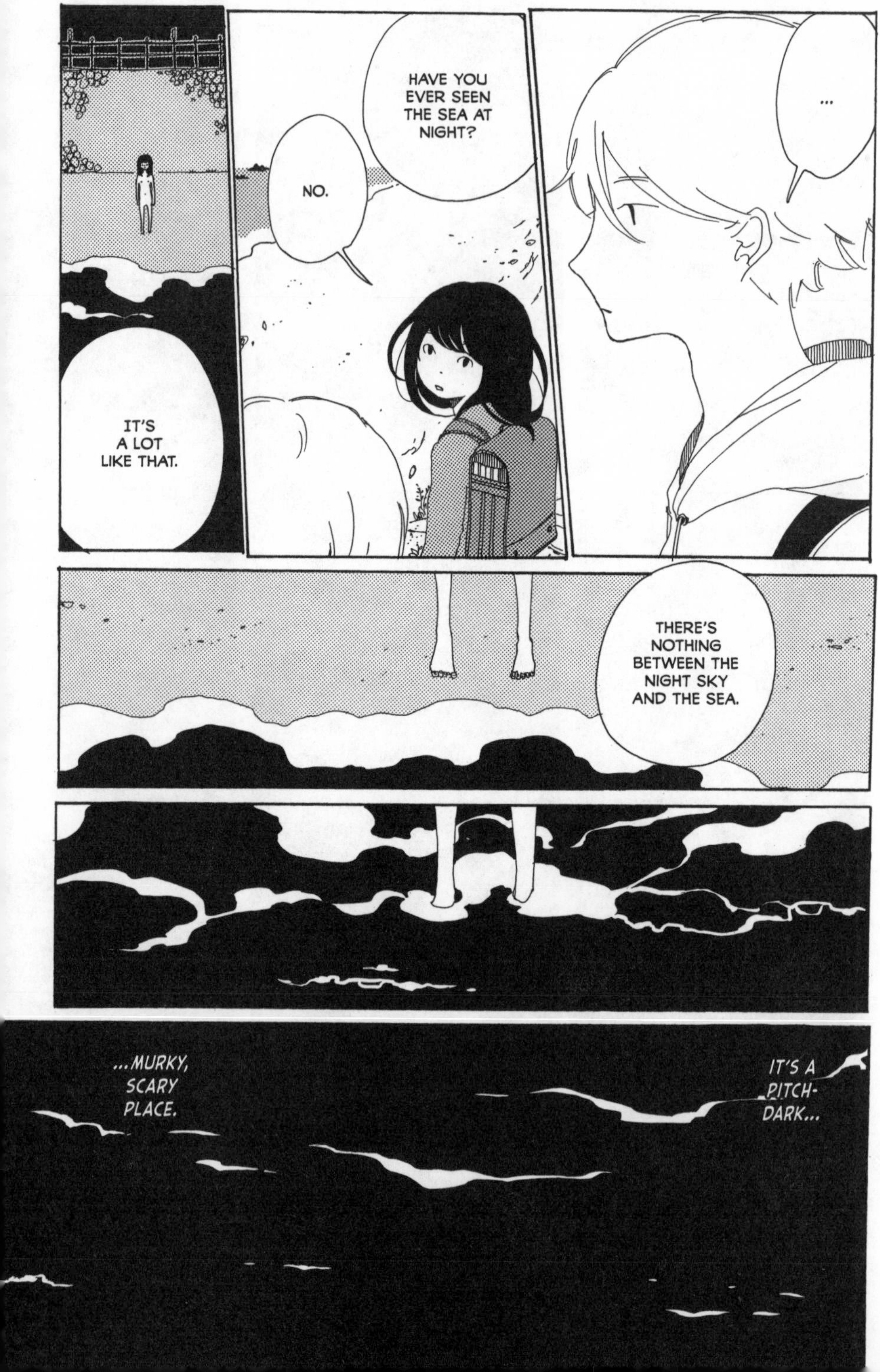
...
HAVE YOU EVER SEEN THE SEA AT NIGHT?
NO.
IT'S A LOT LIKE THAT.
THERE'S NOTHING BETWEEN THE NIGHT SKY AND THE SEA.
IT'S A PITCH-DARK...
...MURKY, SCARY PLACE.

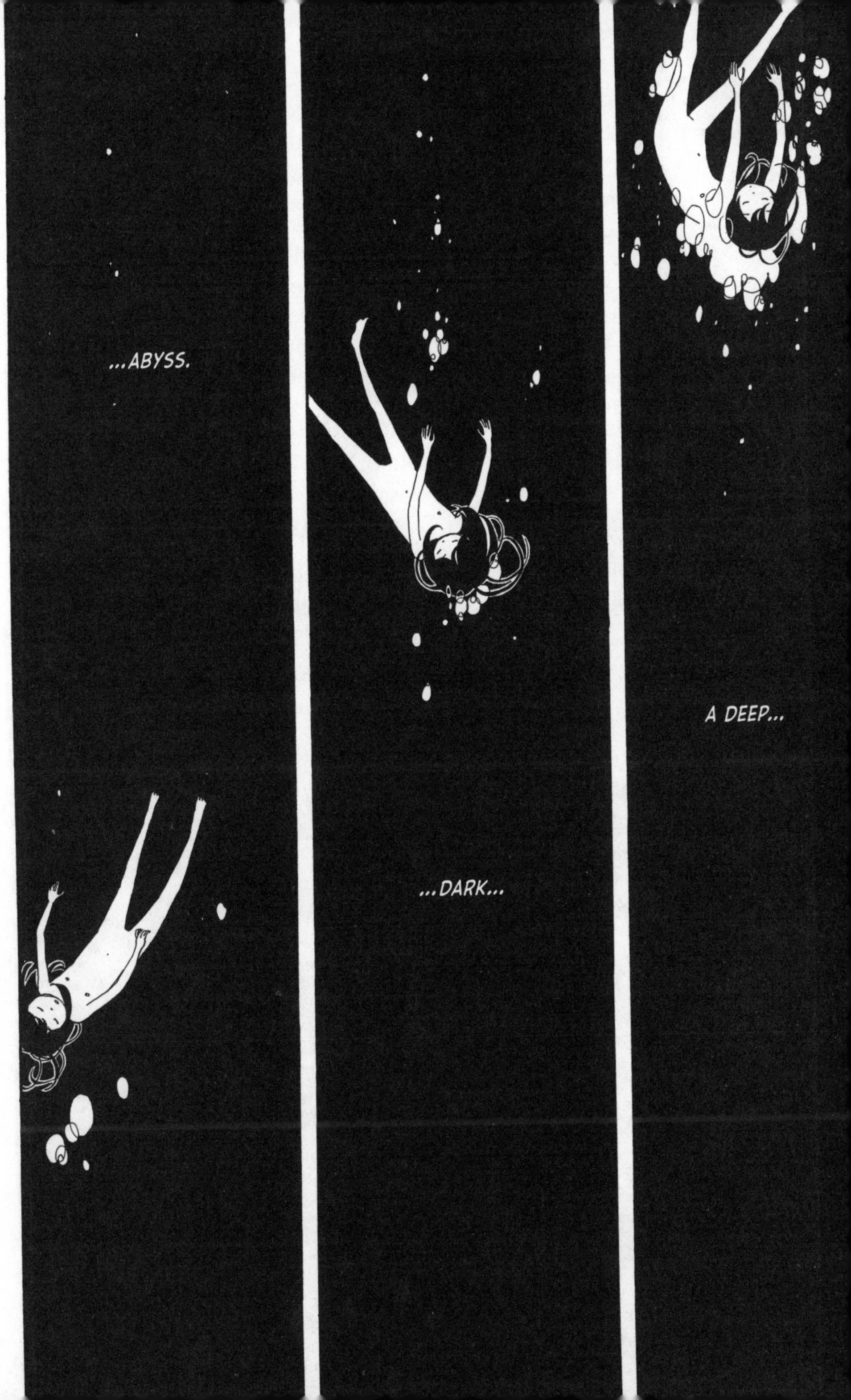
A DEEP...
...DARK...
...ABYSS.

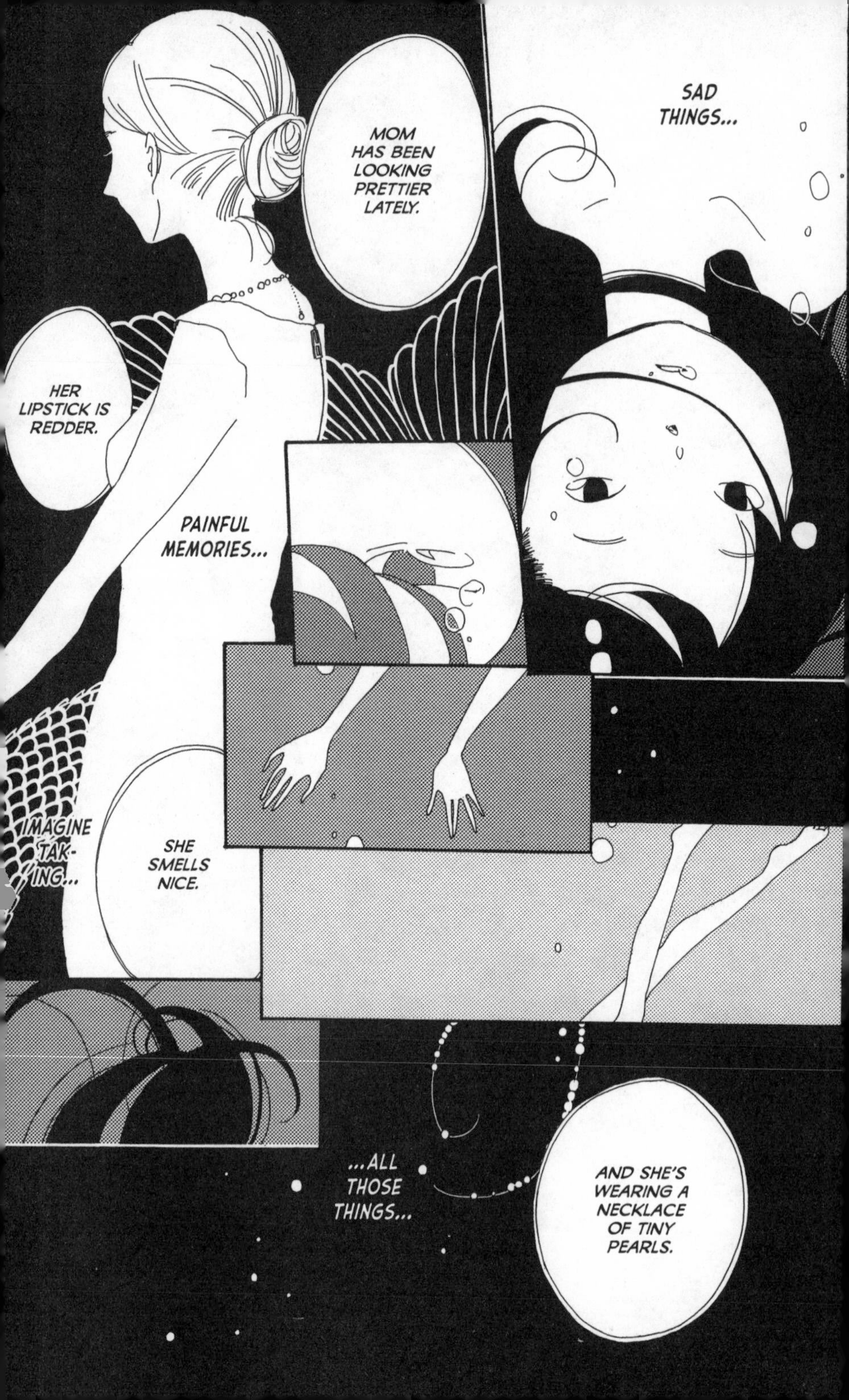
SAD THINGS...
MOM HAS BEEN LOOKING PRETTIER LATELY.
HER LIPSTICK IS REDDER.
PAINFUL MEMORIES...
SHE SMELLS NICE.
IMAGINE TAKING...
AND SHE'S WEARING A NECKLACE OF TINY PEARLS.
...ALL THOSE THINGS...

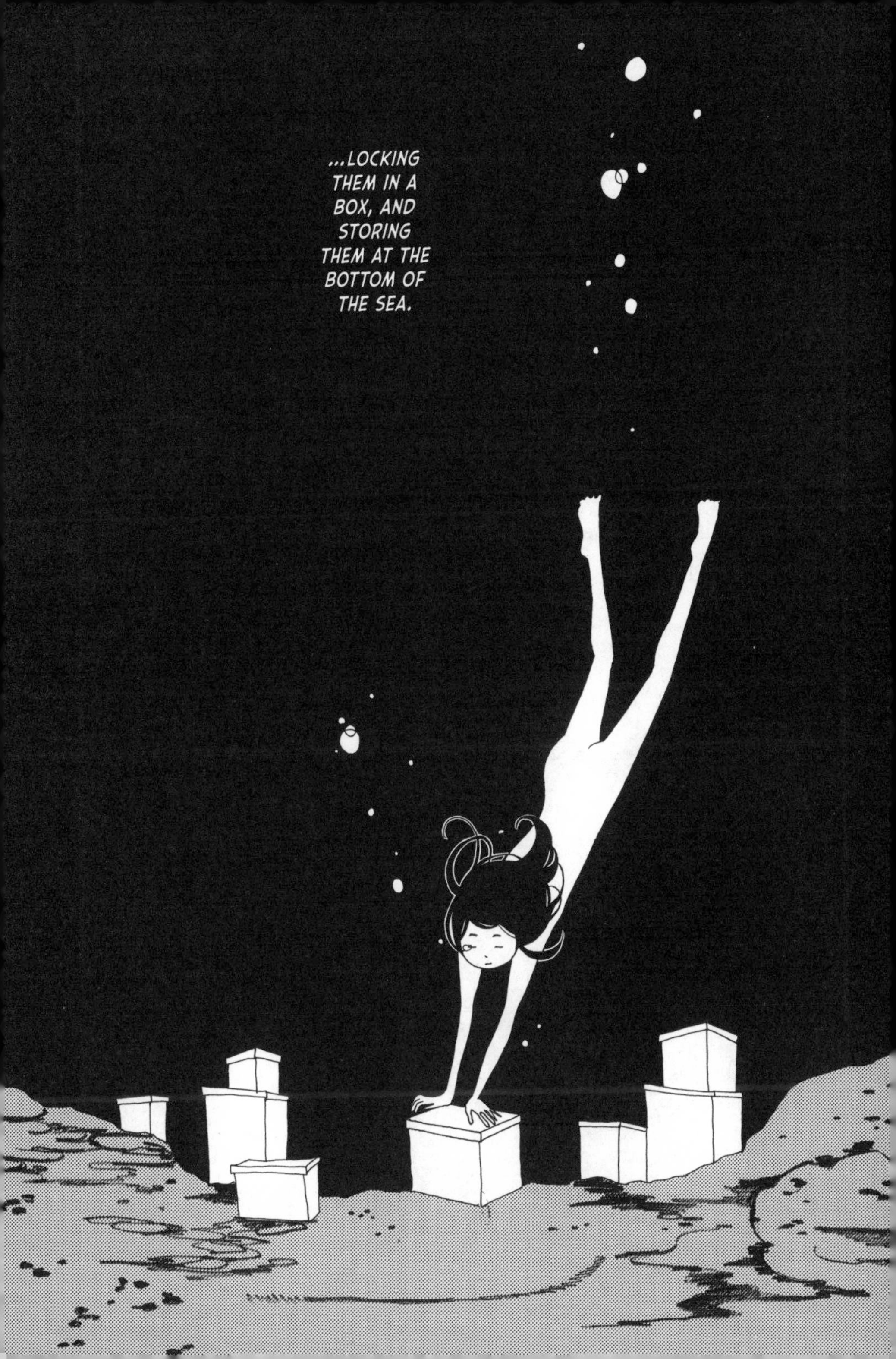
...LOCKING THEM IN A BOX, AND STORING THEM AT THE BOTTOM OF THE SEA.

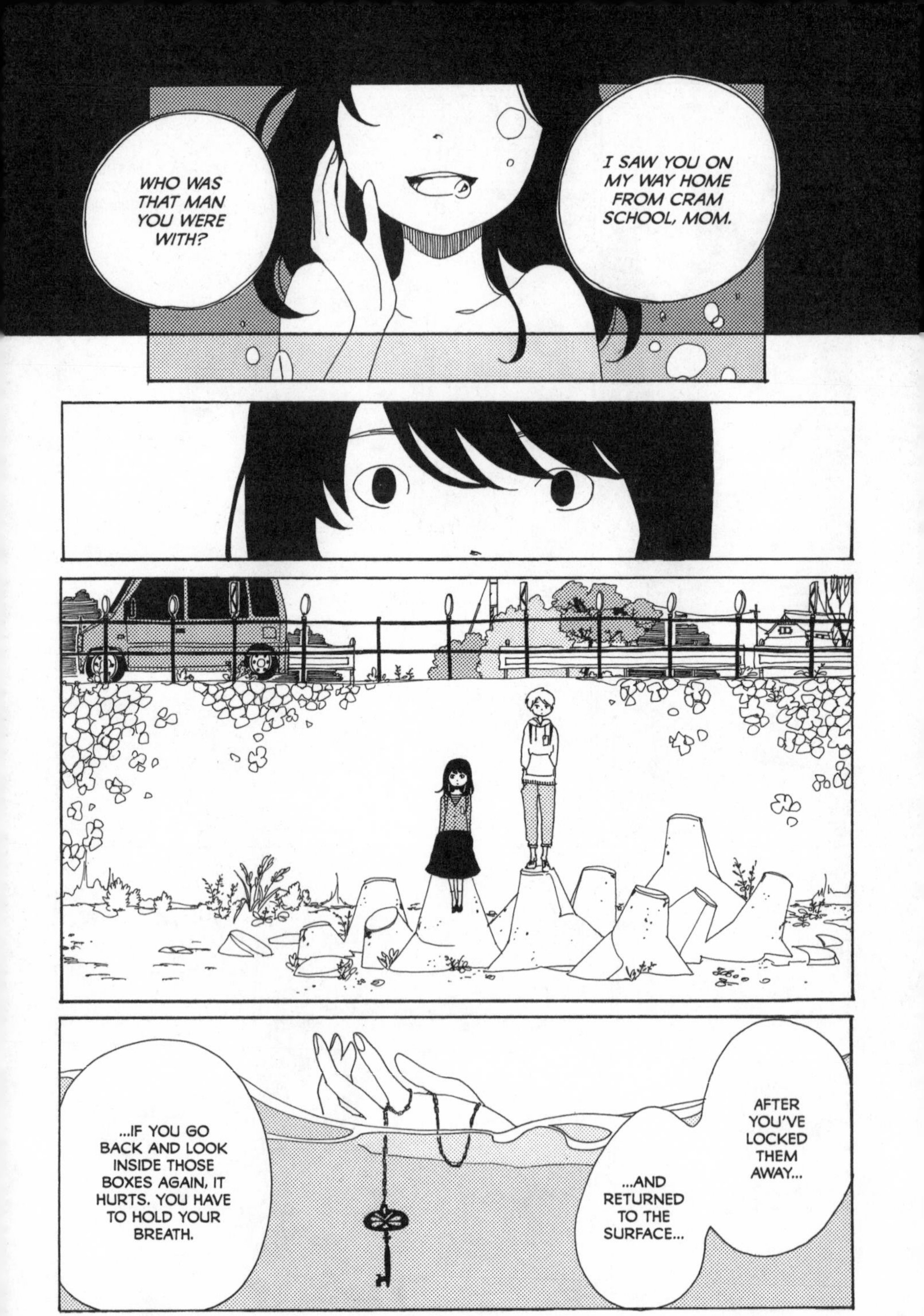
I SAW YOU ON MY WAY HOME FROM CRAM SCHOOL, MOM.
WHO WAS THAT MAN YOU WERE WITH?
AFTER YOU'VE LOCKED THEM AWAY...
...AND RETURNED TO THE SURFACE...
...IF YOU GO BACK AND LOOK INSIDE THOSE BOXES AGAIN, IT HURTS. YOU HAVE TO HOLD YOUR BREATH.

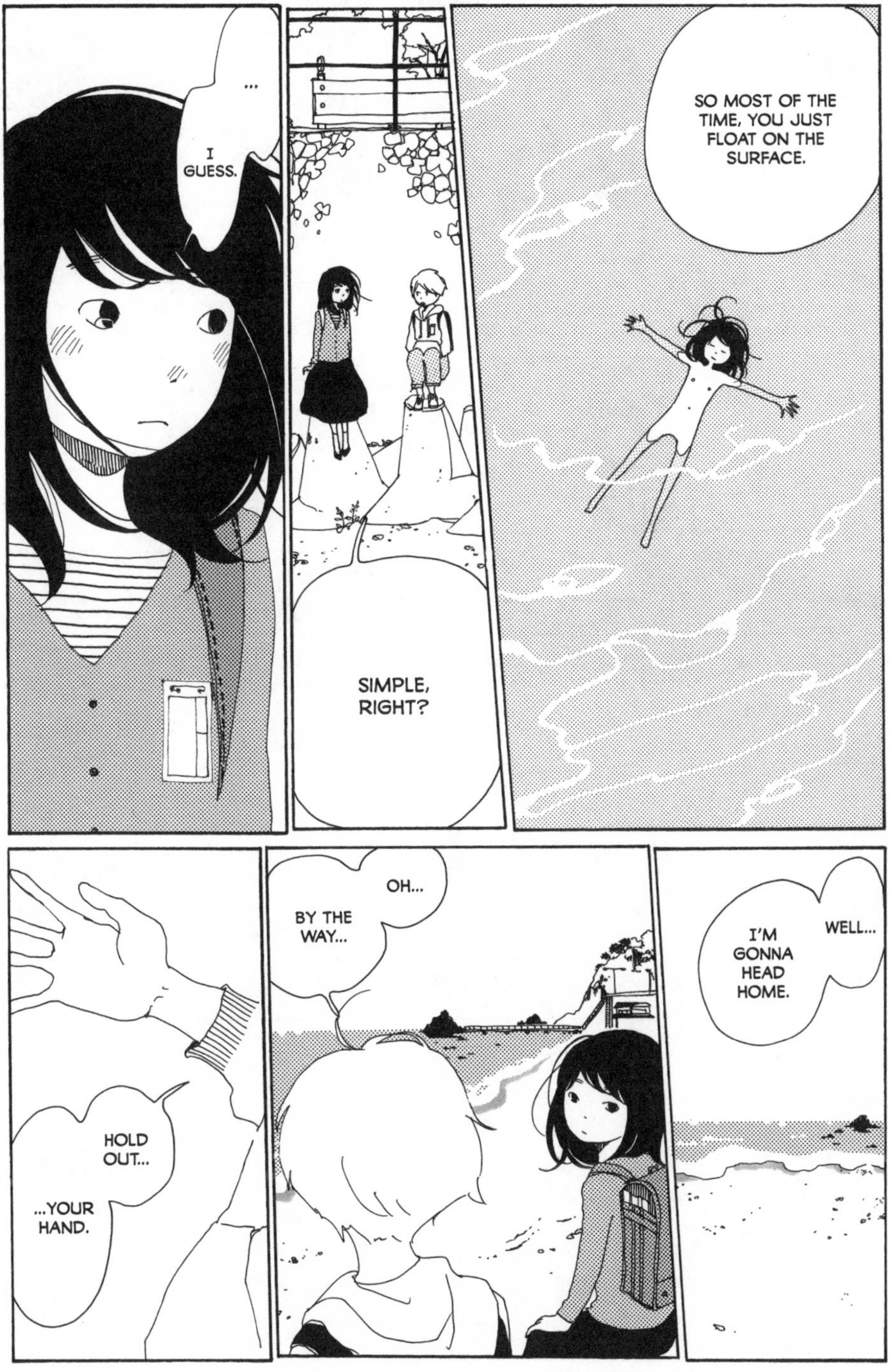
SO MOST OF THE TIME, YOU JUST FLOAT ON THE SURFACE.
SIMPLE, RIGHT?
...
I GUESS.
WELL...
I'M GONNA HEAD HOME.
OH...
BY THE WAY...
HOLD OUT...
...YOUR HAND.

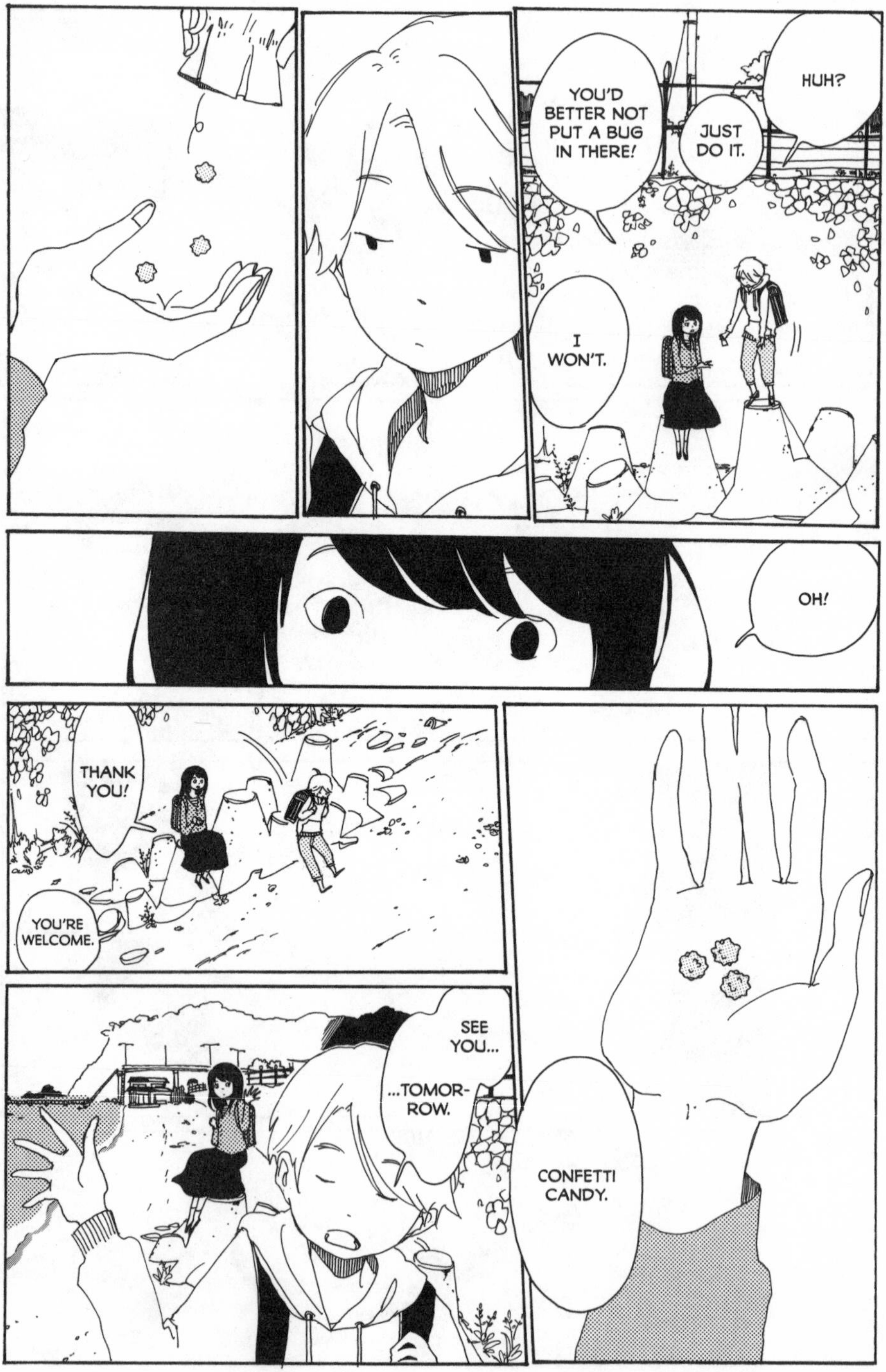
HUH?
JUST DO IT.
YOU'D BETTER NOT PUT A BUG IN THERE!
I WON'T.
OH!
CONFETTI CANDY.
THANK YOU!
YOU'RE WELCOME.
SEE YOU...
...TOMOR-ROW.

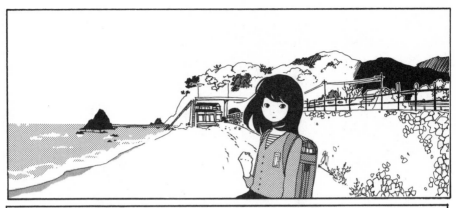

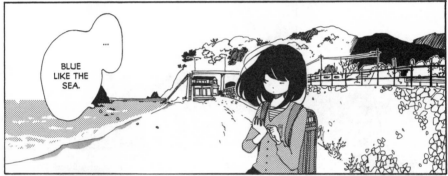

...

BLUE
LIKE THE
SEA.

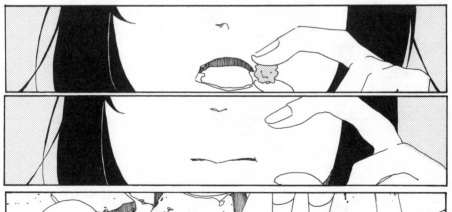

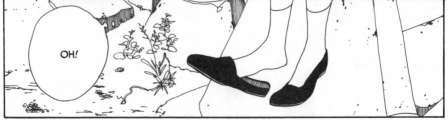

OH!

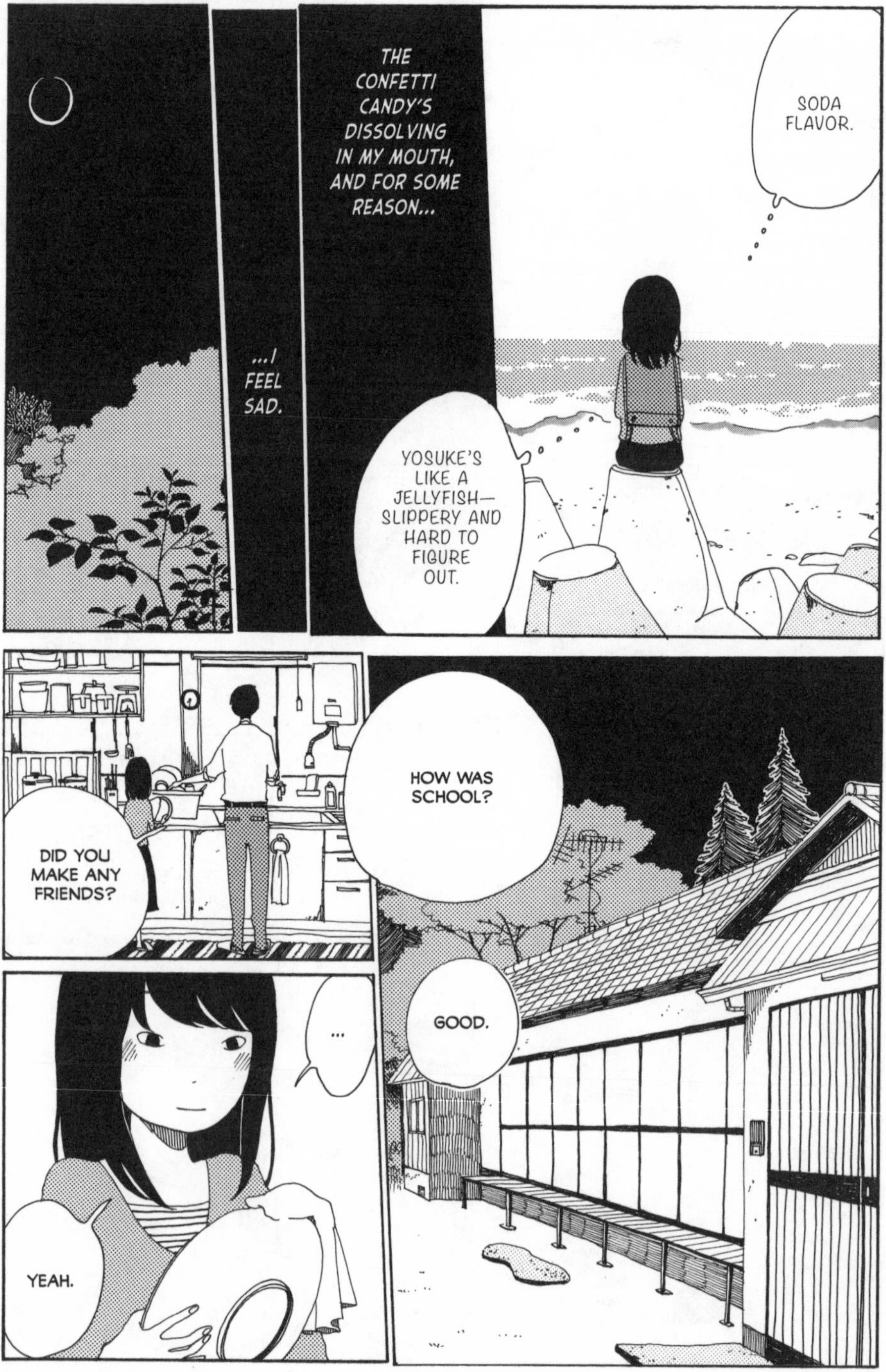
SODA FLAVOR.
YOSUKE'S LIKE A JELLYFISH—SLIPPERY AND HARD TO FIGURE OUT.
THE CONFETTI CANDY'S DISSOLVING IN MY MOUTH, AND FOR SOME REASON...
...I FEEL SAD.
HOW WAS SCHOOL?
GOOD.
DID YOU MAKE ANY FRIENDS?
...
YEAH.

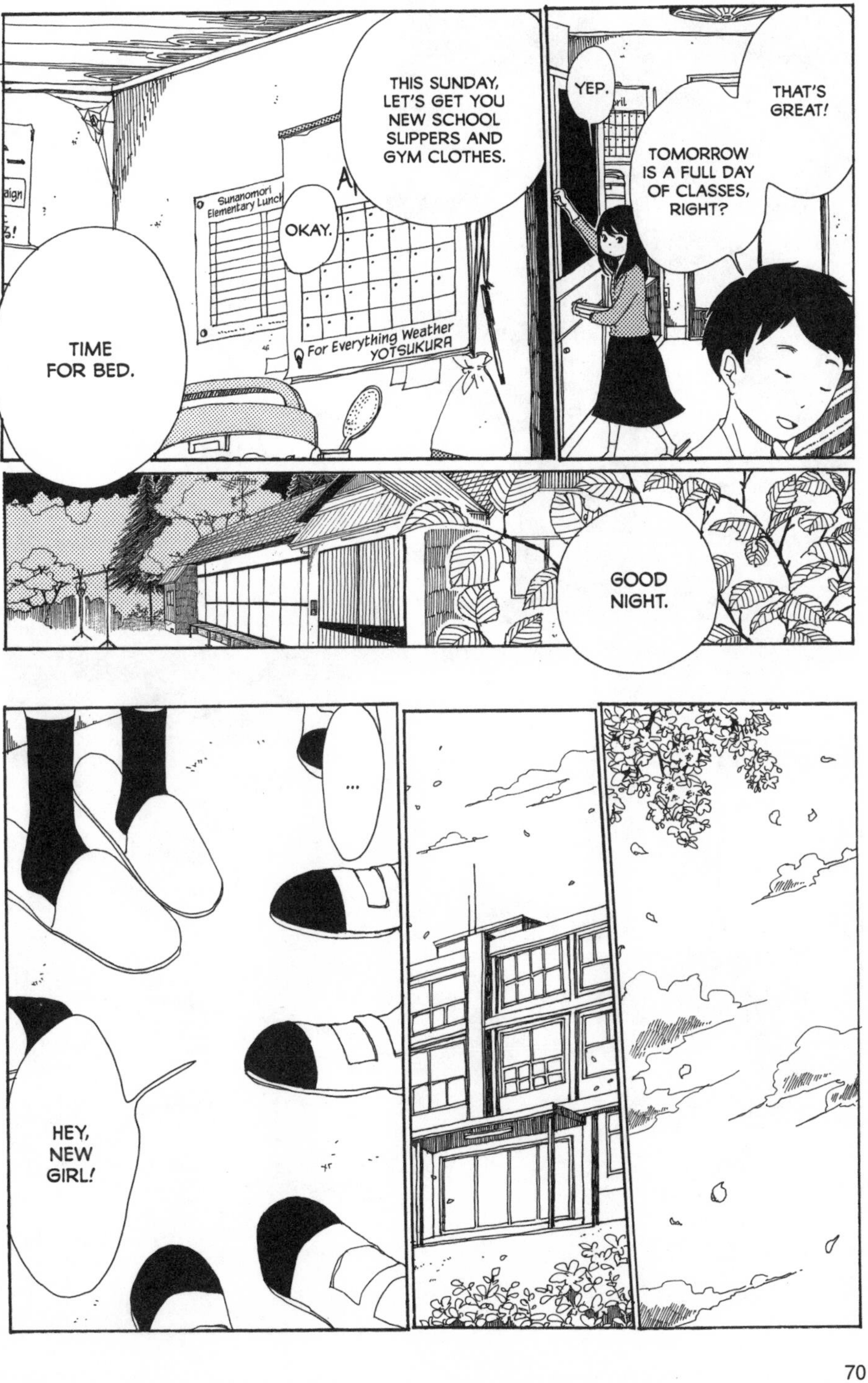
THAT'S GREAT!
TOMORROW IS A FULL DAY OF CLASSES, RIGHT?
YEP.
THIS SUNDAY, LET'S GET YOU NEW SCHOOL SLIPPERS AND GYM CLOTHES.
Sunanomori Elementary Lunch
OKAY.
For Everything Weather YOTSUKURA
TIME FOR BED.
GOOD NIGHT.
...
HEY, NEW GIRL!

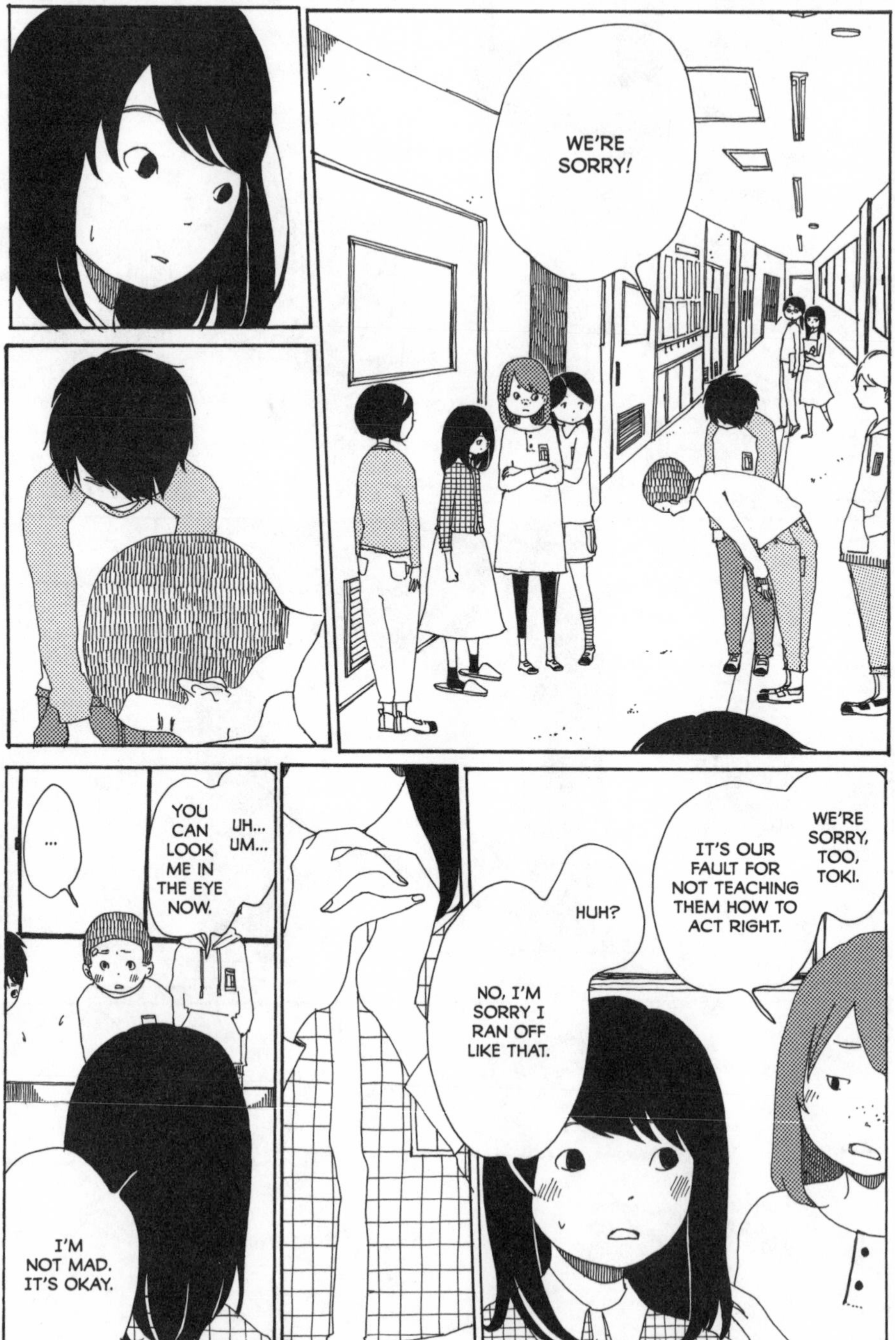
WE'RE SORRY!
WE'RE SORRY, TOO, TOKI.
IT'S OUR FAULT FOR NOT TEACHING THEM HOW TO ACT RIGHT.
HUH?
NO, I'M SORRY I RAN OFF LIKE THAT.
YOU CAN LOOK ME IN THE EYE NOW.
UH... UM...
...
I'M NOT MAD. IT'S OKAY.

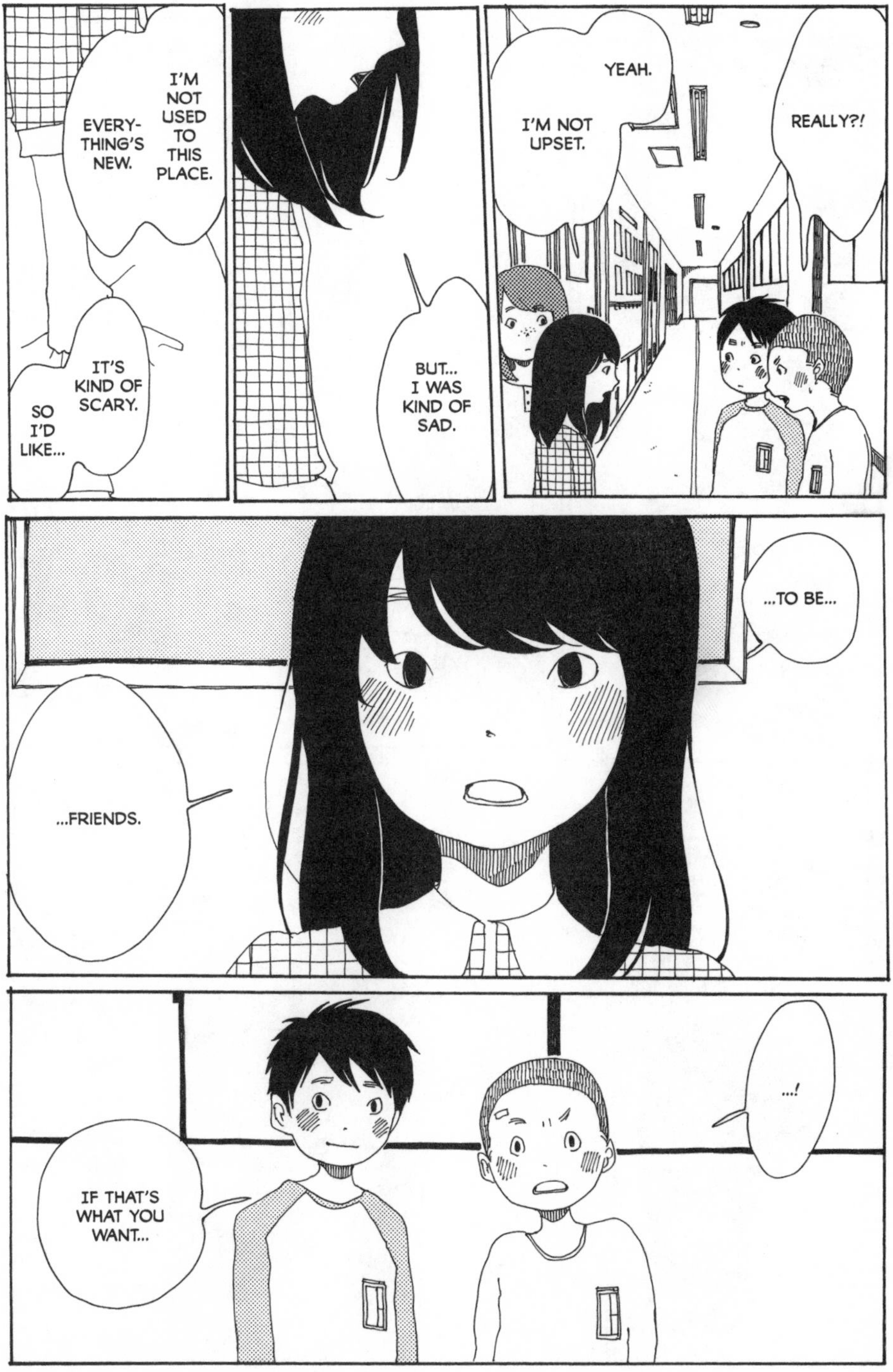
REALLY?!
YEAH.
I'M NOT UPSET.
BUT... I WAS KIND OF SAD.
I'M NOT USED TO THIS PLACE.
EVERY-THING'S NEW.
IT'S KIND OF SCARY.
SO I'D LIKE...
...TO BE...
...FRIENDS.
...!
IF THAT'S WHAT YOU WANT...

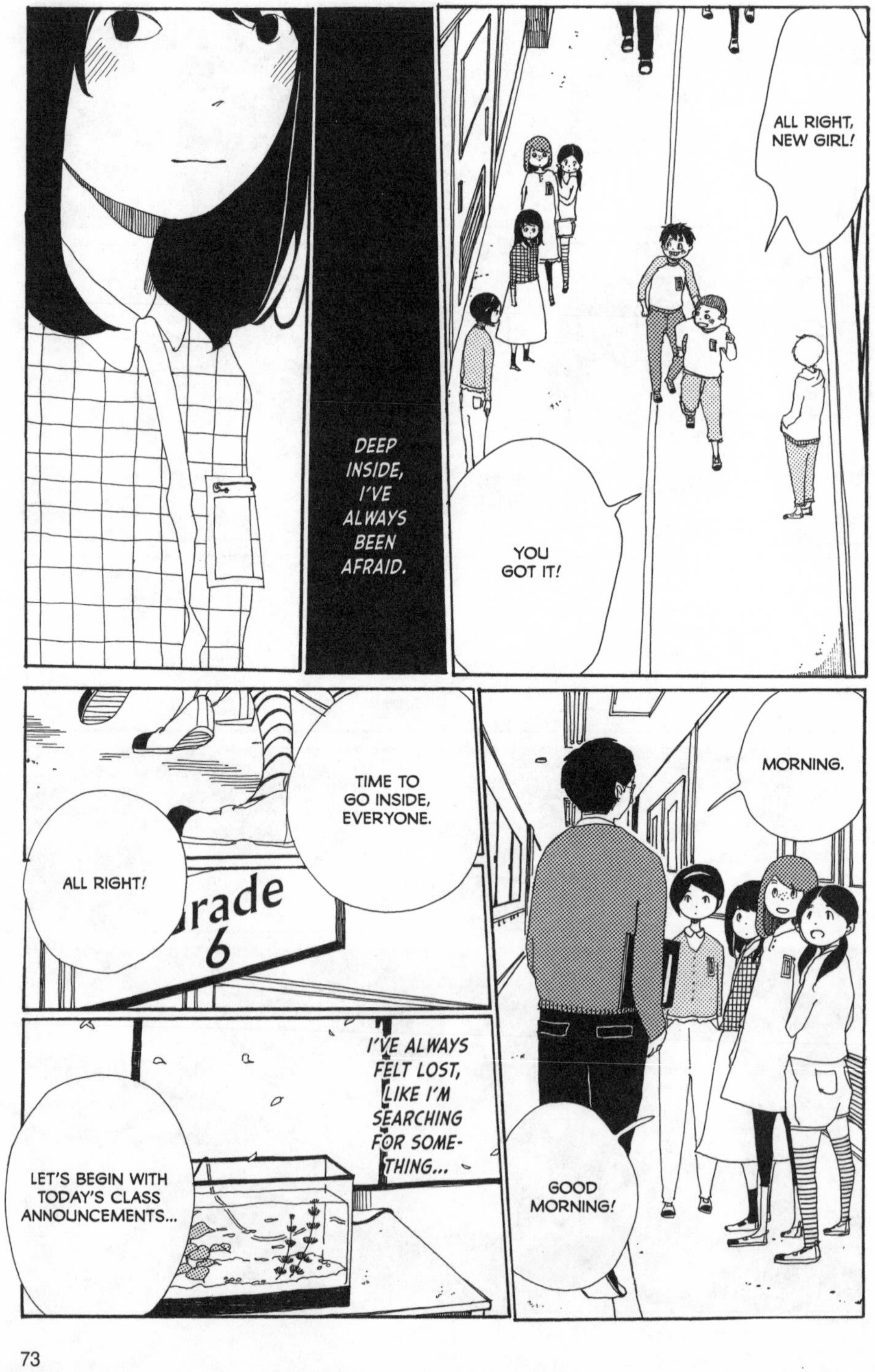
ALL RIGHT, NEW GIRL!
YOU GOT IT!
DEEP INSIDE, I'VE ALWAYS BEEN AFRAID.
MORNING.
GOOD MORNING!
TIME TO GO INSIDE, EVERYONE.
ALL RIGHT!
I'VE ALWAYS FELT LOST, LIKE I'M SEARCHING FOR SOME-THING...
LET'S BEGIN WITH TODAY'S CLASS ANNOUNCEMENTS...

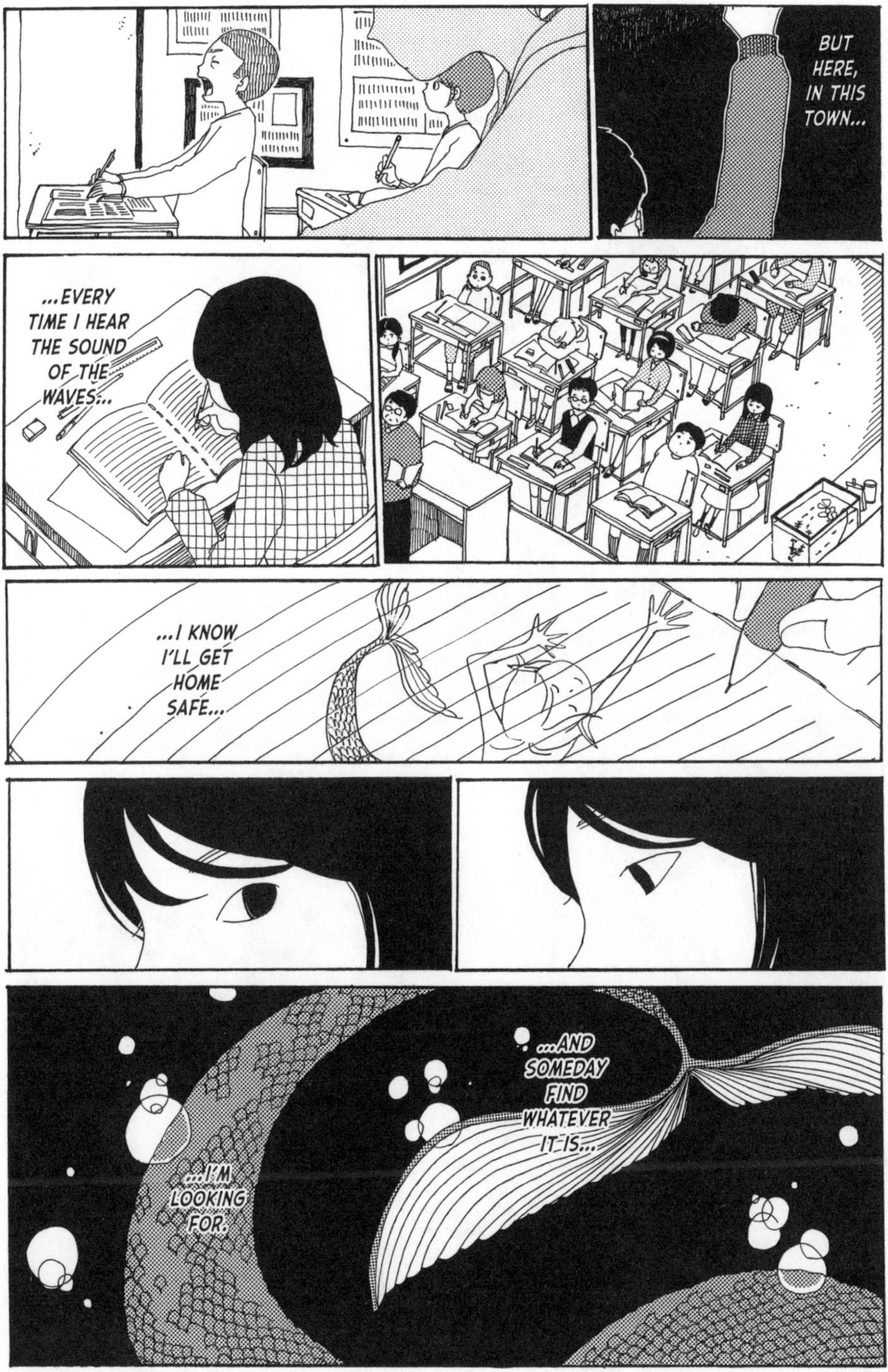
BUT HERE, IN THIS TOWN...
...EVERY TIME I HEAR THE SOUND OF THE WAVES...
...I KNOW I'LL GET HOME SAFE...
...AND SOMEDAY FIND WHATEVER IT IS...
...I'M LOOKING FOR.

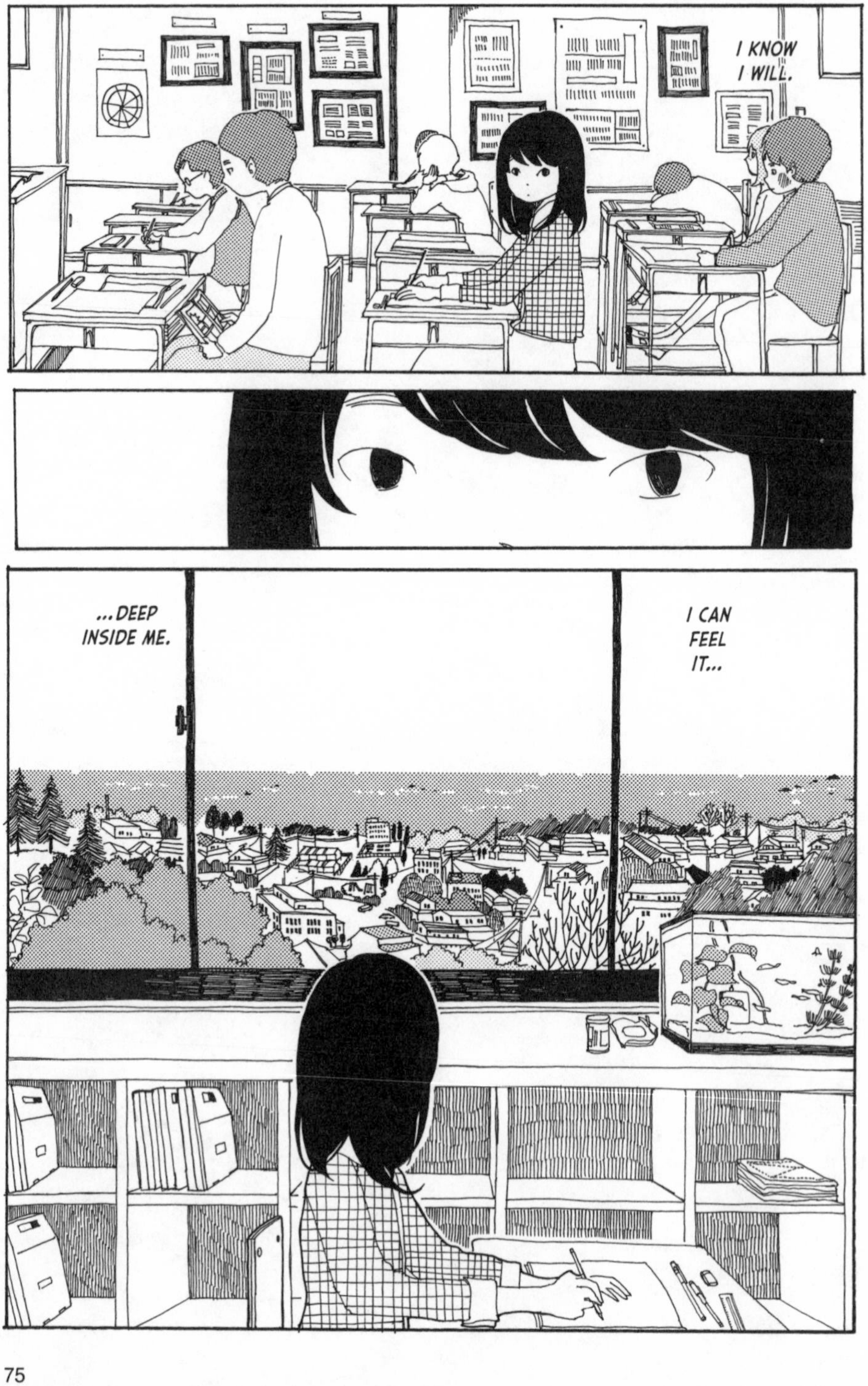
I KNOW I WILL.
I CAN FEEL IT...
...DEEP INSIDE ME.

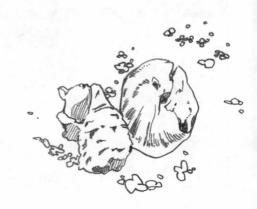

{Three}
Ebb and Flow

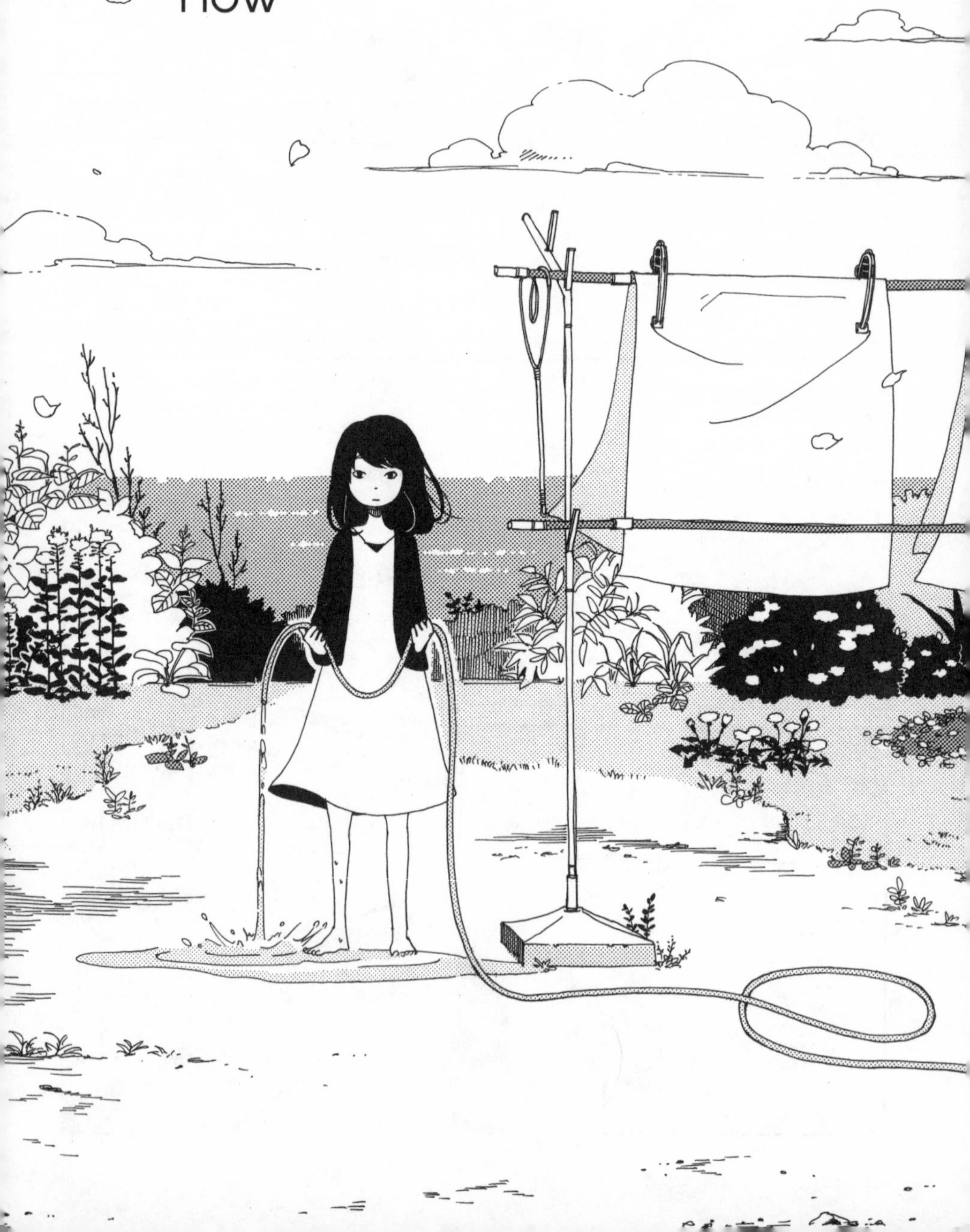

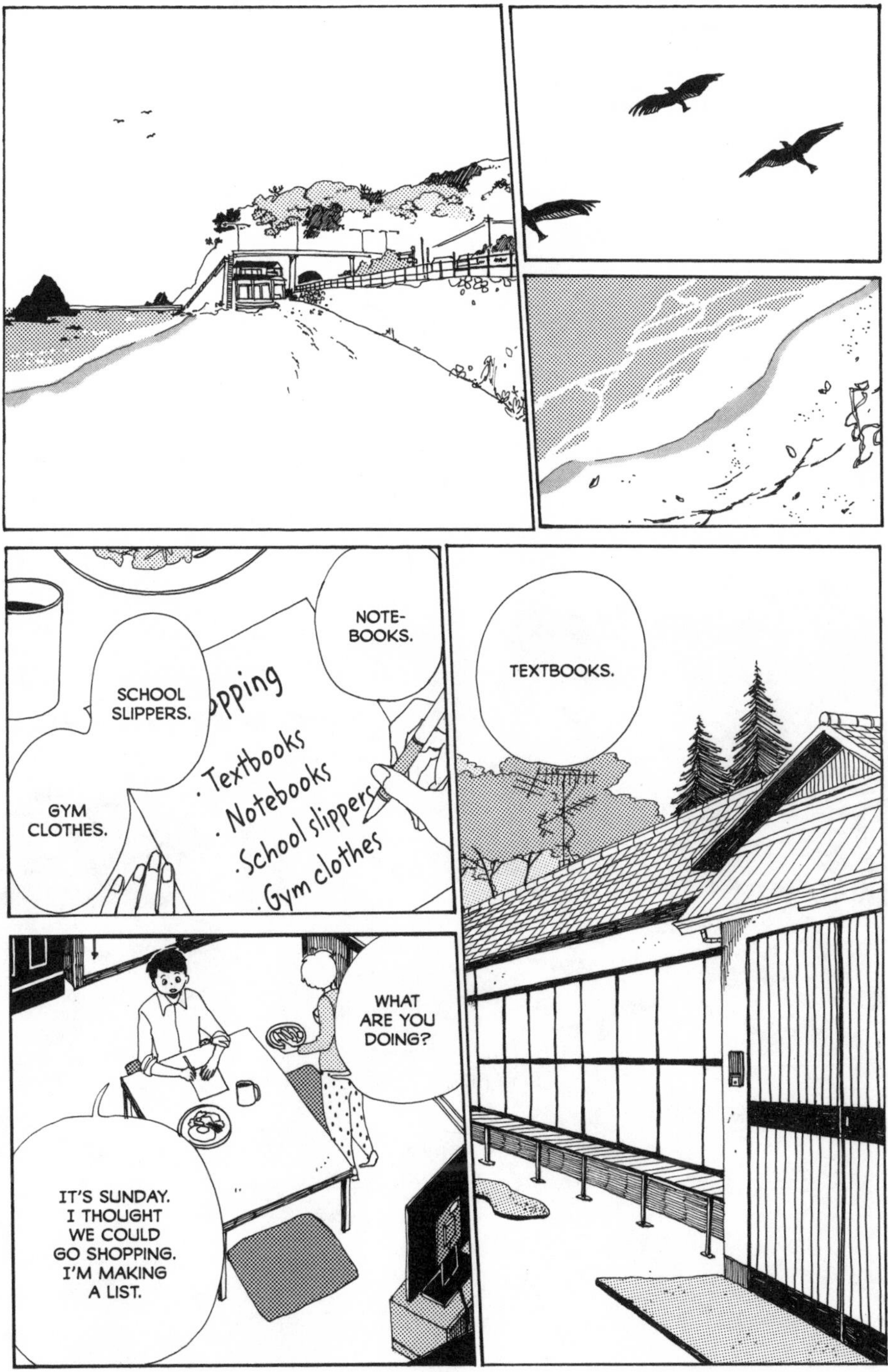
TEXTBOOKS.
NOTE-BOOKS.
SCHOOL SLIPPERS.
GYM CLOTHES.
. Textbooks
. Notebooks
. School slippers
. Gym clothes
WHAT ARE YOU DOING?
IT'S SUNDAY. I THOUGHT WE COULD GO SHOPPING. I'M MAKING A LIST.

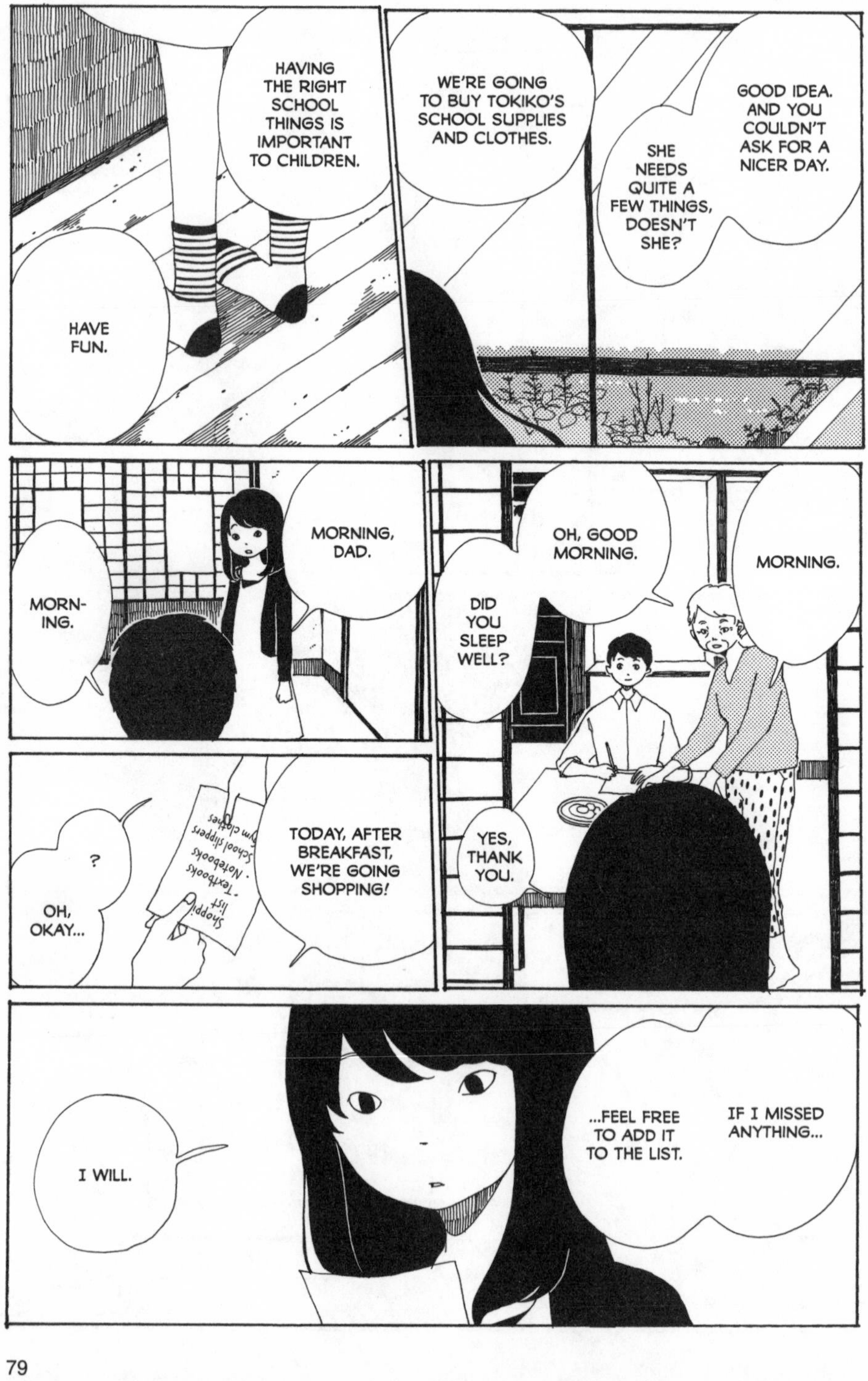
GOOD IDEA. AND YOU COULDN'T ASK FOR A NICER DAY.
WE'RE GOING TO BUY TOKIKO'S SCHOOL SUPPLIES AND CLOTHES.
SHE NEEDS QUITE A FEW THINGS, DOESN'T SHE?
HAVING THE RIGHT SCHOOL THINGS IS IMPORTANT TO CHILDREN.
HAVE FUN.
MORNING.
OH, GOOD MORNING.
DID YOU SLEEP WELL?
YES, THANK YOU.
MORNING, DAD.
MORN-ING.
TODAY, AFTER BREAKFAST, WE'RE GOING SHOPPING!
list
·Textbooks
·Notebooks
School slippers
Gym clothes
?
OH, OKAY...
IF I MISSED ANYTHING...
...FEEL FREE TO ADD IT TO THE LIST.
I WILL.

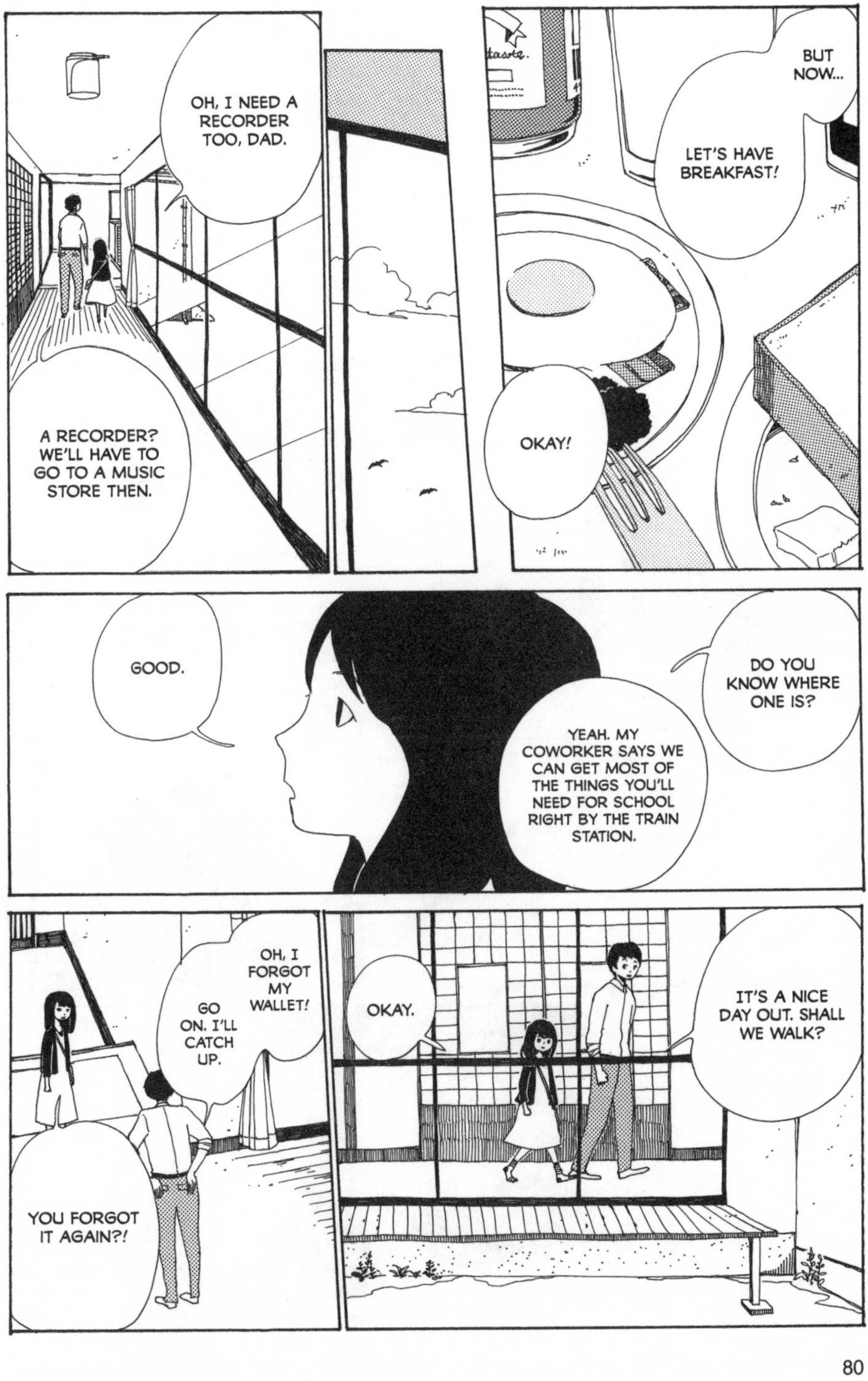
BUT NOW...
LET'S HAVE BREAKFAST!
OKAY!
OH, I NEED A RECORDER TOO, DAD.
A RECORDER? WE'LL HAVE TO GO TO A MUSIC STORE THEN.
DO YOU KNOW WHERE ONE IS?
YEAH. MY COWORKER SAYS WE CAN GET MOST OF THE THINGS YOU'LL NEED FOR SCHOOL RIGHT BY THE TRAIN STATION.
GOOD.
IT'S A NICE DAY OUT. SHALL WE WALK?
OKAY.
OH, I FORGOT MY WALLET!
GO ON. I'LL CATCH UP.
YOU FORGOT IT AGAIN?!

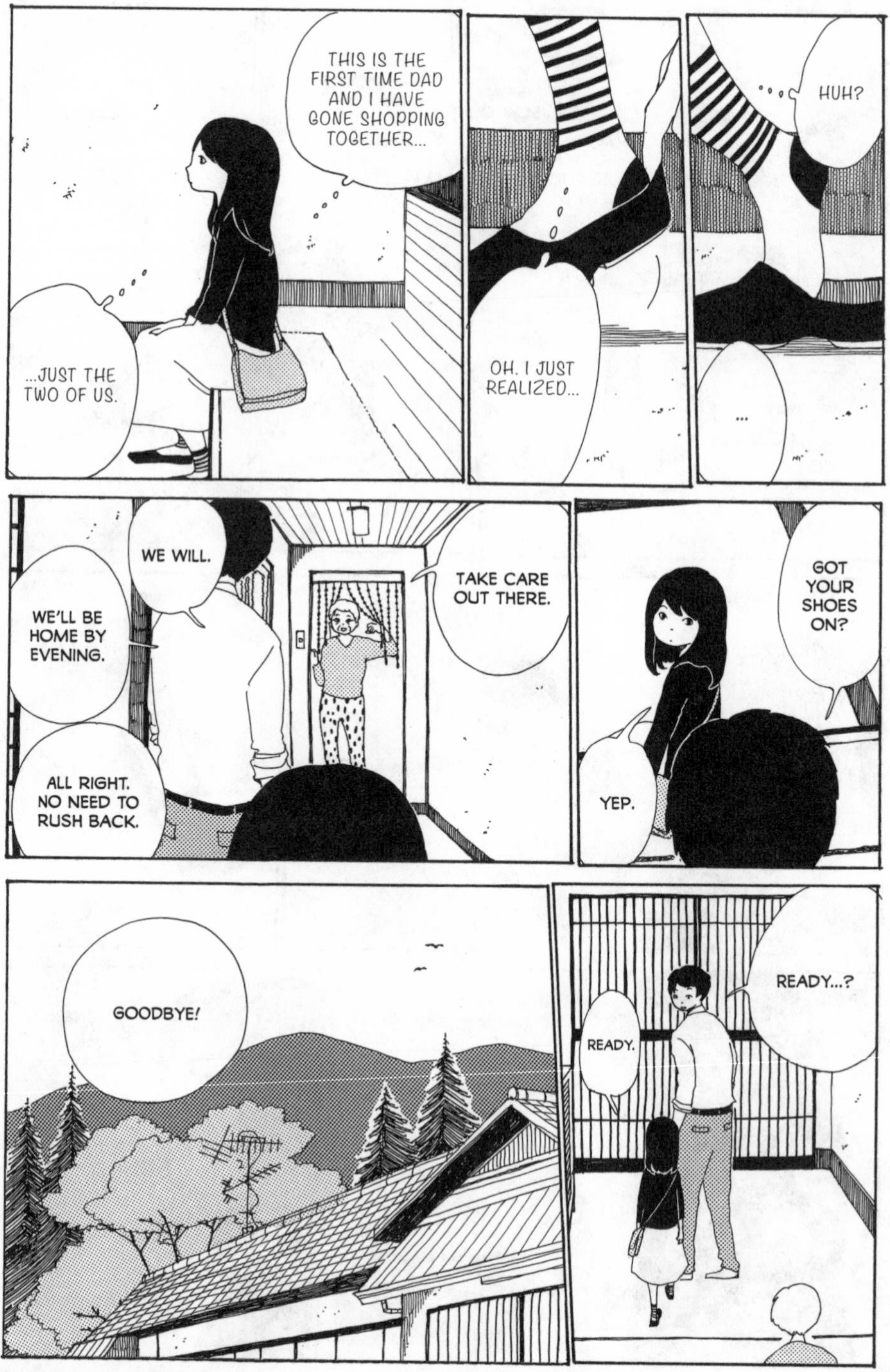
HUH?
...
OH. I JUST REALIZED...
THIS IS THE FIRST TIME DAD AND I HAVE GONE SHOPPING TOGETHER...
...JUST THE TWO OF US.
GOT YOUR SHOES ON?
YEP.
TAKE CARE OUT THERE.
WE WILL.
WE'LL BE HOME BY EVENING.
ALL RIGHT. NO NEED TO RUSH BACK.
READY...?
READY.
GOODBYE!

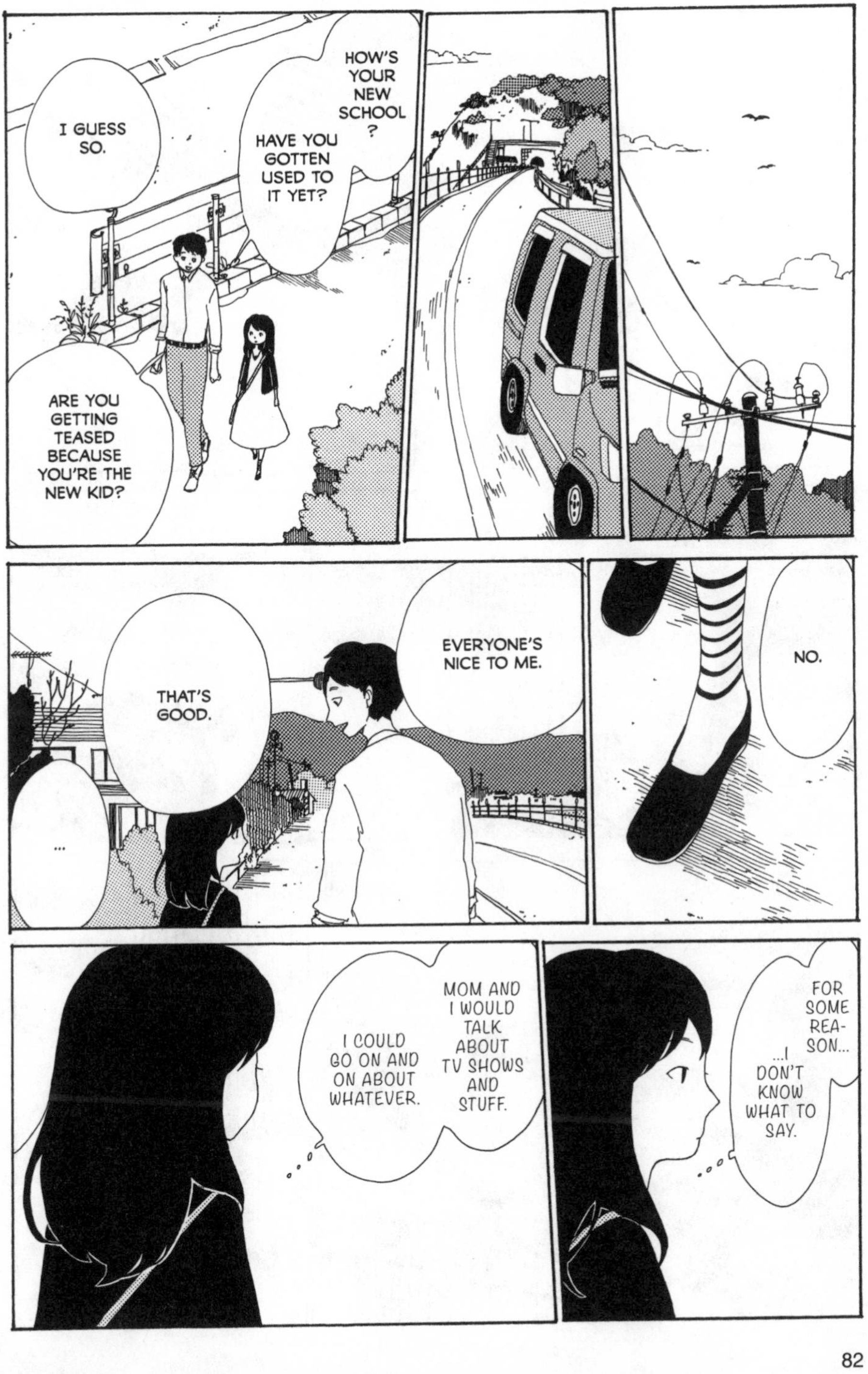
HOW'S YOUR NEW SCHOOL?
HAVE YOU GOTTEN USED TO IT YET?
I GUESS SO.
ARE YOU GETTING TEASED BECAUSE YOU'RE THE NEW KID?
NO.
EVERYONE'S NICE TO ME.
THAT'S GOOD.
...
FOR SOME REA-SON...
...I DON'T KNOW WHAT TO SAY.
MOM AND I WOULD TALK ABOUT TV SHOWS AND STUFF.
I COULD GO ON AND ON ABOUT WHATEVER.

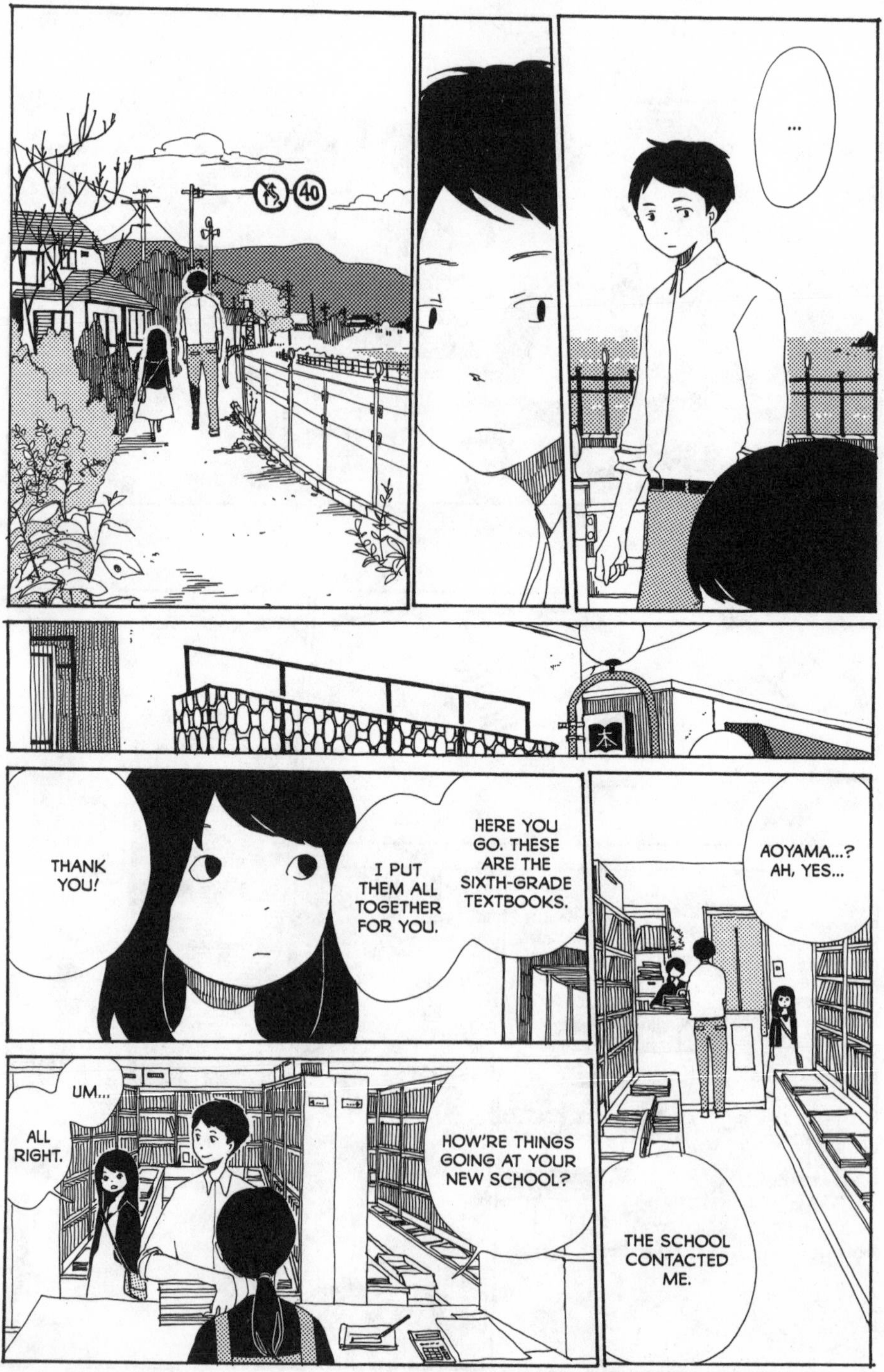
...
40
本
AOYAMA...? AH, YES...
THE SCHOOL CONTACTED ME.
HERE YOU GO. THESE ARE THE SIXTH-GRADE TEXTBOOKS.
I PUT THEM ALL TOGETHER FOR YOU.
THANK YOU!
HOW'RE THINGS GOING AT YOUR NEW SCHOOL?
UM...
ALL RIGHT.

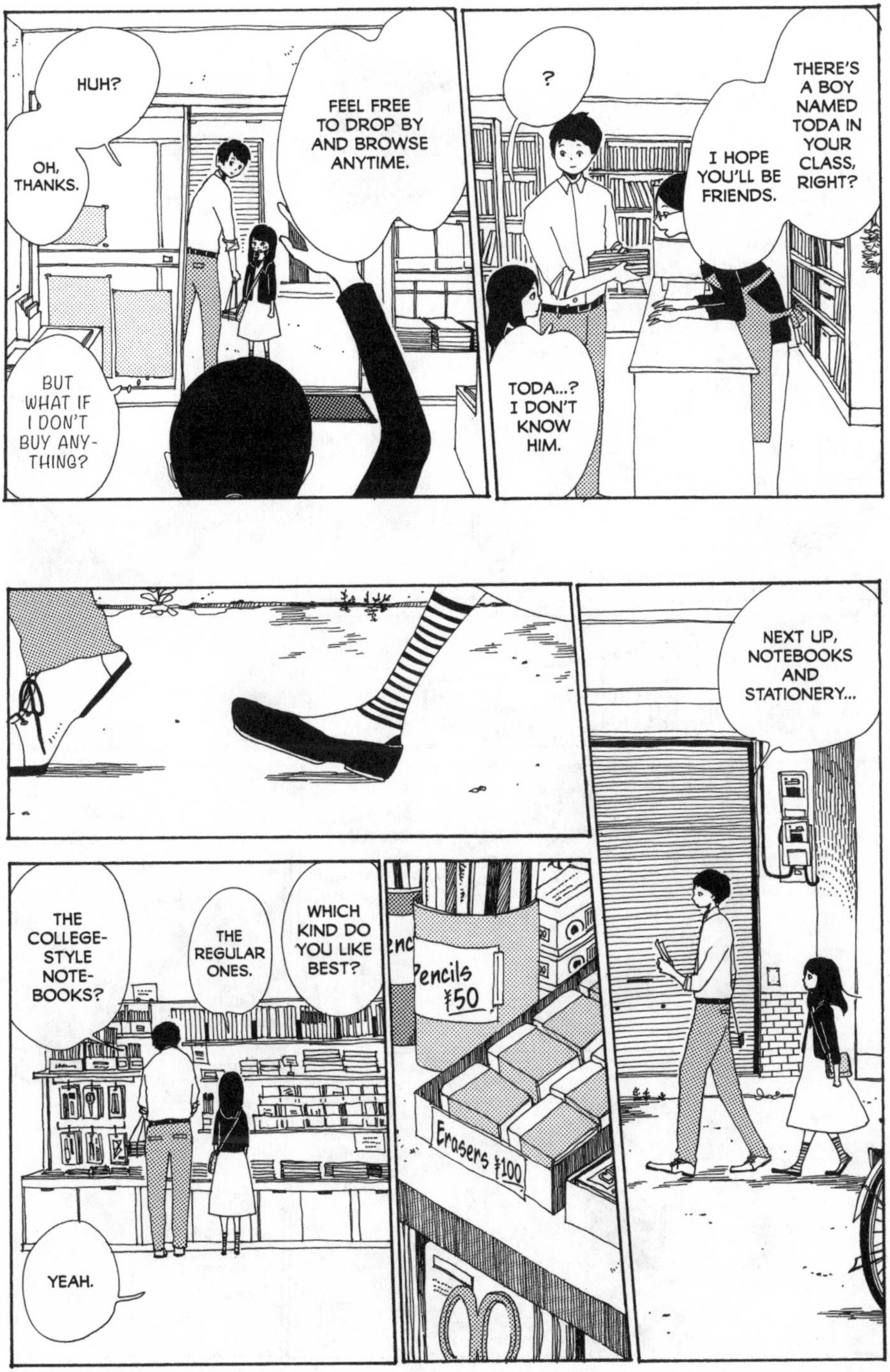
THERE'S A BOY NAMED TODA IN YOUR CLASS, RIGHT?
I HOPE YOU'LL BE FRIENDS.
?
TODA...? I DON'T KNOW HIM.
FEEL FREE TO DROP BY AND BROWSE ANYTIME.
HUH?
OH, THANKS.
BUT WHAT IF I DON'T BUY ANY-THING?
NEXT UP, NOTEBOOKS AND STATIONERY...
Pencils ¥50
Erasers ¥100
WHICH KIND DO YOU LIKE BEST?
THE REGULAR ONES.
THE COLLEGE-STYLE NOTE-BOOKS?
YEAH.

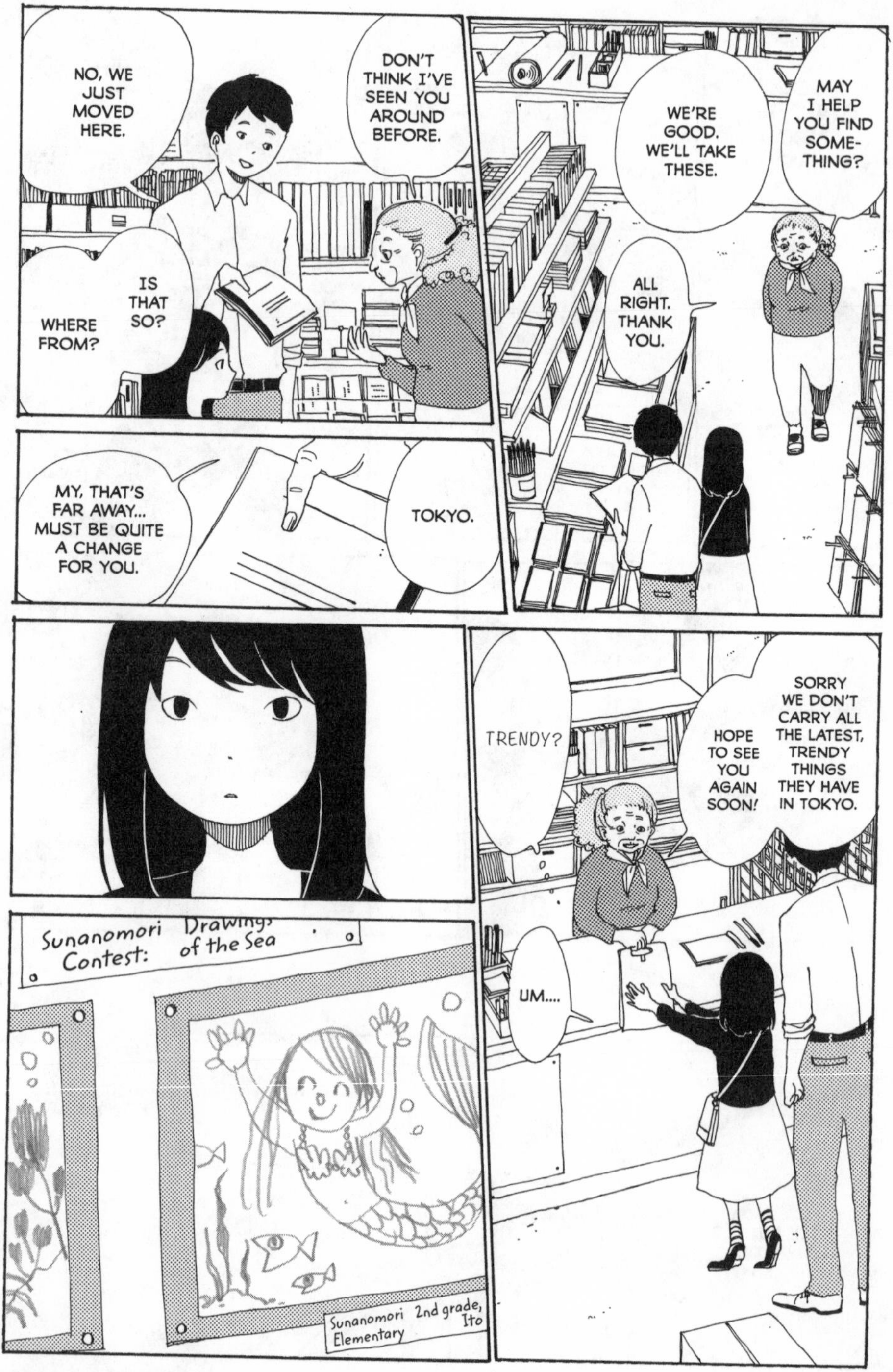
MAY I HELP YOU FIND SOME-THING?
WE'RE GOOD. WE'LL TAKE THESE.
ALL RIGHT. THANK YOU.
DON'T THINK I'VE SEEN YOU AROUND BEFORE.
NO, WE JUST MOVED HERE.
IS THAT SO?
WHERE FROM?
TOKYO.
MY, THAT'S FAR AWAY... MUST BE QUITE A CHANGE FOR YOU.
SORRY WE DON'T CARRY ALL THE LATEST, TRENDY THINGS THEY HAVE IN TOKYO.
HOPE TO SEE YOU AGAIN SOON!
TRENDY?
UM....
Sunanomori Contest: Drawings of the Sea
Sunanomori Elementary 2nd grade, Ito

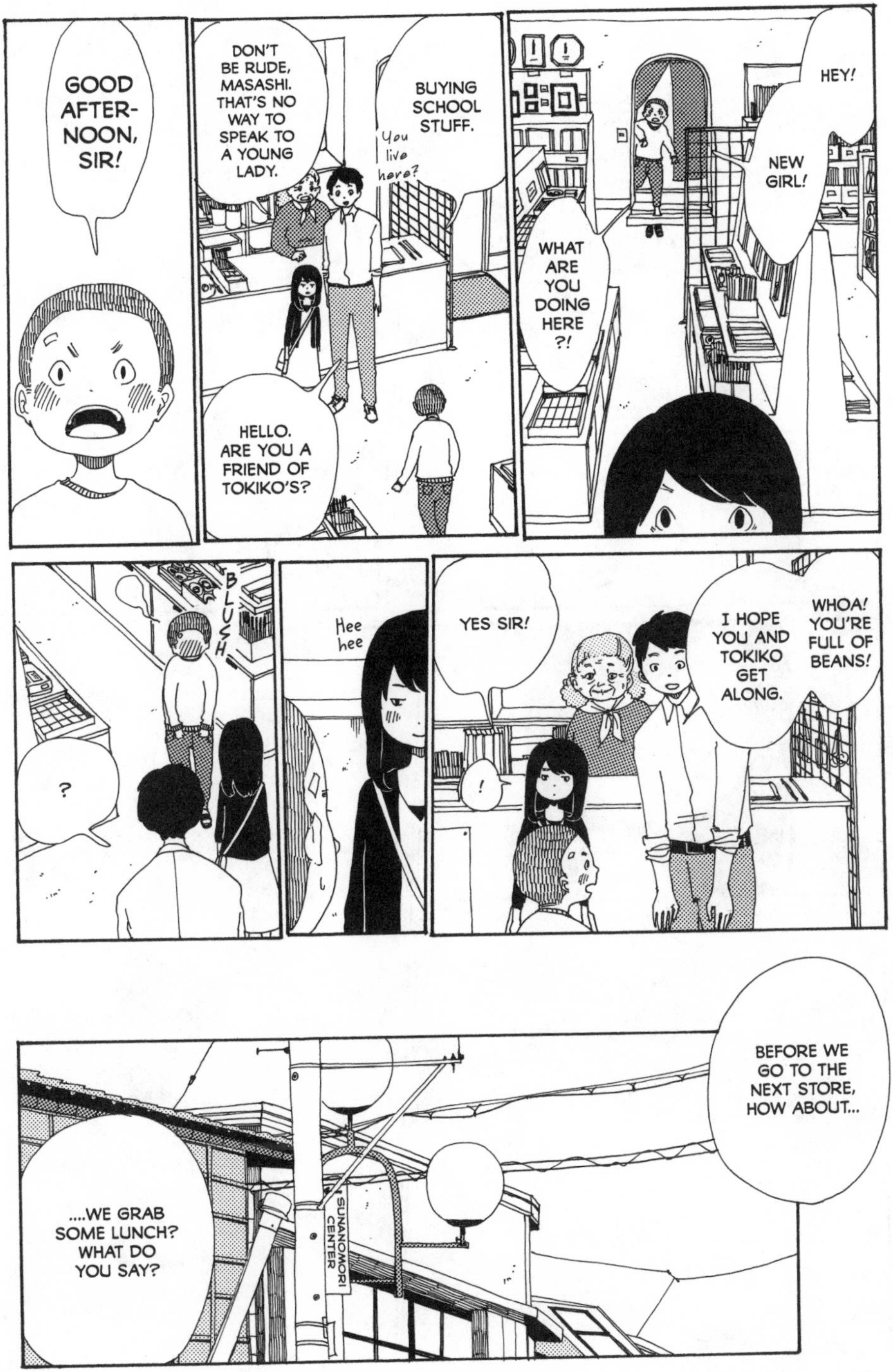
HEY!
NEW GIRL!
WHAT ARE YOU DOING HERE?!
BUYING SCHOOL STUFF.
You live here?
DON'T BE RUDE, MASASHI. THAT'S NO WAY TO SPEAK TO A YOUNG LADY.
HELLO. ARE YOU A FRIEND OF TOKIKO'S?
GOOD AFTER-NOON, SIR!
WHOA! YOU'RE FULL OF BEANS!
I HOPE YOU AND TOKIKO GET ALONG.
YES SIR!
!
Hee hee
BLUSH
?
BEFORE WE GO TO THE NEXT STORE, HOW ABOUT...
SUNANOMORI CENTER
....WE GRAB SOME LUNCH? WHAT DO YOU SAY?

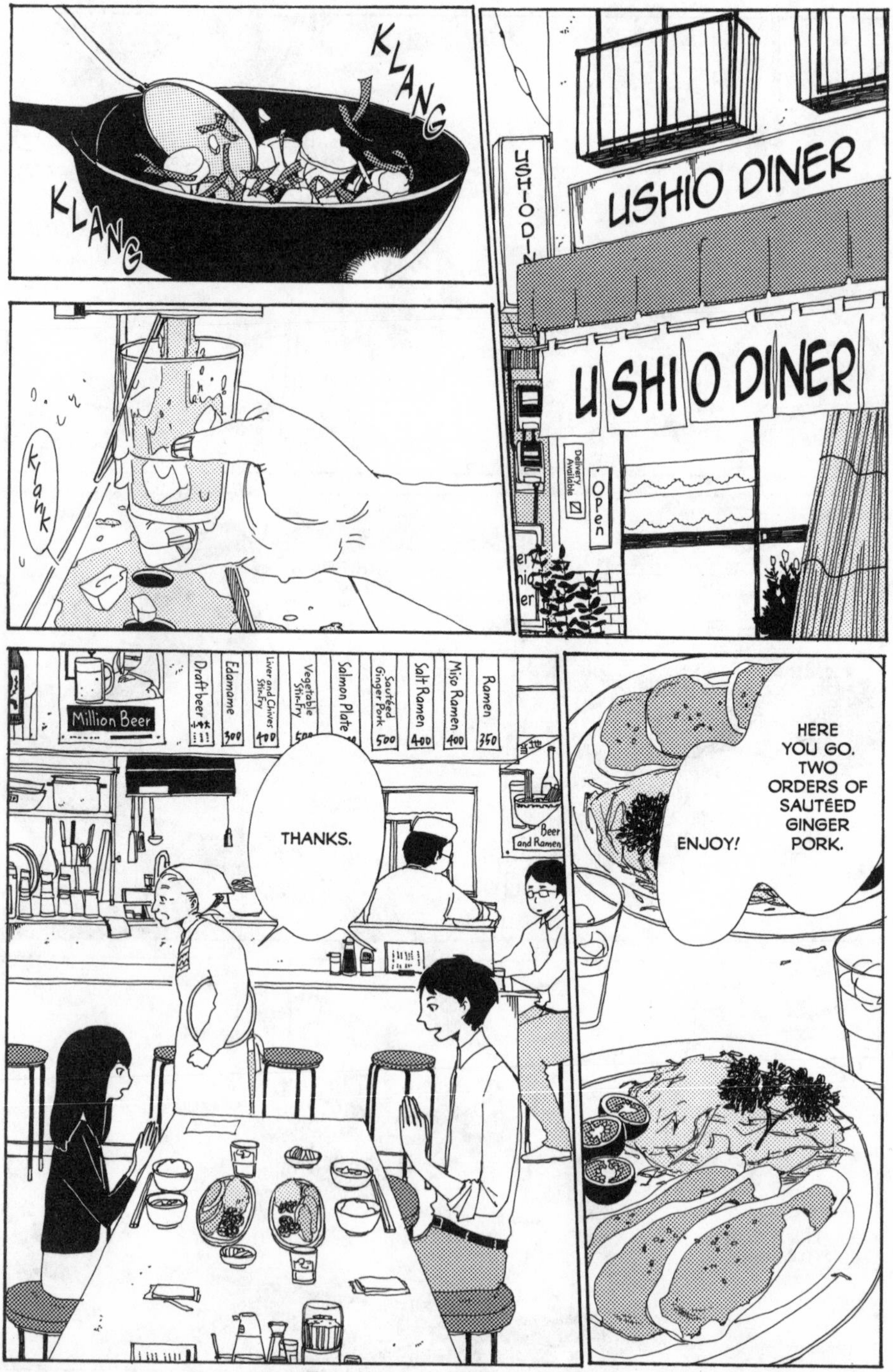
USHIO DIN
USHIO DINER
USHIO DINER
Delivery Available
Open
KLANG
KLANG
klank
Ramen 350
Miso Ramen 400
Salt Ramen 400
Sautéed Ginger Pork 500
Salmon Plate
Vegetable Stir-Fry 500
Liver and Chives Stir-Fry 400
Edamame 300
Draft beer
Million Beer
Beer and Ramen
HERE YOU GO. TWO ORDERS OF SAUTÉED GINGER PORK.
ENJOY!
THANKS.

...
HOW'S YOUR NEW JOB?
GOOD. MY COWORKERS ARE NICE.
GOOD.
UM... WHAT IS IT YOU DO EXACTLY?
THERE'S A FISHING PORT IN THE NEXT TOWN OVER. I WORK AT THE FACTORY THERE.
OH.
IT'S ON THE OTHER SIDE OF THE TUNNEL.
OH.
THERE ARE A LOT OF BIG BOATS OVER THERE.
SEAGULLS TOO.
IT'S A CUTE LITTLE HARBOR.

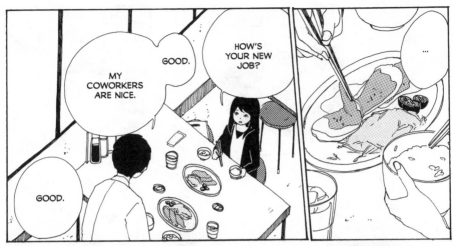

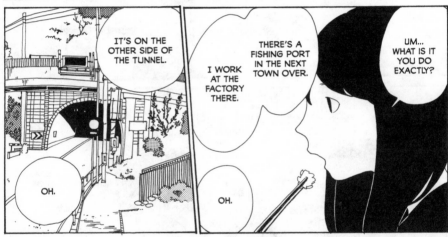

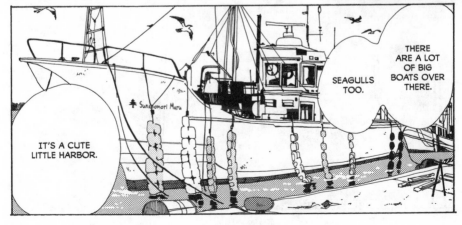

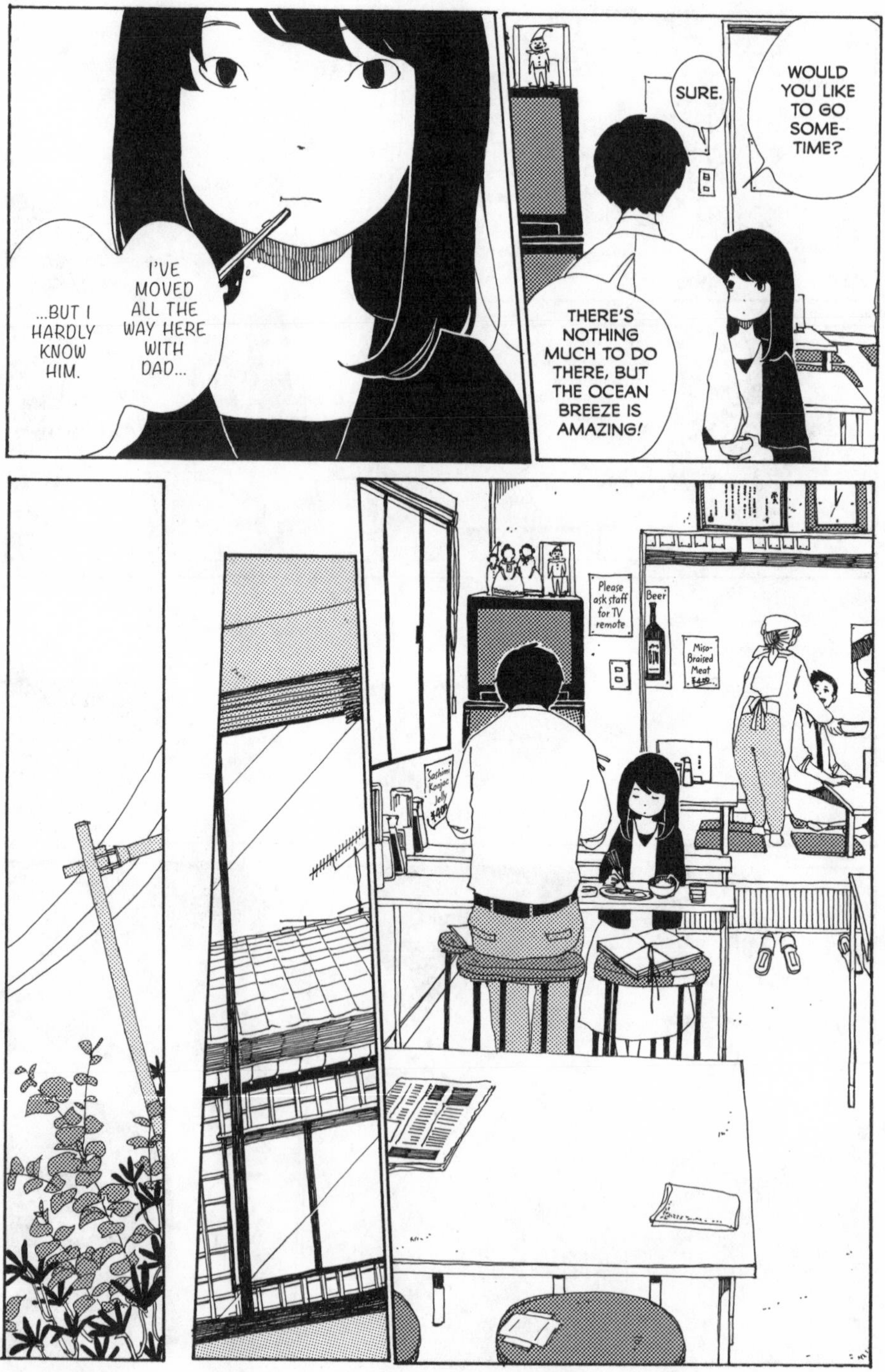
WOULD YOU LIKE TO GO SOME-TIME?
SURE.
THERE'S NOTHING MUCH TO DO THERE, BUT THE OCEAN BREEZE IS AMAZING!
I'VE MOVED ALL THE WAY HERE WITH DAD...
...BUT I HARDLY KNOW HIM.
Please ask staff for TV remote
Beer
Miso-Braised Meat
Sashimi Konjac Jelly

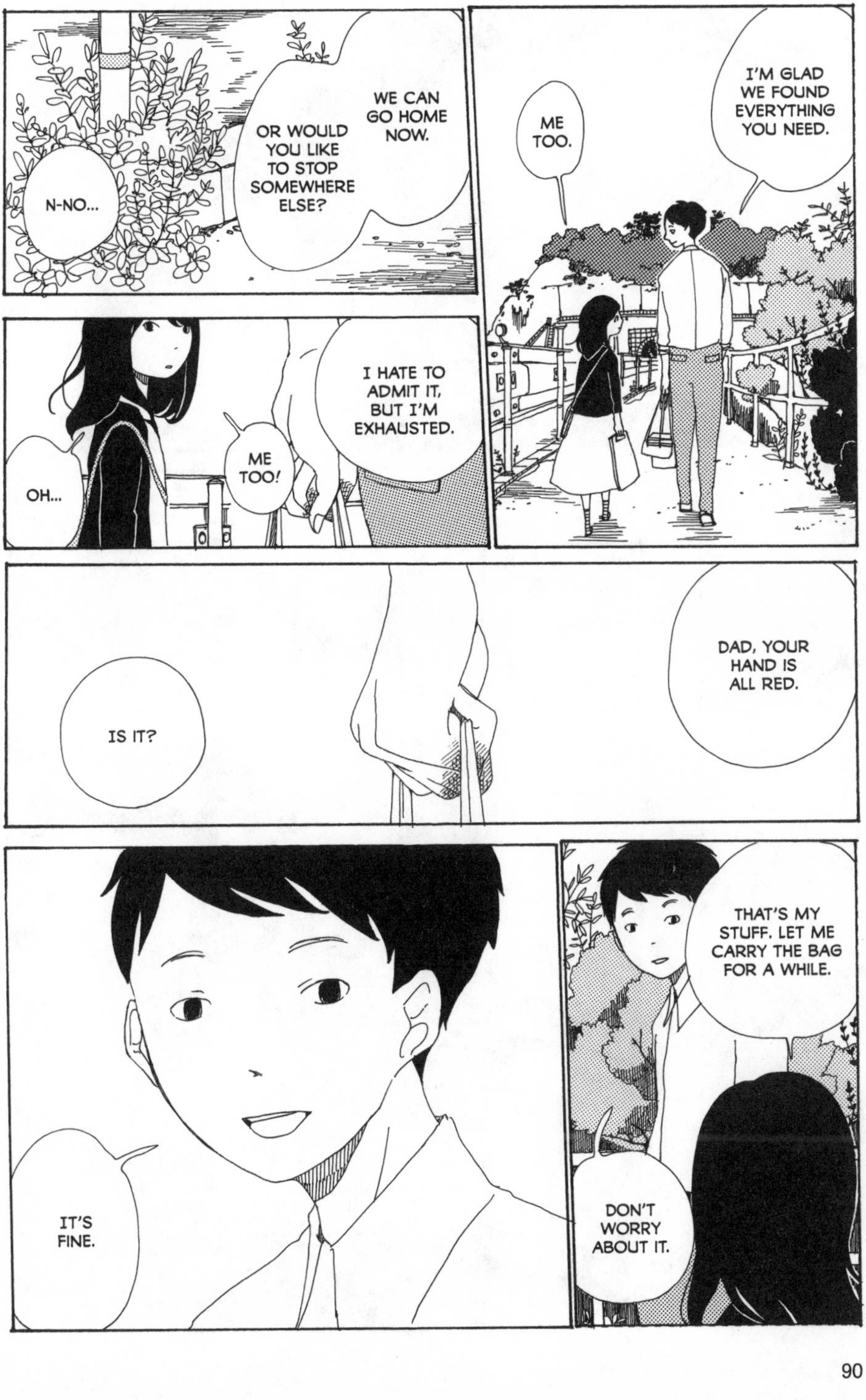
I'M GLAD WE FOUND EVERYTHING YOU NEED.
ME TOO.
WE CAN GO HOME NOW.
OR WOULD YOU LIKE TO STOP SOMEWHERE ELSE?
N-NO...
I HATE TO ADMIT IT, BUT I'M EXHAUSTED.
ME TOO!
OH...
DAD, YOUR HAND IS ALL RED.
IS IT?
THAT'S MY STUFF. LET ME CARRY THE BAG FOR A WHILE.
DON'T WORRY ABOUT IT.
IT'S FINE.

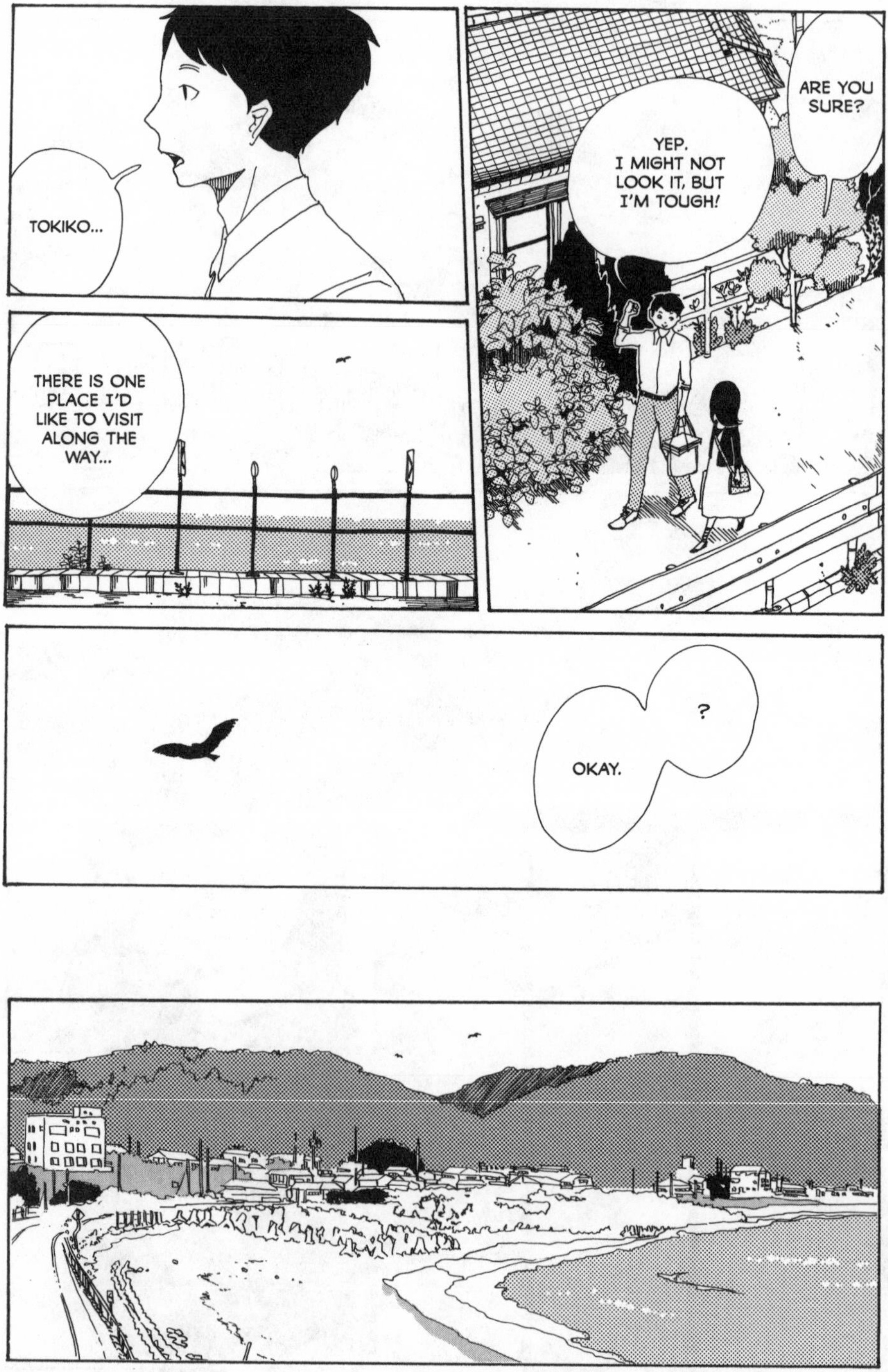
ARE YOU SURE?
YEP. I MIGHT NOT LOOK IT, BUT I'M TOUGH!
TOKIKO...
THERE IS ONE PLACE I'D LIKE TO VISIT ALONG THE WAY...
?
OKAY.

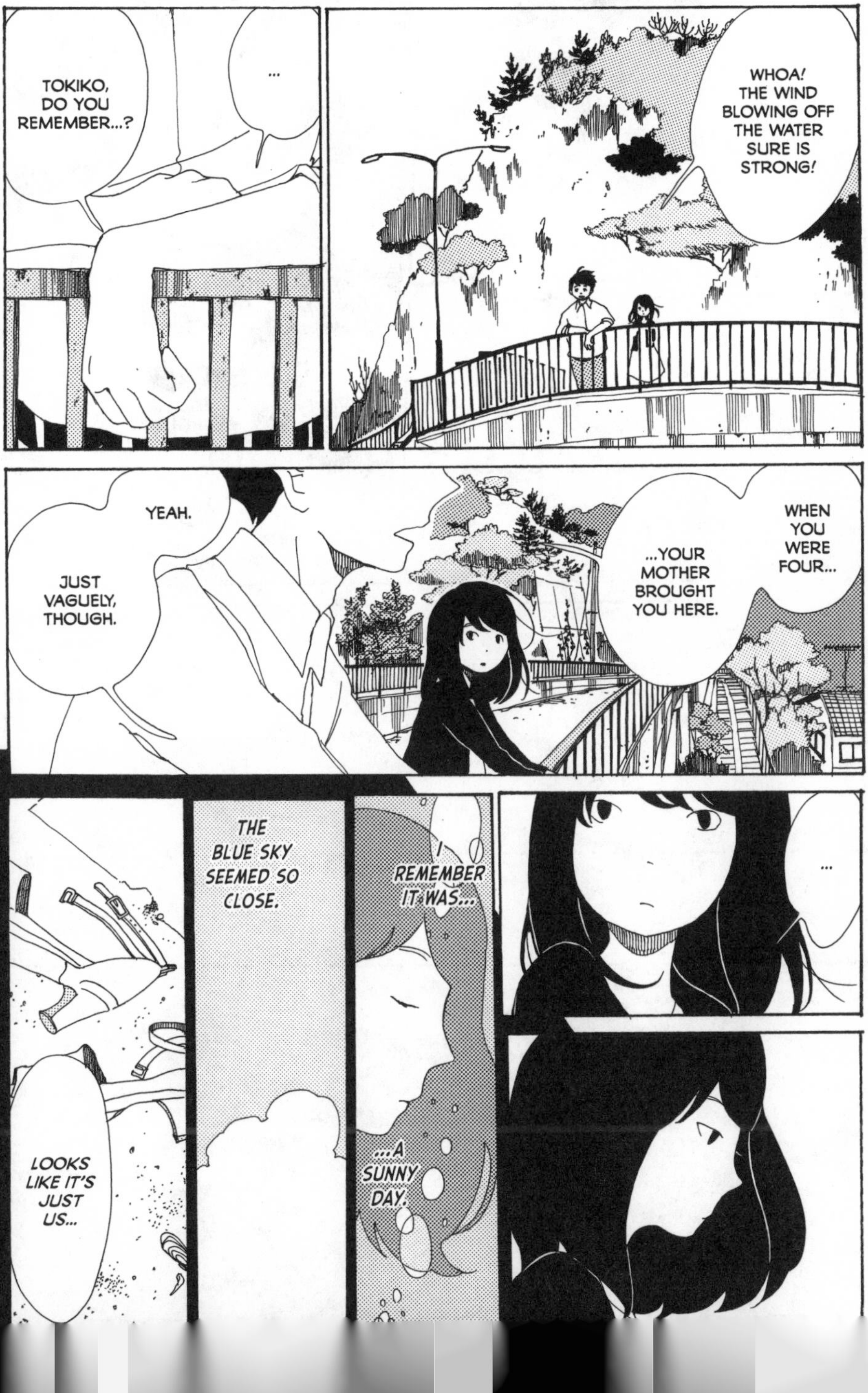
WHOA! THE WIND BLOWING OFF THE WATER SURE IS STRONG!
...
TOKIKO, DO YOU REMEMBER...?
WHEN YOU WERE FOUR...
...YOUR MOTHER BROUGHT YOU HERE.
YEAH.
JUST VAGUELY, THOUGH.
...
I REMEMBER IT WAS...
...A SUNNY DAY.
THE BLUE SKY SEEMED SO CLOSE.
LOOKS LIKE IT'S JUST US...

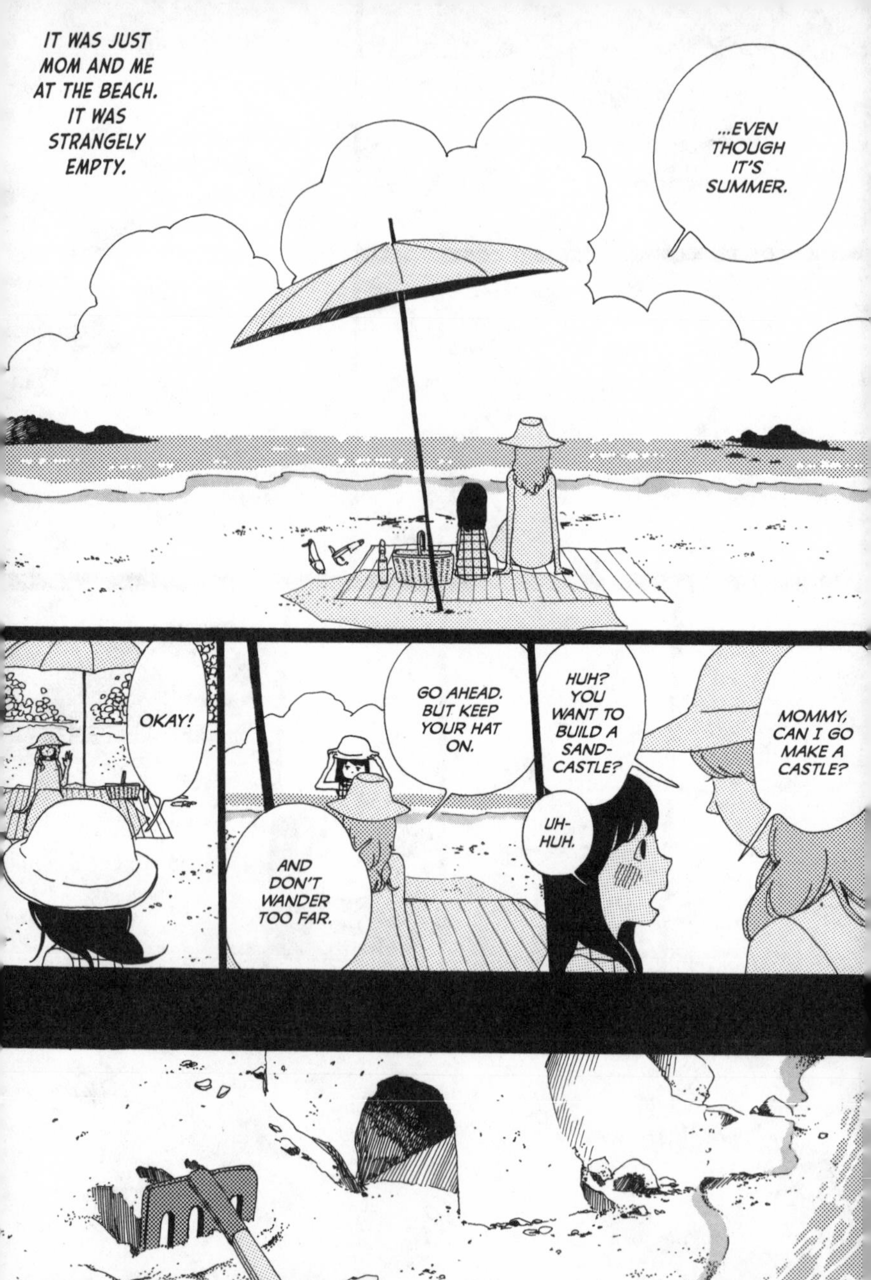
IT WAS JUST MOM AND ME AT THE BEACH. IT WAS STRANGELY EMPTY.
...EVEN THOUGH IT'S SUMMER.
MOMMY, CAN I GO MAKE A CASTLE?
HUH? YOU WANT TO BUILD A SAND-CASTLE?
UH-HUH.
GO AHEAD. BUT KEEP YOUR HAT ON.
AND DON'T WANDER TOO FAR.
OKAY!

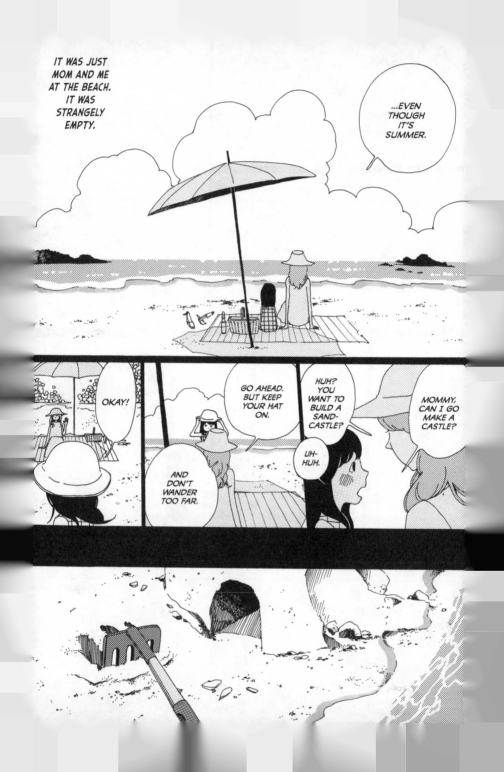

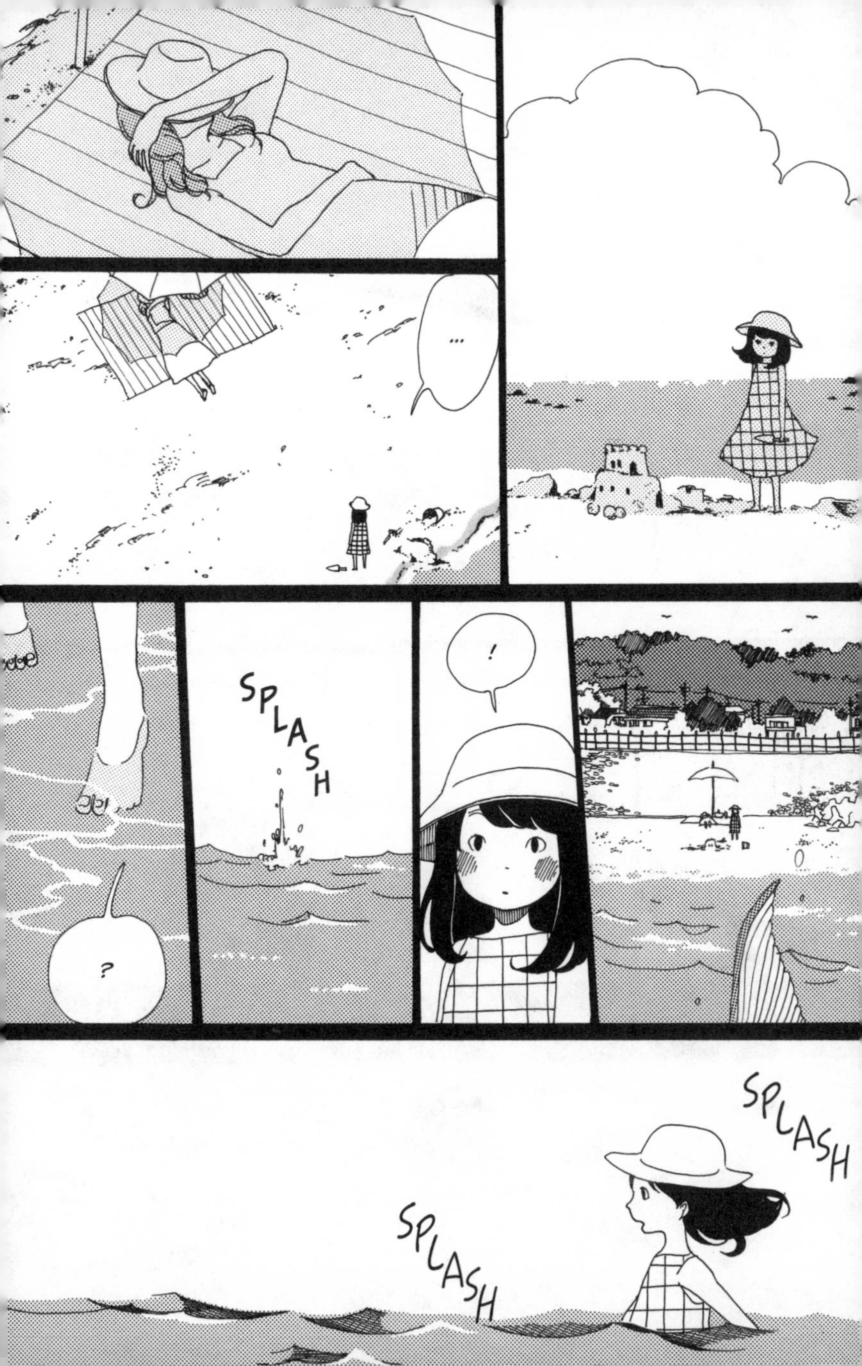
...
!
SPLASH
?
SPLASH
SPLASH

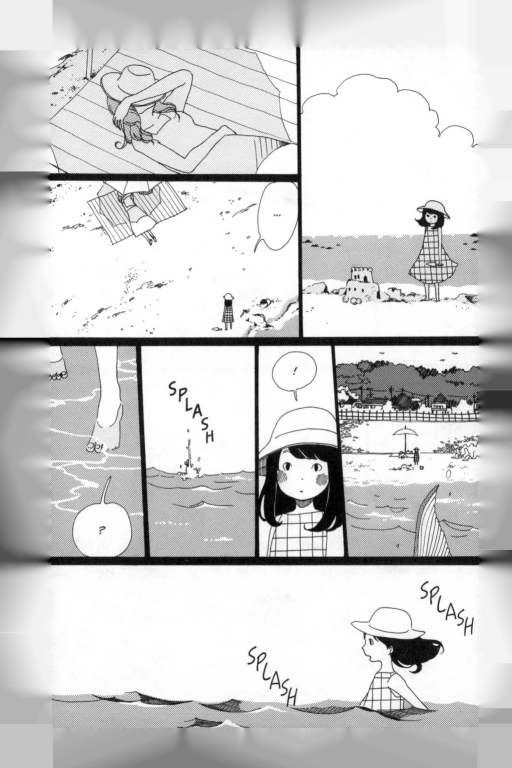

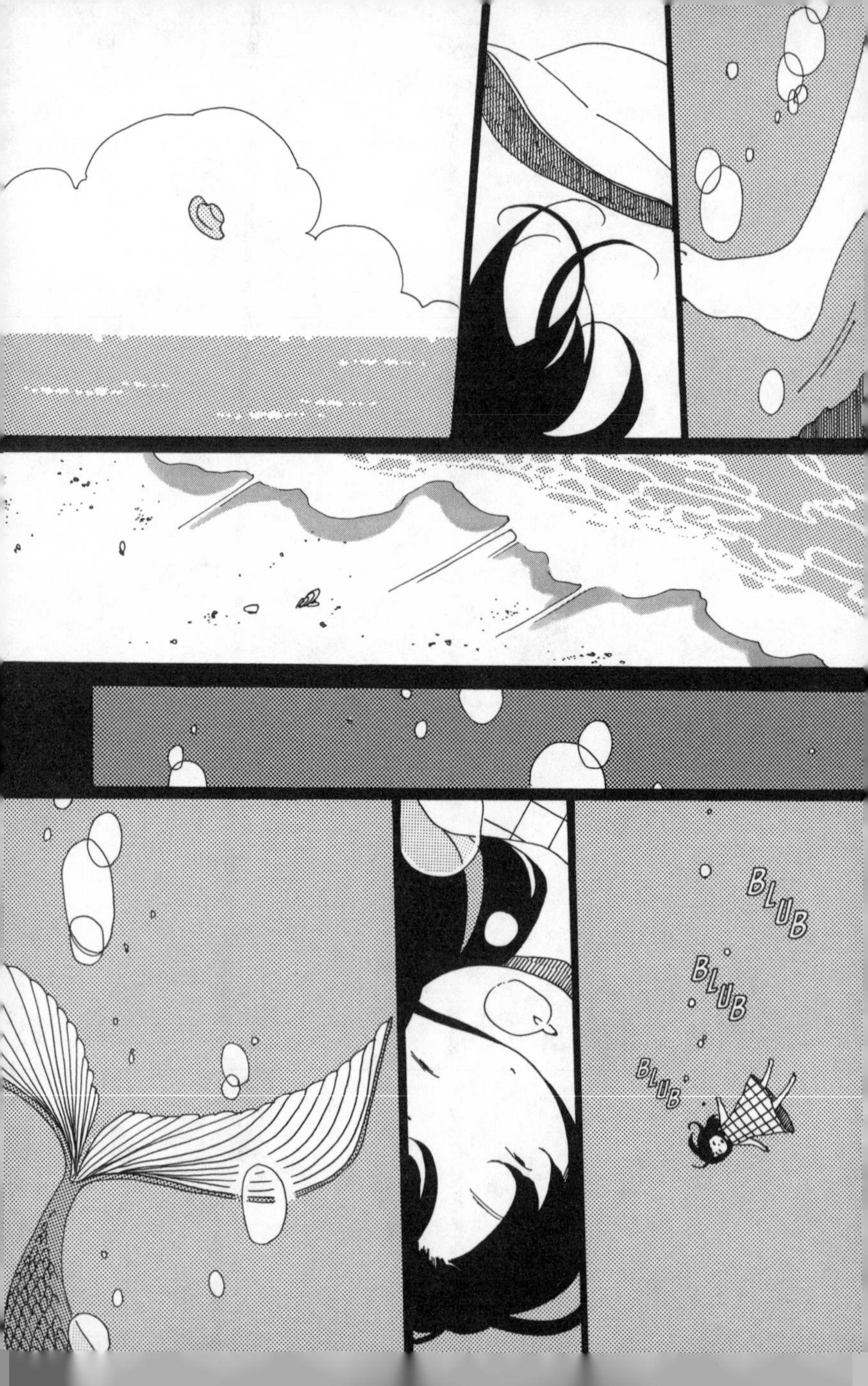
BLUB
BLUB
BLUB

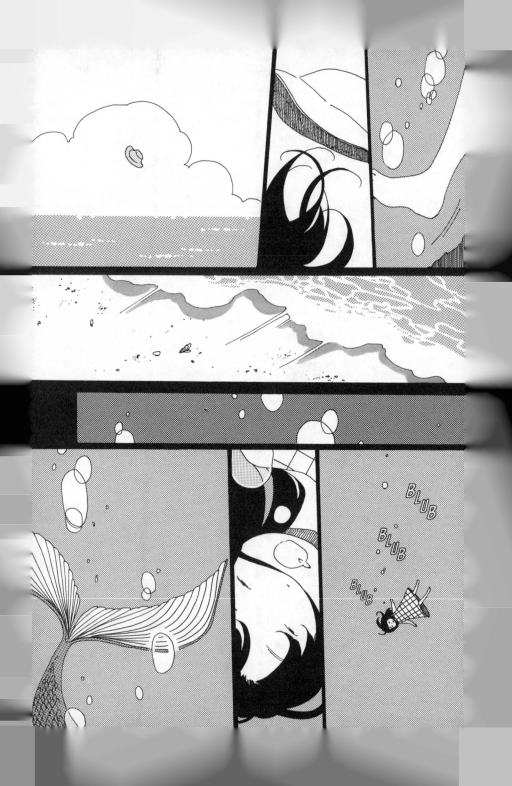

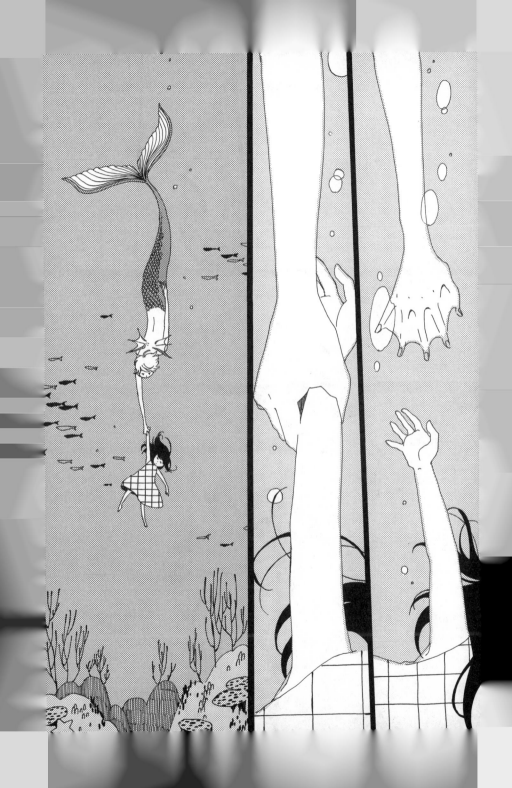

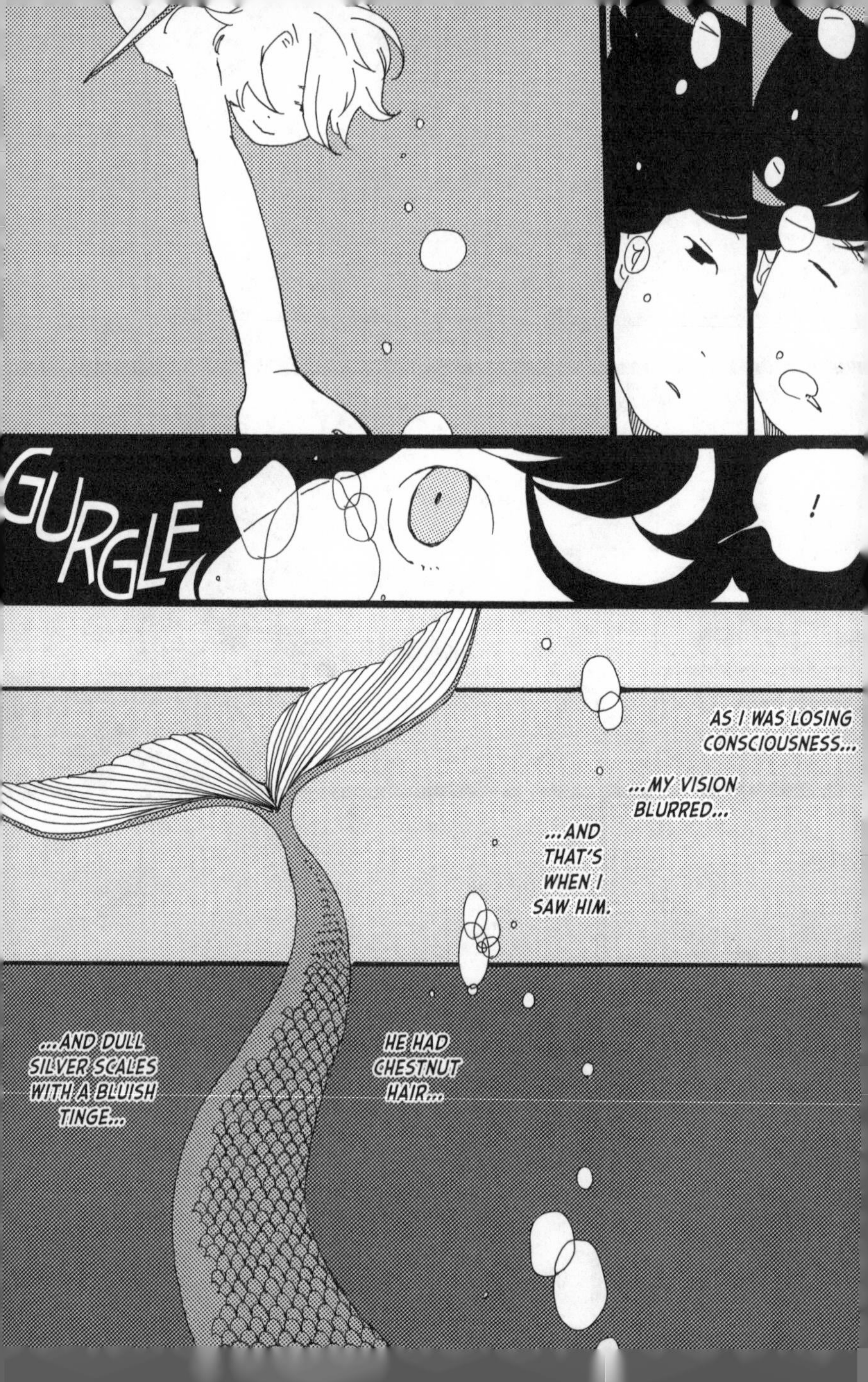
!
GURGLE
AS I WAS LOSING CONSCIOUSNESS...
...MY VISION BLURRED...
...AND THAT'S WHEN I SAW HIM.
HE HAD CHESTNUT HAIR...
...AND DULL SILVER SCALES WITH A BLUISH TINGE...

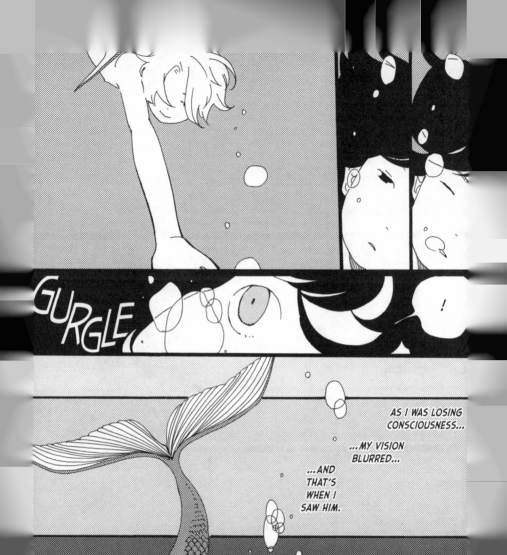

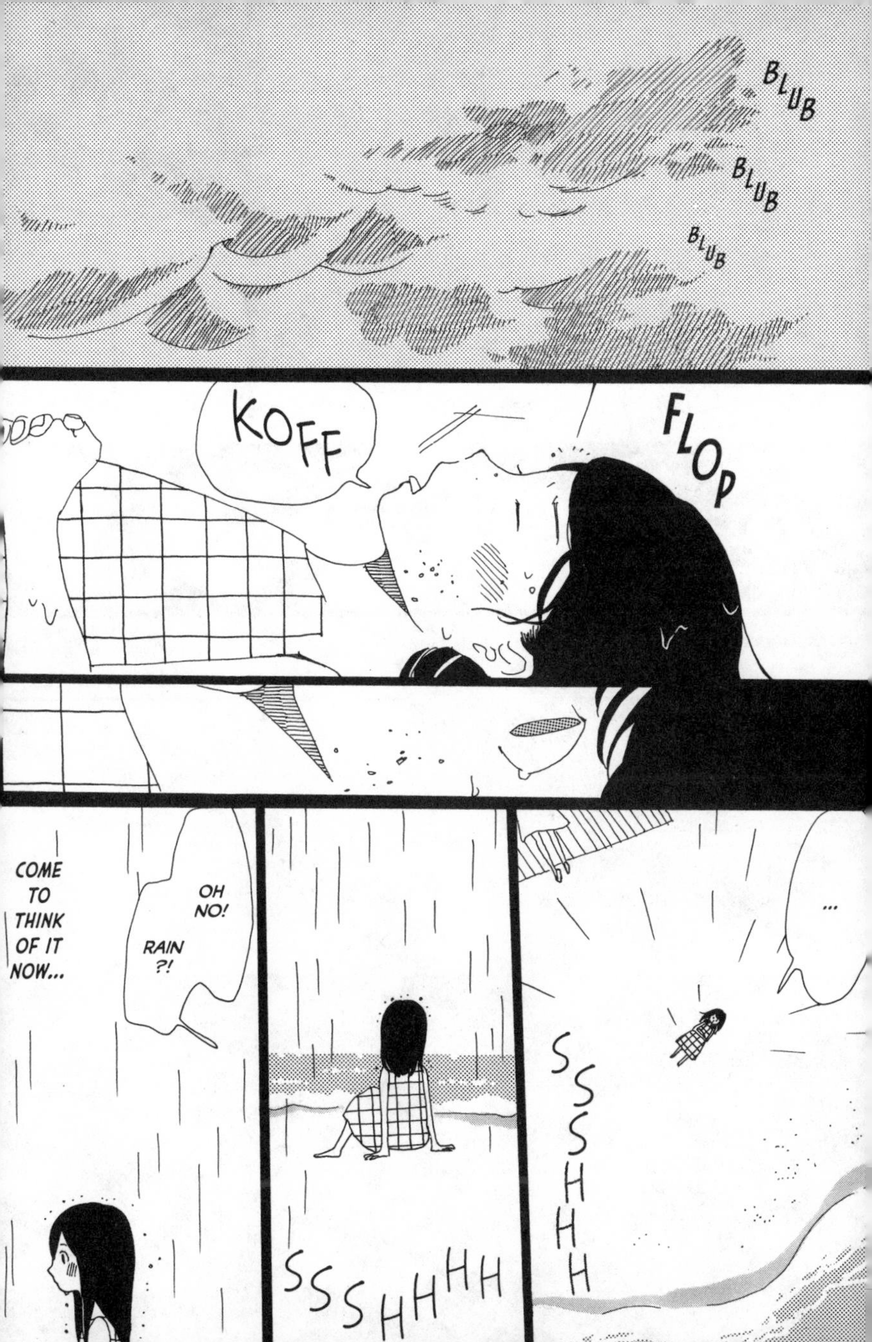

BLUB
BLUB
BLUB
FLOP
KOFF
...
SSSHHHH
SSSHHHH
OH NO! RAIN?!
COME TO THINK OF IT NOW...

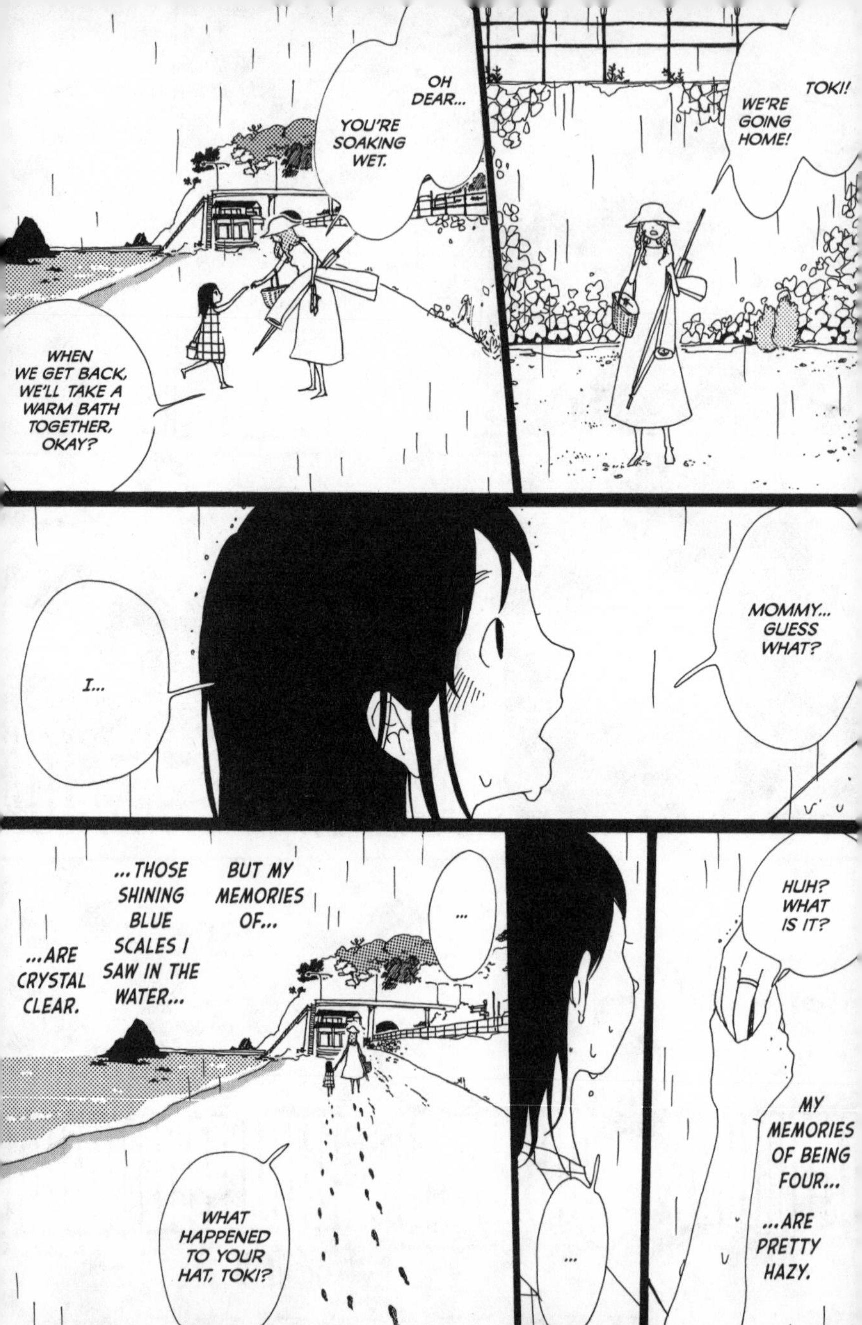
TOKI!
WE'RE GOING HOME!
OH DEAR...
YOU'RE SOAKING WET.
WHEN WE GET BACK, WE'LL TAKE A WARM BATH TOGETHER, OKAY?
MOMMY... GUESS WHAT?
I...
HUH? WHAT IS IT?
MY MEMORIES OF BEING FOUR...
...ARE PRETTY HAZY.
...
...
BUT MY MEMORIES OF...
...THOSE SHINING BLUE SCALES I SAW IN THE WATER...
...ARE CRYSTAL CLEAR.
WHAT HAPPENED TO YOUR HAT, TOKI?

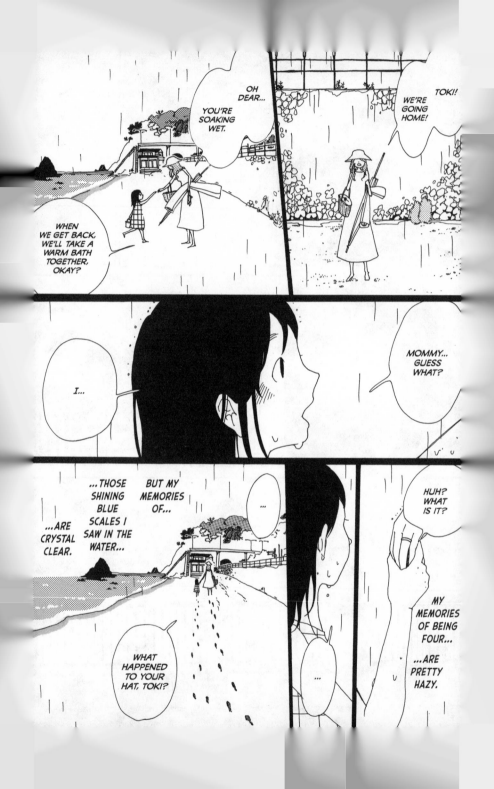

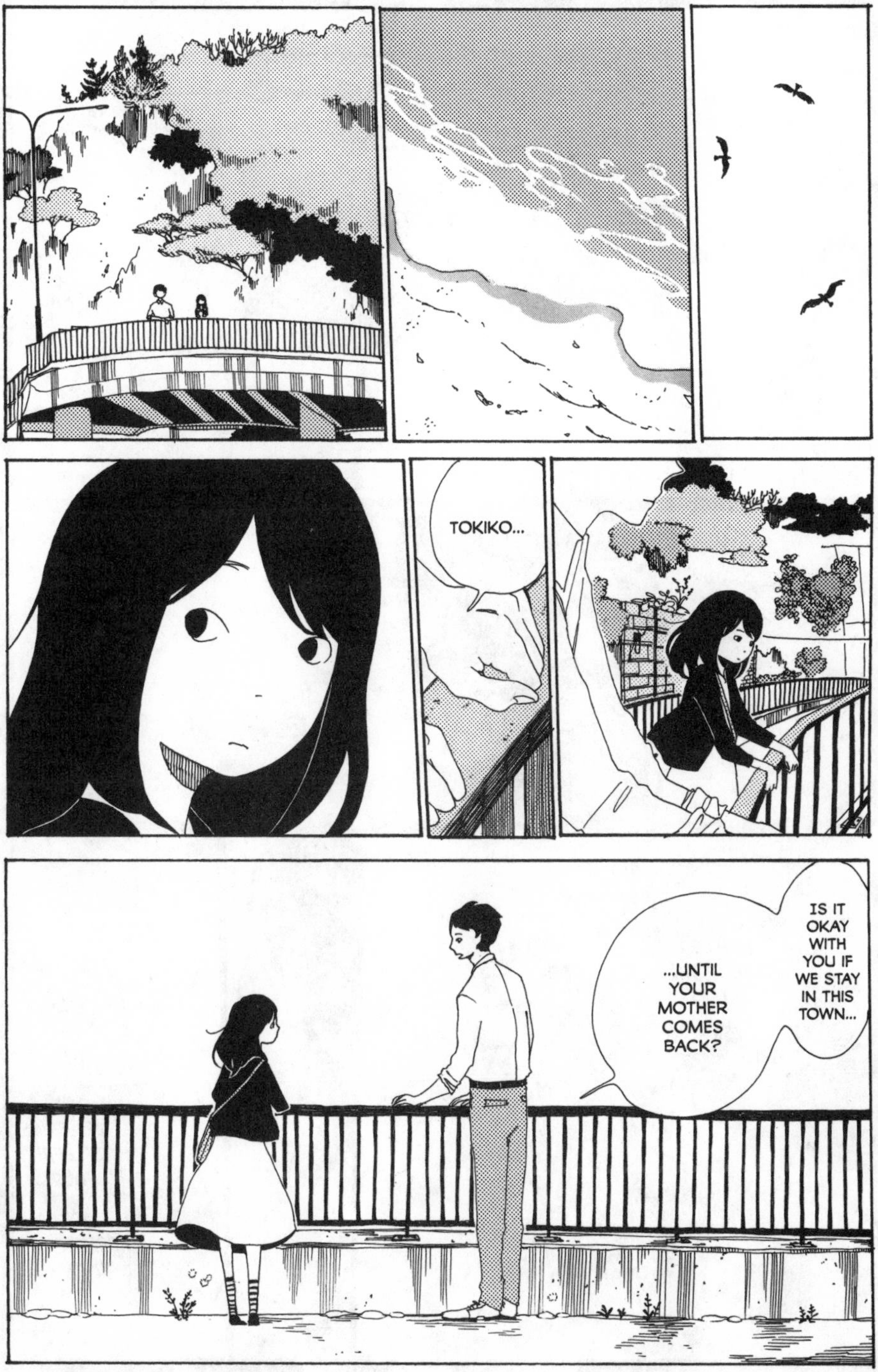
TOKIKO...
IS IT OKAY WITH YOU IF WE STAY IN THIS TOWN...
...UNTIL YOUR MOTHER COMES BACK?

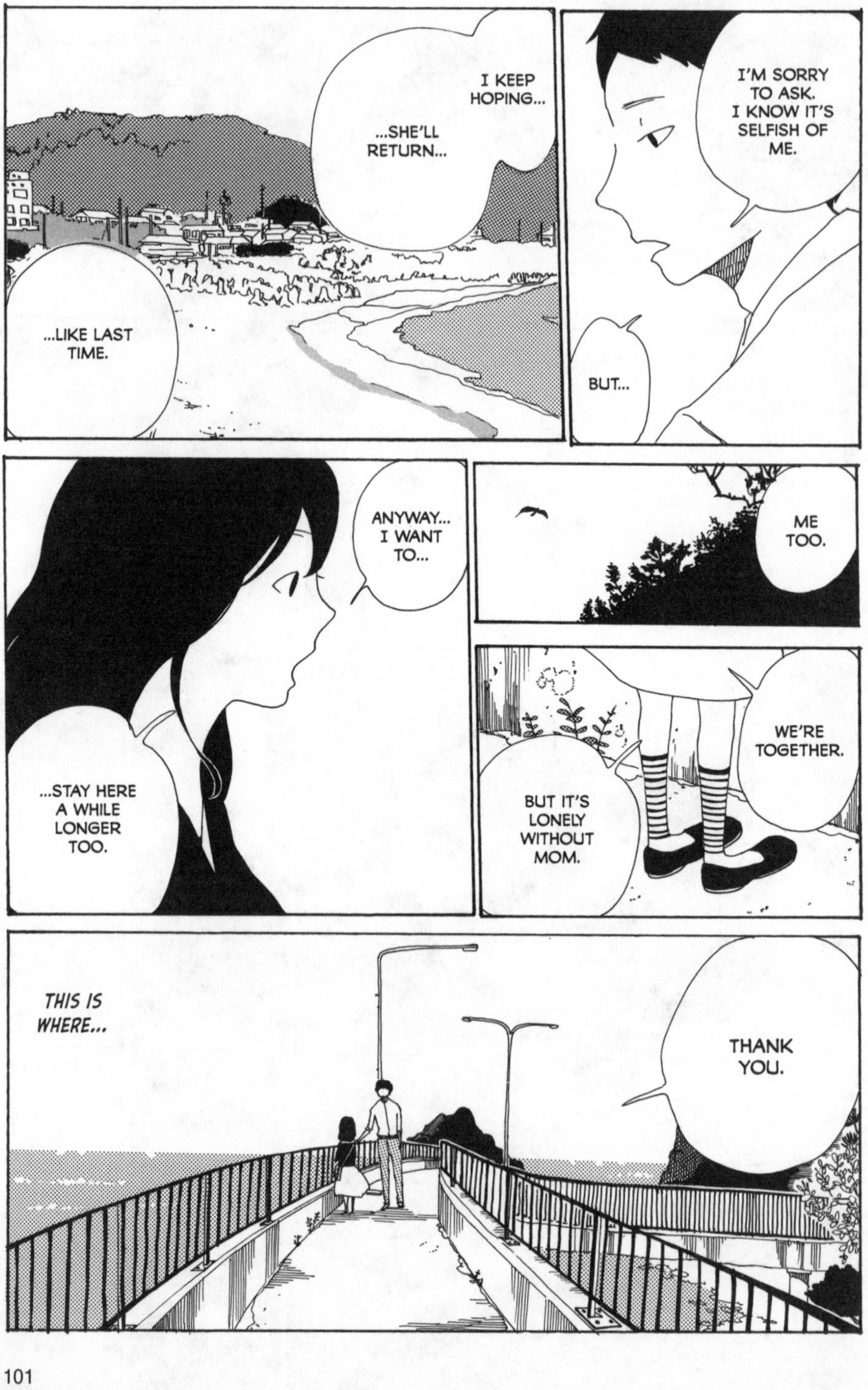
I'M SORRY TO ASK. I KNOW IT'S SELFISH OF ME.
BUT...
I KEEP HOPING...
...SHE'LL RETURN...
...LIKE LAST TIME.
ME TOO.
WE'RE TOGETHER.
BUT IT'S LONELY WITHOUT MOM.
ANYWAY... I WANT TO...
...STAY HERE A WHILE LONGER TOO.
THANK YOU.
THIS IS WHERE...

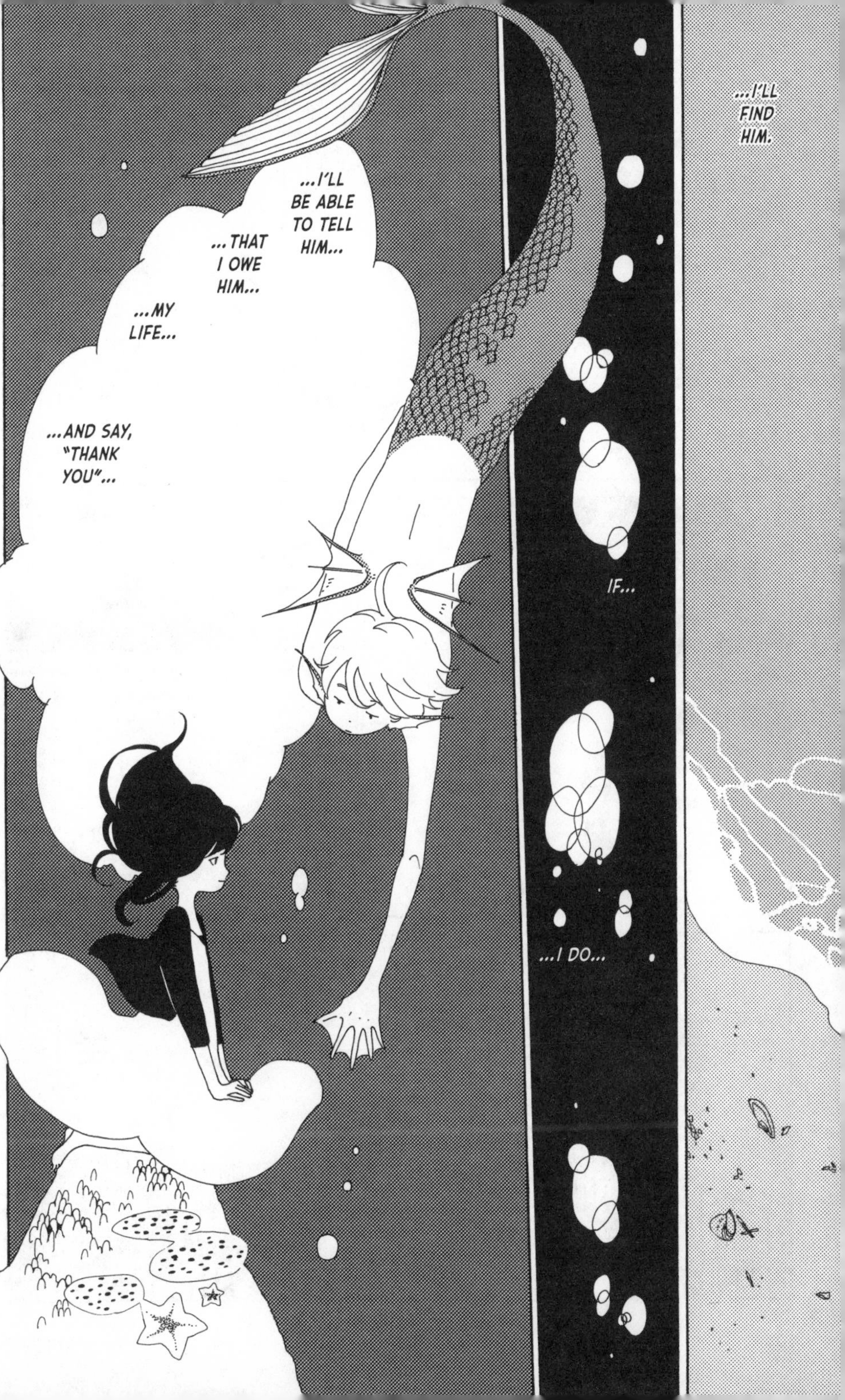
...I'LL FIND HIM.
IF...
...I DO...
...I'LL BE ABLE TO TELL HIM...
...THAT I OWE HIM...
...MY LIFE...
...AND SAY, "THANK YOU"...

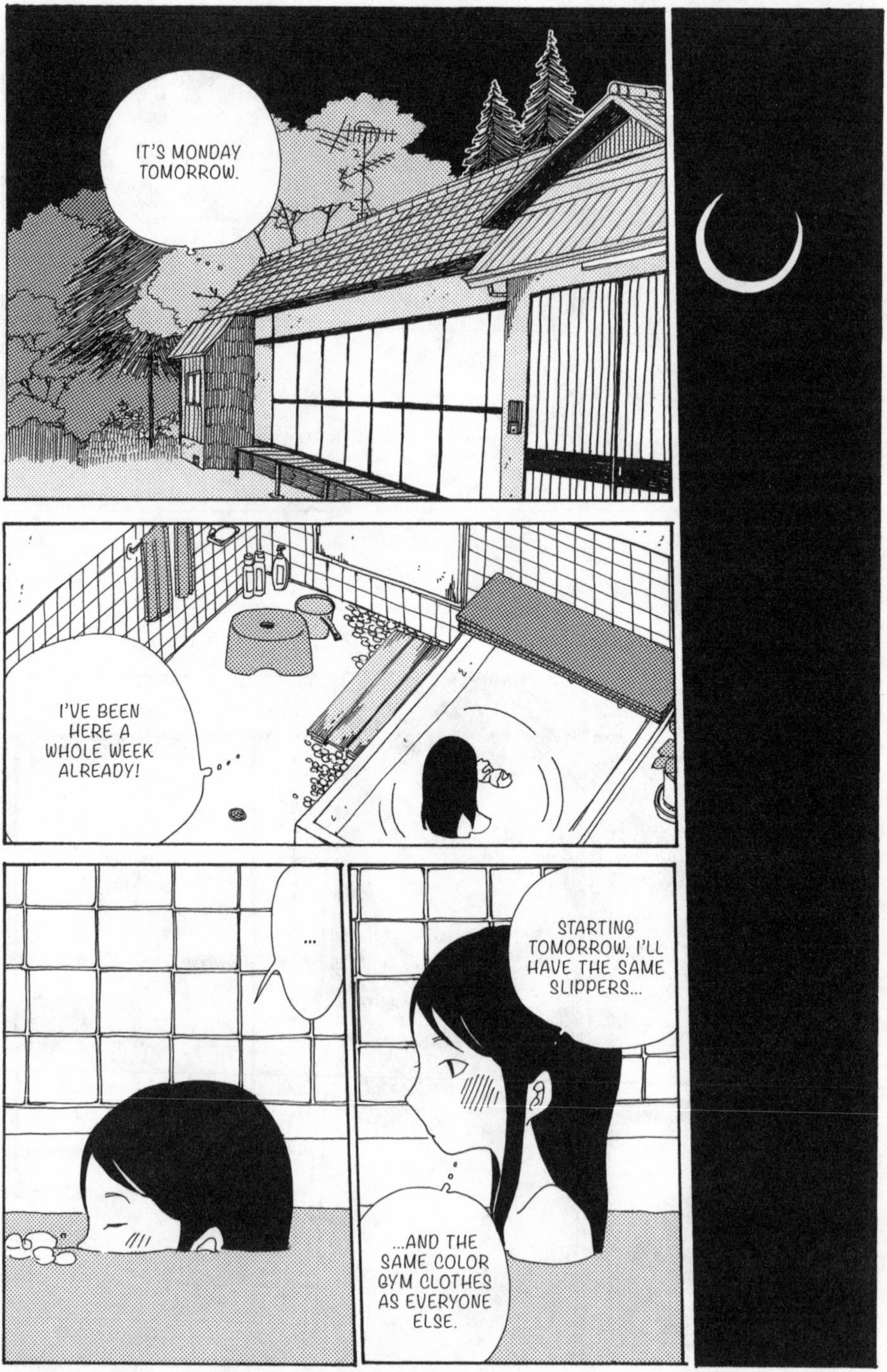
IT'S MONDAY TOMORROW.
I'VE BEEN HERE A WHOLE WEEK ALREADY!
STARTING TOMORROW, I'LL HAVE THE SAME SLIPPERS...
...AND THE SAME COLOR GYM CLOTHES AS EVERYONE ELSE.
...

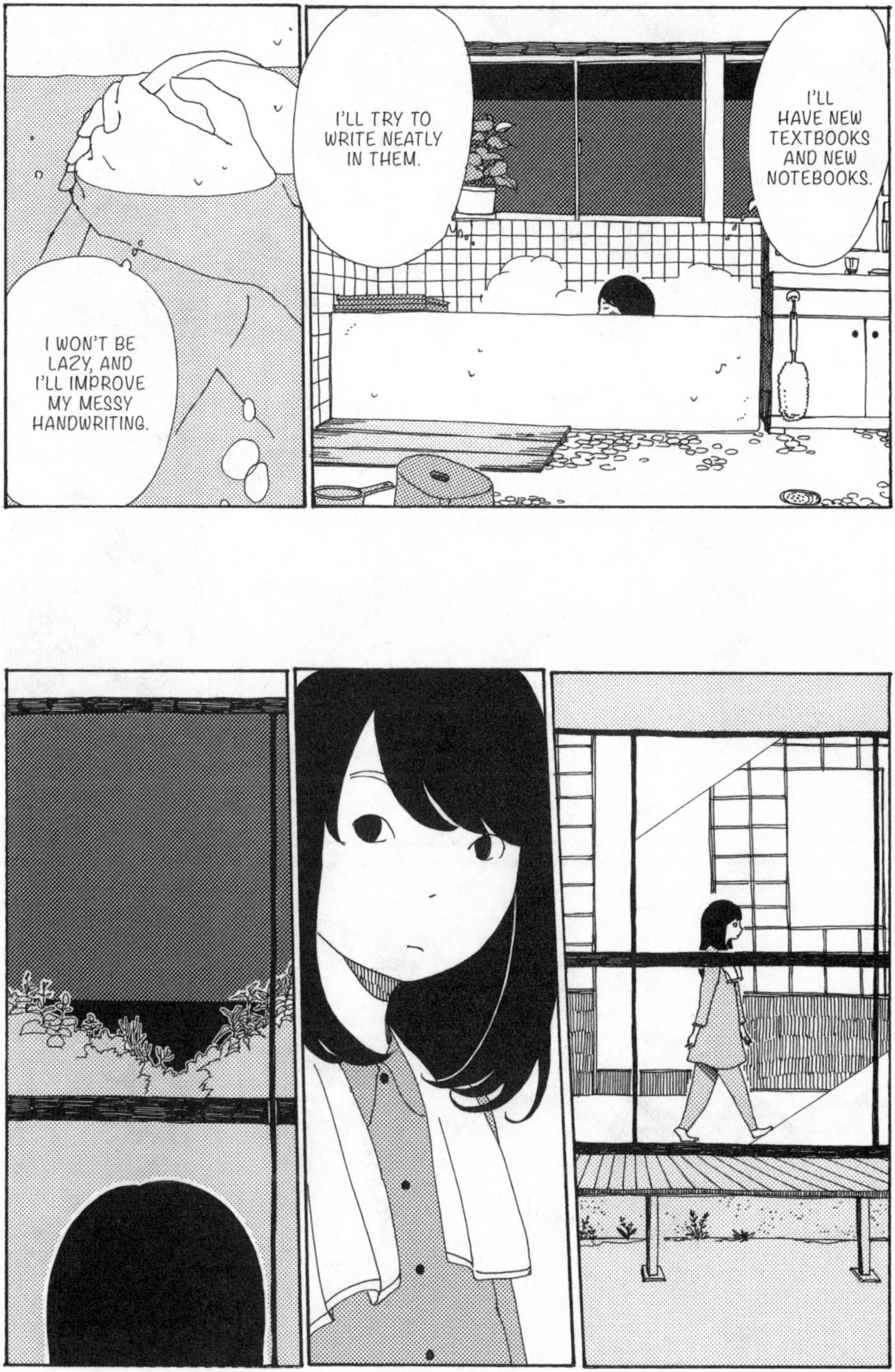
I'LL HAVE NEW TEXTBOOKS AND NEW NOTEBOOKS.
I'LL TRY TO WRITE NEATLY IN THEM.
I WON'T BE LAZY, AND I'LL IMPROVE MY MESSY HANDWRITING.

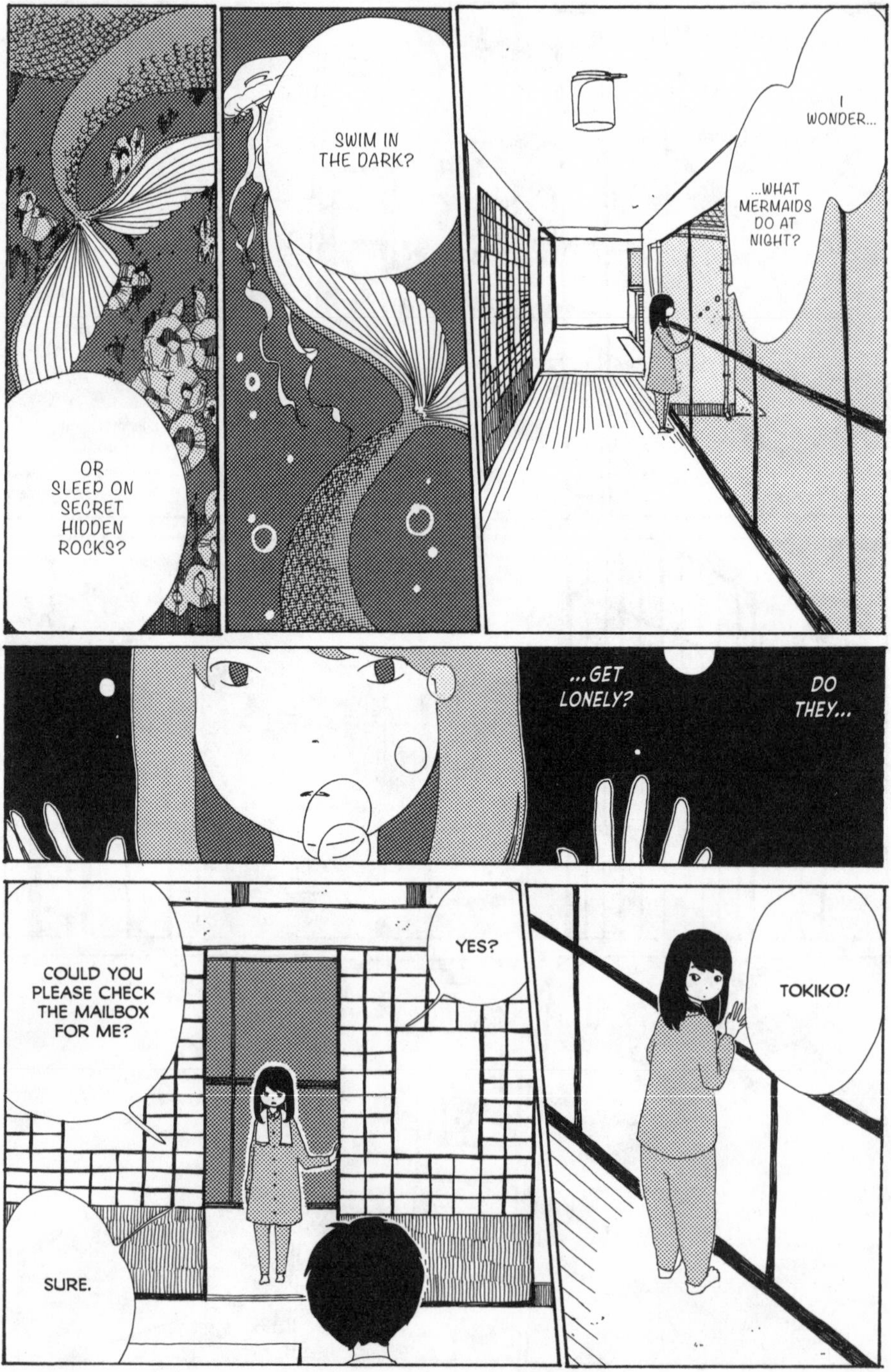
I WONDER...
...WHAT MERMAIDS DO AT NIGHT?
SWIM IN THE DARK?
OR SLEEP ON SECRET HIDDEN ROCKS?
DO THEY...
...GET LONELY?
TOKIKO!
YES?
COULD YOU PLEASE CHECK THE MAILBOX FOR ME?
SURE.

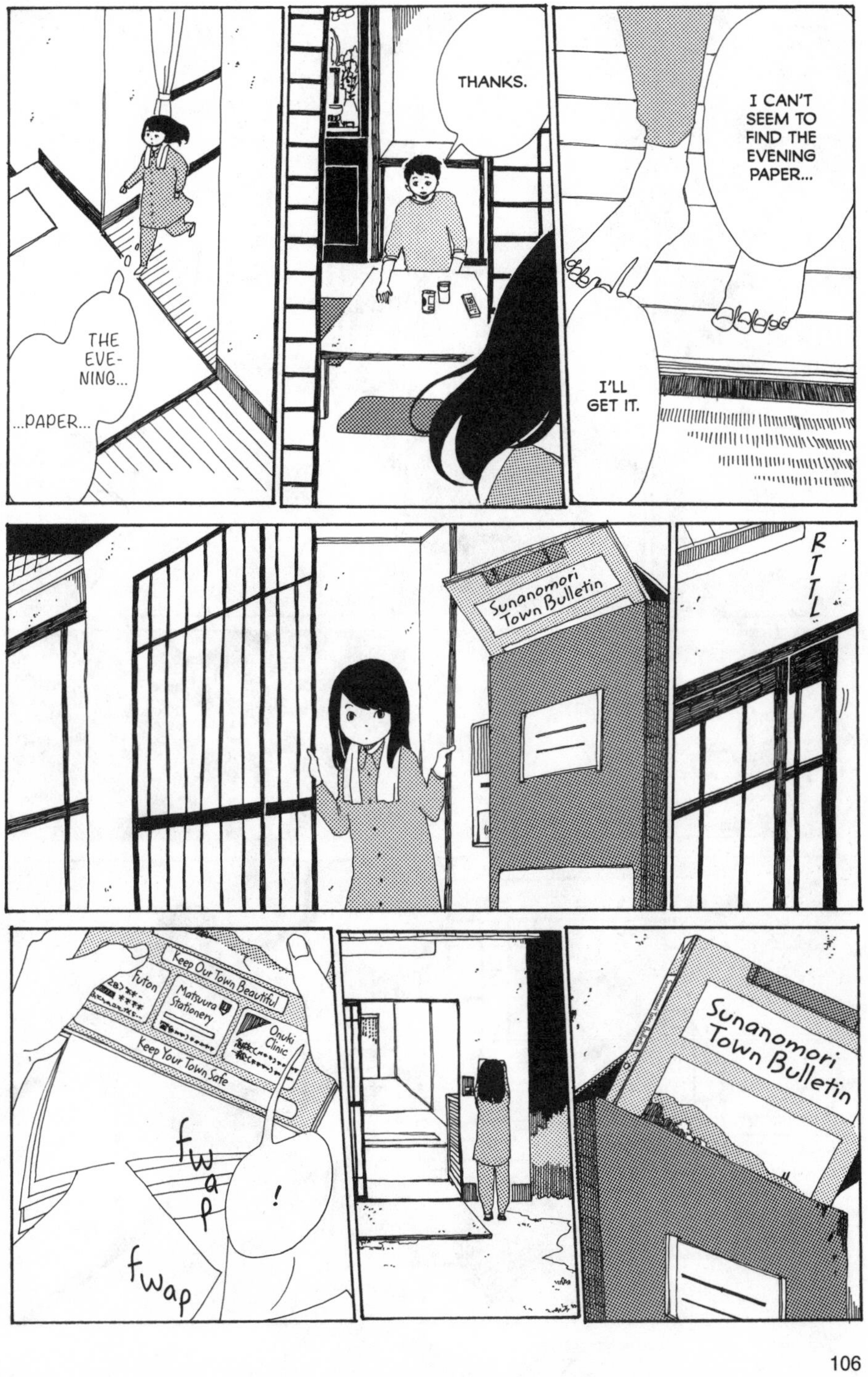
I CAN'T SEEM TO FIND THE EVENING PAPER...
I'LL GET IT.
THANKS.
THE EVE-NING...
...PAPER...
RTTL
Sunanomori Town Bulletin
Sunanomori Town Bulletin
Keep Our Town Beautiful
Futon
Matsuura Stationery
Onuki Clinic
Keep Your Town Safe
fwap
!
fwap

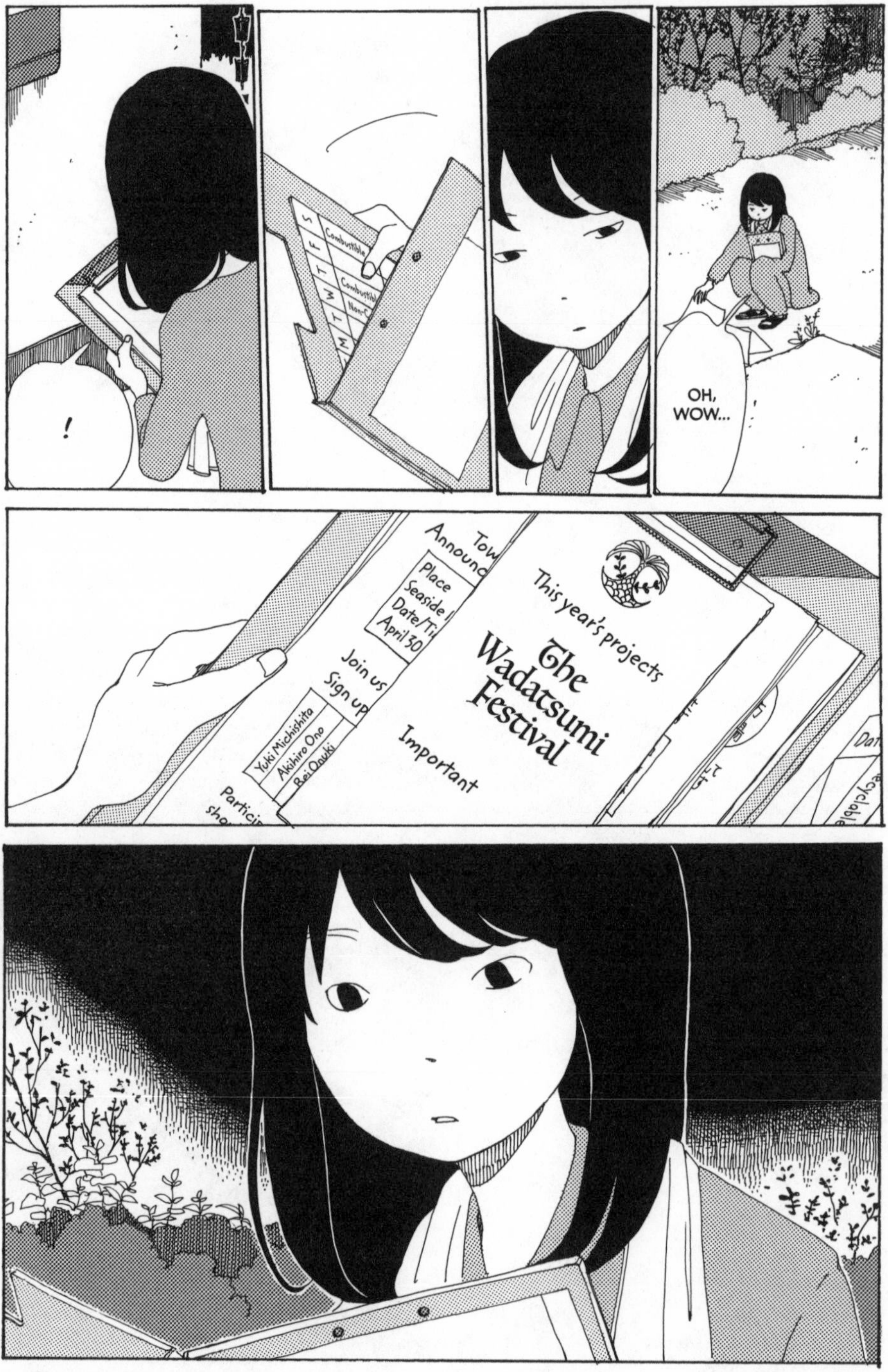
OH, WOW...
Combustible
Combustible
!
This year's projects
The Wadatsumi Festival
Important
Place
Seaside
Date/Ti
April 30
Join us
Sign up
Yuki Michishita
Akihiro Ono
Rei Onuki

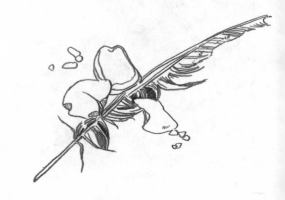

{Four} Secrets of the Deep

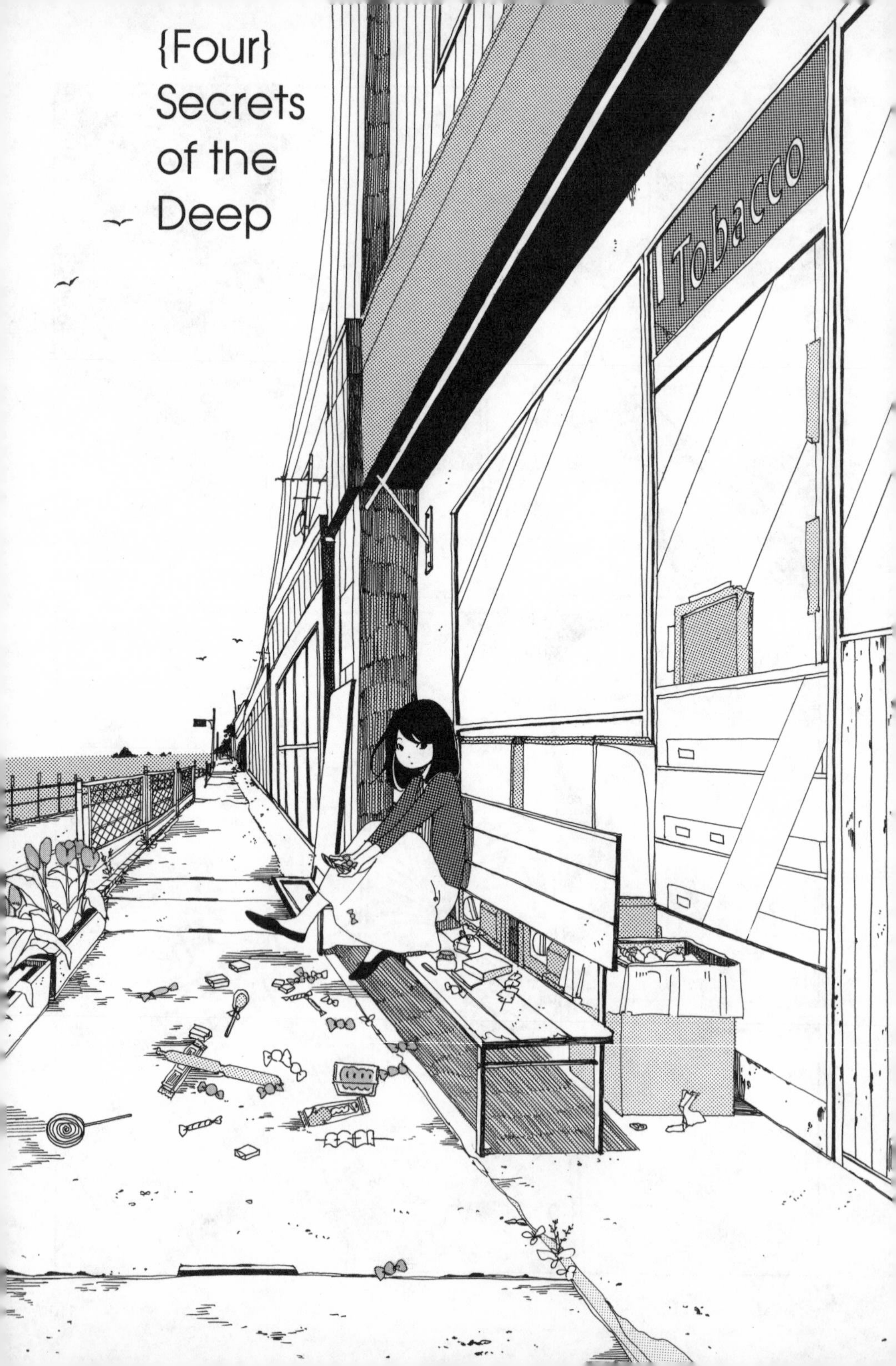
Tobacco

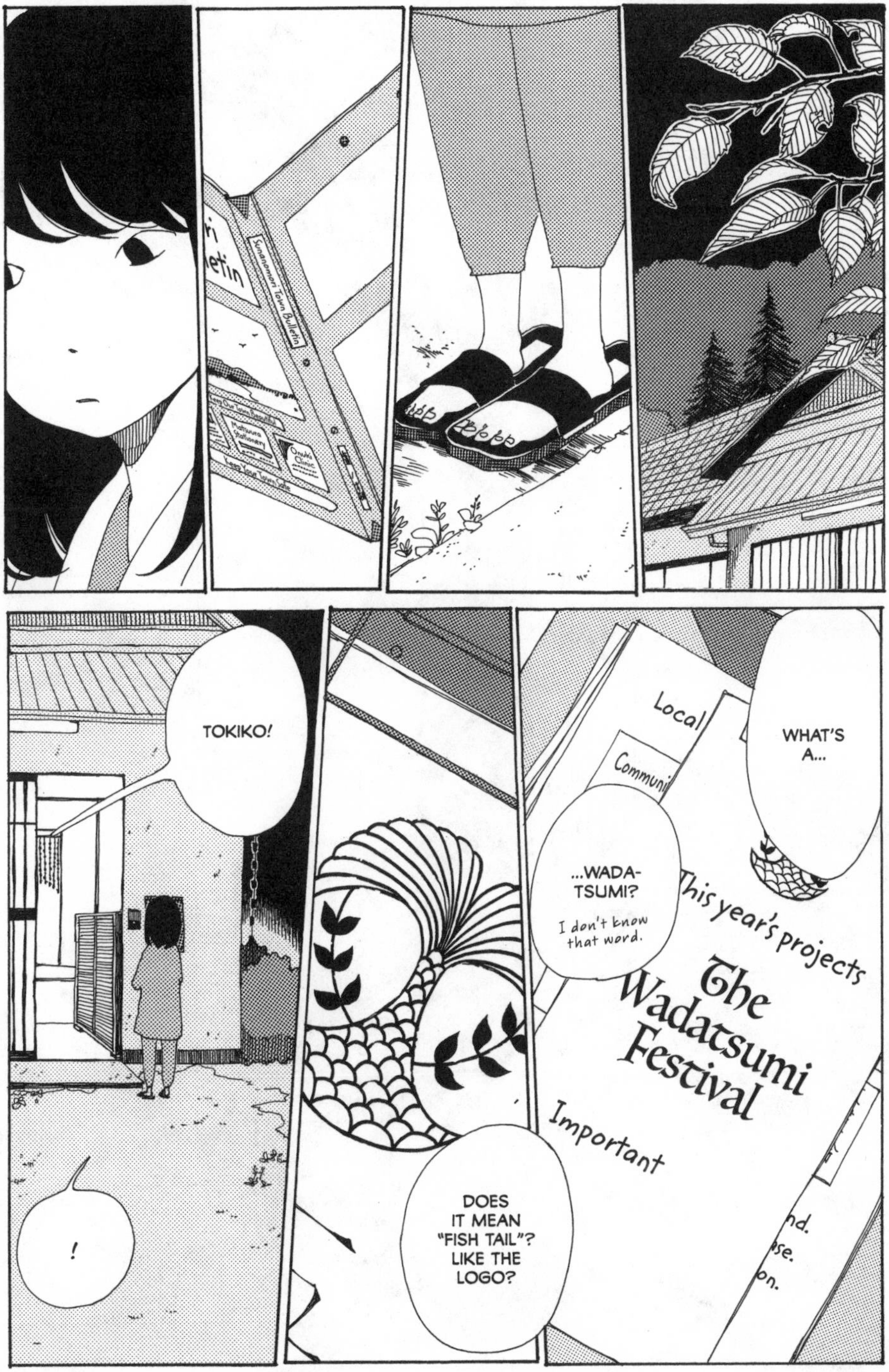
Local
This year's projects
The Wadatsumi Festival
Important
WHAT'S A...
...WADA-TSUMI?
I don't know that word.
DOES IT MEAN "FISH TAIL"? LIKE THE LOGO?
TOKIKO!
!

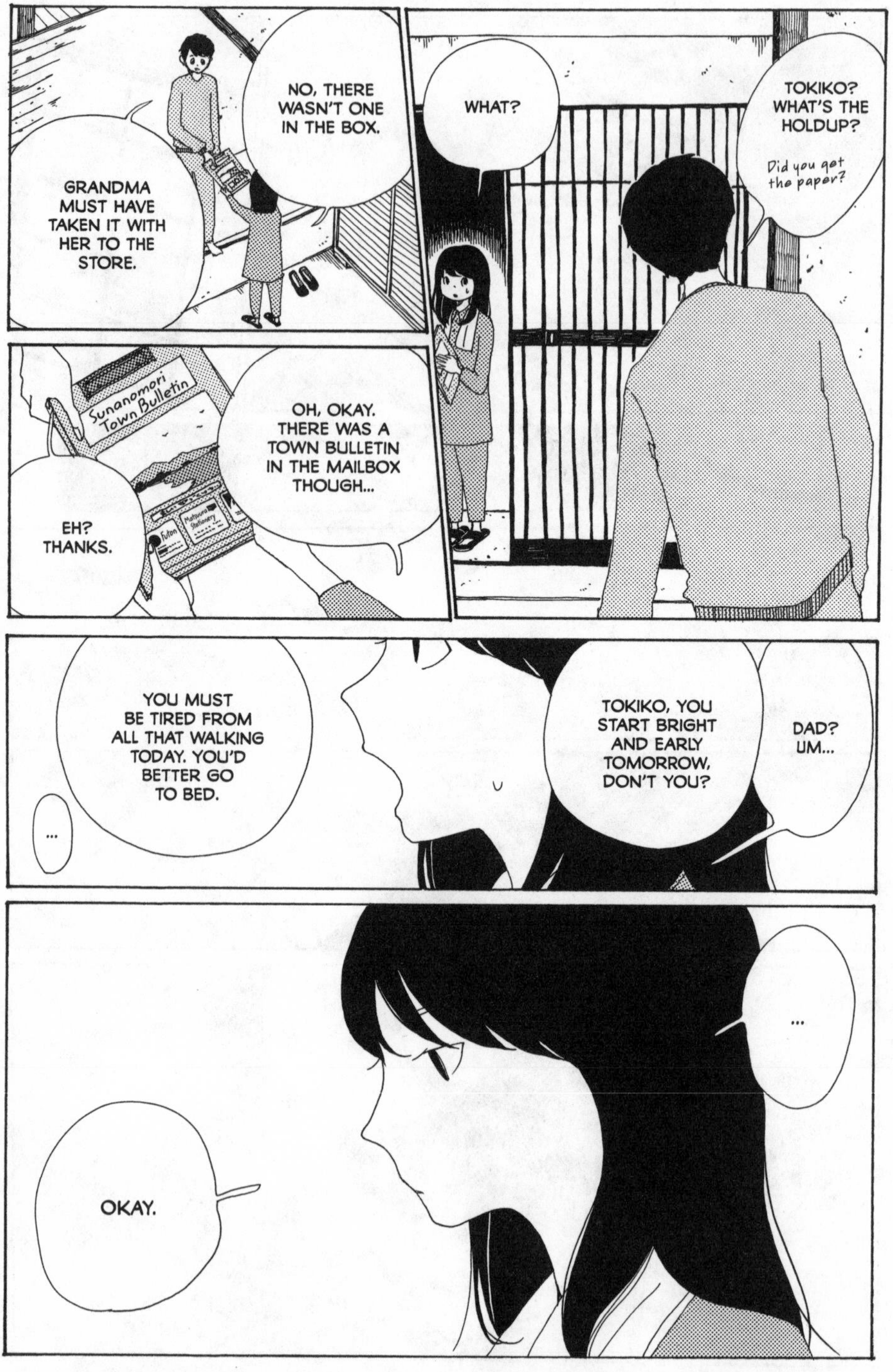
TOKIKO? WHAT'S THE HOLDUP?
Did you get the paper?
WHAT?
NO, THERE WASN'T ONE IN THE BOX.
GRANDMA MUST HAVE TAKEN IT WITH HER TO THE STORE.
OH, OKAY. THERE WAS A TOWN BULLETIN IN THE MAILBOX THOUGH...
Sunanomori Town Bulletin
EH? THANKS.
DAD? UM...
TOKIKO, YOU START BRIGHT AND EARLY TOMORROW, DON'T YOU?
YOU MUST BE TIRED FROM ALL THAT WALKING TODAY. YOU'D BETTER GO TO BED.
...
...
OKAY.

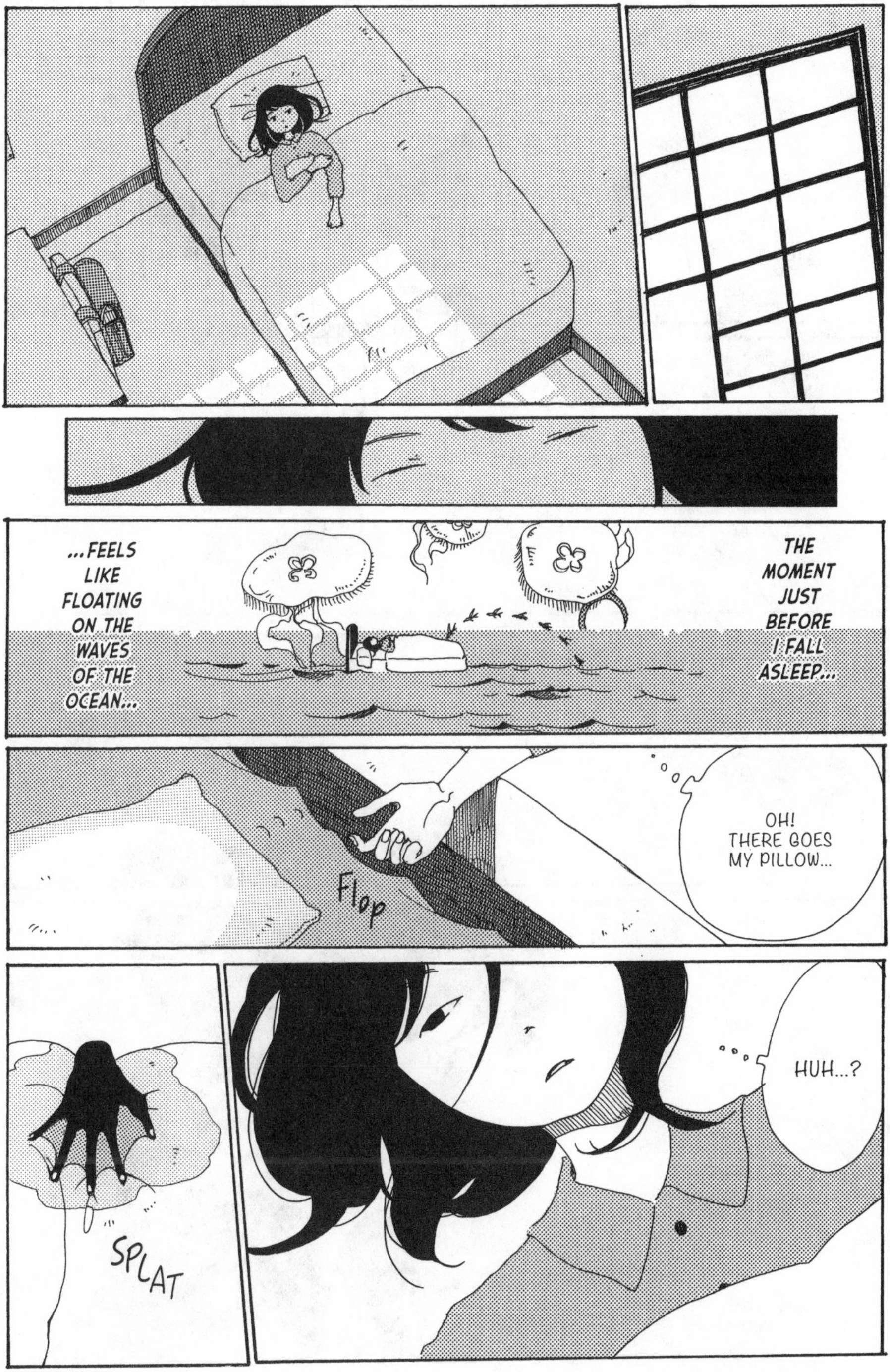
THE MOMENT JUST BEFORE I FALL ASLEEP...
...FEELS LIKE FLOATING ON THE WAVES OF THE OCEAN...
OH! THERE GOES MY PILLOW...
Flop
HUH...?
SPLAT

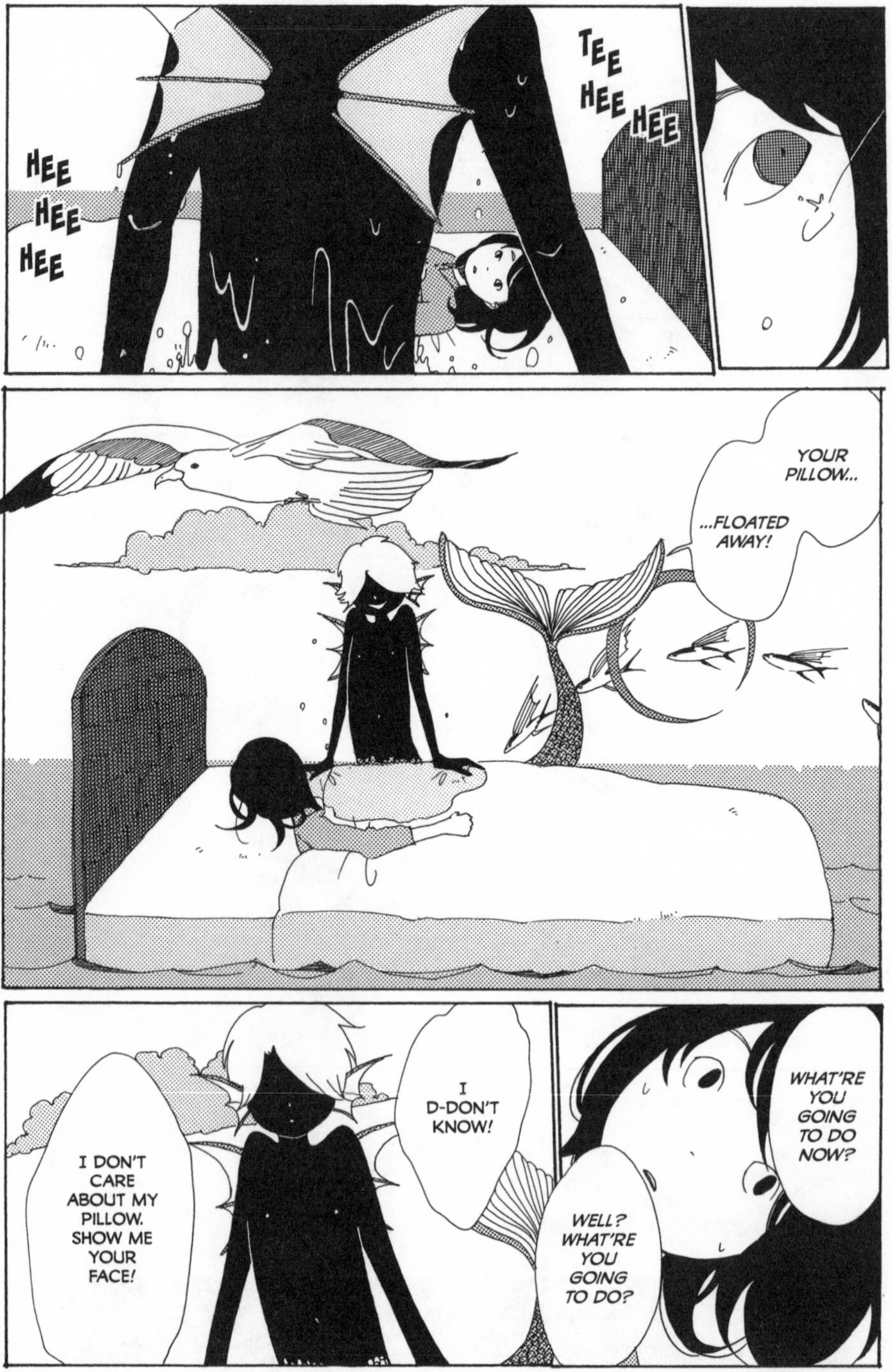
TEE HEE HEE
HEE HEE HEE
YOUR PILLOW...
...FLOATED AWAY!
WHAT'RE YOU GOING TO DO NOW?
WELL? WHAT'RE YOU GOING TO DO?
I D-DON'T KNOW!
I DON'T CARE ABOUT MY PILLOW. SHOW ME YOUR FACE!

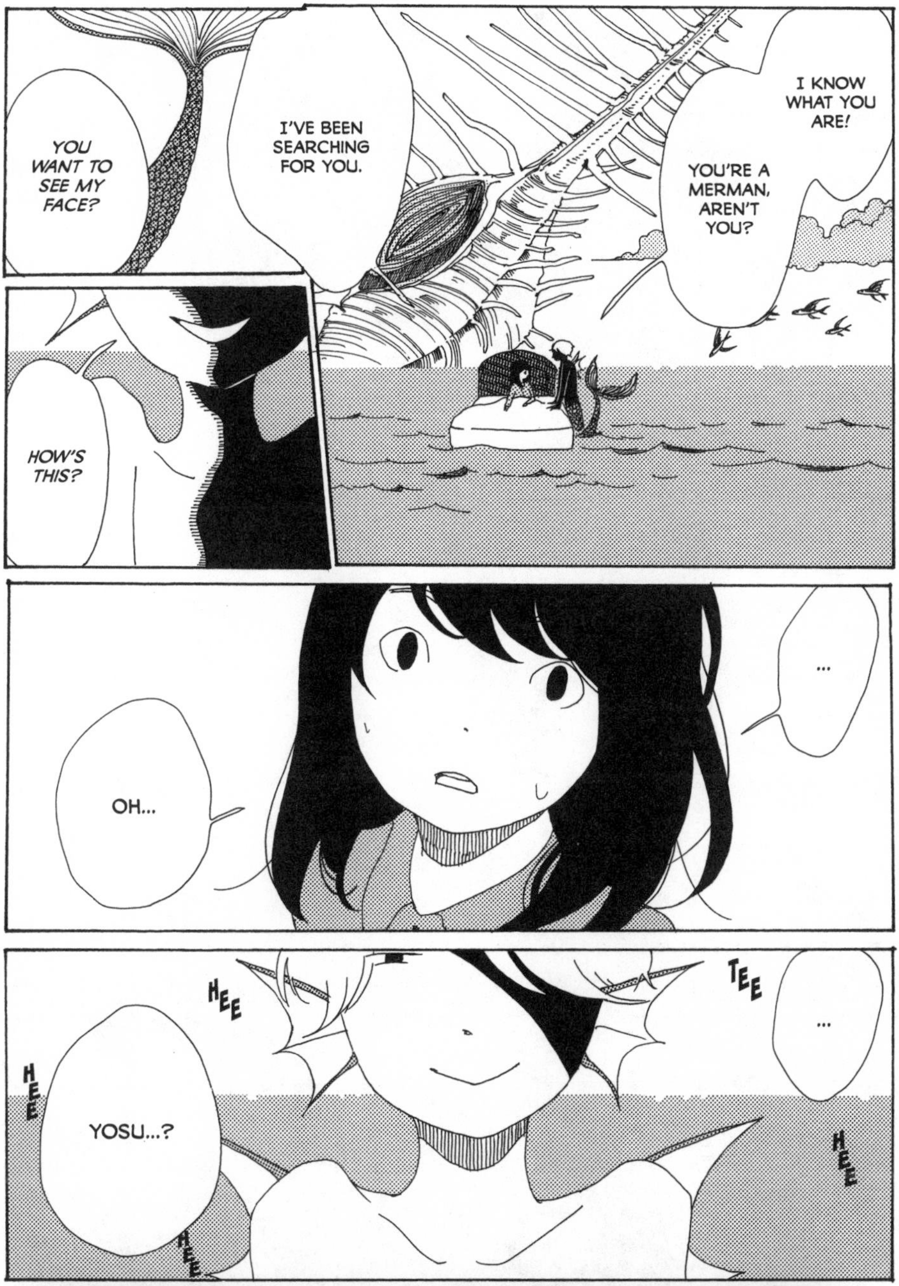
I KNOW WHAT YOU ARE!
YOU'RE A MERMAN, AREN'T YOU?
I'VE BEEN SEARCHING FOR YOU.
YOU WANT TO SEE MY FACE?
HOW'S THIS?
...
OH...
TEE HEE
...
HEE HEE
YOSU...?
HEE HEE
HEE HEE

[redacted]

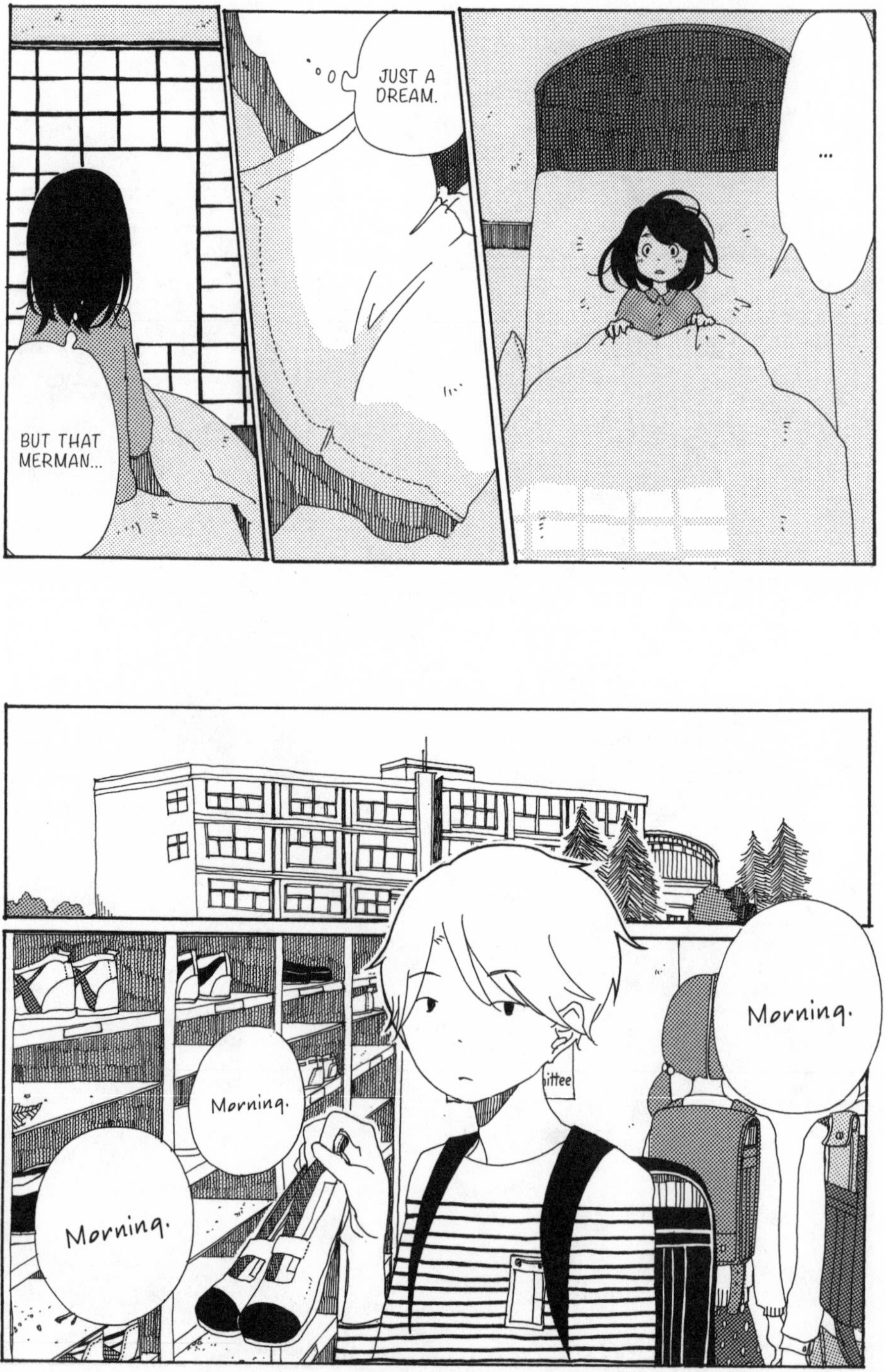
...
JUST A DREAM.
BUT THAT MERMAN...
Morning.
Morning.
Morning.

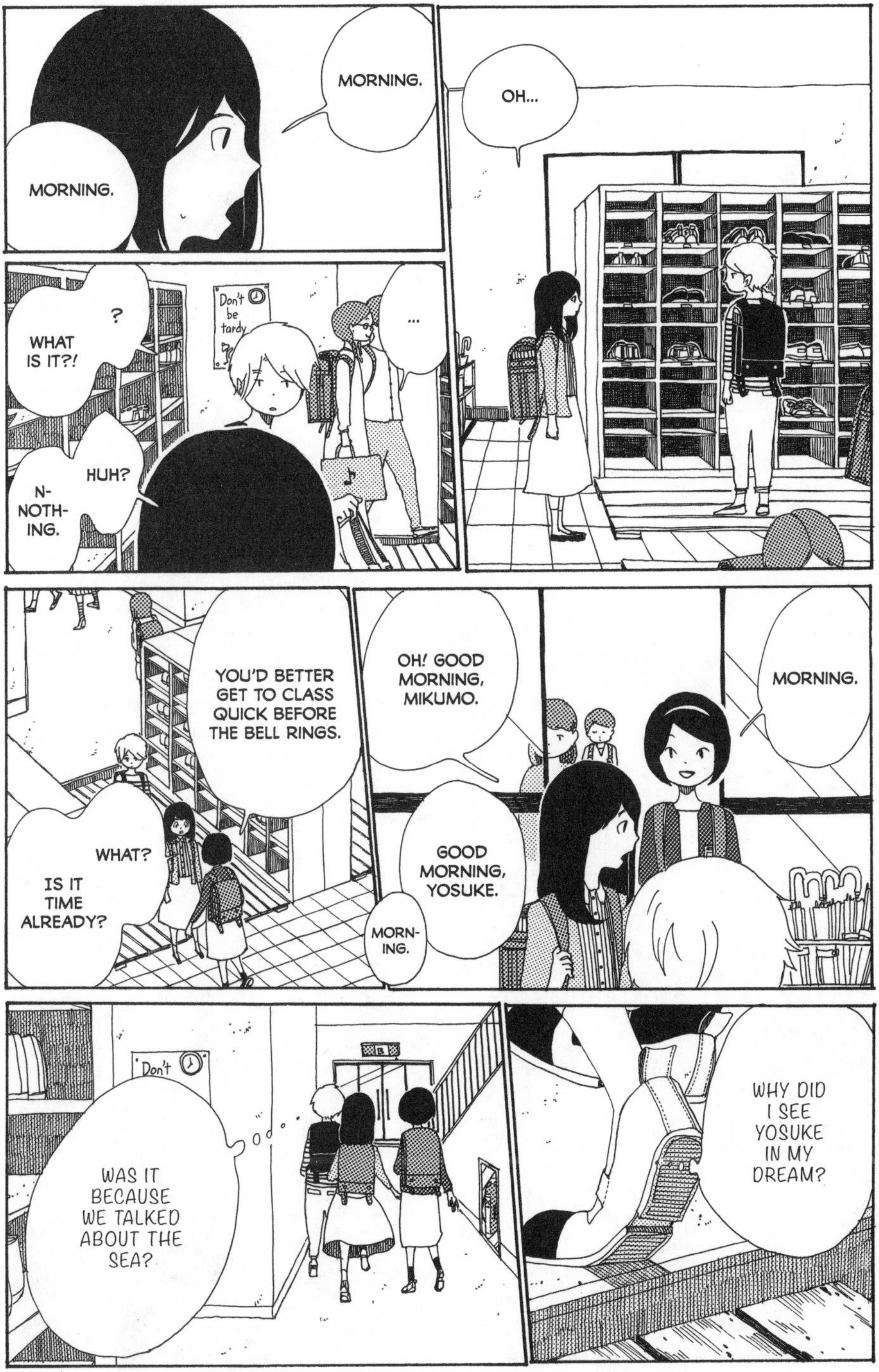
OH...
MORNING.
MORNING.
...
?
WHAT IS IT?!
Don't be tardy
HUH?
N-NOTH-ING.
MORNING.
OH! GOOD MORNING, MIKUMO.
GOOD MORNING, YOSUKE.
MORN-ING.
YOU'D BETTER GET TO CLASS QUICK BEFORE THE BELL RINGS.
WHAT?
IS IT TIME ALREADY?
WHY DID I SEE YOSUKE IN MY DREAM?
Don't
WAS IT BECAUSE WE TALKED ABOUT THE SEA?

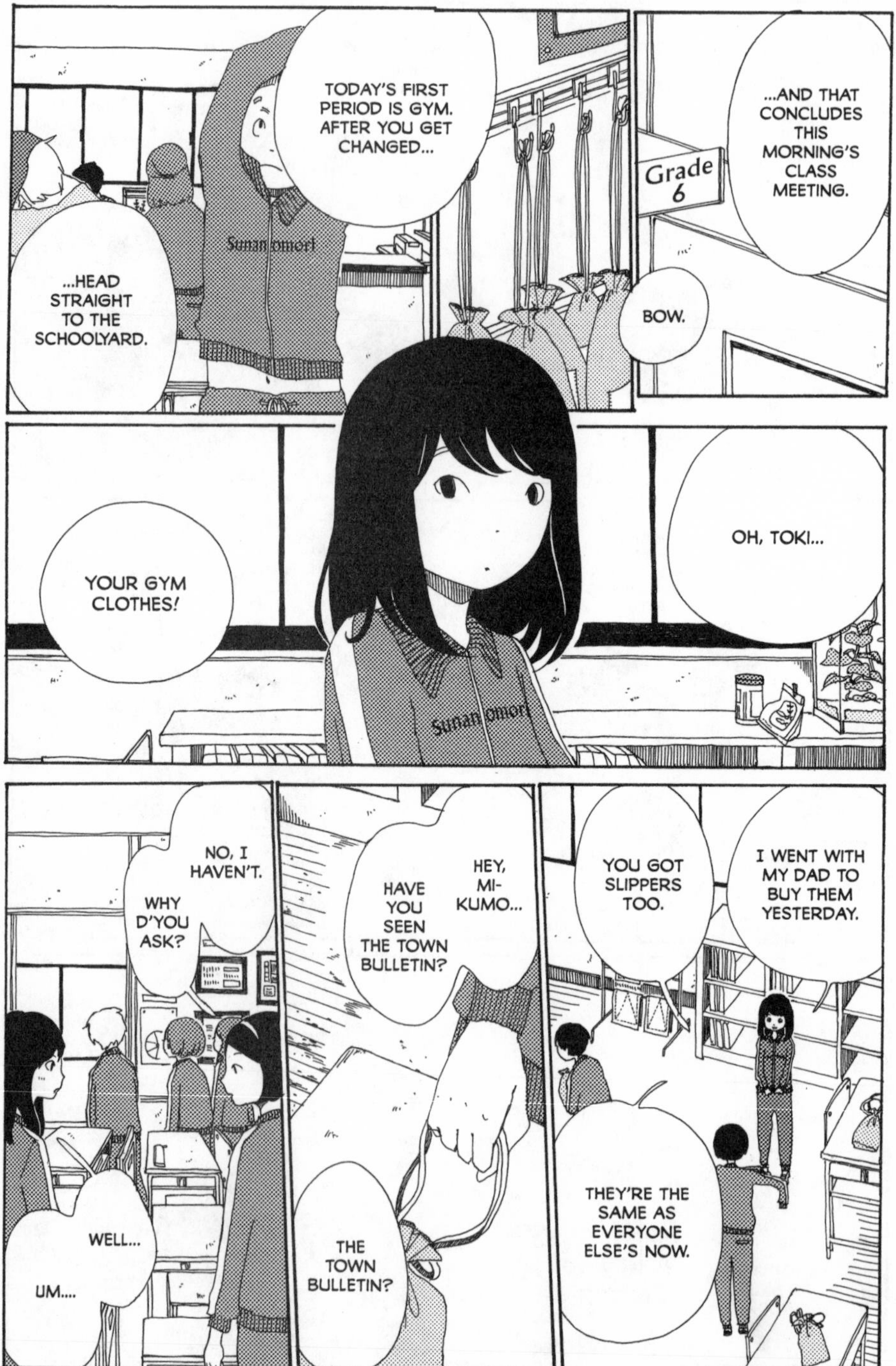
...AND THAT CONCLUDES THIS MORNING'S CLASS MEETING.
Grade 6
BOW.
TODAY'S FIRST PERIOD IS GYM. AFTER YOU GET CHANGED...
...HEAD STRAIGHT TO THE SCHOOLYARD.
Sunan omori
OH, TOKI...
YOUR GYM CLOTHES!
Sunan omori
I WENT WITH MY DAD TO BUY THEM YESTERDAY.
YOU GOT SLIPPERS TOO.
THEY'RE THE SAME AS EVERYONE ELSE'S NOW.
HEY, MI-KUMO...
HAVE YOU SEEN THE TOWN BULLETIN?
THE TOWN BULLETIN?
NO, I HAVEN'T.
WHY D'YOU ASK?
WELL...
UM....

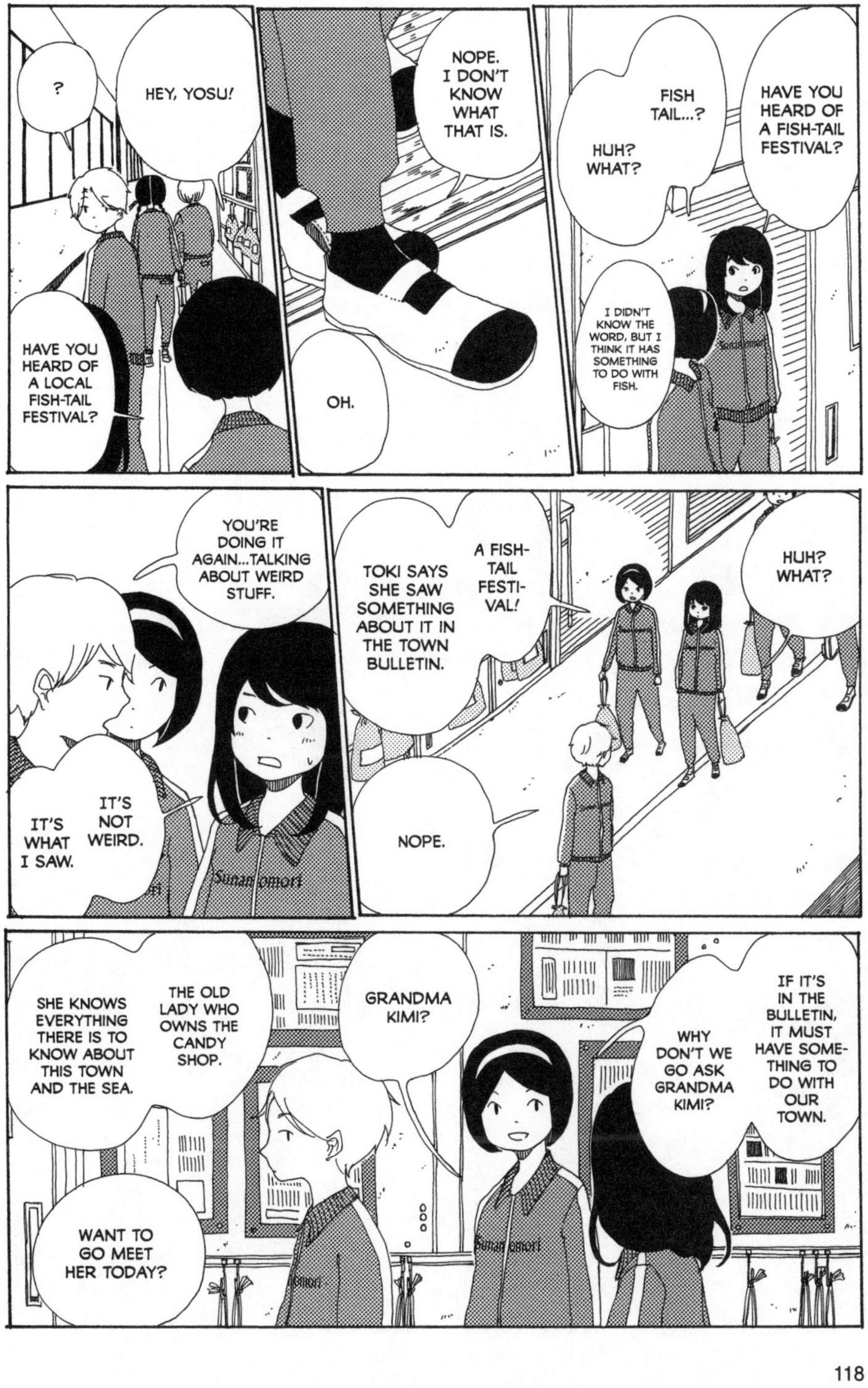
HAVE YOU HEARD OF A FISH-TAIL FESTIVAL?
FISH TAIL...? HUH? WHAT?
I DIDN'T KNOW THE WORD, BUT I THINK IT HAS SOMETHING TO DO WITH FISH.
NOPE. I DON'T KNOW WHAT THAT IS.
OH.
HEY, YOSU!
?
HAVE YOU HEARD OF A LOCAL FISH-TAIL FESTIVAL?
HUH? WHAT?
A FISH-TAIL FESTI-VAL! TOKI SAYS SHE SAW SOMETHING ABOUT IT IN THE TOWN BULLETIN.
NOPE.
YOU'RE DOING IT AGAIN...TALKING ABOUT WEIRD STUFF.
IT'S NOT WEIRD. IT'S WHAT I SAW.
IF IT'S IN THE BULLETIN, IT MUST HAVE SOME-THING TO DO WITH OUR TOWN.
WHY DON'T WE GO ASK GRANDMA KIMI?
GRANDMA KIMI?
THE OLD LADY WHO OWNS THE CANDY SHOP. SHE KNOWS EVERYTHING THERE IS TO KNOW ABOUT THIS TOWN AND THE SEA.
WANT TO GO MEET HER TODAY?

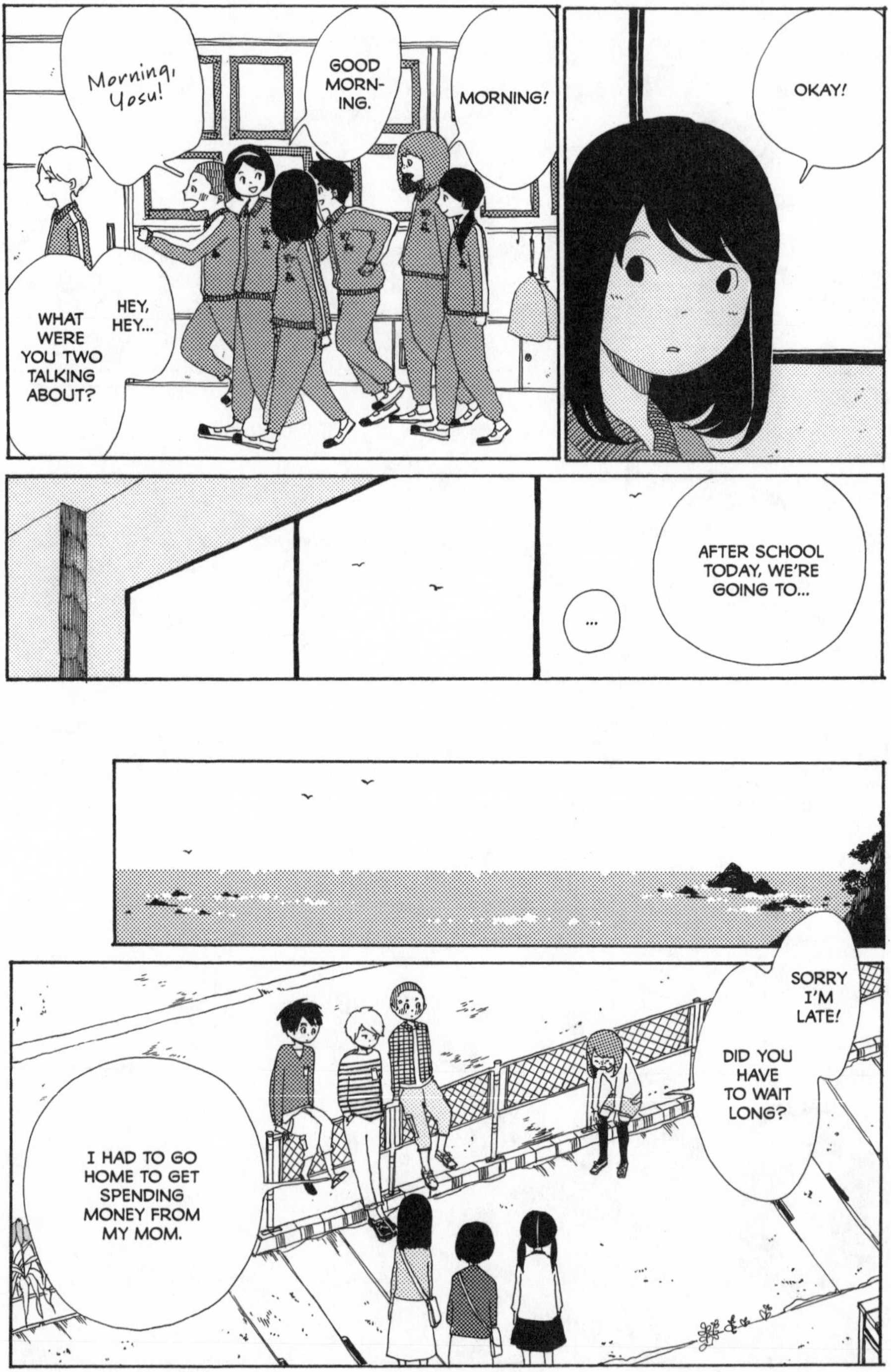
OKAY!
MORNING!
GOOD MORNING.
Morning, Yosu!
HEY, HEY... WHAT WERE YOU TWO TALKING ABOUT?
AFTER SCHOOL TODAY, WE'RE GOING TO...
...
SORRY I'M LATE!
DID YOU HAVE TO WAIT LONG?
I HAD TO GO HOME TO GET SPENDING MONEY FROM MY MOM.

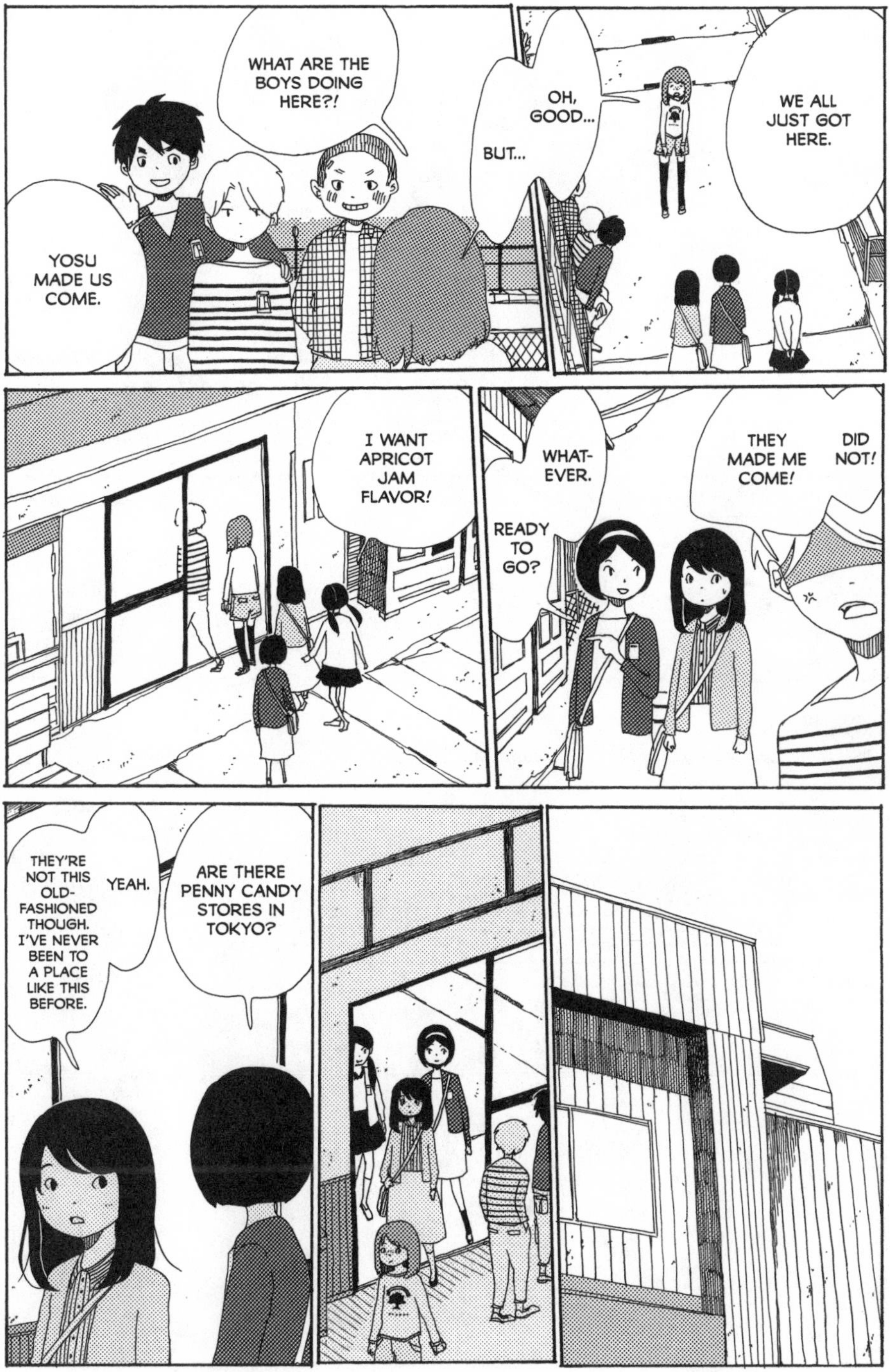
WE ALL JUST GOT HERE.
OH, GOOD...
BUT...
WHAT ARE THE BOYS DOING HERE?!
YOSU MADE US COME.
DID NOT!
THEY MADE ME COME!
WHAT-EVER.
READY TO GO?
I WANT APRICOT JAM FLAVOR!
ARE THERE PENNY CANDY STORES IN TOKYO?
YEAH.
THEY'RE NOT THIS OLD-FASHIONED THOUGH. I'VE NEVER BEEN TO A PLACE LIKE THIS BEFORE.

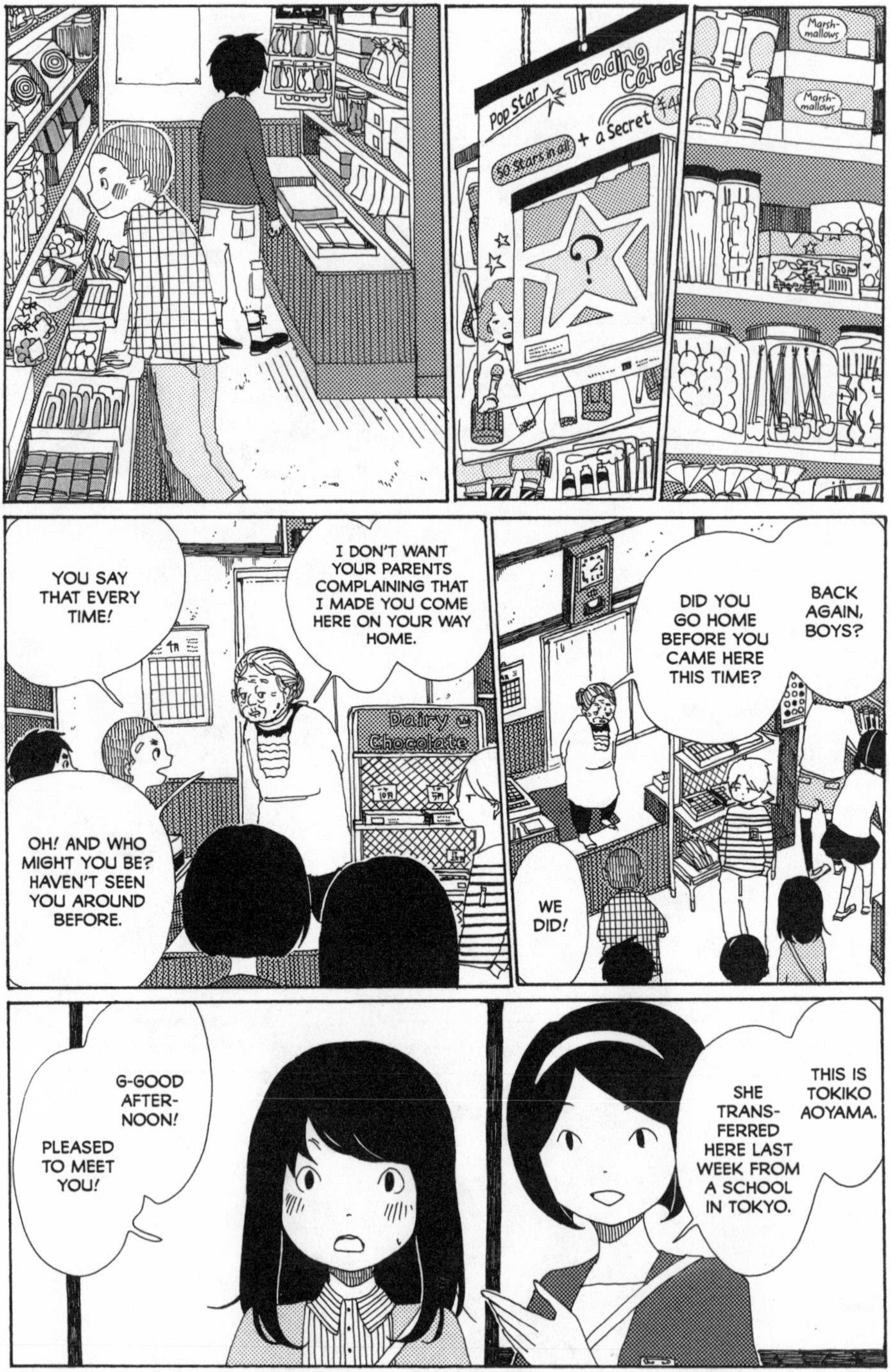
Marsh-mallows
Marsh-mallows
Pop Star
Trading Cards
50 Stars in all
+ a Secret
BACK AGAIN, BOYS?
DID YOU GO HOME BEFORE YOU CAME HERE THIS TIME?
WE DID!
I DON'T WANT YOUR PARENTS COMPLAINING THAT I MADE YOU COME HERE ON YOUR WAY HOME.
YOU SAY THAT EVERY TIME!
Dairy Chocolate
OH! AND WHO MIGHT YOU BE? HAVEN'T SEEN YOU AROUND BEFORE.
THIS IS TOKIKO AOYAMA.
SHE TRANSFERRED HERE LAST WEEK FROM A SCHOOL IN TOKYO.
G-GOOD AFTERNOON!
PLEASED TO MEET YOU!

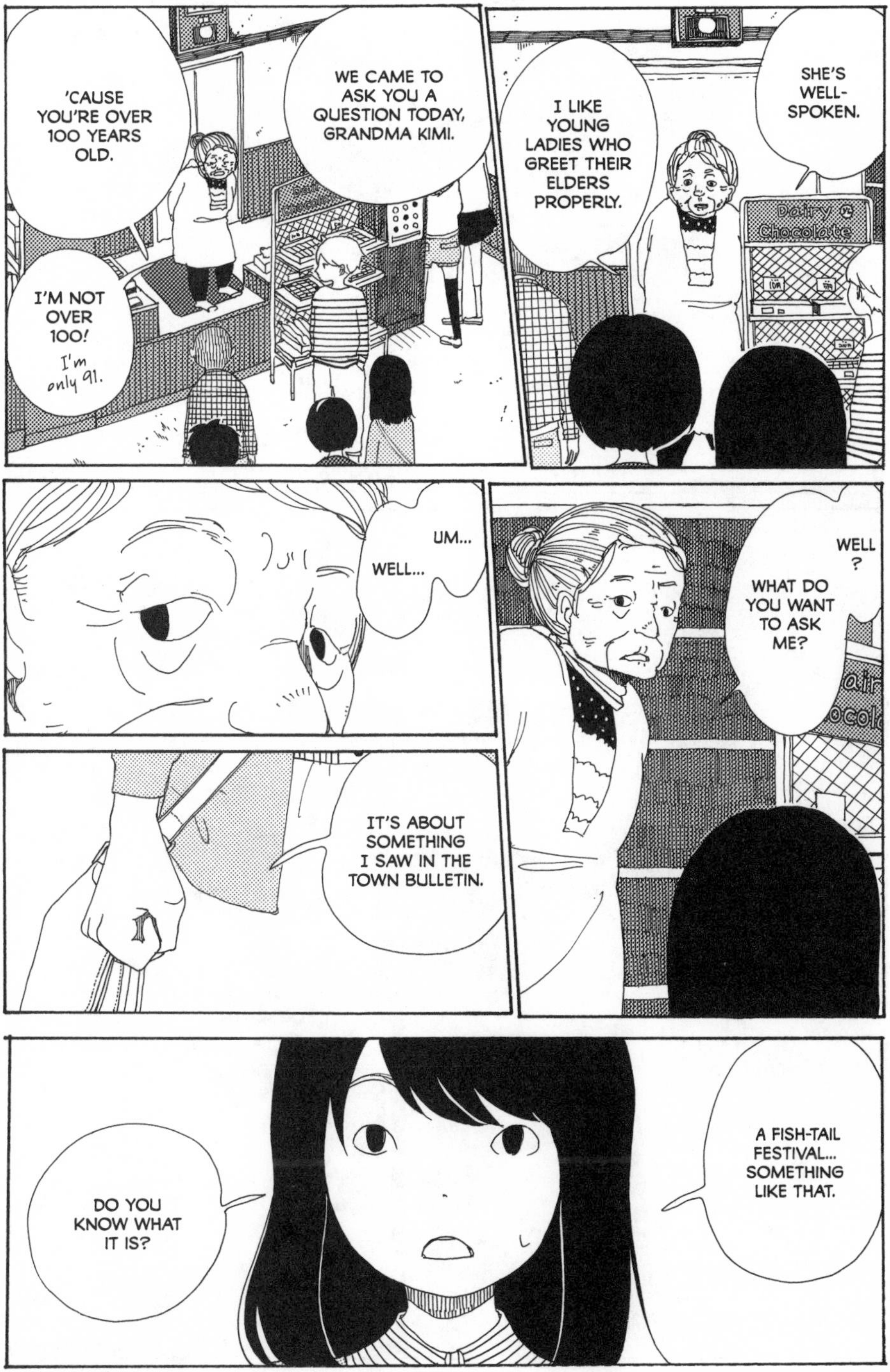
SHE'S WELL-SPOKEN.
I LIKE YOUNG LADIES WHO GREET THEIR ELDERS PROPERLY.
Dairy Chocolate
WE CAME TO ASK YOU A QUESTION TODAY, GRANDMA KIMI.
'CAUSE YOU'RE OVER 100 YEARS OLD.
I'M NOT OVER 100!
I'm only 91.
WELL? WHAT DO YOU WANT TO ASK ME?
UM... WELL...
IT'S ABOUT SOMETHING I SAW IN THE TOWN BULLETIN.
A FISH-TAIL FESTIVAL... SOMETHING LIKE THAT.
DO YOU KNOW WHAT IT IS?

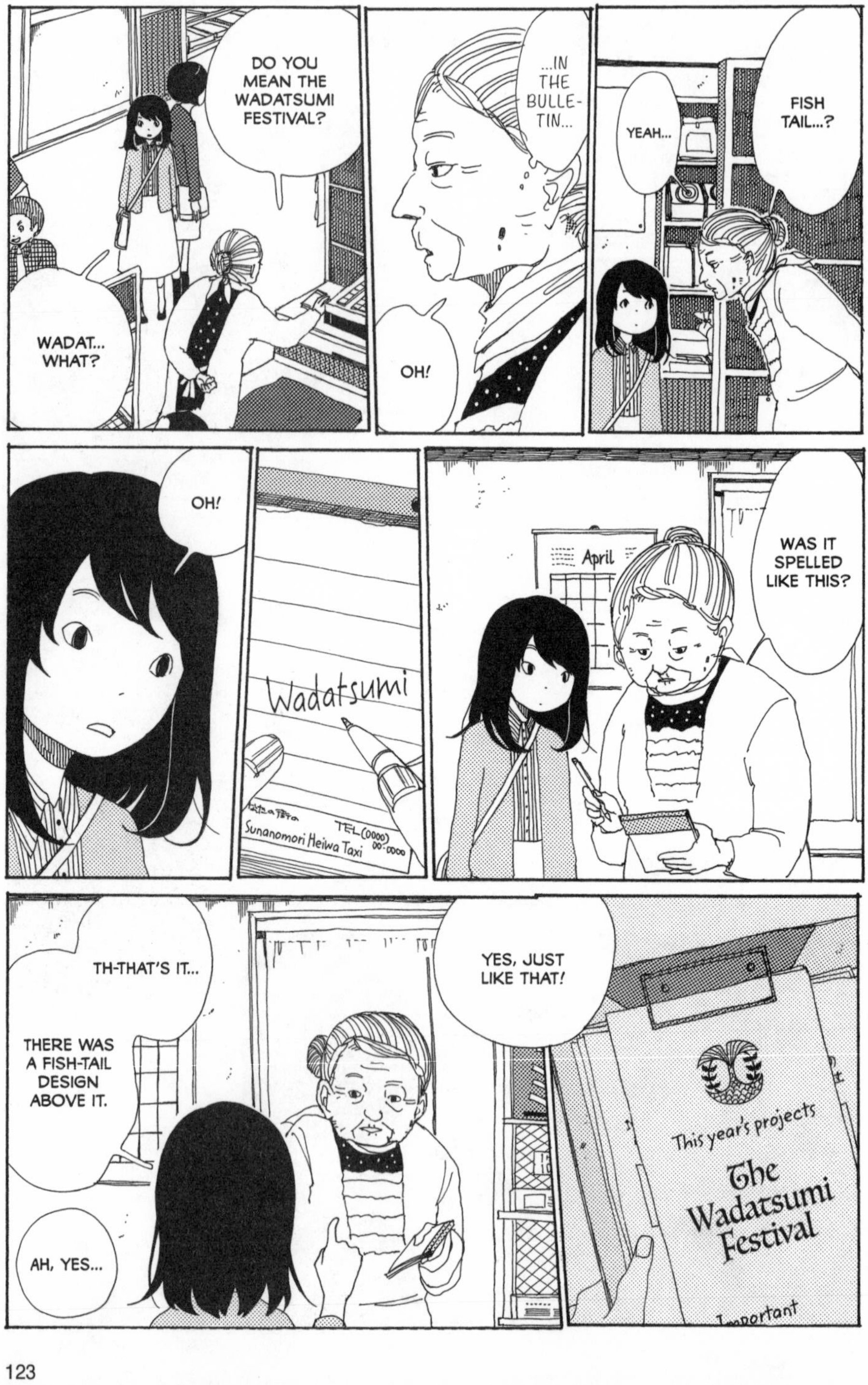
FISH TAIL...?
YEAH...
...IN THE BULLETIN...
OH!
DO YOU MEAN THE WADATSUMI FESTIVAL?
WADAT... WHAT?
WAS IT SPELLED LIKE THIS?
April
Wadatsumi
Sunanomori Heiwa Taxi
TEL(0000) 00-0000
OH!
This year's projects
The Wadatsumi Festival
Important
YES, JUST LIKE THAT!
TH-THAT'S IT...
THERE WAS A FISH-TAIL DESIGN ABOVE IT.
AH, YES...

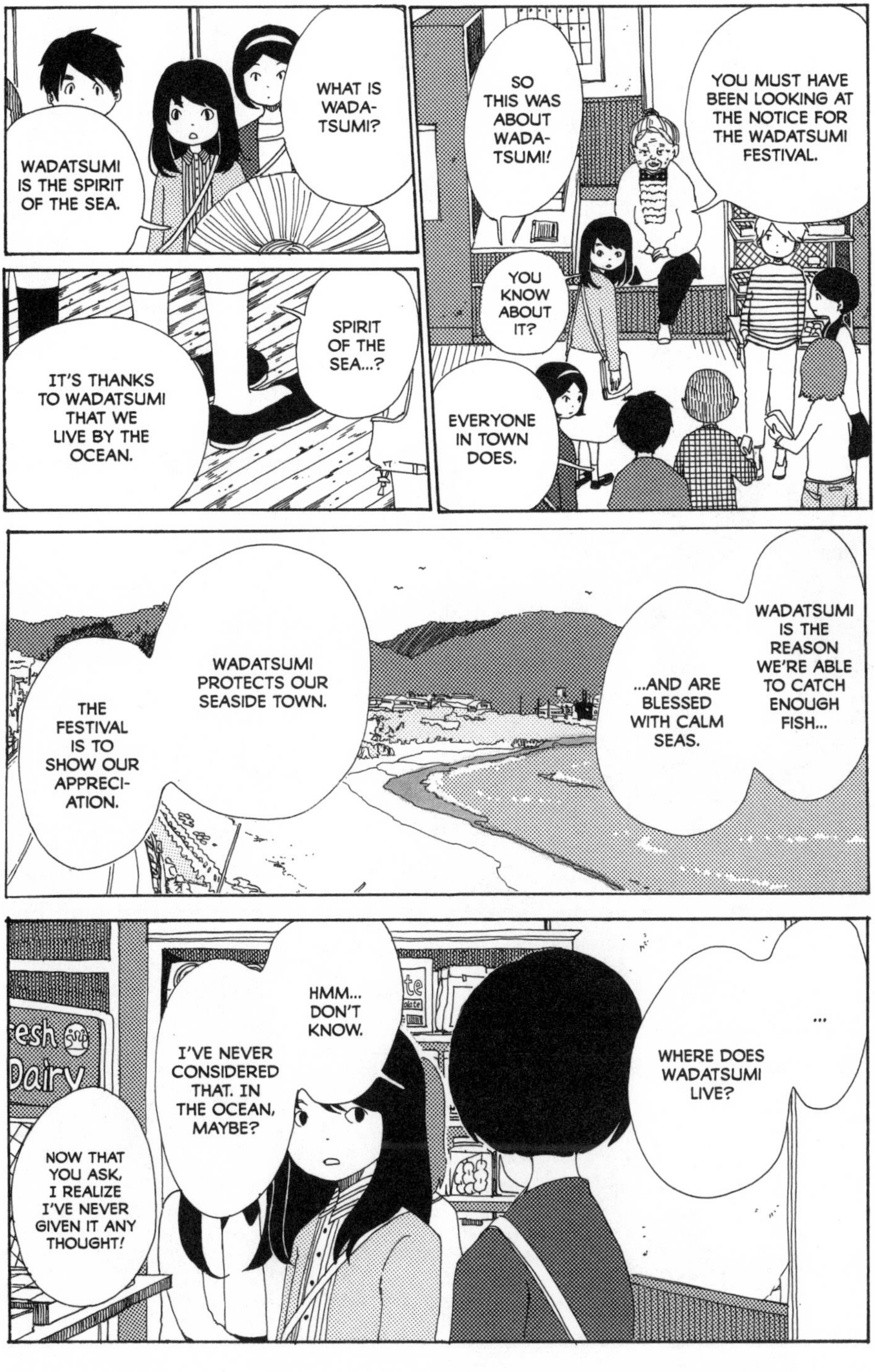
YOU MUST HAVE BEEN LOOKING AT THE NOTICE FOR THE WADATSUMI FESTIVAL.
SO THIS WAS ABOUT WADA-TSUMI!
YOU KNOW ABOUT IT?
EVERYONE IN TOWN DOES.
WHAT IS WADA-TSUMI?
WADATSUMI IS THE SPIRIT OF THE SEA.
SPIRIT OF THE SEA...?
IT'S THANKS TO WADATSUMI THAT WE LIVE BY THE OCEAN.
WADATSUMI IS THE REASON WE'RE ABLE TO CATCH ENOUGH FISH...
...AND ARE BLESSED WITH CALM SEAS.
WADATSUMI PROTECTS OUR SEASIDE TOWN.
THE FESTIVAL IS TO SHOW OUR APPRECI-ATION.
...
WHERE DOES WADATSUMI LIVE?
HMM... DON'T KNOW.
I'VE NEVER CONSIDERED THAT. IN THE OCEAN, MAYBE?
NOW THAT YOU ASK, I REALIZE I'VE NEVER GIVEN IT ANY THOUGHT!

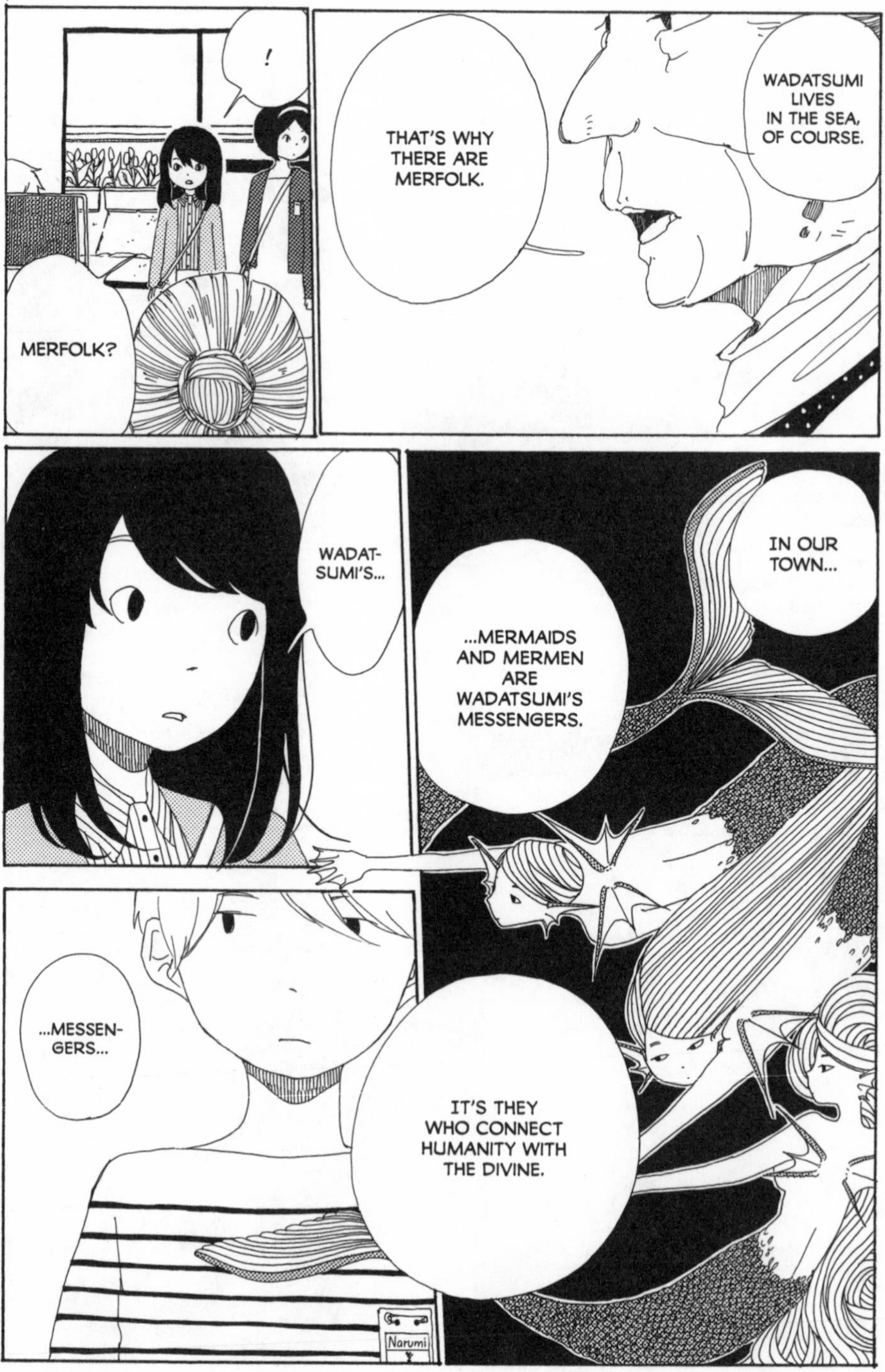
WADATSUMI LIVES IN THE SEA, OF COURSE.
THAT'S WHY THERE ARE MERFOLK.
!
MERFOLK?
IN OUR TOWN...
...MERMAIDS AND MERMEN ARE WADATSUMI'S MESSENGERS.
IT'S THEY WHO CONNECT HUMANITY WITH THE DIVINE.
WADAT-SUMI'S...
...MESSEN-GERS...
Narumi

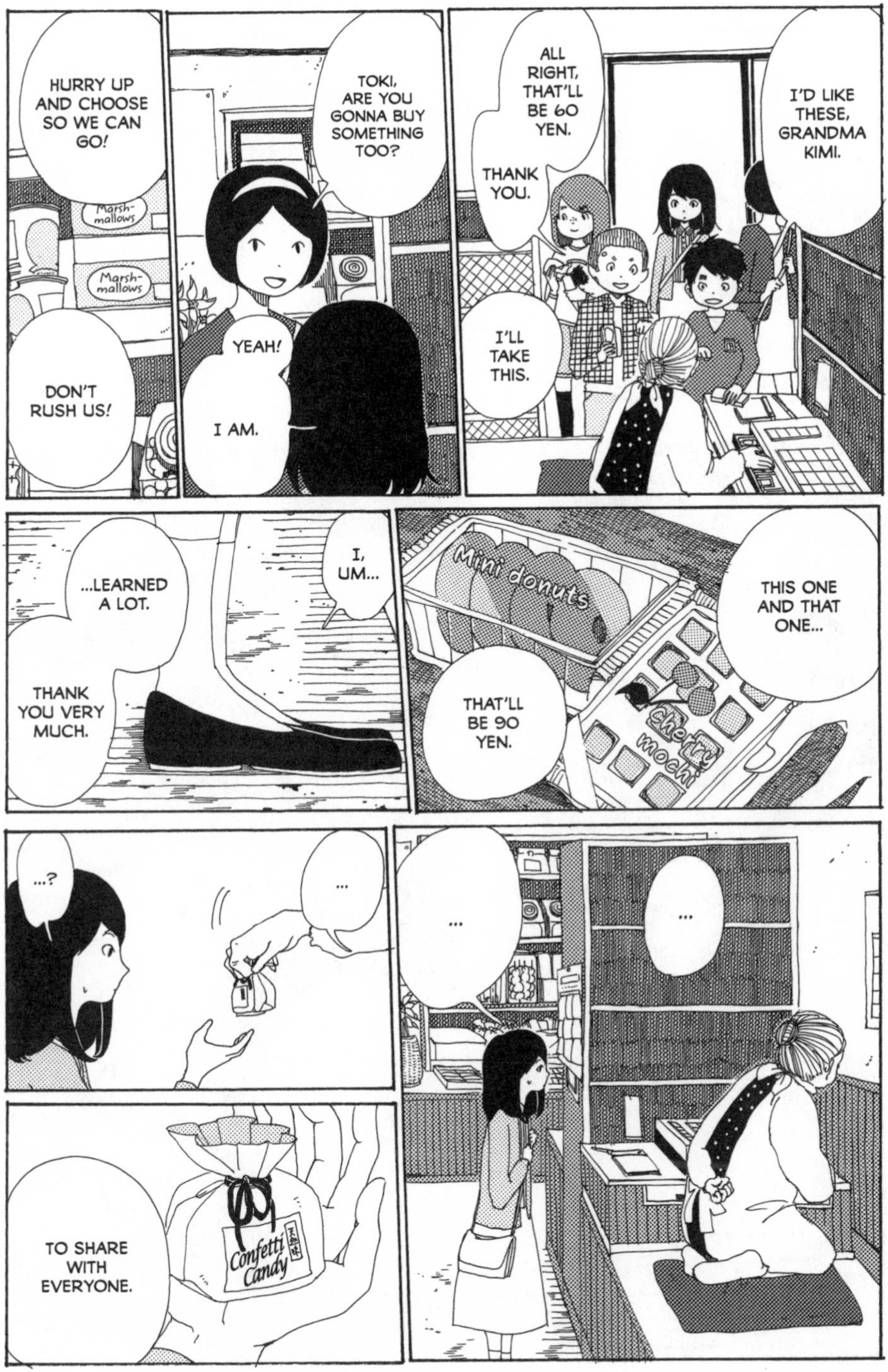
I'D LIKE THESE, GRANDMA KIMI.
ALL RIGHT, THAT'LL BE 60 YEN.
THANK YOU.
I'LL TAKE THIS.
TOKI, ARE YOU GONNA BUY SOMETHING TOO?
YEAH!
I AM.
HURRY UP AND CHOOSE SO WE CAN GO!
Marshmallows
Marshmallows
DON'T RUSH US!
THIS ONE AND THAT ONE...
Mini donuts
Cherry mochi
THAT'LL BE 90 YEN.
I, UM...
...LEARNED A LOT.
THANK YOU VERY MUCH.
...
...
...
...?
Confetti Candy
TO SHARE WITH EVERYONE.

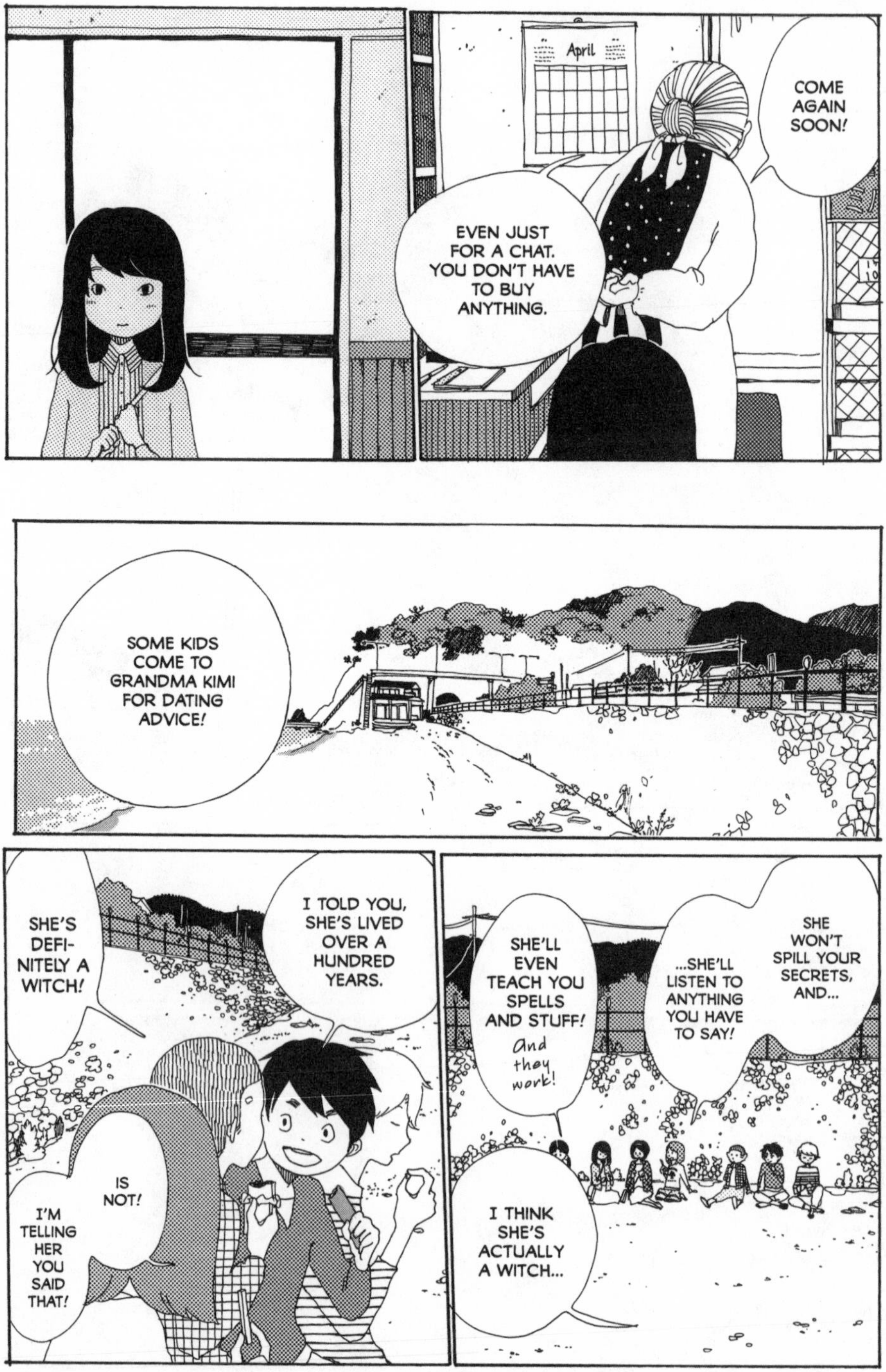
April
COME AGAIN SOON!
EVEN JUST FOR A CHAT. YOU DON'T HAVE TO BUY ANYTHING.
SOME KIDS COME TO GRANDMA KIMI FOR DATING ADVICE!
SHE WON'T SPILL YOUR SECRETS, AND...
...SHE'LL LISTEN TO ANYTHING YOU HAVE TO SAY!
SHE'LL EVEN TEACH YOU SPELLS AND STUFF!
And they work!
I THINK SHE'S ACTUALLY A WITCH...
I TOLD YOU, SHE'S LIVED OVER A HUNDRED YEARS.
SHE'S DEFI-NITELY A WITCH!
IS NOT!
I'M TELLING HER YOU SAID THAT!

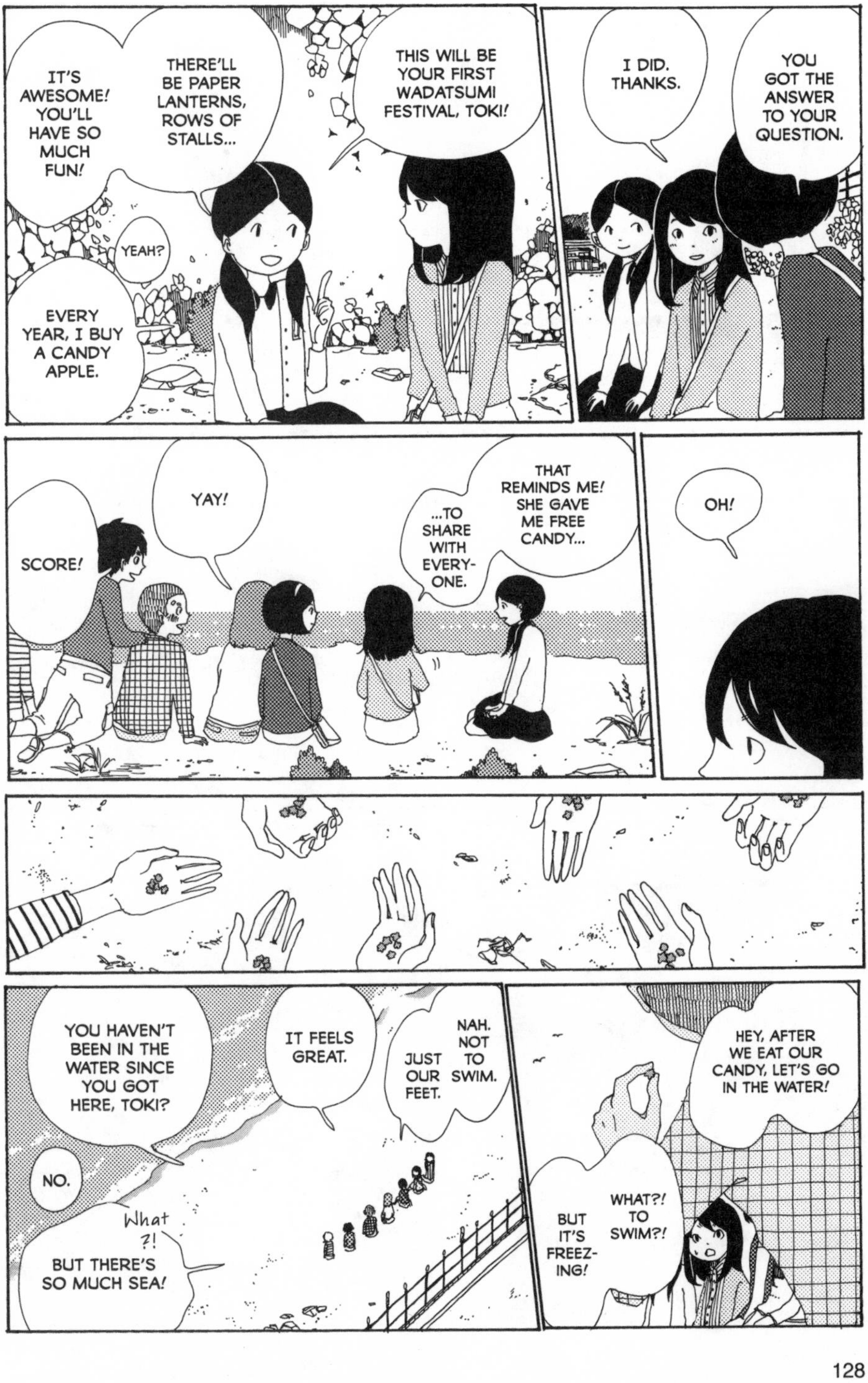
YOU GOT THE ANSWER TO YOUR QUESTION.
I DID. THANKS.
THIS WILL BE YOUR FIRST WADATSUMI FESTIVAL, TOKI!
THERE'LL BE PAPER LANTERNS, ROWS OF STALLS...
IT'S AWESOME! YOU'LL HAVE SO MUCH FUN!
YEAH?
EVERY YEAR, I BUY A CANDY APPLE.
OH!
THAT REMINDS ME! SHE GAVE ME FREE CANDY...
...TO SHARE WITH EVERY-ONE.
YAY!
SCORE!
HEY, AFTER WE EAT OUR CANDY, LET'S GO IN THE WATER!
WHAT?! TO SWIM?!
BUT IT'S FREEZ-ING!
NAH. NOT TO SWIM.
JUST OUR FEET.
IT FEELS GREAT.
YOU HAVEN'T BEEN IN THE WATER SINCE YOU GOT HERE, TOKI?
NO.
What?!
BUT THERE'S SO MUCH SEA!

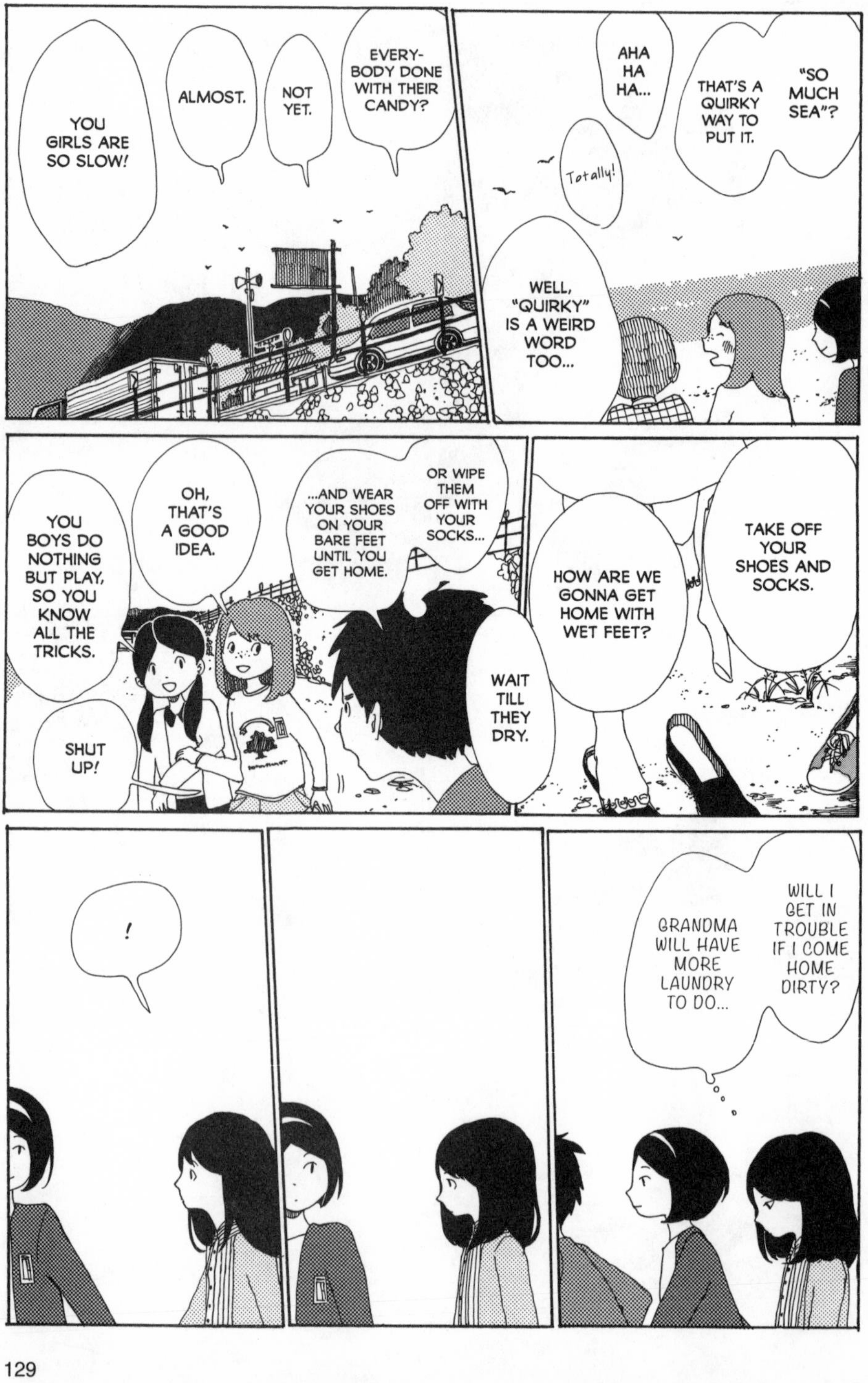
"SO MUCH SEA"?
THAT'S A QUIRKY WAY TO PUT IT.
AHA HA HA...
Totally!
WELL, "QUIRKY" IS A WEIRD WORD TOO...
EVERY-BODY DONE WITH THEIR CANDY?
NOT YET.
ALMOST.
YOU GIRLS ARE SO SLOW!
TAKE OFF YOUR SHOES AND SOCKS.
HOW ARE WE GONNA GET HOME WITH WET FEET?
WAIT TILL THEY DRY.
OR WIPE THEM OFF WITH YOUR SOCKS...
...AND WEAR YOUR SHOES ON YOUR BARE FEET UNTIL YOU GET HOME.
OH, THAT'S A GOOD IDEA.
YOU BOYS DO NOTHING BUT PLAY, SO YOU KNOW ALL THE TRICKS.
SHUT UP!
WILL I GET IN TROUBLE IF I COME HOME DIRTY?
GRANDMA WILL HAVE MORE LAUNDRY TO DO...
!

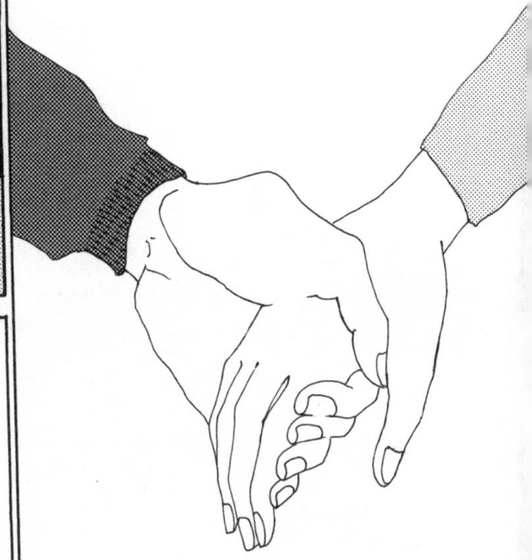

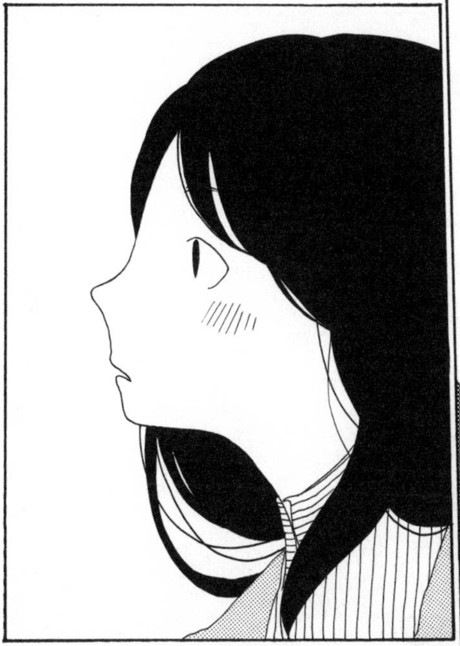

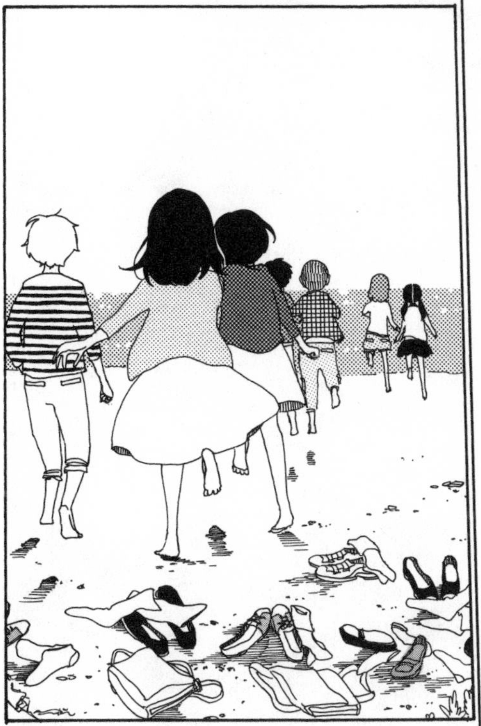

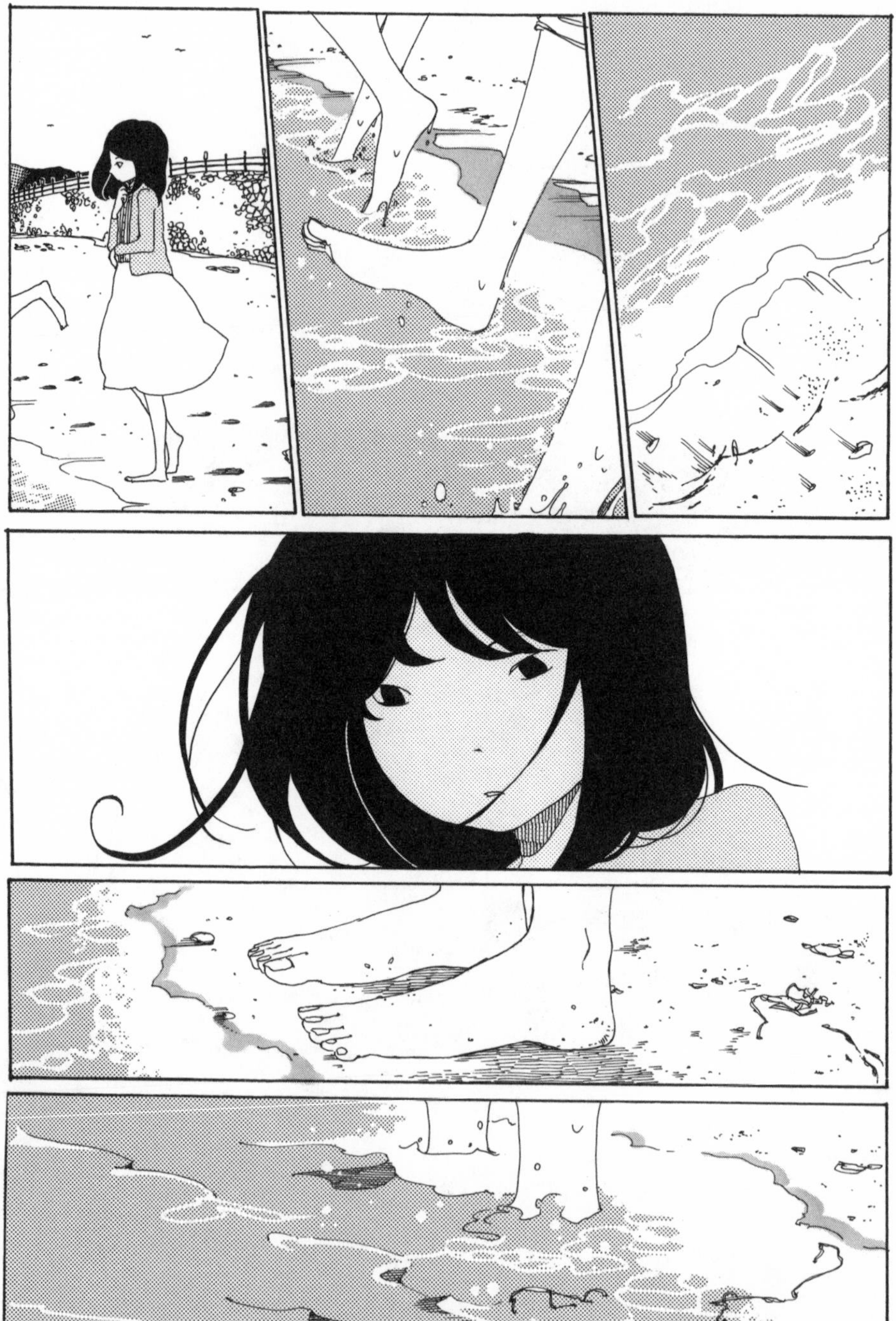

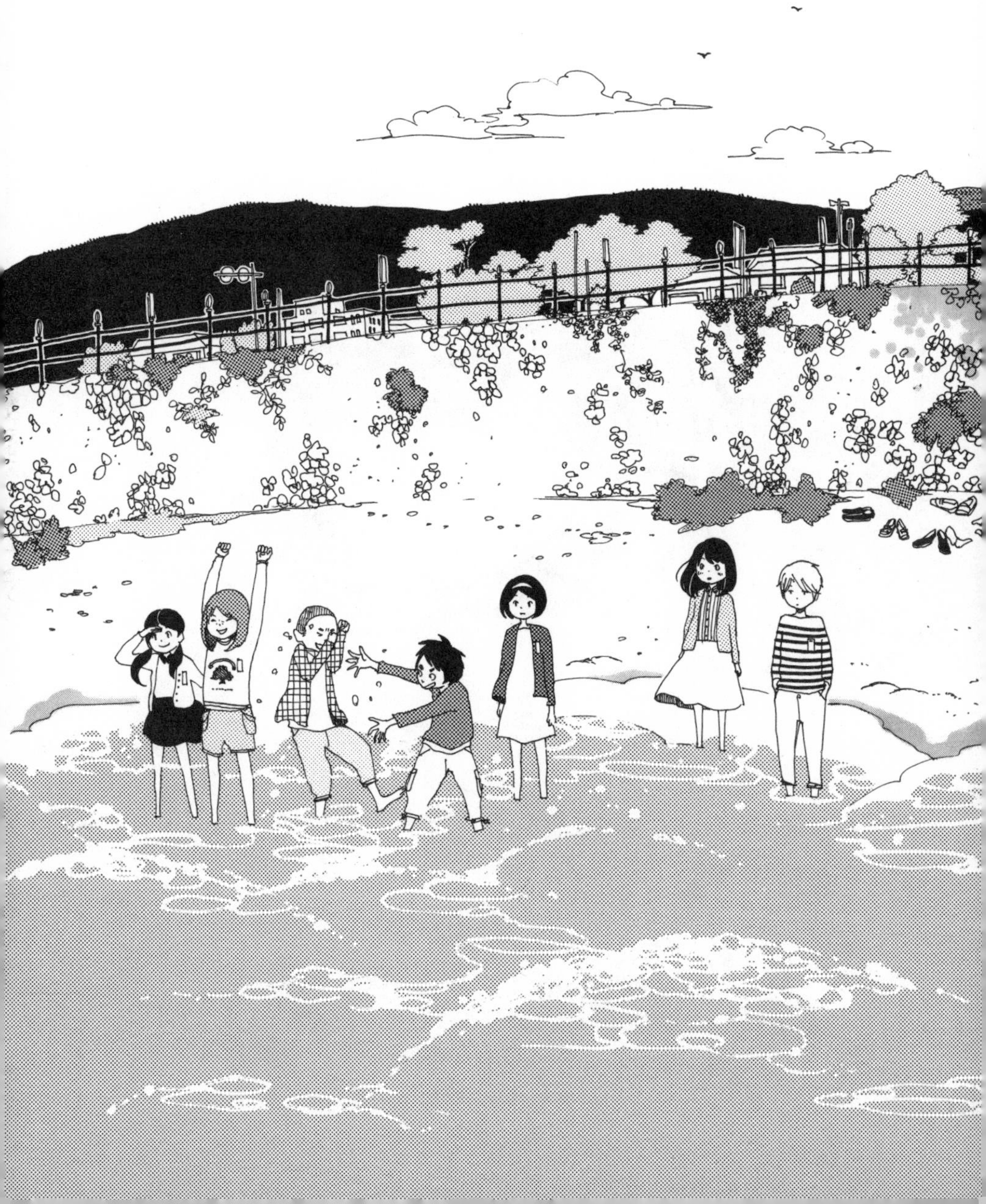

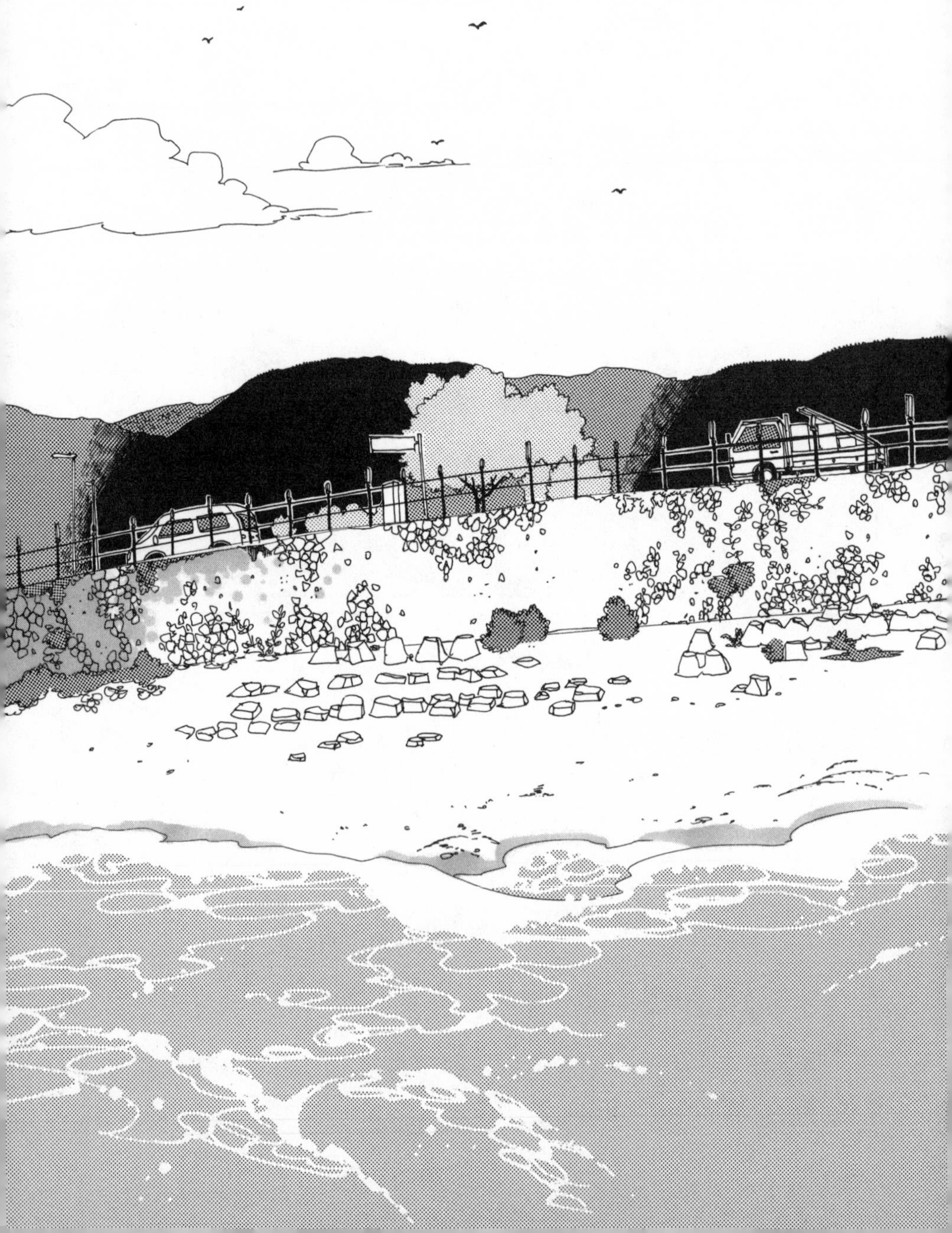

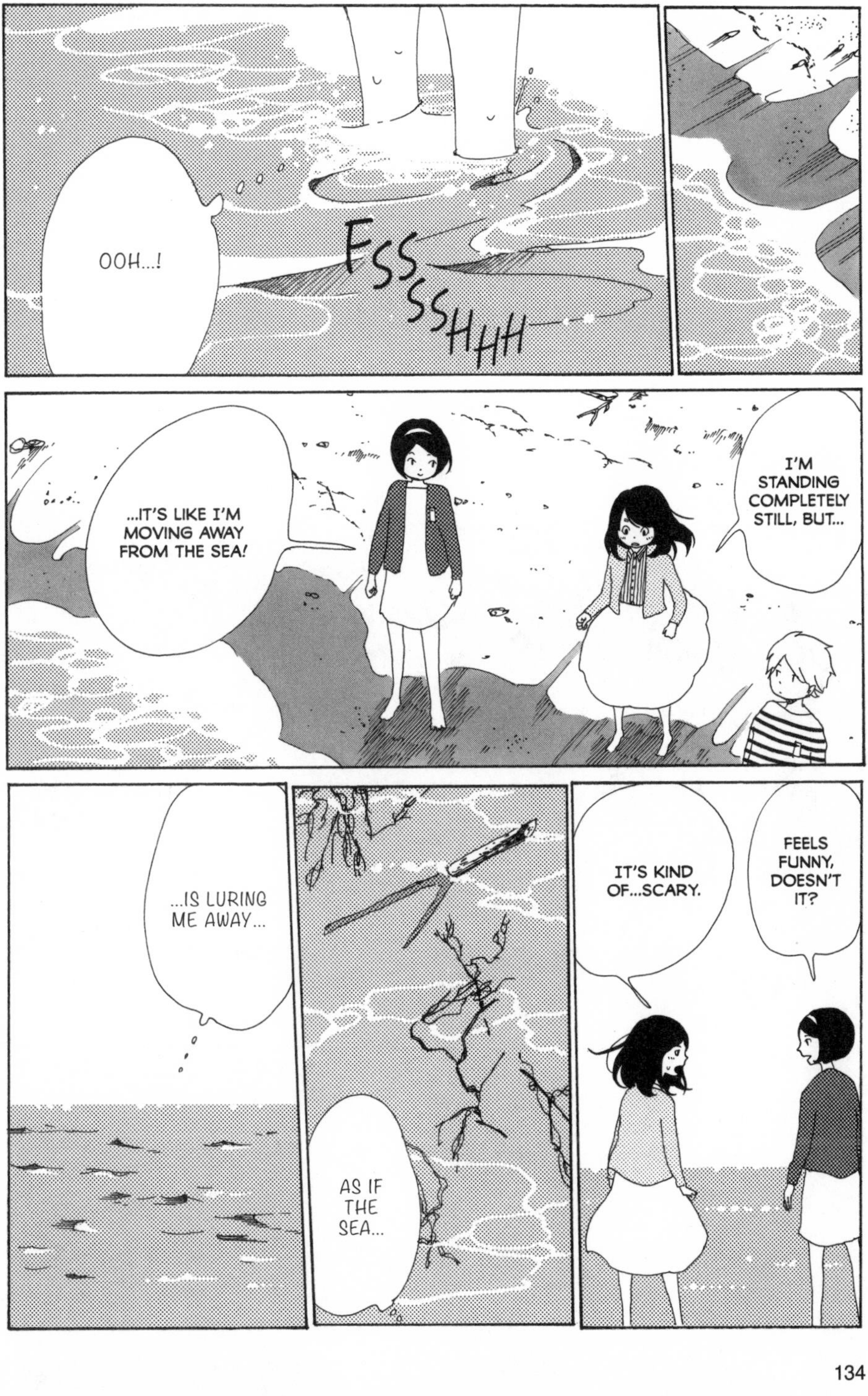
OOH...!
FSSSSHHH
I'M STANDING COMPLETELY STILL, BUT...
...IT'S LIKE I'M MOVING AWAY FROM THE SEA!
FEELS FUNNY, DOESN'T IT?
IT'S KIND OF...SCARY.
AS IF THE SEA...
...IS LURING ME AWAY...

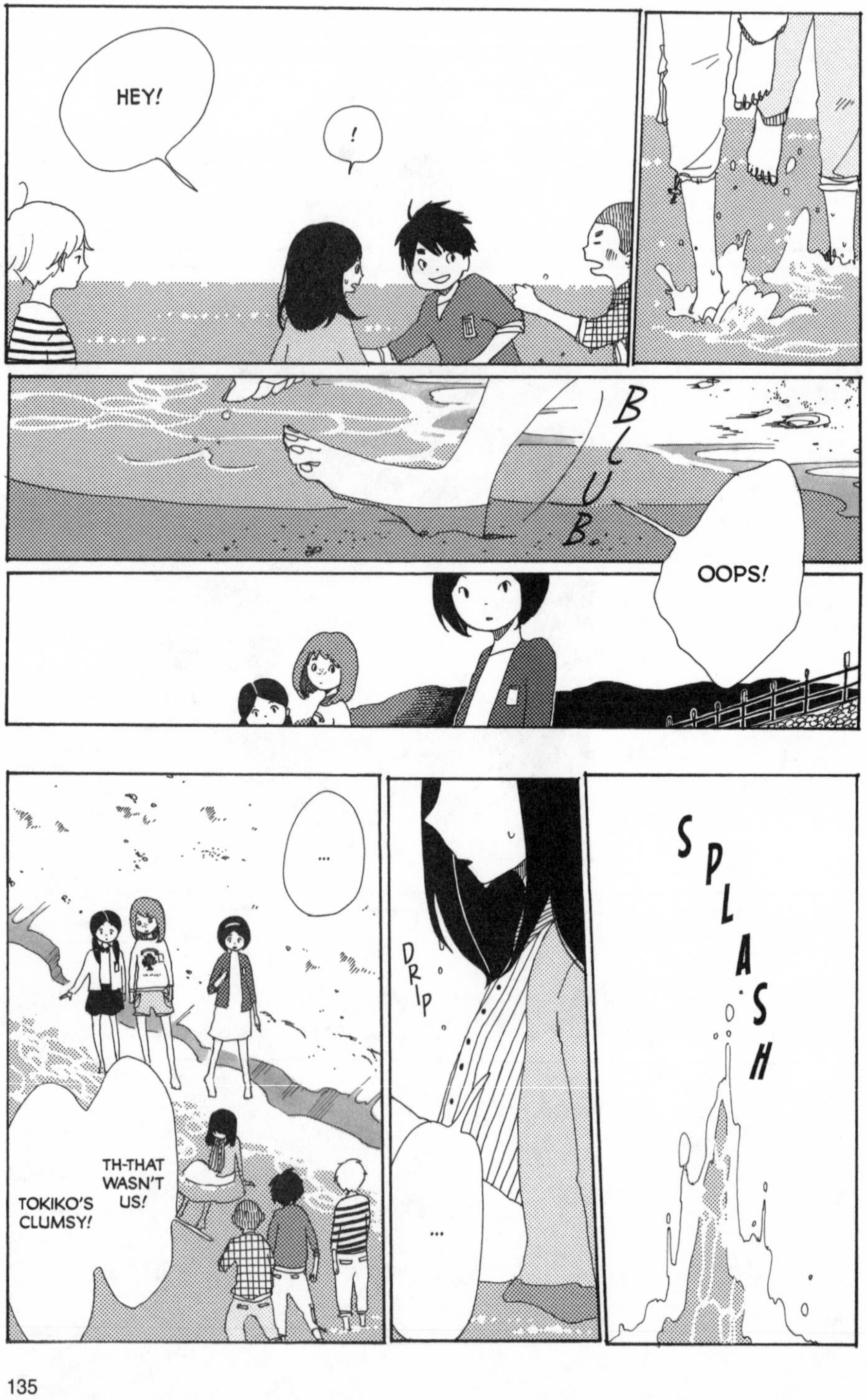
HEY!
!
BLUB
OOPS!
SPLASH
DRIP
...
...
TH-THAT WASN'T US!
TOKIKO'S CLUMSY!

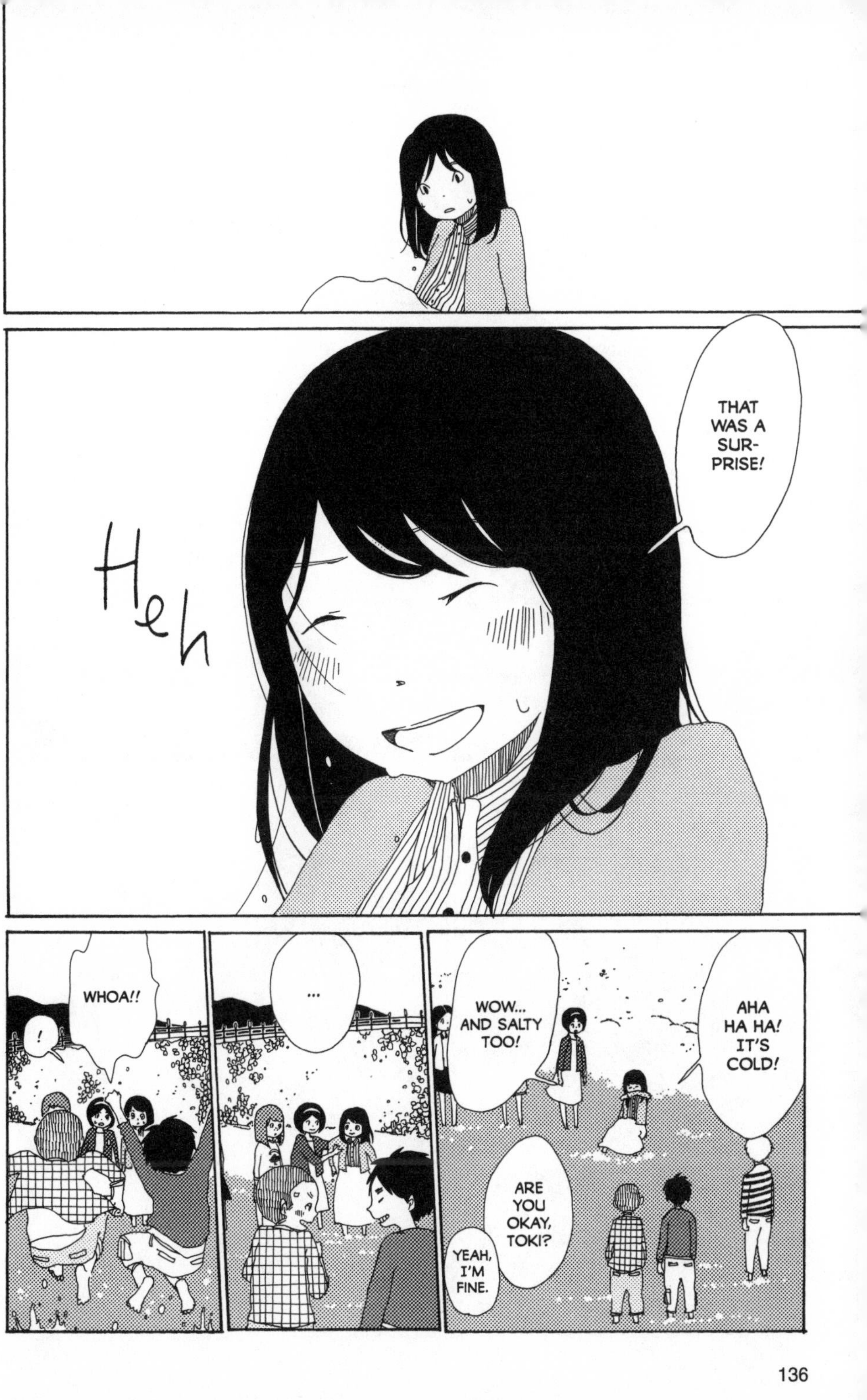
THAT WAS A SUR-PRISE!
Heh
AHA HA HA! IT'S COLD!
WOW... AND SALTY TOO!
ARE YOU OKAY, TOKI?
YEAH, I'M FINE.
...
WHOA!!
!

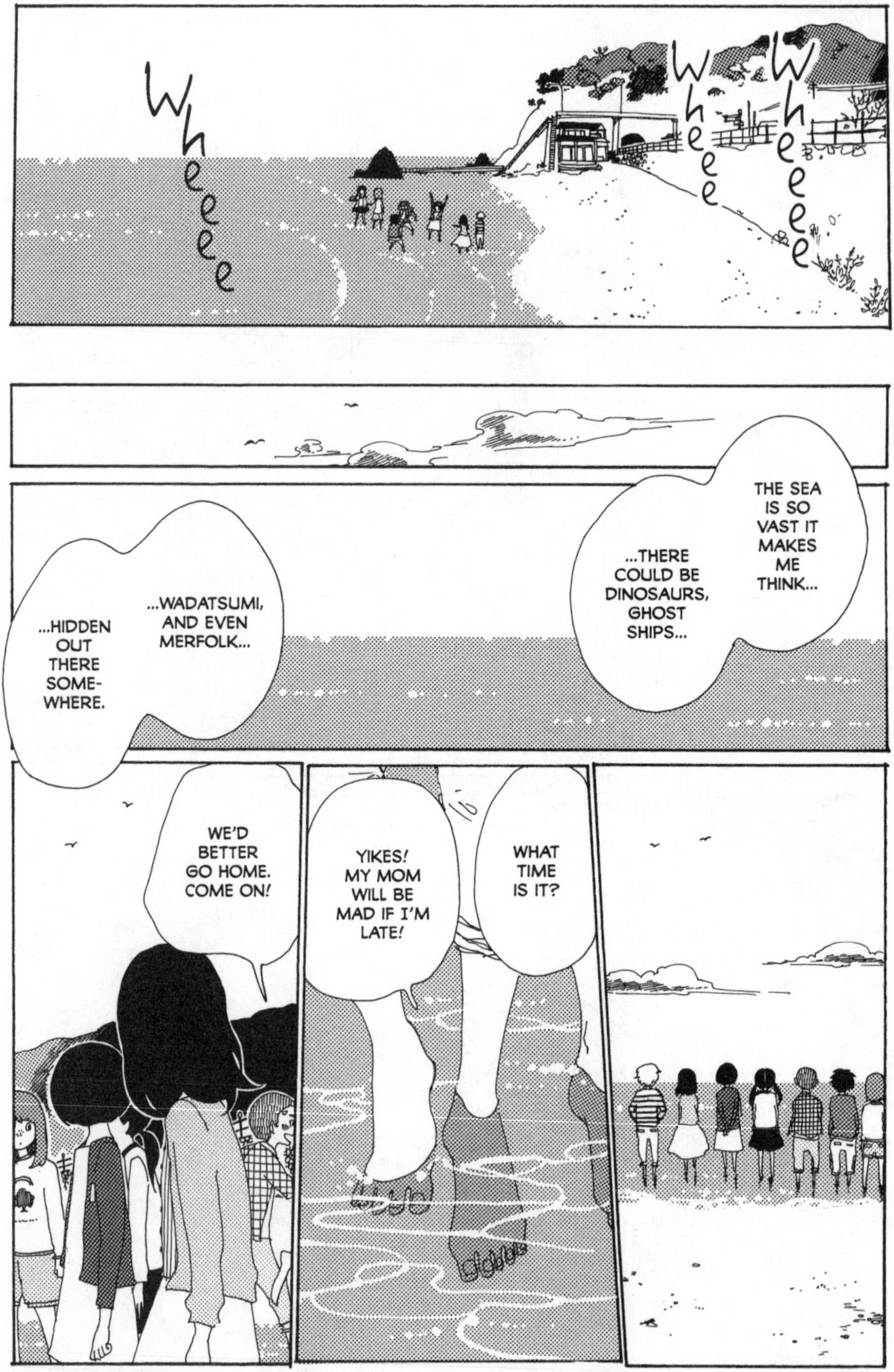
Wheeeee
Wheee
Wheeee
THE SEA IS SO VAST IT MAKES ME THINK...
...THERE COULD BE DINOSAURS, GHOST SHIPS...
...WADATSUMI, AND EVEN MERFOLK...
...HIDDEN OUT THERE SOME-WHERE.
WHAT TIME IS IT?
YIKES! MY MOM WILL BE MAD IF I'M LATE!
WE'D BETTER GO HOME. COME ON!

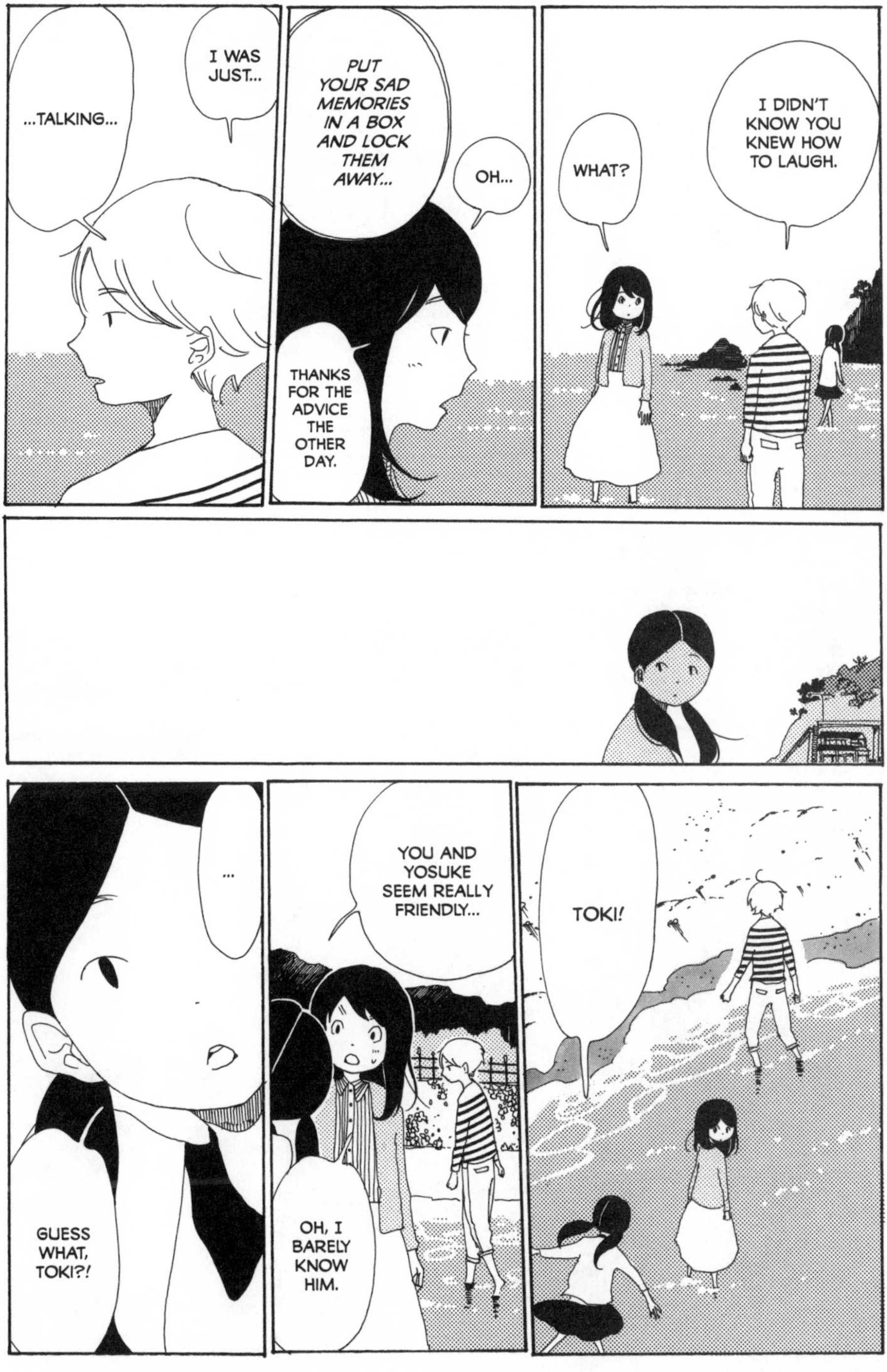
I DIDN'T KNOW YOU KNEW HOW TO LAUGH.
WHAT?
OH...
PUT YOUR SAD MEMORIES IN A BOX AND LOCK THEM AWAY...
THANKS FOR THE ADVICE THE OTHER DAY.
I WAS JUST...
...TALKING...
TOKI!
YOU AND YOSUKE SEEM REALLY FRIENDLY...
OH, I BARELY KNOW HIM.
...
GUESS WHAT, TOKI?!

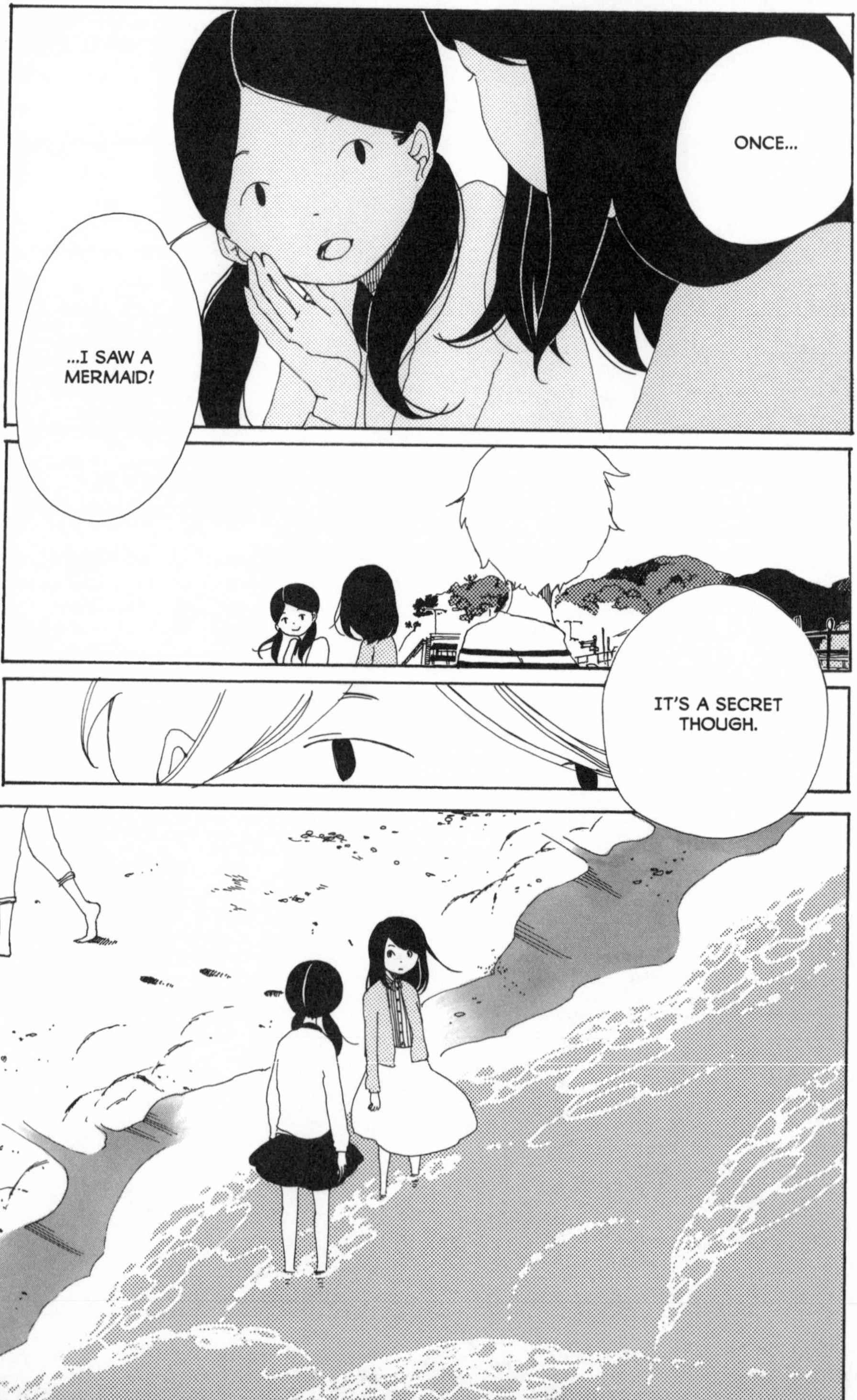
ONCE...
...I SAW A MERMAID!
IT'S A SECRET THOUGH.

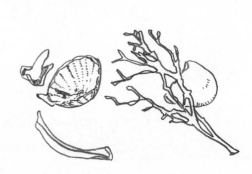

{Five} The Sound of the Sea

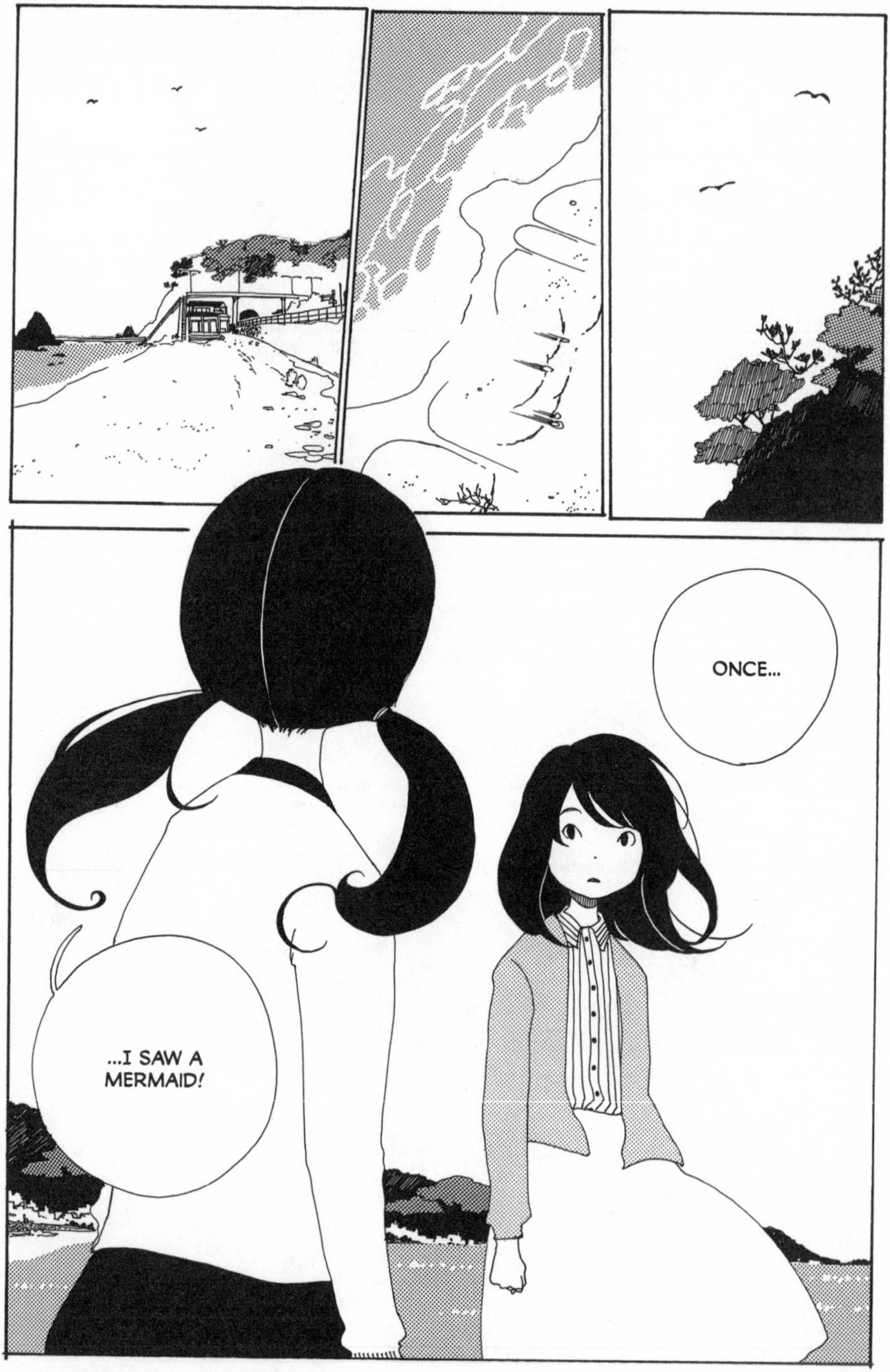
ONCE...
...I SAW A MERMAID!

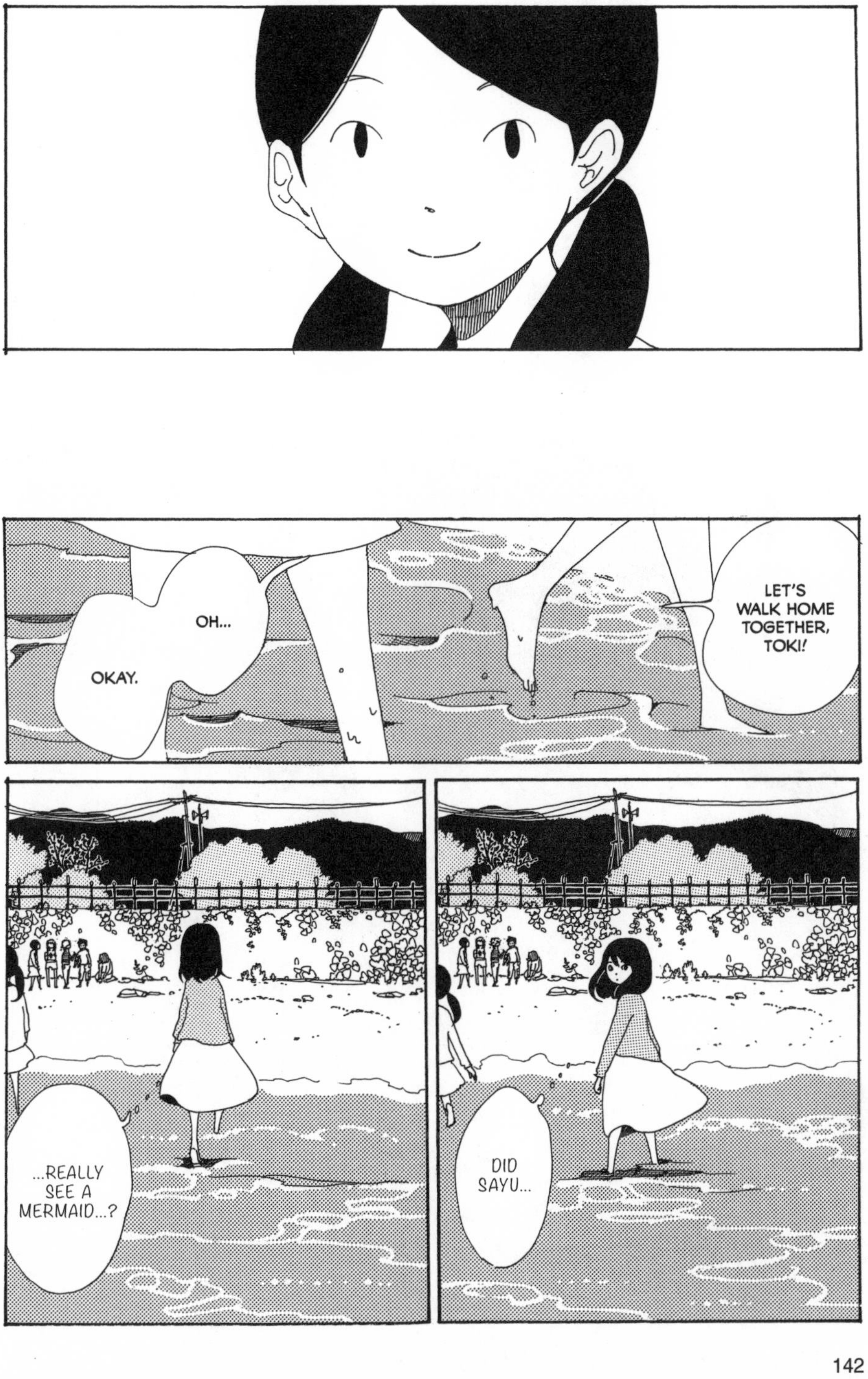
LET'S WALK HOME TOGETHER, TOKI!
OH... OKAY.
DID SAYU...
...REALLY SEE A MERMAID...?

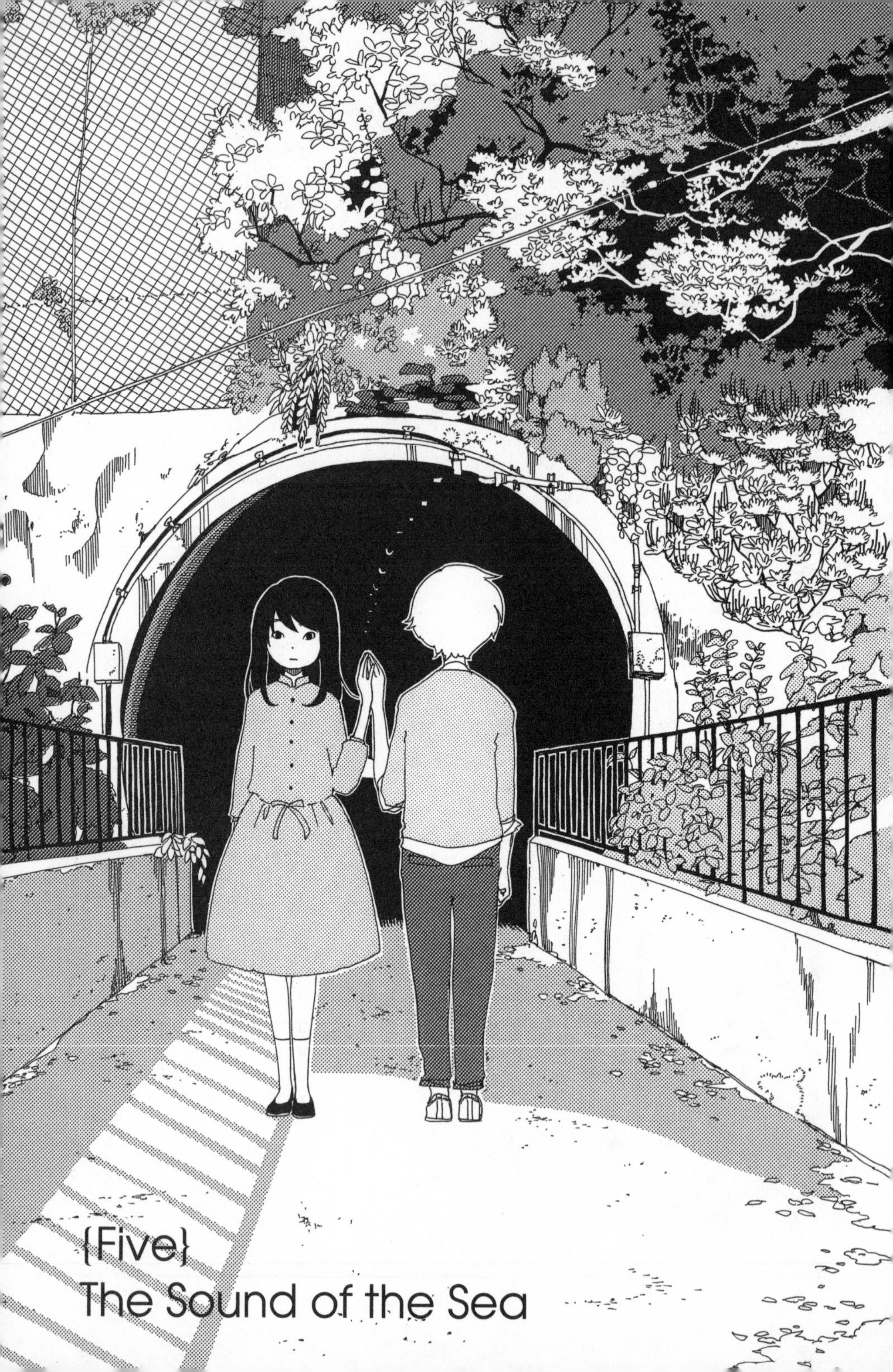

{Five}
The Sound of the Sea

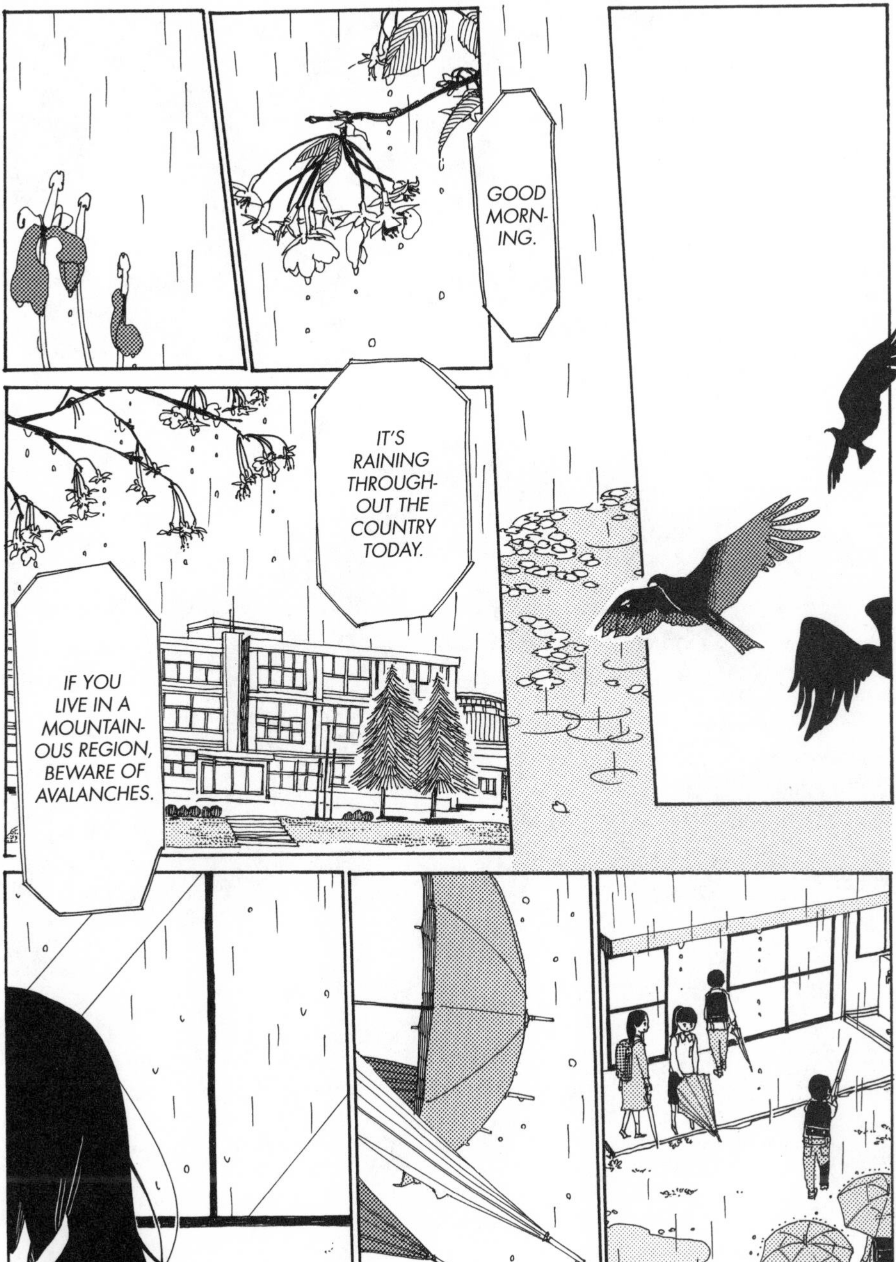
GOOD MORNING.
IT'S RAINING THROUGHOUT THE COUNTRY TODAY.
IF YOU LIVE IN A MOUNTAINOUS REGION, BEWARE OF AVALANCHES.

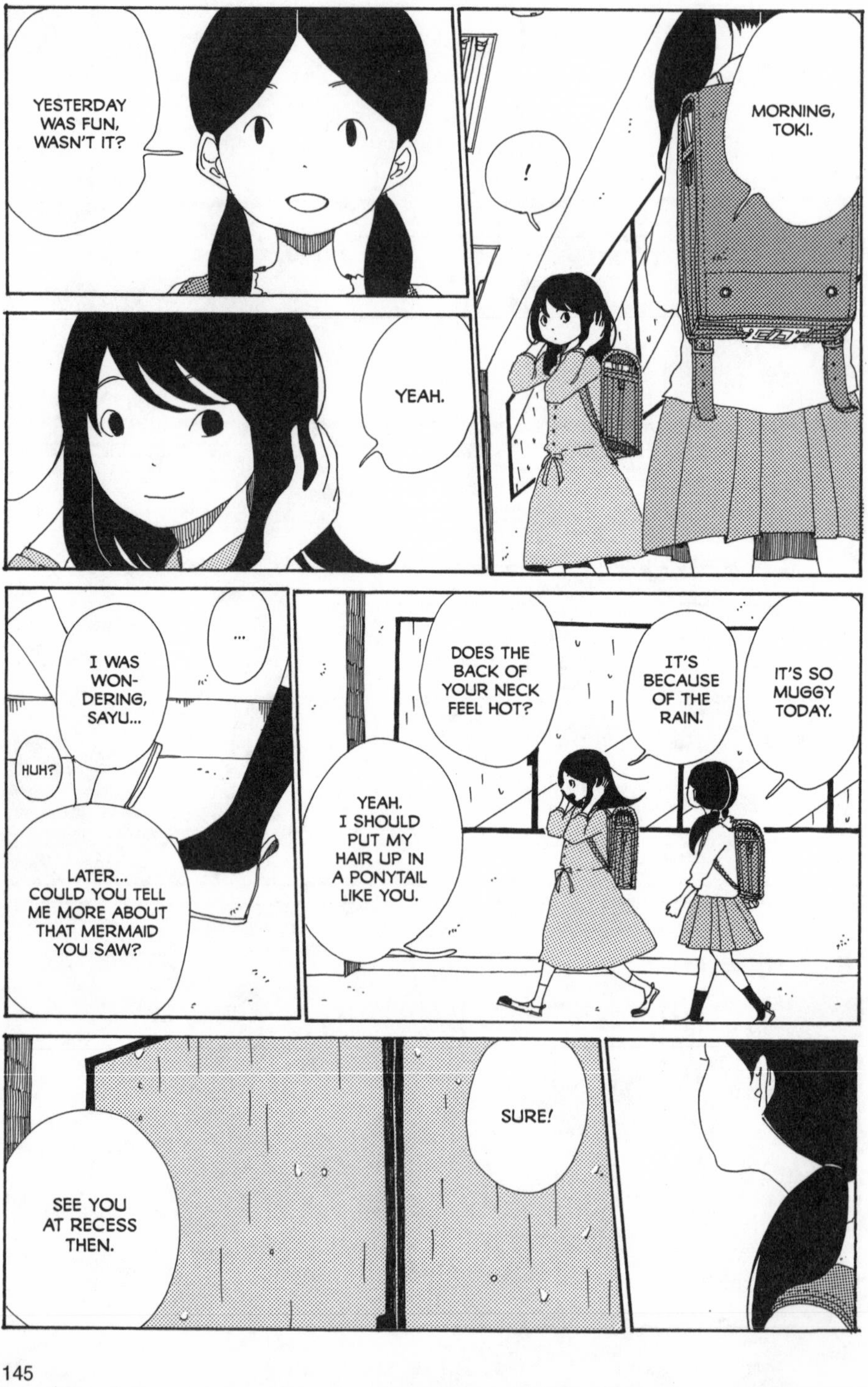
MORNING, TOKI.
!
YESTERDAY WAS FUN, WASN'T IT?
YEAH.
IT'S SO MUGGY TODAY.
IT'S BECAUSE OF THE RAIN.
DOES THE BACK OF YOUR NECK FEEL HOT?
YEAH. I SHOULD PUT MY HAIR UP IN A PONYTAIL LIKE YOU.
...
I WAS WONDERING, SAYU...
HUH?
LATER... COULD YOU TELL ME MORE ABOUT THAT MERMAID YOU SAW?
SURE!
SEE YOU AT RECESS THEN.

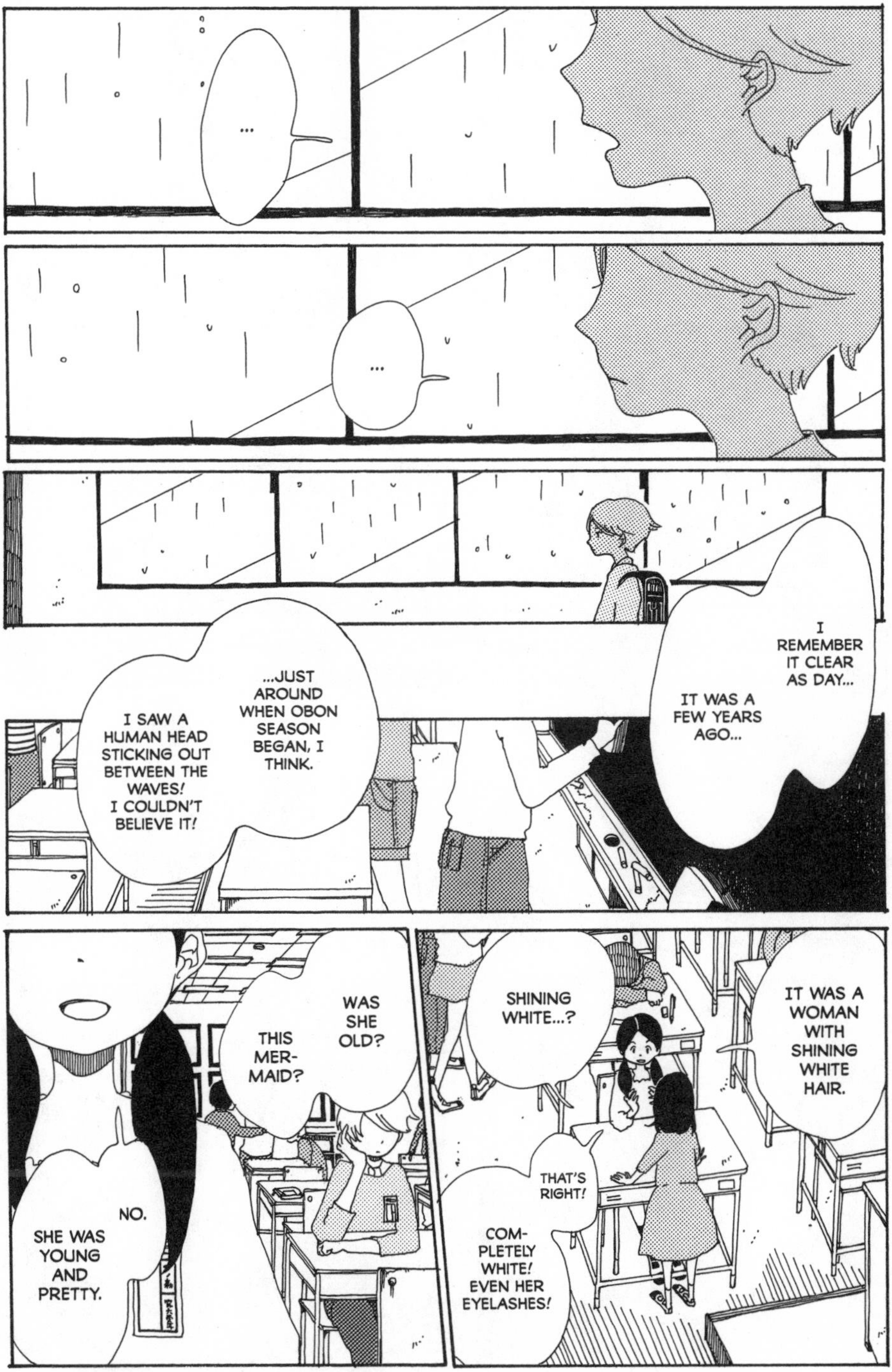
...
...
I REMEMBER IT CLEAR AS DAY...
IT WAS A FEW YEARS AGO...
...JUST AROUND WHEN OBON SEASON BEGAN, I THINK.
I SAW A HUMAN HEAD STICKING OUT BETWEEN THE WAVES! I COULDN'T BELIEVE IT!
IT WAS A WOMAN WITH SHINING WHITE HAIR.
SHINING WHITE...?
THAT'S RIGHT!
COMPLETELY WHITE! EVEN HER EYELASHES!
WAS SHE OLD?
THIS MERMAID?
NO.
SHE WAS YOUNG AND PRETTY.

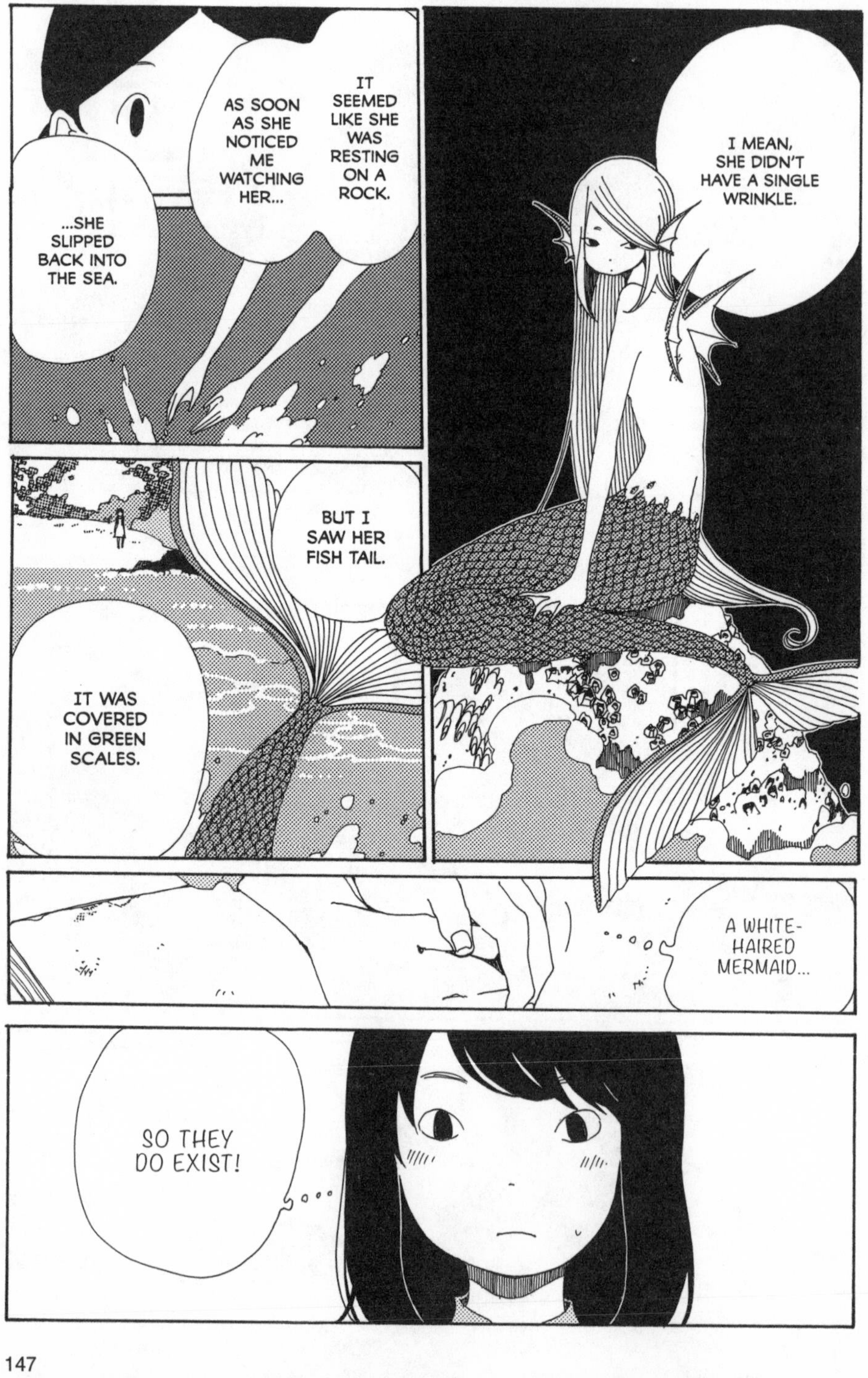
I MEAN, SHE DIDN'T HAVE A SINGLE WRINKLE.
IT SEEMED LIKE SHE WAS RESTING ON A ROCK.
AS SOON AS SHE NOTICED ME WATCHING HER...
...SHE SLIPPED BACK INTO THE SEA.
BUT I SAW HER FISH TAIL.
IT WAS COVERED IN GREEN SCALES.
A WHITE-HAIRED MERMAID...
SO THEY DO EXIST!

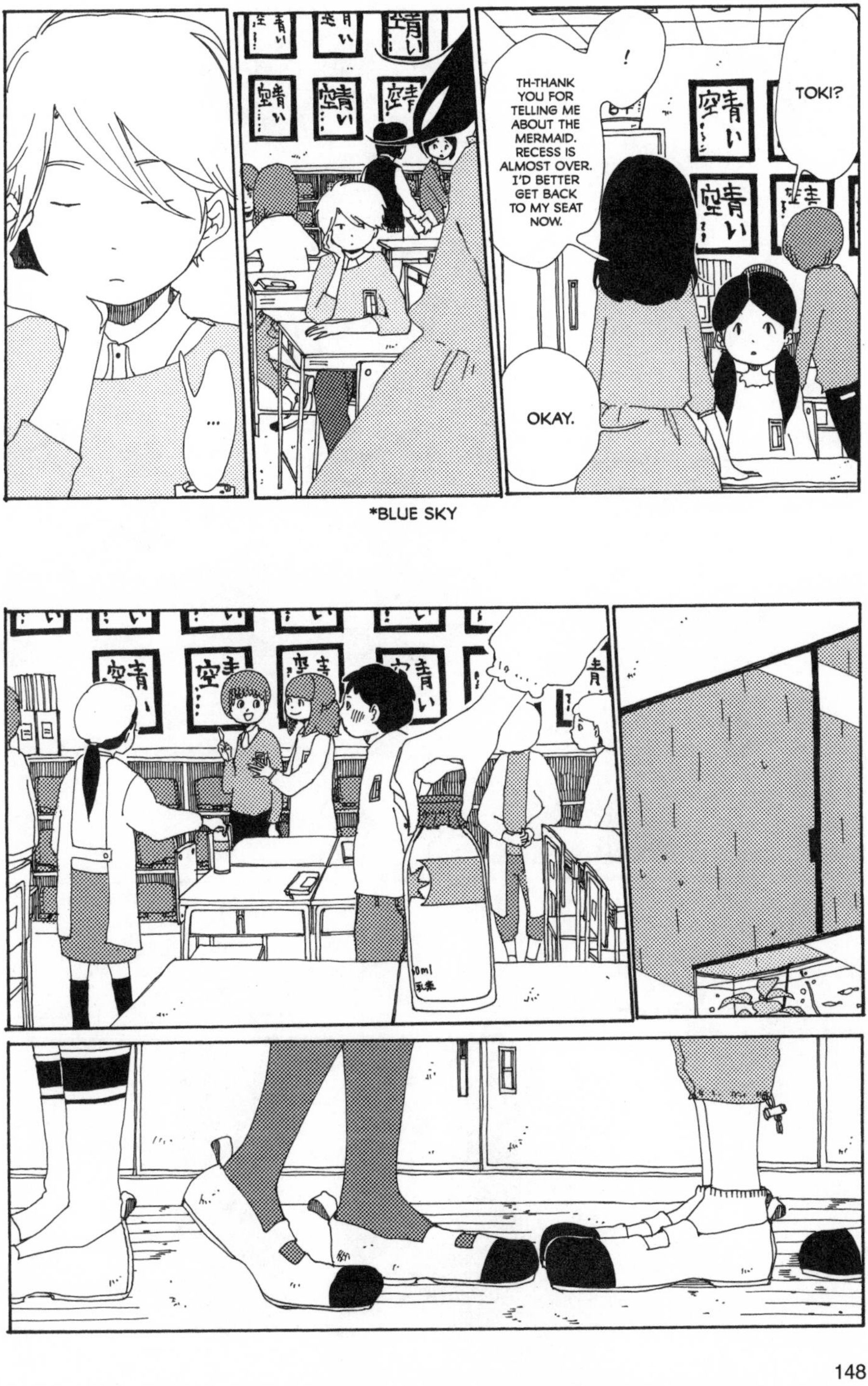
TOKI?
!
TH-THANK YOU FOR TELLING ME ABOUT THE MERMAID. RECESS IS ALMOST OVER. I'D BETTER GET BACK TO MY SEAT NOW.
OKAY.
空青い
...
*BLUE SKY

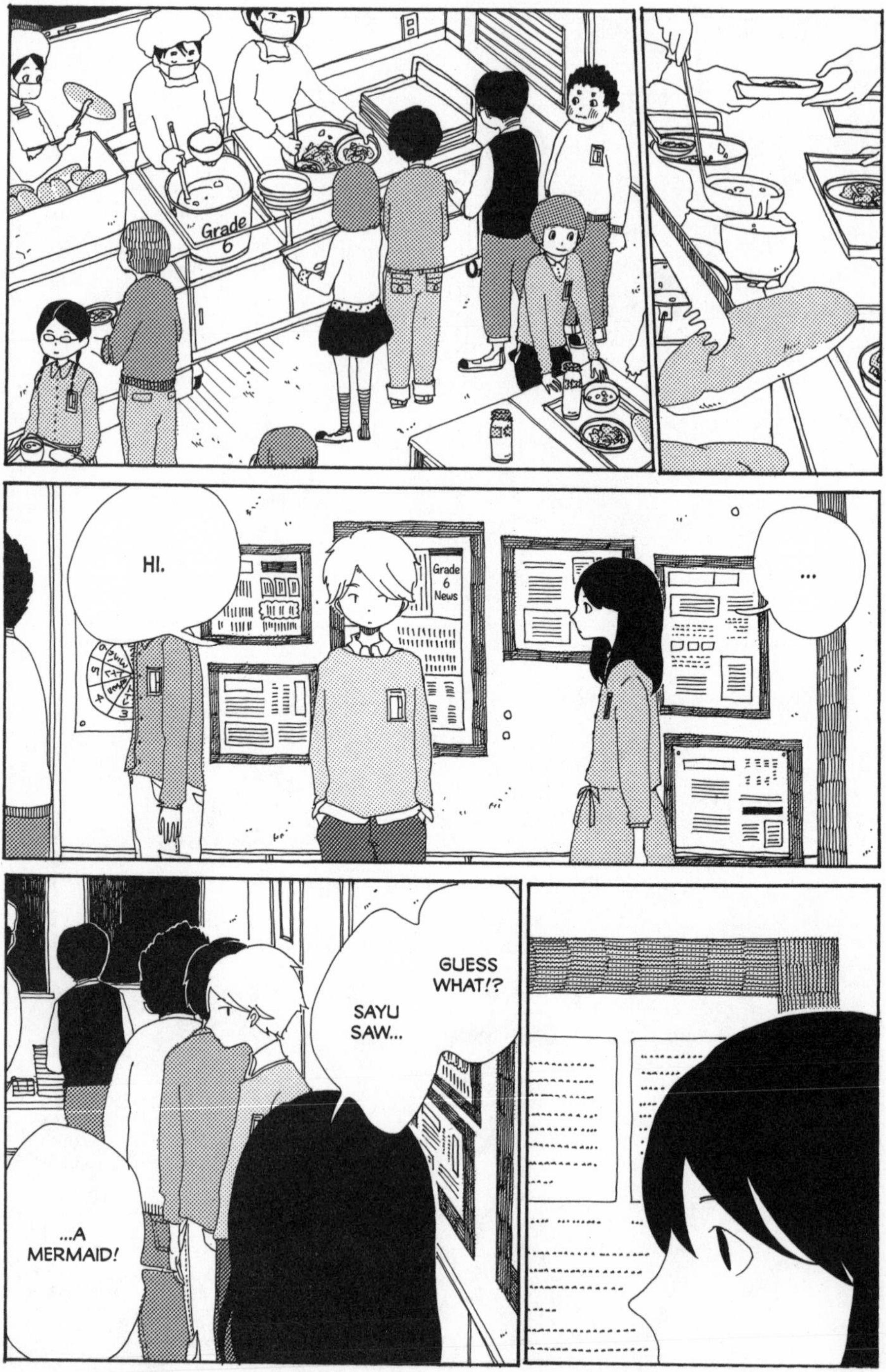
Grade 6
...
Grade 6 News
HI.
GUESS WHAT!?
SAYU SAW...
...A MERMAID!

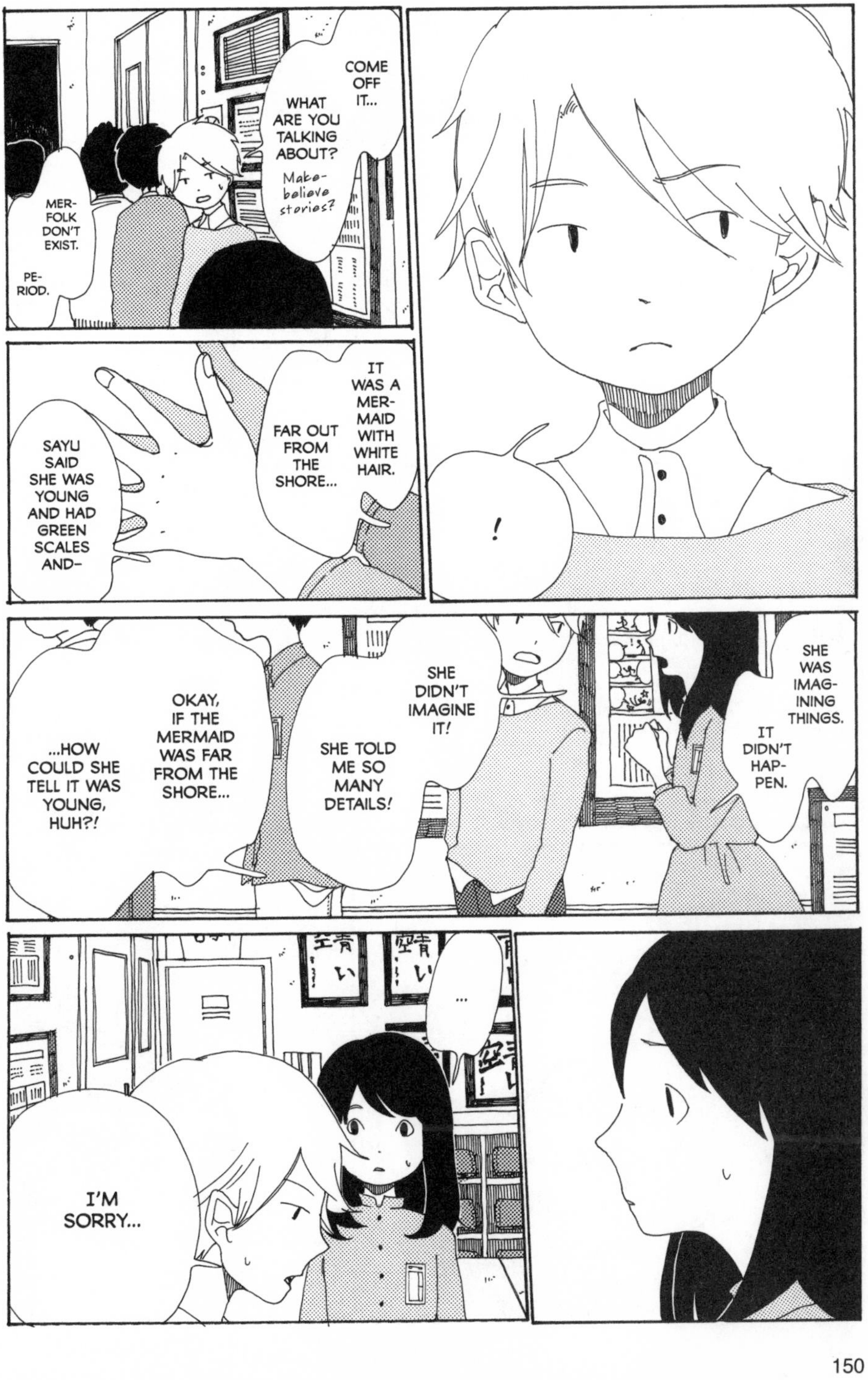
!
COME OFF IT...
WHAT ARE YOU TALKING ABOUT?
Make-believe stories?
MERFOLK DON'T EXIST.
PERIOD.
IT WAS A MERMAID WITH WHITE HAIR.
FAR OUT FROM THE SHORE...
SAYU SAID SHE WAS YOUNG AND HAD GREEN SCALES AND–
SHE WAS IMAGINING THINGS.
IT DIDN'T HAPPEN.
SHE DIDN'T IMAGINE IT!
SHE TOLD ME SO MANY DETAILS!
OKAY, IF THE MERMAID WAS FAR FROM THE SHORE...
...HOW COULD SHE TELL IT WAS YOUNG, HUH?!
...
I'M SORRY...

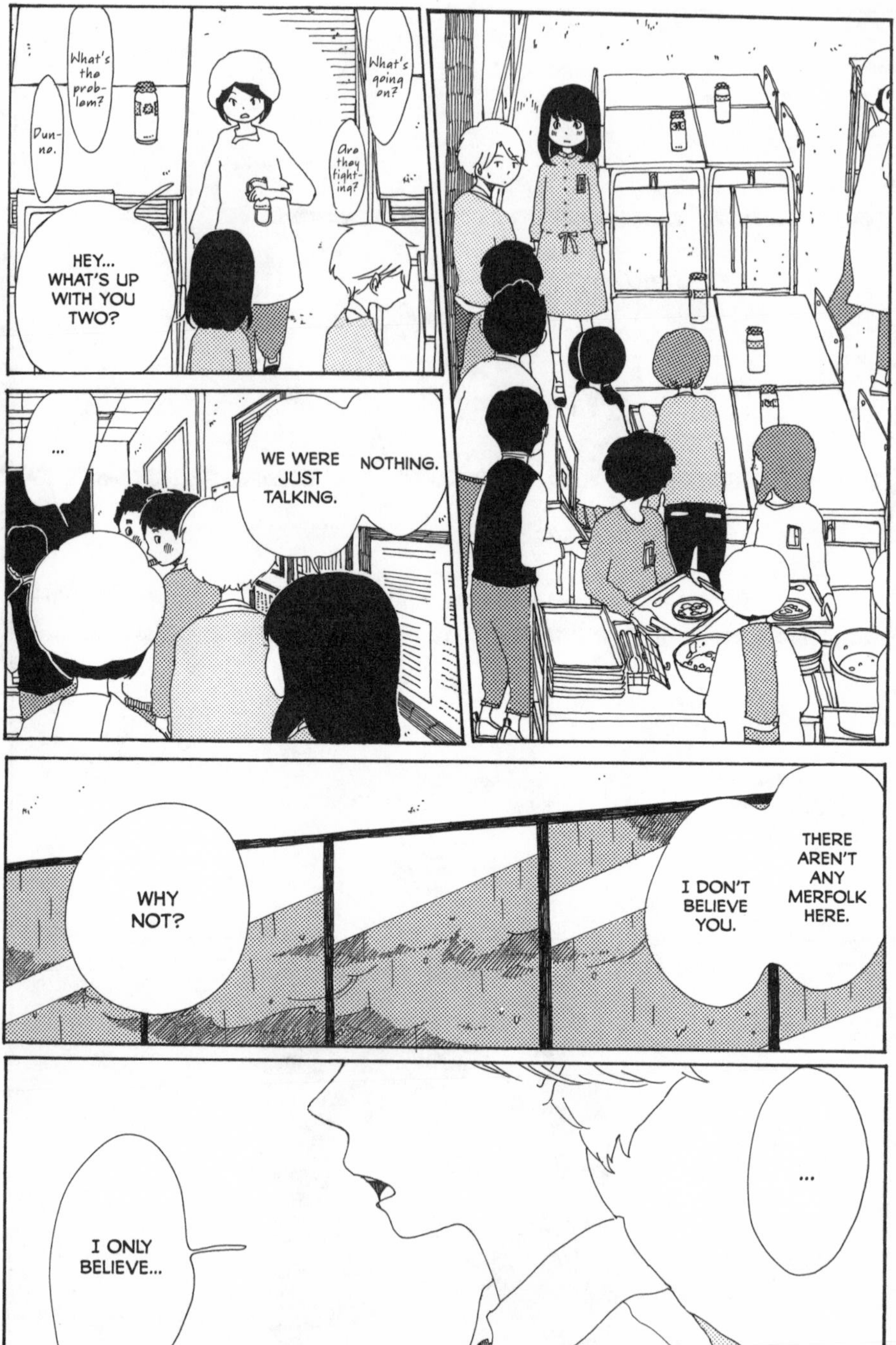
What's going on?
Are they fighting?
What's the problem?
Dunno.
HEY... WHAT'S UP WITH YOU TWO?
NOTHING.
WE WERE JUST TALKING.
...
THERE AREN'T ANY MERFOLK HERE.
I DON'T BELIEVE YOU.
WHY NOT?
...
I ONLY BELIEVE...

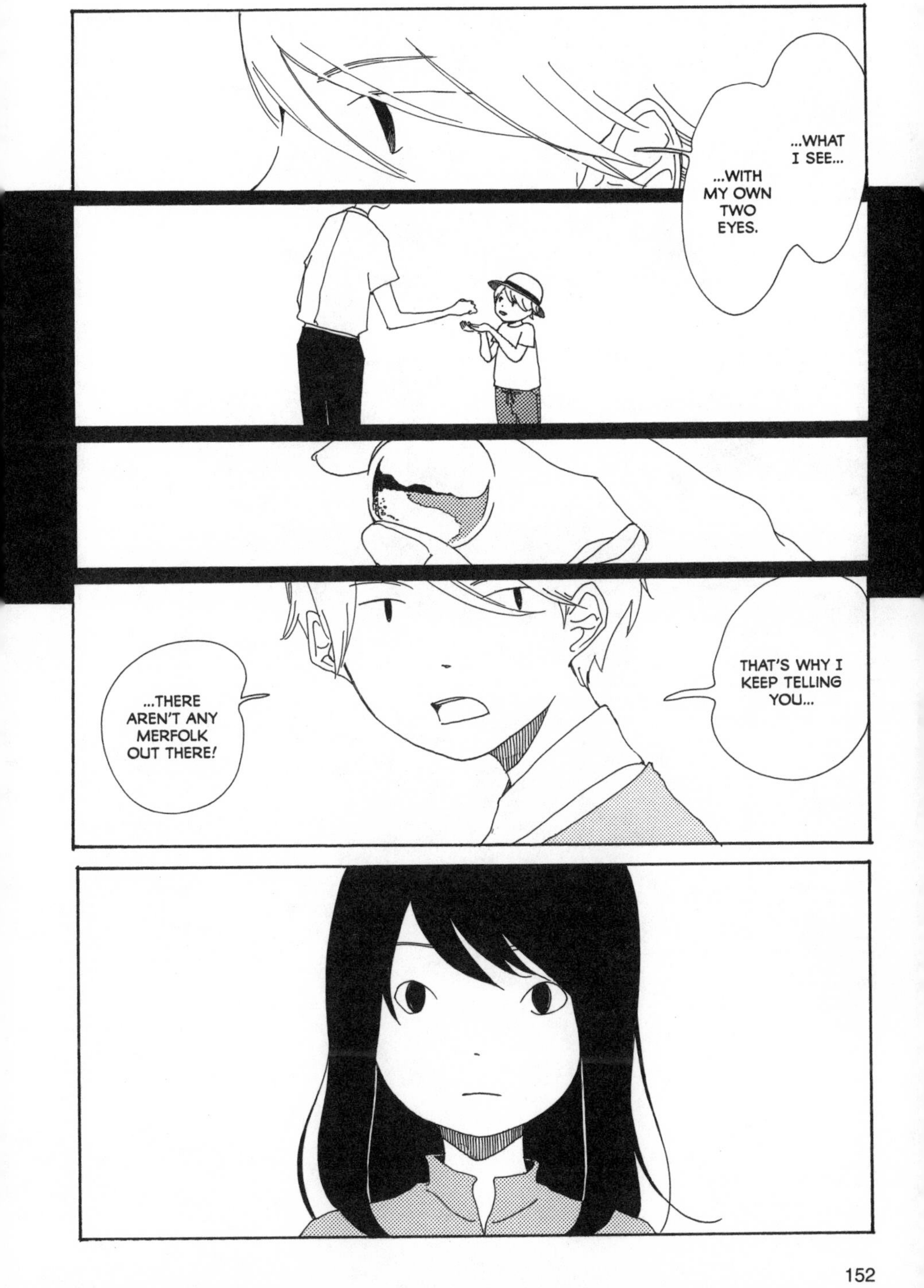
...WHAT I SEE...
...WITH MY OWN TWO EYES.
THAT'S WHY I KEEP TELLING YOU...
...THERE AREN'T ANY MERFOLK OUT THERE!

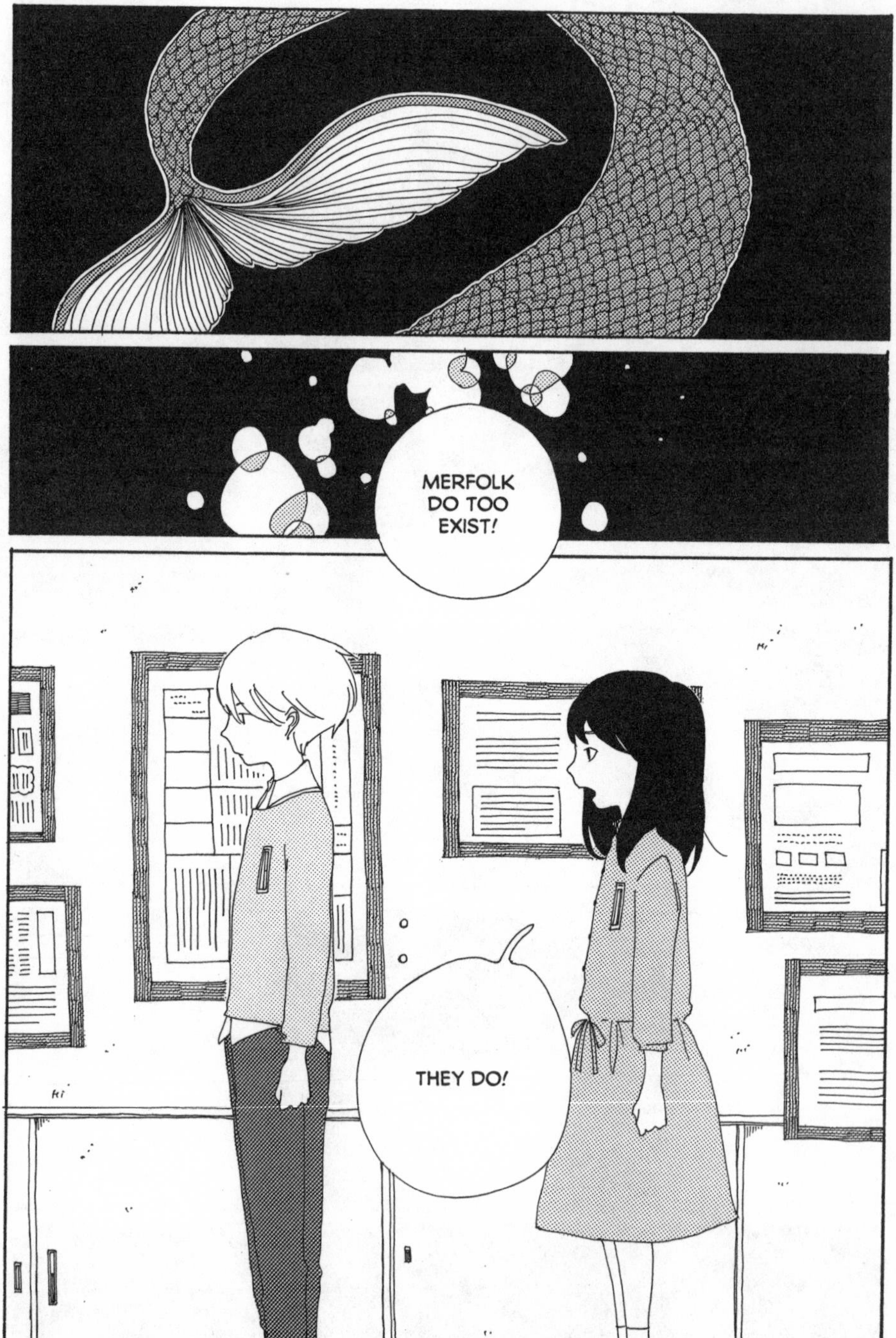
MERFOLK DO TOO EXIST!
THEY DO!

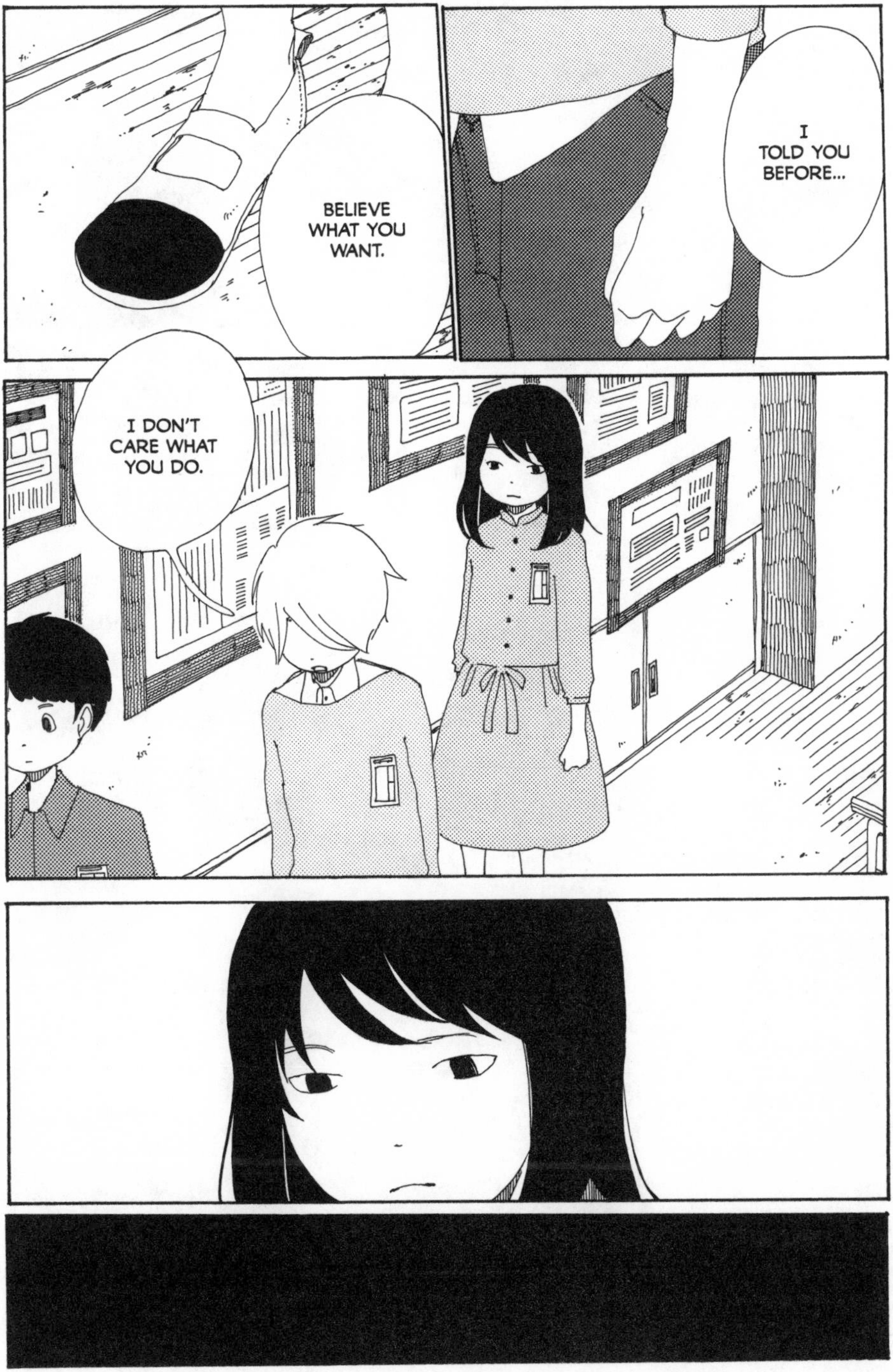
I TOLD YOU BEFORE...
BELIEVE WHAT YOU WANT.
I DON'T CARE WHAT YOU DO.

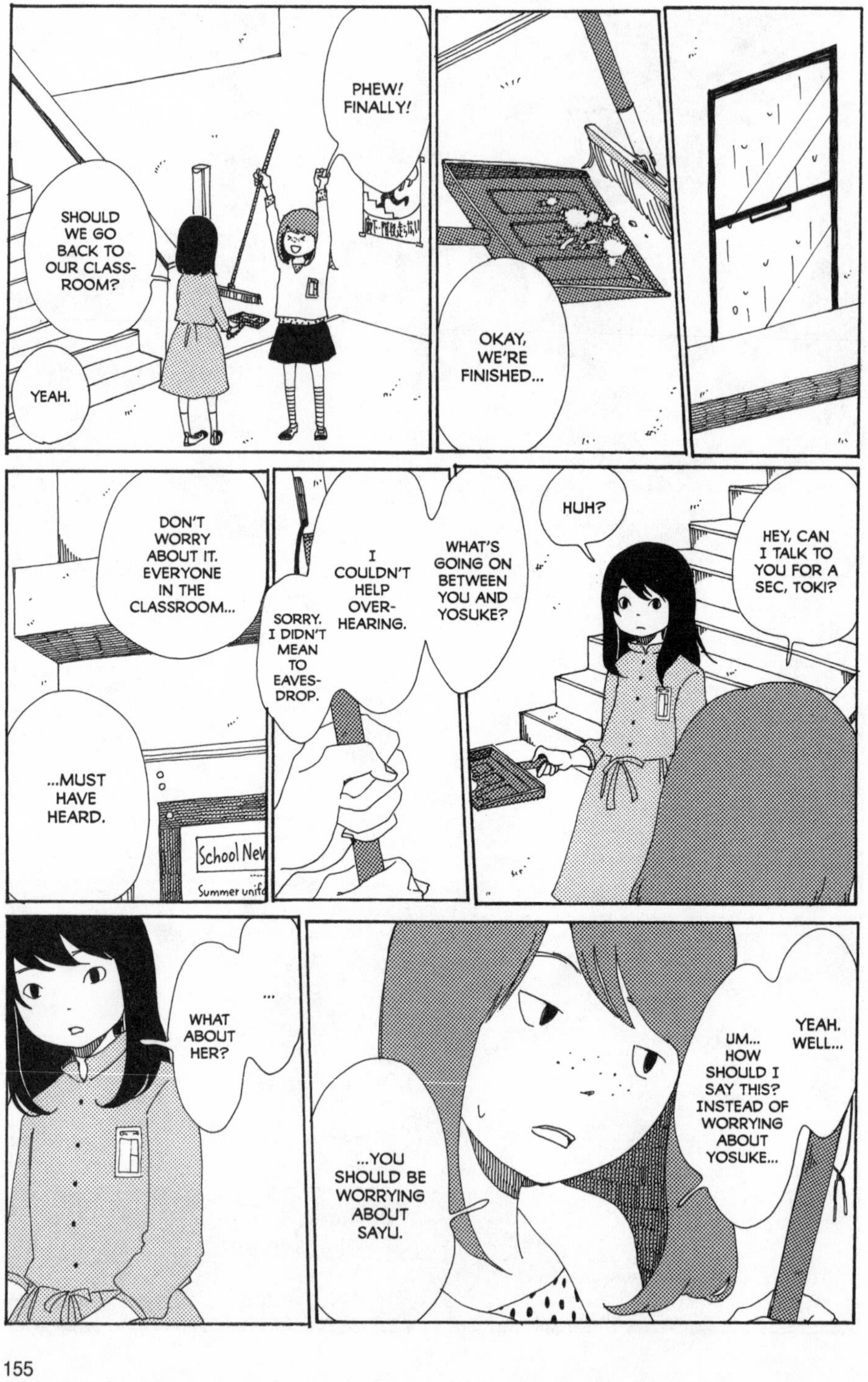

OKAY, WE'RE FINISHED...
PHEW! FINALLY!
SHOULD WE GO BACK TO OUR CLASS-ROOM?
YEAH.
HEY, CAN I TALK TO YOU FOR A SEC, TOKI?
HUH?
WHAT'S GOING ON BETWEEN YOU AND YOSUKE?
I COULDN'T HELP OVER-HEARING.
SORRY. I DIDN'T MEAN TO EAVES-DROP.
DON'T WORRY ABOUT IT. EVERYONE IN THE CLASSROOM...
...MUST HAVE HEARD.
YEAH. WELL...
UM... HOW SHOULD I SAY THIS? INSTEAD OF WORRYING ABOUT YOSUKE...
...YOU SHOULD BE WORRYING ABOUT SAYU.
...
WHAT ABOUT HER?

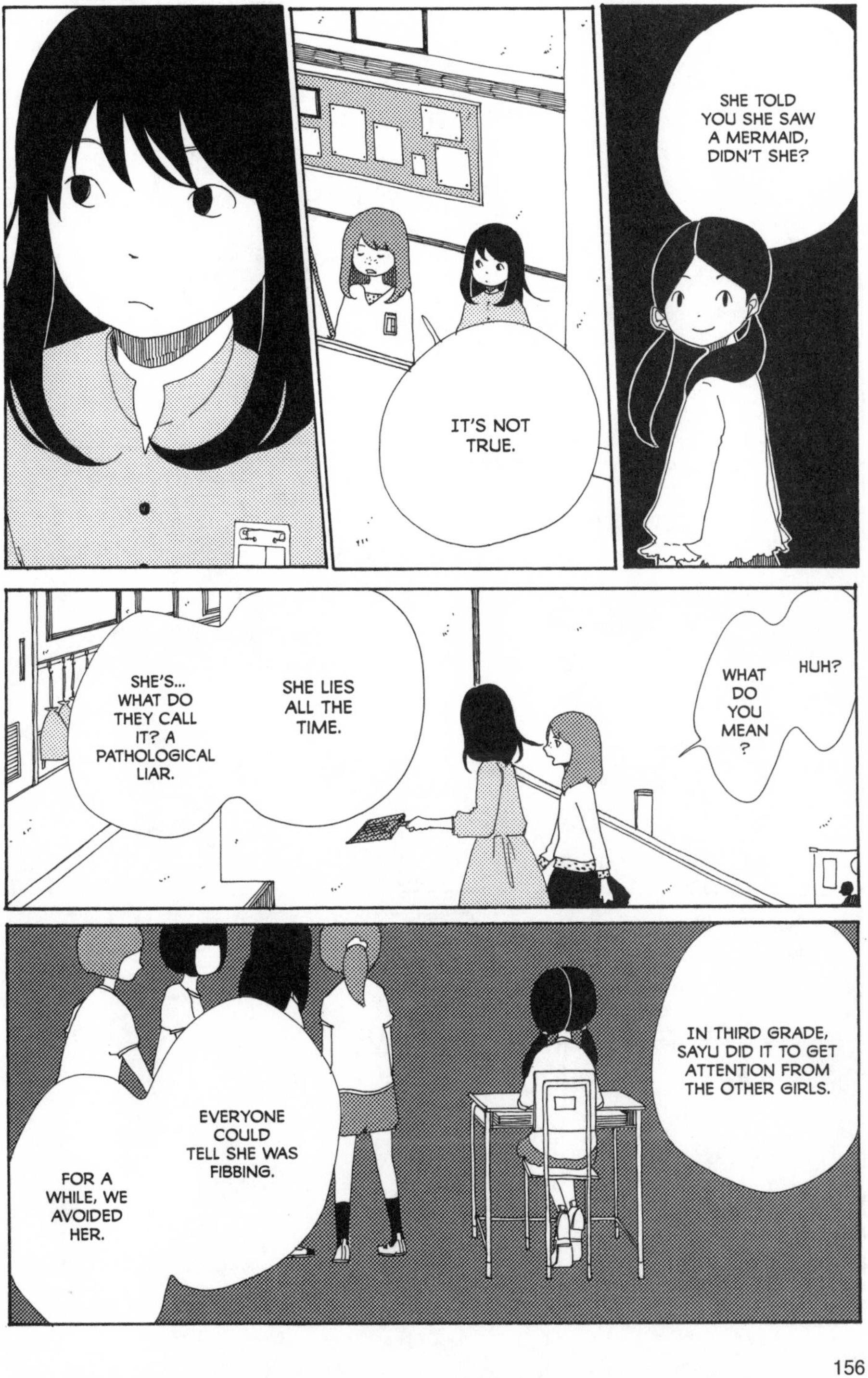
SHE TOLD YOU SHE SAW A MERMAID, DIDN'T SHE?
IT'S NOT TRUE.
HUH?
WHAT DO YOU MEAN?
SHE LIES ALL THE TIME.
SHE'S... WHAT DO THEY CALL IT? A PATHOLOGICAL LIAR.
IN THIRD GRADE, SAYU DID IT TO GET ATTENTION FROM THE OTHER GIRLS.
EVERYONE COULD TELL SHE WAS FIBBING.
FOR A WHILE, WE AVOIDED HER.

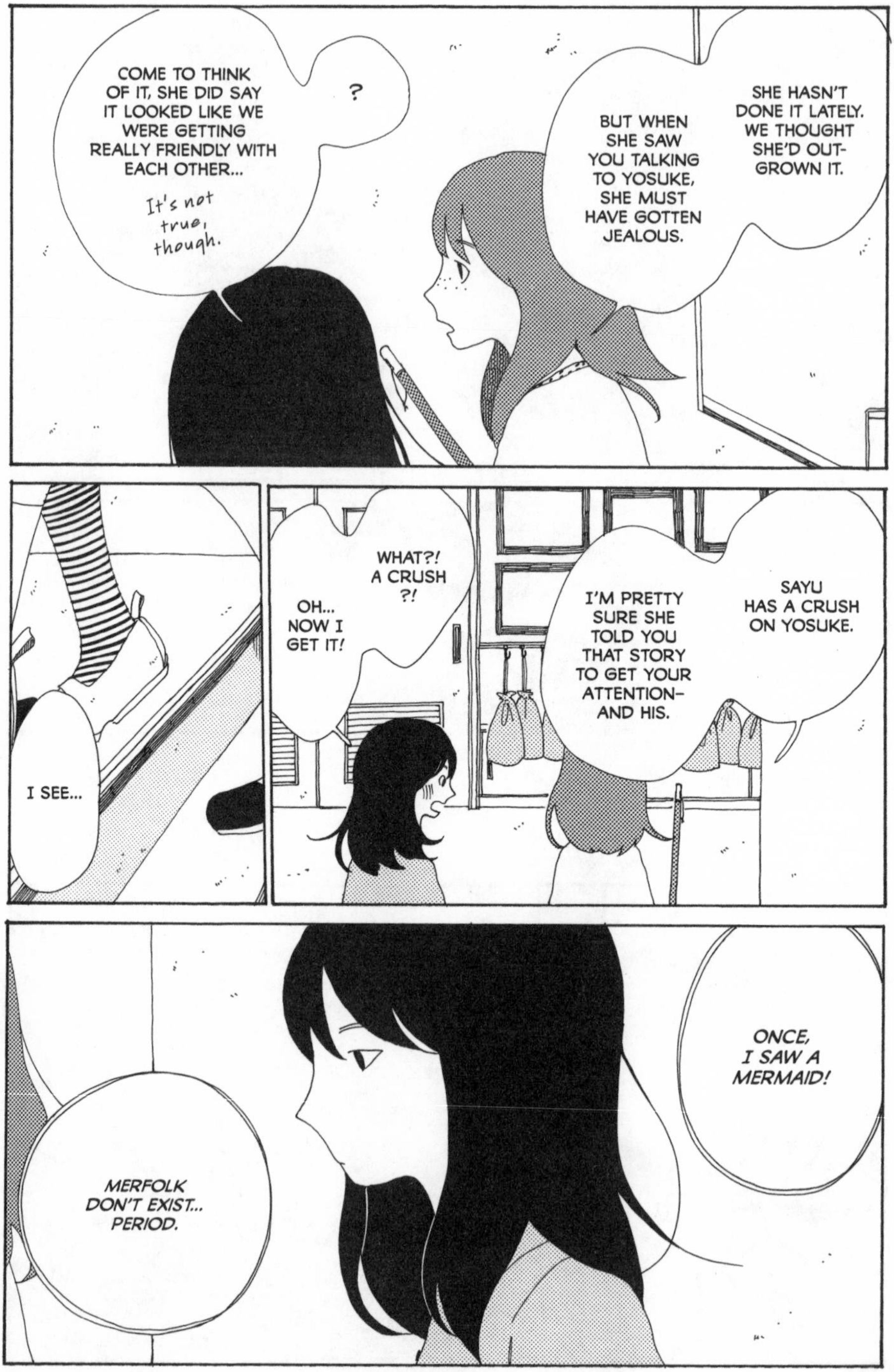
SHE HASN'T DONE IT LATELY. WE THOUGHT SHE'D OUT-GROWN IT.
BUT WHEN SHE SAW YOU TALKING TO YOSUKE, SHE MUST HAVE GOTTEN JEALOUS.
?
COME TO THINK OF IT, SHE DID SAY IT LOOKED LIKE WE WERE GETTING REALLY FRIENDLY WITH EACH OTHER...
It's not true, though.
SAYU HAS A CRUSH ON YOSUKE.
I'M PRETTY SURE SHE TOLD YOU THAT STORY TO GET YOUR ATTENTION— AND HIS.
WHAT?! A CRUSH ?!
OH... NOW I GET IT!
I SEE...
ONCE, I SAW A MERMAID!
MERFOLK DON'T EXIST... PERIOD.

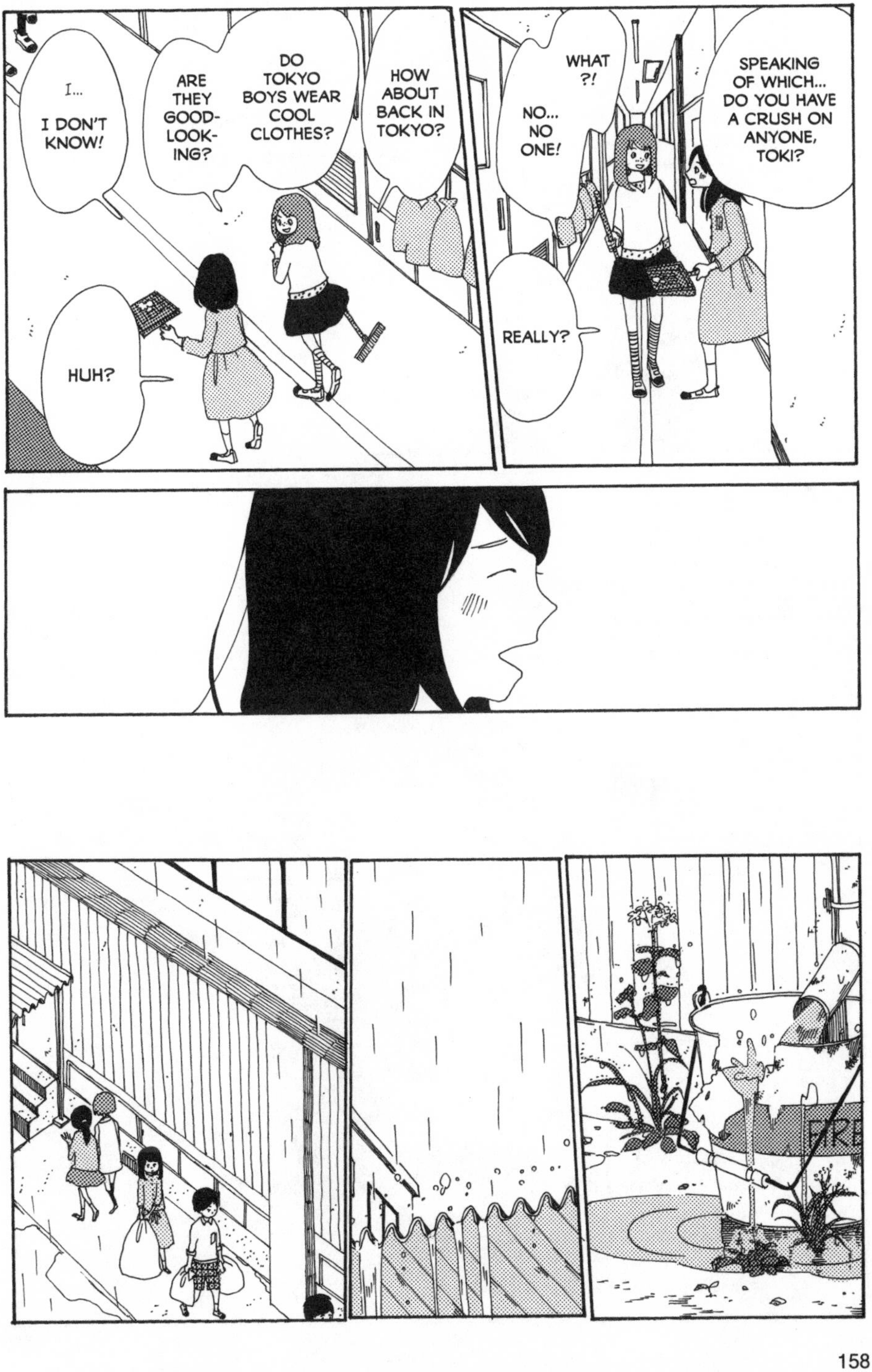
SPEAKING OF WHICH... DO YOU HAVE A CRUSH ON ANYONE, TOKI?
WHAT?!
NO... NO ONE!
REALLY?
HOW ABOUT BACK IN TOKYO?
DO TOKYO BOYS WEAR COOL CLOTHES?
ARE THEY GOOD-LOOKING?
I... I DON'T KNOW!
HUH?
FIRE

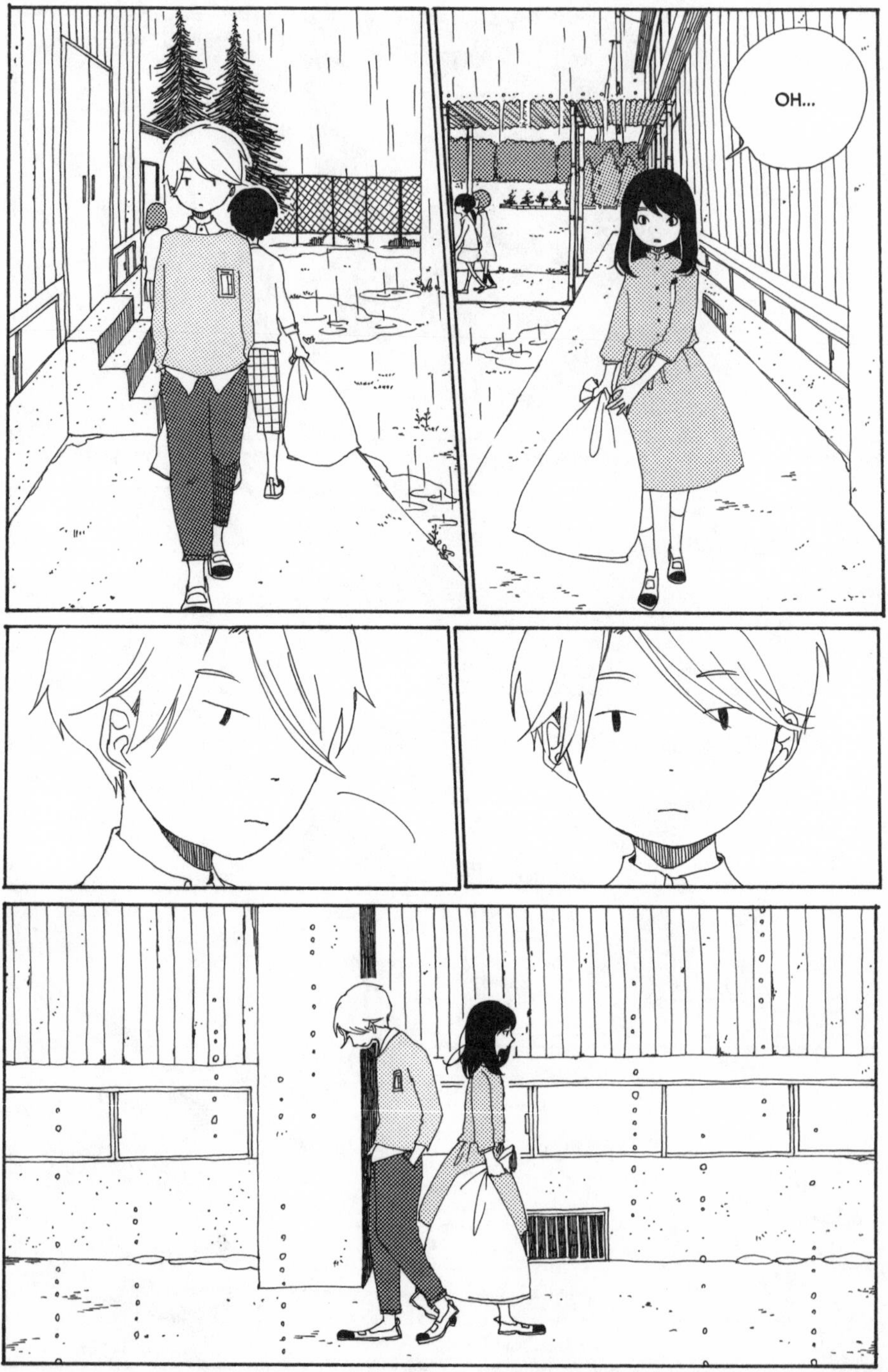
OH...

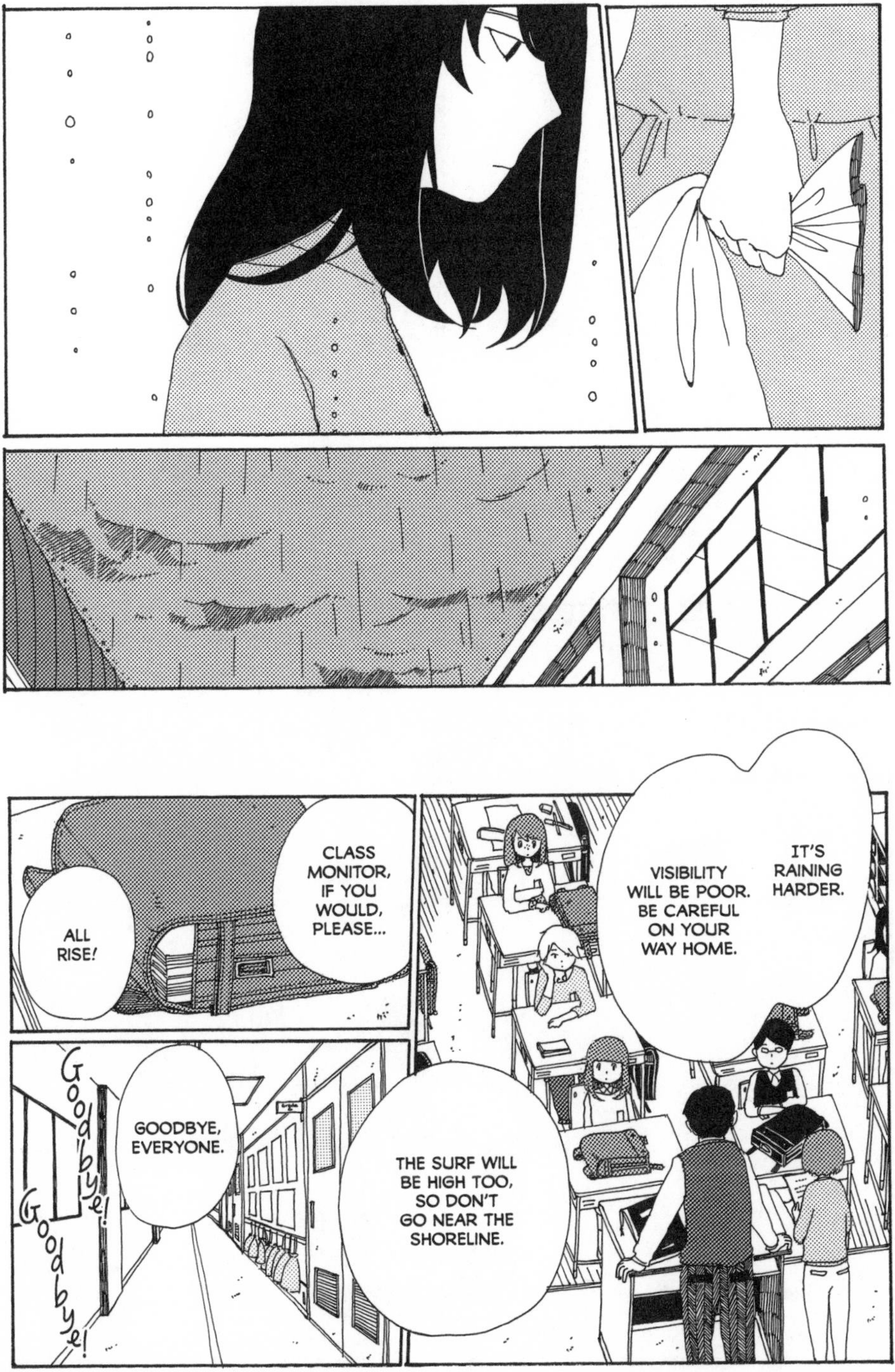
IT'S RAINING HARDER.
VISIBILITY WILL BE POOR. BE CAREFUL ON YOUR WAY HOME.
THE SURF WILL BE HIGH TOO, SO DON'T GO NEAR THE SHORELINE.
CLASS MONITOR, IF YOU WOULD, PLEASE...
ALL RISE!
GOODBYE, EVERYONE.
Goodbye!
Goodbye!

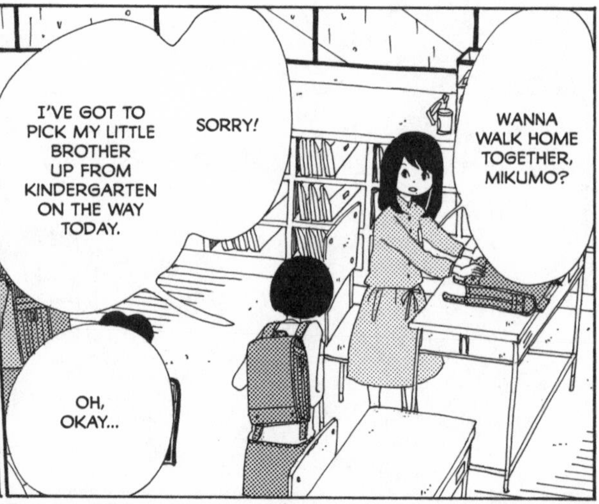
WANNA WALK HOME TOGETHER, MIKUMO?
SORRY!
I'VE GOT TO PICK MY LITTLE BROTHER UP FROM KINDERGARTEN ON THE WAY TODAY.
OH, OKAY...
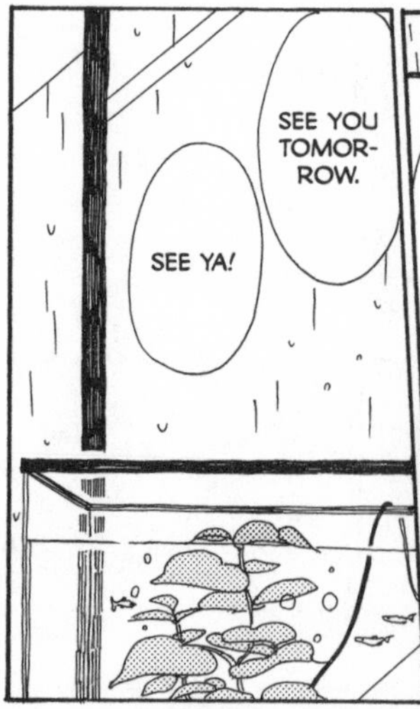
SEE YOU TOMOR-ROW.
SEE YA!
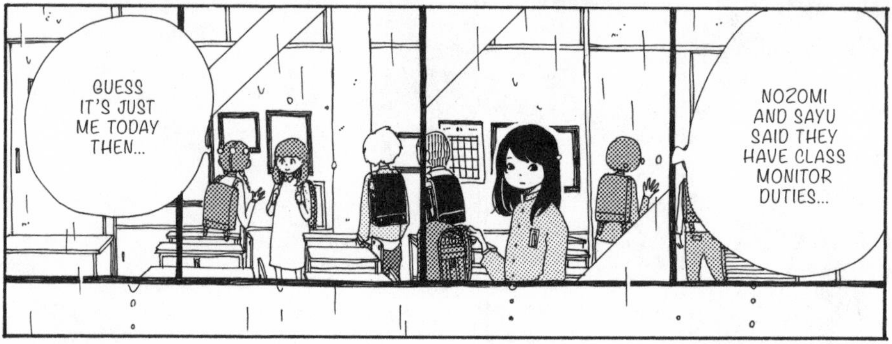
NOZOMI AND SAYU SAID THEY HAVE CLASS MONITOR DUTIES...
GUESS IT'S JUST ME TODAY THEN...
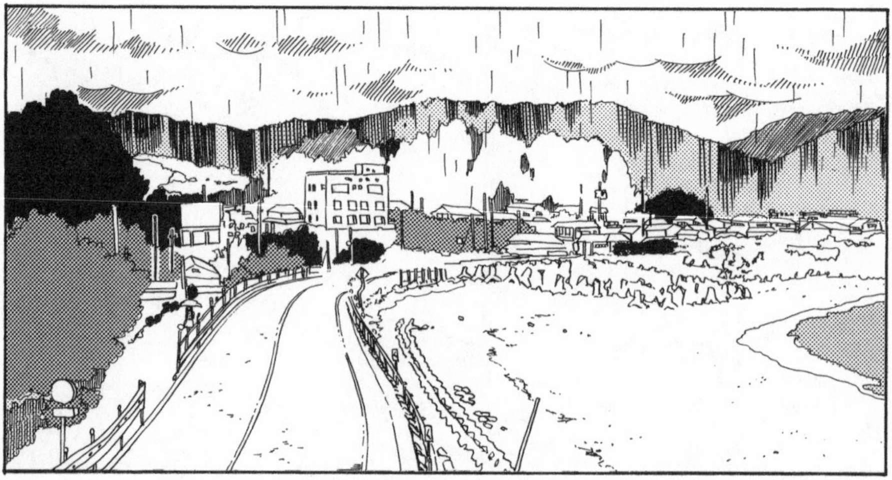

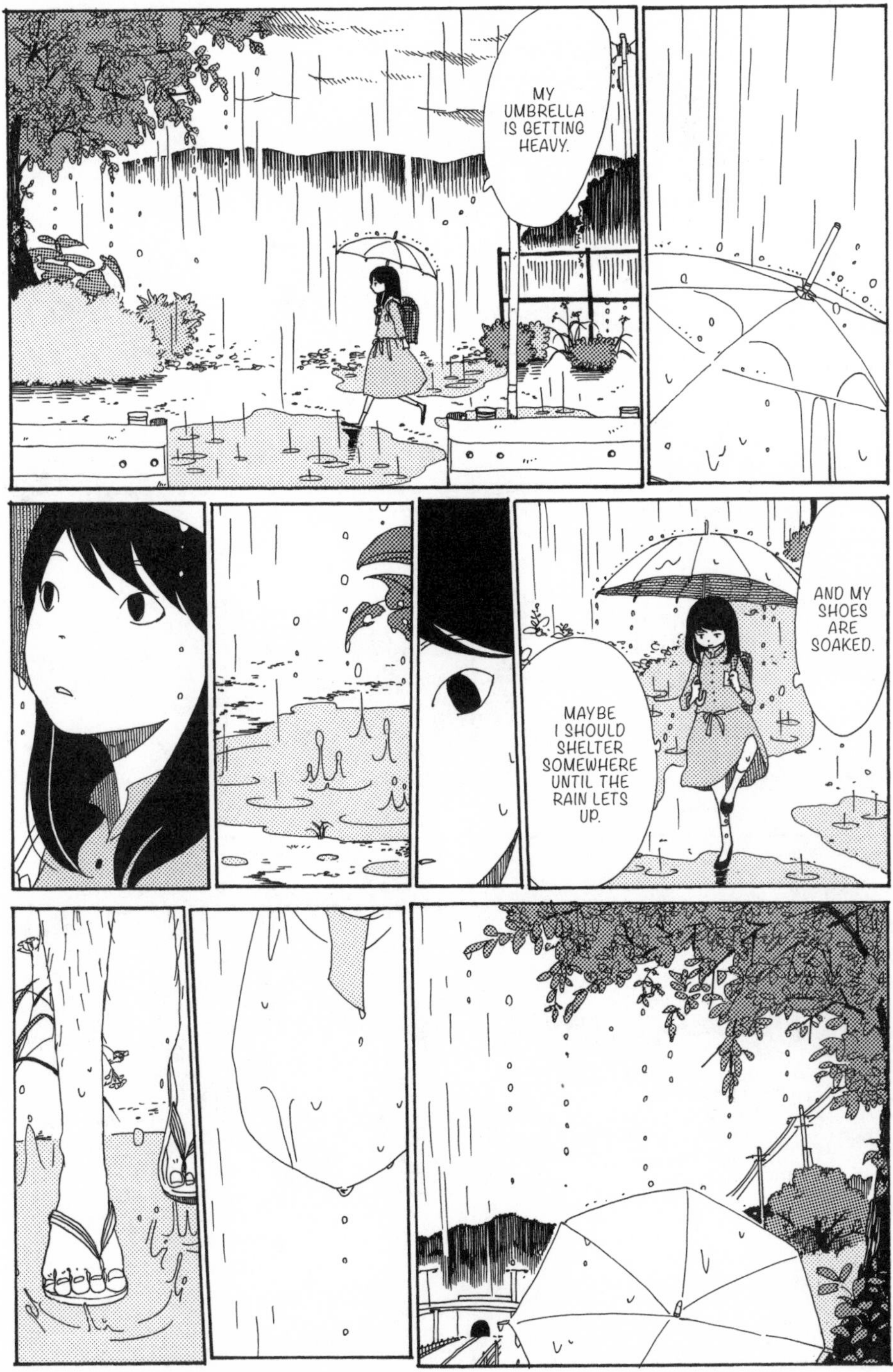
MY UMBRELLA IS GETTING HEAVY.
AND MY SHOES ARE SOAKED.
MAYBE I SHOULD SHELTER SOMEWHERE UNTIL THE RAIN LETS UP.

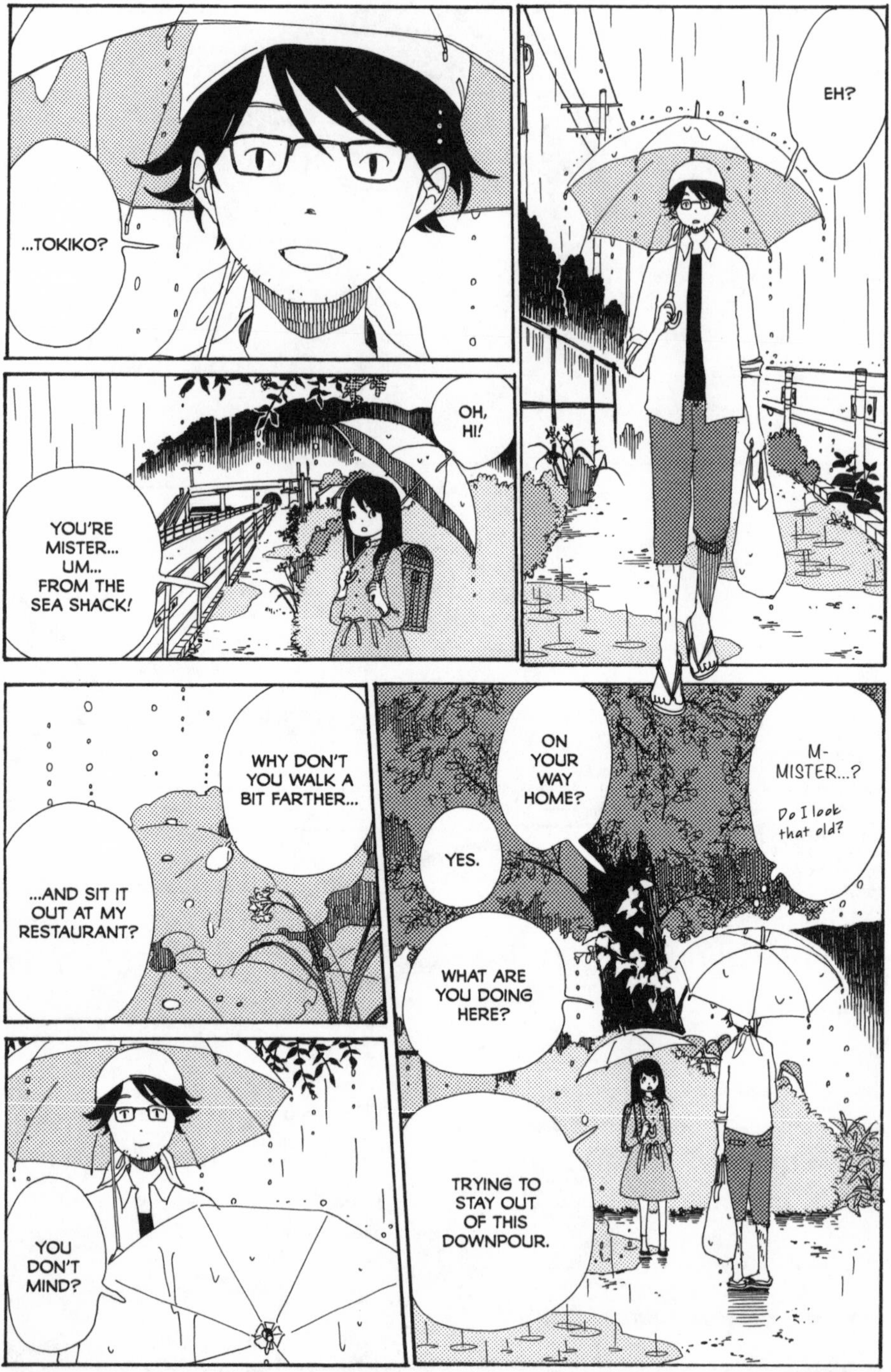
EH?
...TOKIKO?
OH, HI!
YOU'RE MISTER... UM... FROM THE SEA SHACK!
M-MISTER...?
Do I look that old?
ON YOUR WAY HOME?
YES.
WHAT ARE YOU DOING HERE?
TRYING TO STAY OUT OF THIS DOWNPOUR.
WHY DON'T YOU WALK A BIT FARTHER...
...AND SIT IT OUT AT MY RESTAURANT?
YOU DON'T MIND?

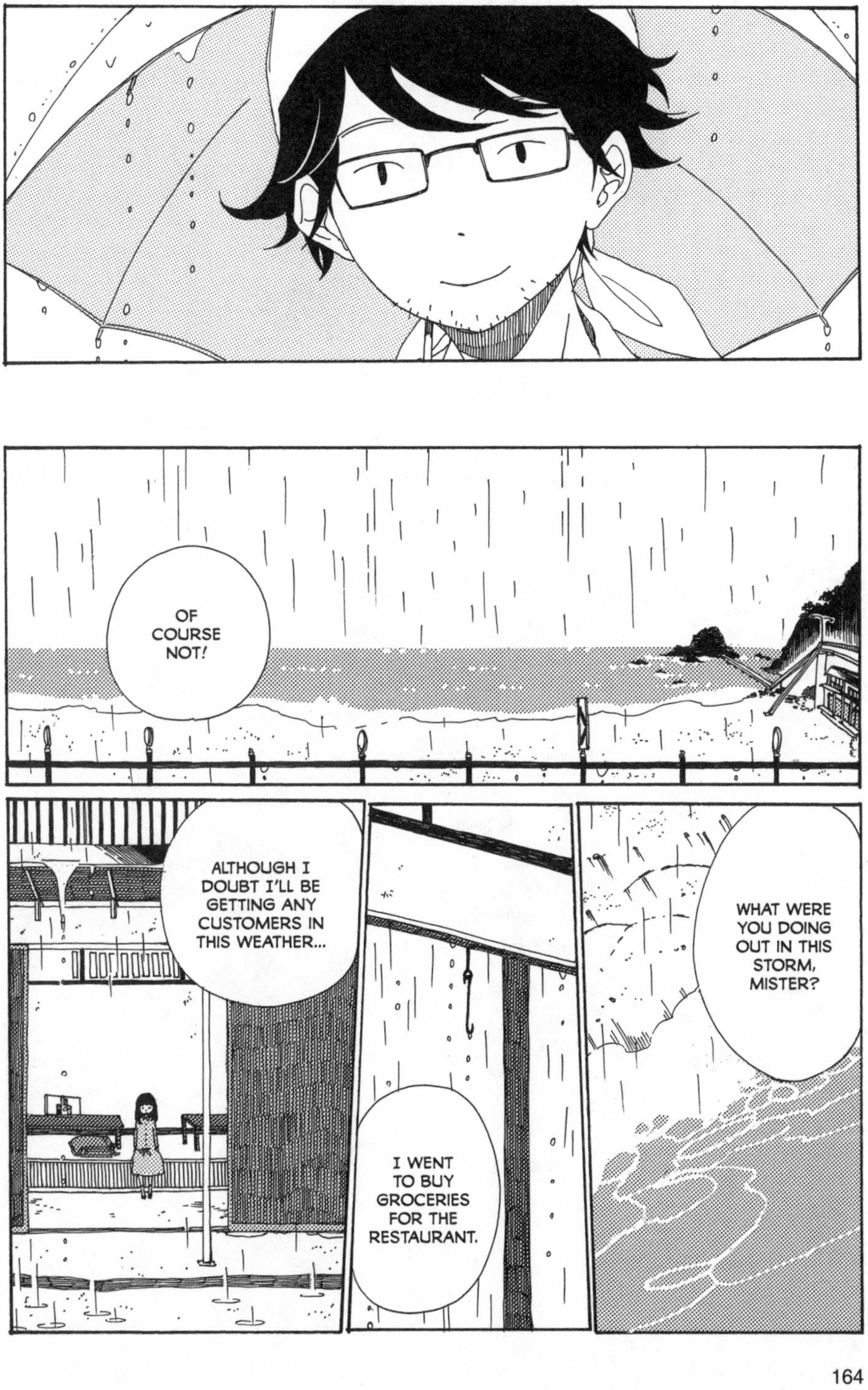
OF COURSE NOT!
WHAT WERE YOU DOING OUT IN THIS STORM, MISTER?
I WENT TO BUY GROCERIES FOR THE RESTAURANT.
ALTHOUGH I DOUBT I'LL BE GETTING ANY CUSTOMERS IN THIS WEATHER...

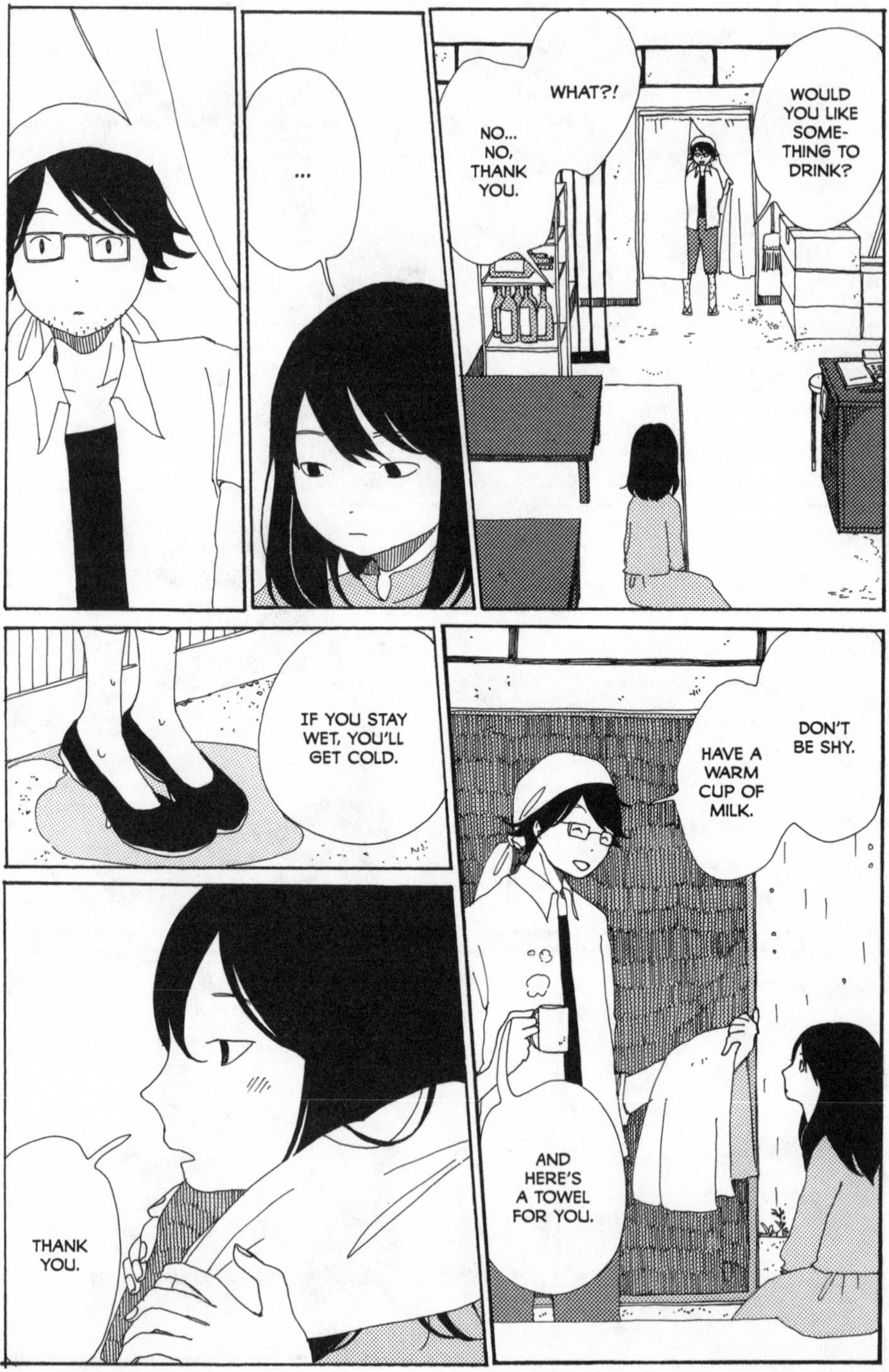
WOULD YOU LIKE SOME-THING TO DRINK?
WHAT?!
NO... NO, THANK YOU.
...
DON'T BE SHY.
HAVE A WARM CUP OF MILK.
AND HERE'S A TOWEL FOR YOU.
IF YOU STAY WET, YOU'LL GET COLD.
THANK YOU.

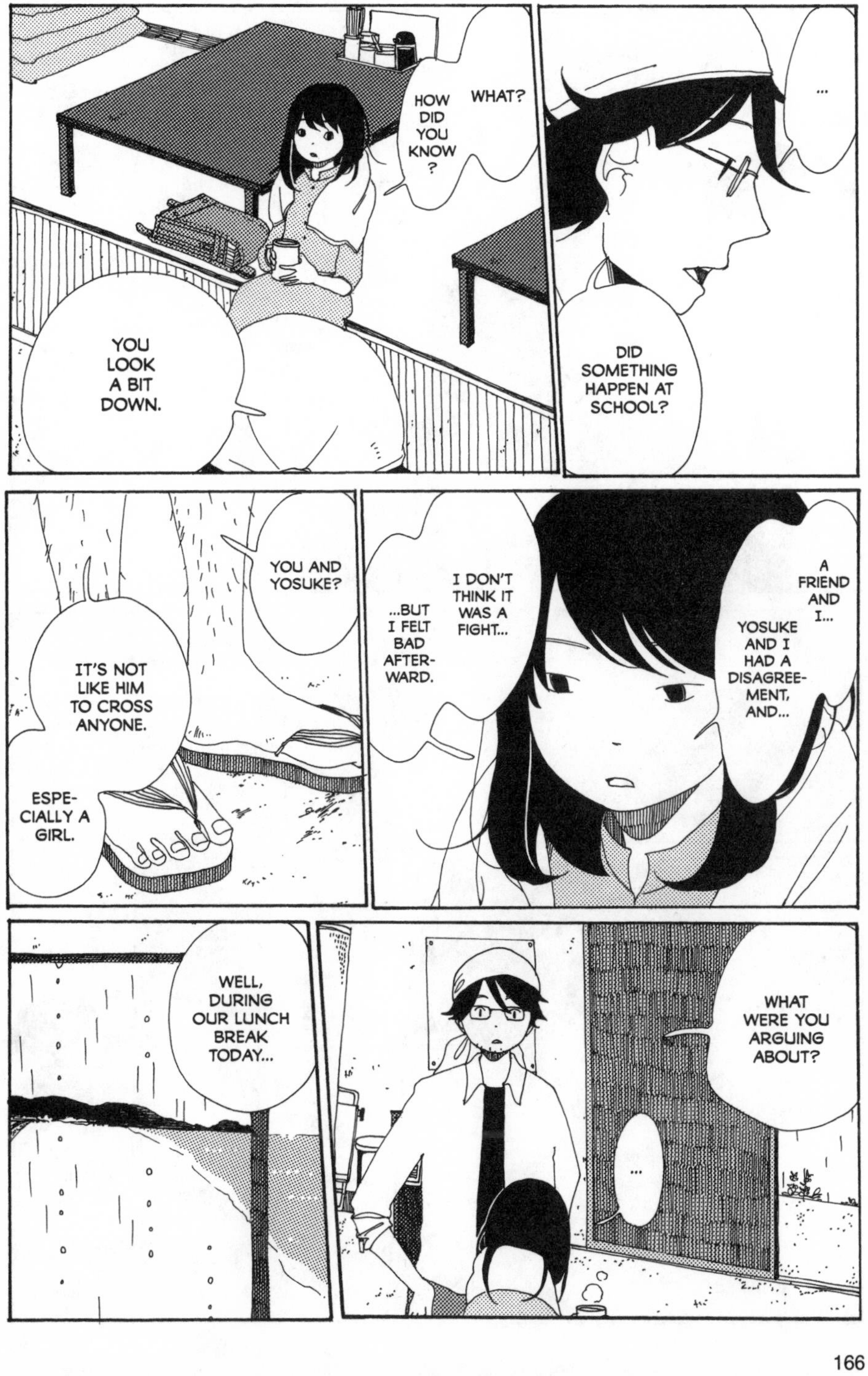
...
DID SOMETHING HAPPEN AT SCHOOL?
WHAT?
HOW DID YOU KNOW?
YOU LOOK A BIT DOWN.
A FRIEND AND I...
YOSUKE AND I HAD A DISAGREEMENT, AND...
I DON'T THINK IT WAS A FIGHT...
...BUT I FELT BAD AFTERWARD.
YOU AND YOSUKE?
IT'S NOT LIKE HIM TO CROSS ANYONE.
ESPECIALLY A GIRL.
WHAT WERE YOU ARGUING ABOUT?
...
WELL, DURING OUR LUNCH BREAK TODAY...

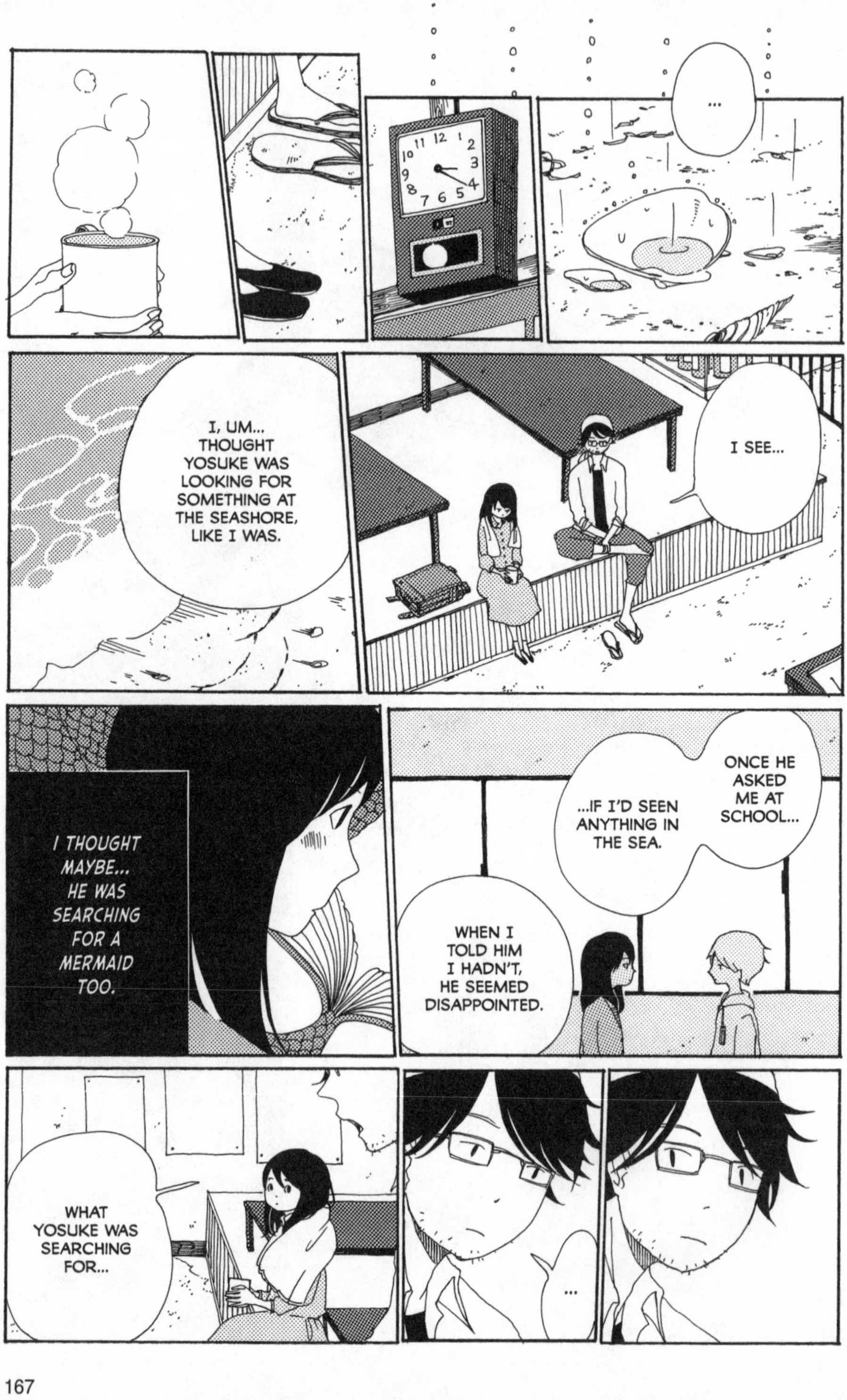
...
I SEE...
I, UM... THOUGHT YOSUKE WAS LOOKING FOR SOMETHING AT THE SEASHORE, LIKE I WAS.
ONCE HE ASKED ME AT SCHOOL...
...IF I'D SEEN ANYTHING IN THE SEA.
WHEN I TOLD HIM I HADN'T, HE SEEMED DISAPPOINTED.
I THOUGHT MAYBE... HE WAS SEARCHING FOR A MERMAID TOO.
...
WHAT YOSUKE WAS SEARCHING FOR...

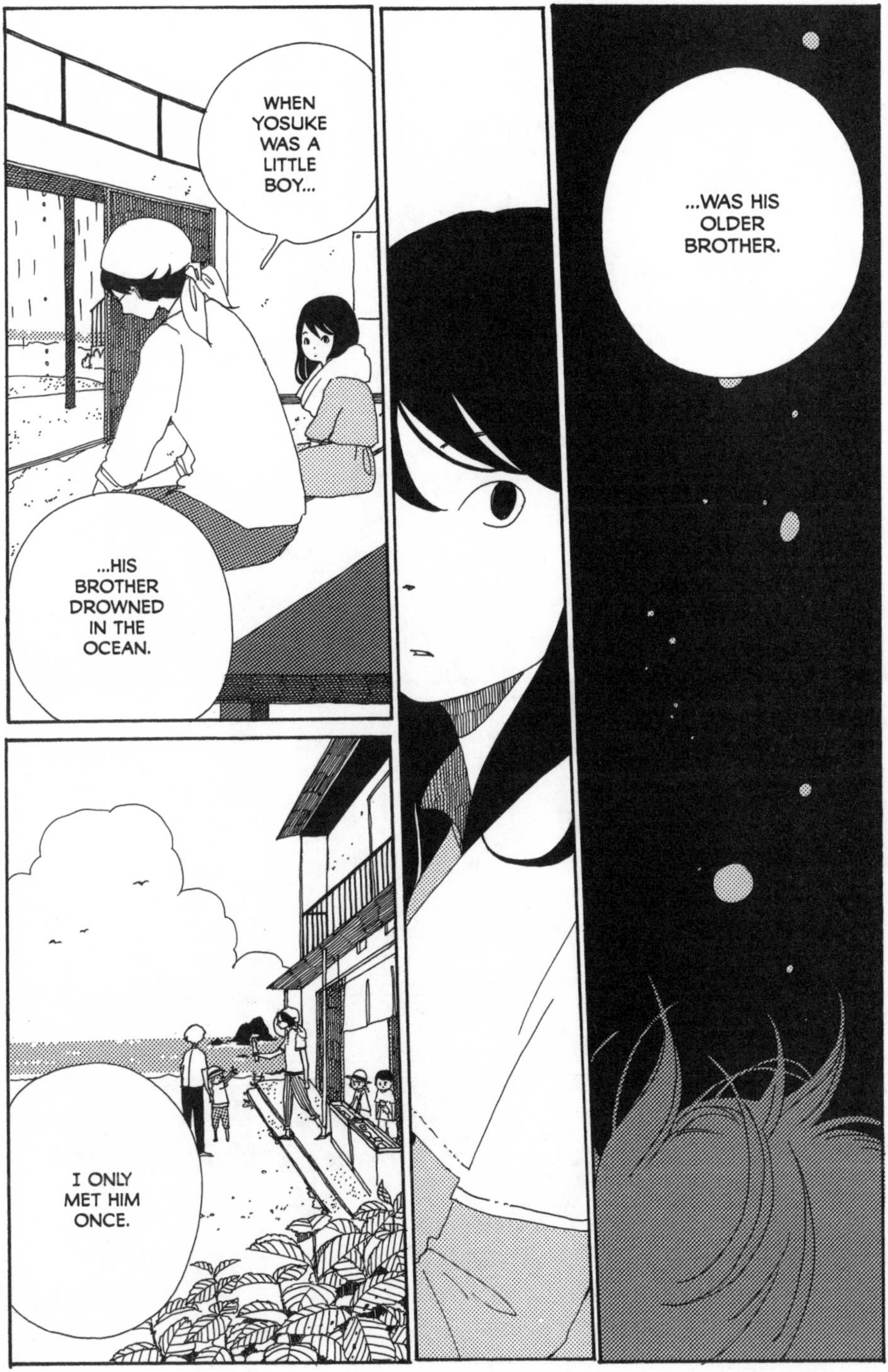
...WAS HIS OLDER BROTHER.
WHEN YOSUKE WAS A LITTLE BOY...
...HIS BROTHER DROWNED IN THE OCEAN.
I ONLY MET HIM ONCE.

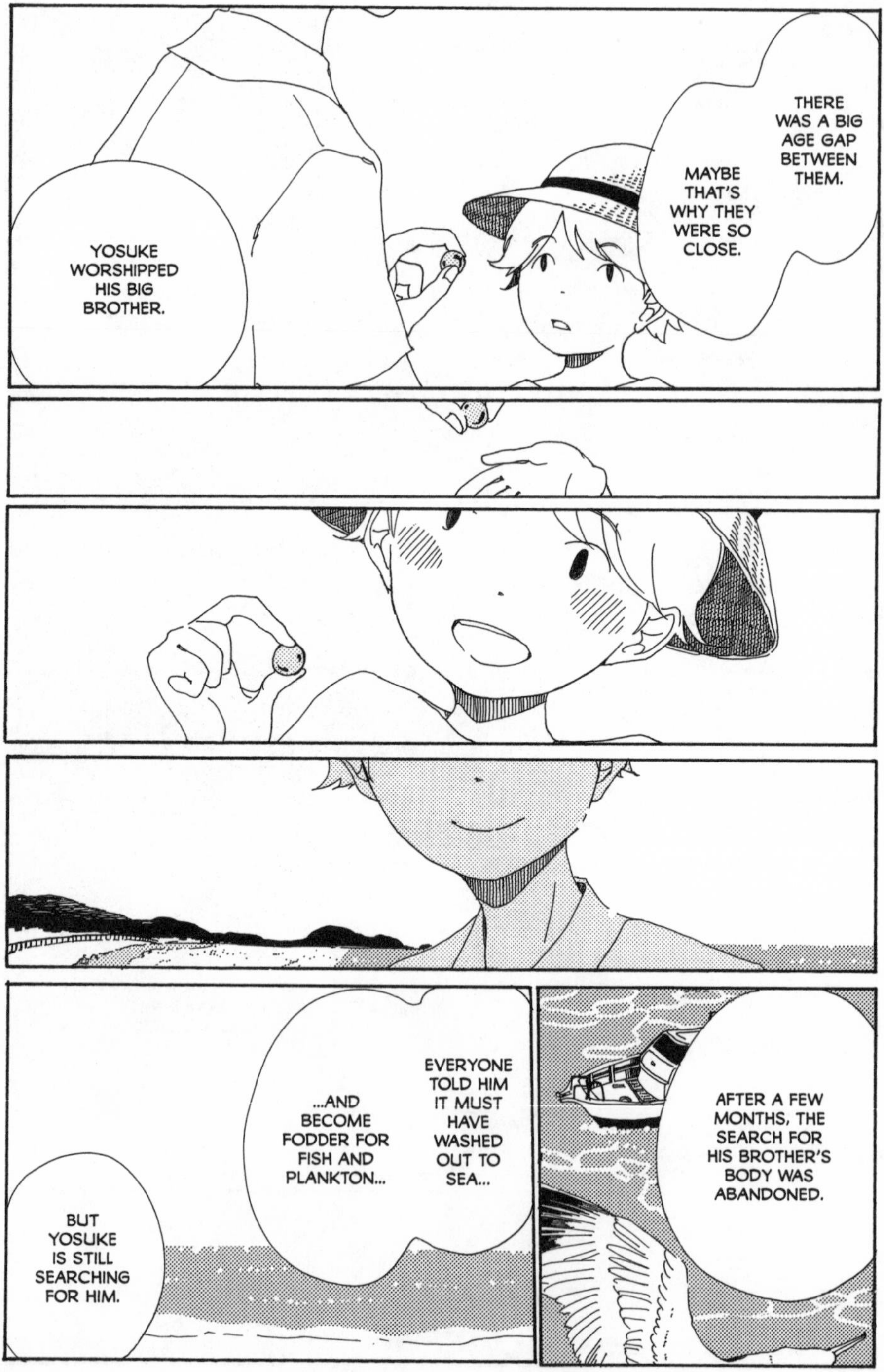
THERE WAS A BIG AGE GAP BETWEEN THEM.
MAYBE THAT'S WHY THEY WERE SO CLOSE.
YOSUKE WORSHIPPED HIS BIG BROTHER.
AFTER A FEW MONTHS, THE SEARCH FOR HIS BROTHER'S BODY WAS ABANDONED.
EVERYONE TOLD HIM IT MUST HAVE WASHED OUT TO SEA...
...AND BECOME FODDER FOR FISH AND PLANKTON...
BUT YOSUKE IS STILL SEARCHING FOR HIM.

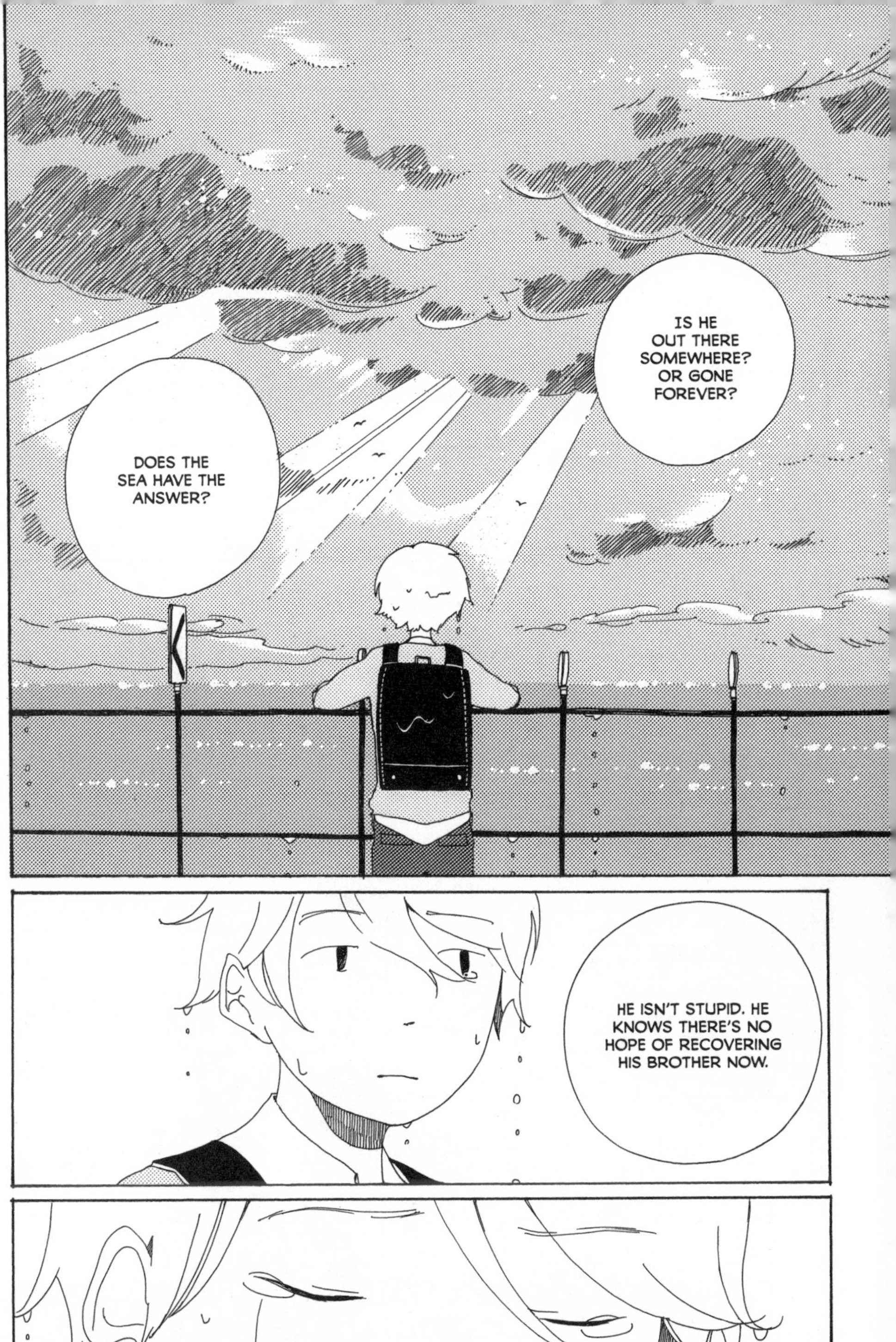
IS HE OUT THERE SOMEWHERE? OR GONE FOREVER?
DOES THE SEA HAVE THE ANSWER?
HE ISN'T STUPID. HE KNOWS THERE'S NO HOPE OF RECOVERING HIS BROTHER NOW.

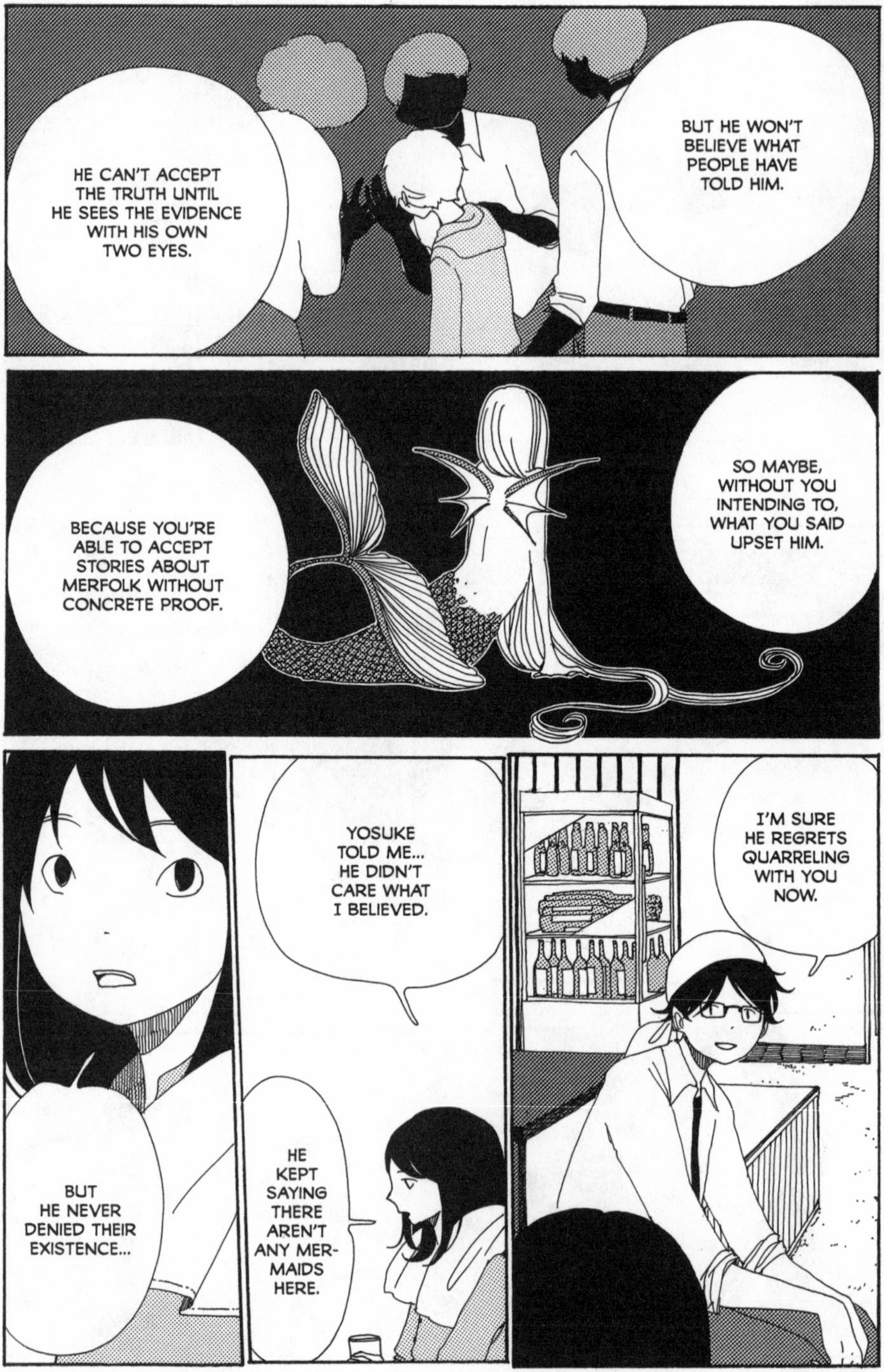
BUT HE WON'T BELIEVE WHAT PEOPLE HAVE TOLD HIM.
HE CAN'T ACCEPT THE TRUTH UNTIL HE SEES THE EVIDENCE WITH HIS OWN TWO EYES.
SO MAYBE, WITHOUT YOU INTENDING TO, WHAT YOU SAID UPSET HIM.
BECAUSE YOU'RE ABLE TO ACCEPT STORIES ABOUT MERFOLK WITHOUT CONCRETE PROOF.
I'M SURE HE REGRETS QUARRELING WITH YOU NOW.
YOSUKE TOLD ME... HE DIDN'T CARE WHAT I BELIEVED.
HE KEPT SAYING THERE AREN'T ANY MER-MAIDS HERE.
BUT HE NEVER DENIED THEIR EXISTENCE...

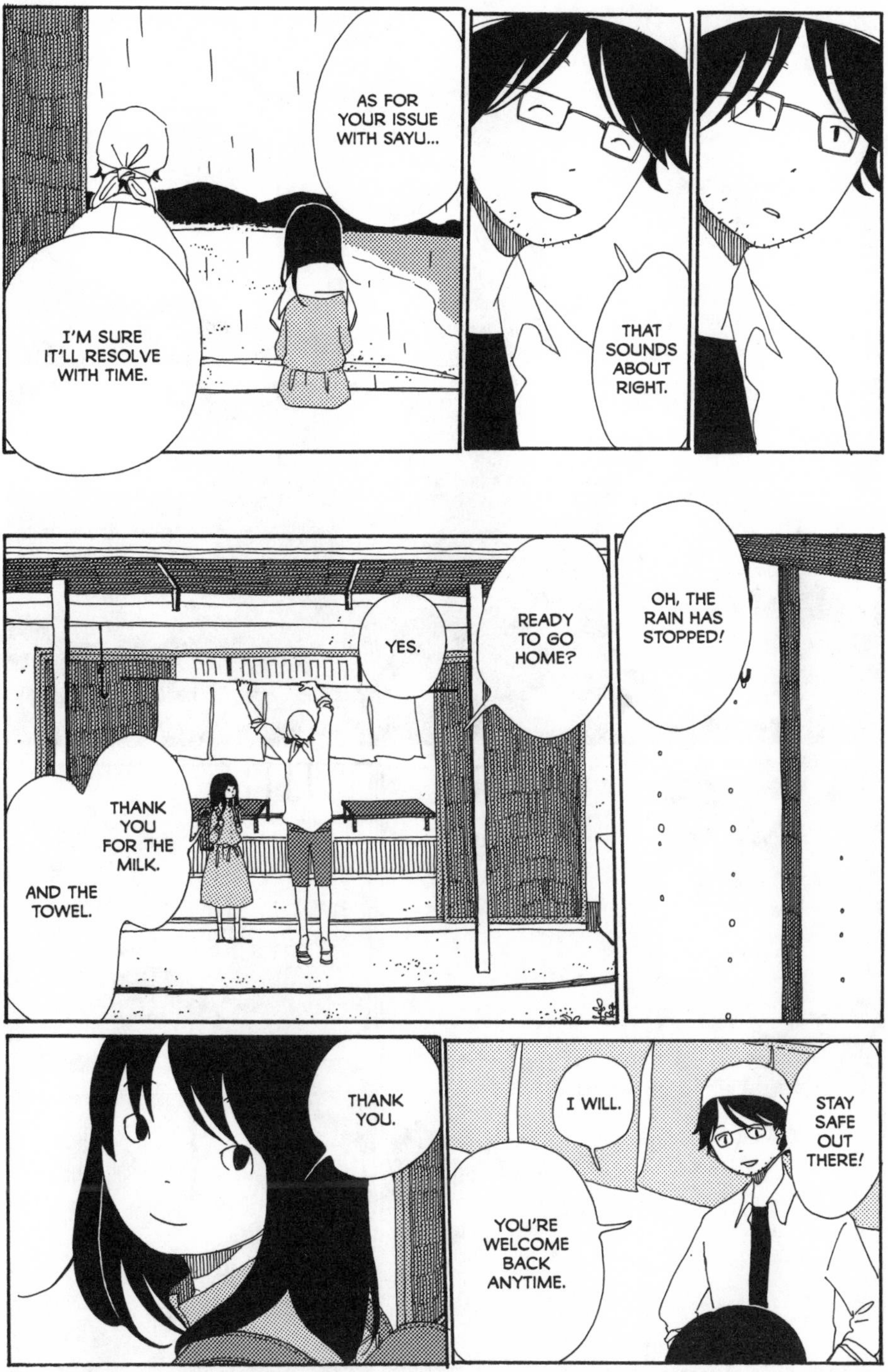
THAT SOUNDS ABOUT RIGHT.
AS FOR YOUR ISSUE WITH SAYU...
I'M SURE IT'LL RESOLVE WITH TIME.
OH, THE RAIN HAS STOPPED!
READY TO GO HOME?
YES.
THANK YOU FOR THE MILK.
AND THE TOWEL.
STAY SAFE OUT THERE!
I WILL.
YOU'RE WELCOME BACK ANYTIME.
THANK YOU.

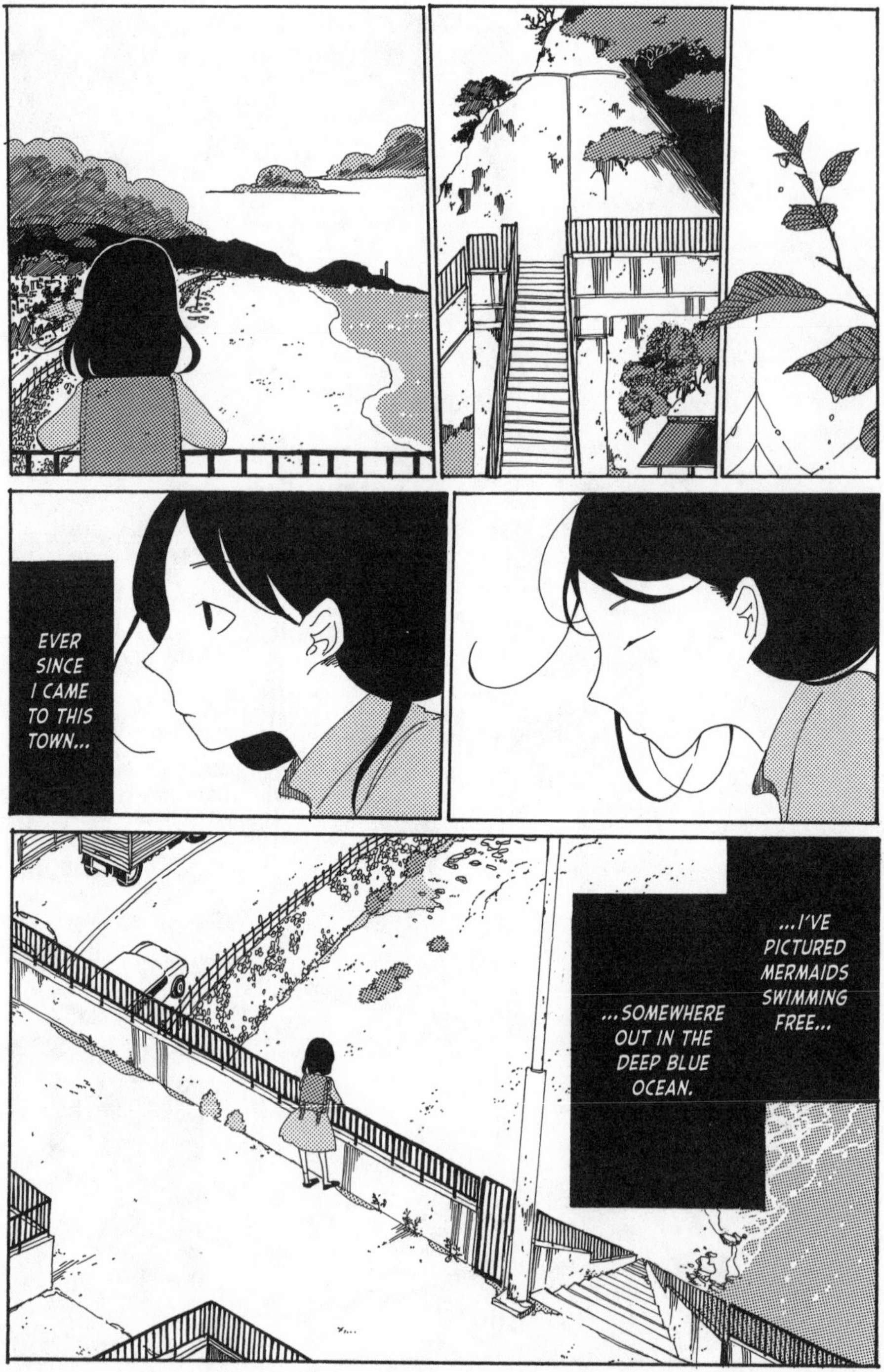
EVER SINCE I CAME TO THIS TOWN...
...I'VE PICTURED MERMAIDS SWIMMING FREE...
...SOMEWHERE OUT IN THE DEEP BLUE OCEAN.

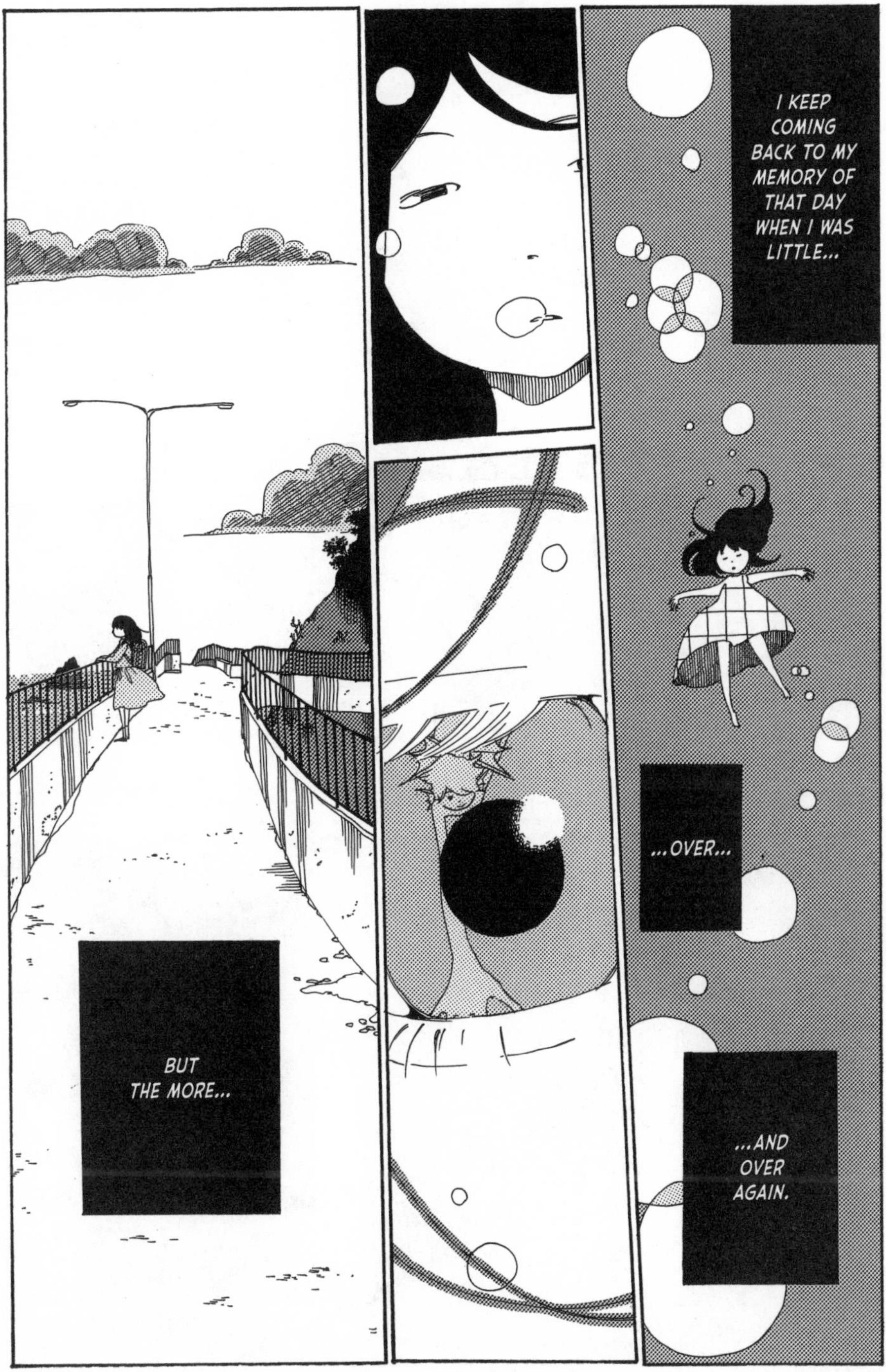
I KEEP COMING BACK TO MY MEMORY OF THAT DAY WHEN I WAS LITTLE...
...OVER...
...AND OVER AGAIN.
BUT THE MORE...

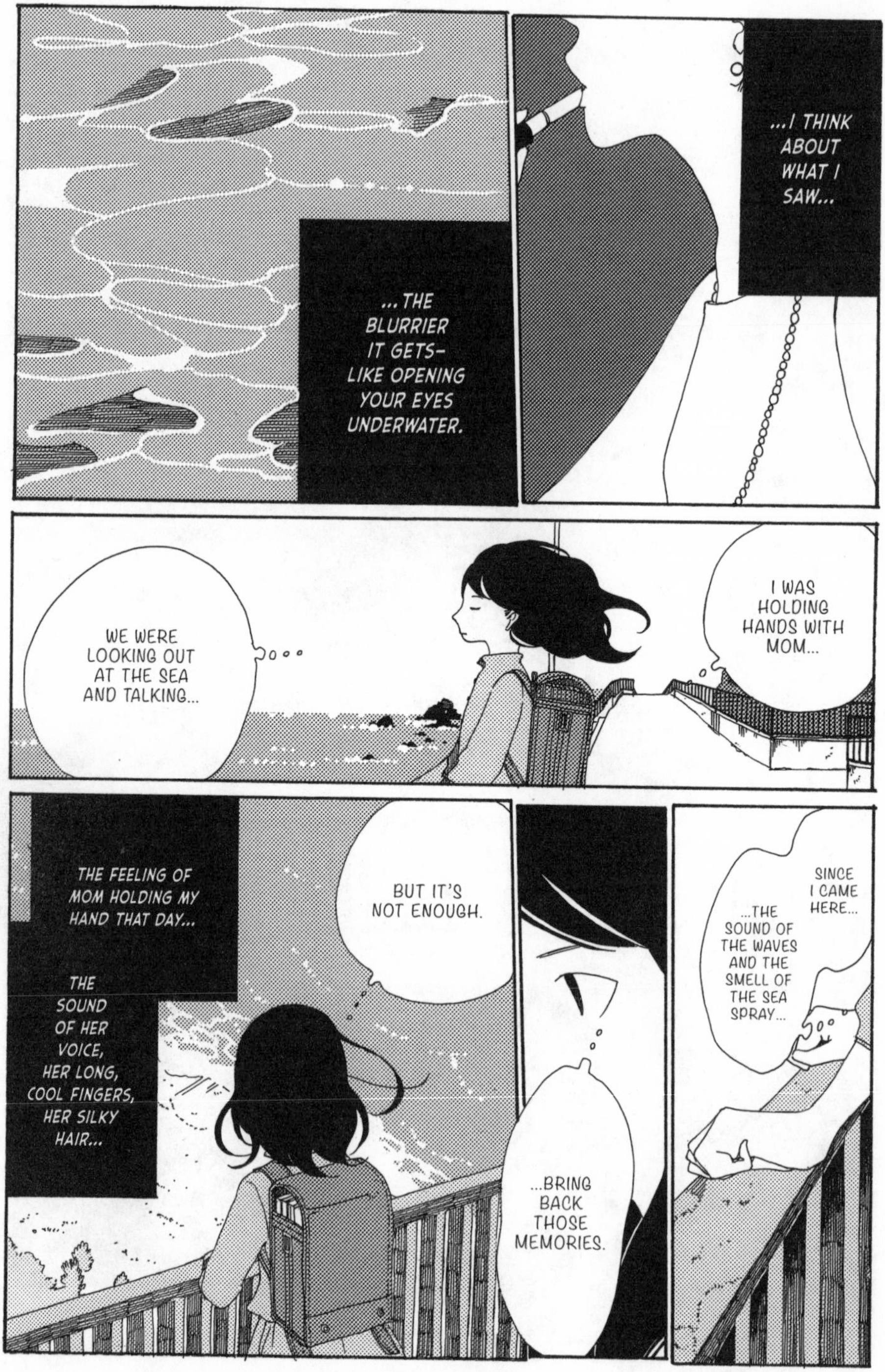
...I THINK ABOUT WHAT I SAW...
...THE BLURRIER IT GETS— LIKE OPENING YOUR EYES UNDERWATER.
I WAS HOLDING HANDS WITH MOM...
WE WERE LOOKING OUT AT THE SEA AND TALKING...
SINCE I CAME HERE...
...THE SOUND OF THE WAVES AND THE SMELL OF THE SEA SPRAY...
...BRING BACK THOSE MEMORIES.
BUT IT'S NOT ENOUGH.
THE FEELING OF MOM HOLDING MY HAND THAT DAY...
THE SOUND OF HER VOICE, HER LONG, COOL FINGERS, HER SILKY HAIR...

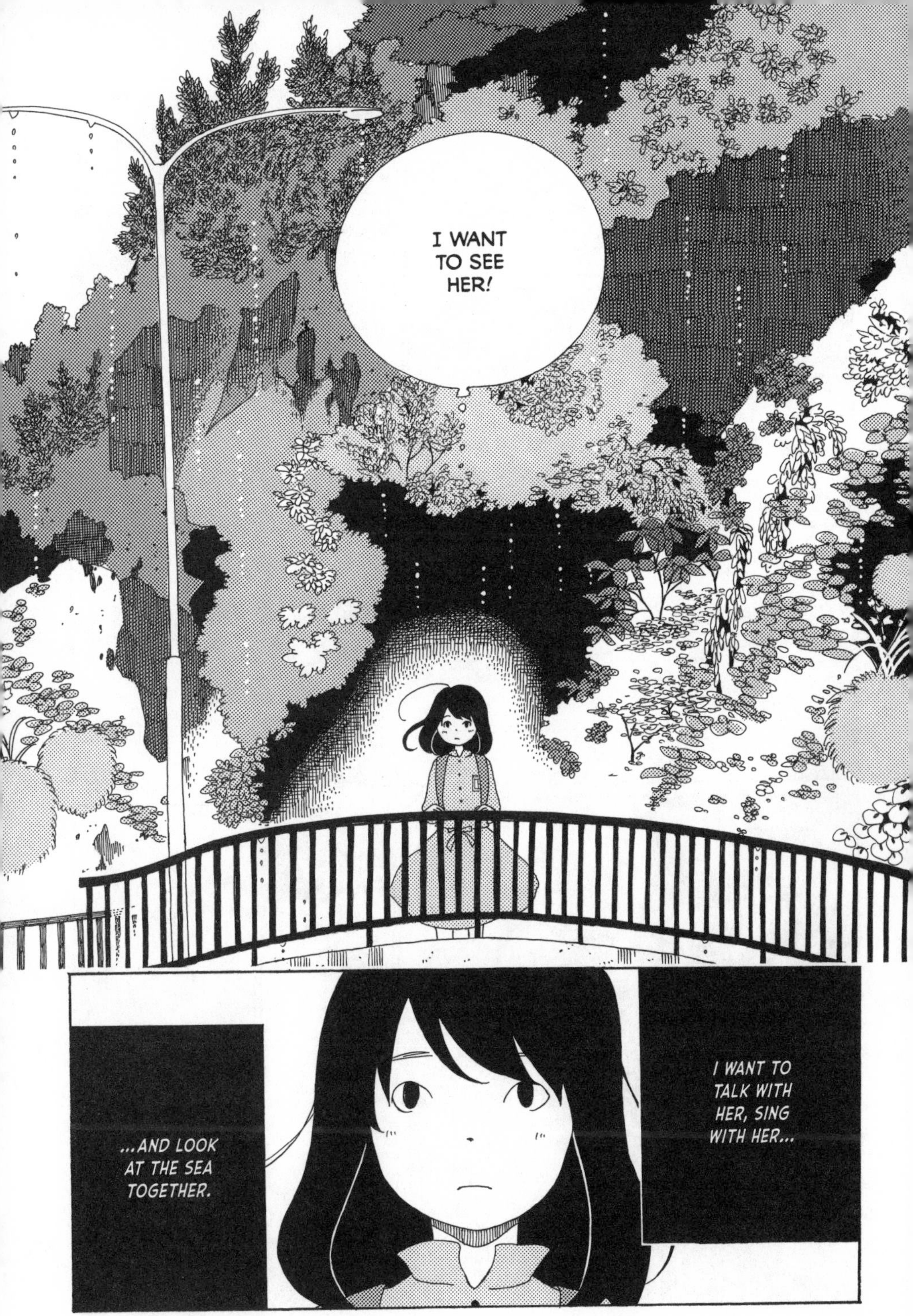
I WANT TO SEE HER!
I WANT TO TALK WITH HER, SING WITH HER...
...AND LOOK AT THE SEA TOGETHER.

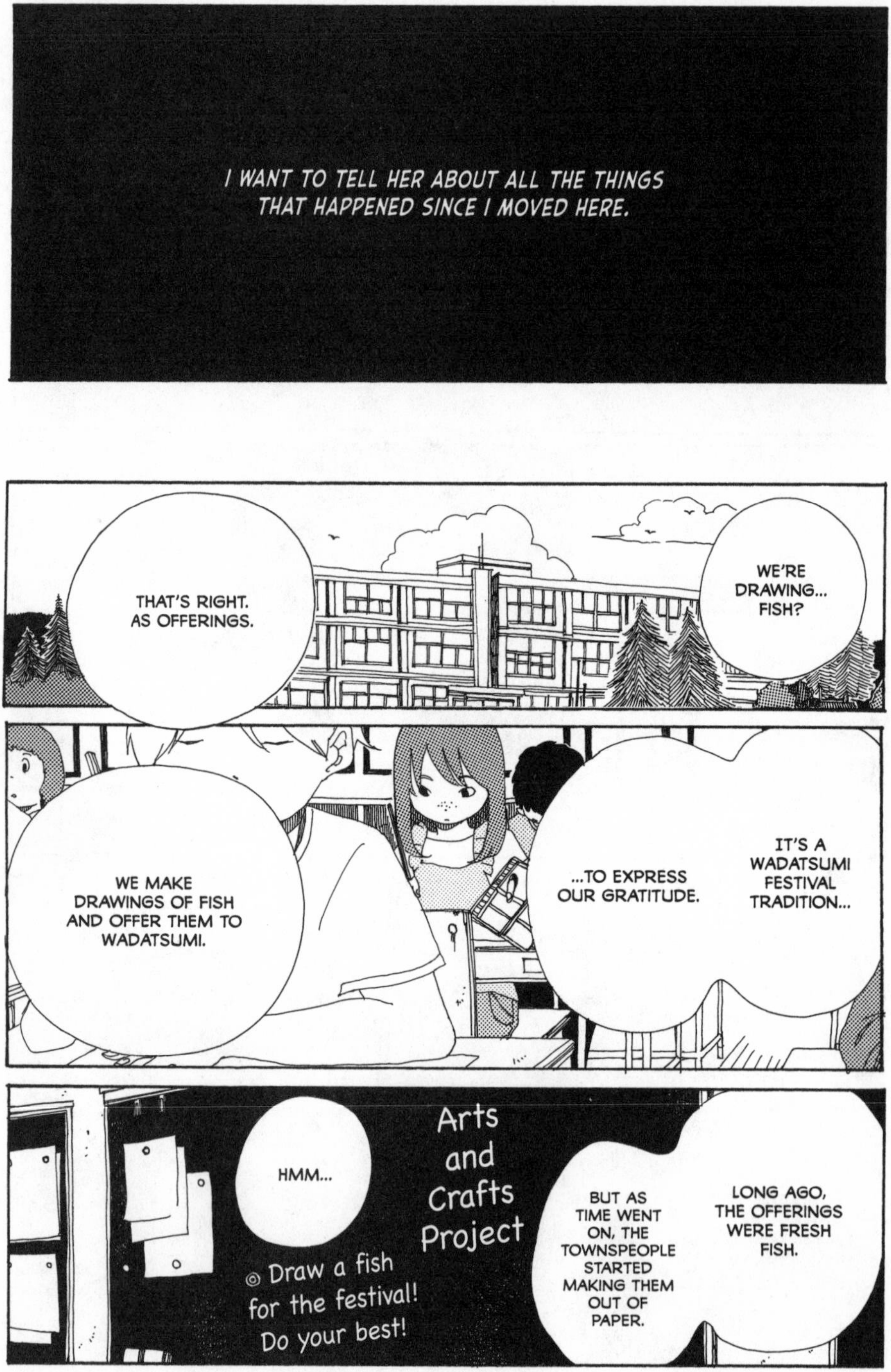
I WANT TO TELL HER ABOUT ALL THE THINGS THAT HAPPENED SINCE I MOVED HERE.
WE'RE DRAWING... FISH?
THAT'S RIGHT. AS OFFERINGS.
IT'S A WADATSUMI FESTIVAL TRADITION...
...TO EXPRESS OUR GRATITUDE.
WE MAKE DRAWINGS OF FISH AND OFFER THEM TO WADATSUMI.
LONG AGO, THE OFFERINGS WERE FRESH FISH.
BUT AS TIME WENT ON, THE TOWNSPEOPLE STARTED MAKING THEM OUT OF PAPER.
Arts and Crafts Project
◎ Draw a fish for the festival! Do your best!
HMM...

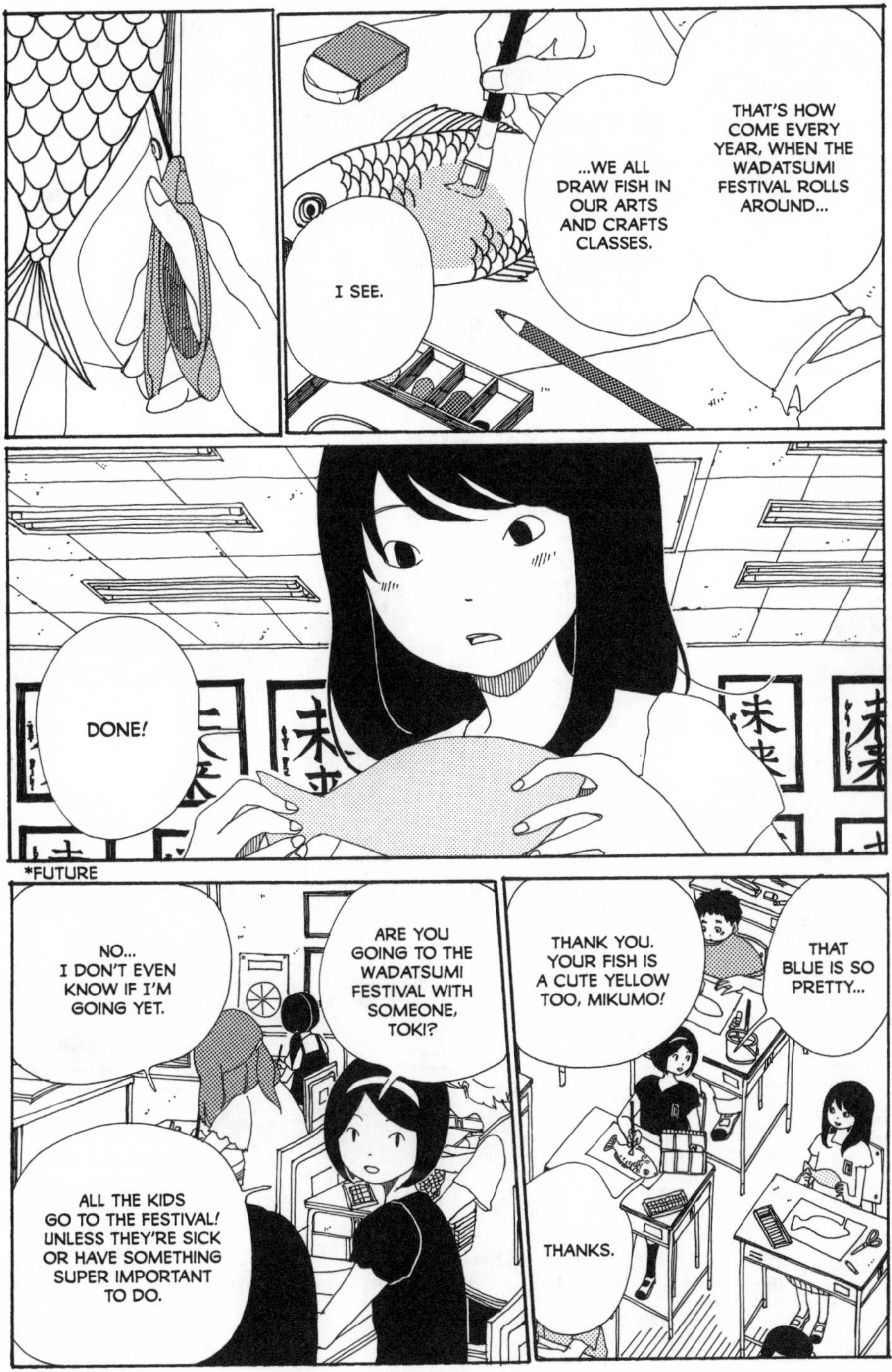
THAT'S HOW COME EVERY YEAR, WHEN THE WADATSUMI FESTIVAL ROLLS AROUND...
...WE ALL DRAW FISH IN OUR ARTS AND CRAFTS CLASSES.
I SEE.
DONE!
*FUTURE
THAT BLUE IS SO PRETTY...
THANK YOU. YOUR FISH IS A CUTE YELLOW TOO, MIKUMO!
THANKS.
ARE YOU GOING TO THE WADATSUMI FESTIVAL WITH SOMEONE, TOKI?
NO... I DON'T EVEN KNOW IF I'M GOING YET.
ALL THE KIDS GO TO THE FESTIVAL! UNLESS THEY'RE SICK OR HAVE SOMETHING SUPER IMPORTANT TO DO.

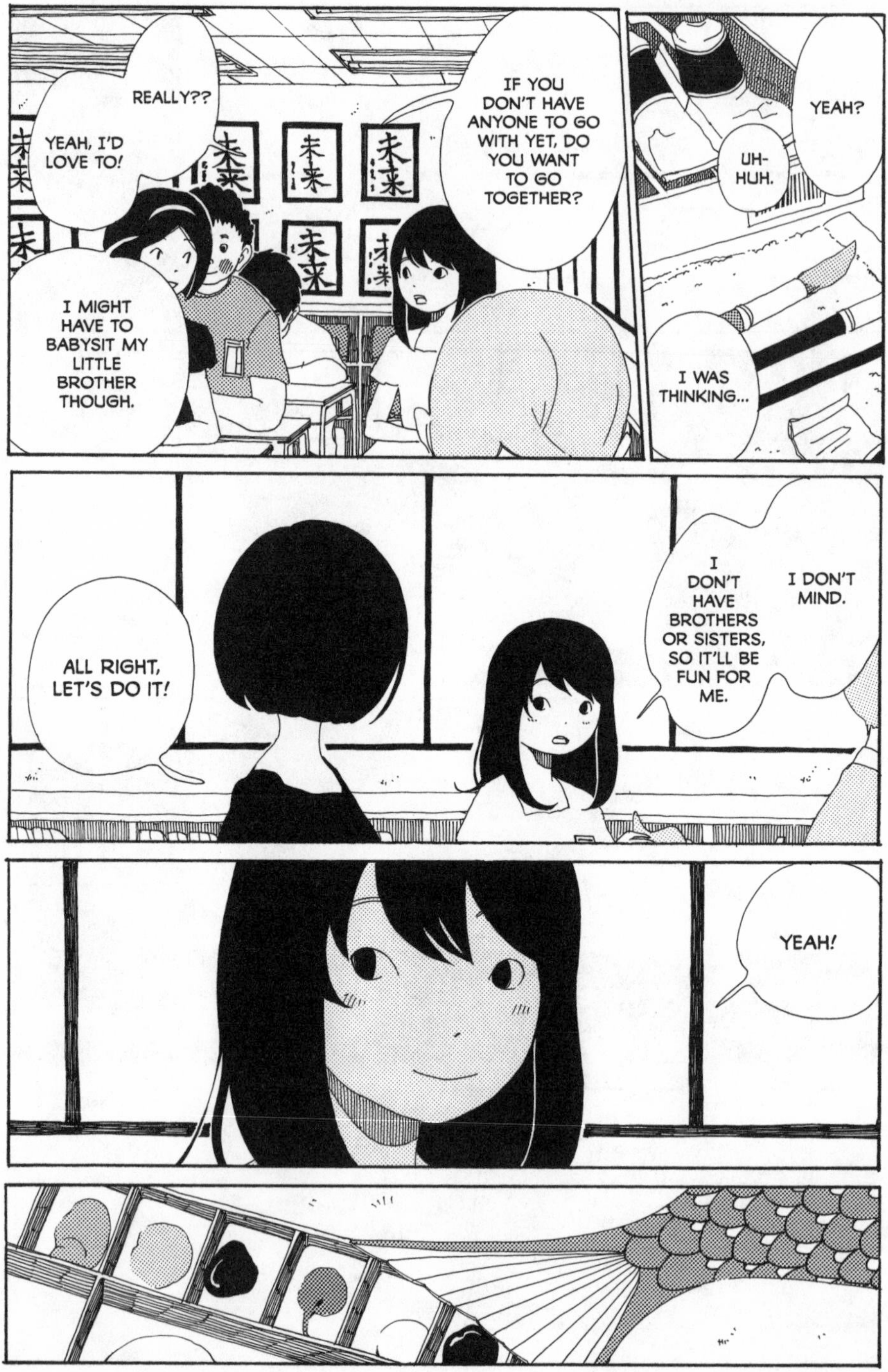
YEAH?
UH-HUH.
I WAS THINKING...
IF YOU DON'T HAVE ANYONE TO GO WITH YET, DO YOU WANT TO GO TOGETHER?
REALLY??
YEAH, I'D LOVE TO!
I MIGHT HAVE TO BABYSIT MY LITTLE BROTHER THOUGH.
I DON'T MIND.
I DON'T HAVE BROTHERS OR SISTERS, SO IT'LL BE FUN FOR ME.
ALL RIGHT, LET'S DO IT!
YEAH!

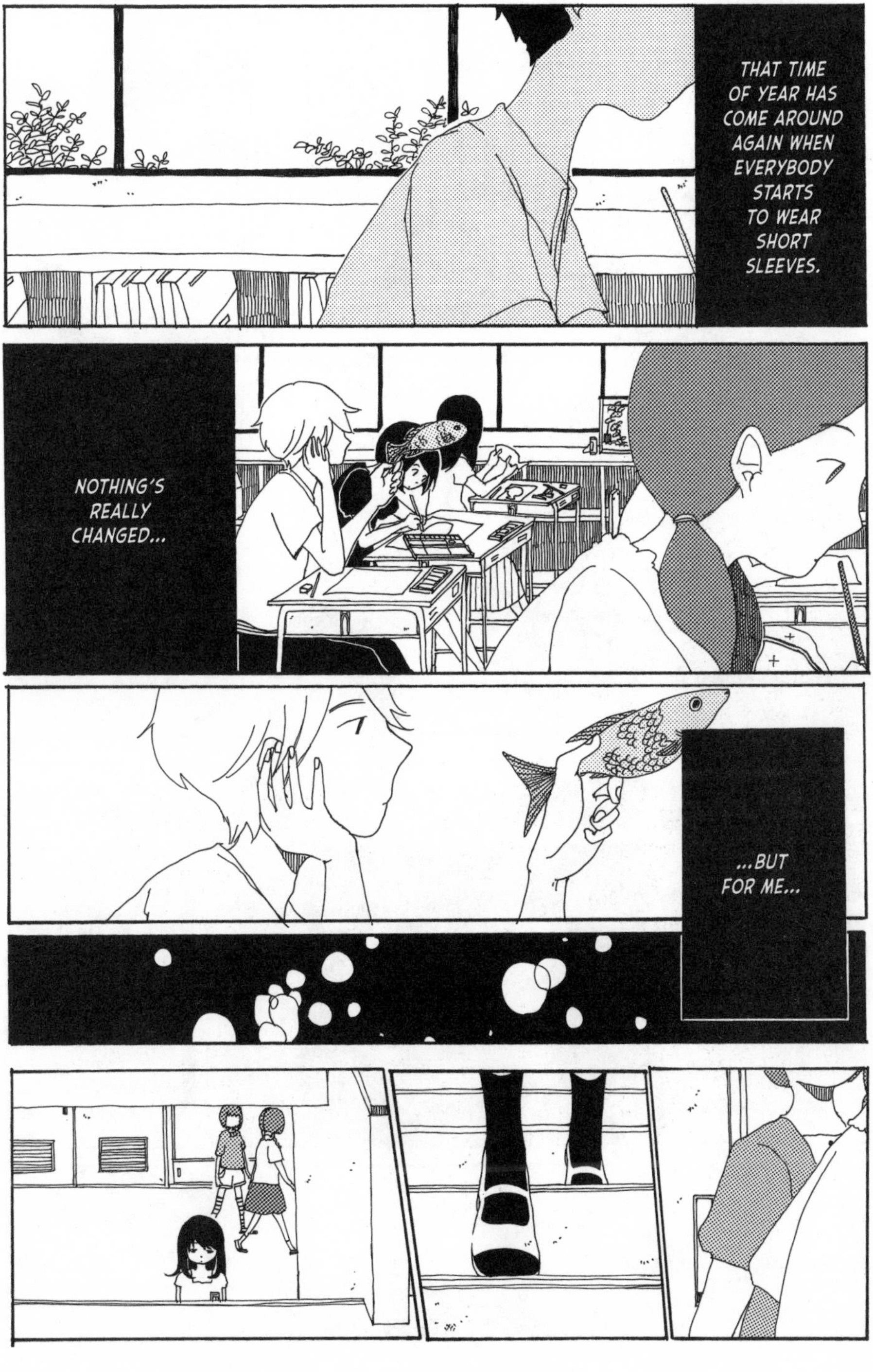
THAT TIME OF YEAR HAS COME AROUND AGAIN WHEN EVERYBODY STARTS TO WEAR SHORT SLEEVES.
NOTHING'S REALLY CHANGED...
...BUT FOR ME...

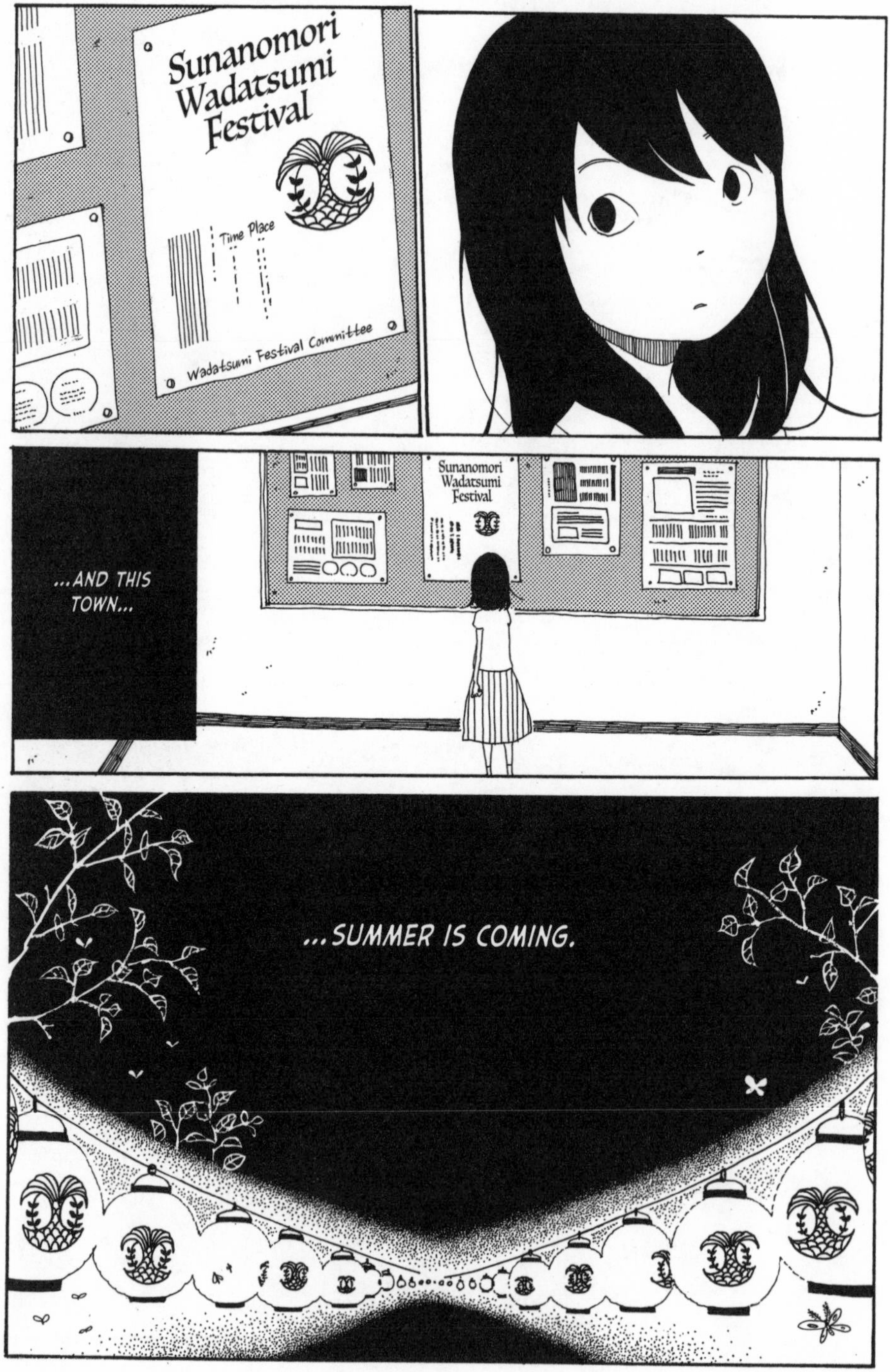
Sunanomori Wadatsumi Festival
Time Place
Wadatsumi Festival Committee
...AND THIS TOWN...
Sunanomori Wadatsumi Festival
...SUMMER IS COMING.

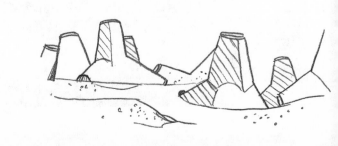

Bonus: A Day in the Life of Yosuke Narumi

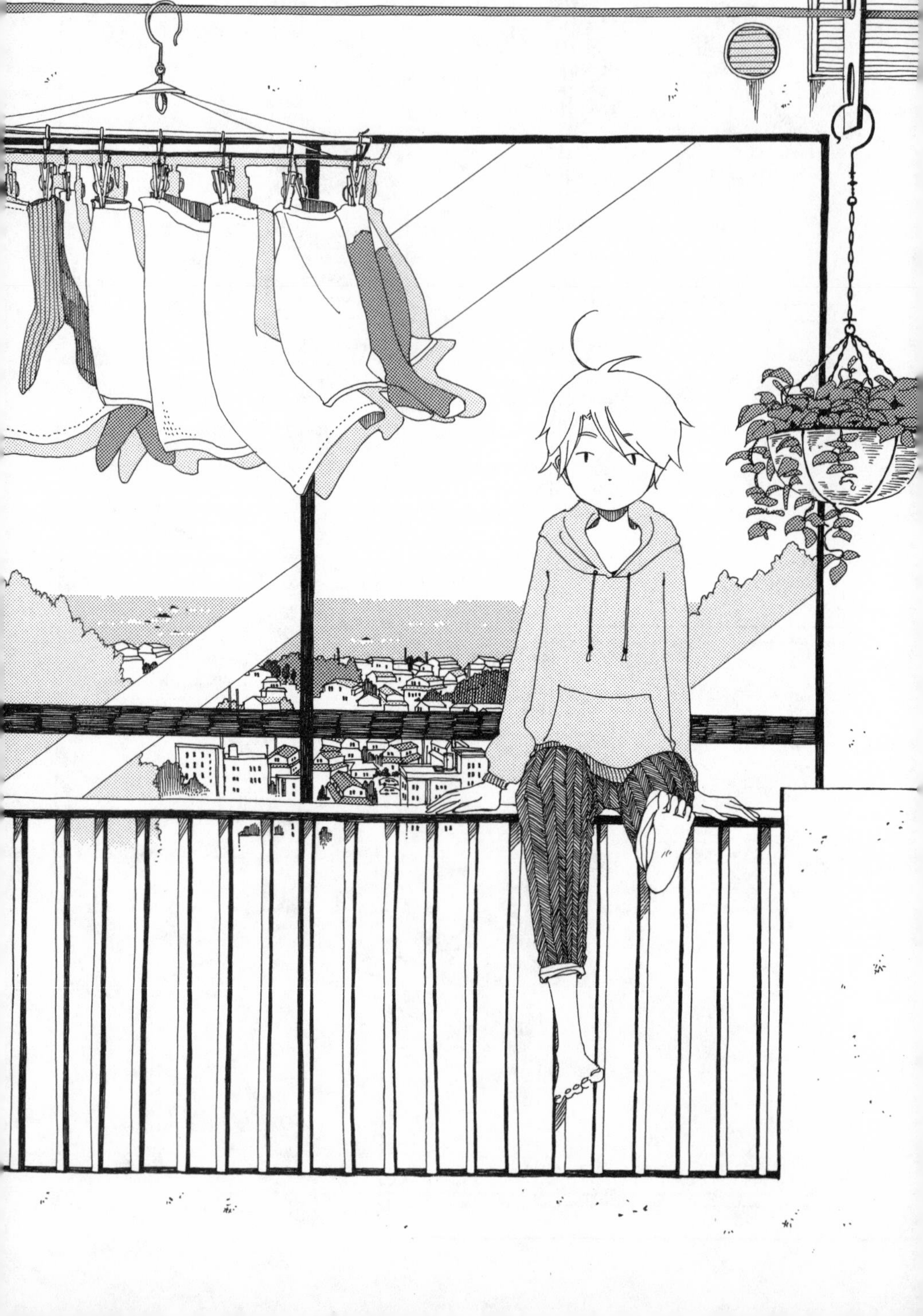

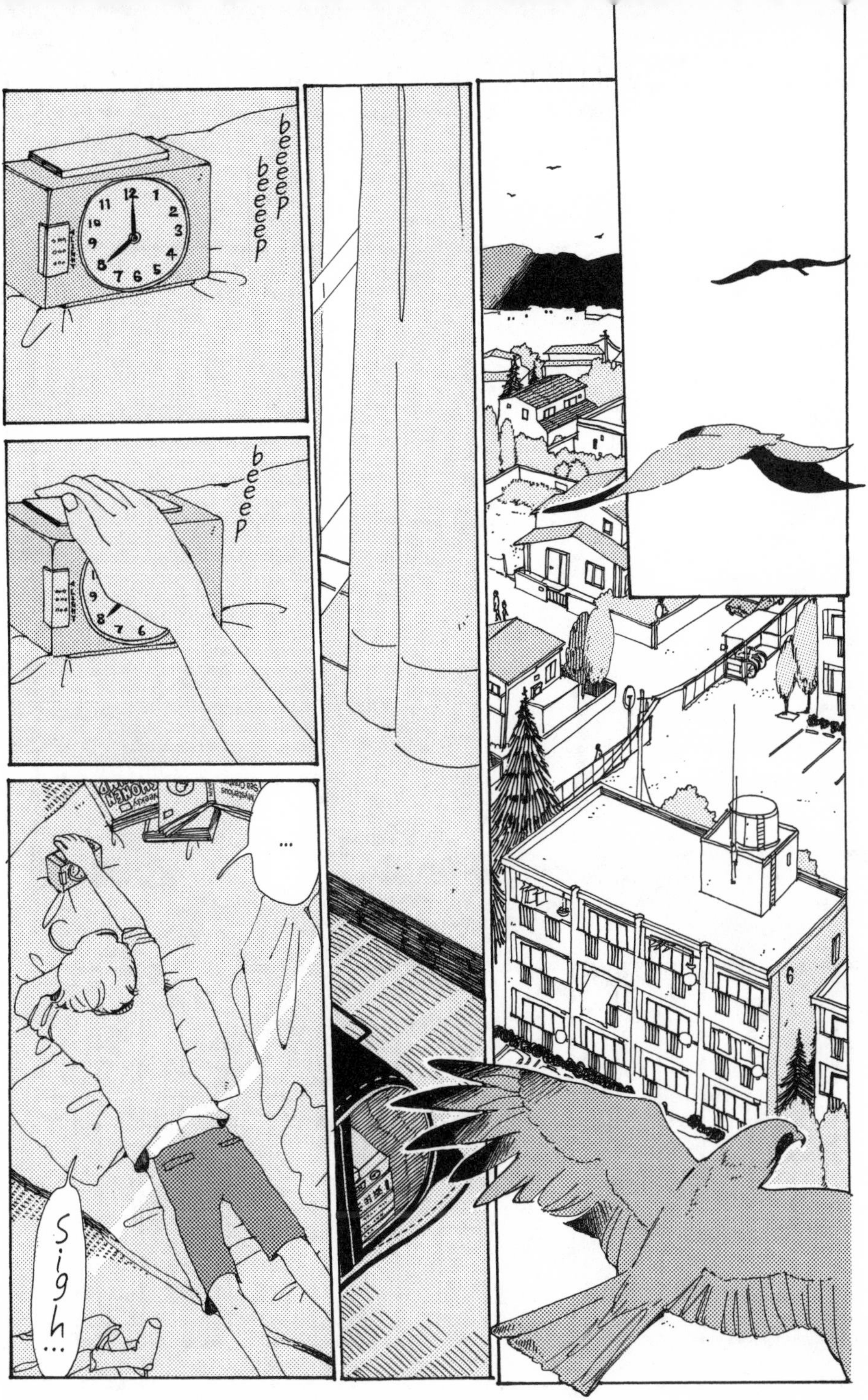
beeeep beeeep
beeep
...
Sigh...

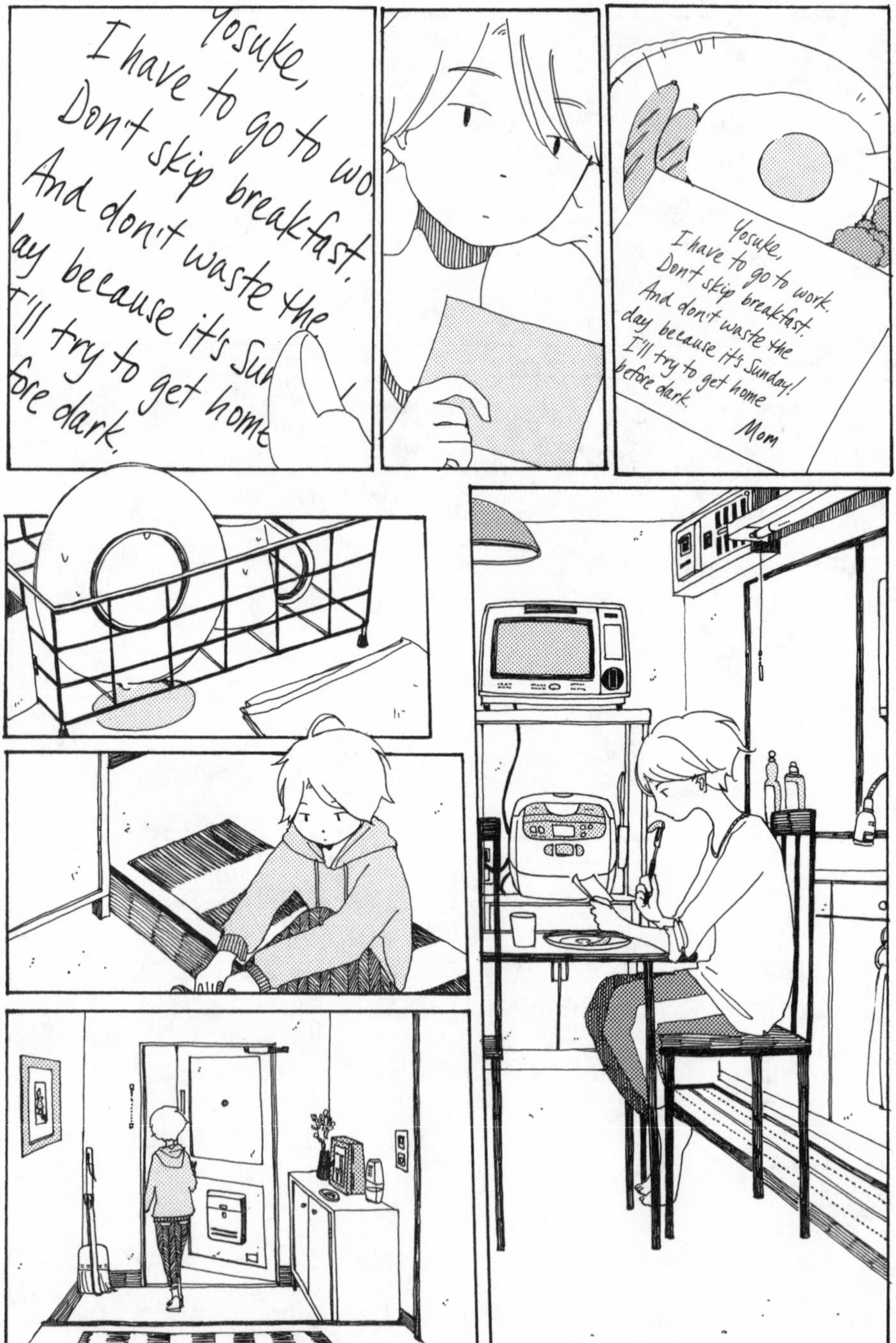
Yosuke,
I have to go to work.
Don't skip breakfast.
And don't waste the
day because it's Sunday!
I'll try to get home
before dark.
Mom
Yosuke,
I have to go to wo
Don't skip breakfast.
And don't waste the
ay because it's Su
'll try to get hom
fore dark.

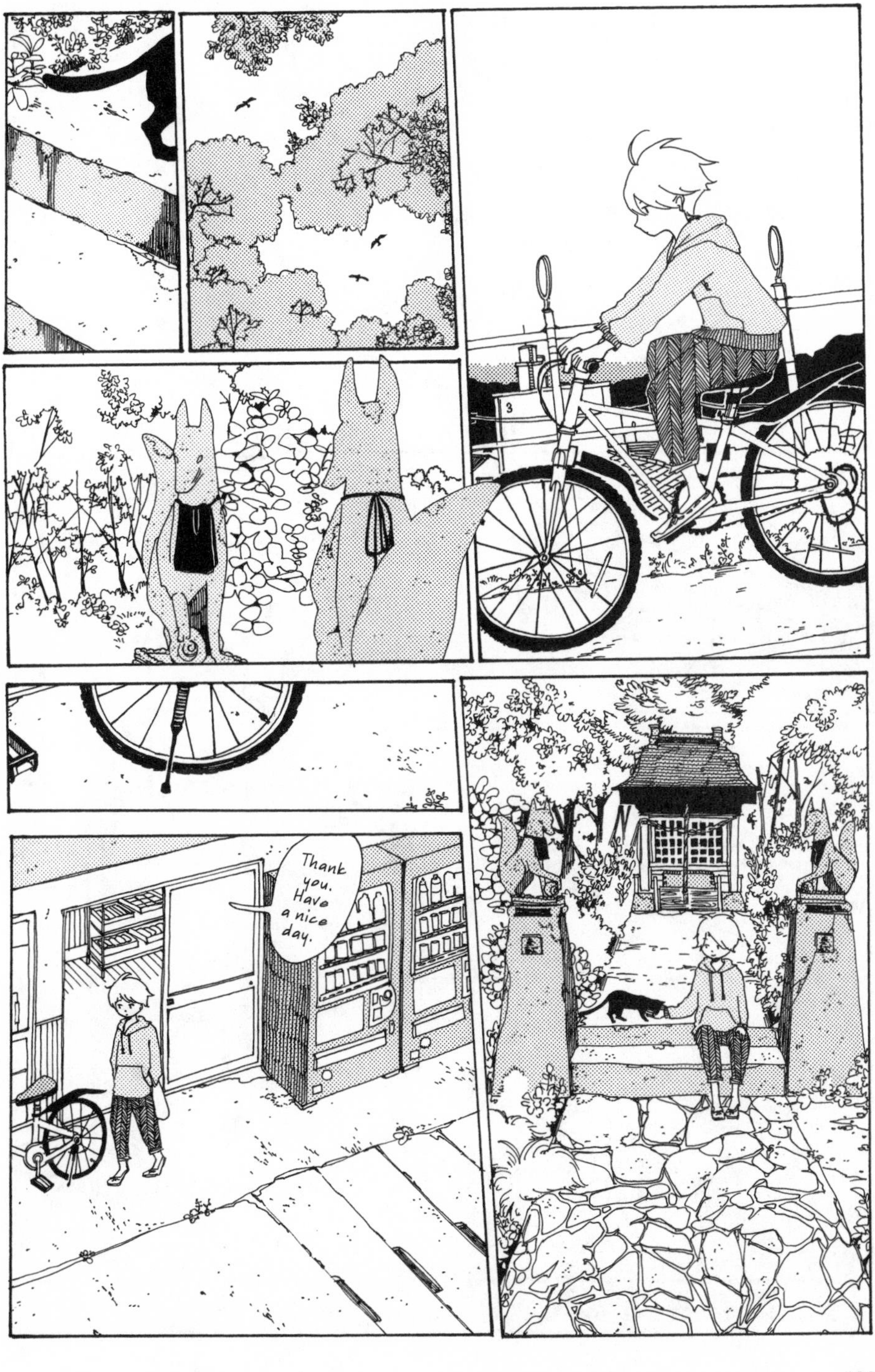
Thank you. Have a nice day.

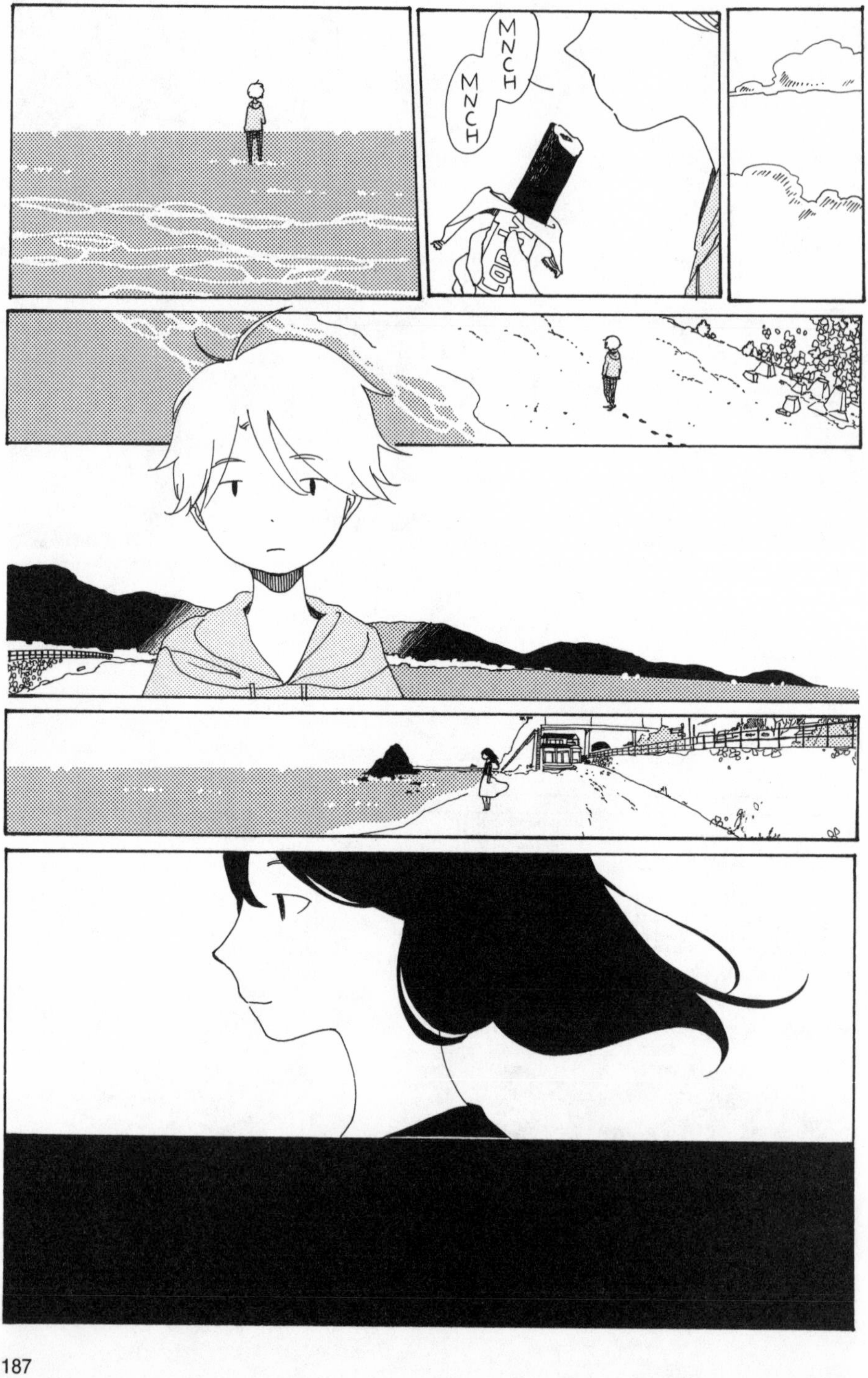
MNCH
MNCH

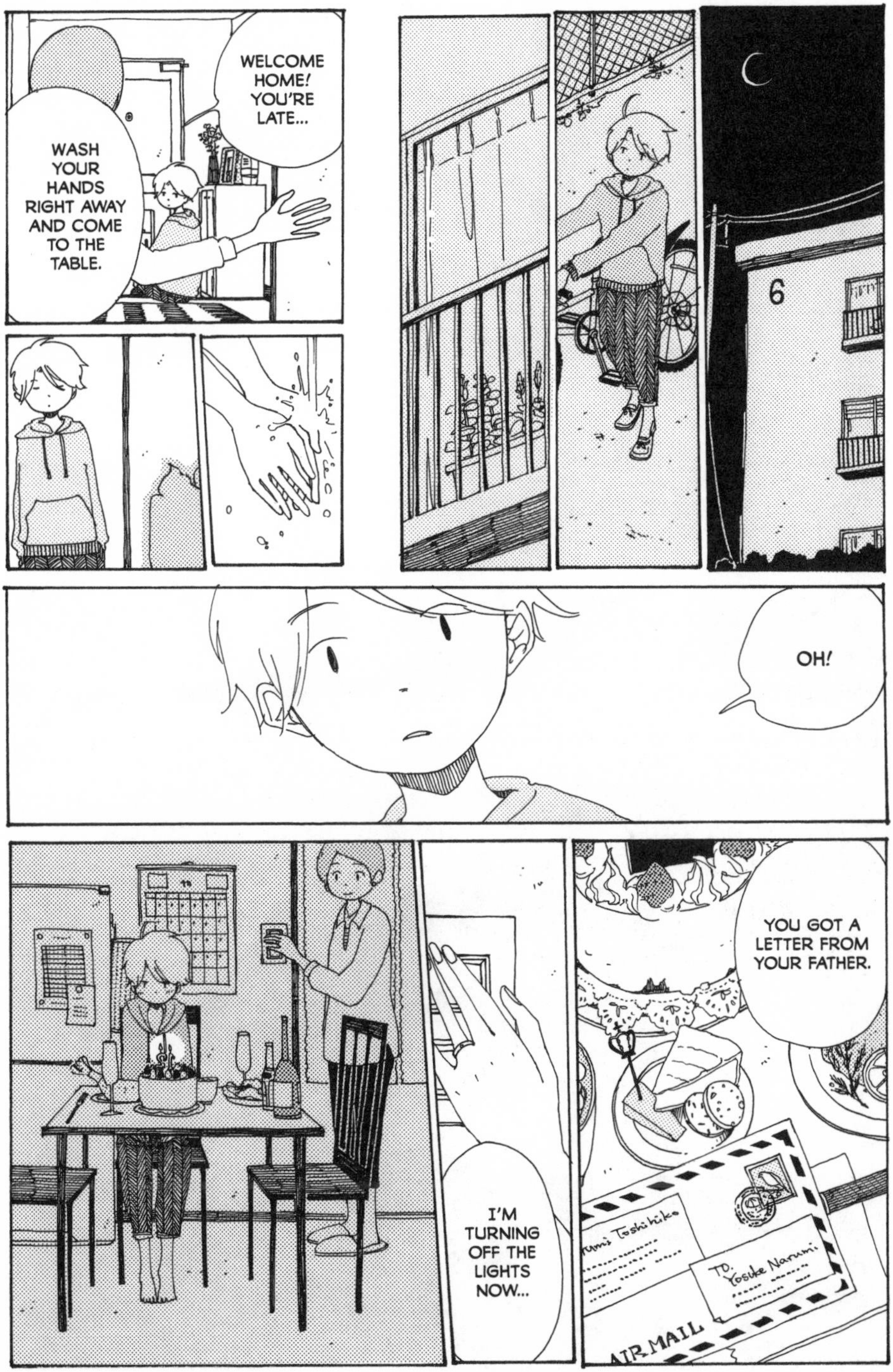
WELCOME HOME! YOU'RE LATE...
WASH YOUR HANDS RIGHT AWAY AND COME TO THE TABLE.
OH!
YOU GOT A LETTER FROM YOUR FATHER.
TO. Yosuke Narumi
AIR MAIL
I'M TURNING OFF THE LIGHTS NOW...

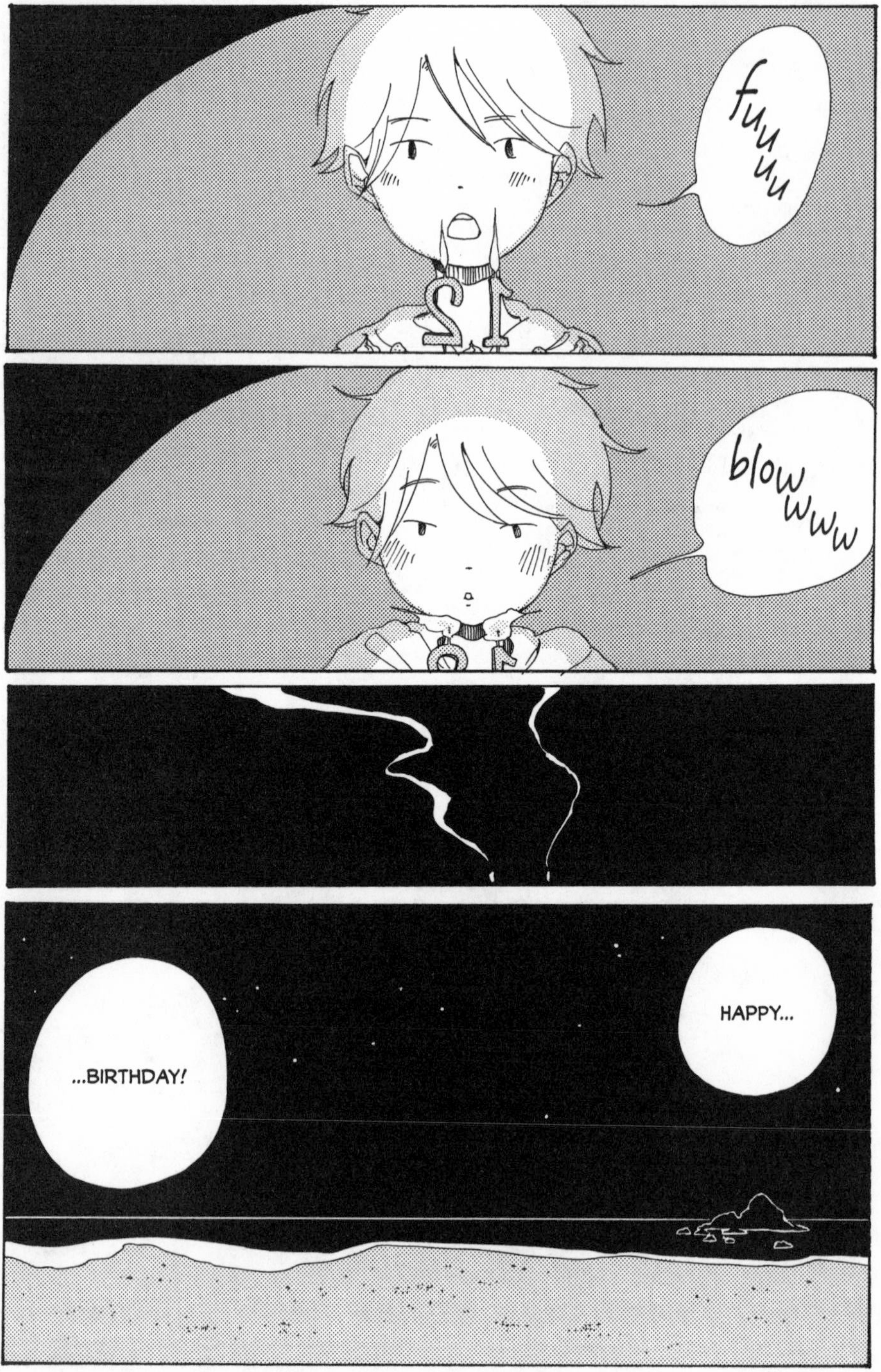
fuuuu
blowwww
HAPPY...
...BIRTHDAY!

A Day in the Life of Yosuke Narumi – The End

A Note from the Author

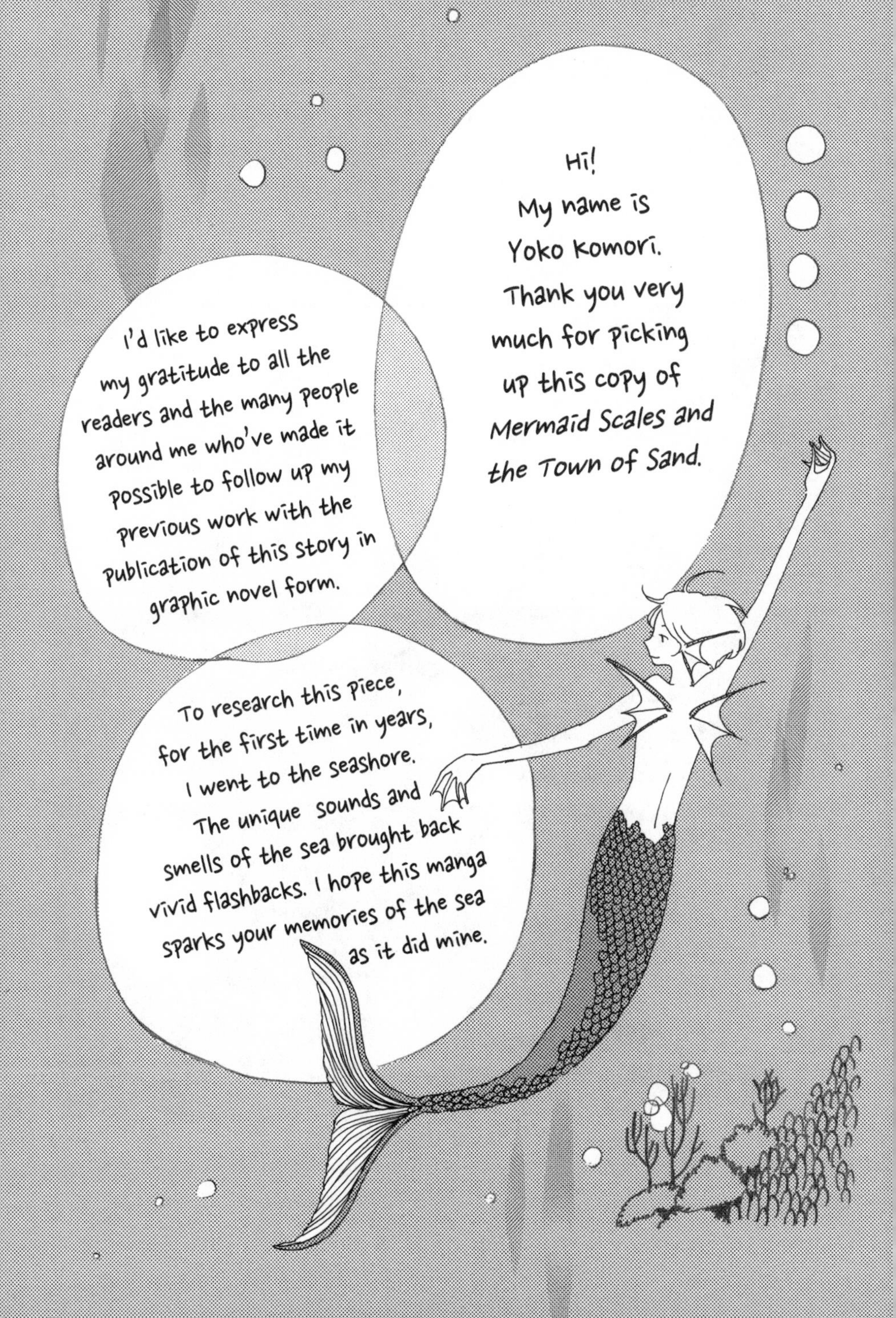
Hi! My name is Yoko Komori. Thank you very much for picking up this copy of *Mermaid Scales and the Town of Sand*.
I'd like to express my gratitude to all the readers and the many people around me who've made it possible to follow up my previous work with the publication of this story in graphic novel form.
To research this piece, for the first time in years, I went to the seashore. The unique sounds and smells of the sea brought back vivid flashbacks. I hope this manga sparks your memories of the sea as it did mine.

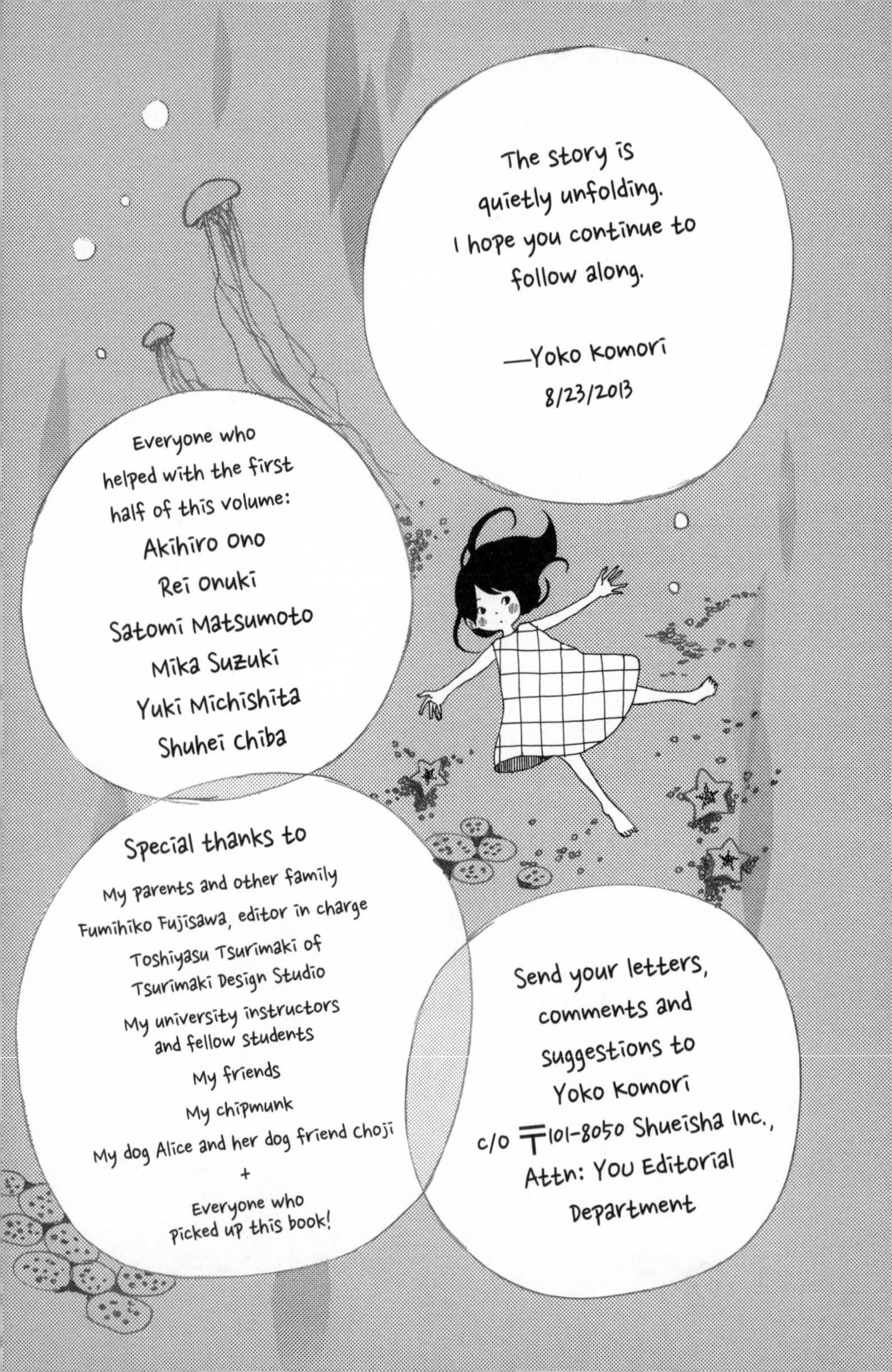
The story is
quietly unfolding.
I hope you continue to
follow along.
—Yoko Komori
8/23/2013
Everyone who
helped with the first
half of this volume:
Akihiro Ono
Rei Onuki
Satomi Matsumoto
Mika Suzuki
Yuki Michishita
Shuhei Chiba
Send your letters,
comments and
suggestions to
Yoko Komori
c/o 〒101-8050 Shueisha Inc.,
Attn: You Editorial
Department
Special thanks to
My parents and other family
Fumihiko Fujisawa, editor in charge
Toshiyasu Tsurimaki of
Tsurimaki Design Studio
My university instructors
and fellow students
My friends
My chipmunk
My dog Alice and her dog friend Choji
+
Everyone who
picked up this book!

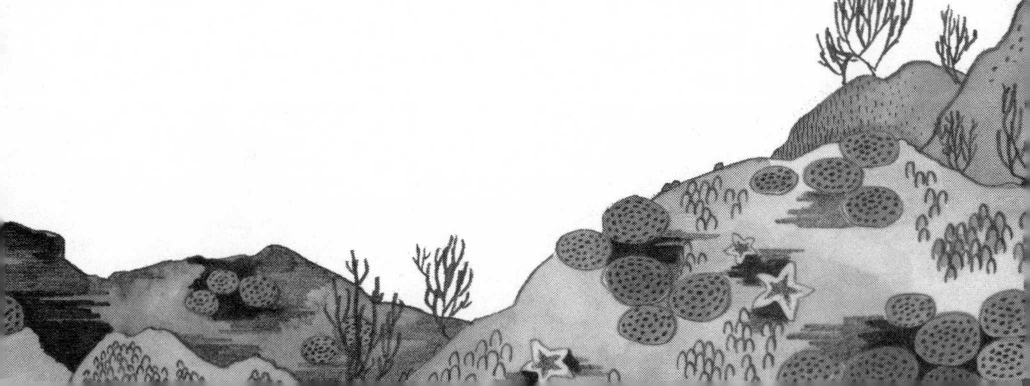

{Six} The Monster in the Tunnel

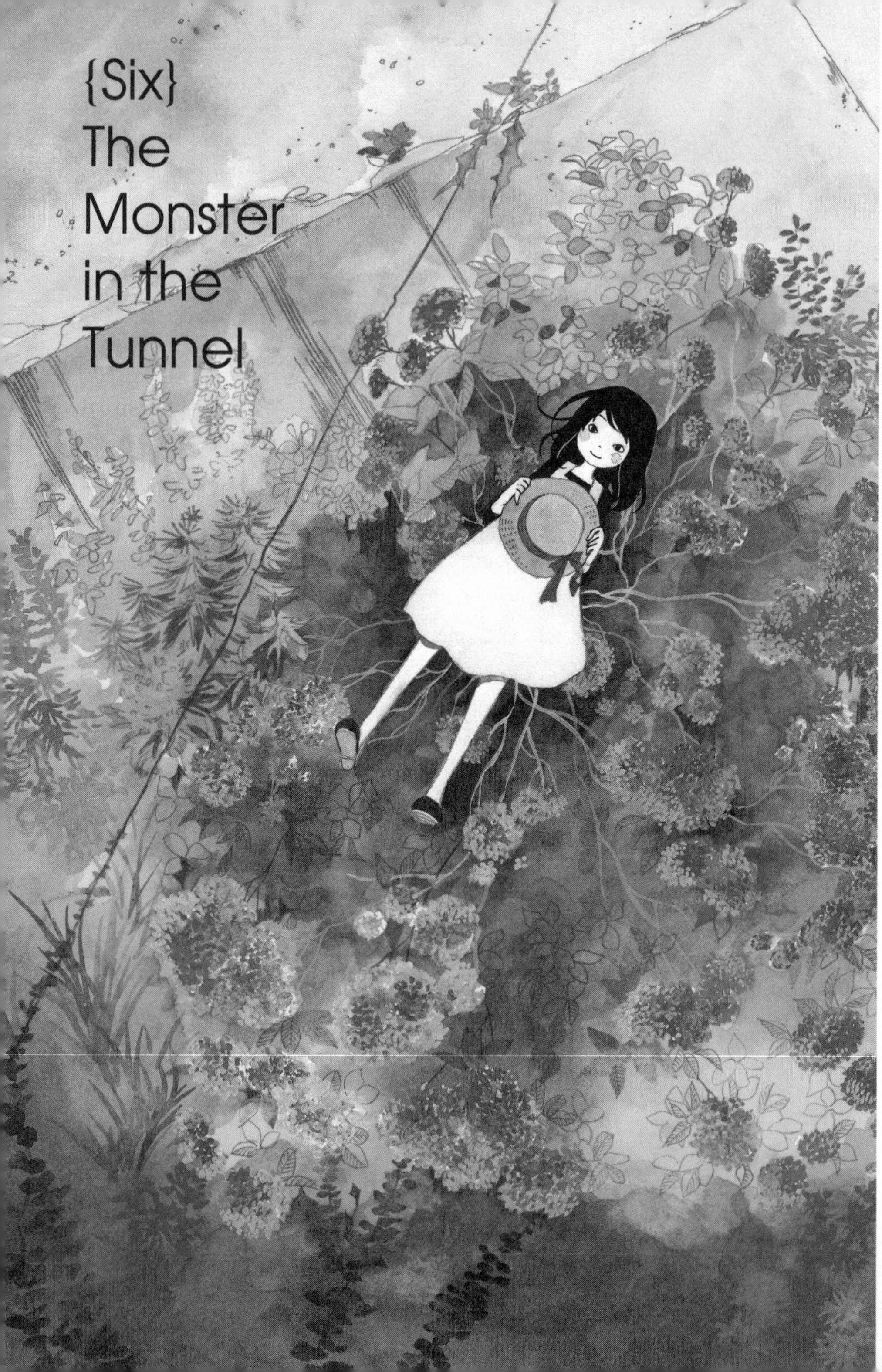

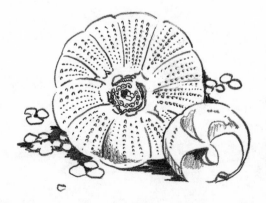

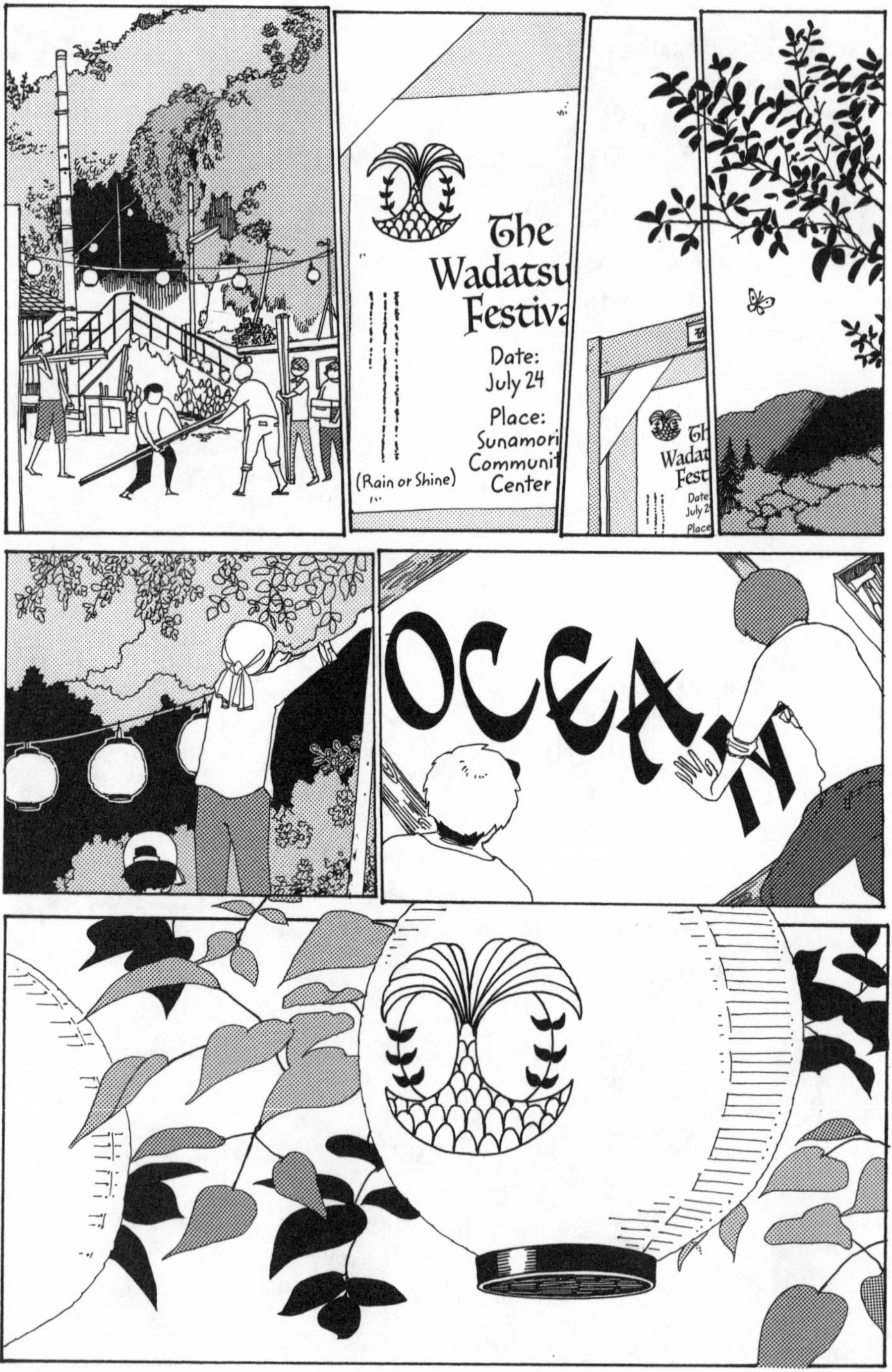

The
Wadat
Fest
Date
July 24
Place
The
Wadatsu
Festiva
Date:
July 24
Place:
Sunamori
Communit
Center
(Rain or Shine)
OCEAN

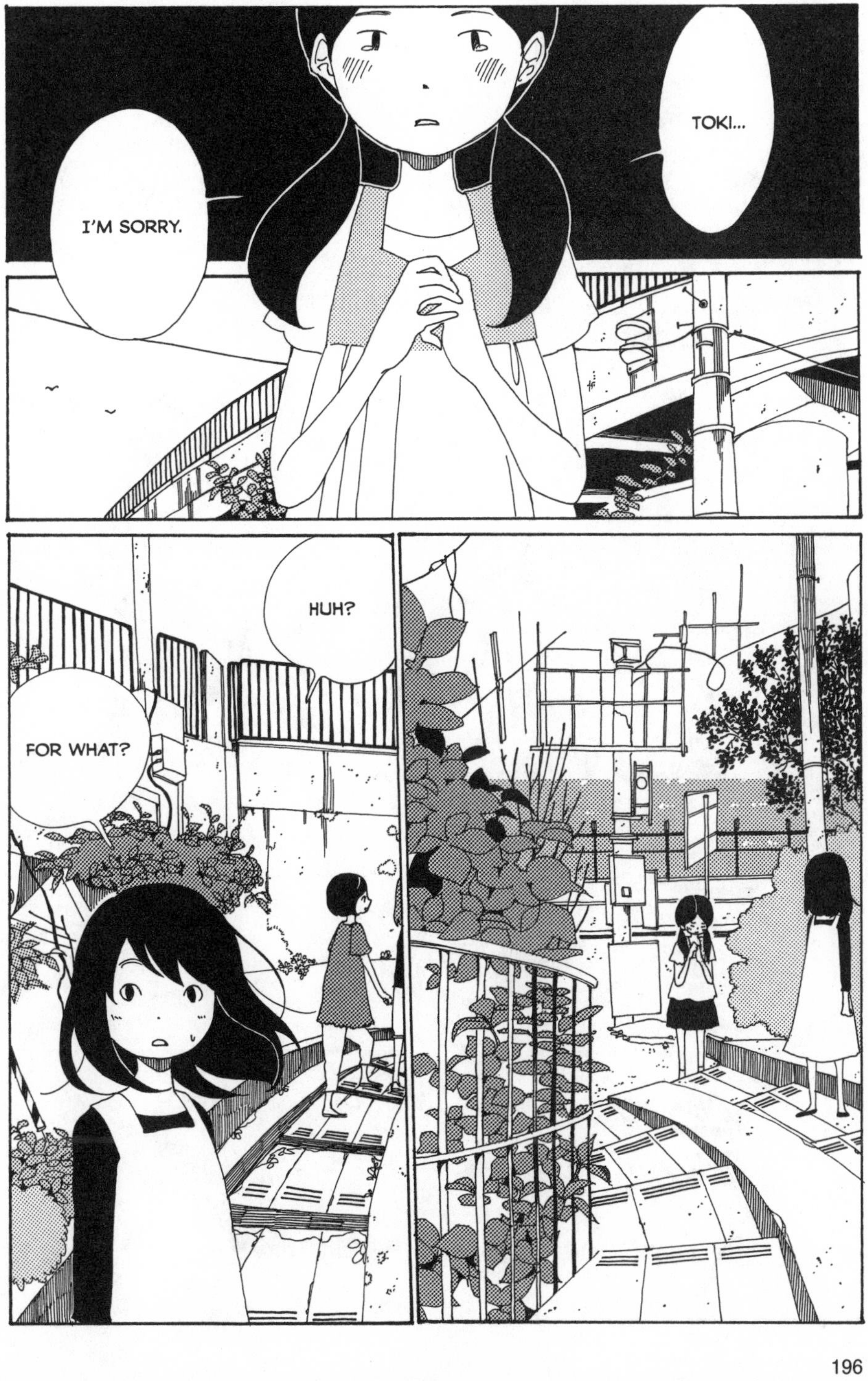
TOKI...
I'M SORRY.
HUH?
FOR WHAT?

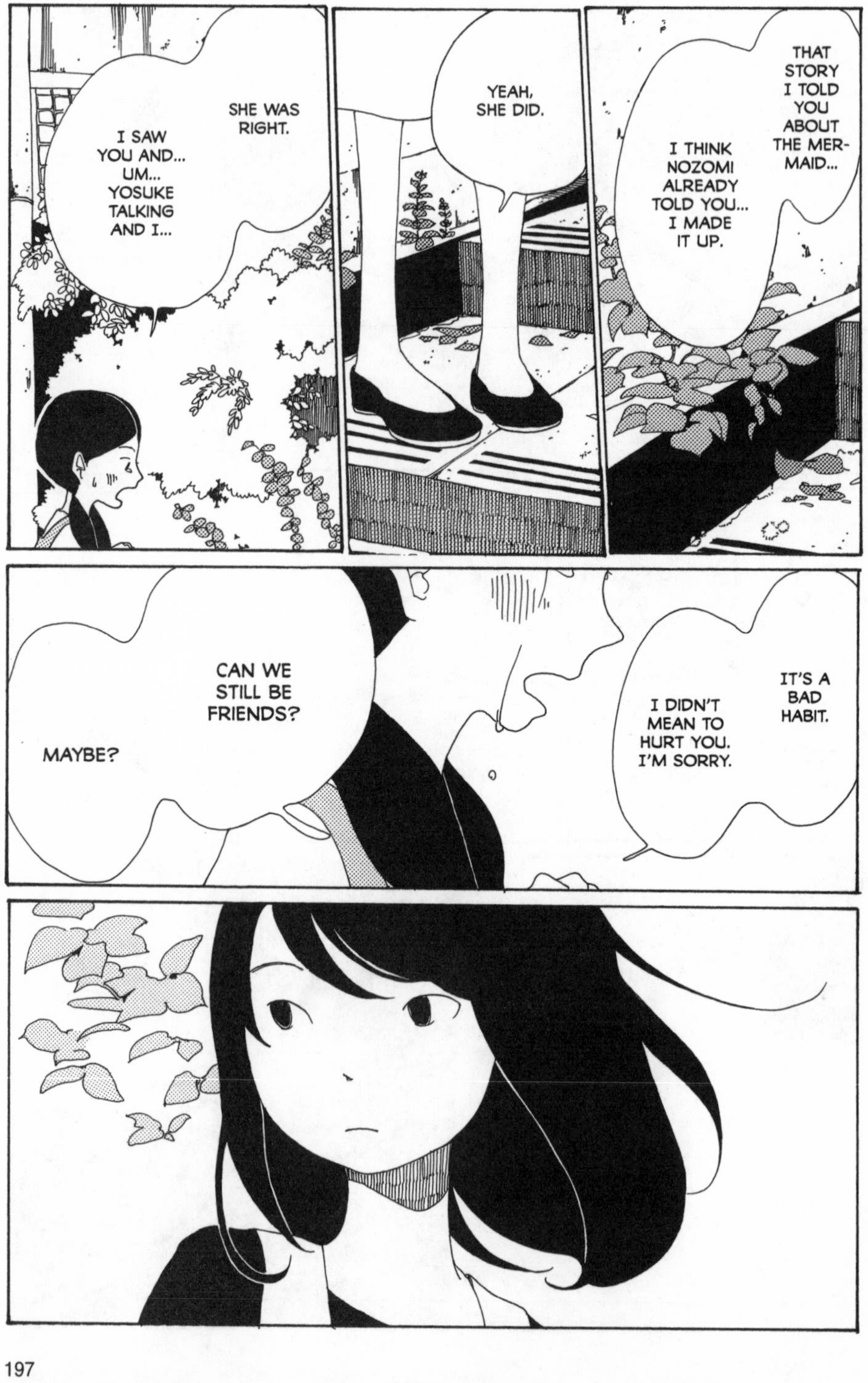
THAT STORY I TOLD YOU ABOUT THE MER-MAID...
I THINK NOZOMI ALREADY TOLD YOU... I MADE IT UP.
YEAH, SHE DID.
SHE WAS RIGHT.
I SAW YOU AND... UM... YOSUKE TALKING AND I...
IT'S A BAD HABIT.
I DIDN'T MEAN TO HURT YOU. I'M SORRY.
CAN WE STILL BE FRIENDS?
MAYBE?

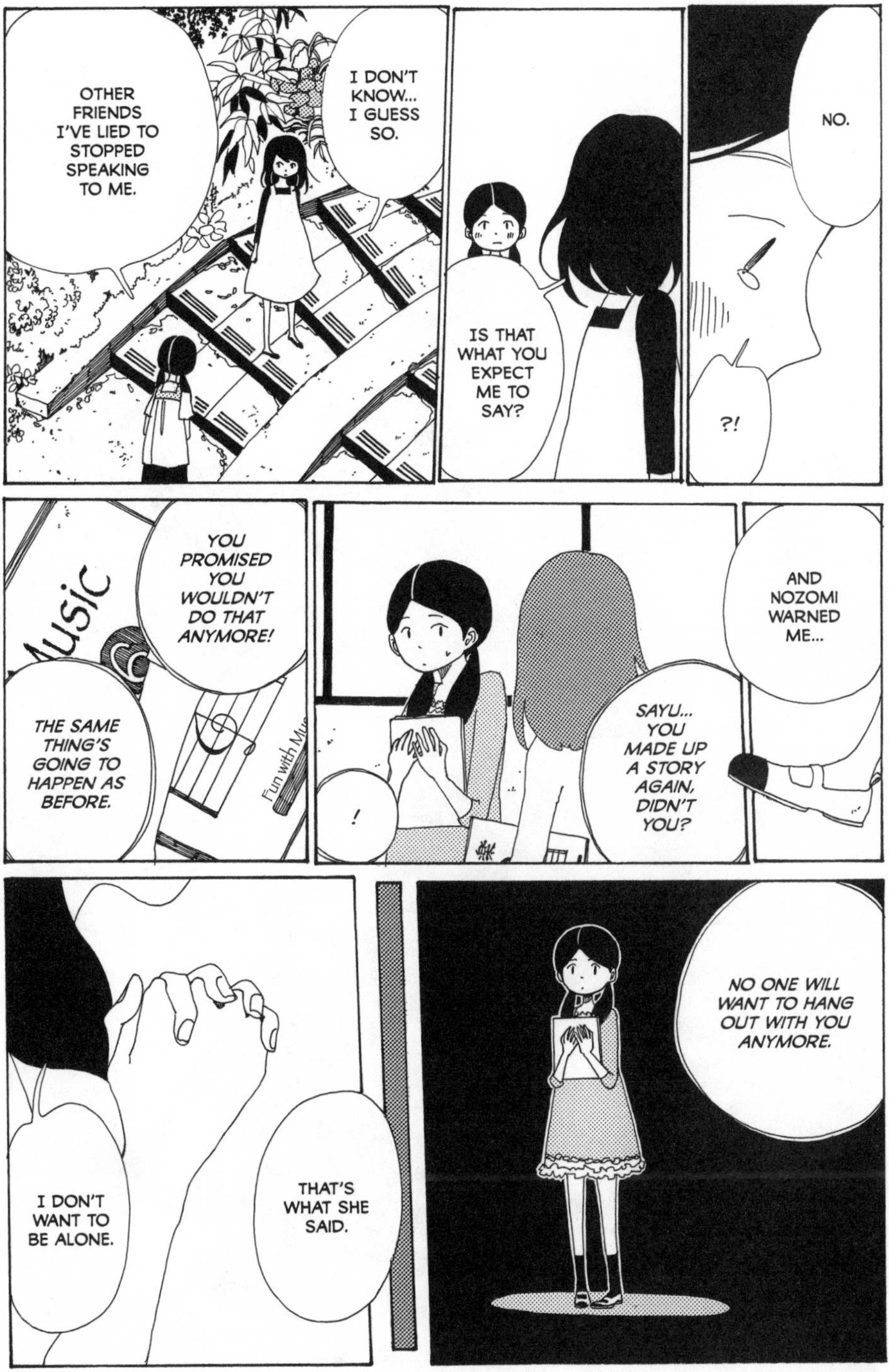
NO.
?!
IS THAT WHAT YOU EXPECT ME TO SAY?
I DON'T KNOW... I GUESS SO.
OTHER FRIENDS I'VE LIED TO STOPPED SPEAKING TO ME.
AND NOZOMI WARNED ME...
SAYU... YOU MADE UP A STORY AGAIN, DIDN'T YOU?
!
YOU PROMISED YOU WOULDN'T DO THAT ANYMORE!
Music
THE SAME THING'S GOING TO HAPPEN AS BEFORE.
NO ONE WILL WANT TO HANG OUT WITH YOU ANYMORE.
THAT'S WHAT SHE SAID.
I DON'T WANT TO BE ALONE.

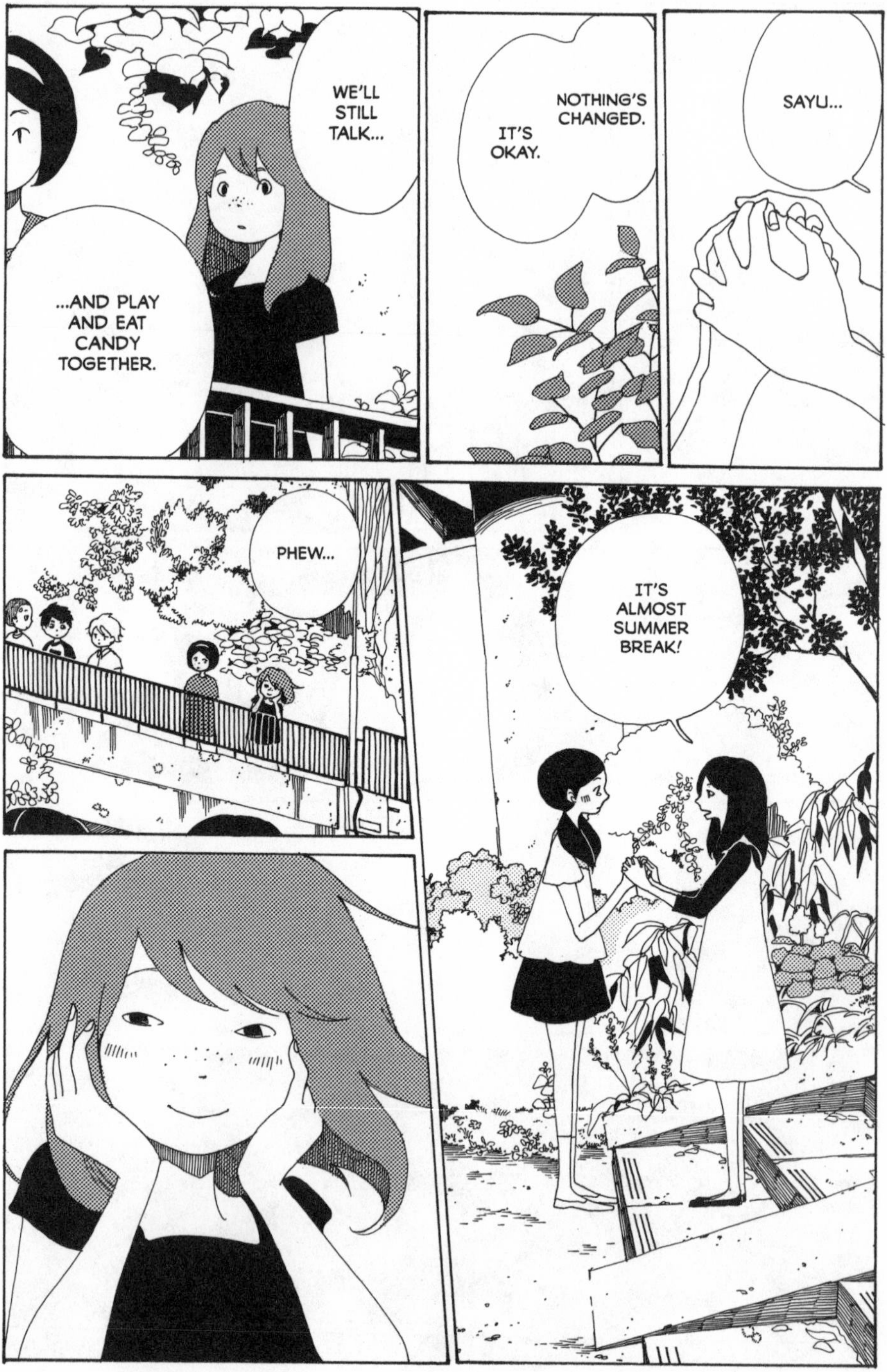
SAYU...
NOTHING'S CHANGED.
IT'S OKAY.
WE'LL STILL TALK...
...AND PLAY AND EAT CANDY TOGETHER.
IT'S ALMOST SUMMER BREAK!
PHEW...

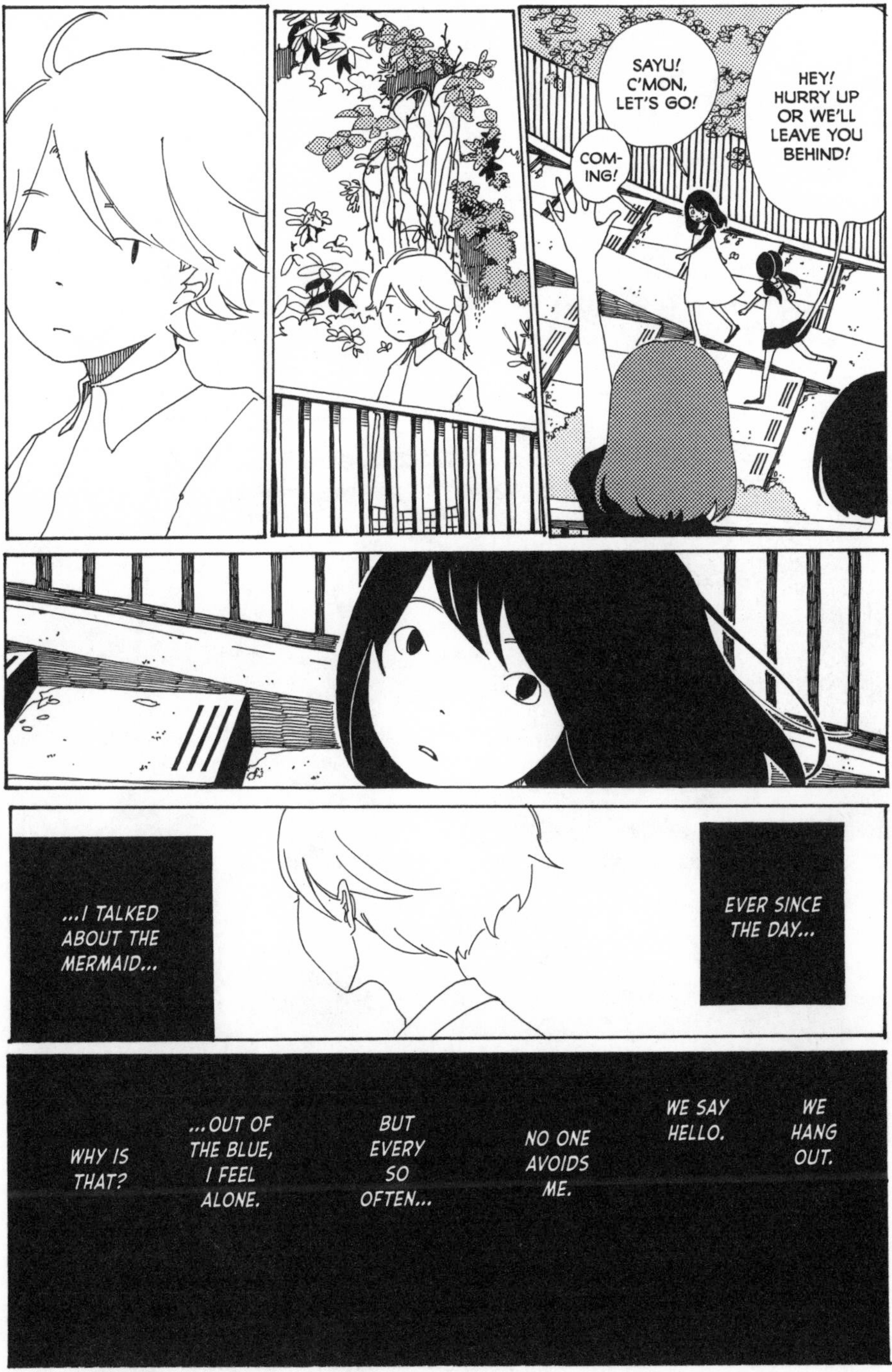
HEY! HURRY UP OR WE'LL LEAVE YOU BEHIND!
SAYU! C'MON, LET'S GO!
COM-ING!
EVER SINCE THE DAY...
...I TALKED ABOUT THE MERMAID...
WE HANG OUT.
WE SAY HELLO.
NO ONE AVOIDS ME.
BUT EVERY SO OFTEN...
...OUT OF THE BLUE, I FEEL ALONE.
WHY IS THAT?

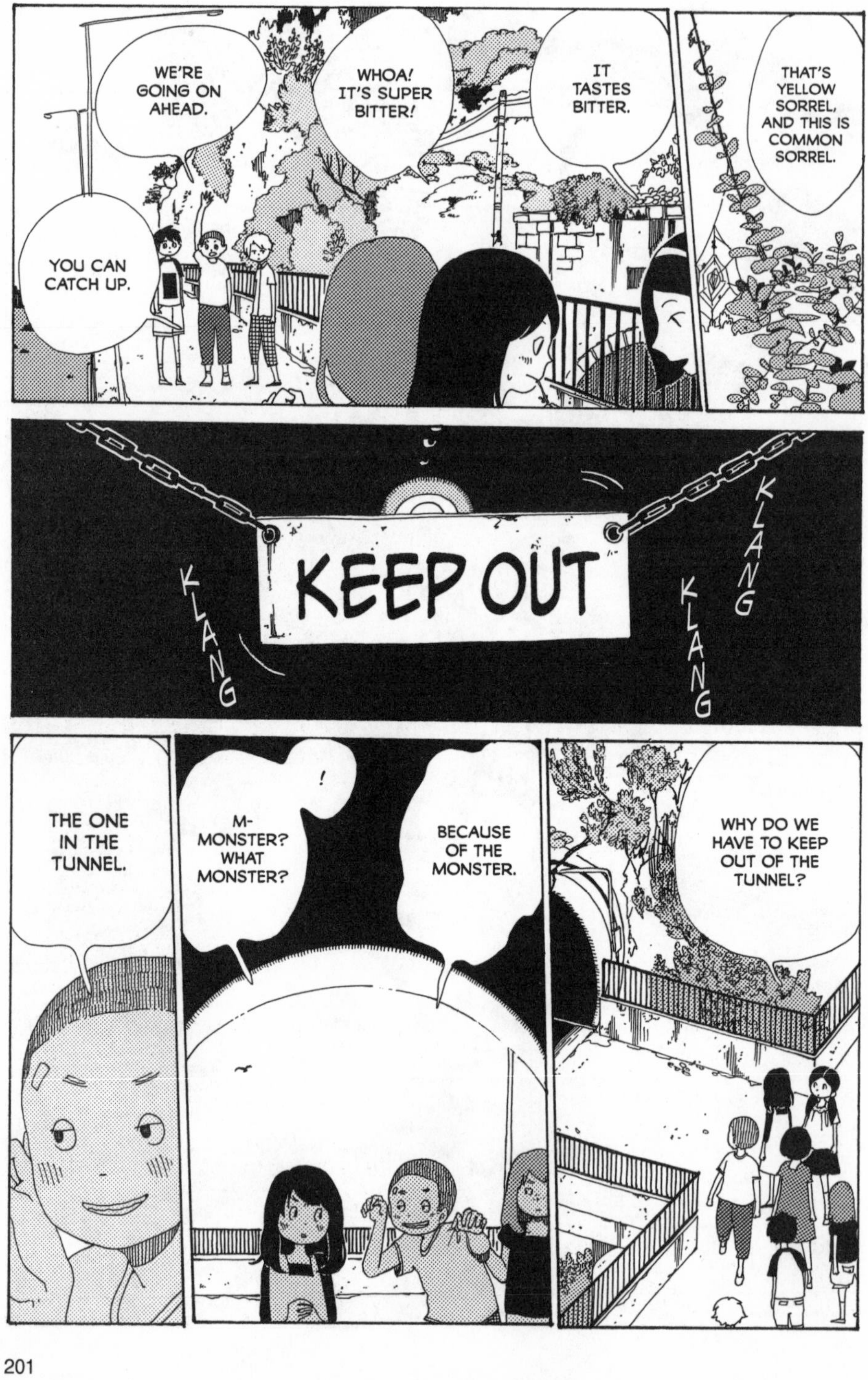
THAT'S YELLOW SORREL, AND THIS IS COMMON SORREL.
IT TASTES BITTER.
WHOA! IT'S SUPER BITTER!
WE'RE GOING ON AHEAD.
YOU CAN CATCH UP.
KLANG
KLANG
KEEP OUT
KLANG
WHY DO WE HAVE TO KEEP OUT OF THE TUNNEL?
!
BECAUSE OF THE MONSTER.
M-MONSTER? WHAT MONSTER?
THE ONE IN THE TUNNEL.

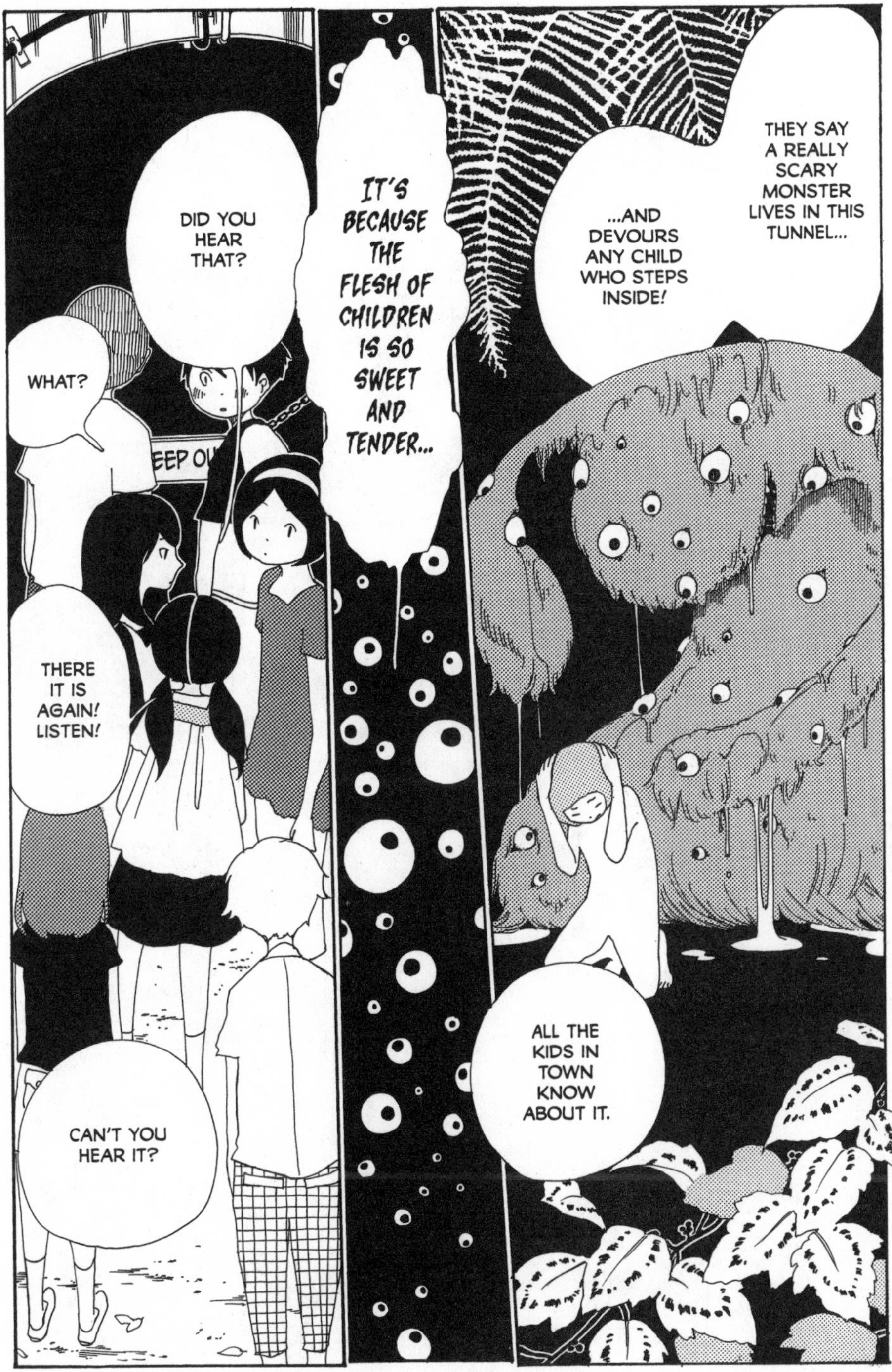
THEY SAY A REALLY SCARY MONSTER LIVES IN THIS TUNNEL...
...AND DEVOURS ANY CHILD WHO STEPS INSIDE!
ALL THE KIDS IN TOWN KNOW ABOUT IT.
IT'S BECAUSE THE FLESH OF CHILDREN IS SO SWEET AND TENDER...
DID YOU HEAR THAT?
WHAT?
THERE IT IS AGAIN! LISTEN!
CAN'T YOU HEAR IT?

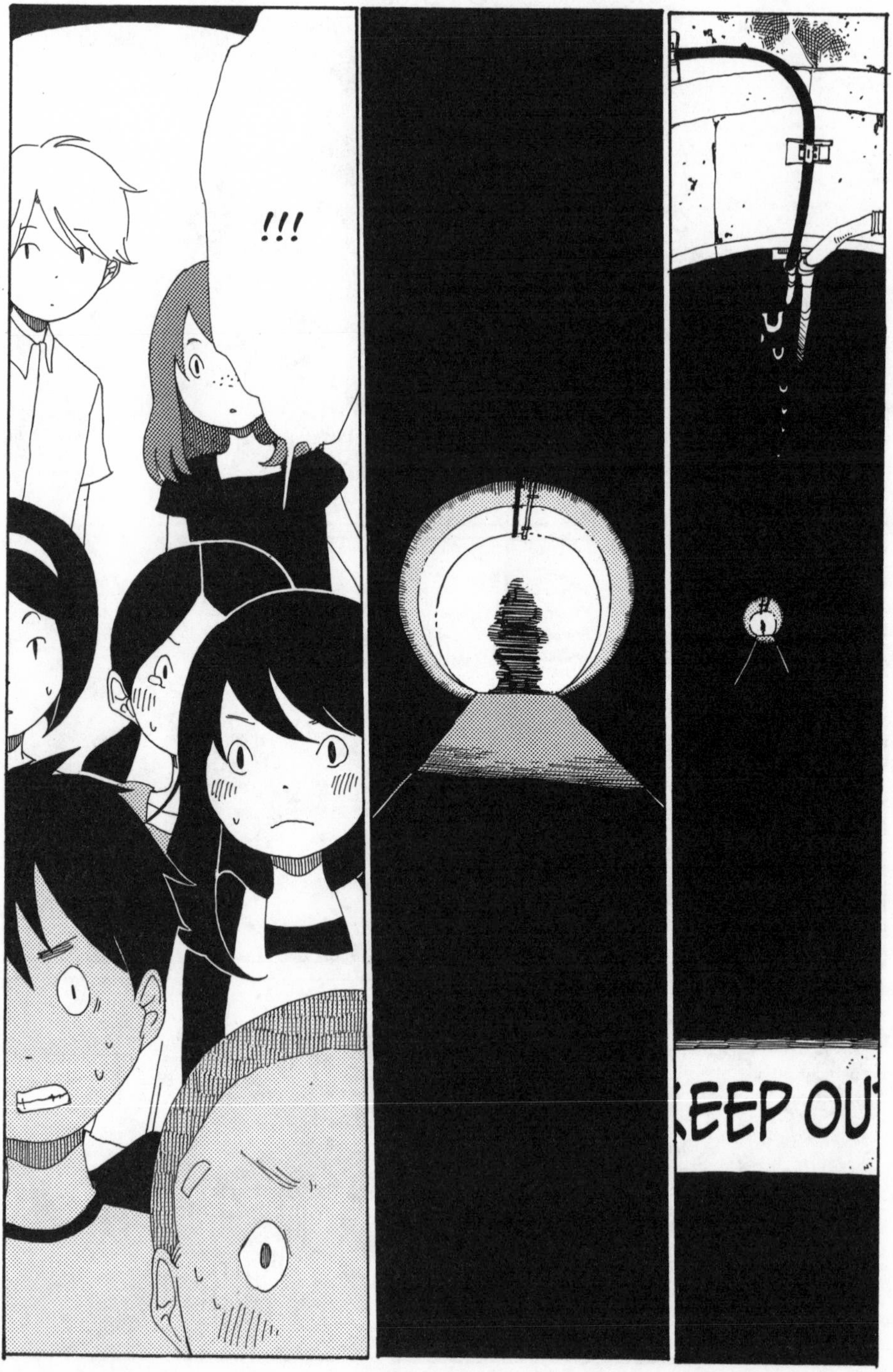
KEEP OUT
!!!

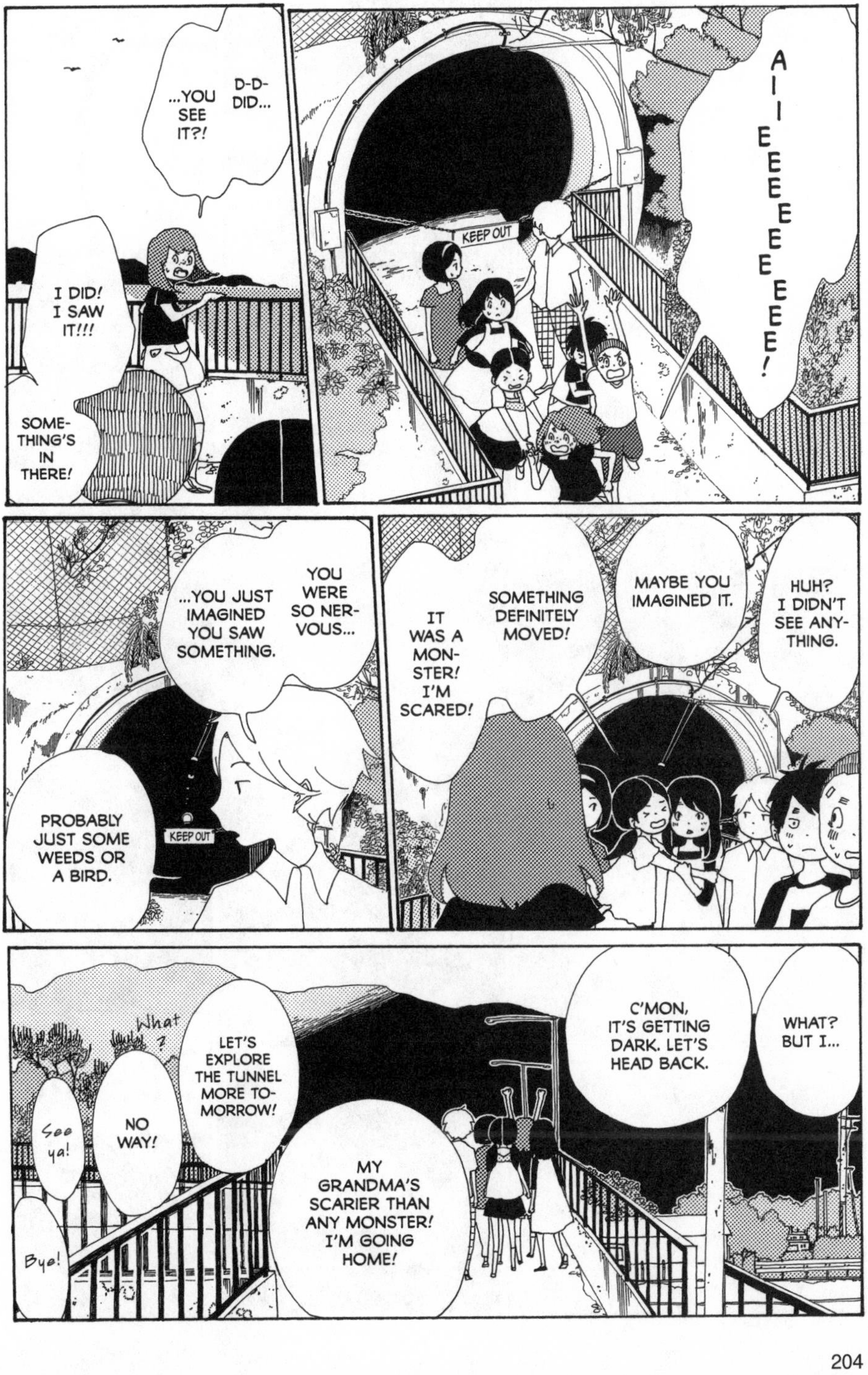
AIIEEEEEEEEE!
D-D-DID...
...YOU SEE IT?!
I DID! I SAW IT!!!
SOMETHING'S IN THERE!
KEEP OUT
HUH? I DIDN'T SEE ANYTHING.
MAYBE YOU IMAGINED IT.
SOMETHING DEFINITELY MOVED!
IT WAS A MONSTER! I'M SCARED!
YOU WERE SO NERVOUS...
...YOU JUST IMAGINED YOU SAW SOMETHING.
PROBABLY JUST SOME WEEDS OR A BIRD.
KEEP OUT
WHAT? BUT I...
C'MON, IT'S GETTING DARK. LET'S HEAD BACK.
MY GRANDMA'S SCARIER THAN ANY MONSTER! I'M GOING HOME!
LET'S EXPLORE THE TUNNEL MORE TOMORROW!
What?
NO WAY!
See ya!
Bye!

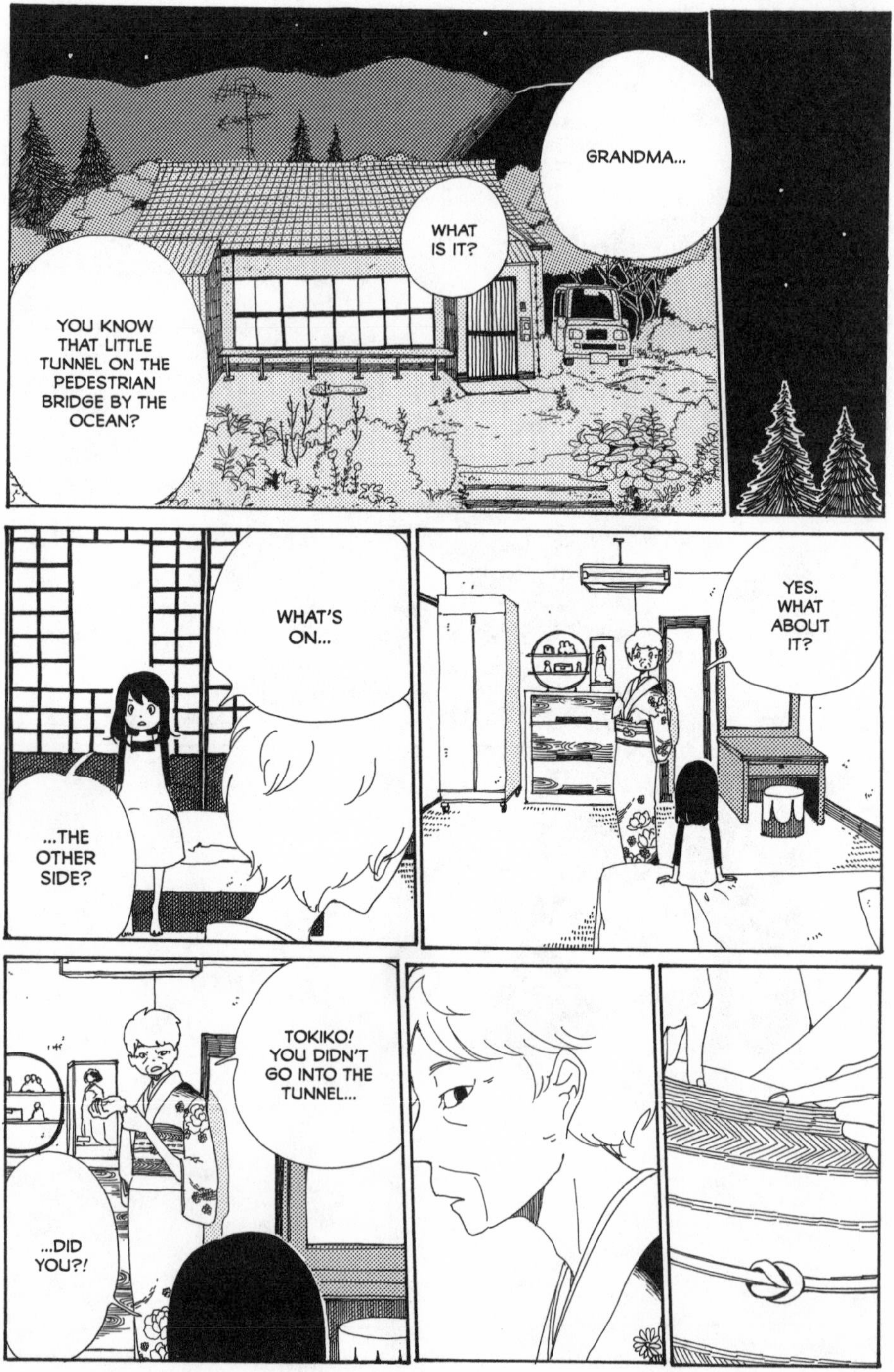

GRANDMA...
WHAT IS IT?
YOU KNOW THAT LITTLE TUNNEL ON THE PEDESTRIAN BRIDGE BY THE OCEAN?
YES. WHAT ABOUT IT?
WHAT'S ON...
...THE OTHER SIDE?
TOKIKO! YOU DIDN'T GO INTO THE TUNNEL...
...DID YOU?!

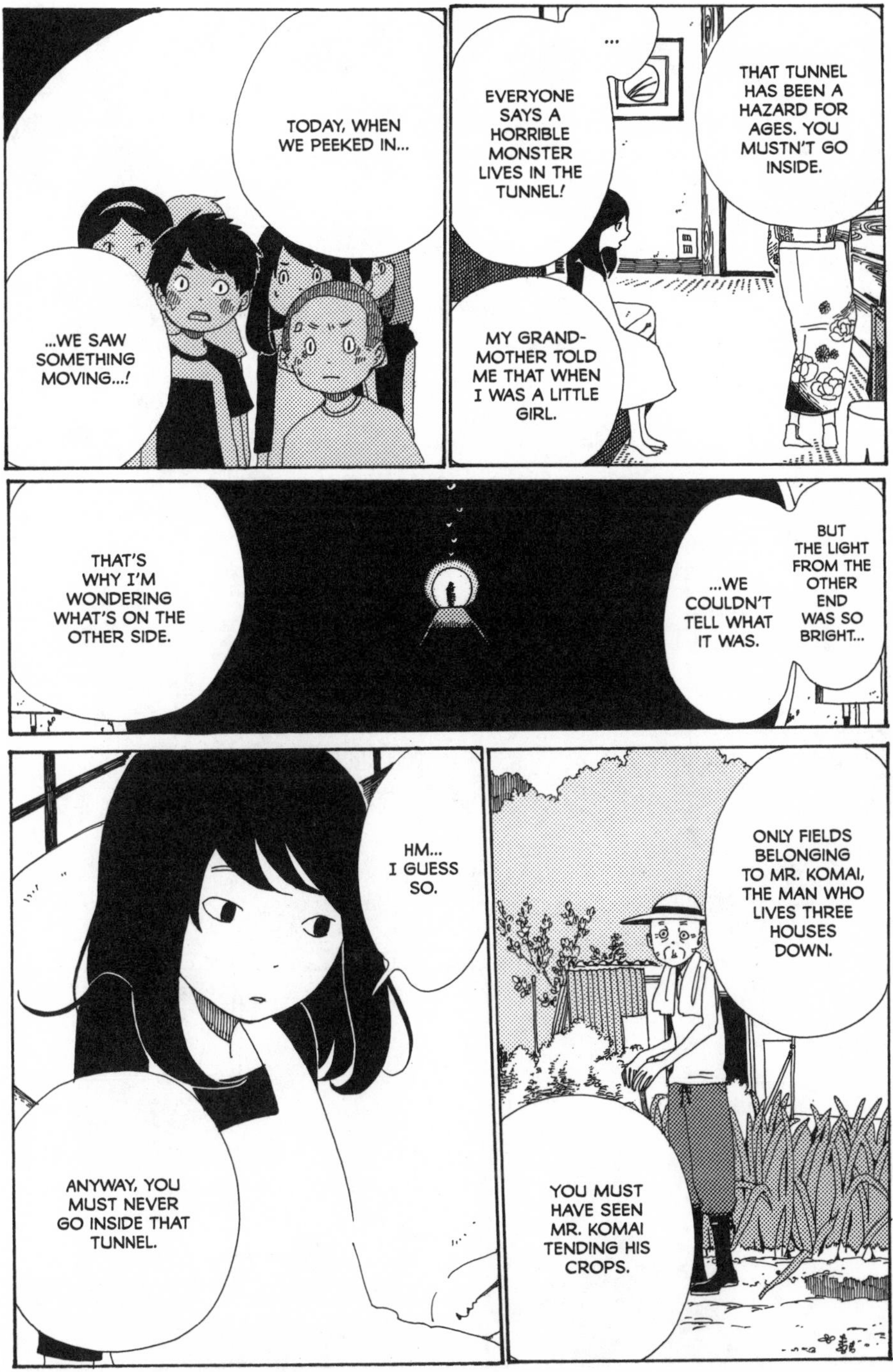
THAT TUNNEL HAS BEEN A HAZARD FOR AGES. YOU MUSTN'T GO INSIDE.
...
EVERYONE SAYS A HORRIBLE MONSTER LIVES IN THE TUNNEL!
MY GRAND-MOTHER TOLD ME THAT WHEN I WAS A LITTLE GIRL.
TODAY, WHEN WE PEEKED IN...
...WE SAW SOMETHING MOVING...!
BUT THE LIGHT FROM THE OTHER END WAS SO BRIGHT...
...WE COULDN'T TELL WHAT IT WAS.
THAT'S WHY I'M WONDERING WHAT'S ON THE OTHER SIDE.
ONLY FIELDS BELONGING TO MR. KOMAI, THE MAN WHO LIVES THREE HOUSES DOWN.
YOU MUST HAVE SEEN MR. KOMAI TENDING HIS CROPS.
HM... I GUESS SO.
ANYWAY, YOU MUST NEVER GO INSIDE THAT TUNNEL.

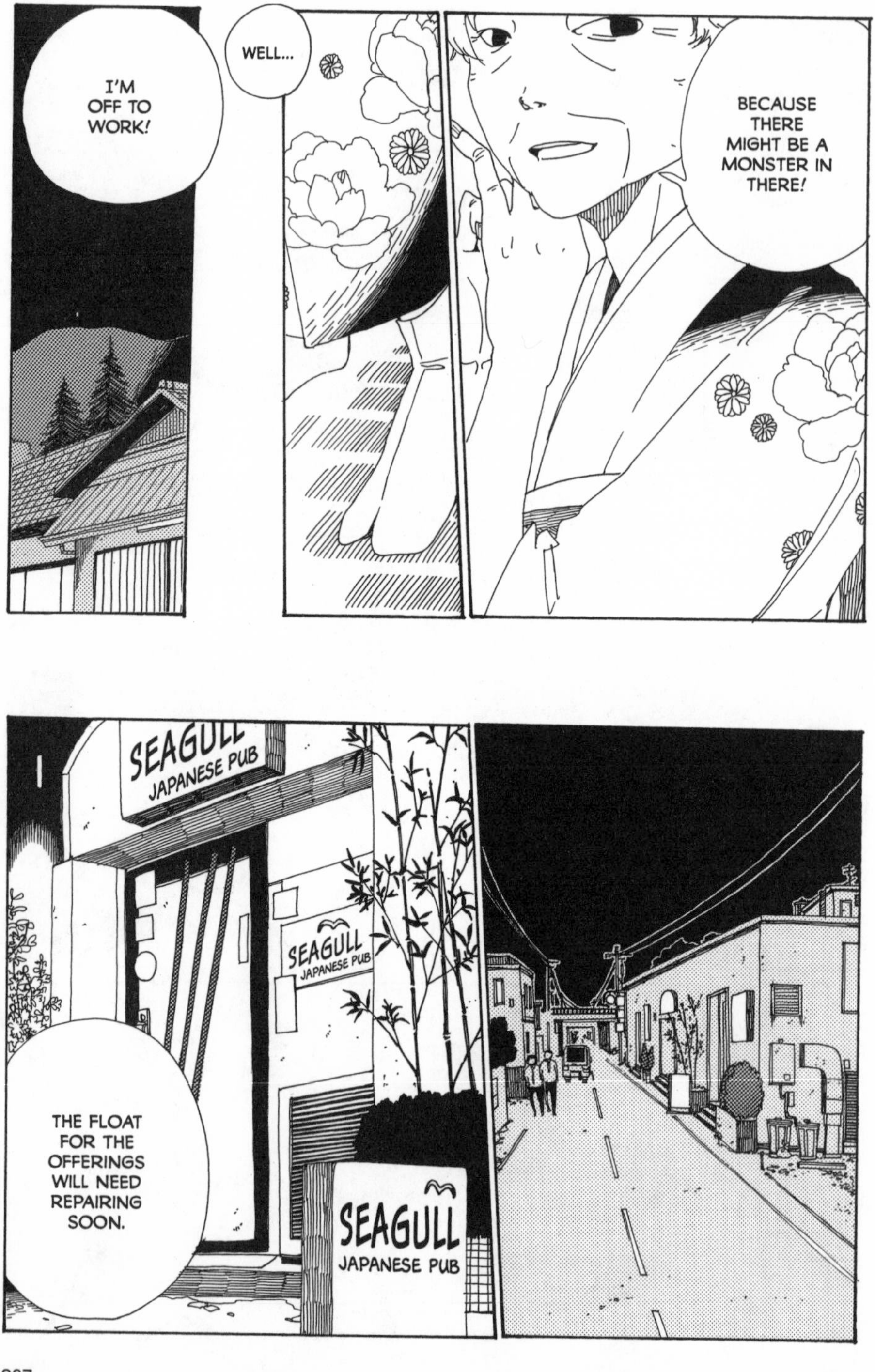
BECAUSE THERE MIGHT BE A MONSTER IN THERE!
WELL...
I'M OFF TO WORK!
SEAGULL JAPANESE PUB
SEAGULL JAPANESE PUB
SEAGULL JAPANESE PUB
THE FLOAT FOR THE OFFERINGS WILL NEED REPAIRING SOON.

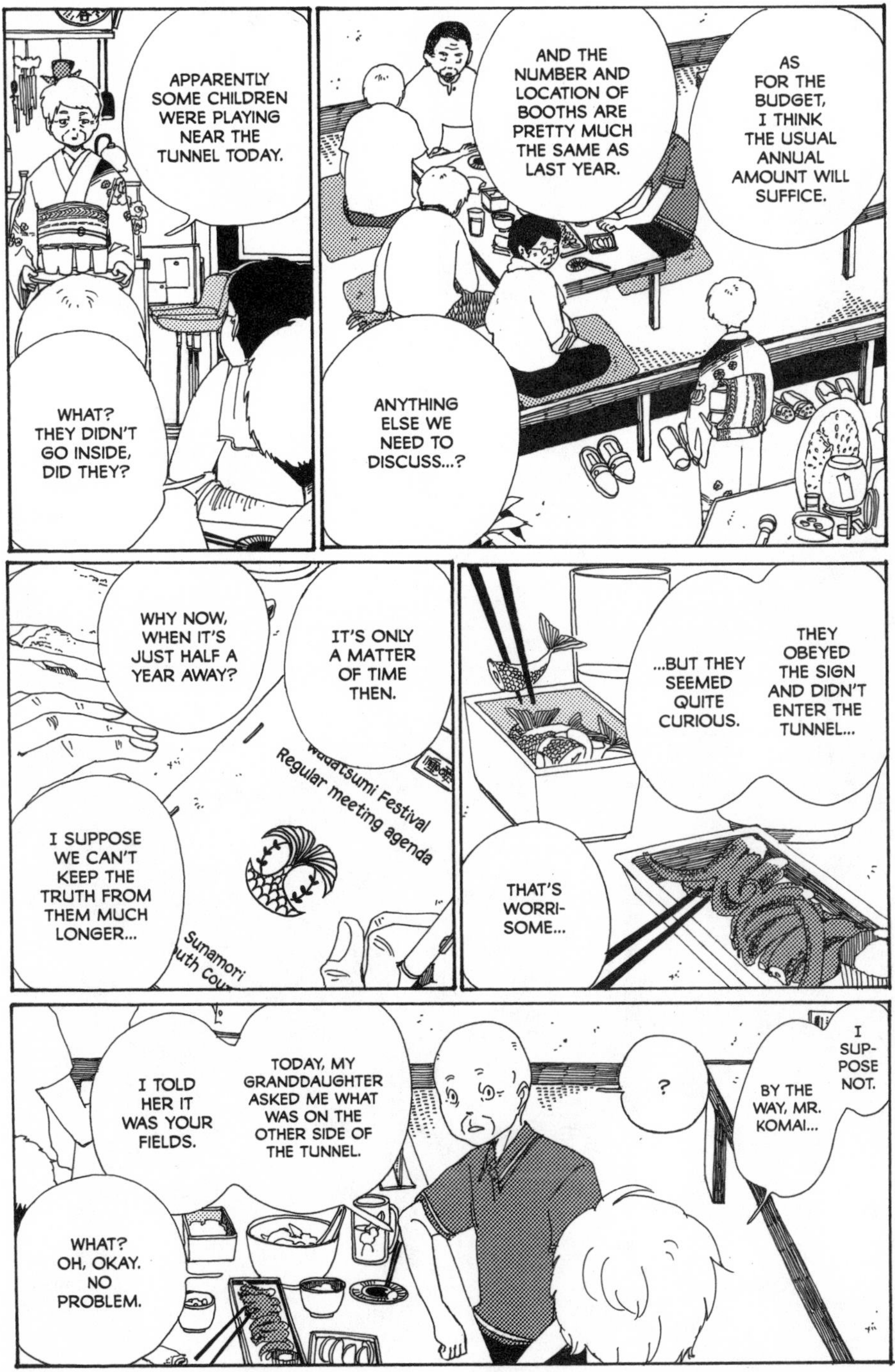
AS FOR THE BUDGET, I THINK THE USUAL ANNUAL AMOUNT WILL SUFFICE.
AND THE NUMBER AND LOCATION OF BOOTHS ARE PRETTY MUCH THE SAME AS LAST YEAR.
ANYTHING ELSE WE NEED TO DISCUSS...?
APPARENTLY SOME CHILDREN WERE PLAYING NEAR THE TUNNEL TODAY.
WHAT? THEY DIDN'T GO INSIDE, DID THEY?
THEY OBEYED THE SIGN AND DIDN'T ENTER THE TUNNEL...
...BUT THEY SEEMED QUITE CURIOUS.
THAT'S WORRI-SOME...
IT'S ONLY A MATTER OF TIME THEN.
WHY NOW, WHEN IT'S JUST HALF A YEAR AWAY?
Festival
Regular meeting agenda
Sunamori
I SUPPOSE WE CAN'T KEEP THE TRUTH FROM THEM MUCH LONGER...
I SUPPOSE NOT.
BY THE WAY, MR. KOMAI...
?
TODAY, MY GRANDDAUGHTER ASKED ME WHAT WAS ON THE OTHER SIDE OF THE TUNNEL.
I TOLD HER IT WAS YOUR FIELDS.
WHAT? OH, OKAY. NO PROBLEM.

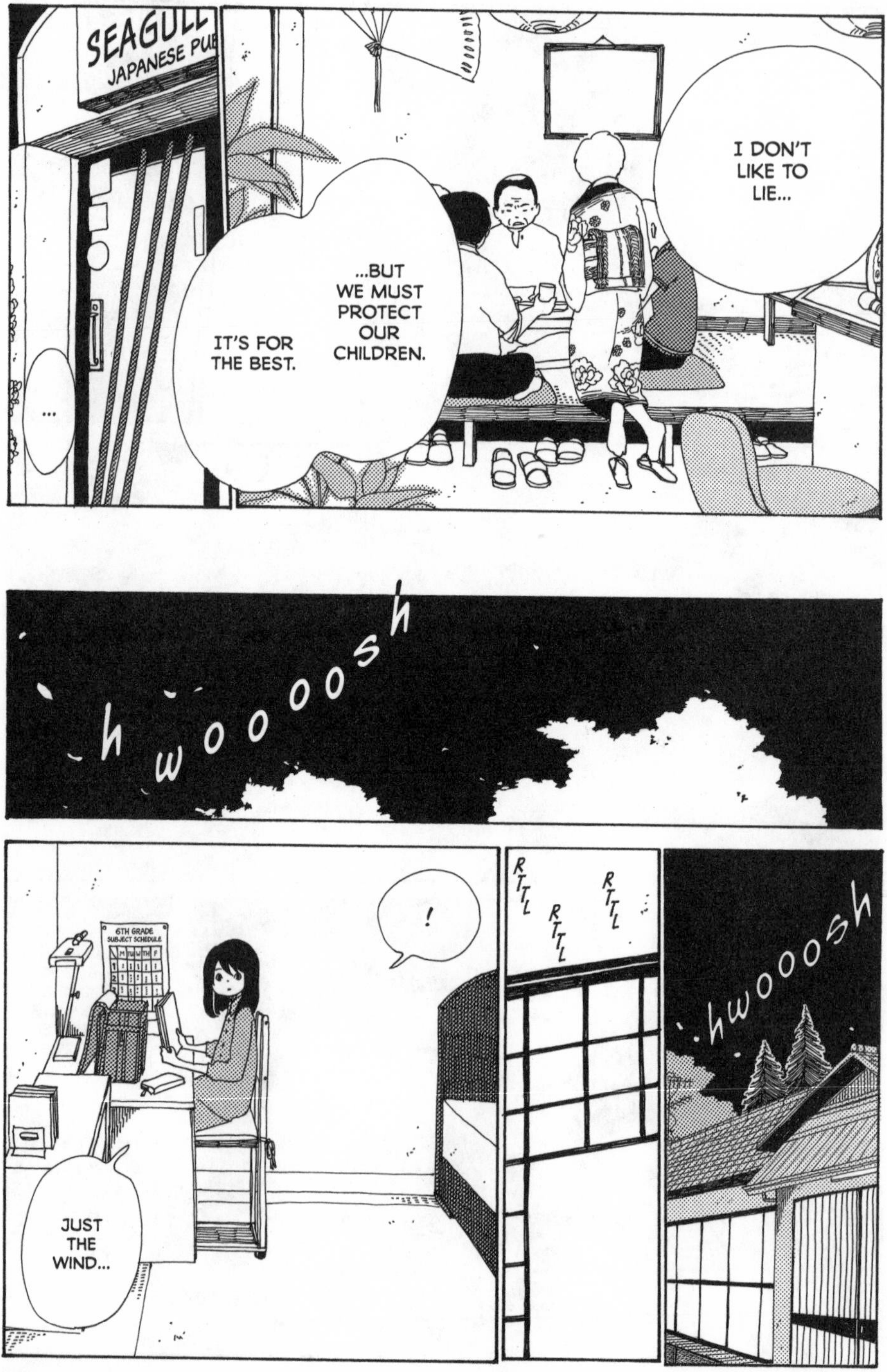
I DON'T LIKE TO LIE...
...BUT WE MUST PROTECT OUR CHILDREN.
IT'S FOR THE BEST.
SEAGULL
JAPANESE PUB
...
hwooosh
hwooosh
RTTL
RTTL
RTTL
!
6TH GRADE SUBJECT SCHEDULE
JUST THE WIND...

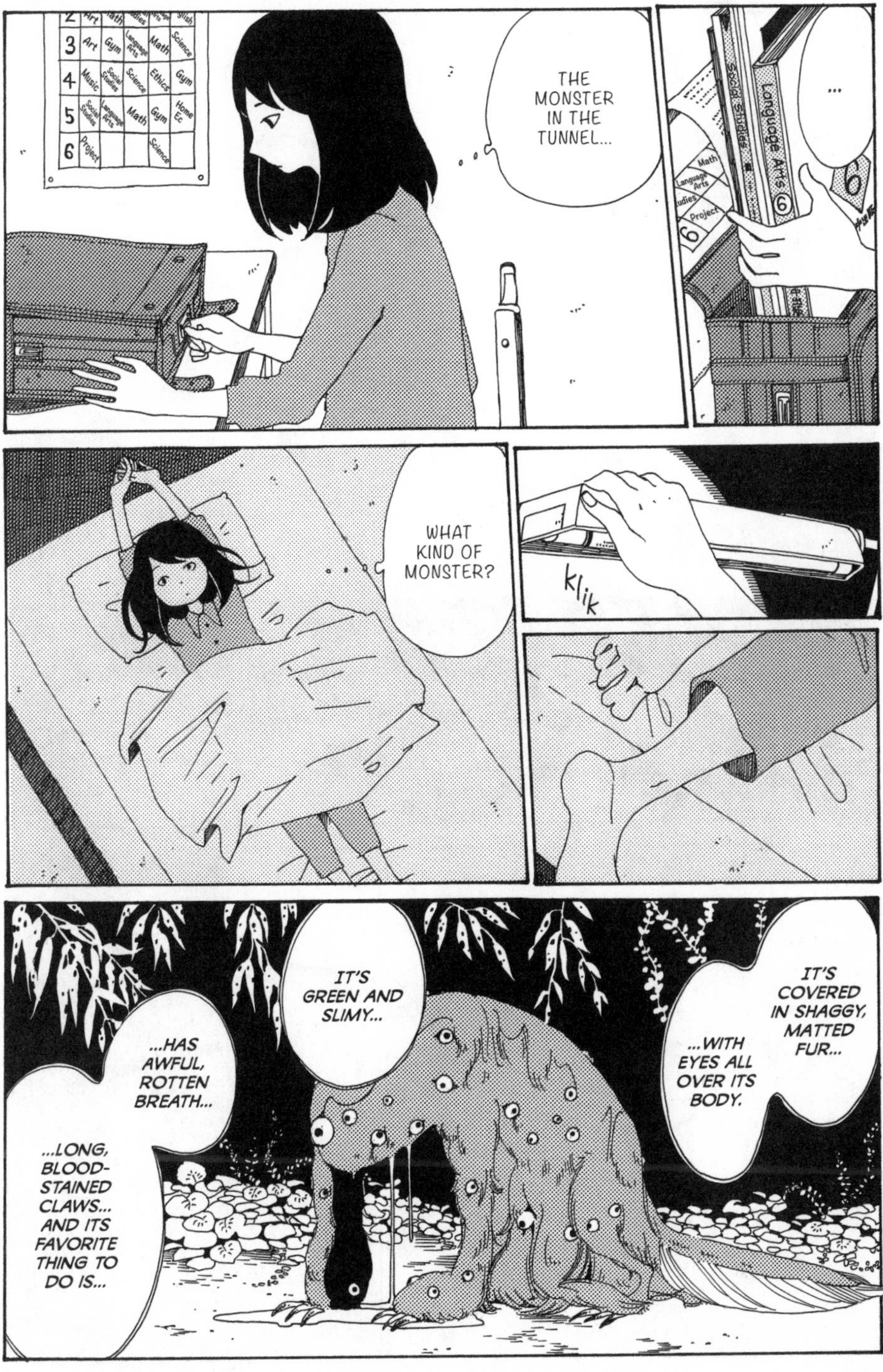
...
THE MONSTER IN THE TUNNEL...
KLIK
WHAT KIND OF MONSTER?
IT'S COVERED IN SHAGGY, MATTED FUR...
...WITH EYES ALL OVER ITS BODY.
IT'S GREEN AND SLIMY...
...HAS AWFUL, ROTTEN BREATH...
...LONG, BLOOD-STAINED CLAWS... AND ITS FAVORITE THING TO DO IS...

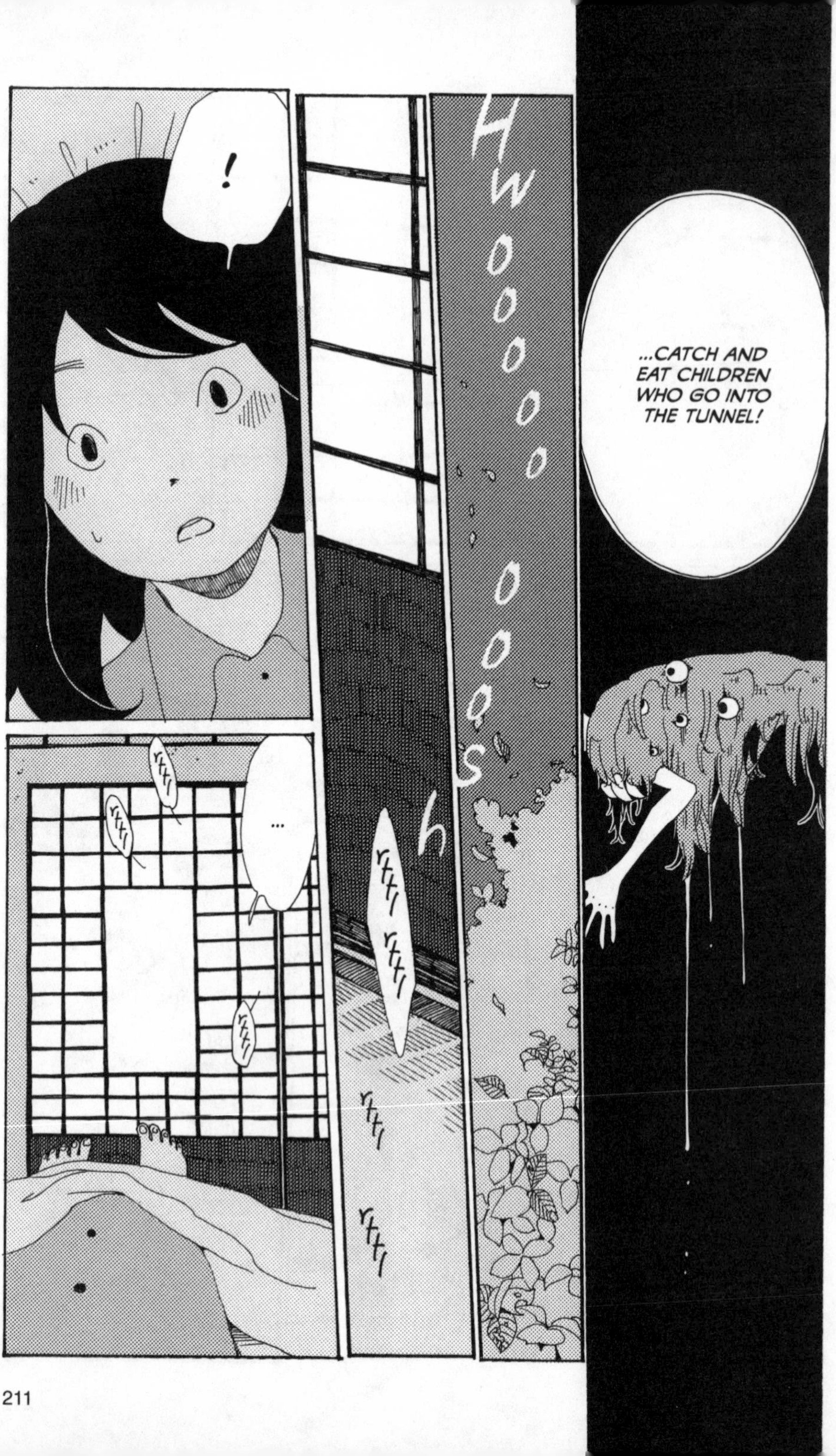
...CATCH AND EAT CHILDREN WHO GO INTO THE TUNNEL!
HWOOOOOOOOSh
rttl rttl
rttl
rttl
!
...
...
rttl
rttl
rttl

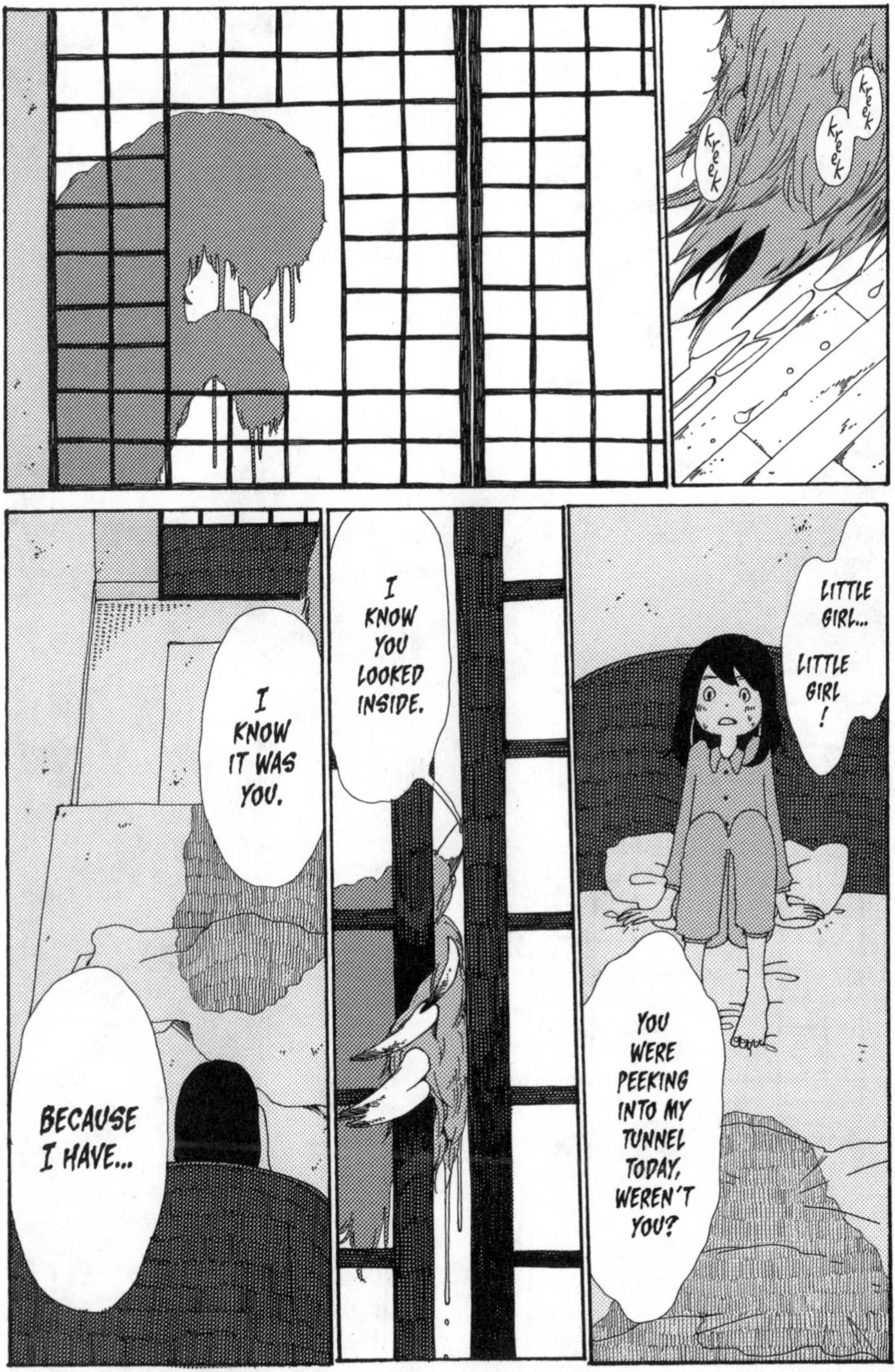
kreek
kreek
kreek
LITTLE GIRL... LITTLE GIRL!
YOU WERE PEEKING INTO MY TUNNEL TODAY, WEREN'T YOU?
I KNOW YOU LOOKED INSIDE.
I KNOW IT WAS YOU.
BECAUSE I HAVE...

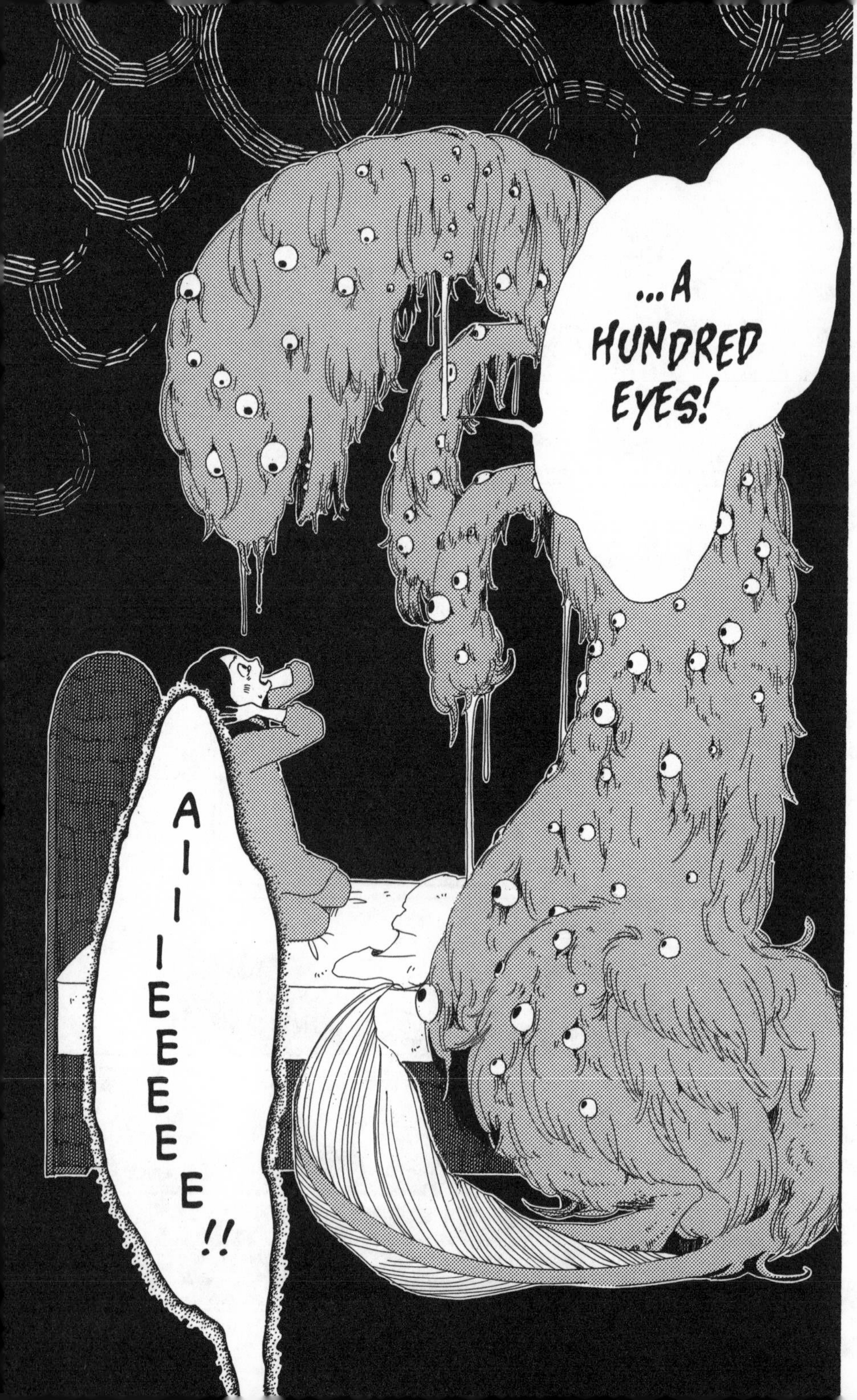
...A HUNDRED EYES!
AIIIEEEEE!!

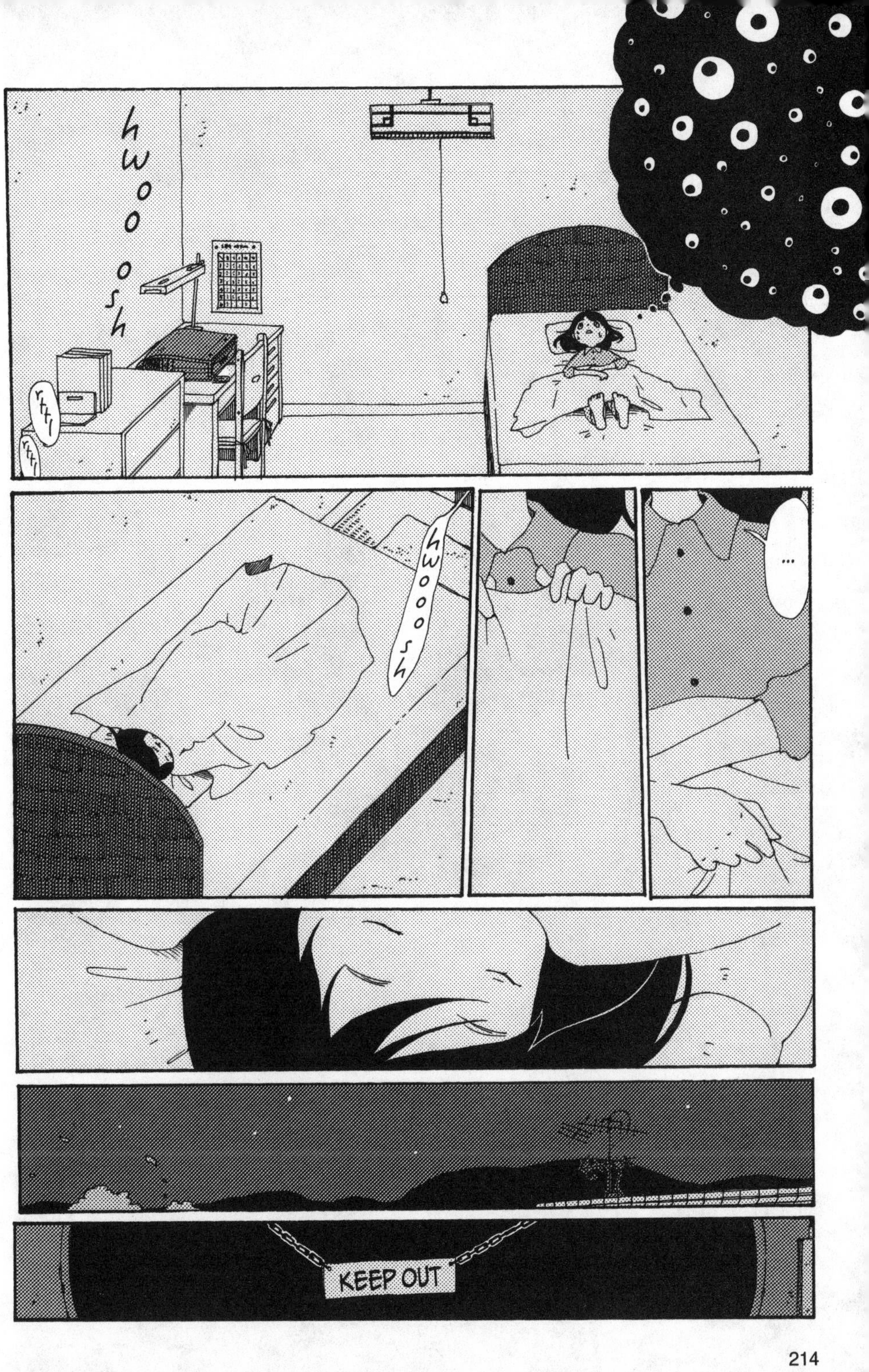
hwooosh
rxxl
rxxl
...
hwooo sh
KEEP OUT

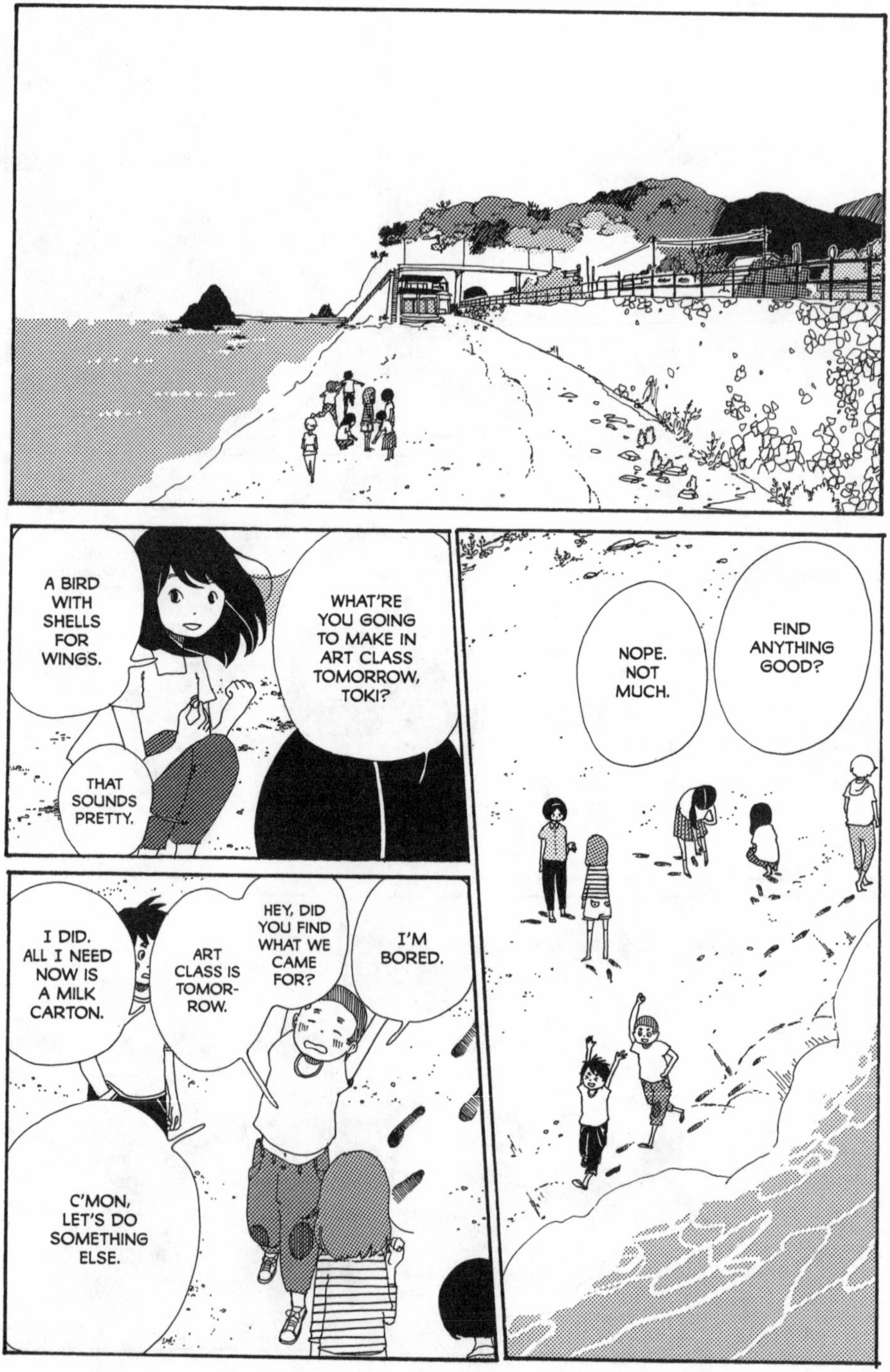
FIND ANYTHING GOOD?
NOPE. NOT MUCH.
WHAT'RE YOU GOING TO MAKE IN ART CLASS TOMORROW, TOKI?
A BIRD WITH SHELLS FOR WINGS.
THAT SOUNDS PRETTY.
I'M BORED.
HEY, DID YOU FIND WHAT WE CAME FOR?
ART CLASS IS TOMOR-ROW.
I DID. ALL I NEED NOW IS A MILK CARTON.
C'MON, LET'S DO SOMETHING ELSE.

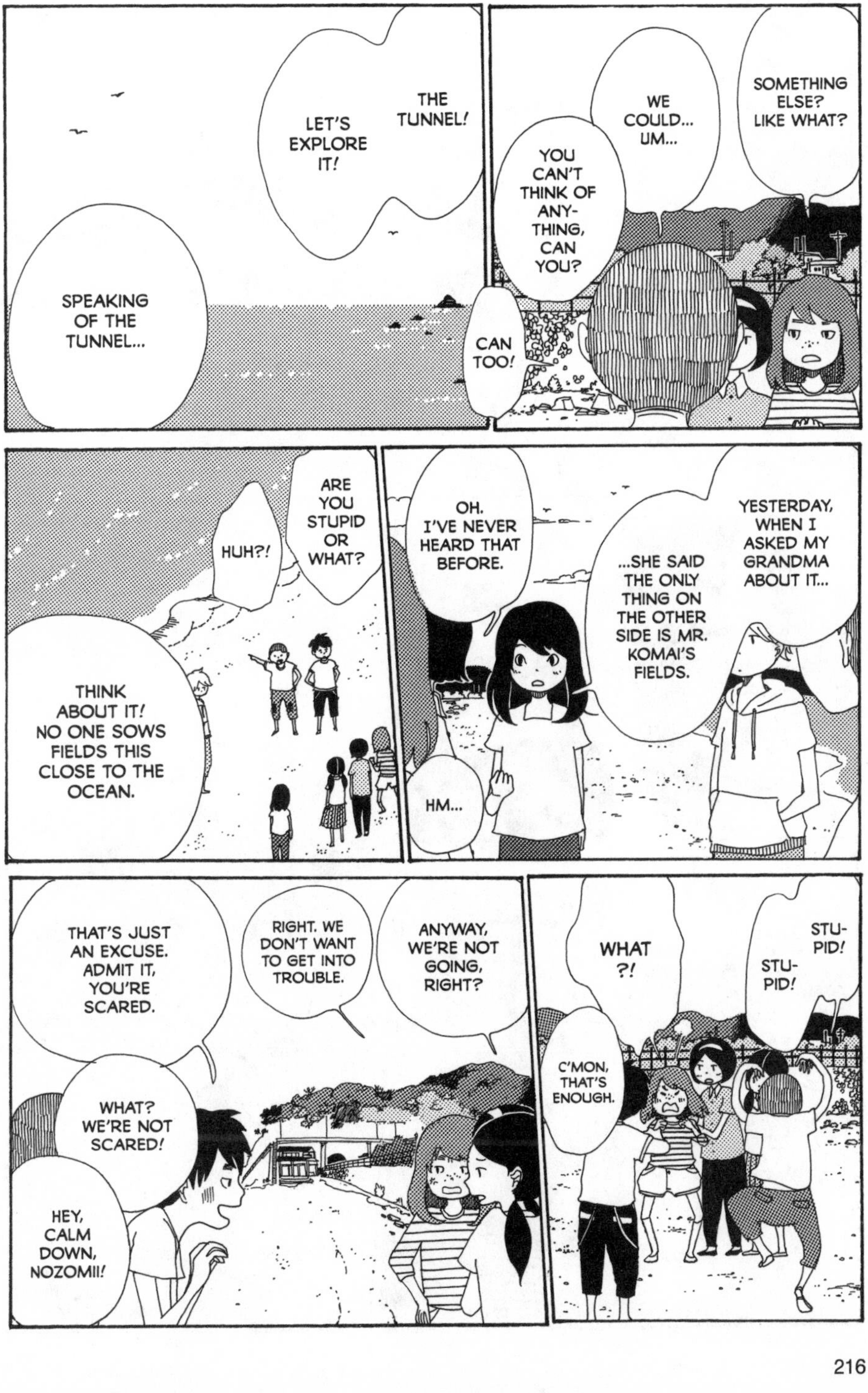
SOMETHING ELSE? LIKE WHAT?
WE COULD... UM...
YOU CAN'T THINK OF ANY-THING, CAN YOU?
CAN TOO!
THE TUNNEL!
LET'S EXPLORE IT!
SPEAKING OF THE TUNNEL...
YESTERDAY, WHEN I ASKED MY GRANDMA ABOUT IT...
...SHE SAID THE ONLY THING ON THE OTHER SIDE IS MR. KOMAI'S FIELDS.
OH. I'VE NEVER HEARD THAT BEFORE.
HM...
ARE YOU STUPID OR WHAT?
HUH?!
THINK ABOUT IT! NO ONE SOWS FIELDS THIS CLOSE TO THE OCEAN.
STU-PID!
STU-PID!
WHAT?!
C'MON, THAT'S ENOUGH.
ANYWAY, WE'RE NOT GOING, RIGHT?
RIGHT. WE DON'T WANT TO GET INTO TROUBLE.
THAT'S JUST AN EXCUSE. ADMIT IT, YOU'RE SCARED.
WHAT? WE'RE NOT SCARED!
HEY, CALM DOWN, NOZOMII!

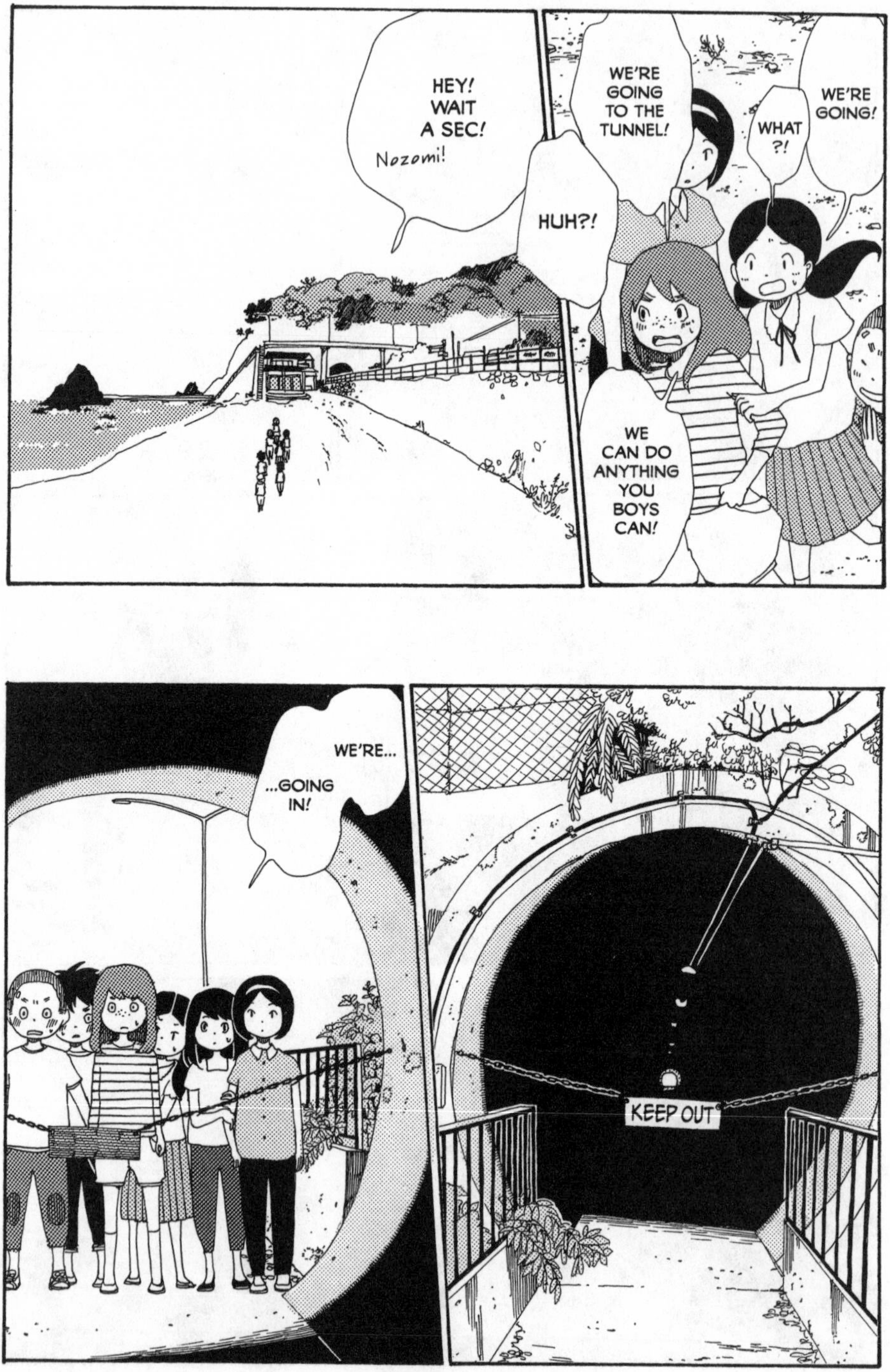

WE'RE GOING!
WHAT?!
WE'RE GOING TO THE TUNNEL!
HUH?!
WE CAN DO ANYTHING YOU BOYS CAN!
HEY! WAIT A SEC!
Nozomi!
KEEP OUT
WE'RE...
...GOING IN!

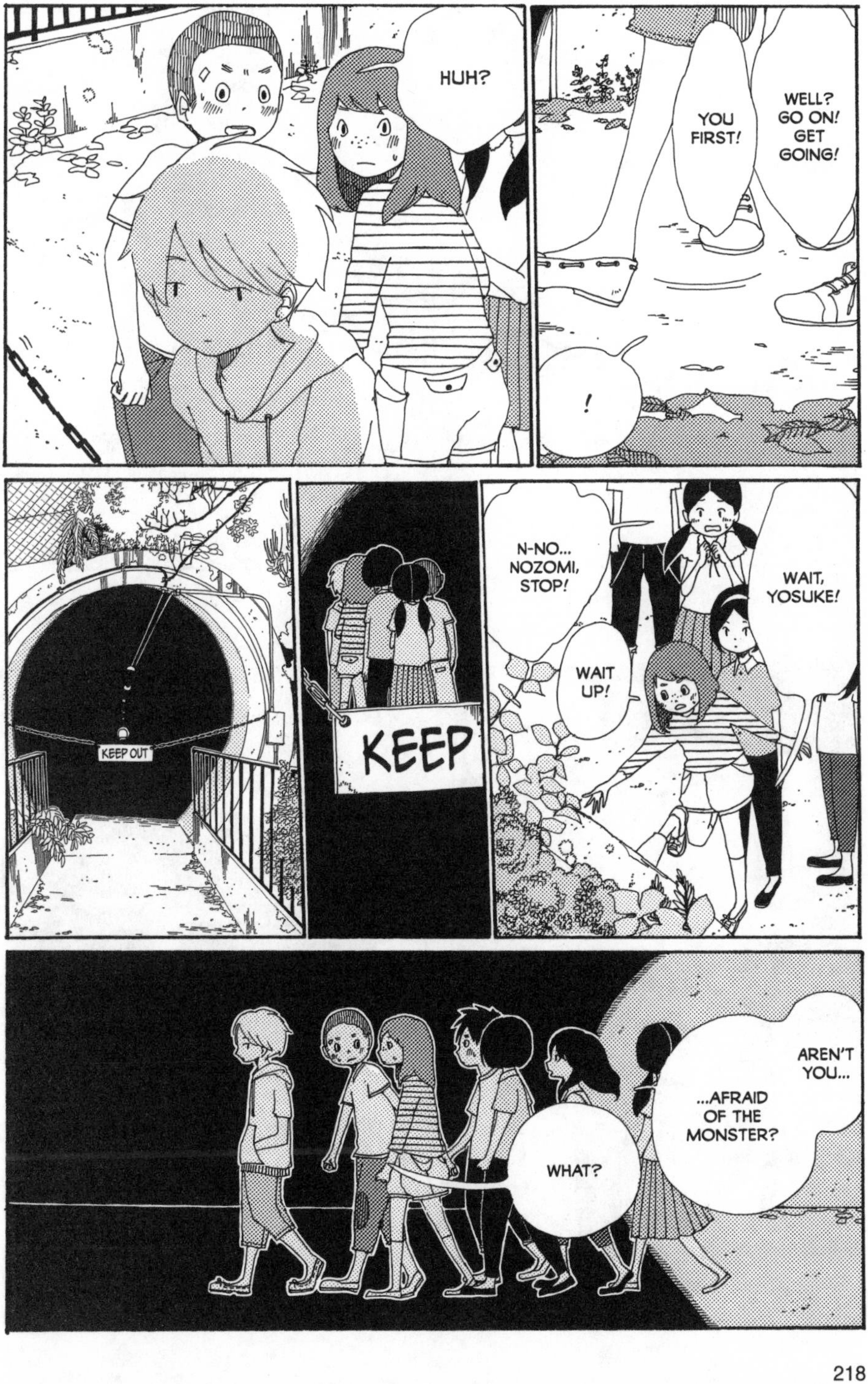

WELL? GO ON! GET GOING!
YOU FIRST!
!
HUH?
WAIT, YOSUKE!
N-NO... NOZOMI, STOP!
WAIT UP!
KEEP
KEEP OUT
AREN'T YOU...
...AFRAID OF THE MONSTER?
WHAT?

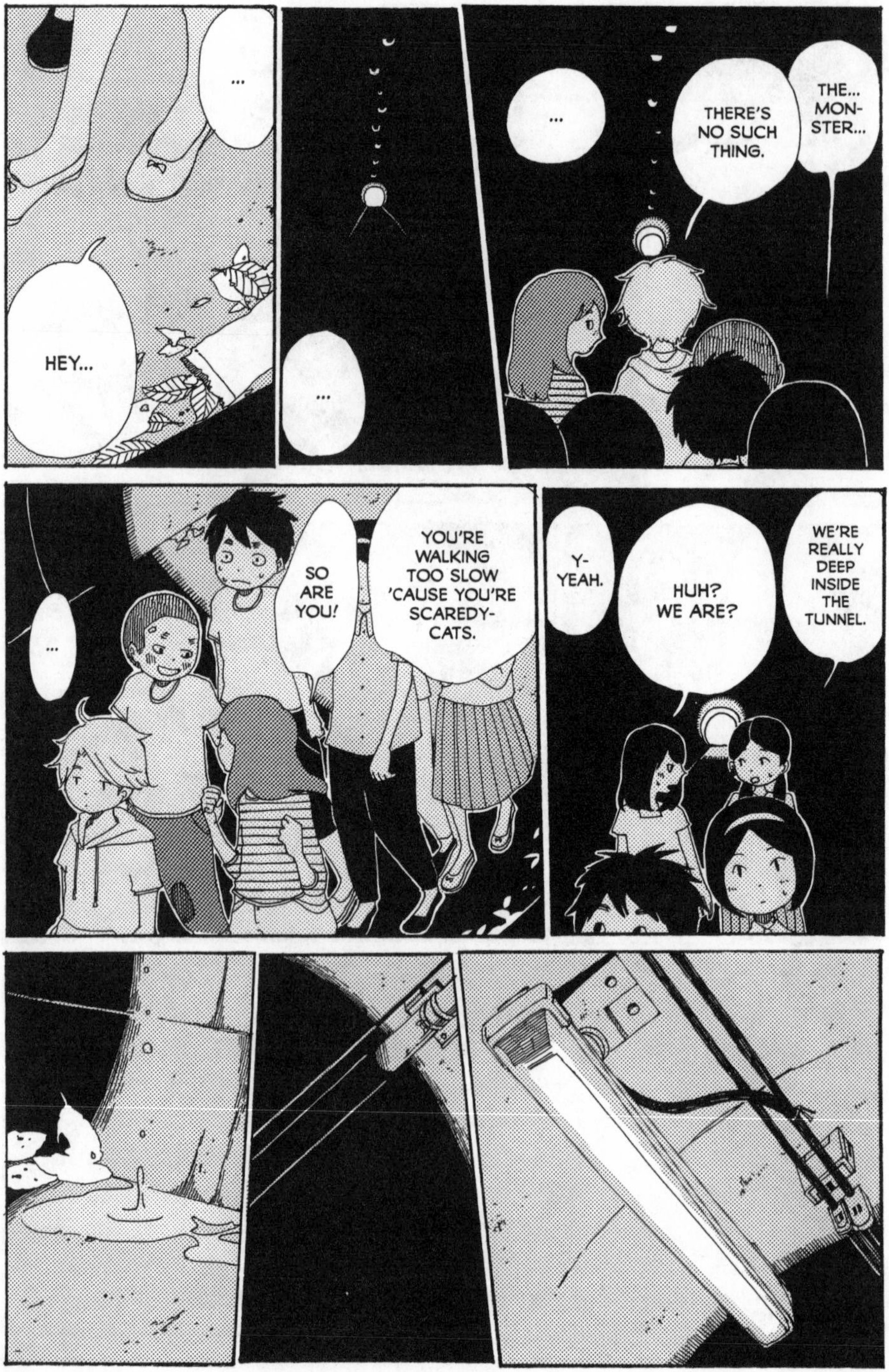
THE... MON-STER...
THERE'S NO SUCH THING.
...
...
...
HEY...
WE'RE REALLY DEEP INSIDE THE TUNNEL.
HUH? WE ARE?
Y-YEAH.
YOU'RE WALKING TOO SLOW 'CAUSE YOU'RE SCAREDY-CATS.
SO ARE YOU!
...

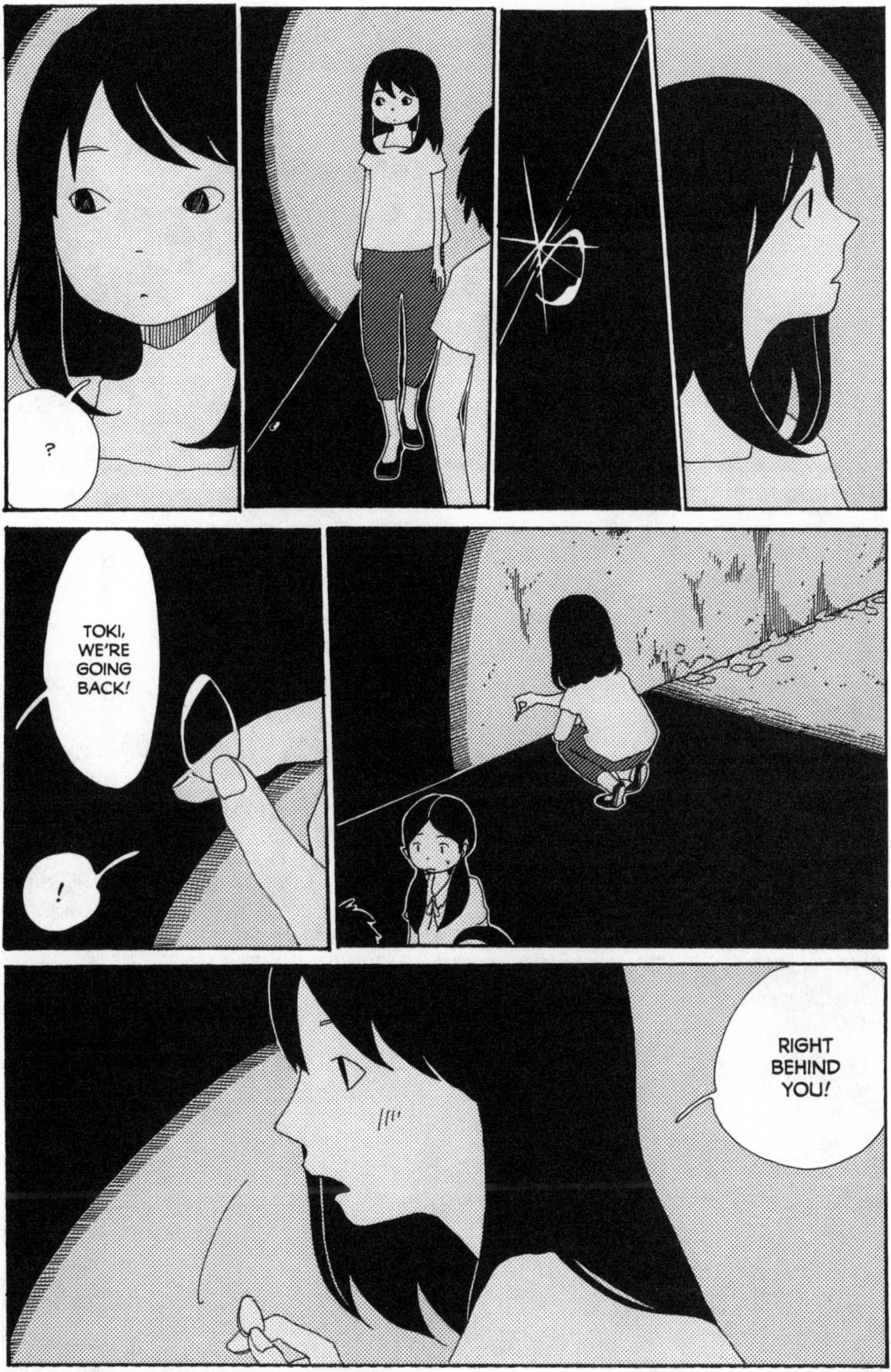
?
TOKI, WE'RE GOING BACK!
!
RIGHT BEHIND YOU!

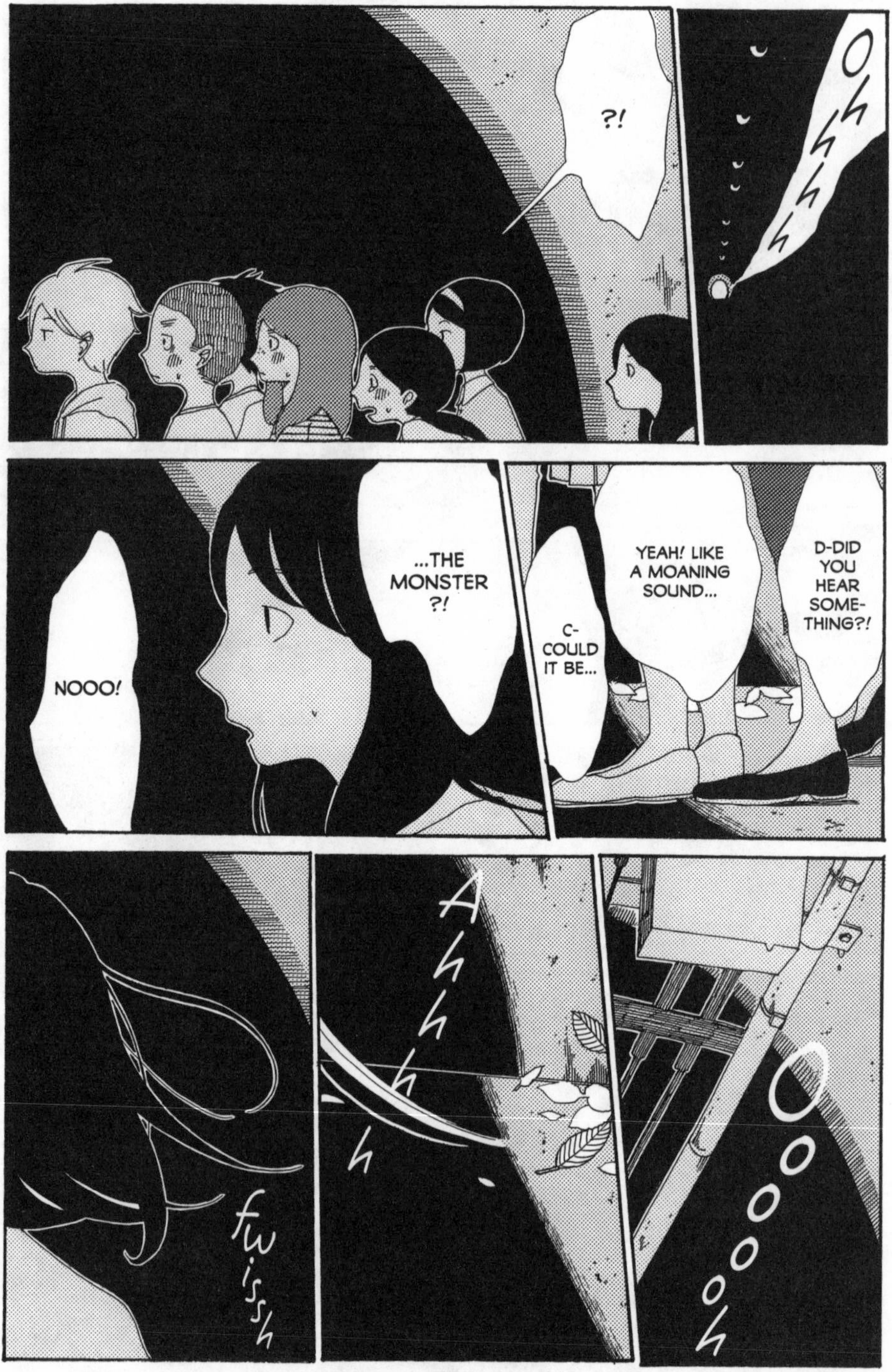
Ohhhhh
?!
D-DID YOU HEAR SOME-THING?!
YEAH! LIKE A MOANING SOUND...
C-COULD IT BE...
...THE MONSTER?!
NOOO!
Ooooooh
Ahhhhh
fwissh

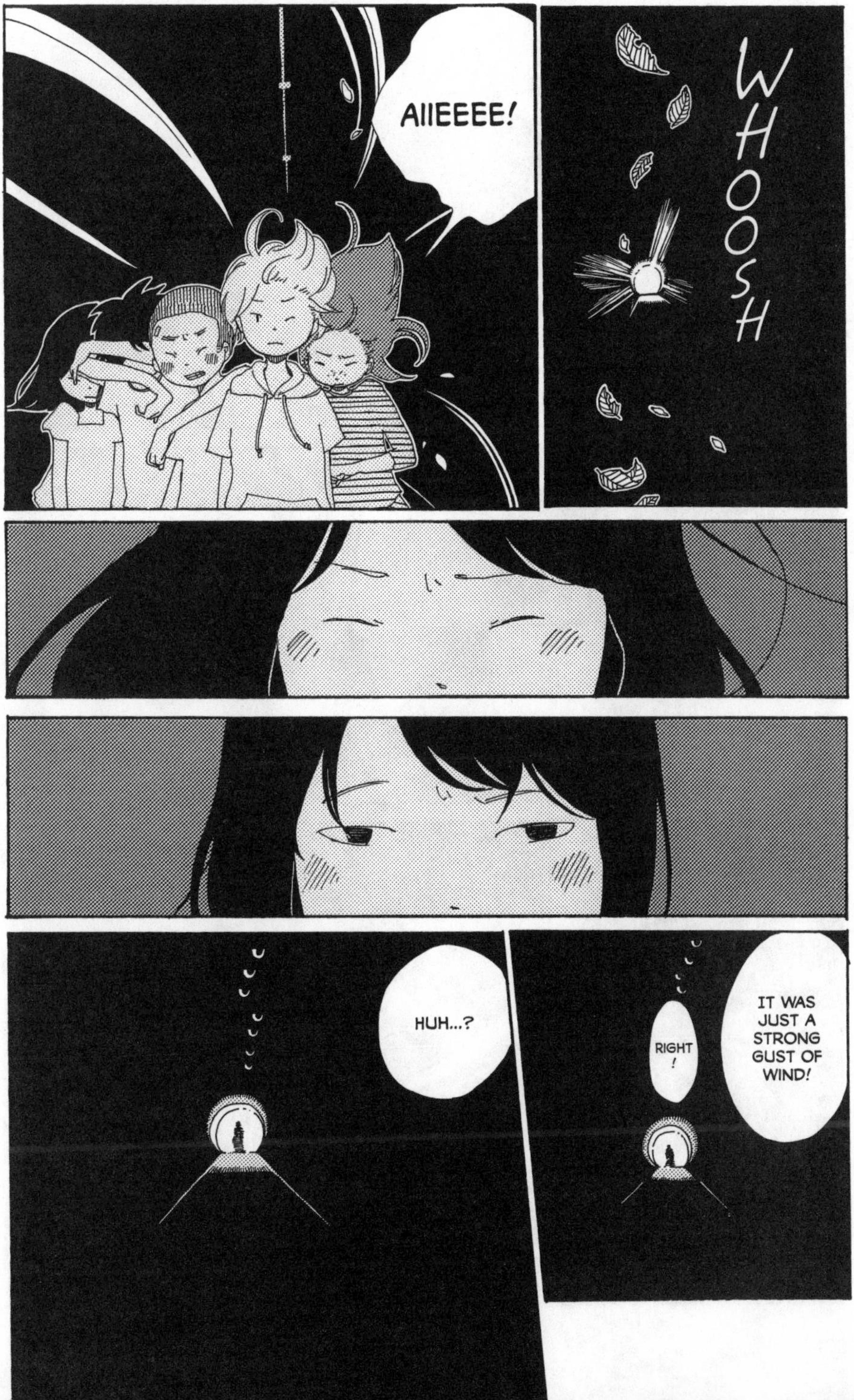
WHOOSH
AIIEEEE!
IT WAS JUST A STRONG GUST OF WIND!
RIGHT!
HUH...?

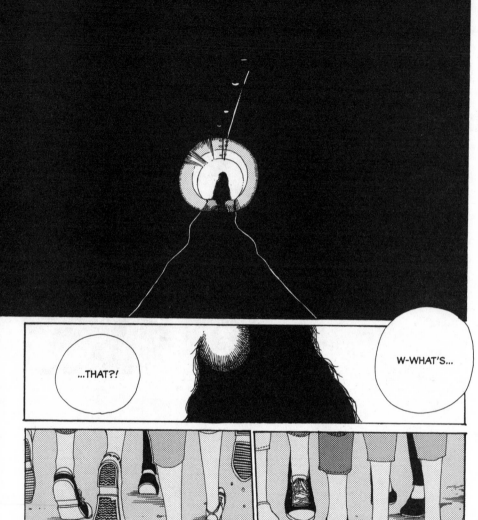

...THAT?!

W-WHAT'S...

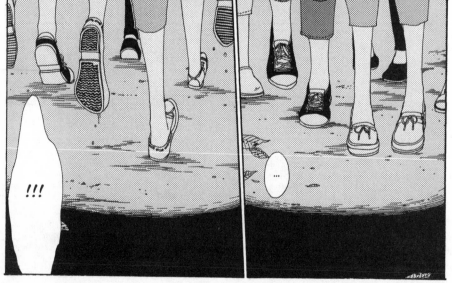

!!!

...

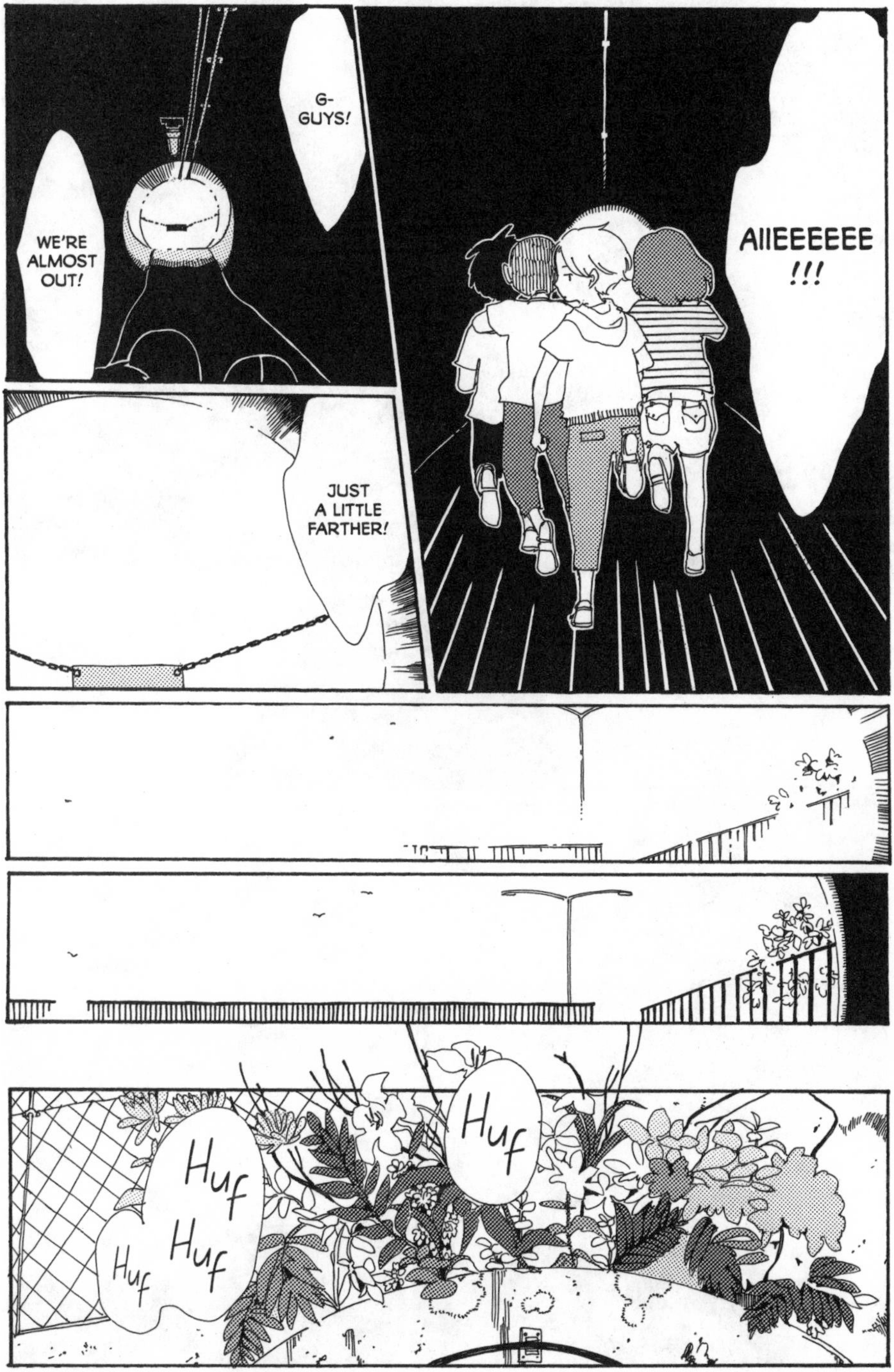
AIIEEEEEE!!!
G-GUYS!
WE'RE ALMOST OUT!
JUST A LITTLE FARTHER!
Huf
Huf Huf
Huf

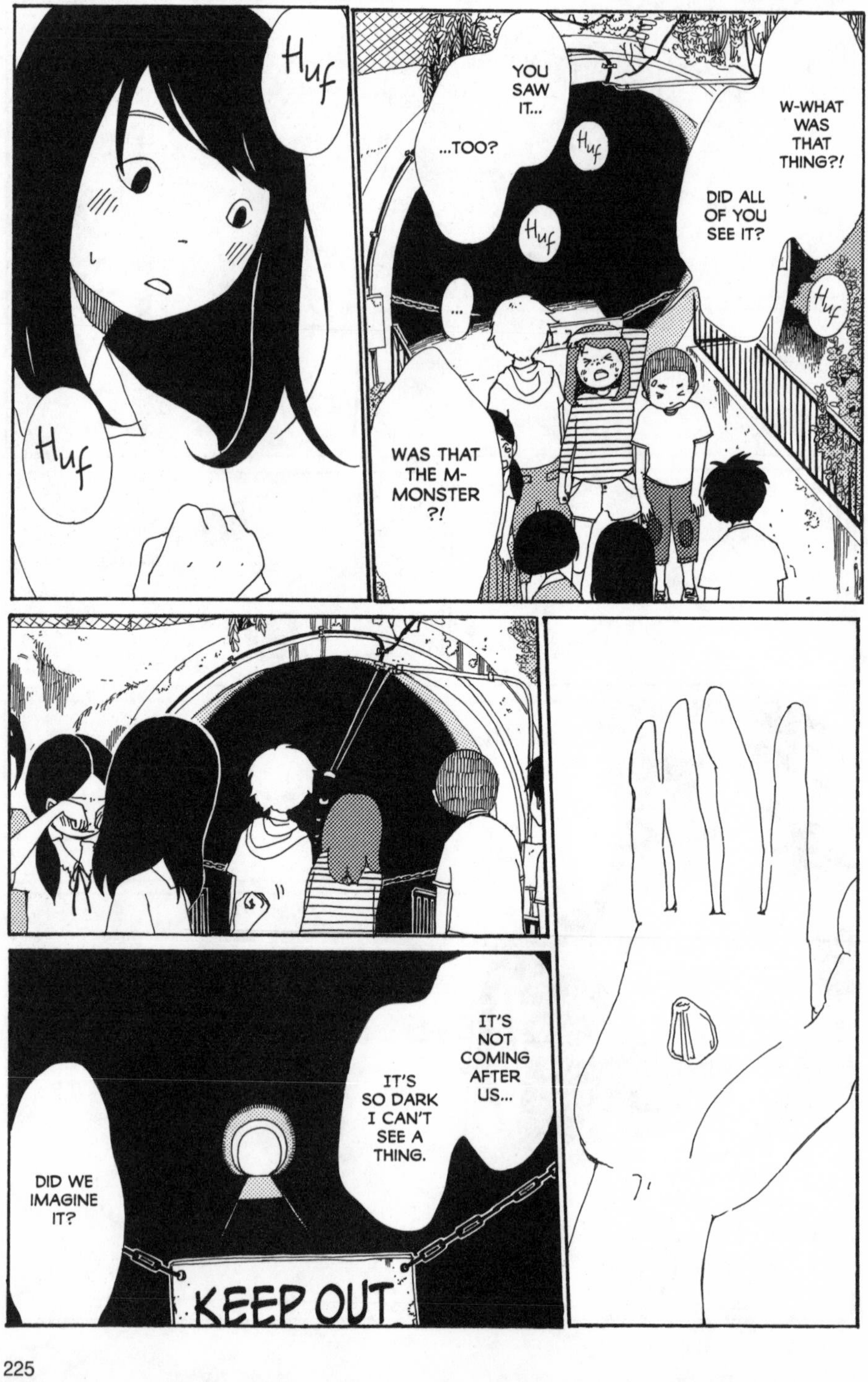
W-WHAT WAS THAT THING?!
DID ALL OF YOU SEE IT?
Huf
YOU SAW IT...
...TOO?
Huf
Huf
...
WAS THAT THE M-MONSTER?!
Huf
Huf
IT'S NOT COMING AFTER US...
IT'S SO DARK I CAN'T SEE A THING.
DID WE IMAGINE IT?
KEEP OUT

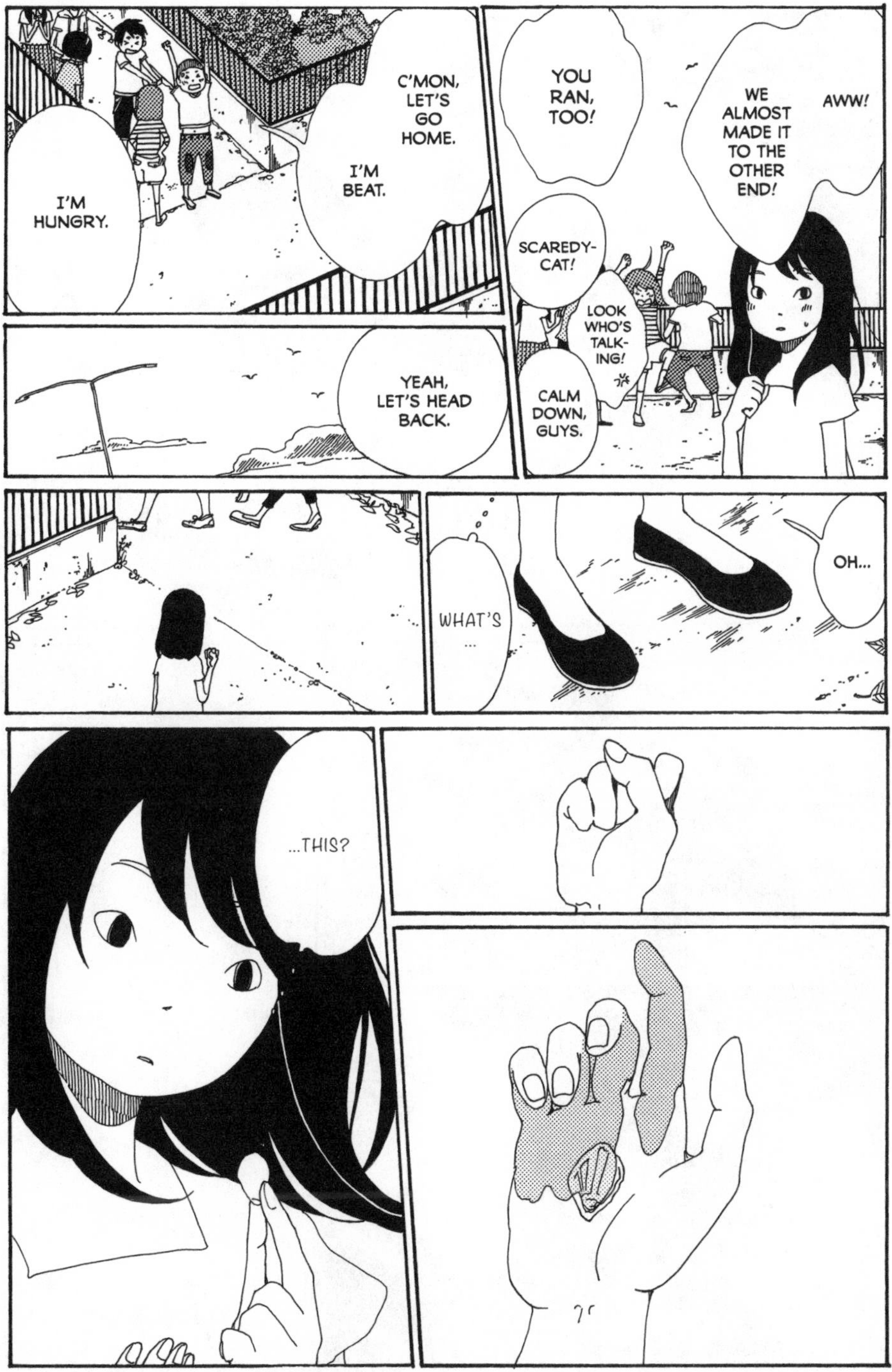
AWW!
WE ALMOST MADE IT TO THE OTHER END!
YOU RAN, TOO!
SCAREDY-CAT!
LOOK WHO'S TALKING!
CALM DOWN, GUYS.
C'MON, LET'S GO HOME.
I'M BEAT.
I'M HUNGRY.
YEAH, LET'S HEAD BACK.
OH...
WHAT'S ...
...THIS?

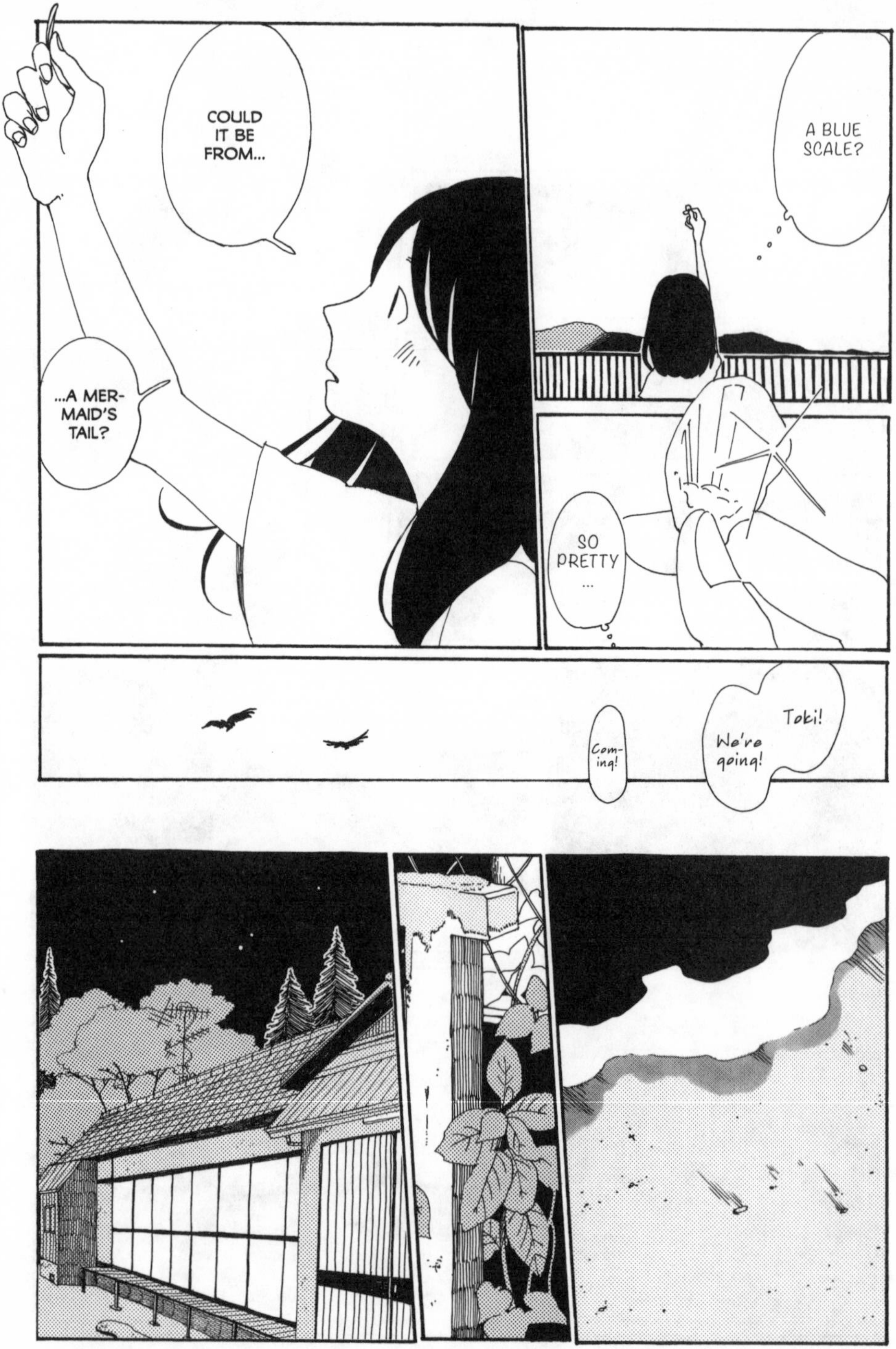
A BLUE SCALE?
SO PRETTY ...
COULD IT BE FROM...
...A MERMAID'S TAIL?
Toki! We're going!
Coming!

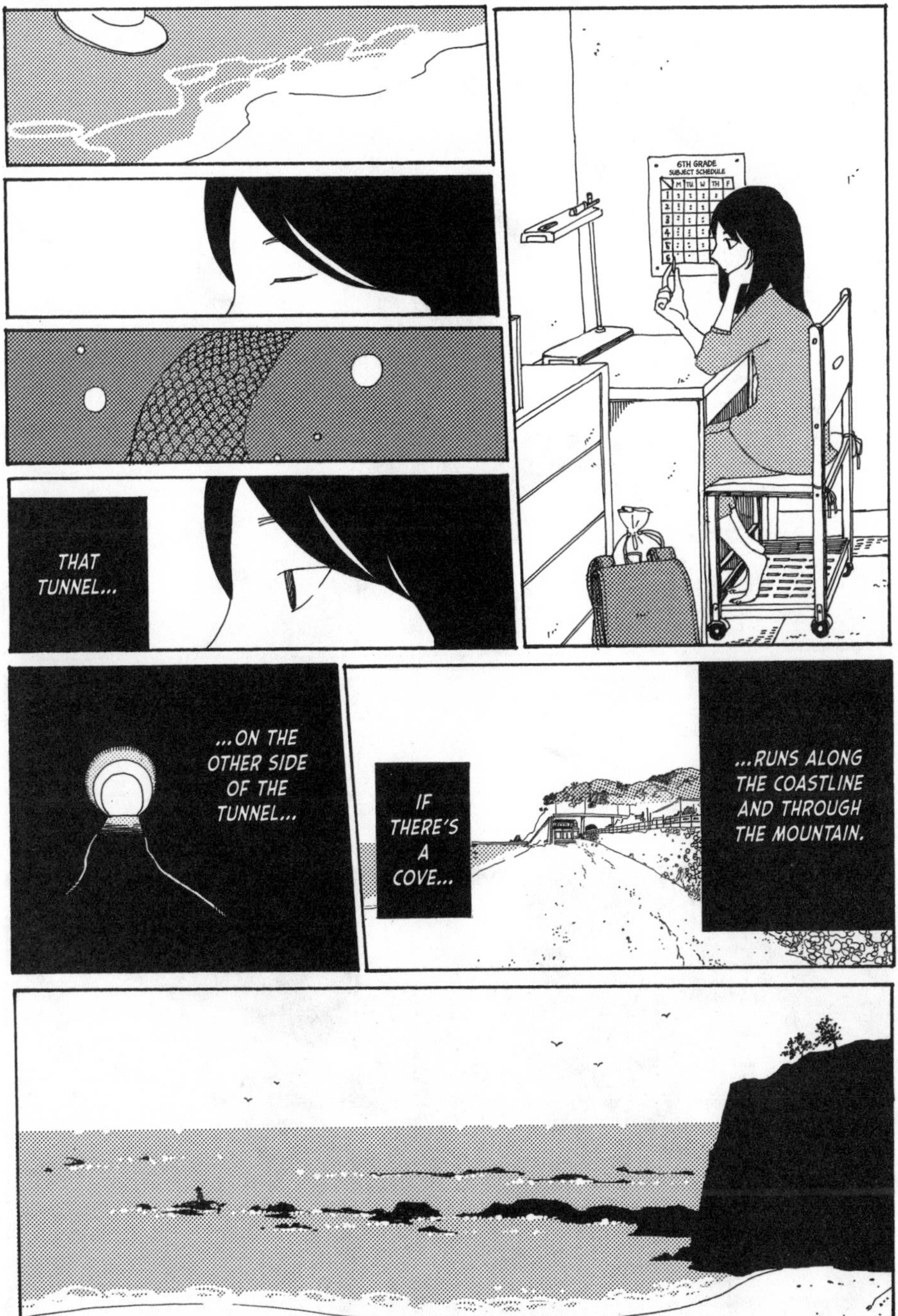
6TH GRADE
SUBJECT SCHEDULE
M TU W TH F
THAT TUNNEL...
...RUNS ALONG THE COASTLINE AND THROUGH THE MOUNTAIN.
IF THERE'S A COVE...
...ON THE OTHER SIDE OF THE TUNNEL...

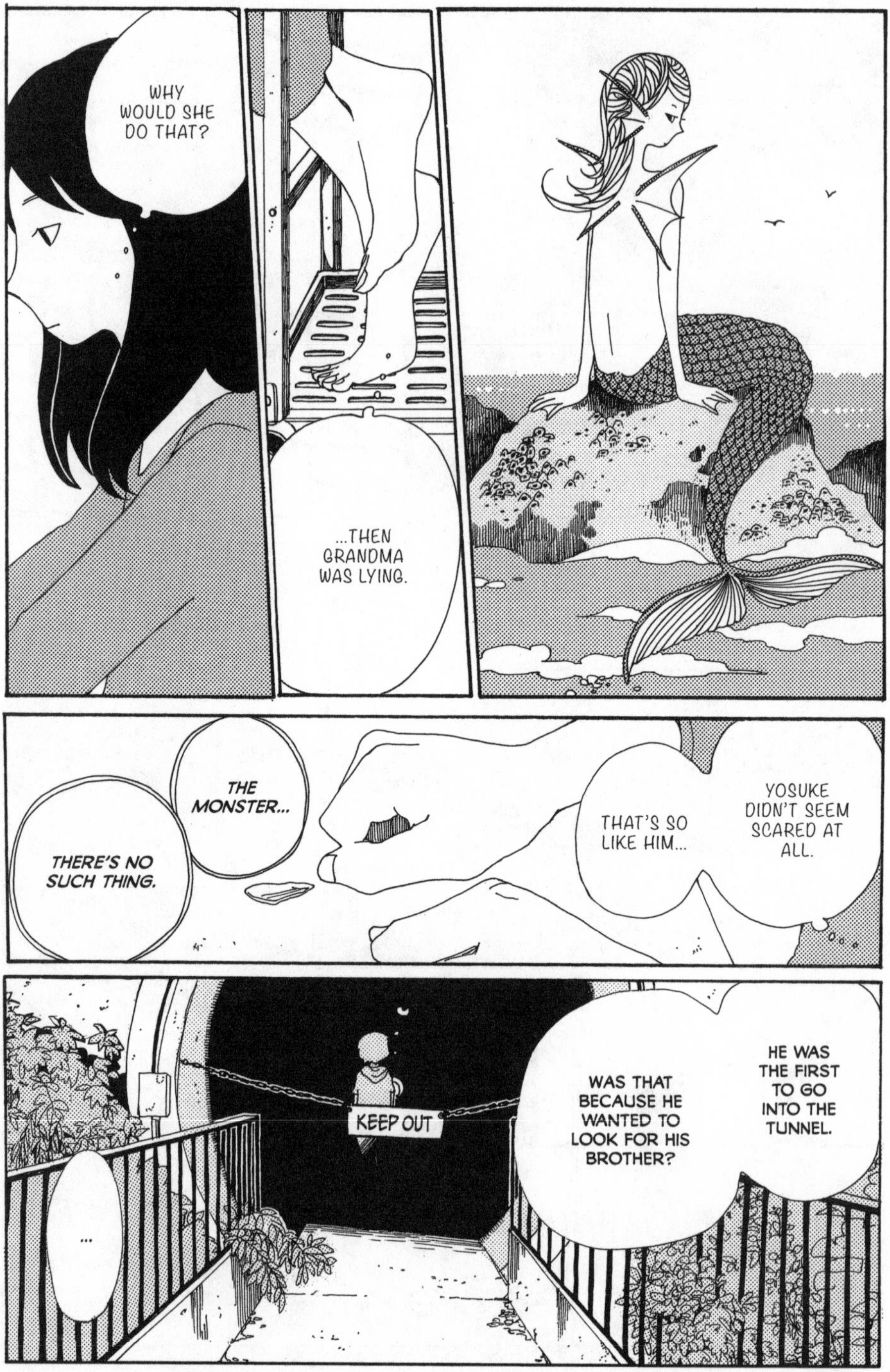
...THEN GRANDMA WAS LYING.
WHY WOULD SHE DO THAT?
YOSUKE DIDN'T SEEM SCARED AT ALL.
THAT'S SO LIKE HIM...
THE MONSTER...
THERE'S NO SUCH THING.
HE WAS THE FIRST TO GO INTO THE TUNNEL.
WAS THAT BECAUSE HE WANTED TO LOOK FOR HIS BROTHER?
KEEP OUT
...

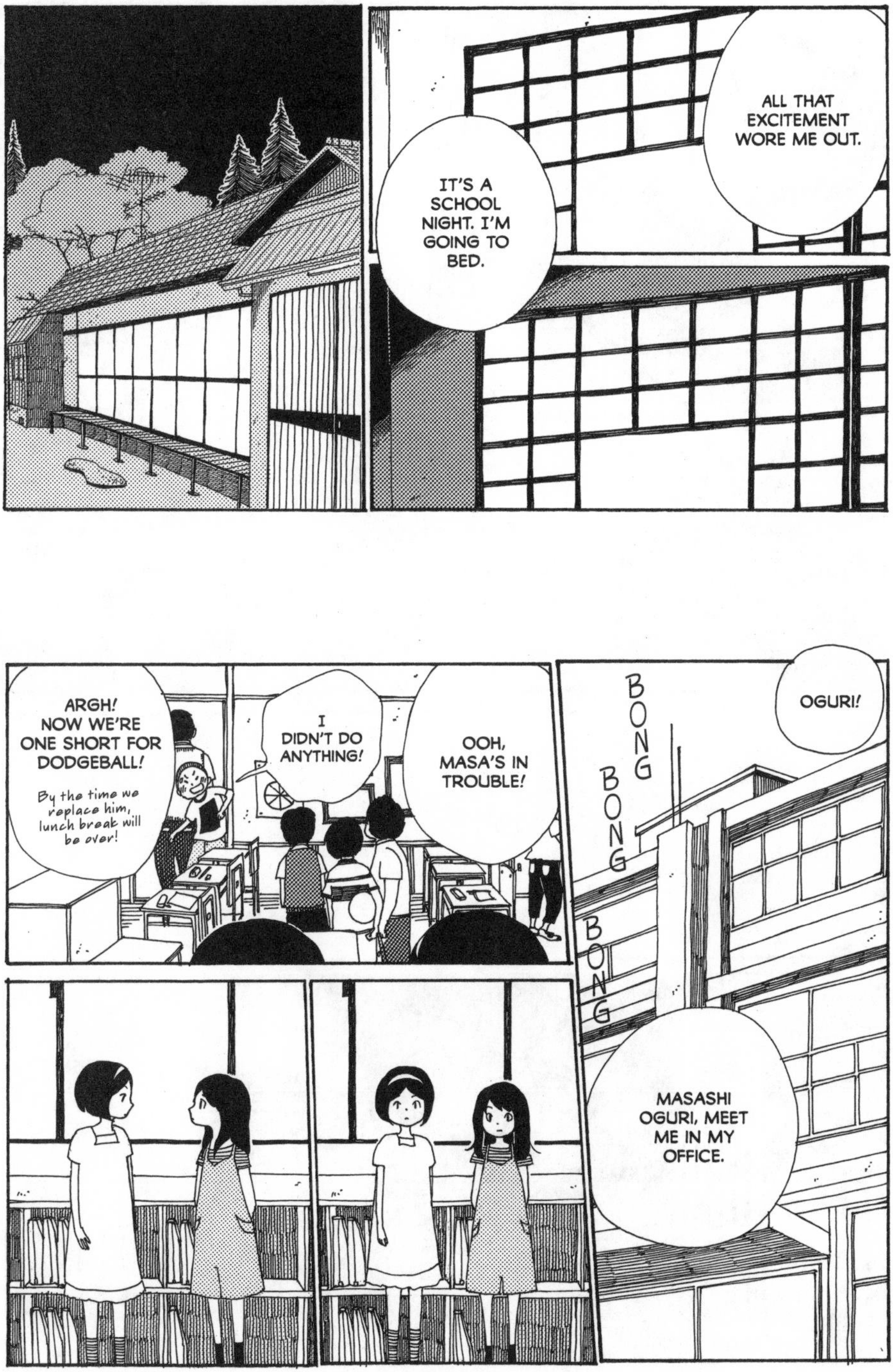
ALL THAT EXCITEMENT WORE ME OUT.
IT'S A SCHOOL NIGHT. I'M GOING TO BED.
BONG BONG BONG
OGURI!
MASASHI OGURI, MEET ME IN MY OFFICE.
OOH, MASA'S IN TROUBLE!
I DIDN'T DO ANYTHING!
ARGH! NOW WE'RE ONE SHORT FOR DODGEBALL!
By the time we replace him, lunch break will be over!

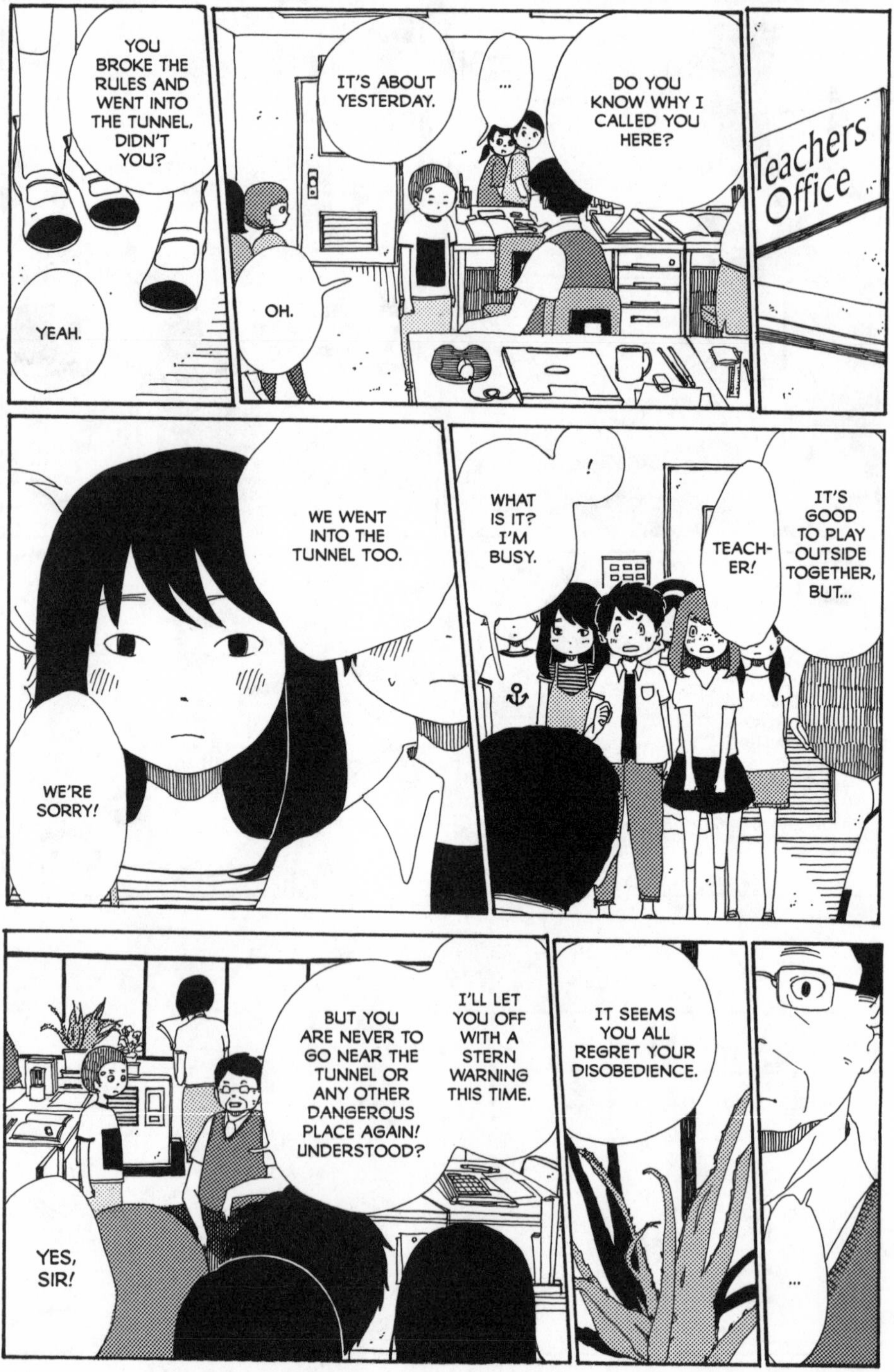
Teachers Office
DO YOU KNOW WHY I CALLED YOU HERE?
...
IT'S ABOUT YESTERDAY.
OH.
YOU BROKE THE RULES AND WENT INTO THE TUNNEL, DIDN'T YOU?
YEAH.
IT'S GOOD TO PLAY OUTSIDE TOGETHER, BUT...
TEACH-ER!
!
WHAT IS IT? I'M BUSY.
WE WENT INTO THE TUNNEL TOO.
WE'RE SORRY!
...
IT SEEMS YOU ALL REGRET YOUR DISOBEDIENCE.
I'LL LET YOU OFF WITH A STERN WARNING THIS TIME.
BUT YOU ARE NEVER TO GO NEAR THE TUNNEL OR ANY OTHER DANGEROUS PLACE AGAIN! UNDERSTOOD?
YES, SIR!

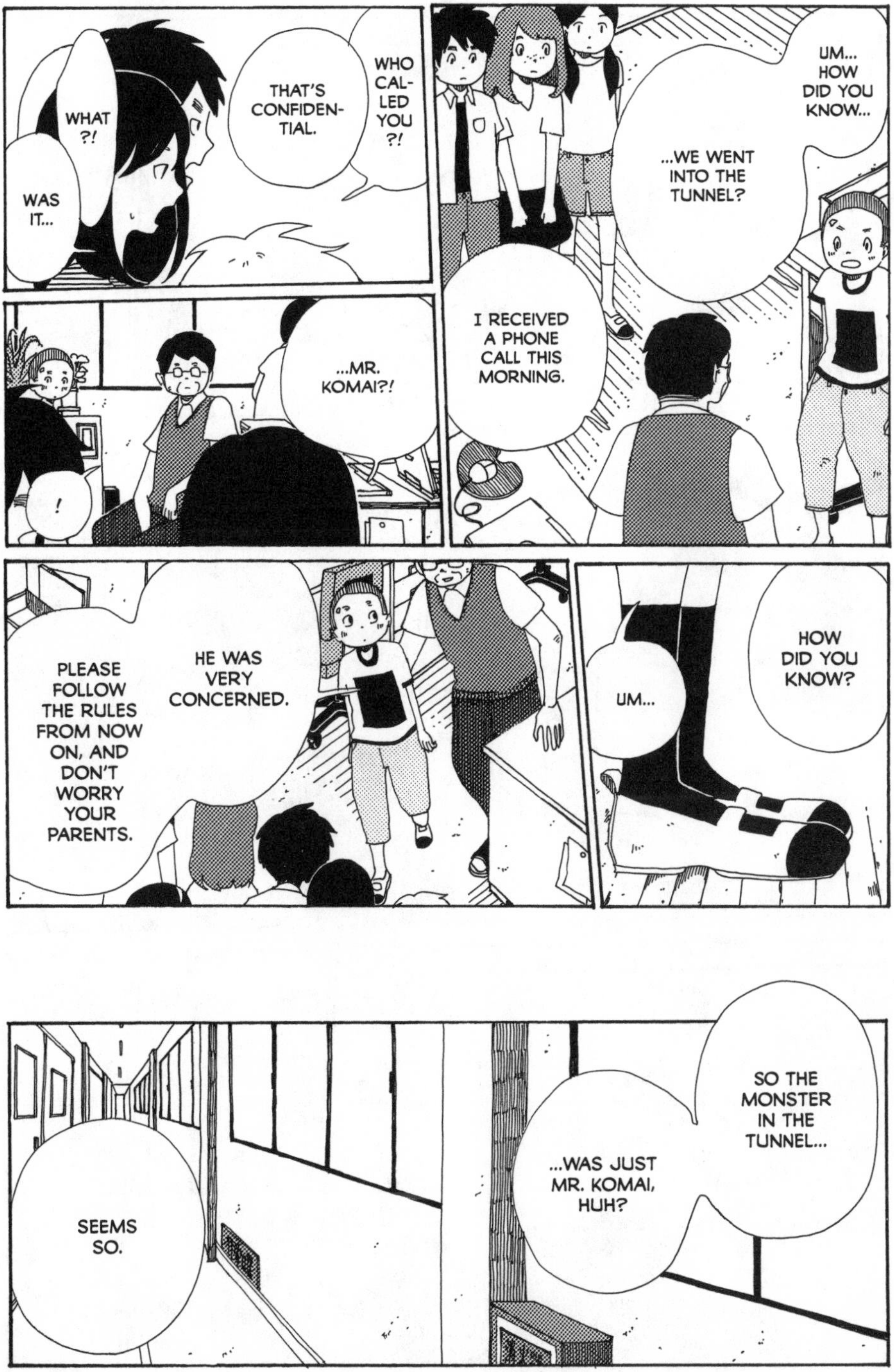
UM... HOW DID YOU KNOW...
...WE WENT INTO THE TUNNEL?
I RECEIVED A PHONE CALL THIS MORNING.
WHO CALLED YOU ?!
THAT'S CONFIDENTIAL.
WHAT ?!
WAS IT...
...MR. KOMAI?!
!
HOW DID YOU KNOW?
UM...
HE WAS VERY CONCERNED.
PLEASE FOLLOW THE RULES FROM NOW ON, AND DON'T WORRY YOUR PARENTS.
SO THE MONSTER IN THE TUNNEL...
...WAS JUST MR. KOMAI, HUH?
SEEMS SO.

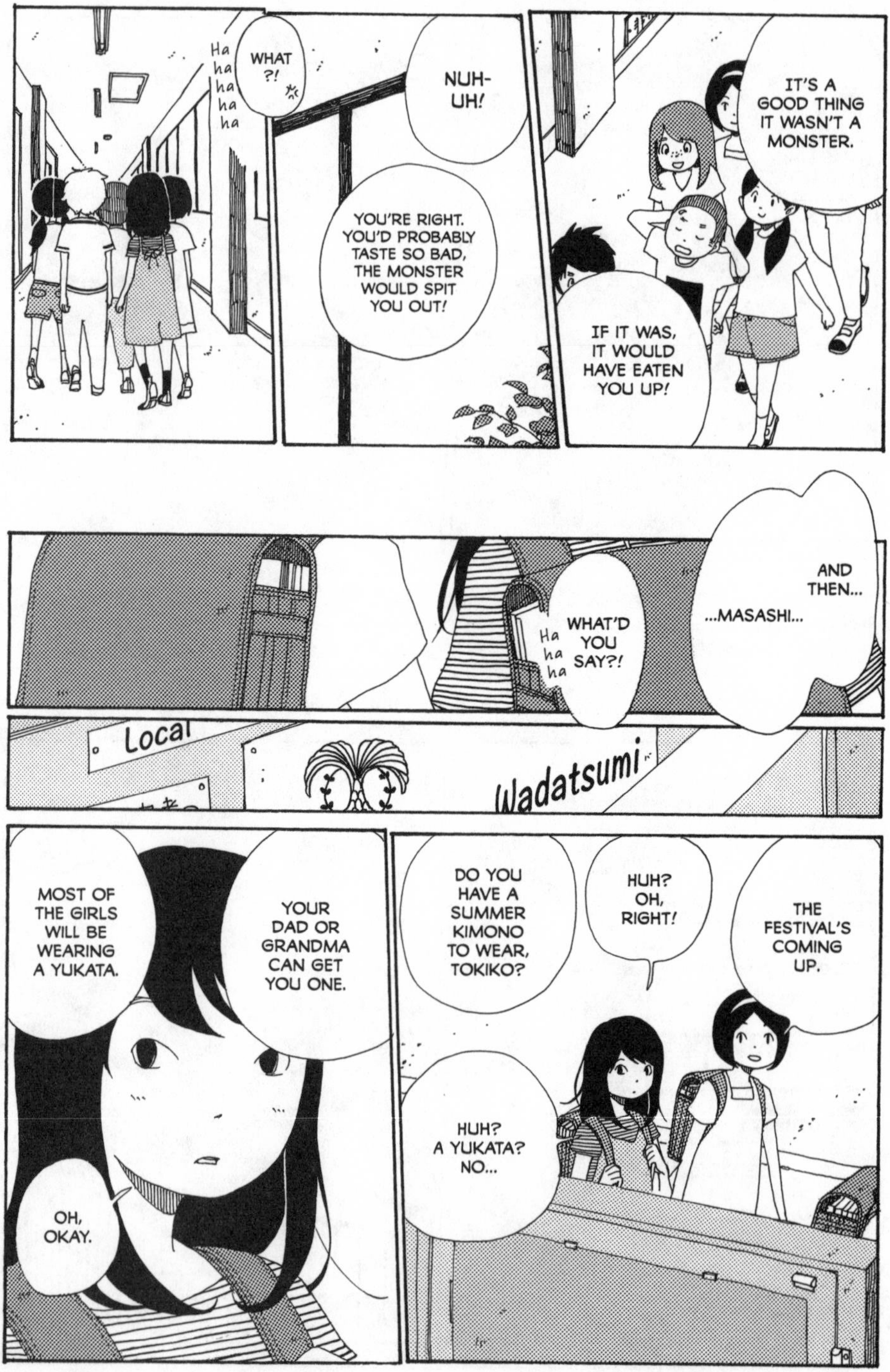
IT'S A GOOD THING IT WASN'T A MONSTER.
IF IT WAS, IT WOULD HAVE EATEN YOU UP!
NUH-UH!
YOU'RE RIGHT. YOU'D PROBABLY TASTE SO BAD, THE MONSTER WOULD SPIT YOU OUT!
WHAT?!
Ha ha ha ha ha
AND THEN...
...MASASHI...
WHAT'D YOU SAY?!
Ha ha ha
Wadatsumi
Local
THE FESTIVAL'S COMING UP.
HUH? OH, RIGHT!
DO YOU HAVE A SUMMER KIMONO TO WEAR, TOKIKO?
HUH? A YUKATA? NO...
YOUR DAD OR GRANDMA CAN GET YOU ONE.
MOST OF THE GIRLS WILL BE WEARING A YUKATA.
OH, OKAY.

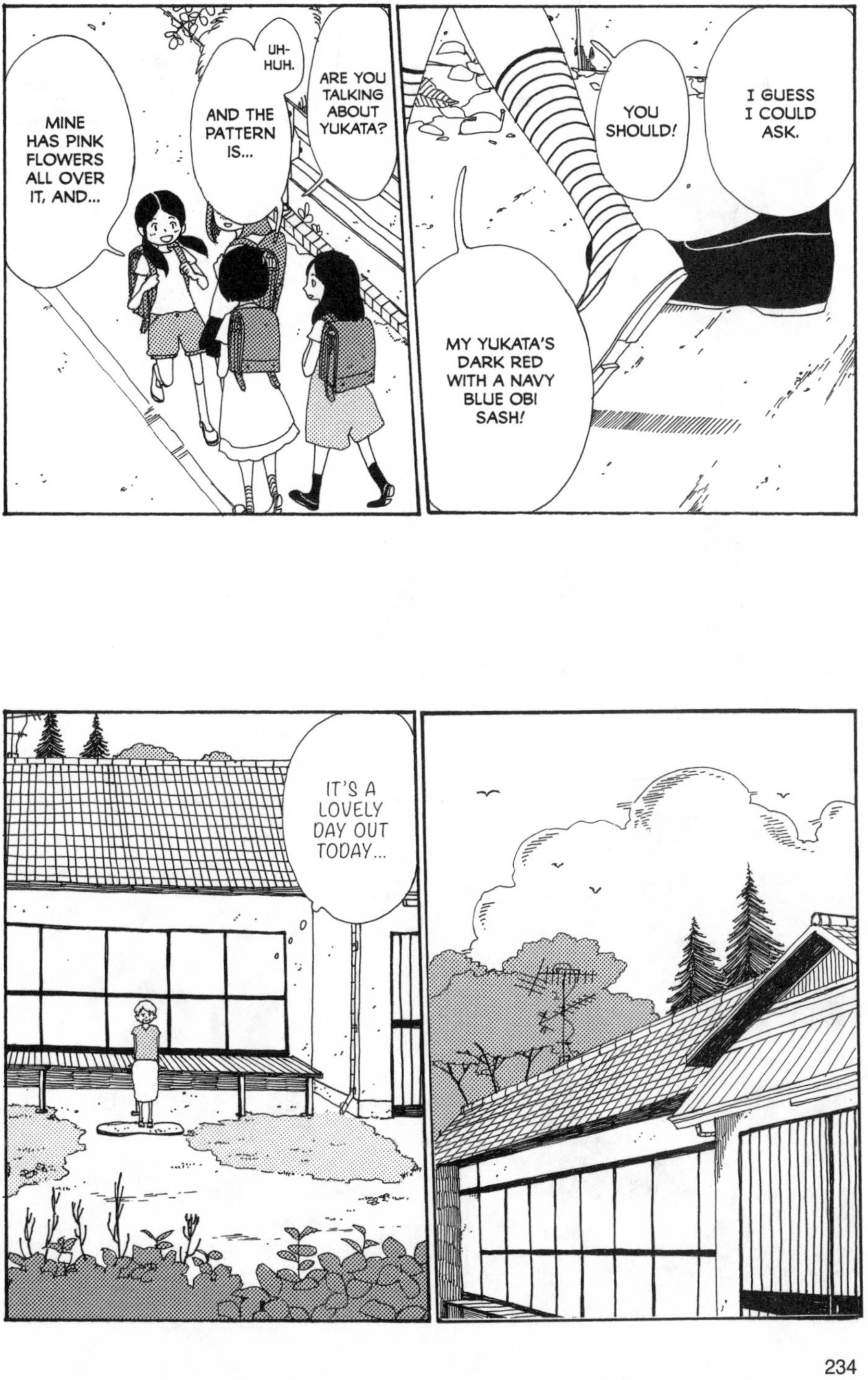
I GUESS I COULD ASK.
YOU SHOULD!
MY YUKATA'S DARK RED WITH A NAVY BLUE OBI SASH!
ARE YOU TALKING ABOUT YUKATA?
UH-HUH.
AND THE PATTERN IS...
MINE HAS PINK FLOWERS ALL OVER IT, AND...
IT'S A LOVELY DAY OUT TODAY...

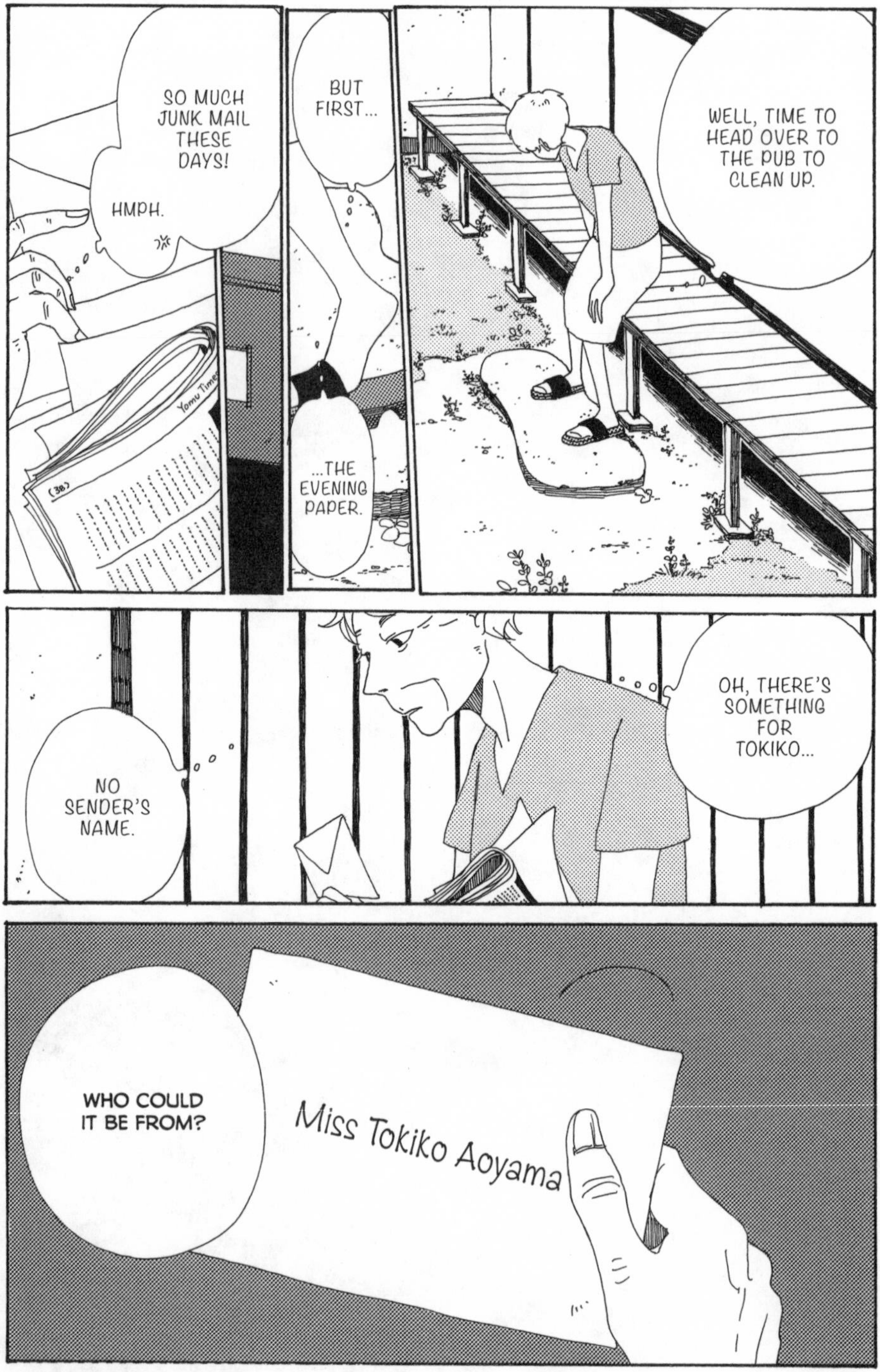
WELL, TIME TO HEAD OVER TO THE PUB TO CLEAN UP.
BUT FIRST...
...THE EVENING PAPER.
SO MUCH JUNK MAIL THESE DAYS!
HMPH.
Yomu Times
(38)
OH, THERE'S SOMETHING FOR TOKIKO...
NO SENDER'S NAME.
Miss Tokiko Aoyama
WHO COULD IT BE FROM?

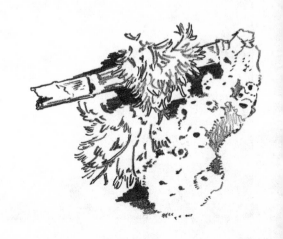

{Seven} Tide of Tears

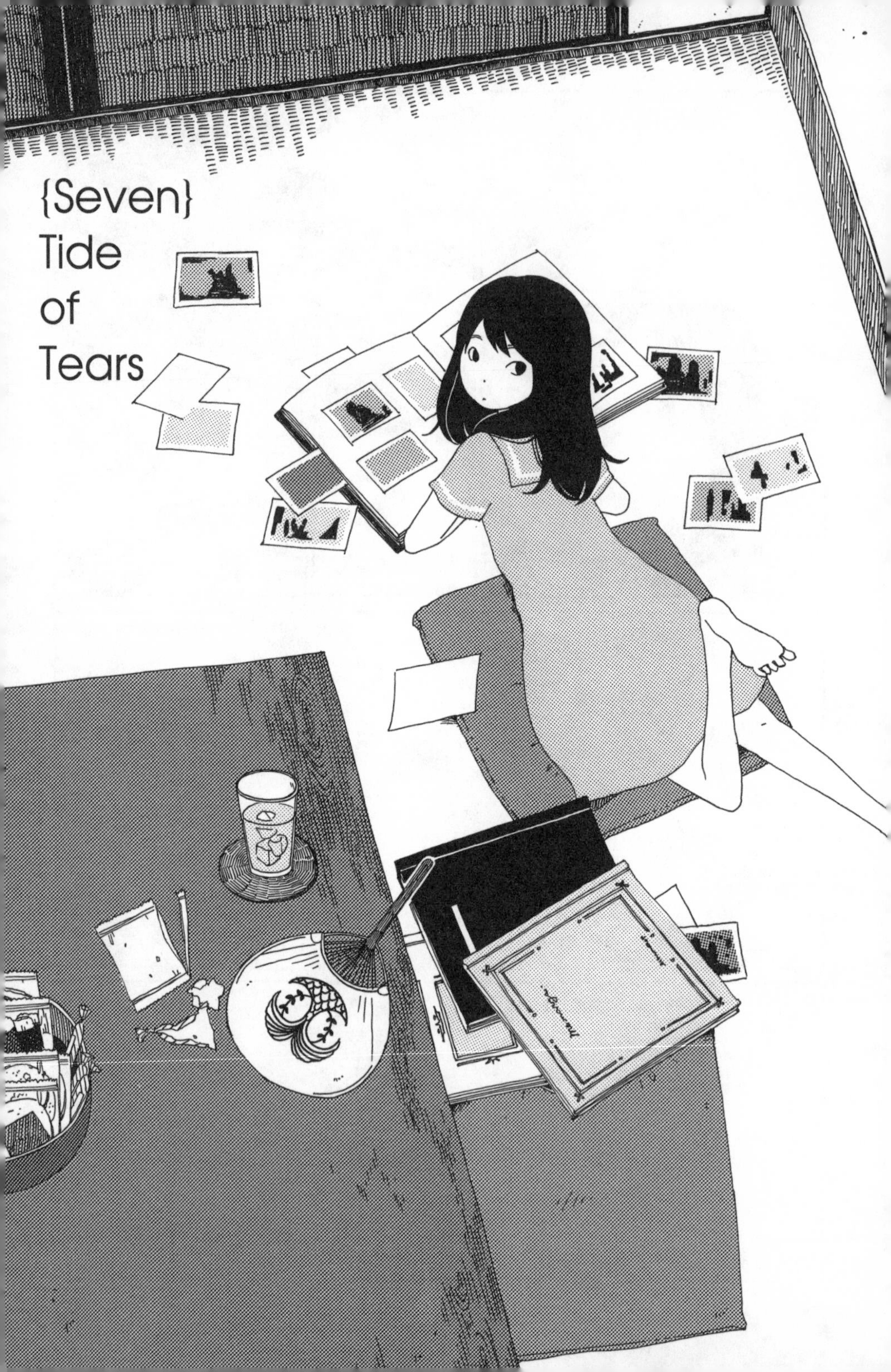

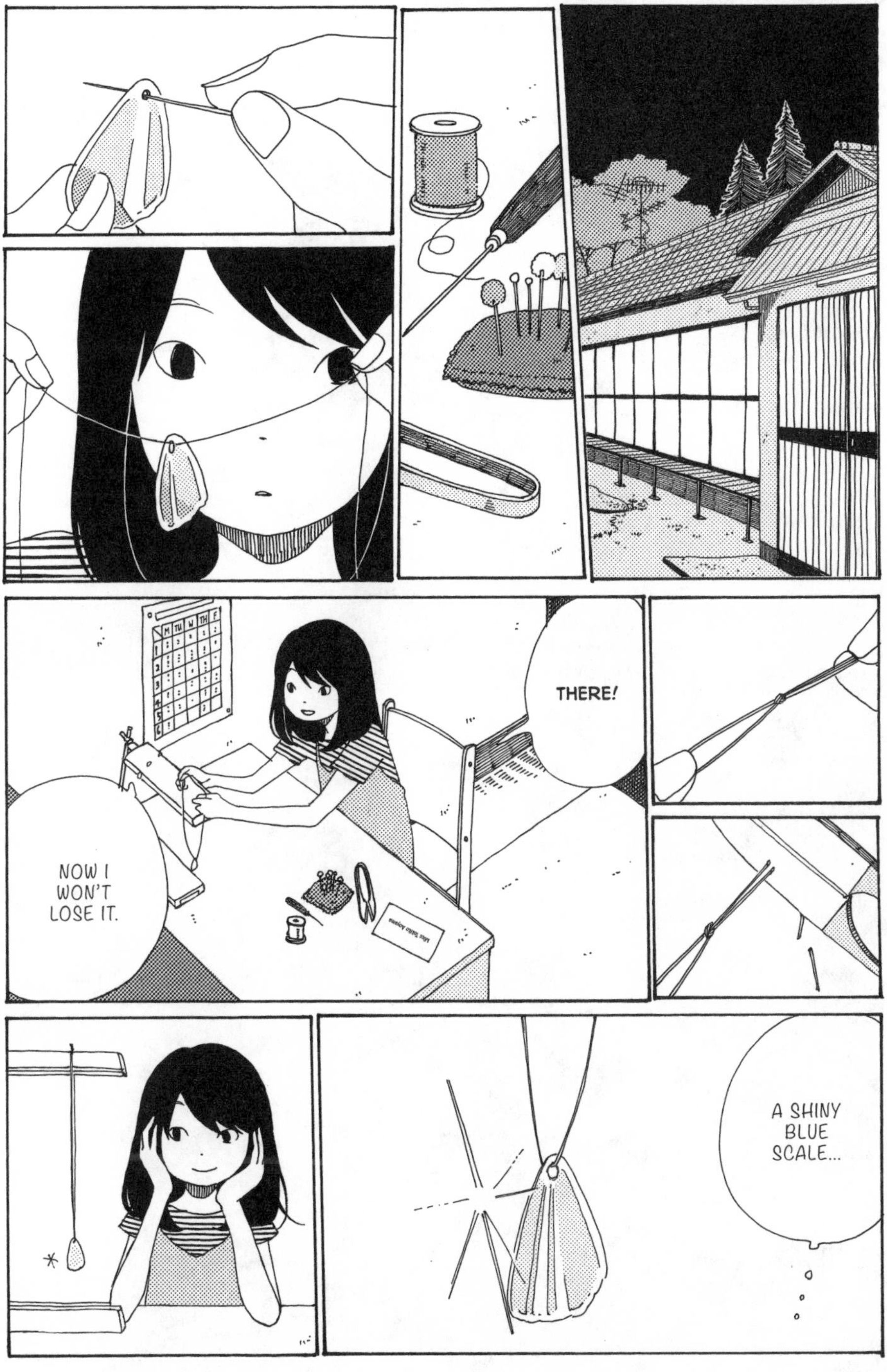
THERE!
NOW I WON'T LOSE IT.
A SHINY BLUE SCALE...

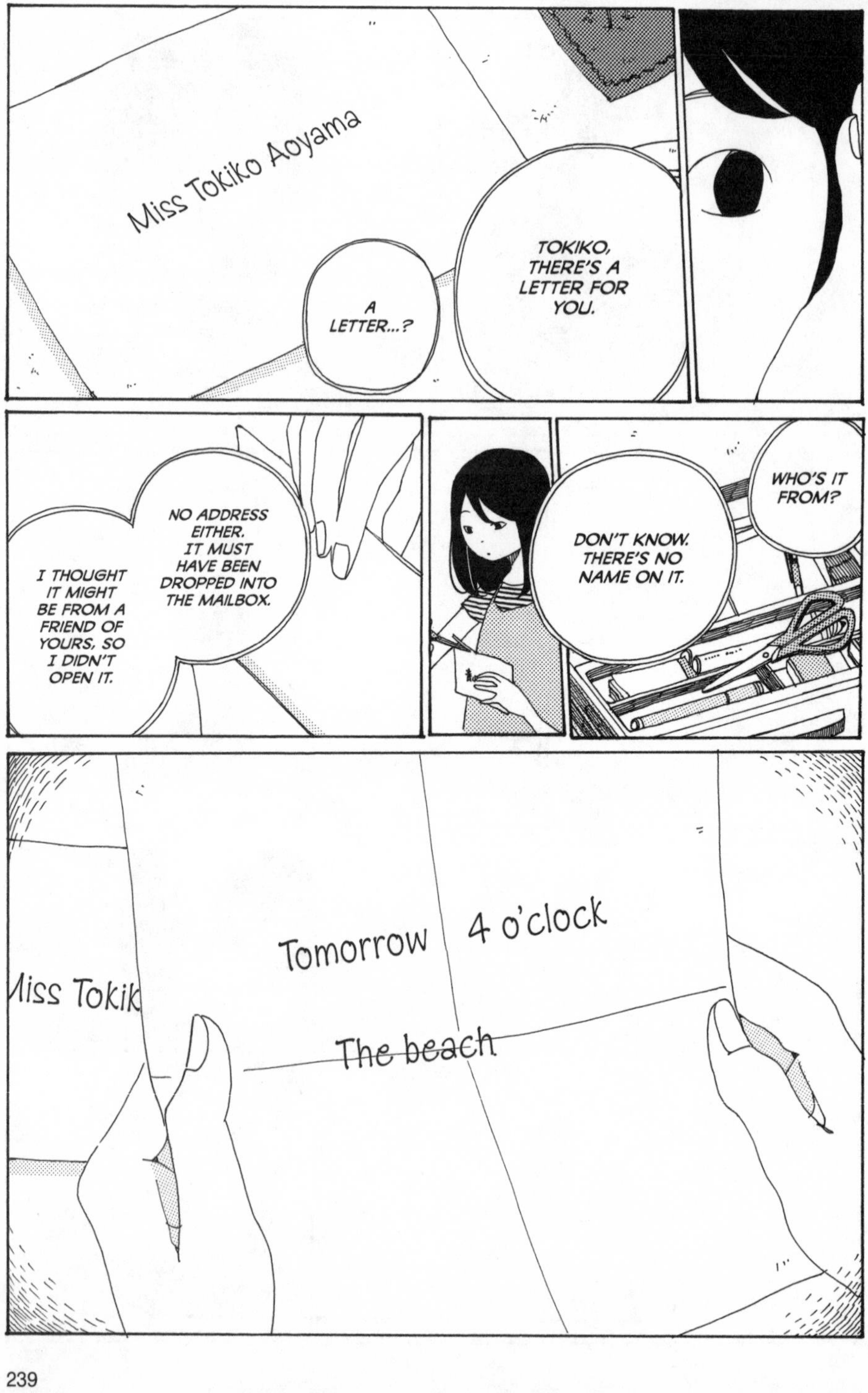
TOKIKO, THERE'S A LETTER FOR YOU.
A LETTER...?
Miss Tokiko Aoyama
WHO'S IT FROM?
DON'T KNOW. THERE'S NO NAME ON IT.
NO ADDRESS EITHER. IT MUST HAVE BEEN DROPPED INTO THE MAILBOX.
I THOUGHT IT MIGHT BE FROM A FRIEND OF YOURS, SO I DIDN'T OPEN IT.
Tomorrow 4 o'clock
The beach

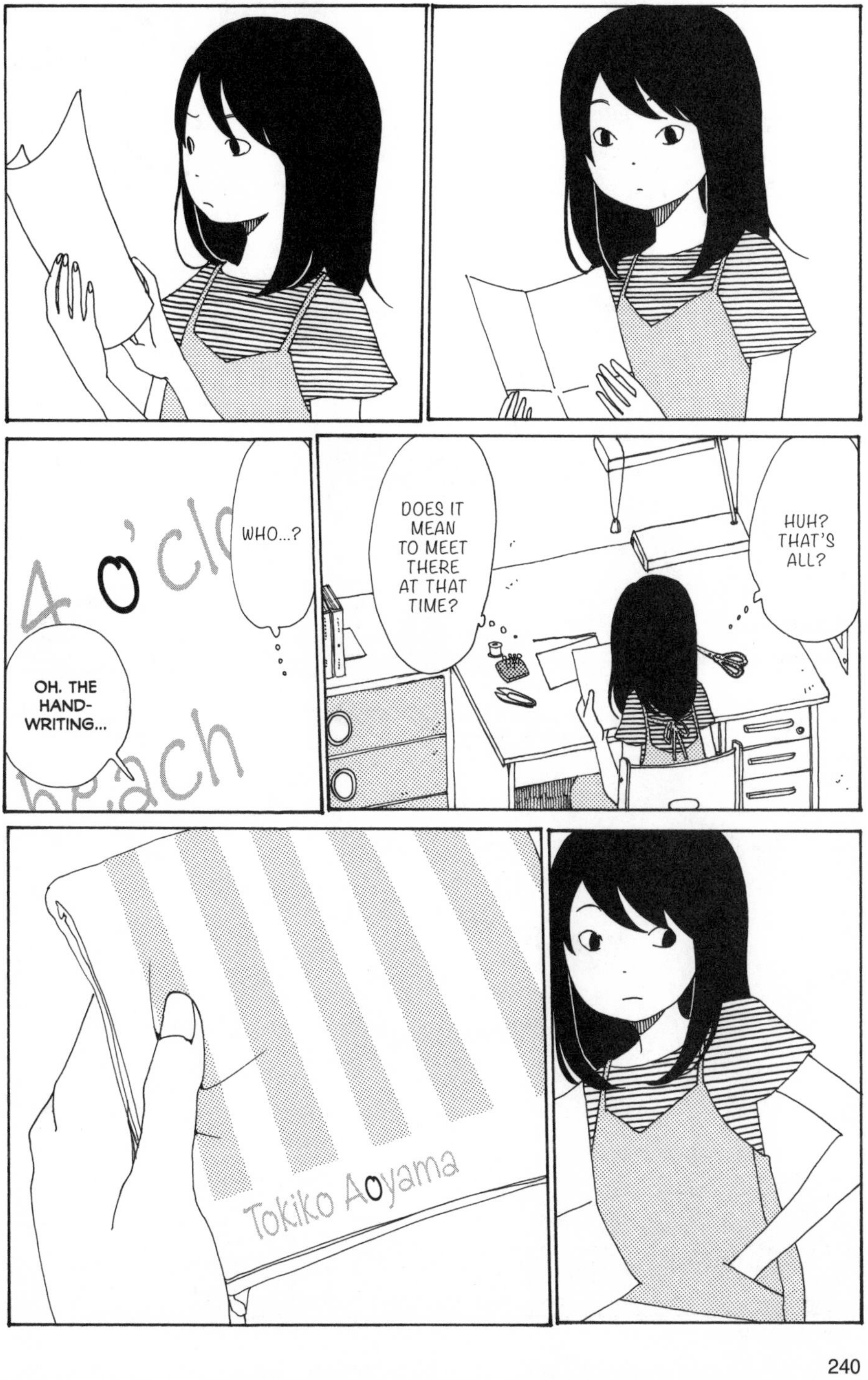
HUH? THAT'S ALL?
DOES IT MEAN TO MEET THERE AT THAT TIME?
WHO...?
4 o'clo
beach
OH. THE HAND-WRITING...
Tokiko Aoyama

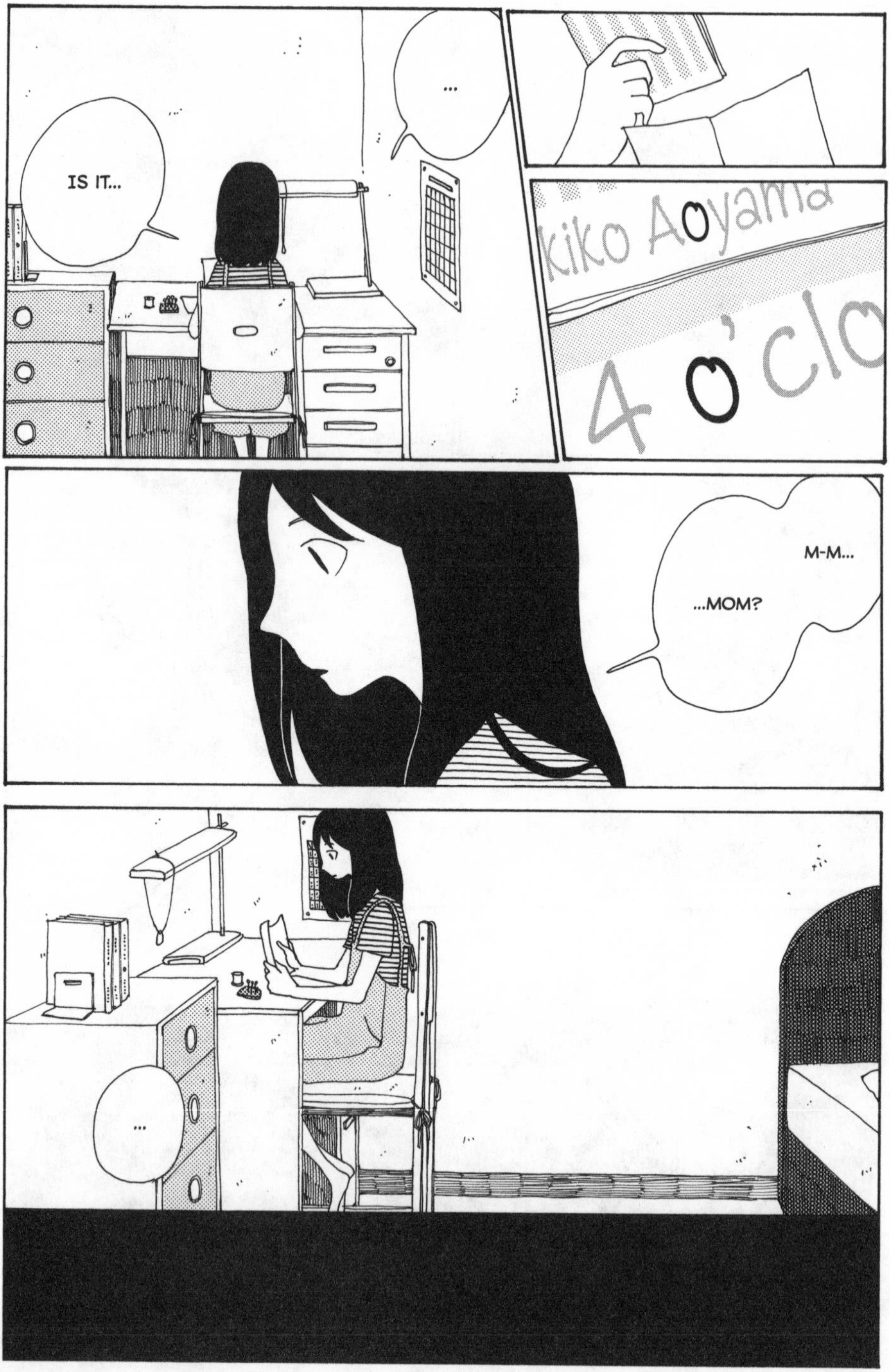
kiko Aoyama
4 o'clo
...
IS IT...
M-M...
...MOM?
...

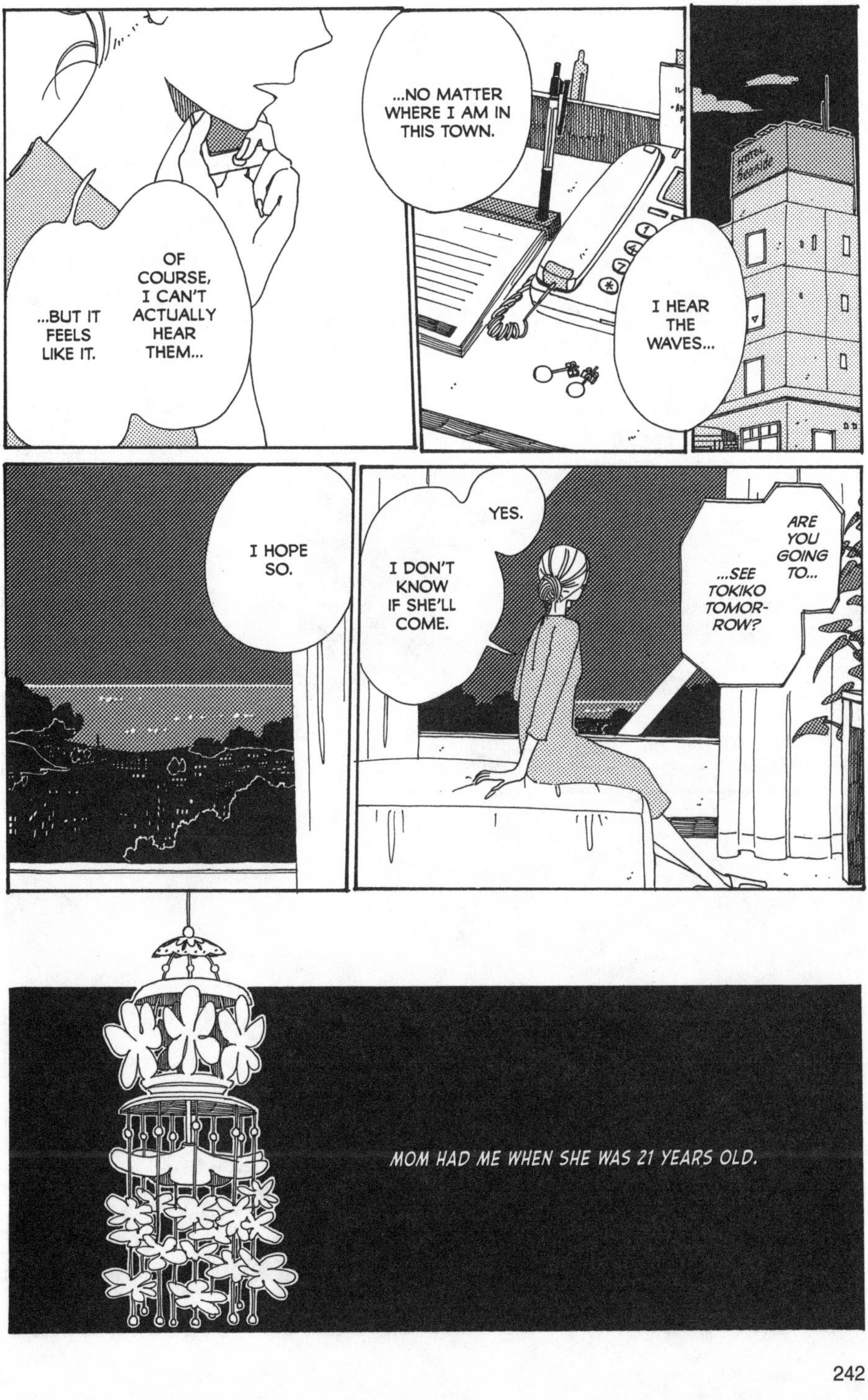
I HEAR THE WAVES...
...NO MATTER WHERE I AM IN THIS TOWN.
OF COURSE, I CAN'T ACTUALLY HEAR THEM...
...BUT IT FEELS LIKE IT.
ARE YOU GOING TO...
...SEE TOKIKO TOMOR-ROW?
YES.
I DON'T KNOW IF SHE'LL COME.
I HOPE SO.
MOM HAD ME WHEN SHE WAS 21 YEARS OLD.

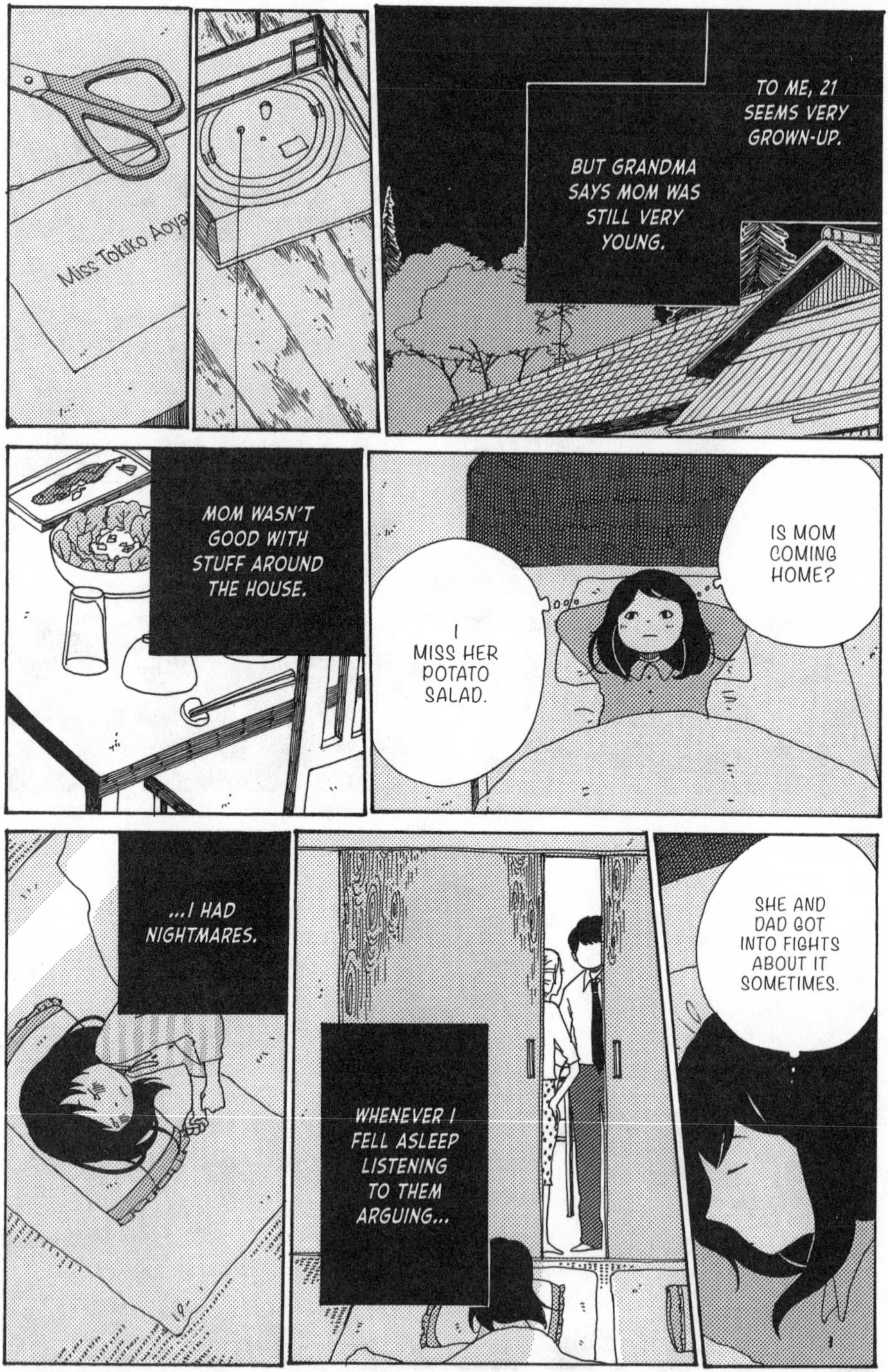
TO ME, 21 SEEMS VERY GROWN-UP.
BUT GRANDMA SAYS MOM WAS STILL VERY YOUNG.
Miss Tokiko Aoya
IS MOM COMING HOME?
I MISS HER POTATO SALAD.
MOM WASN'T GOOD WITH STUFF AROUND THE HOUSE.
SHE AND DAD GOT INTO FIGHTS ABOUT IT SOMETIMES.
WHENEVER I FELL ASLEEP LISTENING TO THEM ARGUING...
...I HAD NIGHTMARES.

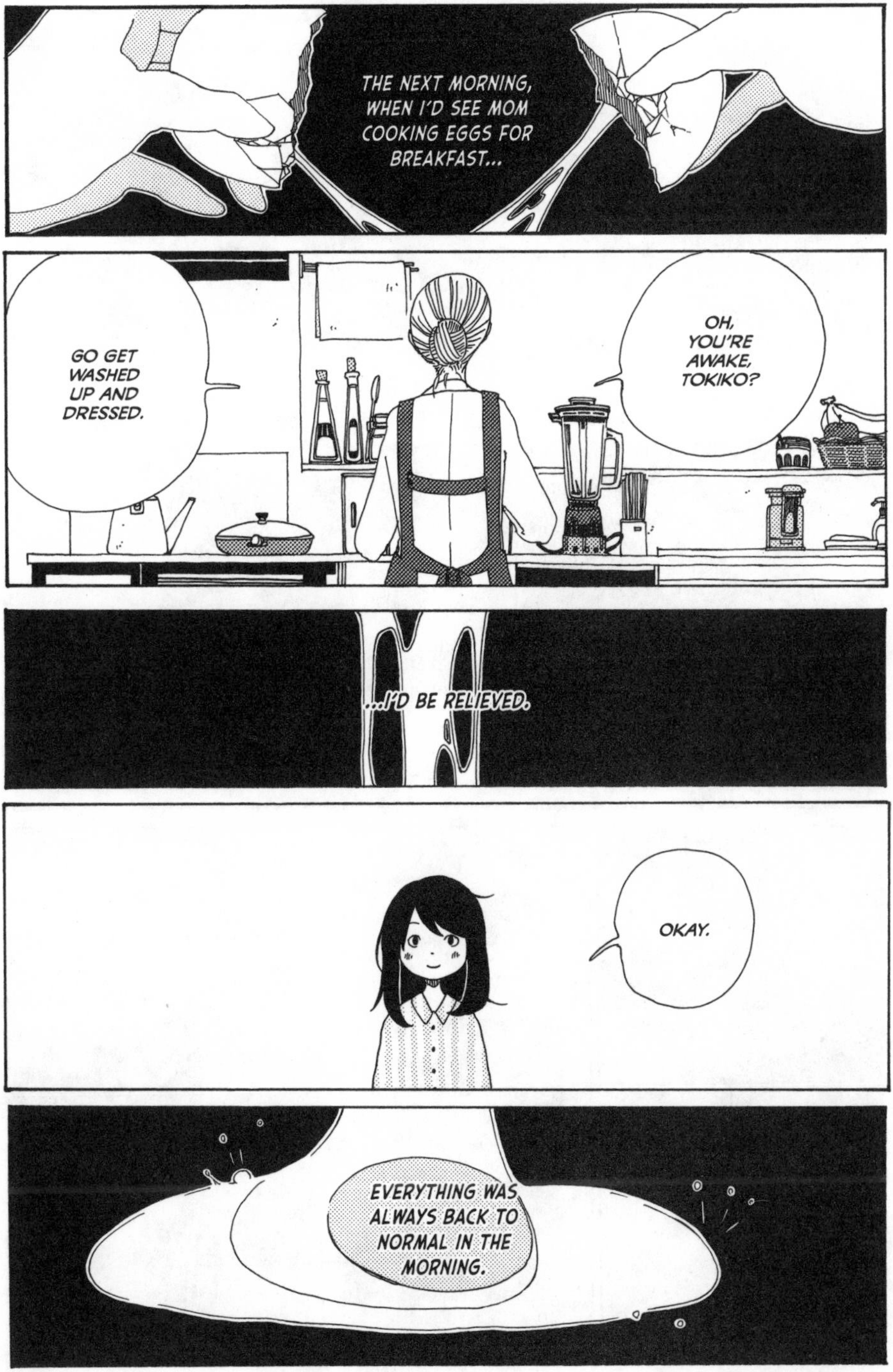
THE NEXT MORNING, WHEN I'D SEE MOM COOKING EGGS FOR BREAKFAST...
OH, YOU'RE AWAKE, TOKIKO?
GO GET WASHED UP AND DRESSED.
...I'D BE RELIEVED.
OKAY.
EVERYTHING WAS ALWAYS BACK TO NORMAL IN THE MORNING.

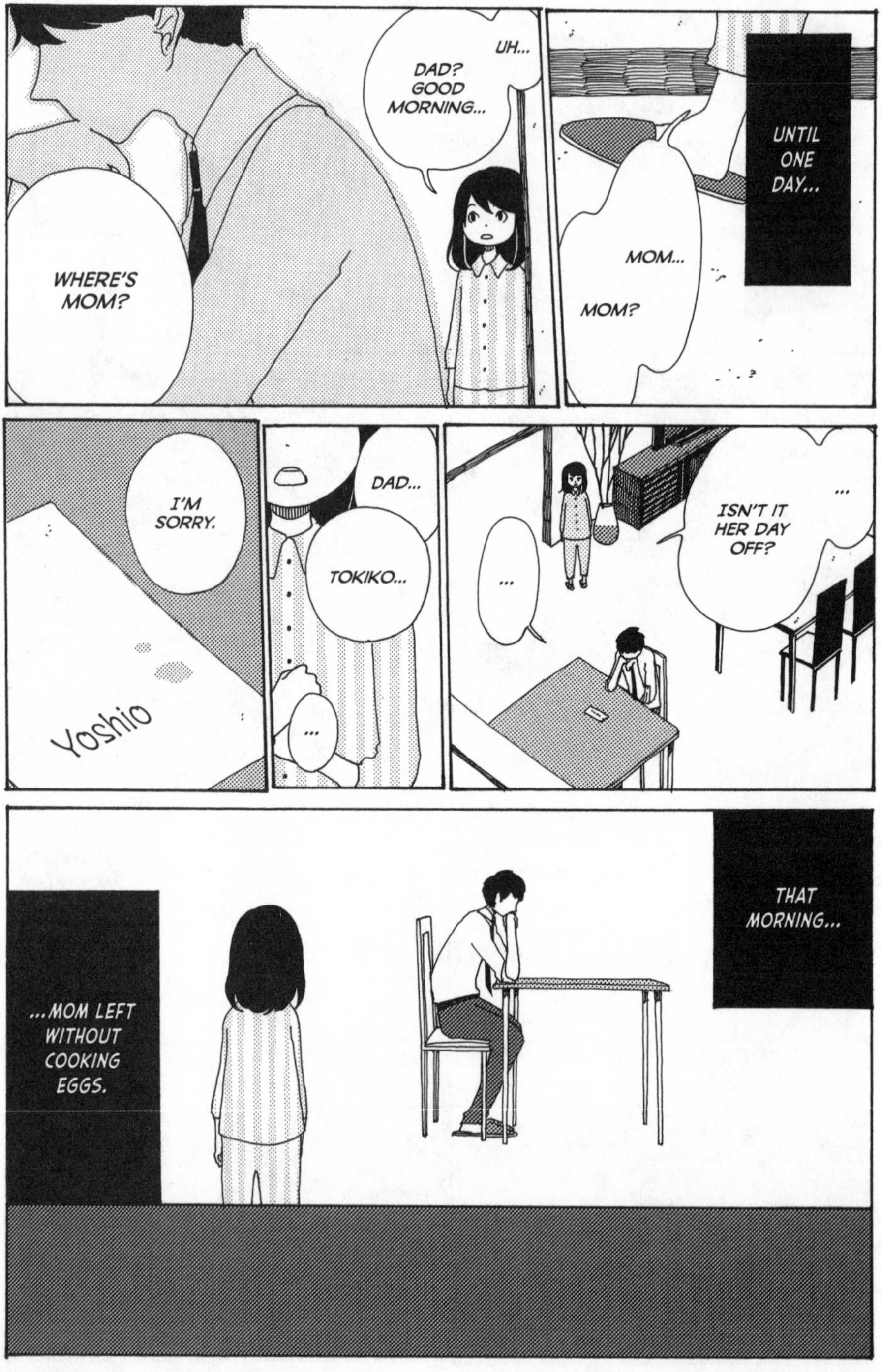
UNTIL ONE DAY...
MOM...
MOM?
UH...
DAD? GOOD MORNING...
WHERE'S MOM?
...
ISN'T IT HER DAY OFF?
...
DAD...
TOKIKO...
...
I'M SORRY.
Yoshio
THAT MORNING...
...MOM LEFT WITHOUT COOKING EGGS.

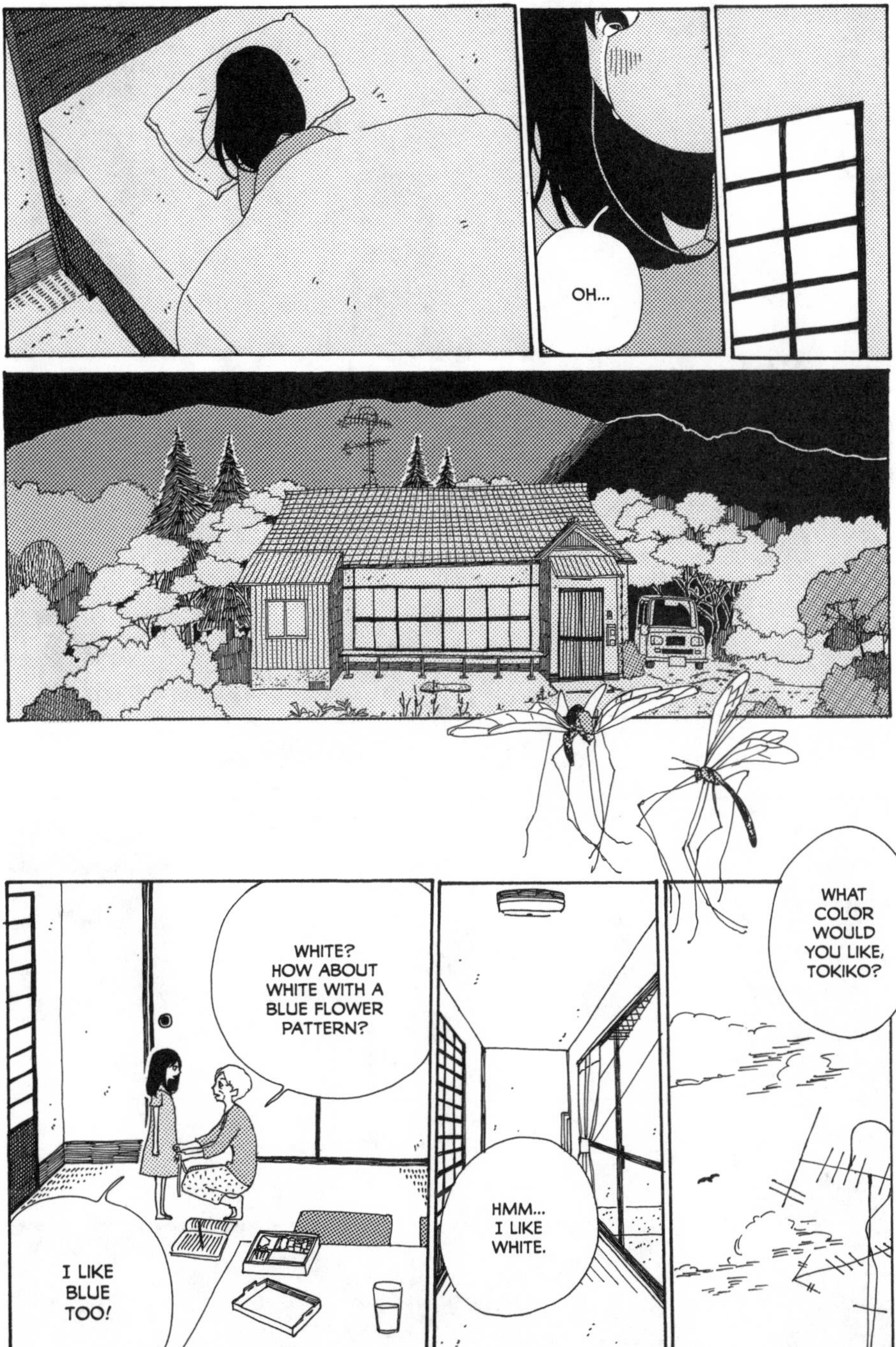
OH...
WHAT COLOR WOULD YOU LIKE, TOKIKO?
HMM... I LIKE WHITE.
WHITE? HOW ABOUT WHITE WITH A BLUE FLOWER PATTERN?
I LIKE BLUE TOO!

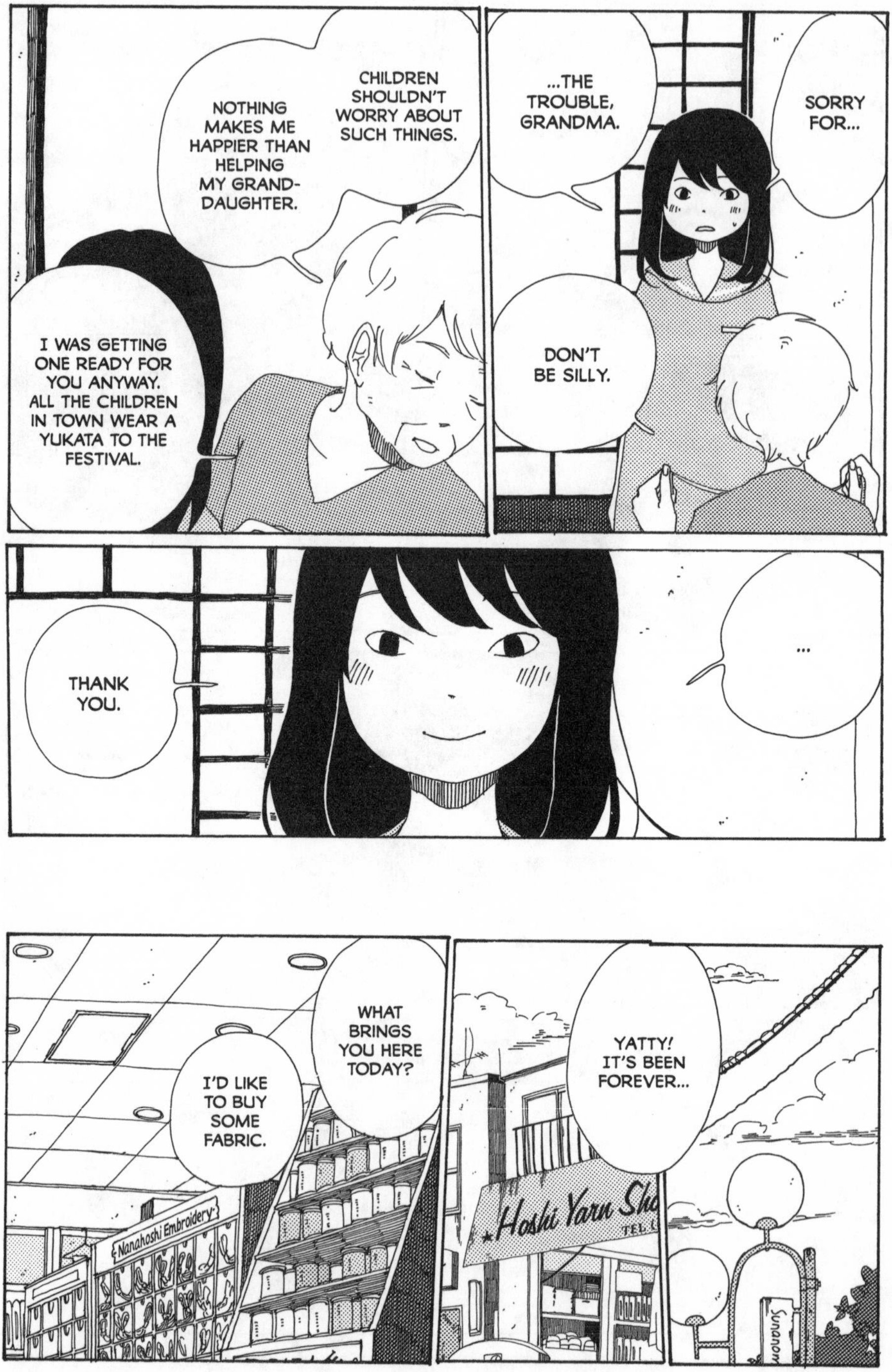
SORRY FOR...
...THE TROUBLE, GRANDMA.
DON'T BE SILLY.
CHILDREN SHOULDN'T WORRY ABOUT SUCH THINGS.
NOTHING MAKES ME HAPPIER THAN HELPING MY GRAND-DAUGHTER.
I WAS GETTING ONE READY FOR YOU ANYWAY. ALL THE CHILDREN IN TOWN WEAR A YUKATA TO THE FESTIVAL.
...
THANK YOU.
YATTY! IT'S BEEN FOREVER...
WHAT BRINGS YOU HERE TODAY?
I'D LIKE TO BUY SOME FABRIC.
Nanahoshi Embroidery

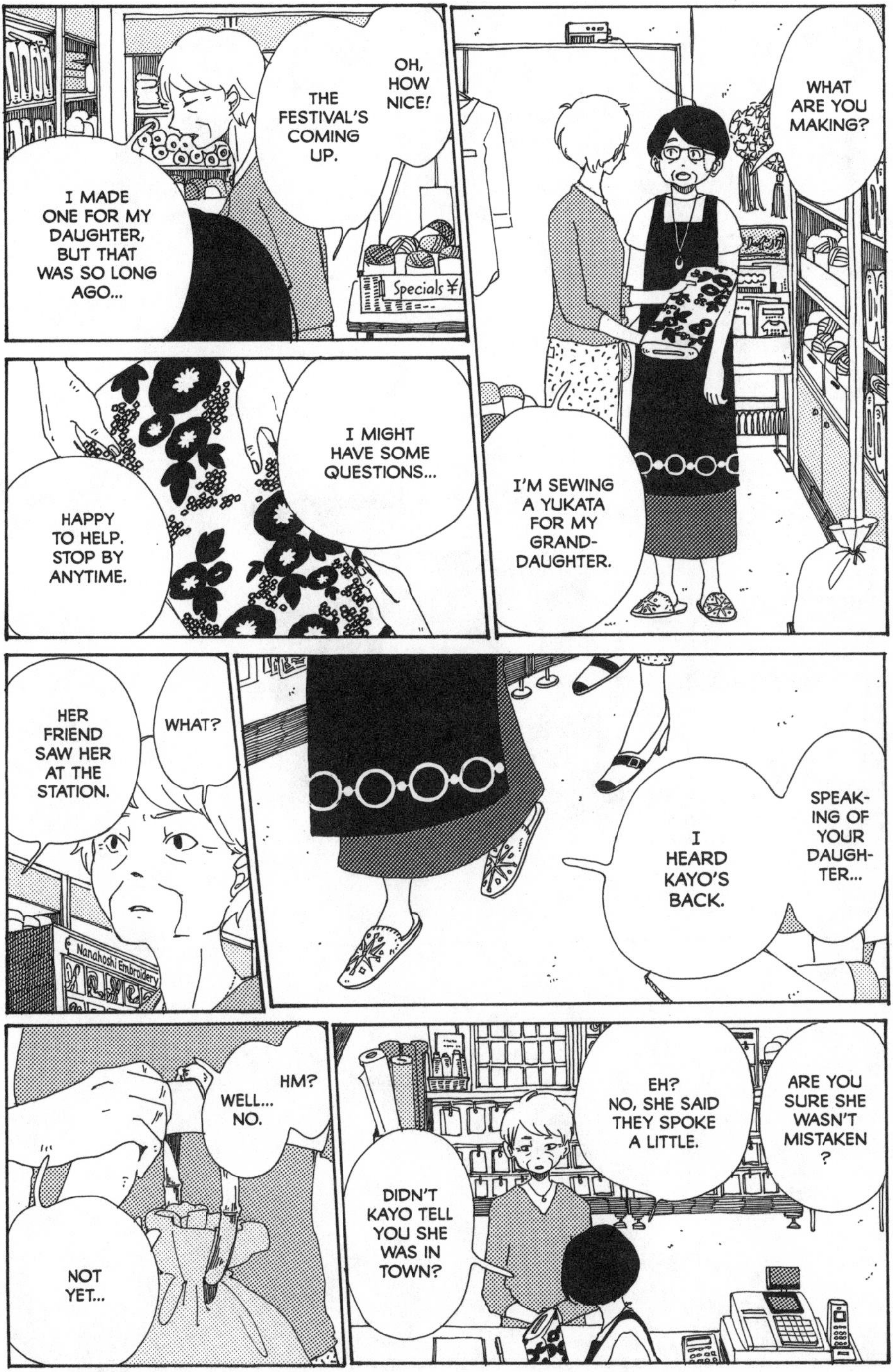
WHAT ARE YOU MAKING?
I'M SEWING A YUKATA FOR MY GRAND-DAUGHTER.
OH, HOW NICE!
THE FESTIVAL'S COMING UP.
I MADE ONE FOR MY DAUGHTER, BUT THAT WAS SO LONG AGO...
Specials ¥
I MIGHT HAVE SOME QUESTIONS...
HAPPY TO HELP. STOP BY ANYTIME.
SPEAK-ING OF YOUR DAUGH-TER...
I HEARD KAYO'S BACK.
WHAT?
HER FRIEND SAW HER AT THE STATION.
Nanahoshi Embroidery
ARE YOU SURE SHE WASN'T MISTAKEN?
EH? NO, SHE SAID THEY SPOKE A LITTLE.
DIDN'T KAYO TELL YOU SHE WAS IN TOWN?
HM?
WELL... NO.
NOT YET...

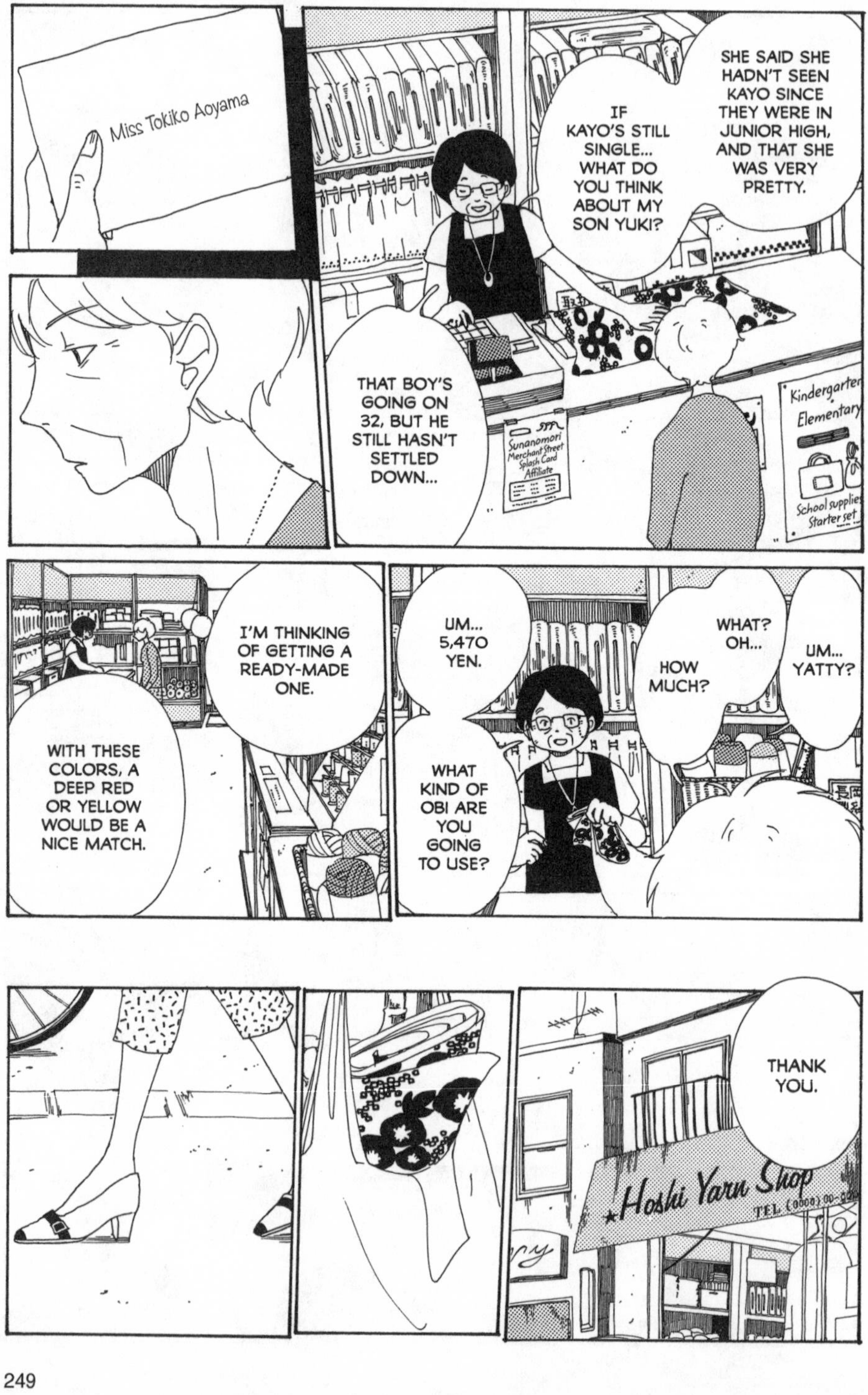
SHE SAID SHE HADN'T SEEN KAYO SINCE THEY WERE IN JUNIOR HIGH, AND THAT SHE WAS VERY PRETTY.
IF KAYO'S STILL SINGLE... WHAT DO YOU THINK ABOUT MY SON YUKI?
Kindergarten
Elementary
School supplies
Starter set
Sunanomori
Merchant Street
Splash Card
Affiliate
THAT BOY'S GOING ON 32, BUT HE STILL HASN'T SETTLED DOWN...
Miss Tokiko Aoyama
UM... YATTY?
WHAT? OH...
HOW MUCH?
UM... 5,470 YEN.
WHAT KIND OF OBI ARE YOU GOING TO USE?
I'M THINKING OF GETTING A READY-MADE ONE.
WITH THESE COLORS, A DEEP RED OR YELLOW WOULD BE A NICE MATCH.
THANK YOU.
Hoshi Yarn Shop

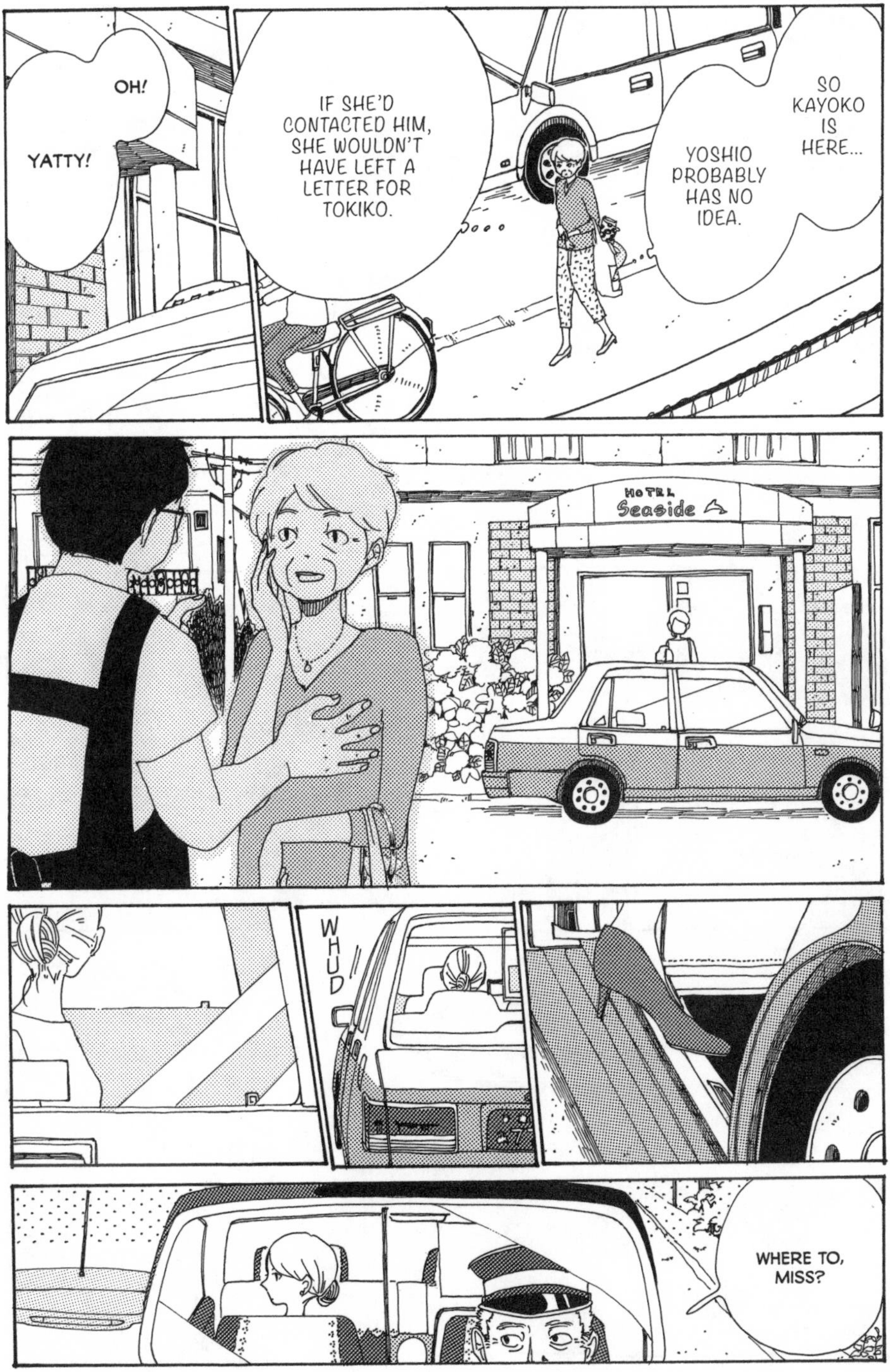
SO KAYOKO IS HERE...
YOSHIO PROBABLY HAS NO IDEA.
IF SHE'D CONTACTED HIM, SHE WOULDN'T HAVE LEFT A LETTER FOR TOKIKO.
OH!
YATTY!
WHUD
WHERE TO, MISS?

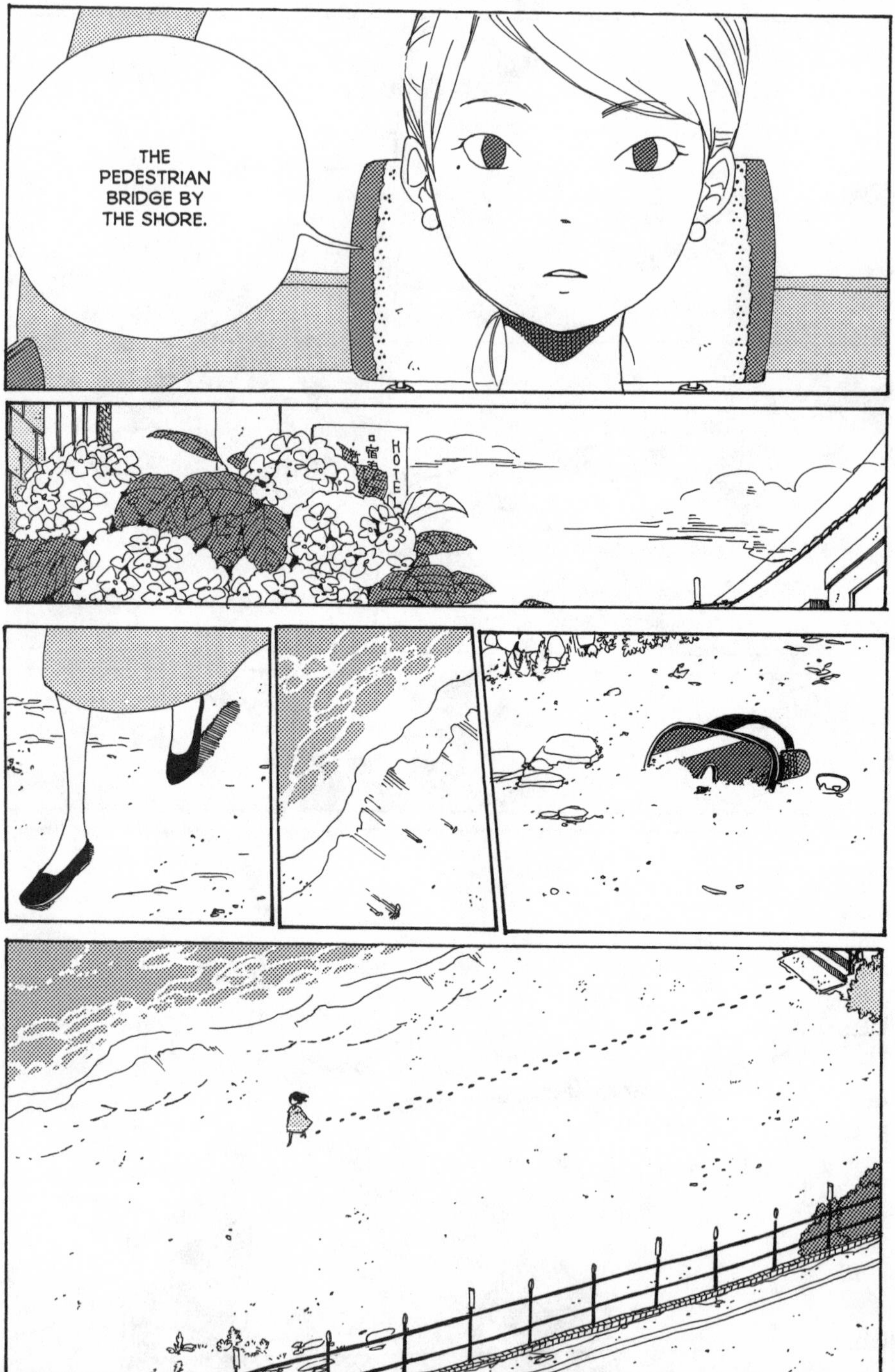
THE PEDESTRIAN BRIDGE BY THE SHORE.

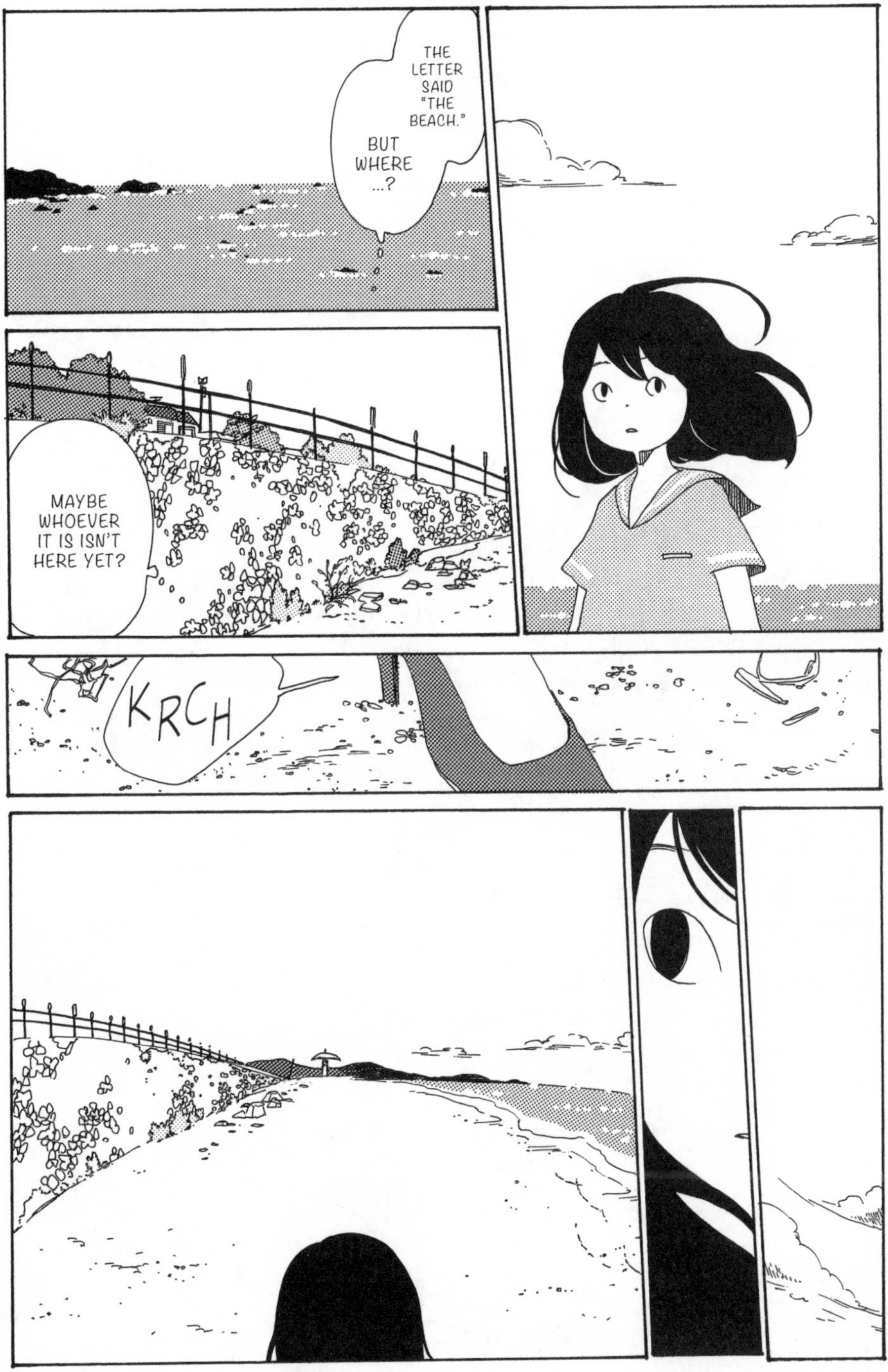
THE LETTER SAID "THE BEACH."
BUT WHERE ...?
MAYBE WHOEVER IT IS ISN'T HERE YET?
KRCH

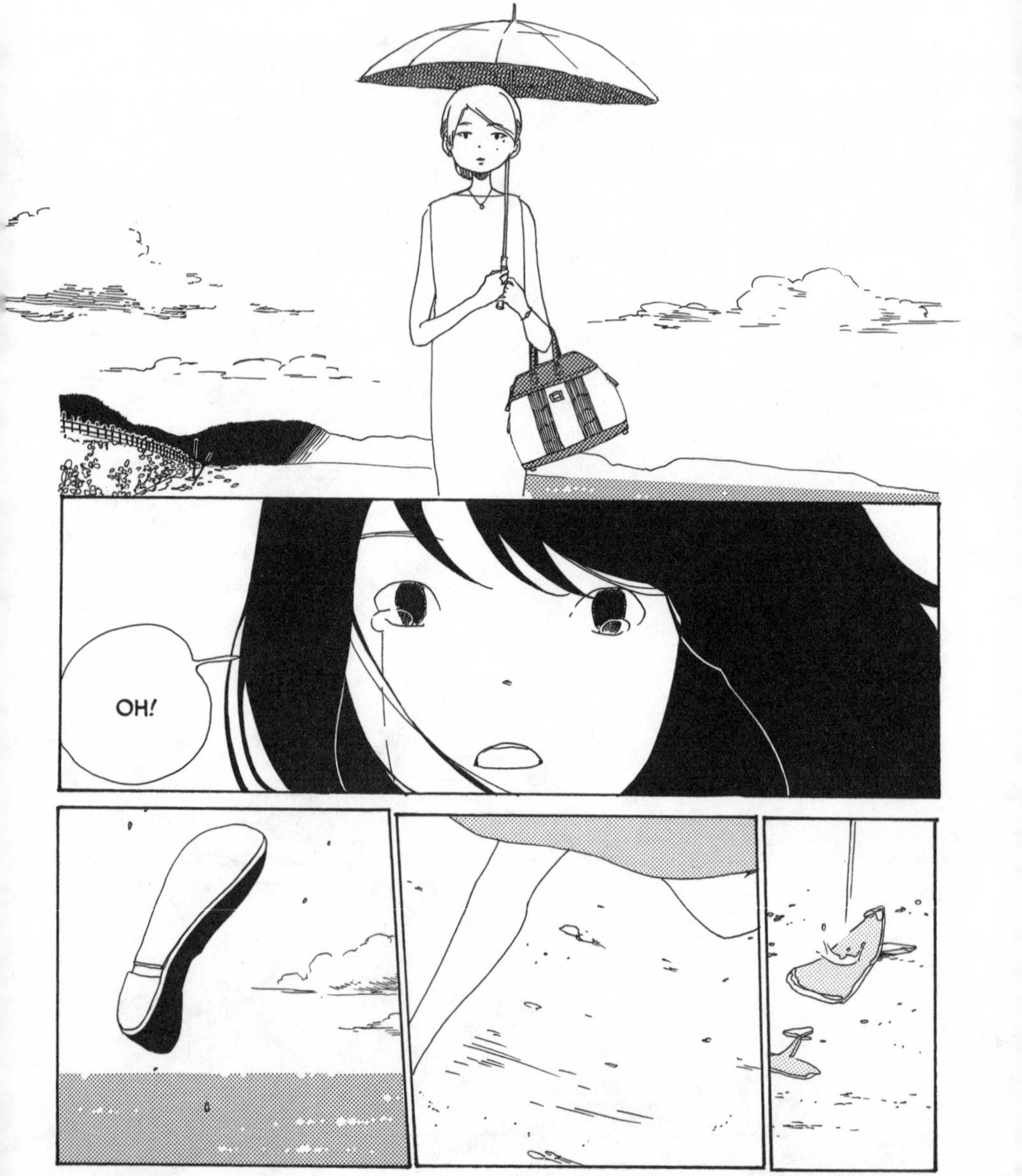
OH!

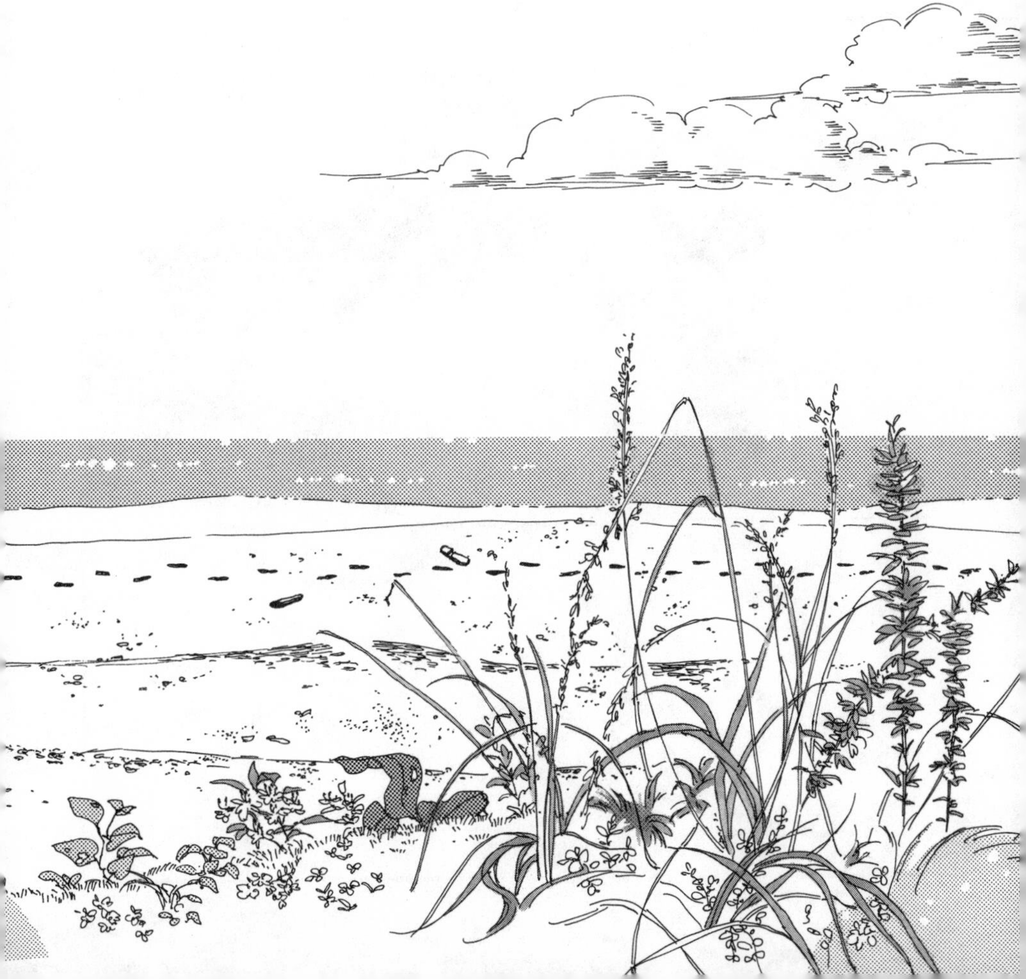

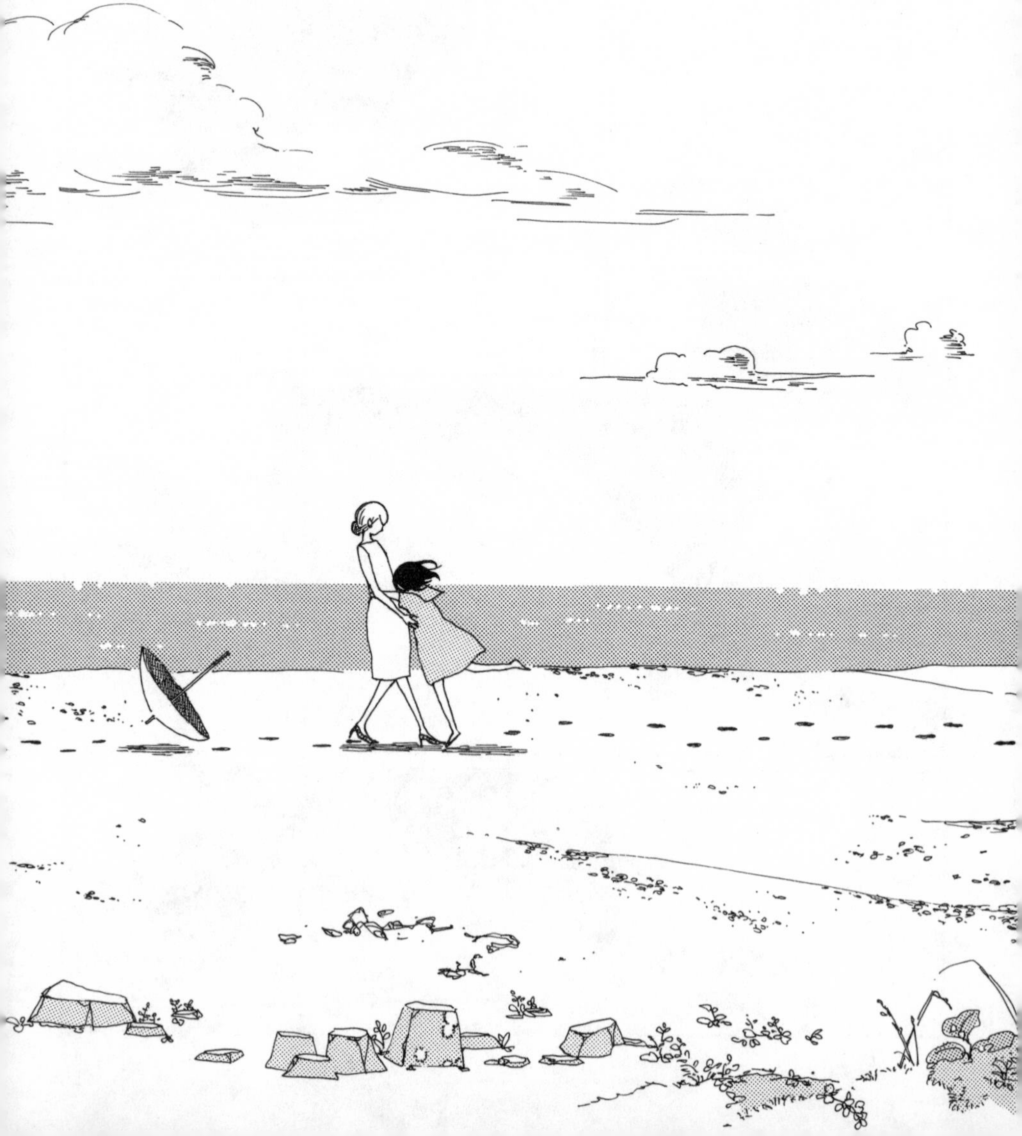

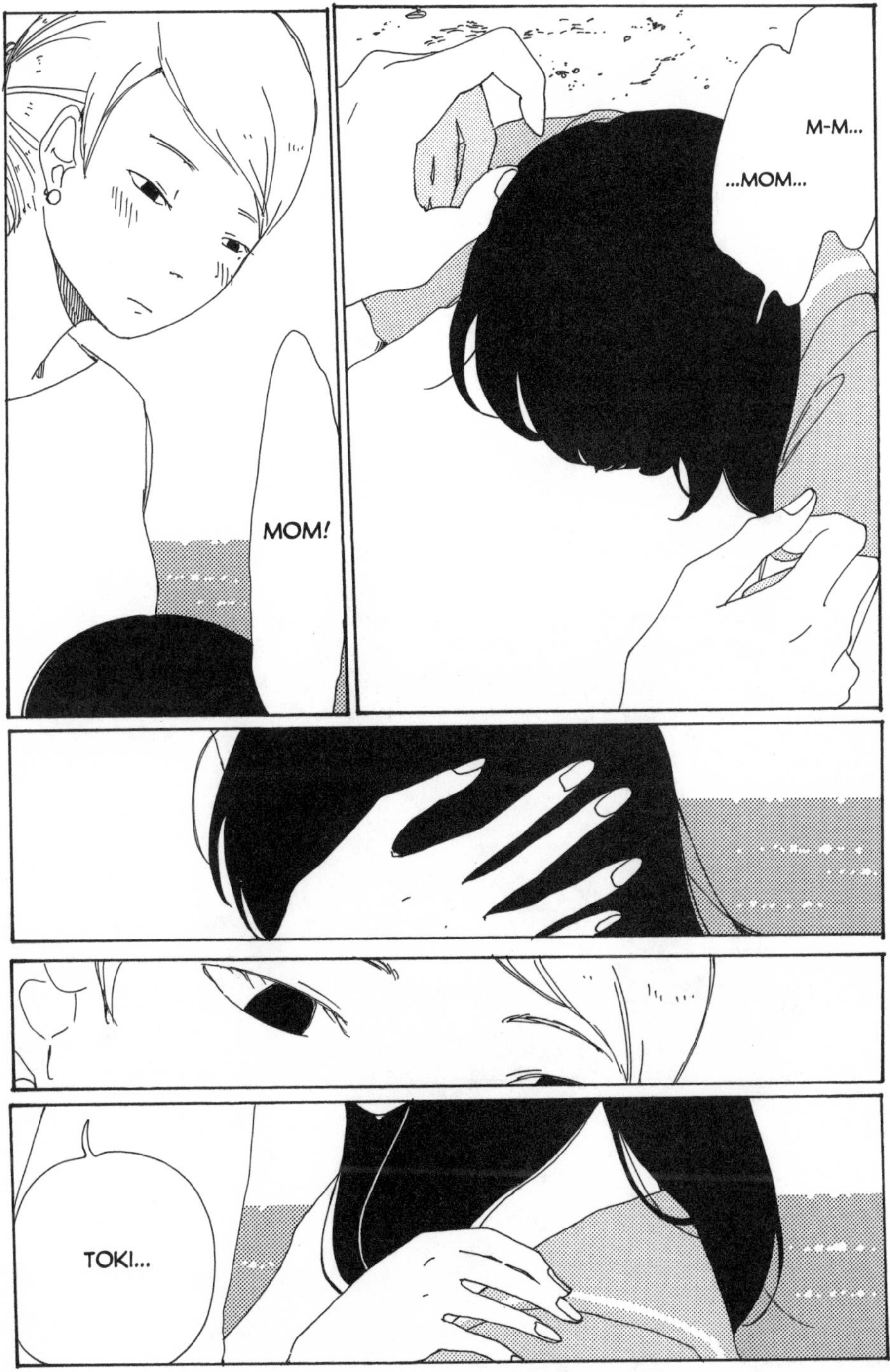
M-M...
...MOM...
MOM!
TOKI...

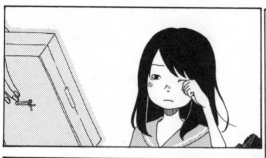

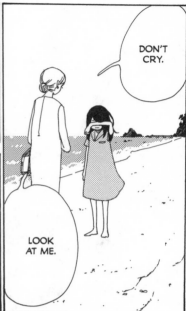

DON'T CRY.

LOOK AT ME.

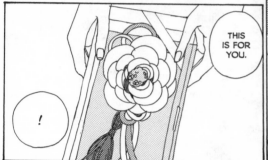

THIS IS FOR YOU.

!

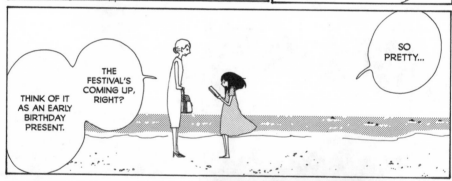

SO PRETTY...

THE FESTIVAL'S COMING UP, RIGHT?

THINK OF IT AS AN EARLY BIRTHDAY PRESENT.

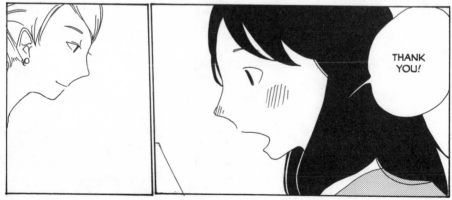

THANK YOU!

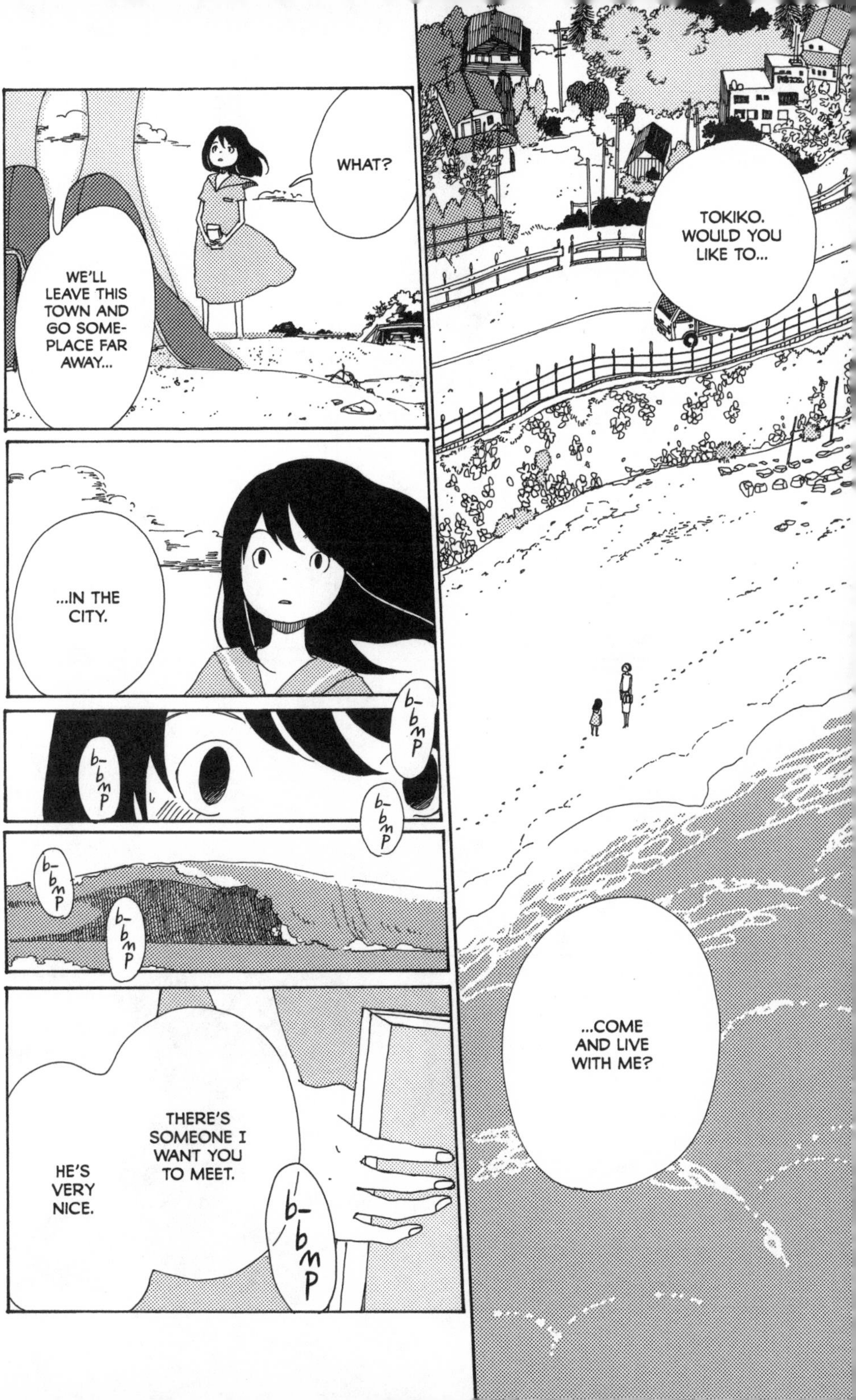
TOKIKO. WOULD YOU LIKE TO...
...COME AND LIVE WITH ME?
WHAT?
WE'LL LEAVE THIS TOWN AND GO SOME-PLACE FAR AWAY...
...IN THE CITY.
b-bmp
b-bmp
b-bmp
b-bmp
b-bmp
THERE'S SOMEONE I WANT YOU TO MEET.
HE'S VERY NICE.
b-bmp

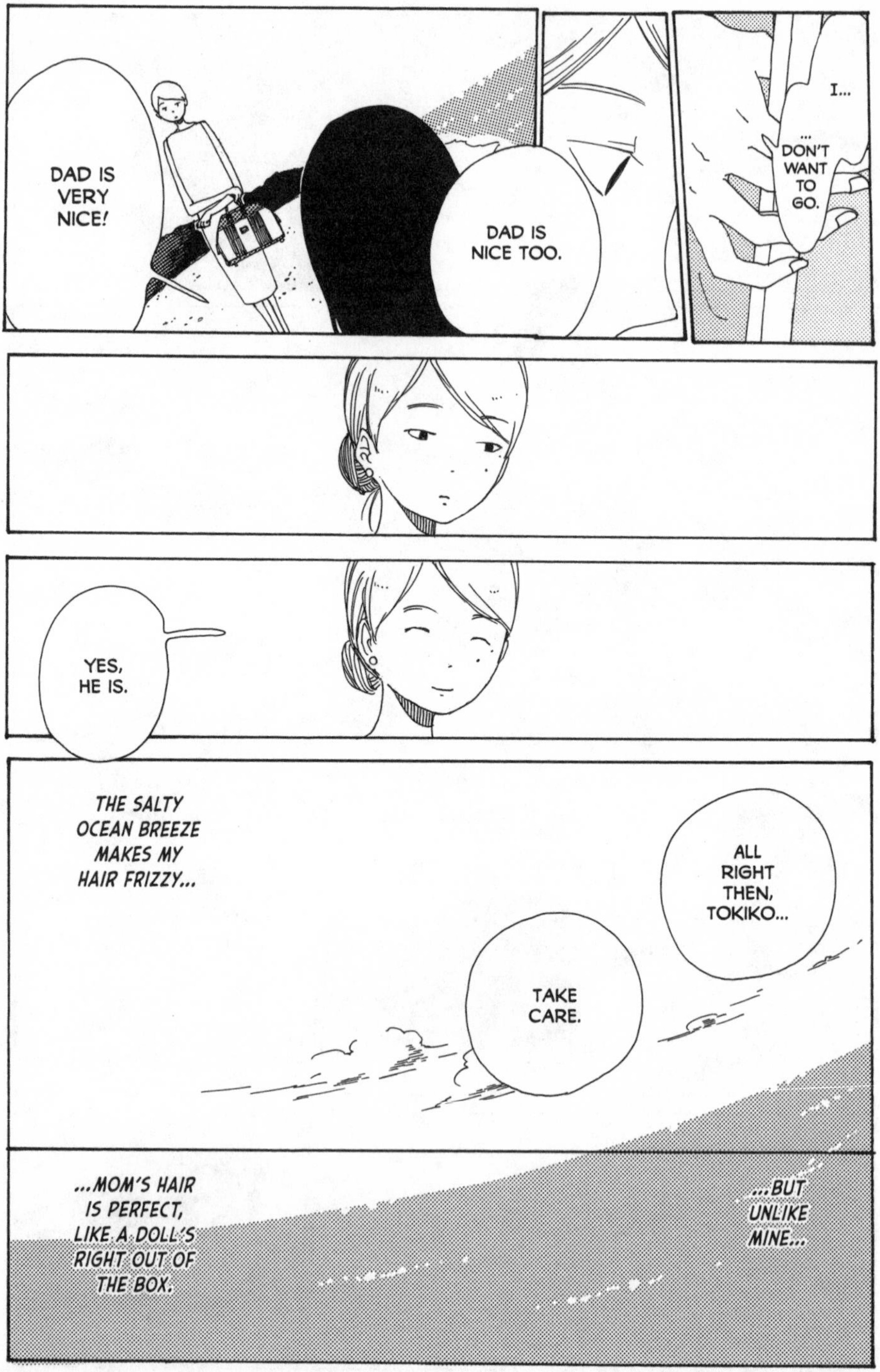
I...
...DON'T WANT TO GO.
DAD IS NICE TOO.
DAD IS VERY NICE!
YES, HE IS.
ALL RIGHT THEN, TOKIKO...
TAKE CARE.
THE SALTY OCEAN BREEZE MAKES MY HAIR FRIZZY...
...BUT UNLIKE MINE...
...MOM'S HAIR IS PERFECT, LIKE A DOLL'S RIGHT OUT OF THE BOX.

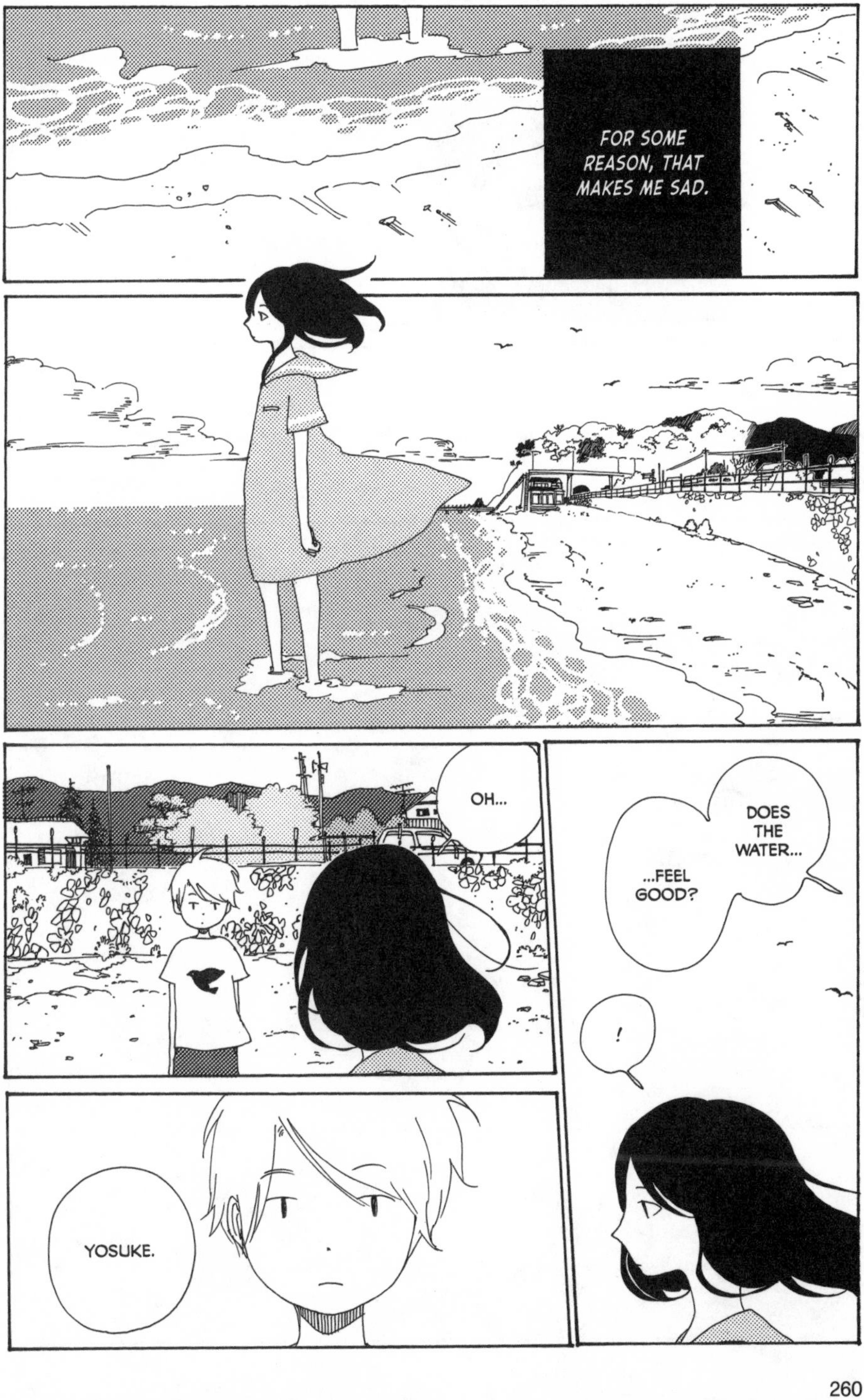
FOR SOME REASON, THAT MAKES ME SAD.
DOES THE WATER...
...FEEL GOOD?
!
OH...
YOSUKE.

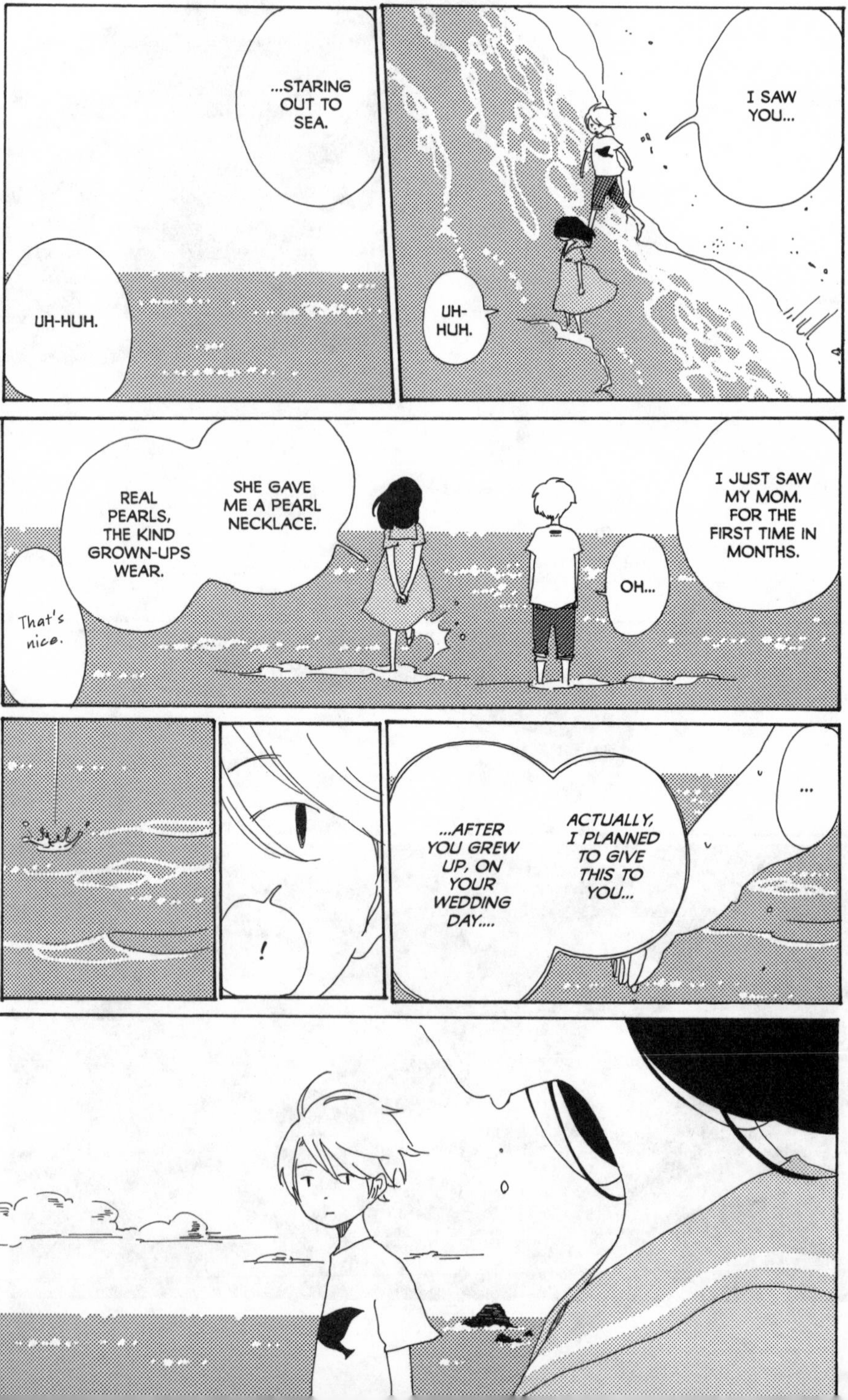
I SAW YOU...
UH-HUH.
...STARING OUT TO SEA.
UH-HUH.
I JUST SAW MY MOM. FOR THE FIRST TIME IN MONTHS.
OH...
SHE GAVE ME A PEARL NECKLACE.
REAL PEARLS, THE KIND GROWN-UPS WEAR.
That's nice.
...
ACTUALLY, I PLANNED TO GIVE THIS TO YOU...
...AFTER YOU GREW UP, ON YOUR WEDDING DAY....
!

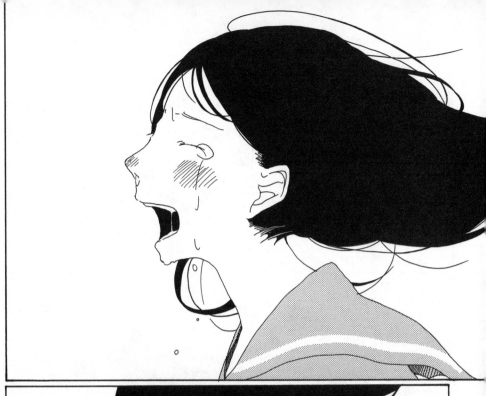

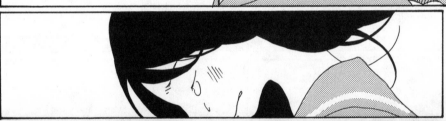

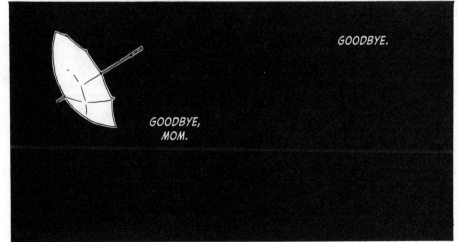

GOODBYE.

GOODBYE,
MOM.

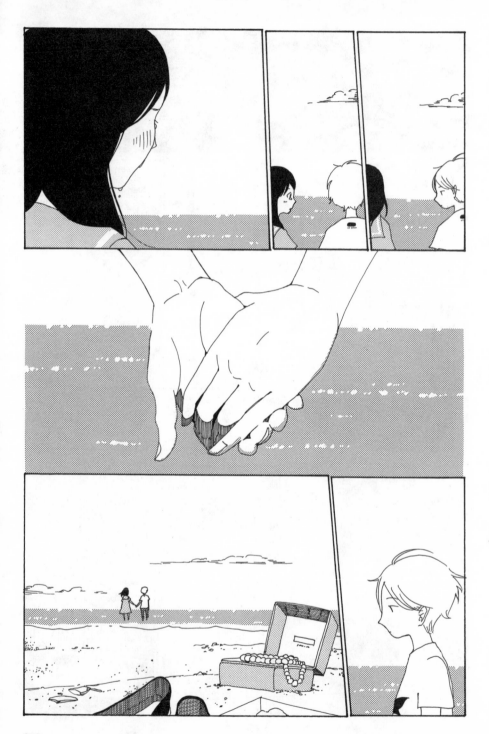

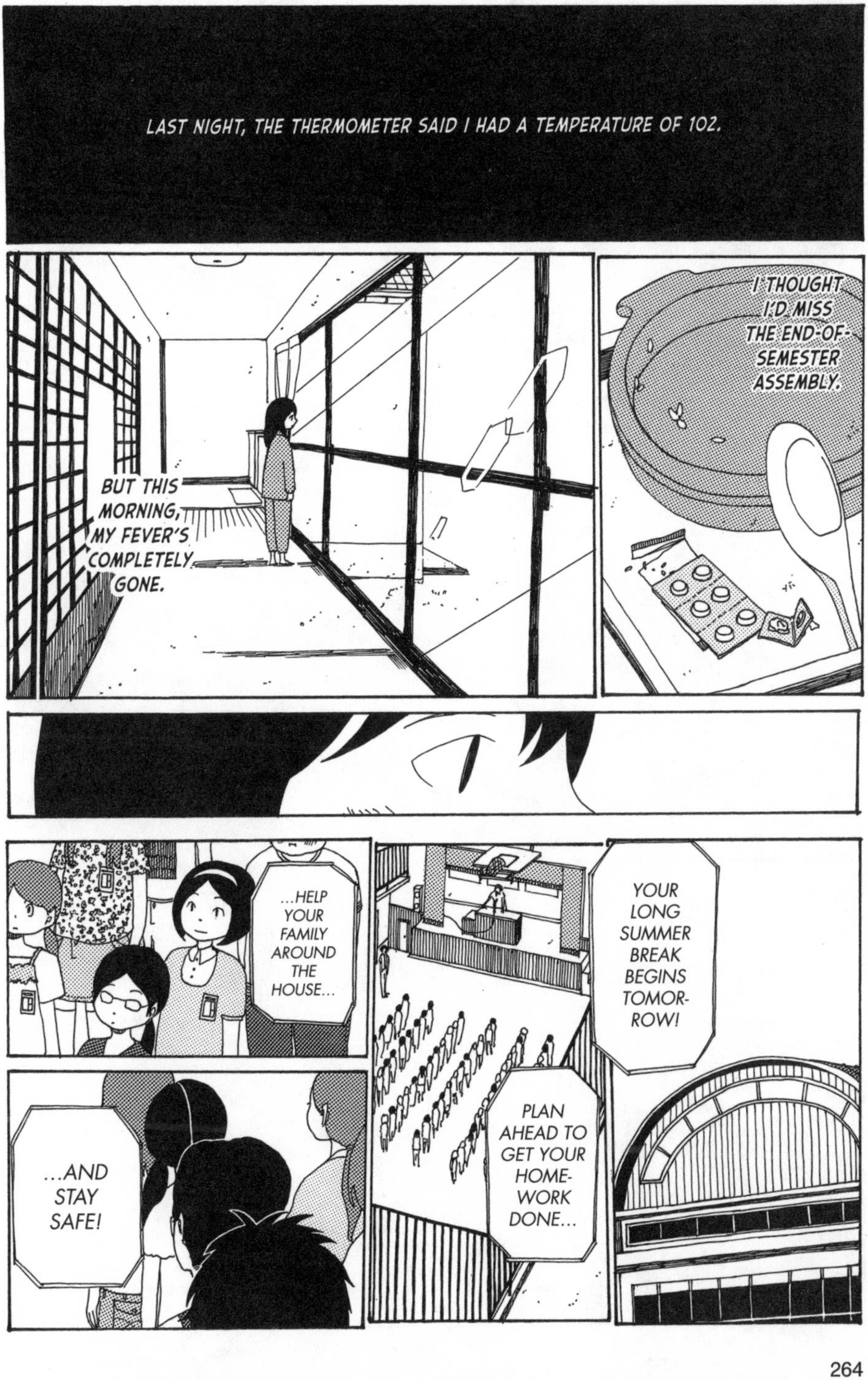
LAST NIGHT, THE THERMOMETER SAID I HAD A TEMPERATURE OF 102.
I THOUGHT I'D MISS THE END-OF-SEMESTER ASSEMBLY.
BUT THIS MORNING, MY FEVER'S COMPLETELY GONE.
YOUR LONG SUMMER BREAK BEGINS TOMORROW!
PLAN AHEAD TO GET YOUR HOMEWORK DONE...
...HELP YOUR FAMILY AROUND THE HOUSE...
...AND STAY SAFE!

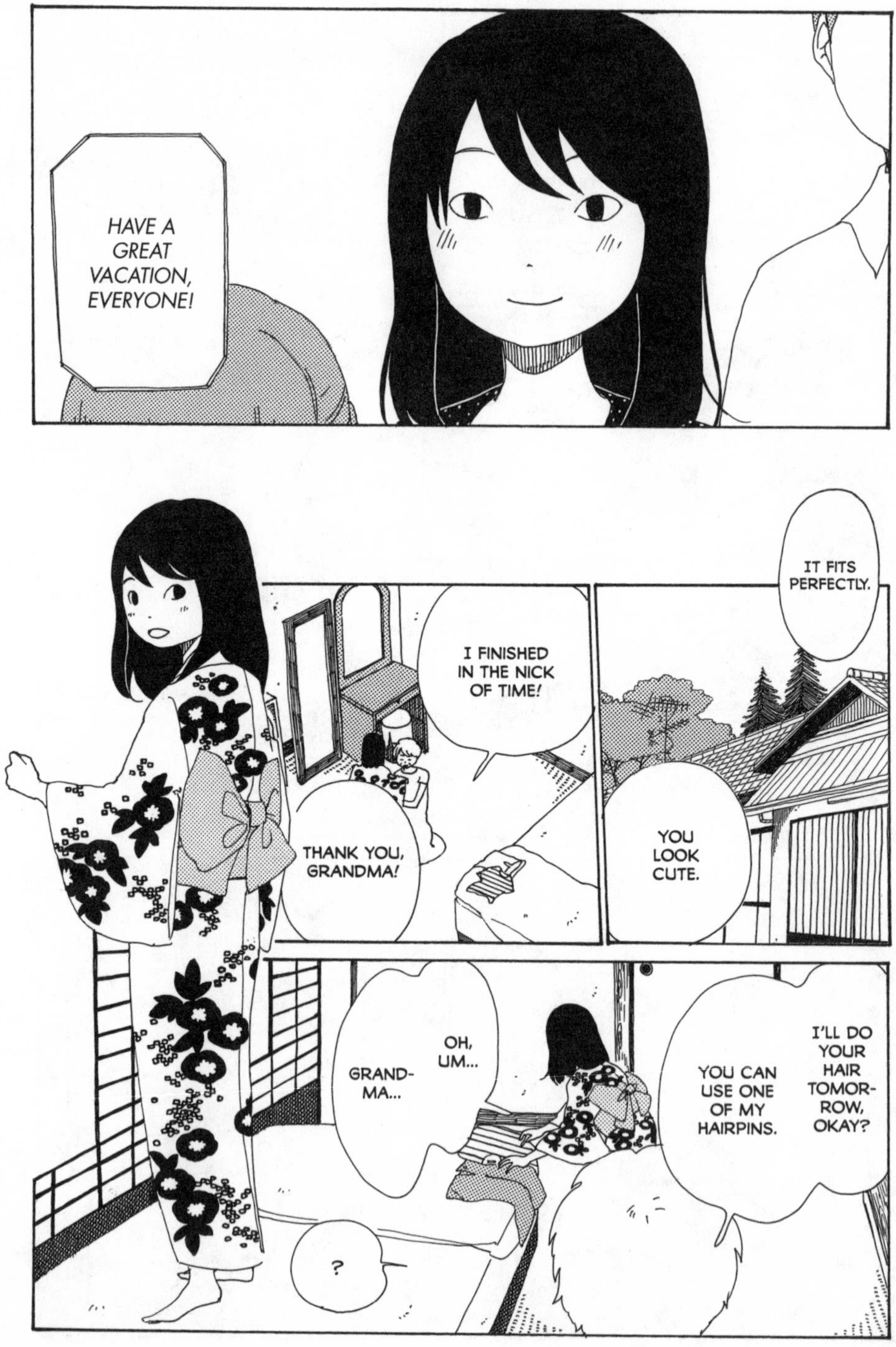
HAVE A GREAT VACATION, EVERYONE!
IT FITS PERFECTLY.
YOU LOOK CUTE.
I FINISHED IN THE NICK OF TIME!
THANK YOU, GRANDMA!
I'LL DO YOUR HAIR TOMOR-ROW, OKAY?
YOU CAN USE ONE OF MY HAIRPINS.
OH, UM...
GRAND-MA...
?

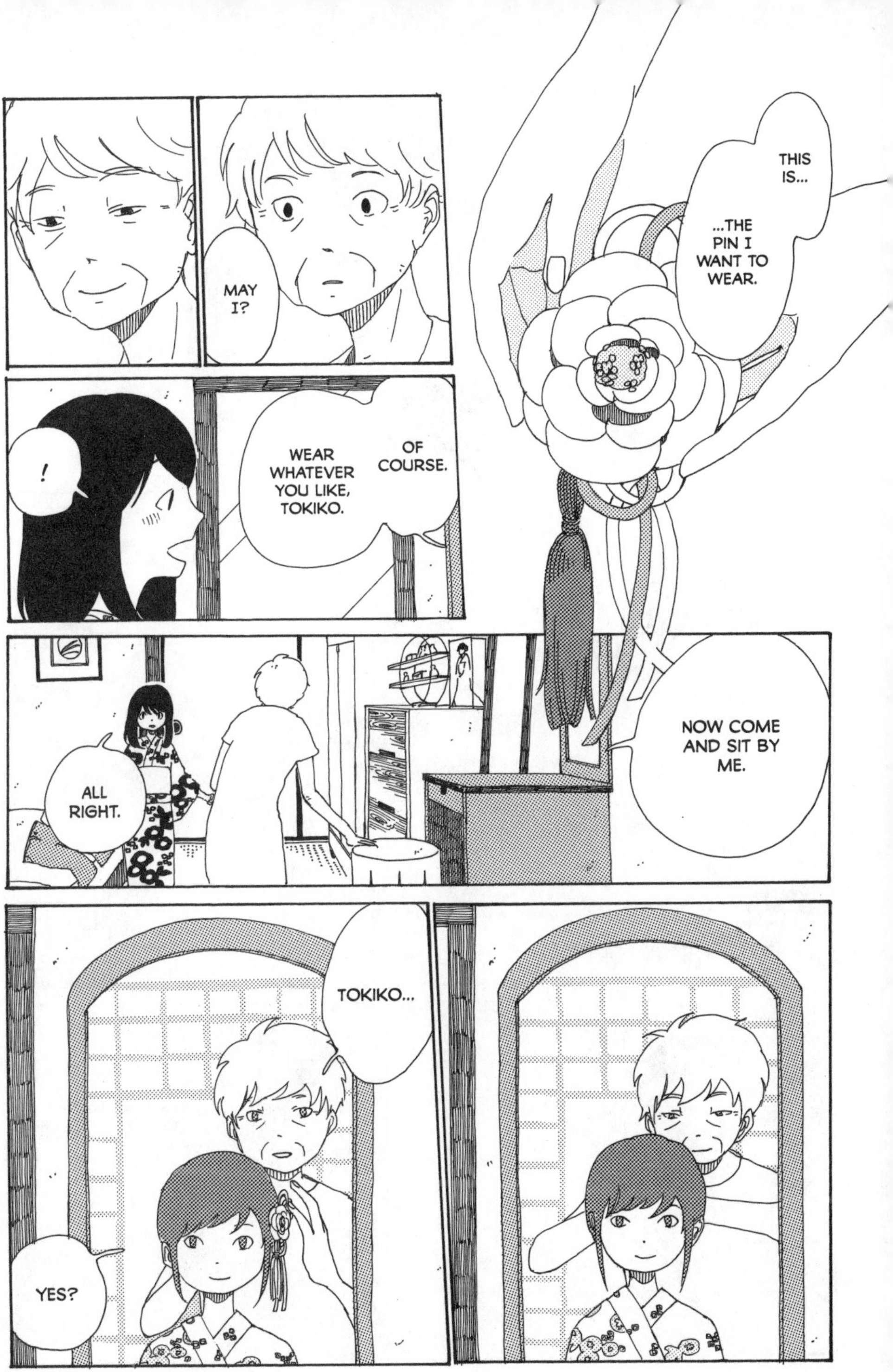
THIS IS...
...THE PIN I WANT TO WEAR.
MAY I?
OF COURSE.
WEAR WHATEVER YOU LIKE, TOKIKO.
!
NOW COME AND SIT BY ME.
ALL RIGHT.
TOKIKO...
YES?

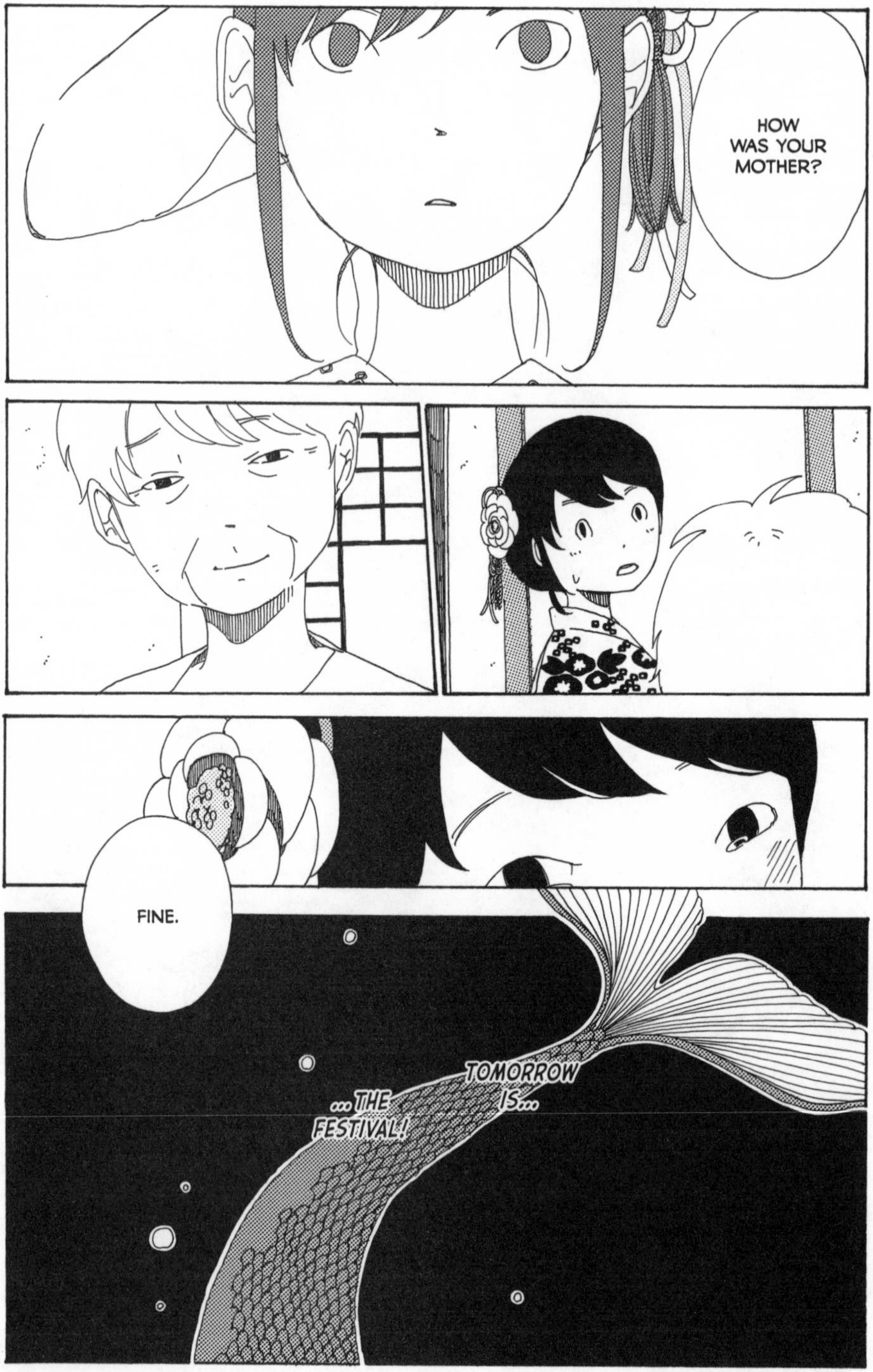
HOW WAS YOUR MOTHER?
FINE.
TOMORROW IS...
...THE FESTIVAL!

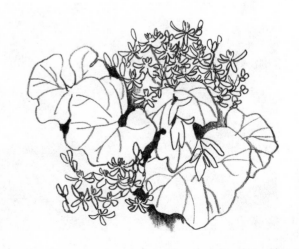

{Eight} Abyss

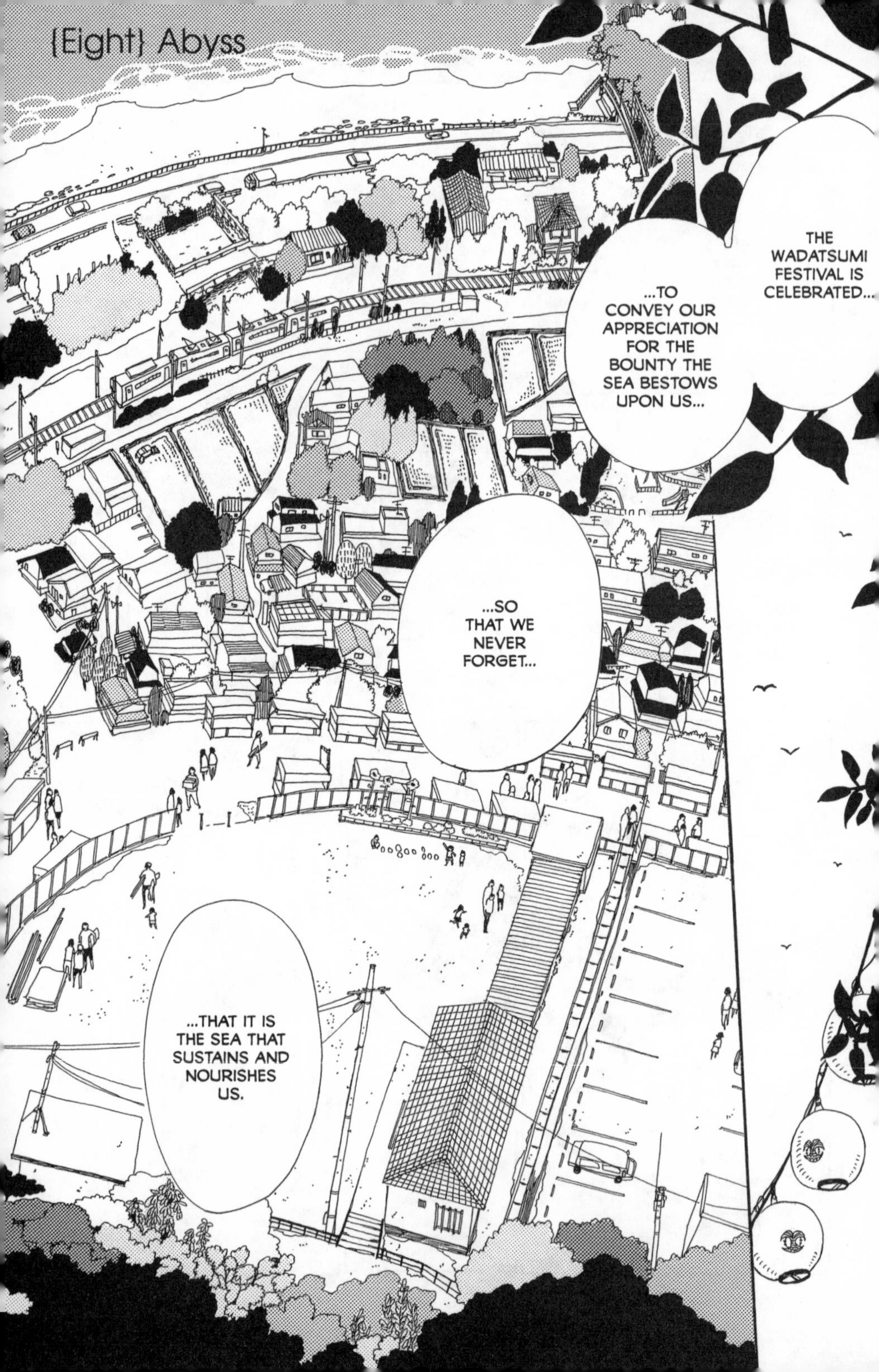
THE WADATSUMI FESTIVAL IS CELEBRATED...
...TO CONVEY OUR APPRECIATION FOR THE BOUNTY THE SEA BESTOWS UPON US...
...SO THAT WE NEVER FORGET...
...THAT IT IS THE SEA THAT SUSTAINS AND NOURISHES US.

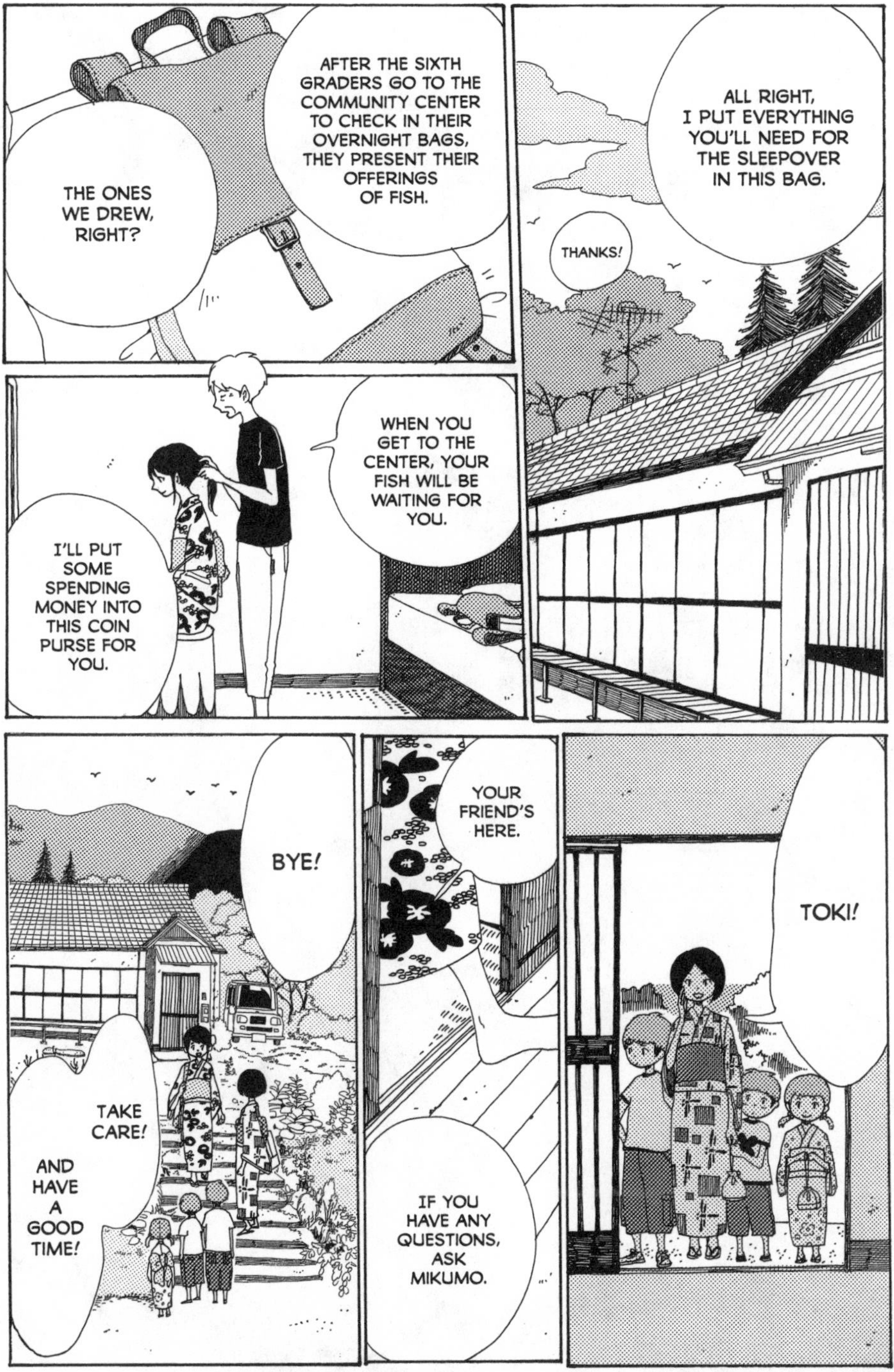
ALL RIGHT, I PUT EVERYTHING YOU'LL NEED FOR THE SLEEPOVER IN THIS BAG.
THANKS!
AFTER THE SIXTH GRADERS GO TO THE COMMUNITY CENTER TO CHECK IN THEIR OVERNIGHT BAGS, THEY PRESENT THEIR OFFERINGS OF FISH.
THE ONES WE DREW, RIGHT?
WHEN YOU GET TO THE CENTER, YOUR FISH WILL BE WAITING FOR YOU.
I'LL PUT SOME SPENDING MONEY INTO THIS COIN PURSE FOR YOU.
TOKI!
YOUR FRIEND'S HERE.
IF YOU HAVE ANY QUESTIONS, ASK MIKUMO.
BYE!
TAKE CARE!
AND HAVE A GOOD TIME!

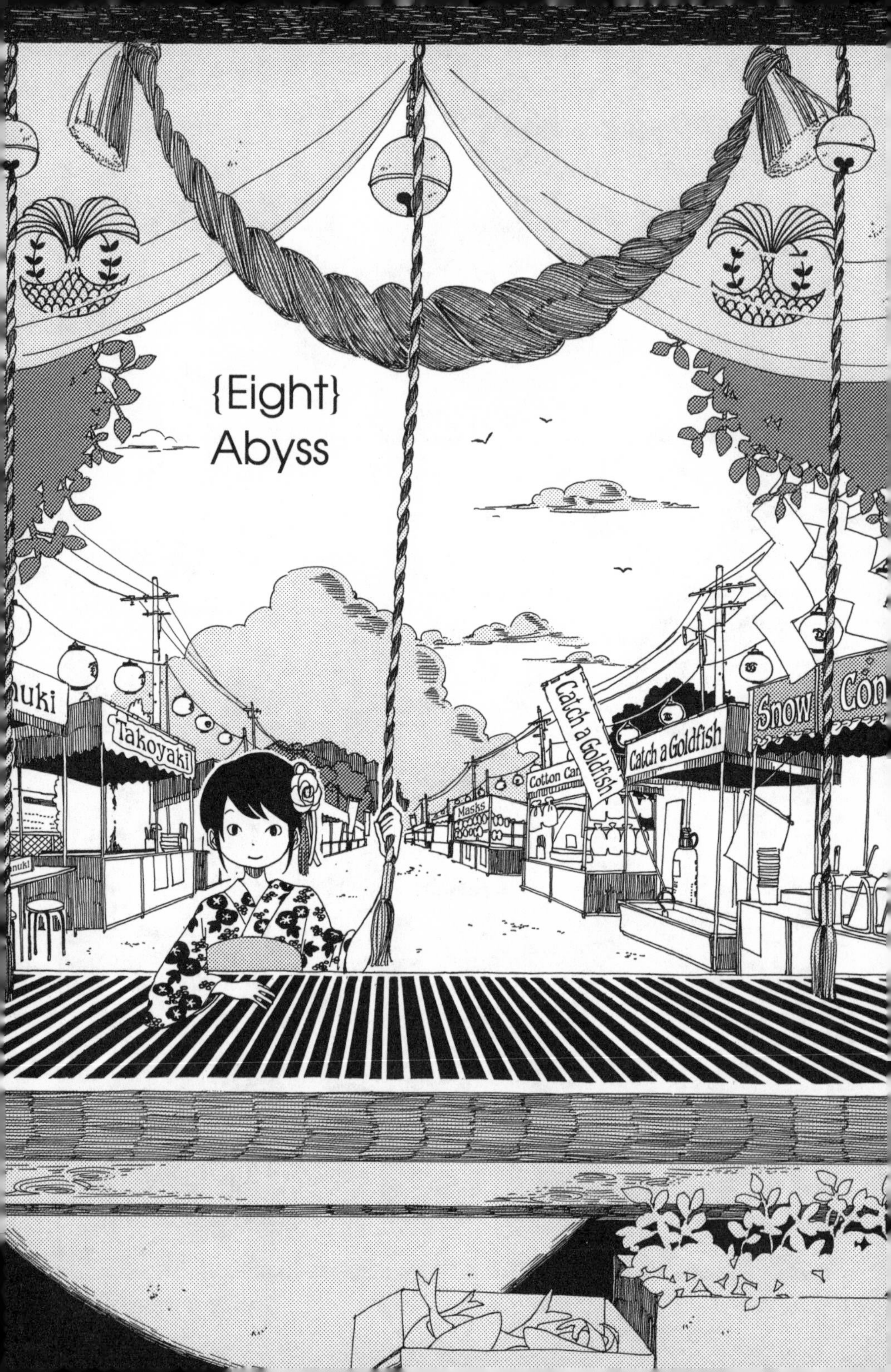
{Eight}
Abyss
Takoyaki
Catch a Goldfish
Catch a Goldfish
Masks

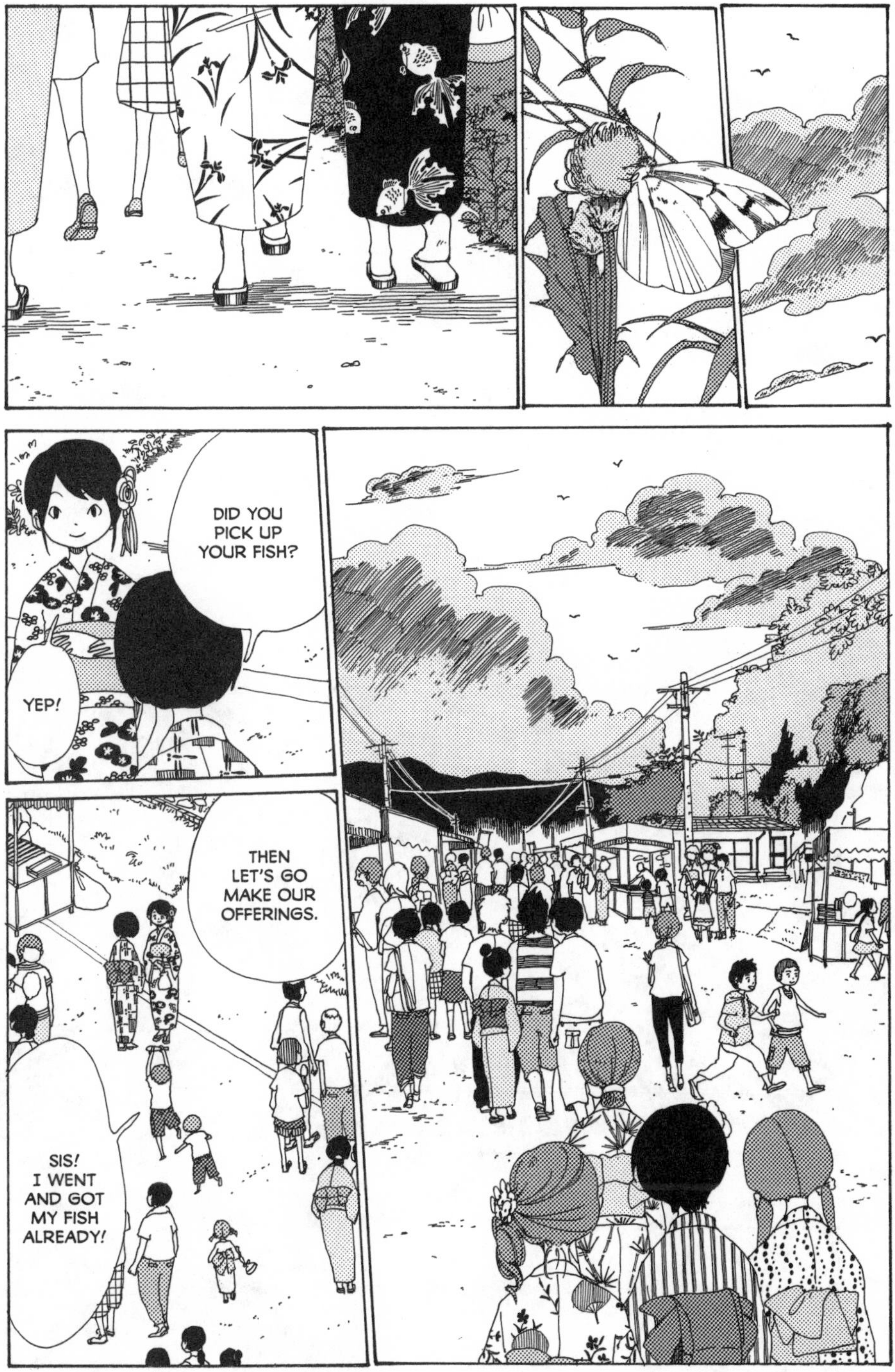
DID YOU PICK UP YOUR FISH?
YEP!
THEN LET'S GO MAKE OUR OFFERINGS.
SIS! I WENT AND GOT MY FISH ALREADY!

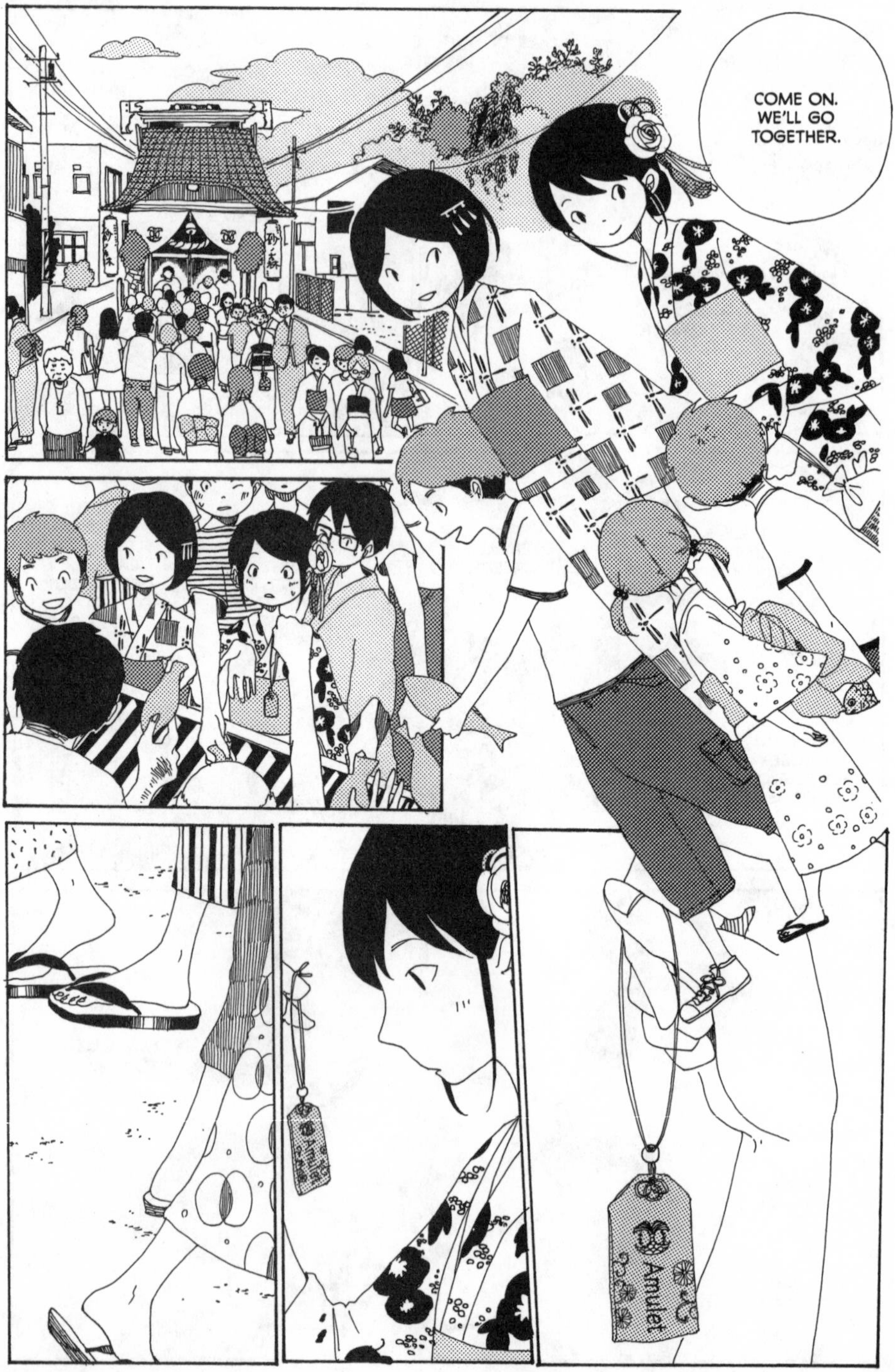
COME ON. WE'LL GO TOGETHER.
Amulet

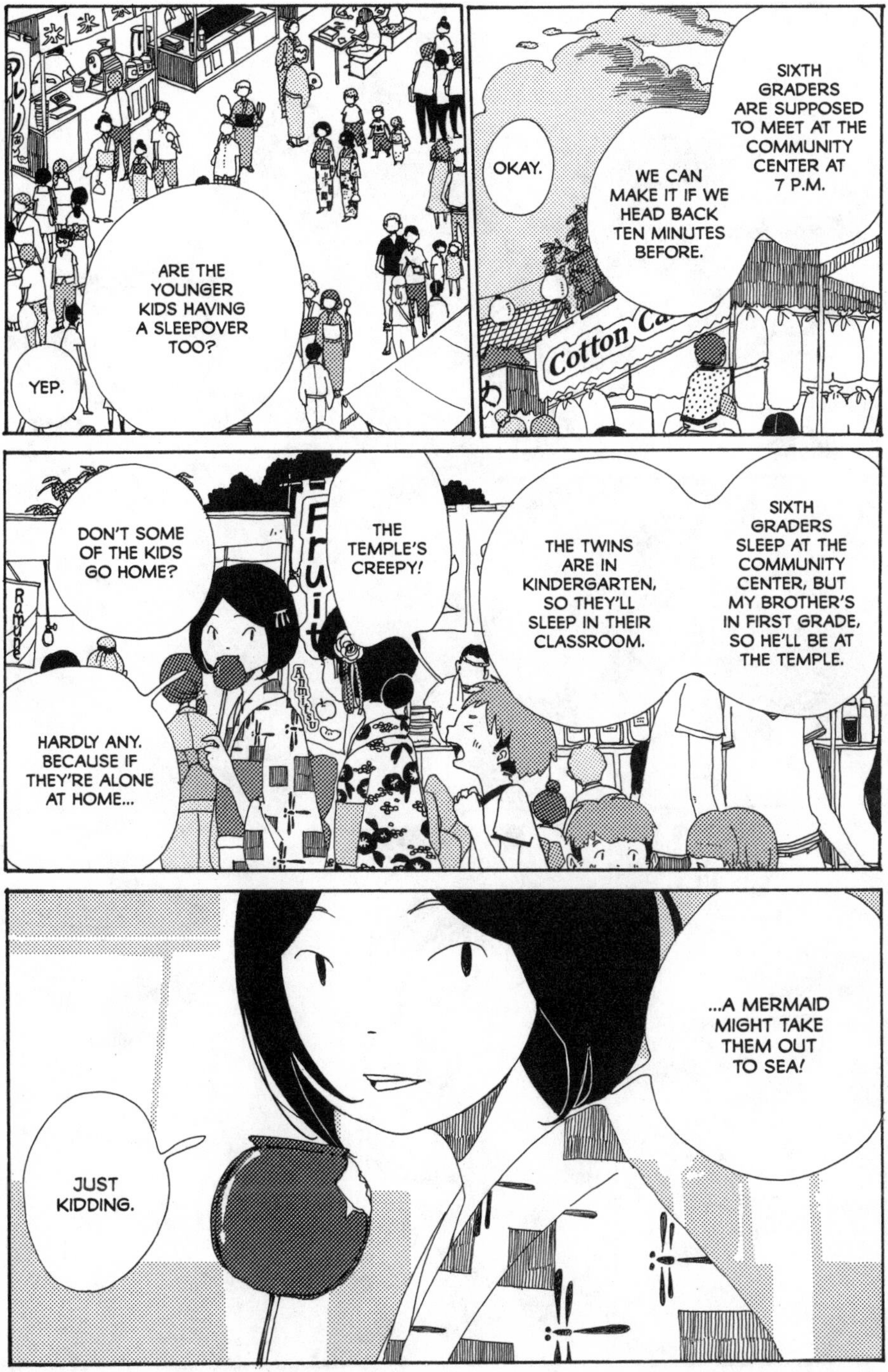
SIXTH GRADERS ARE SUPPOSED TO MEET AT THE COMMUNITY CENTER AT 7 P.M.
WE CAN MAKE IT IF WE HEAD BACK TEN MINUTES BEFORE.
OKAY.
ARE THE YOUNGER KIDS HAVING A SLEEPOVER TOO?
YEP.
SIXTH GRADERS SLEEP AT THE COMMUNITY CENTER, BUT MY BROTHER'S IN FIRST GRADE, SO HE'LL BE AT THE TEMPLE.
THE TWINS ARE IN KINDERGARTEN, SO THEY'LL SLEEP IN THEIR CLASSROOM.
THE TEMPLE'S CREEPY!
Fruit
Anmitsu
Ramune
DON'T SOME OF THE KIDS GO HOME?
HARDLY ANY. BECAUSE IF THEY'RE ALONE AT HOME...
...A MERMAID MIGHT TAKE THEM OUT TO SEA!
JUST KIDDING.

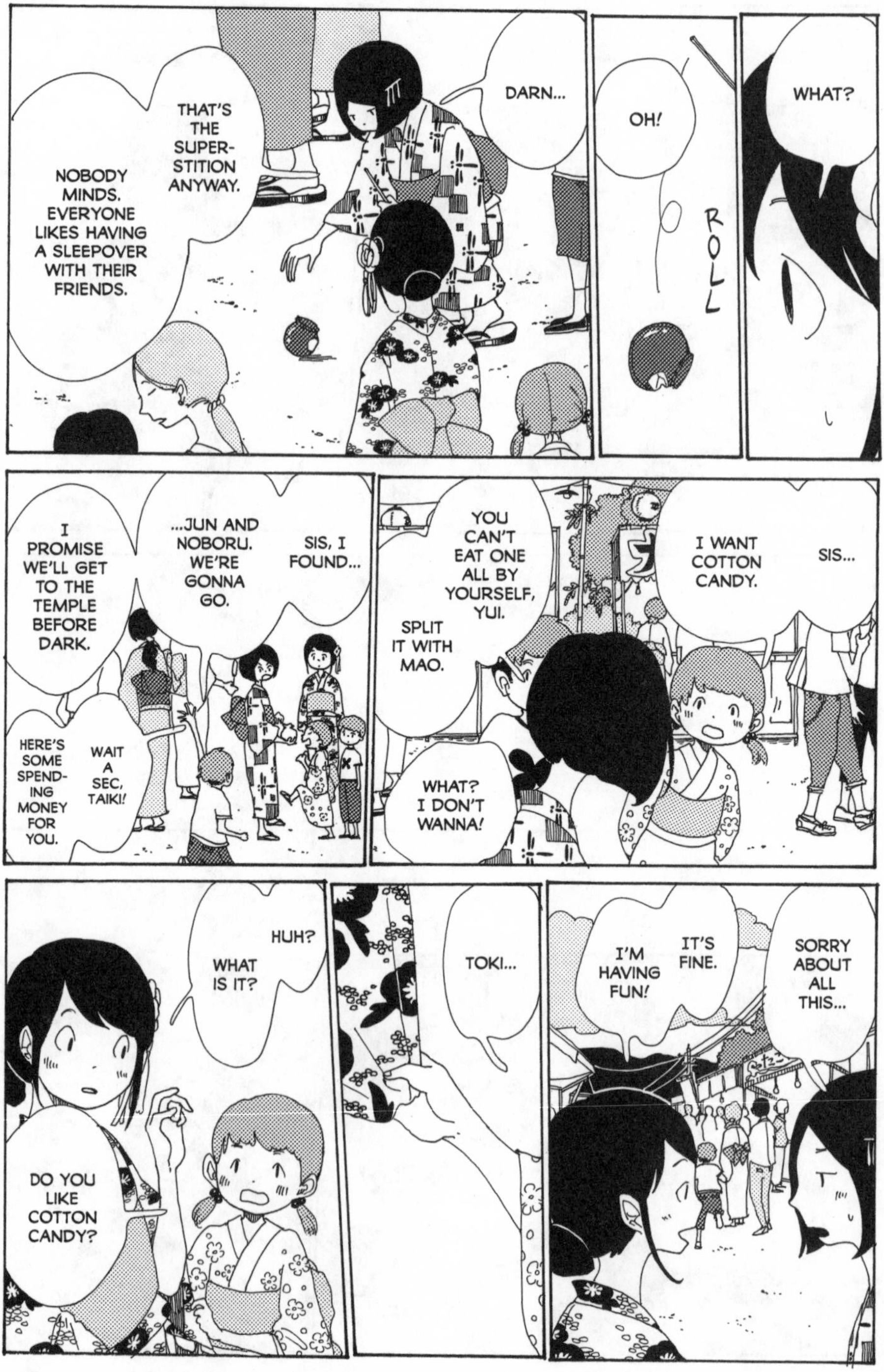
WHAT?
OH!
ROLL
DARN...
THAT'S THE SUPERSTITION ANYWAY.
NOBODY MINDS. EVERYONE LIKES HAVING A SLEEPOVER WITH THEIR FRIENDS.
SIS...
I WANT COTTON CANDY.
YOU CAN'T EAT ONE ALL BY YOURSELF, YUI.
SPLIT IT WITH MAO.
WHAT? I DON'T WANNA!
SIS, I FOUND...
...JUN AND NOBORU. WE'RE GONNA GO.
I PROMISE WE'LL GET TO THE TEMPLE BEFORE DARK.
WAIT A SEC, TAIKI!
HERE'S SOME SPENDING MONEY FOR YOU.
SORRY ABOUT ALL THIS...
IT'S FINE.
I'M HAVING FUN!
TOKI...
HUH?
WHAT IS IT?
DO YOU LIKE COTTON CANDY?

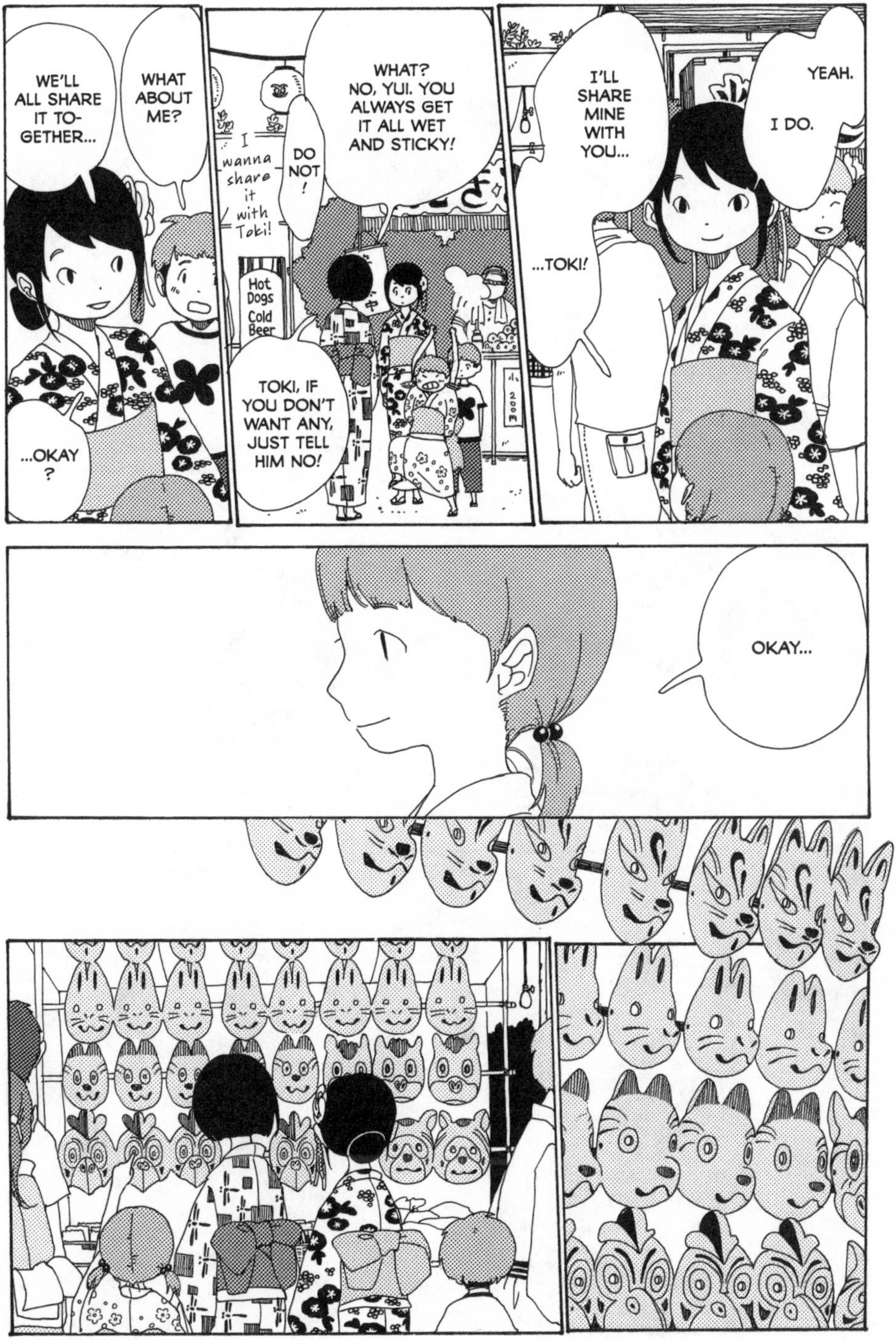
YEAH. I DO.
I'LL SHARE MINE WITH YOU...
...TOKI!
WHAT? NO, YUI. YOU ALWAYS GET IT ALL WET AND STICKY!
DO NOT!
I wanna share it with Toki!
Hot Dogs Cold Beer
TOKI, IF YOU DON'T WANT ANY, JUST TELL HIM NO!
WHAT ABOUT ME?
WE'LL ALL SHARE IT TO-GETHER...
...OKAY?
OKAY...

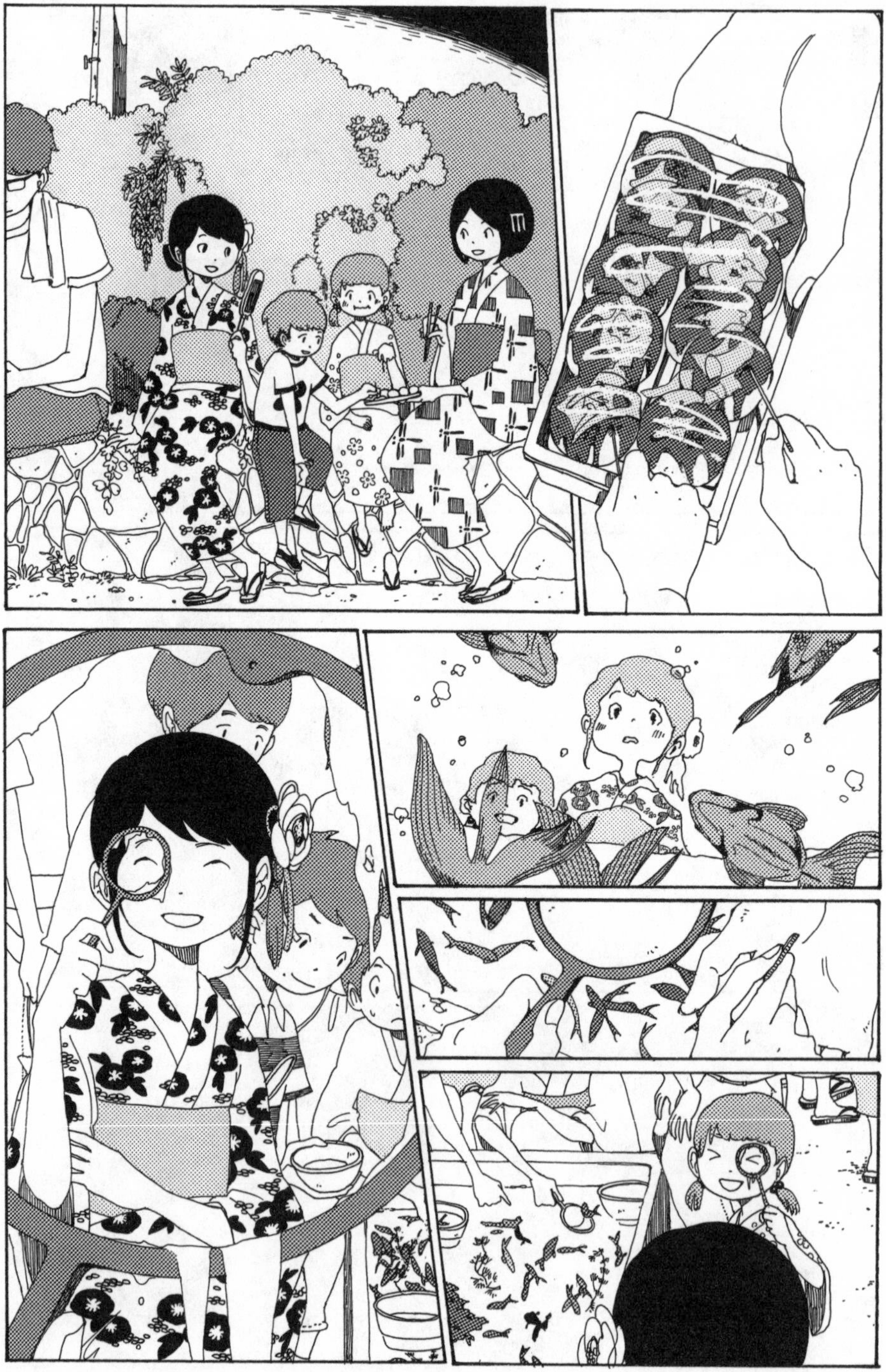

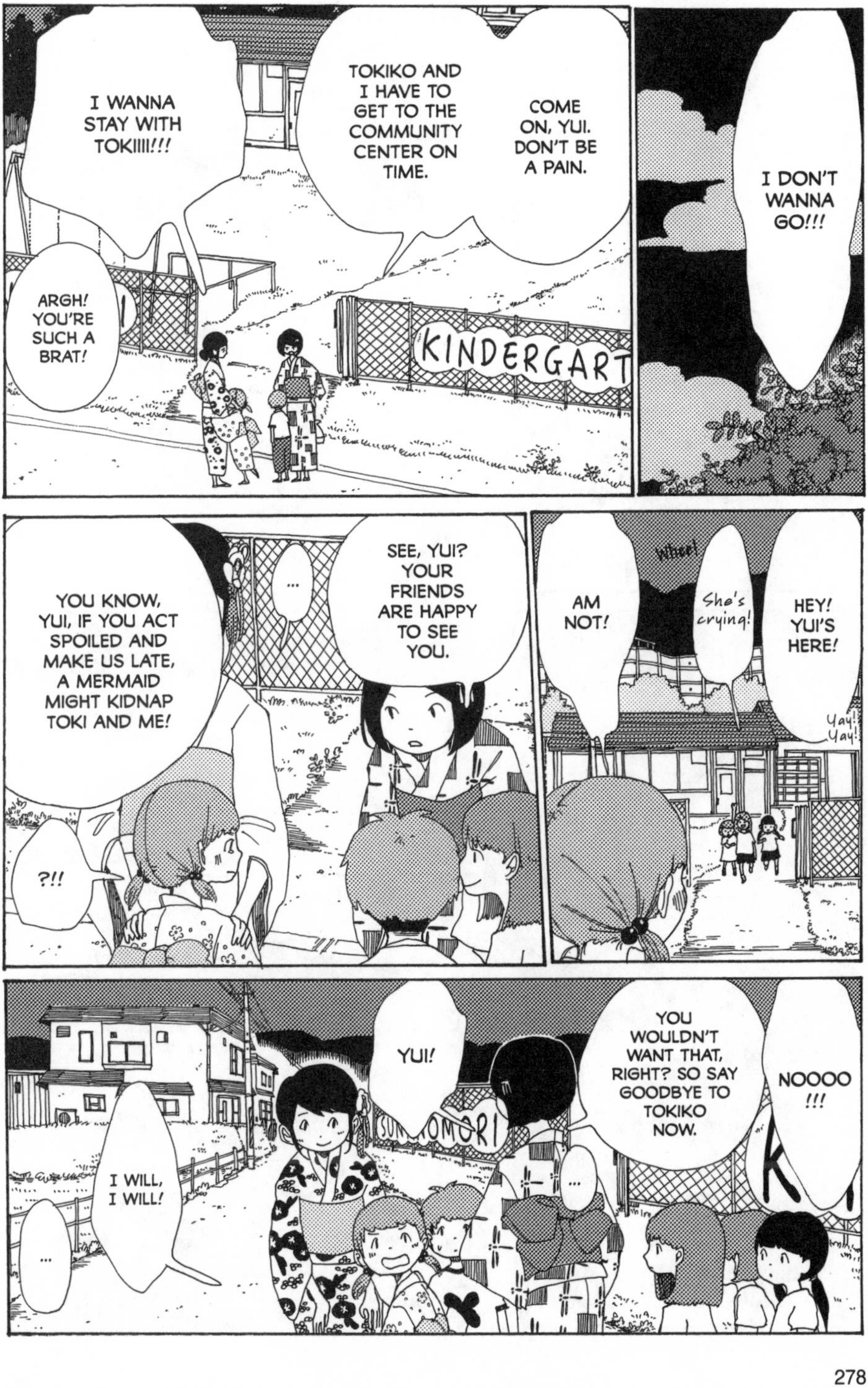
I DON'T WANNA GO!!!
COME ON, YUI. DON'T BE A PAIN.
TOKIKO AND I HAVE TO GET TO THE COMMUNITY CENTER ON TIME.
I WANNA STAY WITH TOKIIII!!!
ARGH! YOU'RE SUCH A BRAT!
KINDERGART
HEY! YUI'S HERE!
Yay! Yay!
She's crying!
Whee!
AM NOT!
SEE, YUI? YOUR FRIENDS ARE HAPPY TO SEE YOU.
...
YOU KNOW, YUI, IF YOU ACT SPOILED AND MAKE US LATE, A MERMAID MIGHT KIDNAP TOKI AND ME!
?!!
NOOOO !!!
YOU WOULDN'T WANT THAT, RIGHT? SO SAY GOODBYE TO TOKIKO NOW.
...
YUI!
I WILL, I WILL!
...

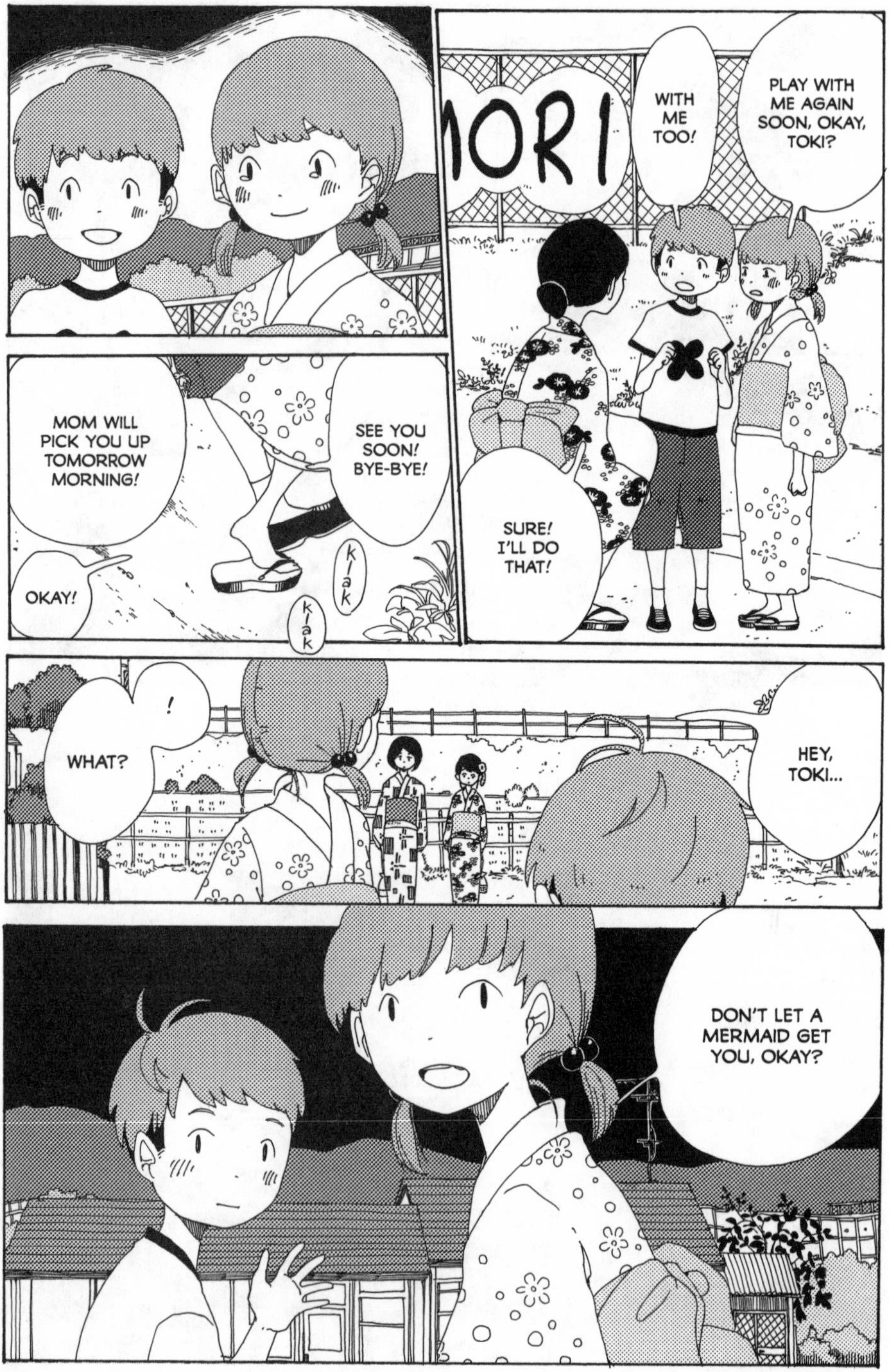
PLAY WITH ME AGAIN SOON, OKAY, TOKI?
WITH ME TOO!
MORI
SURE! I'LL DO THAT!
SEE YOU SOON! BYE-BYE!
MOM WILL PICK YOU UP TOMORROW MORNING!
OKAY!
klak
klak
HEY, TOKI...
!
WHAT?
DON'T LET A MERMAID GET YOU, OKAY?

C'MON, TOKI.
WE NEED TO GET GOING.
TOKI...?
WHAT?!
RIGHT...
COMING!
SETTLE DOWN, EVERYONE...
NIGHT IS FALLING, SO I'LL GO OVER THE RULES.
THIS YEAR, AS ALWAYS...
...YOU NEED TO REMEMBER...
...NOT TO STEP FOOT OUTSIDE THIS ROOM.

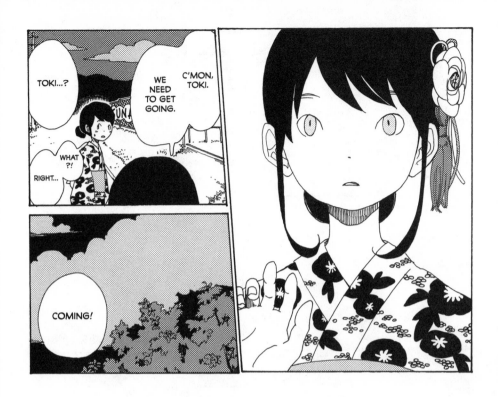

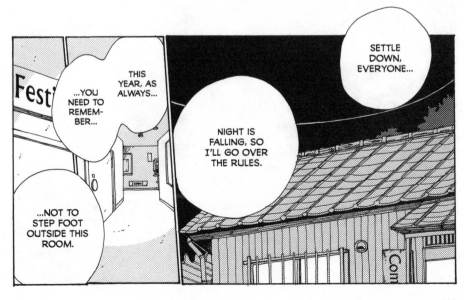

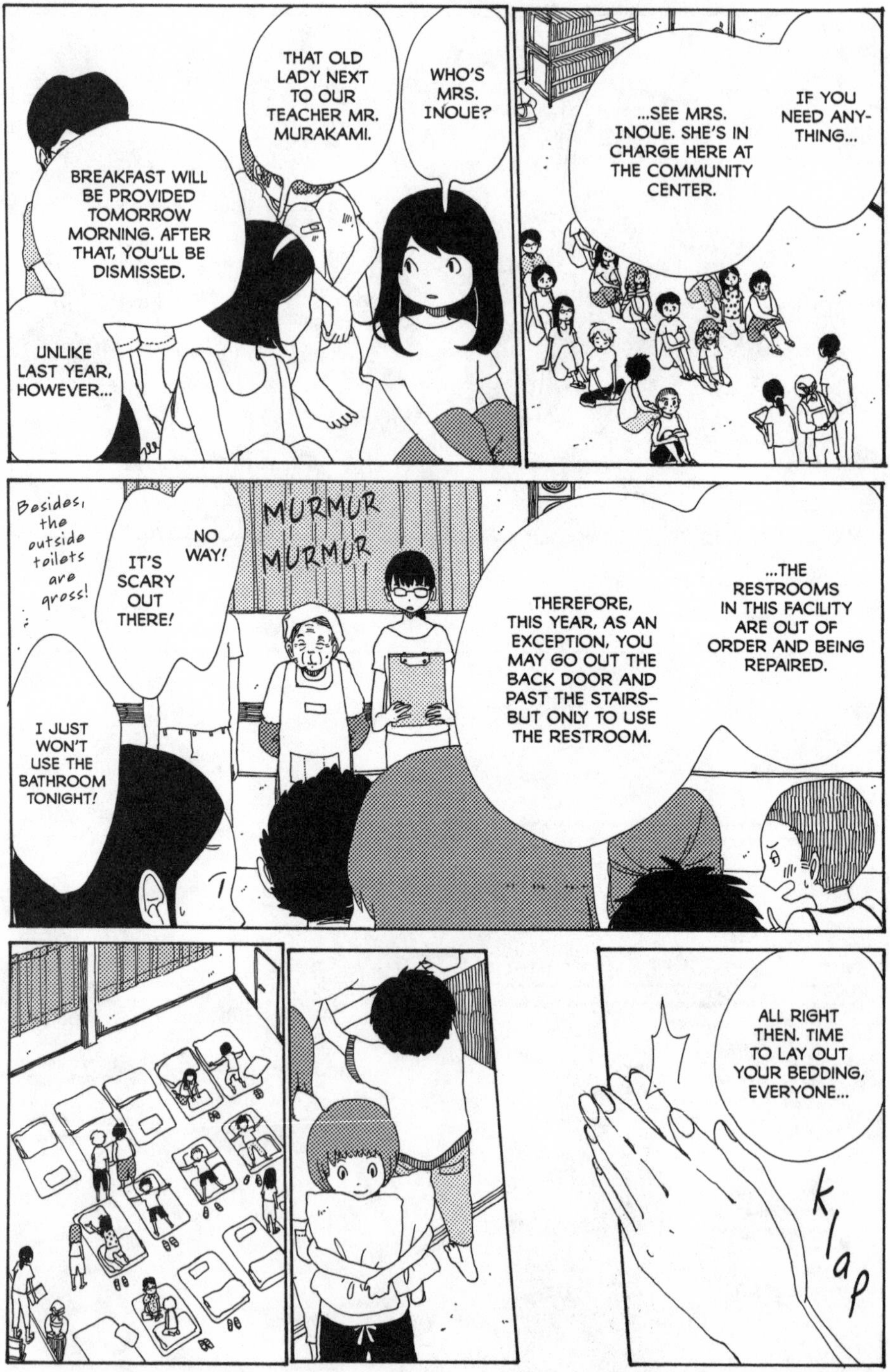
IF YOU NEED ANY-THING...
...SEE MRS. INOUE. SHE'S IN CHARGE HERE AT THE COMMUNITY CENTER.
WHO'S MRS. INOUE?
THAT OLD LADY NEXT TO OUR TEACHER MR. MURAKAMI.
BREAKFAST WILL BE PROVIDED TOMORROW MORNING. AFTER THAT, YOU'LL BE DISMISSED.
UNLIKE LAST YEAR, HOWEVER...
...THE RESTROOMS IN THIS FACILITY ARE OUT OF ORDER AND BEING REPAIRED.
THEREFORE, THIS YEAR, AS AN EXCEPTION, YOU MAY GO OUT THE BACK DOOR AND PAST THE STAIRS- BUT ONLY TO USE THE RESTROOM.
MURMUR MURMUR
NO WAY!
IT'S SCARY OUT THERE!
Besides, the outside toilets are gross!
I JUST WON'T USE THE BATHROOM TONIGHT!
ALL RIGHT THEN. TIME TO LAY OUT YOUR BEDDING, EVERYONE...
klap

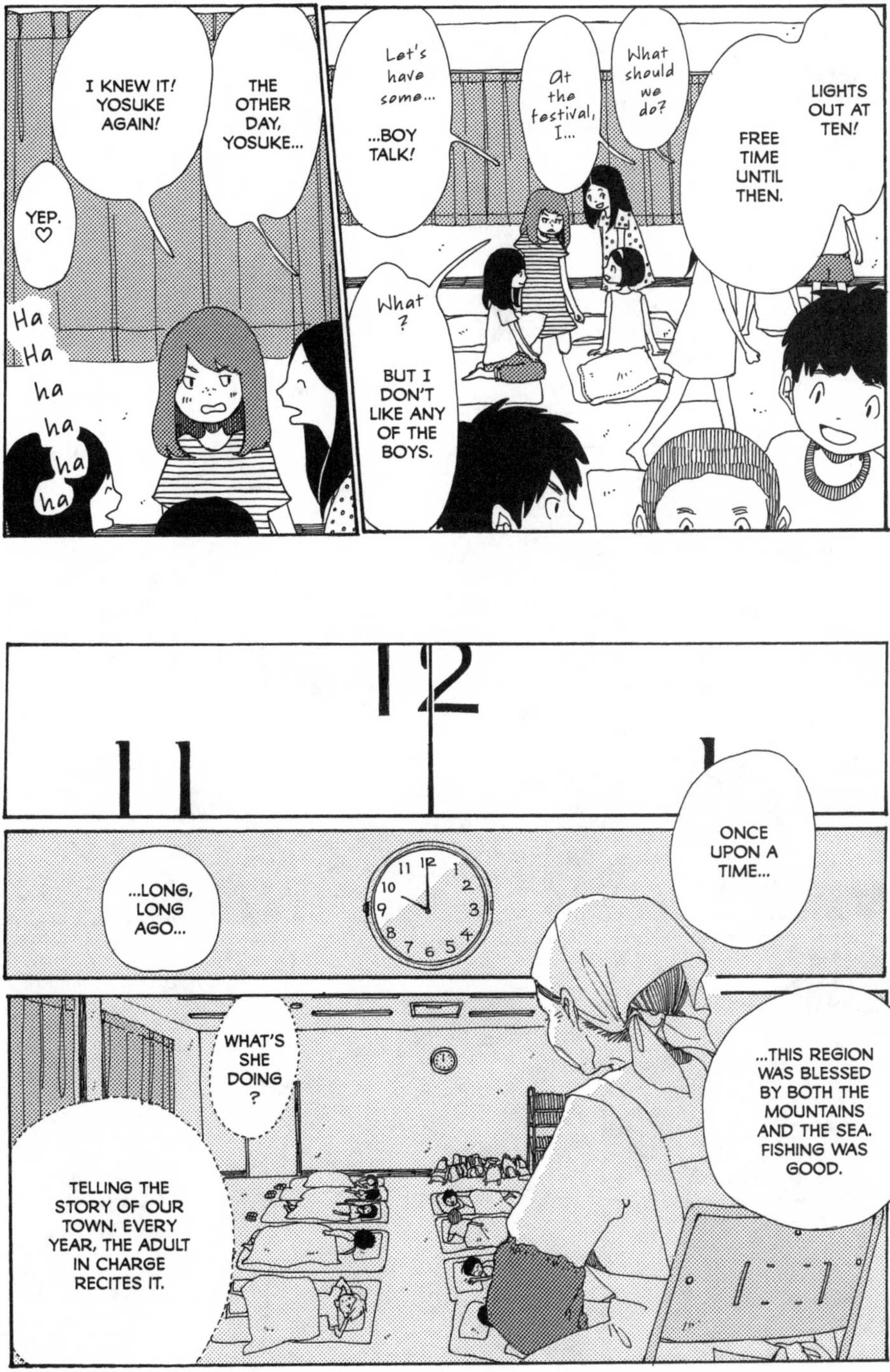
LIGHTS OUT AT TEN!
FREE TIME UNTIL THEN.
What should we do?
At the festival, I...
Let's have some... ...BOY TALK!
What? BUT I DON'T LIKE ANY OF THE BOYS.
THE OTHER DAY, YOSUKE...
I KNEW IT! YOSUKE AGAIN!
YEP. ♡
Ha Ha ha ha ha ha
ONCE UPON A TIME...
...LONG, LONG AGO...
...THIS REGION WAS BLESSED BY BOTH THE MOUNTAINS AND THE SEA. FISHING WAS GOOD.
WHAT'S SHE DOING?
TELLING THE STORY OF OUR TOWN. EVERY YEAR, THE ADULT IN CHARGE RECITES IT.

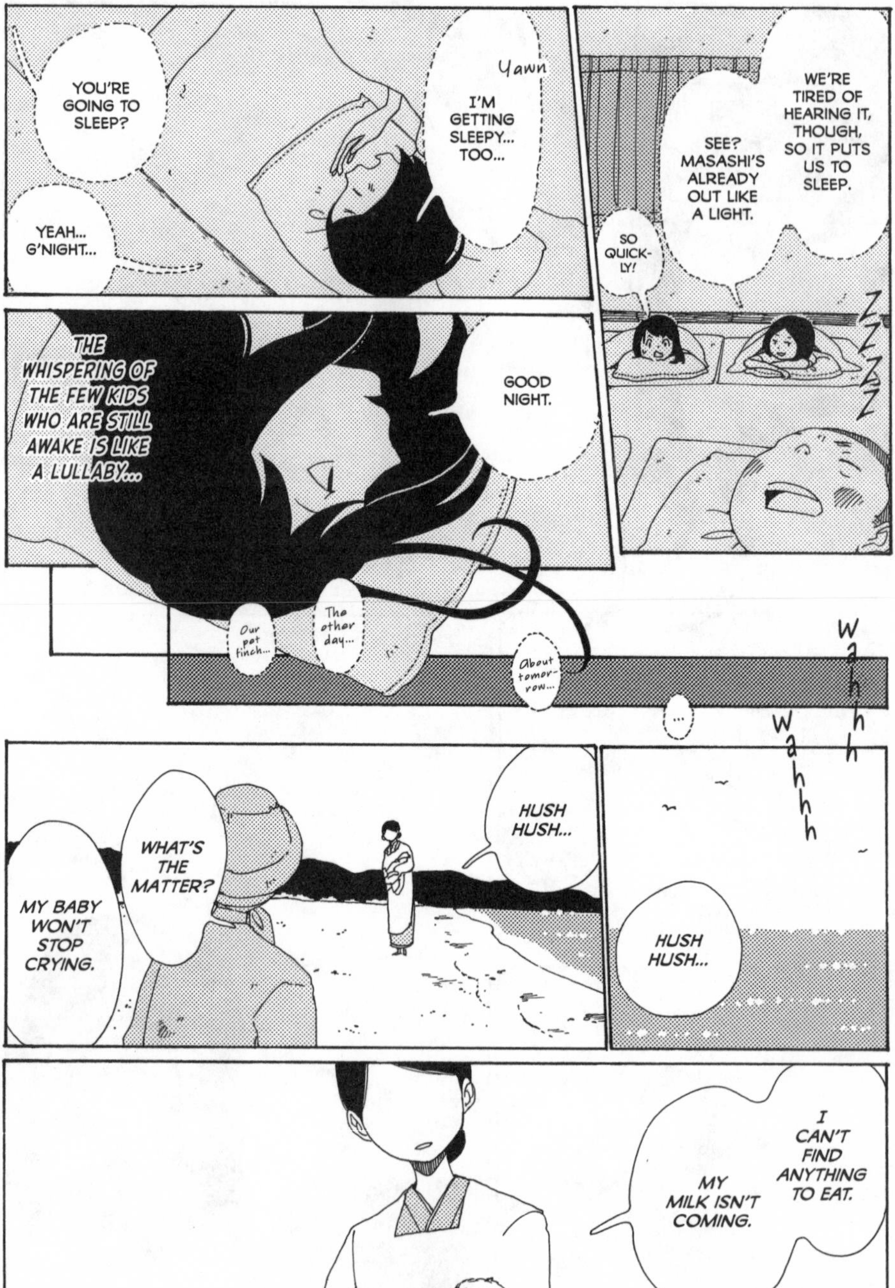
WE'RE TIRED OF HEARING IT, THOUGH, SO IT PUTS US TO SLEEP.
SEE? MASASHI'S ALREADY OUT LIKE A LIGHT.
SO QUICKLY!
ZZZZZ
Yawn
I'M GETTING SLEEPY... TOO...
YOU'RE GOING TO SLEEP?
YEAH... G'NIGHT...
GOOD NIGHT.
THE WHISPERING OF THE FEW KIDS WHO ARE STILL AWAKE IS LIKE A LULLABY...
About tomor-row...
The other day...
Our pet finch...
Wahhh
...
Wahhh
HUSH HUSH...
HUSH HUSH...
WHAT'S THE MATTER?
MY BABY WON'T STOP CRYING.
I CAN'T FIND ANYTHING TO EAT.
MY MILK ISN'T COMING.

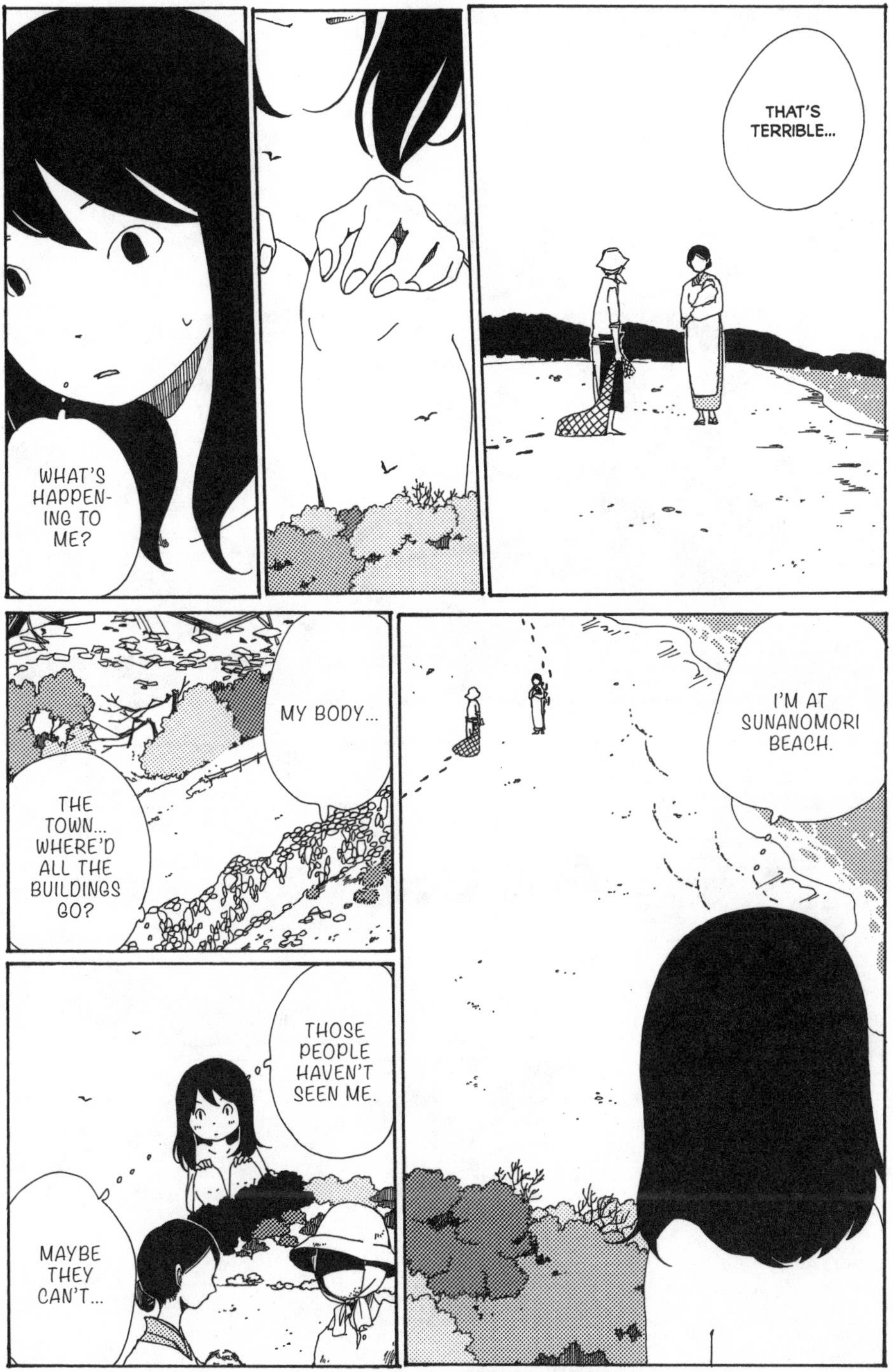
THAT'S TERRIBLE...
WHAT'S HAPPENING TO ME?
I'M AT SUNANOMORI BEACH.
MY BODY...
THE TOWN... WHERE'D ALL THE BUILDINGS GO?
THOSE PEOPLE HAVEN'T SEEN ME.
MAYBE THEY CAN'T...

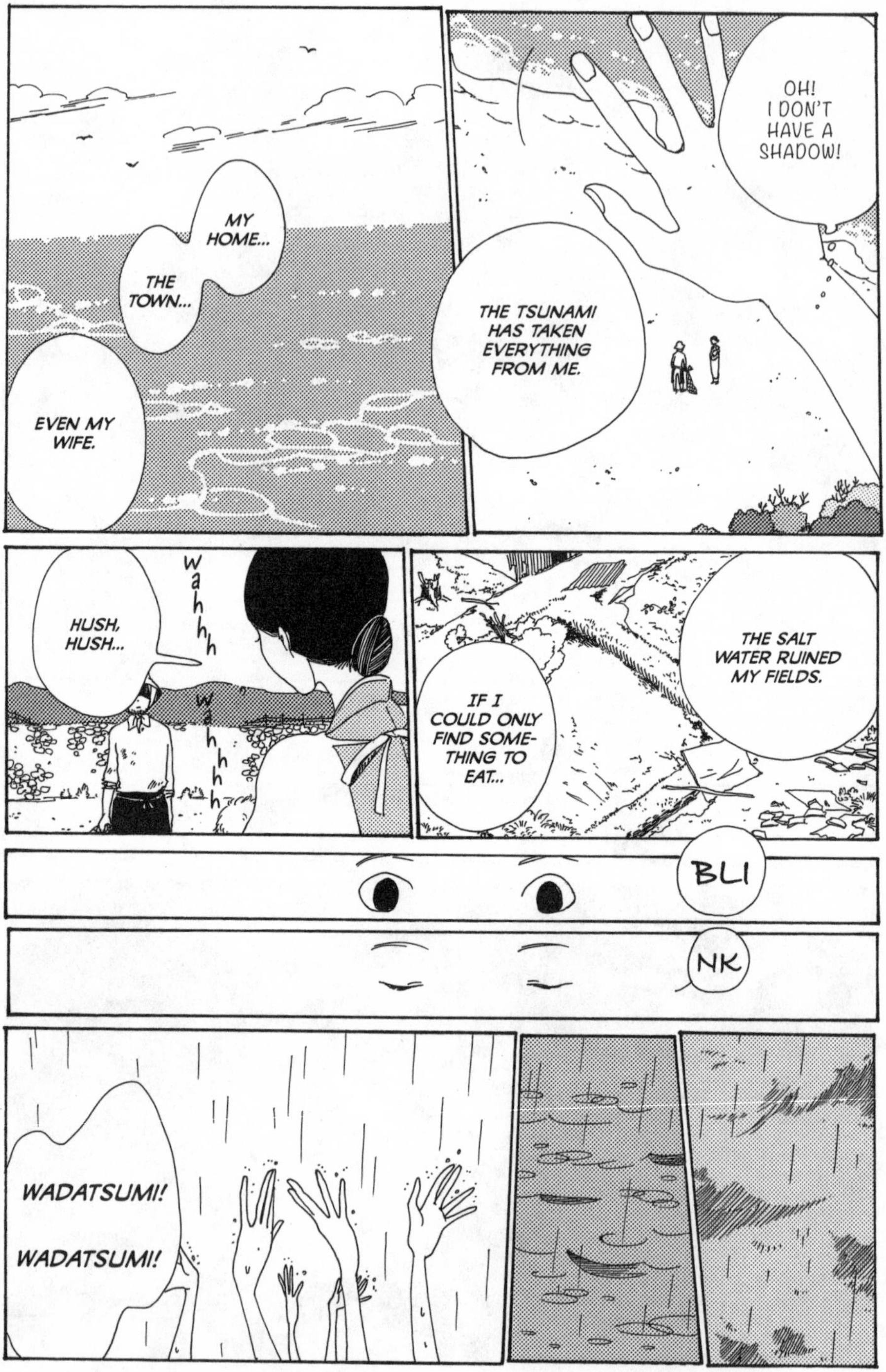

OH! I DON'T HAVE A SHADOW!
THE TSUNAMI HAS TAKEN EVERYTHING FROM ME.
MY HOME...
THE TOWN...
EVEN MY WIFE.
THE SALT WATER RUINED MY FIELDS.
IF I COULD ONLY FIND SOME-THING TO EAT...
wahhh
HUSH, HUSH...
wahhhhh
BLI
NK
WADATSUMI!
WADATSUMI!

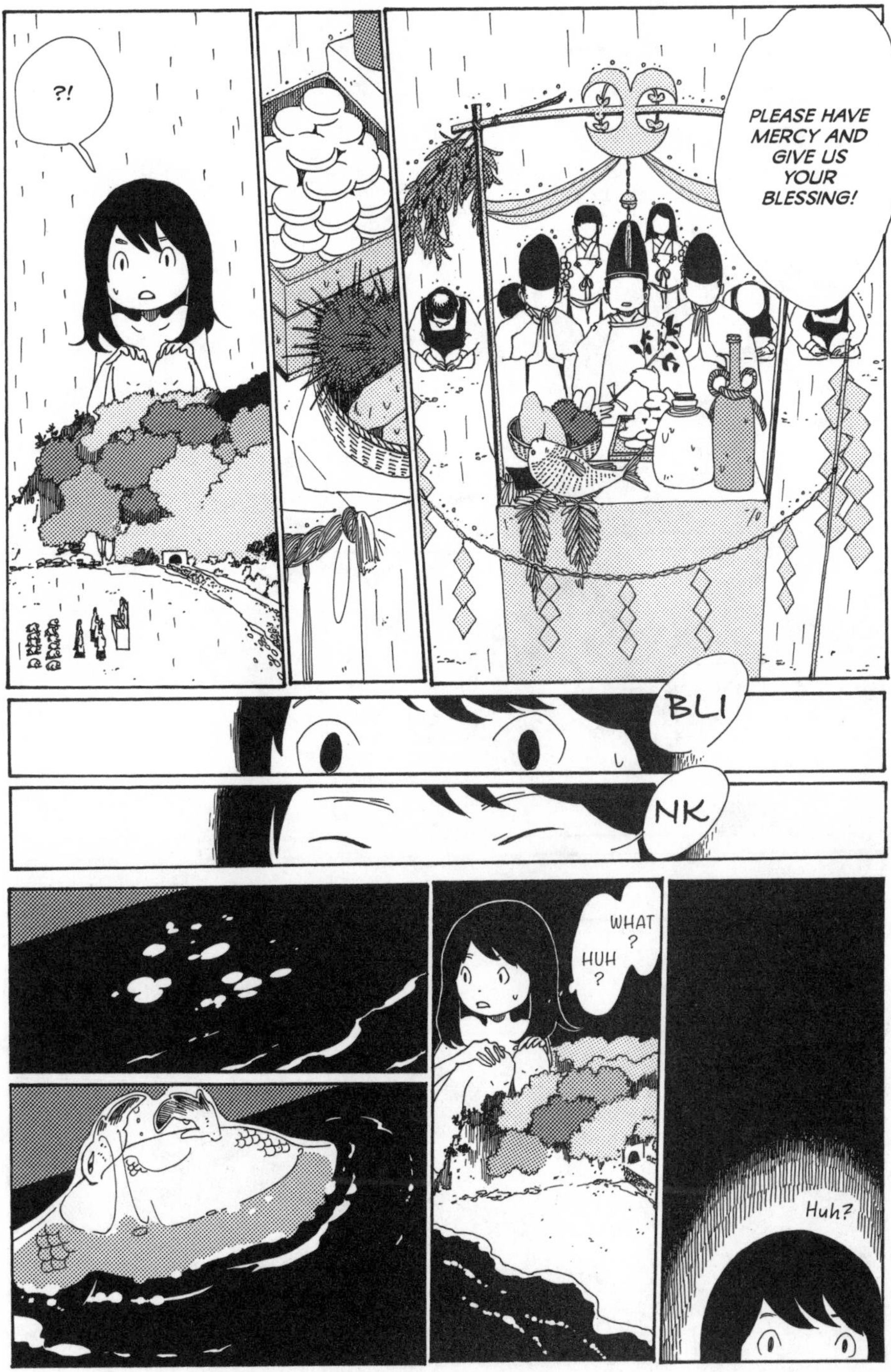
PLEASE HAVE MERCY AND GIVE US YOUR BLESSING!
?!
BLI
NK
Huh?
WHAT ?
HUH ?

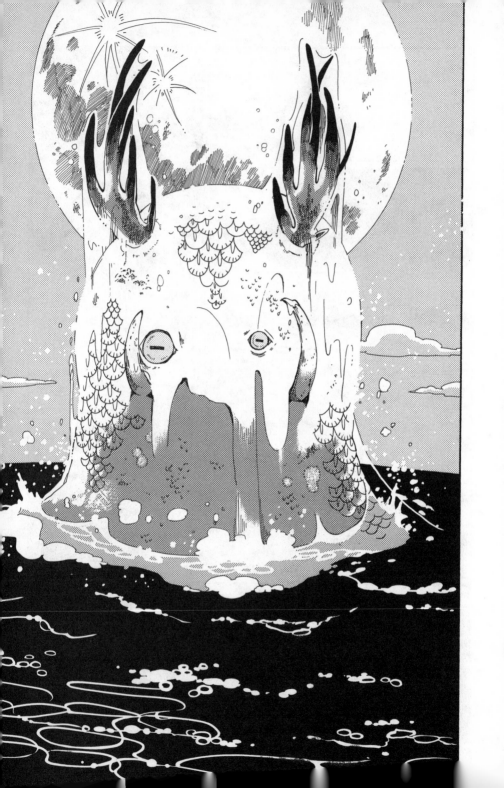

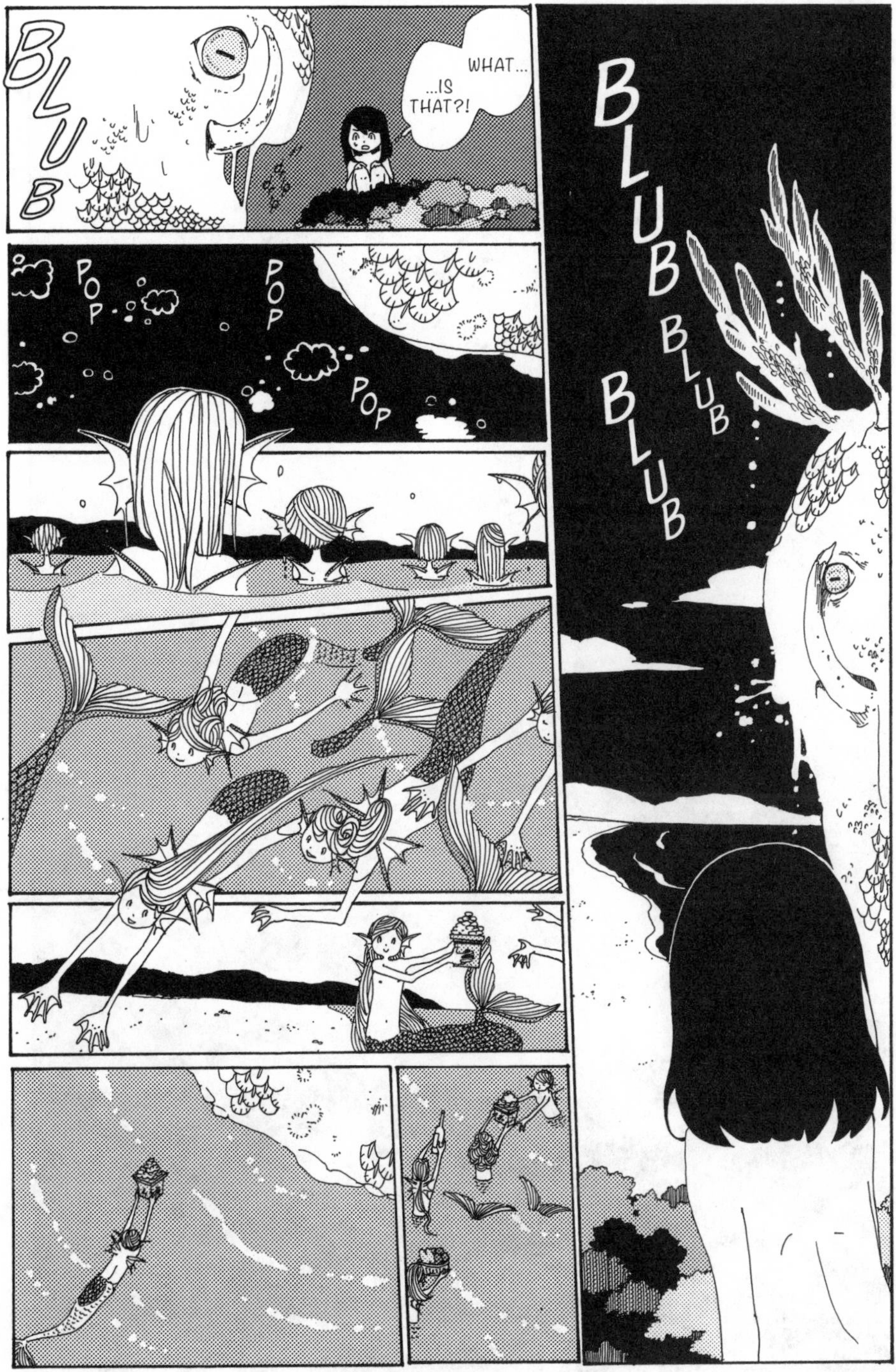
BLUB
BLUB
BLUB
WHAT... ...IS THAT?!
BLUB
POP
POP
POP

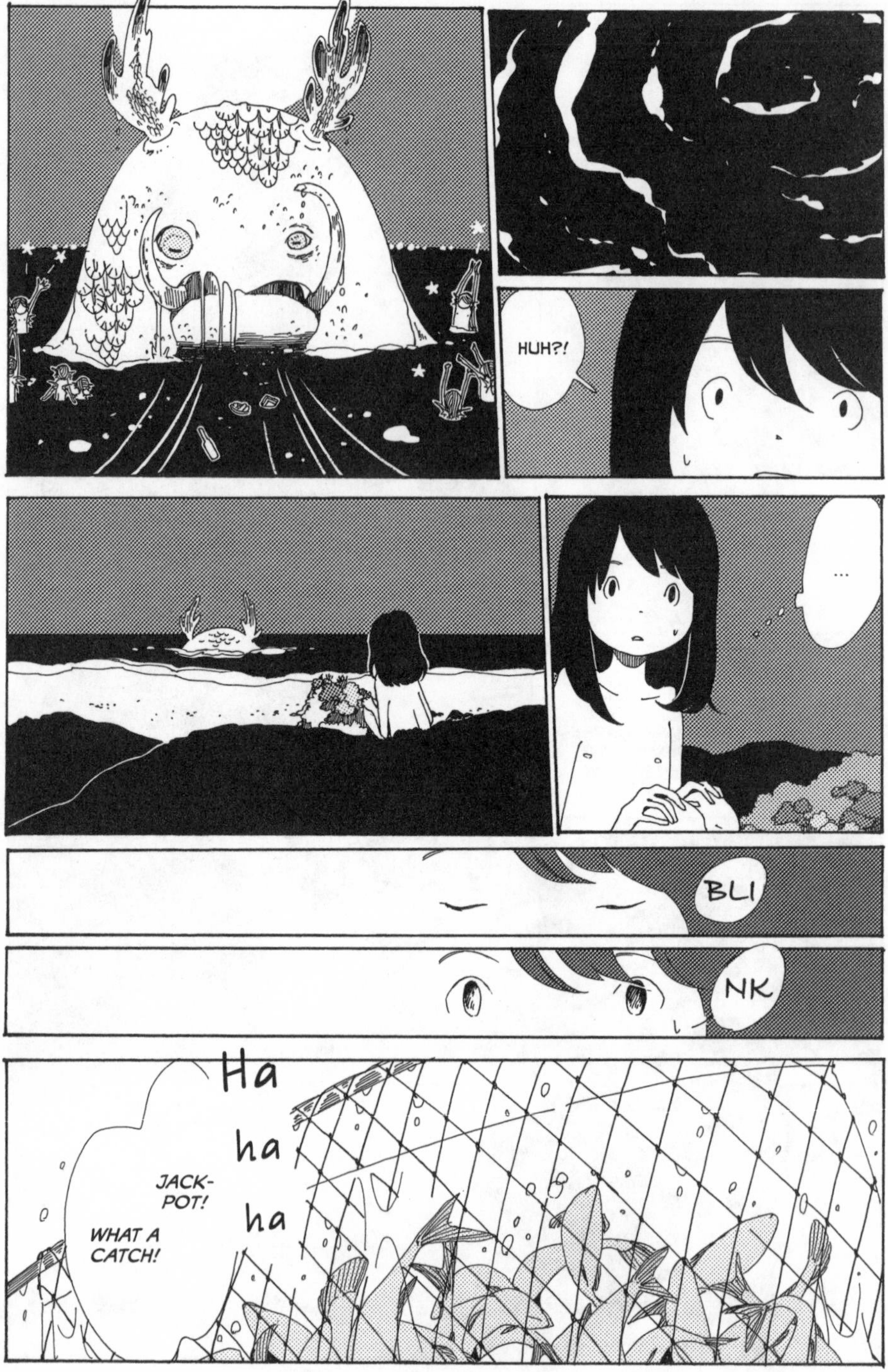
HUH?!
...
BLI
NK
Ha ha ha
JACK-POT! WHAT A CATCH!

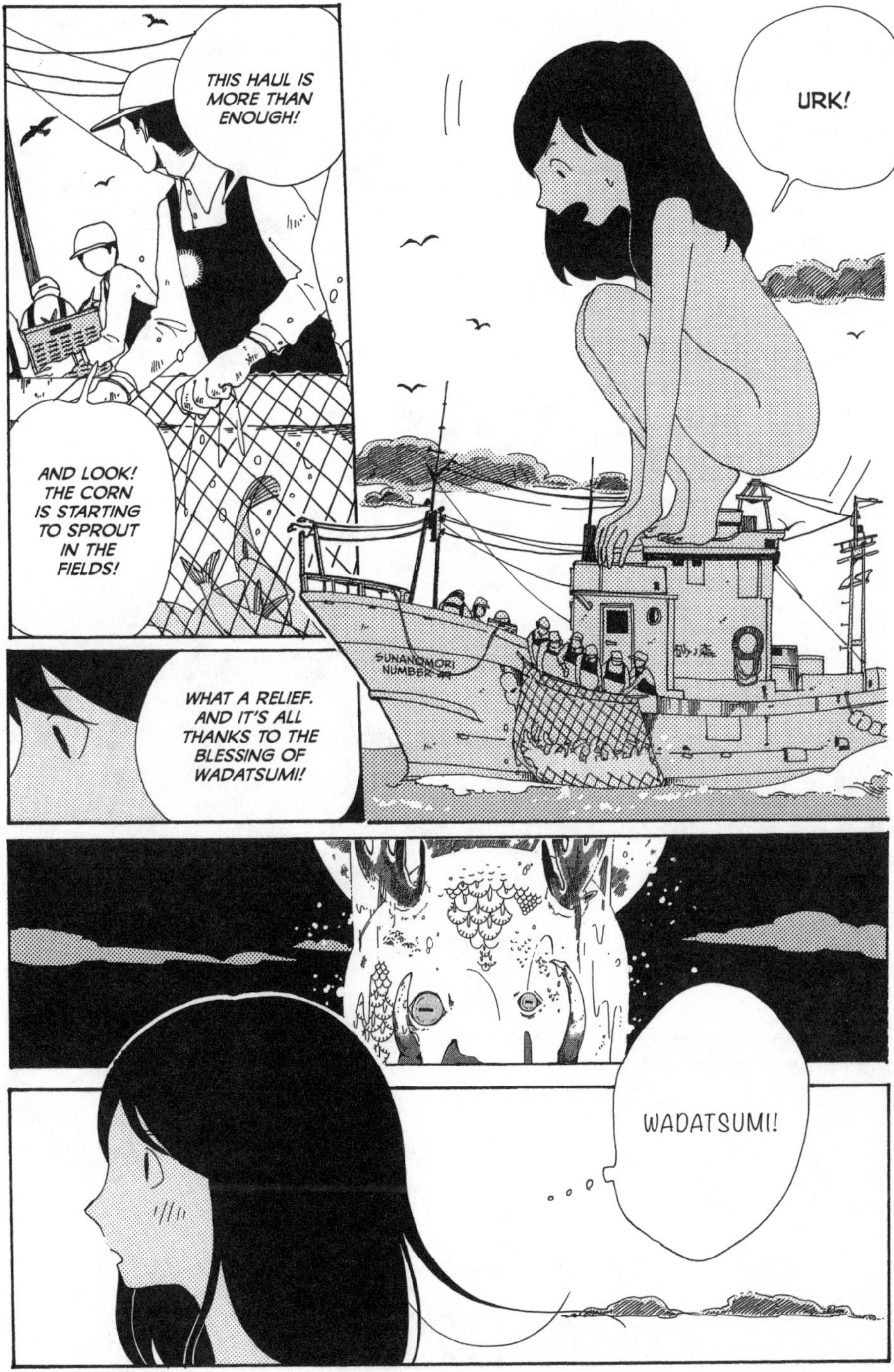
URK!
THIS HAUL IS MORE THAN ENOUGH!
AND LOOK! THE CORN IS STARTING TO SPROUT IN THE FIELDS!
WHAT A RELIEF. AND IT'S ALL THANKS TO THE BLESSING OF WADATSUMI!
SUNANOMORI NUMBER
WADATSUMI!

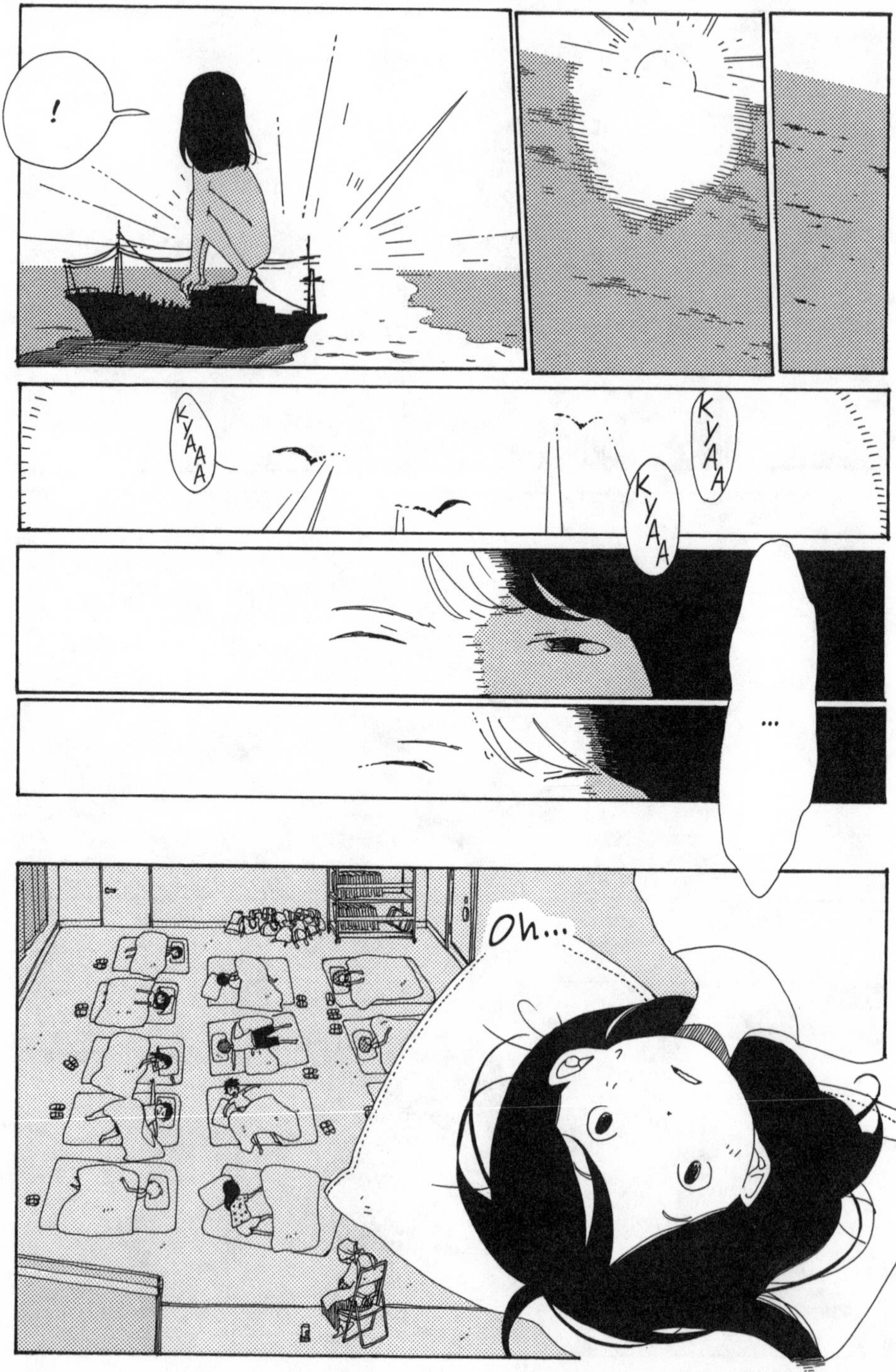
!
KYAAA
KYAAA
KYAAA
...
Oh...

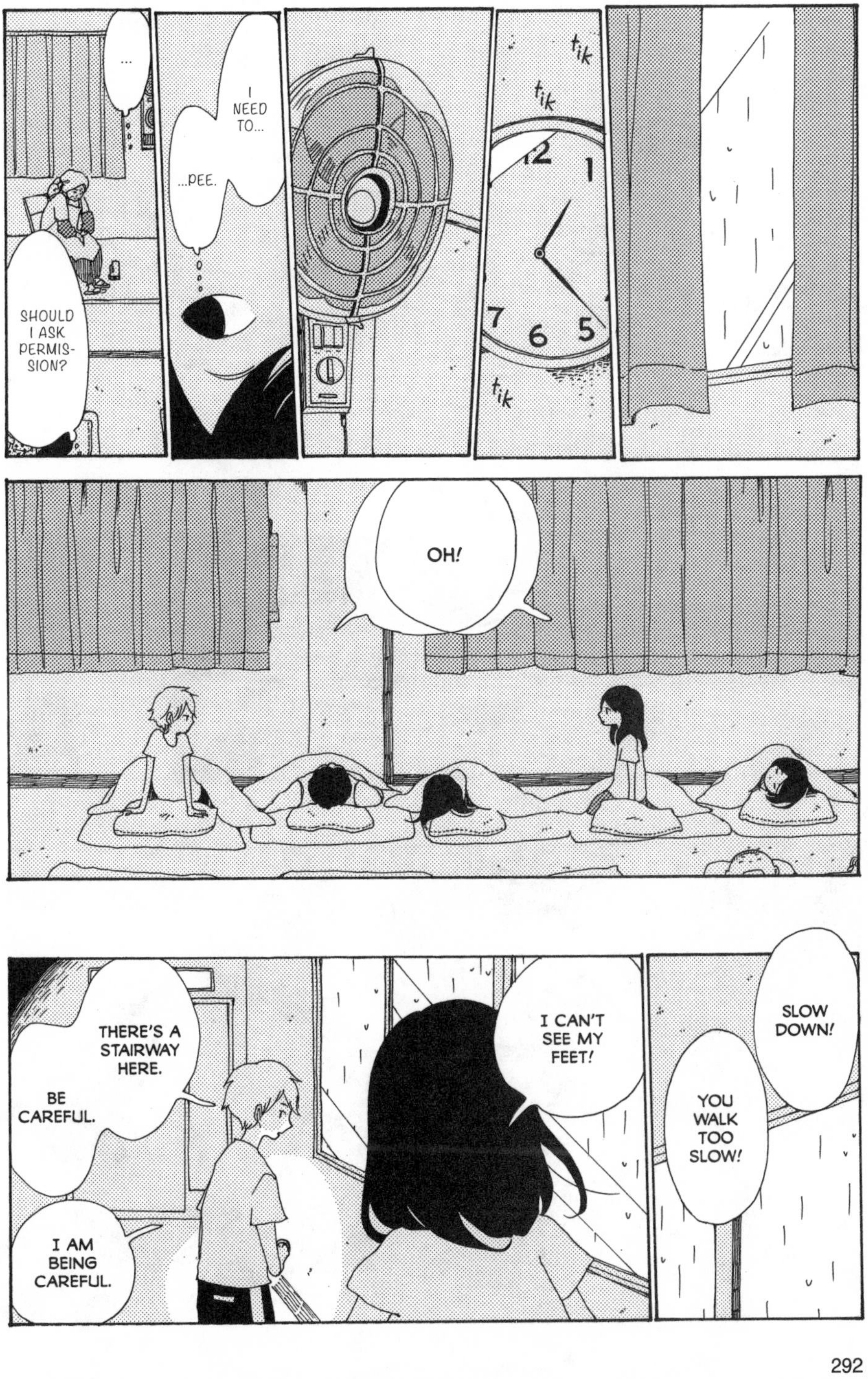
tik
tik
tik
I NEED TO...
...PEE.
...
SHOULD I ASK PERMISSION?
OH!
SLOW DOWN!
YOU WALK TOO SLOW!
I CAN'T SEE MY FEET!
THERE'S A STAIRWAY HERE.
BE CAREFUL.
I AM BEING CAREFUL.

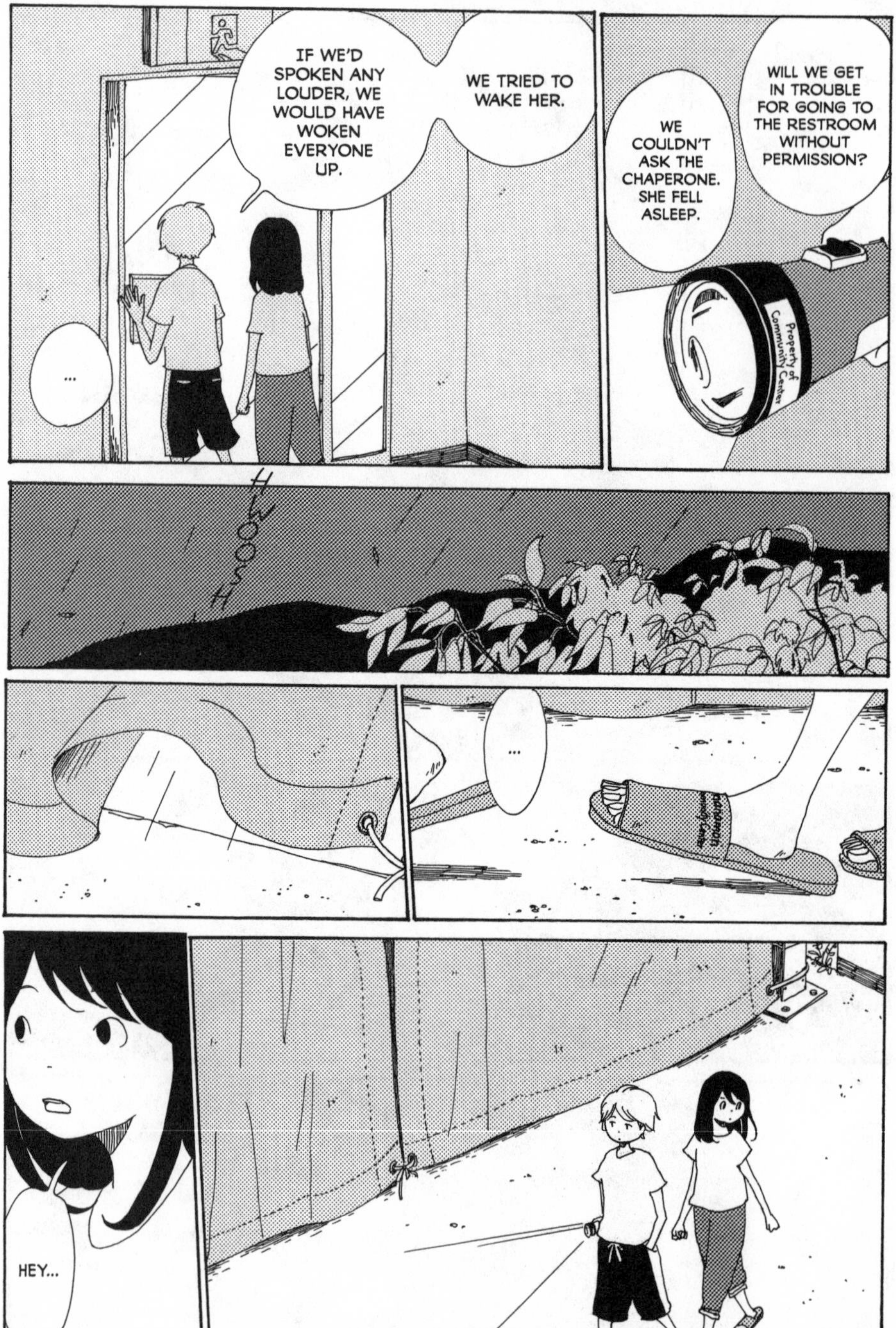
WILL WE GET IN TROUBLE FOR GOING TO THE RESTROOM WITHOUT PERMISSION?
WE COULDN'T ASK THE CHAPERONE. SHE FELL ASLEEP.
Property of Community Center
WE TRIED TO WAKE HER.
IF WE'D SPOKEN ANY LOUDER, WE WOULD HAVE WOKEN EVERYONE UP.
...
HWOOSH
...
HEY...

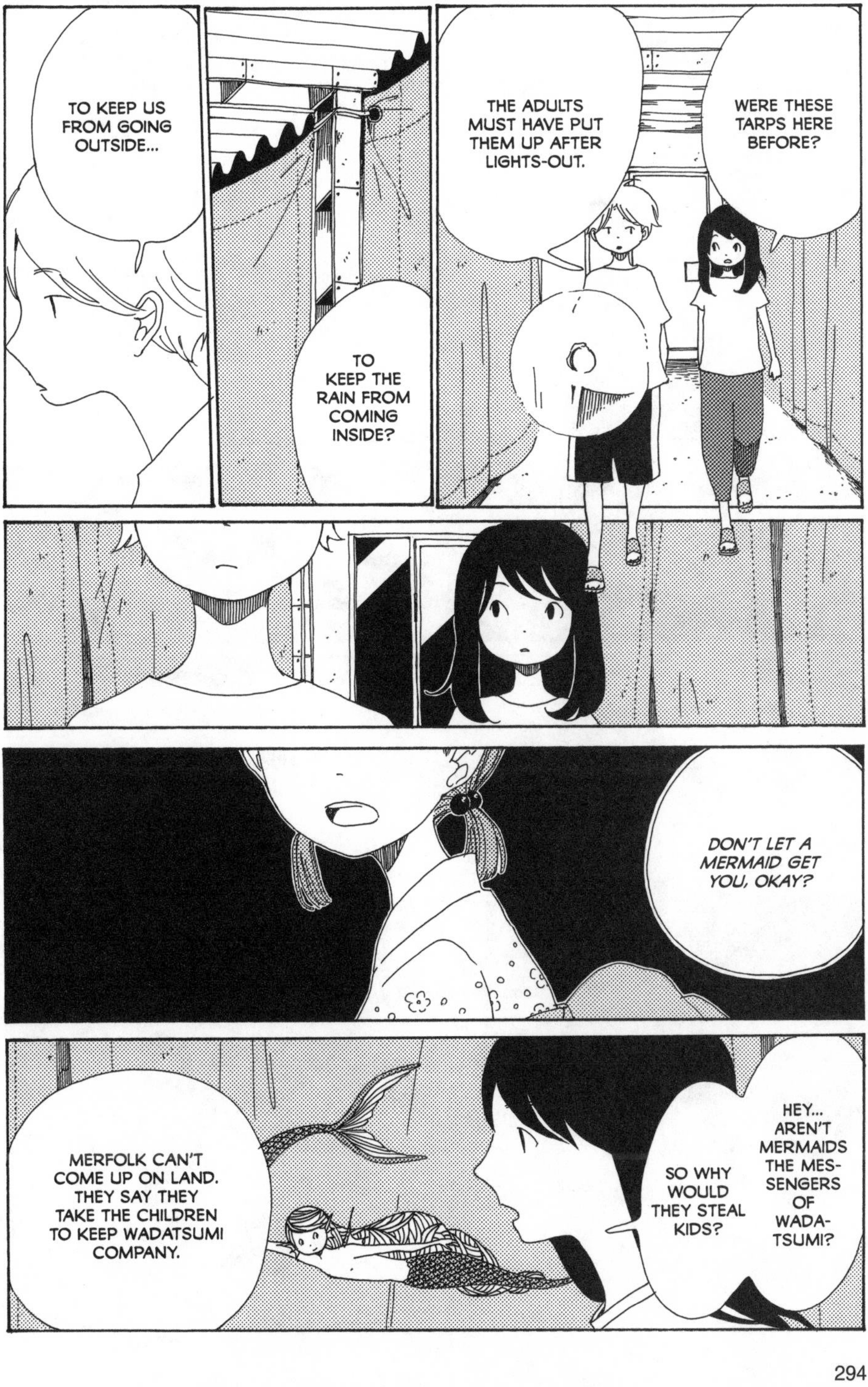
WERE THESE TARPS HERE BEFORE?
THE ADULTS MUST HAVE PUT THEM UP AFTER LIGHTS-OUT.
TO KEEP THE RAIN FROM COMING INSIDE?
TO KEEP US FROM GOING OUTSIDE...
DON'T LET A MERMAID GET YOU, OKAY?
HEY... AREN'T MERMAIDS THE MES-SENGERS OF WADA-TSUMI?
SO WHY WOULD THEY STEAL KIDS?
MERFOLK CAN'T COME UP ON LAND. THEY SAY THEY TAKE THE CHILDREN TO KEEP WADATSUMI COMPANY.

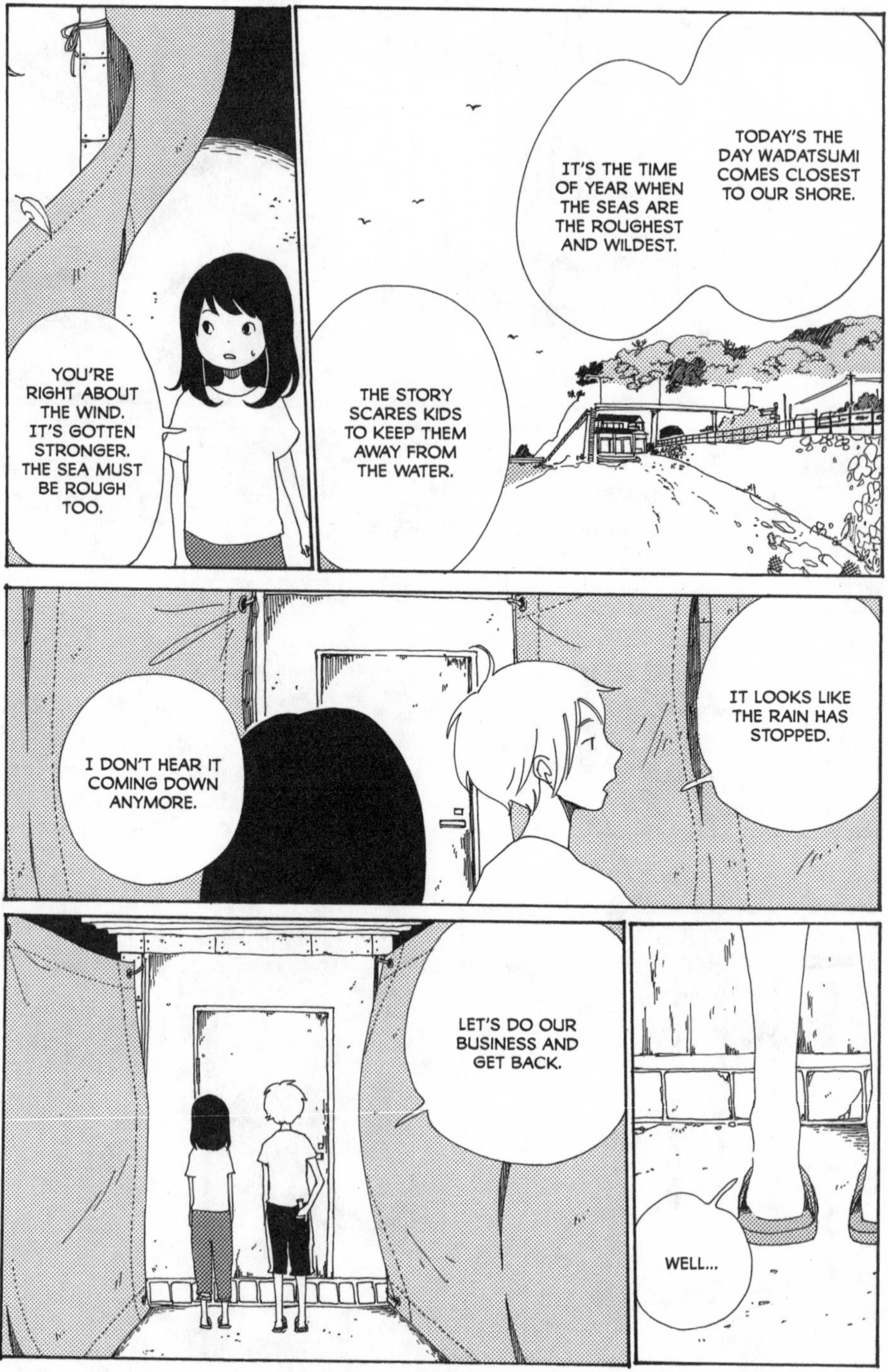
TODAY'S THE DAY WADATSUMI COMES CLOSEST TO OUR SHORE.
IT'S THE TIME OF YEAR WHEN THE SEAS ARE THE ROUGHEST AND WILDEST.
THE STORY SCARES KIDS TO KEEP THEM AWAY FROM THE WATER.
YOU'RE RIGHT ABOUT THE WIND. IT'S GOTTEN STRONGER. THE SEA MUST BE ROUGH TOO.
IT LOOKS LIKE THE RAIN HAS STOPPED.
I DON'T HEAR IT COMING DOWN ANYMORE.
WELL...
LET'S DO OUR BUSINESS AND GET BACK.

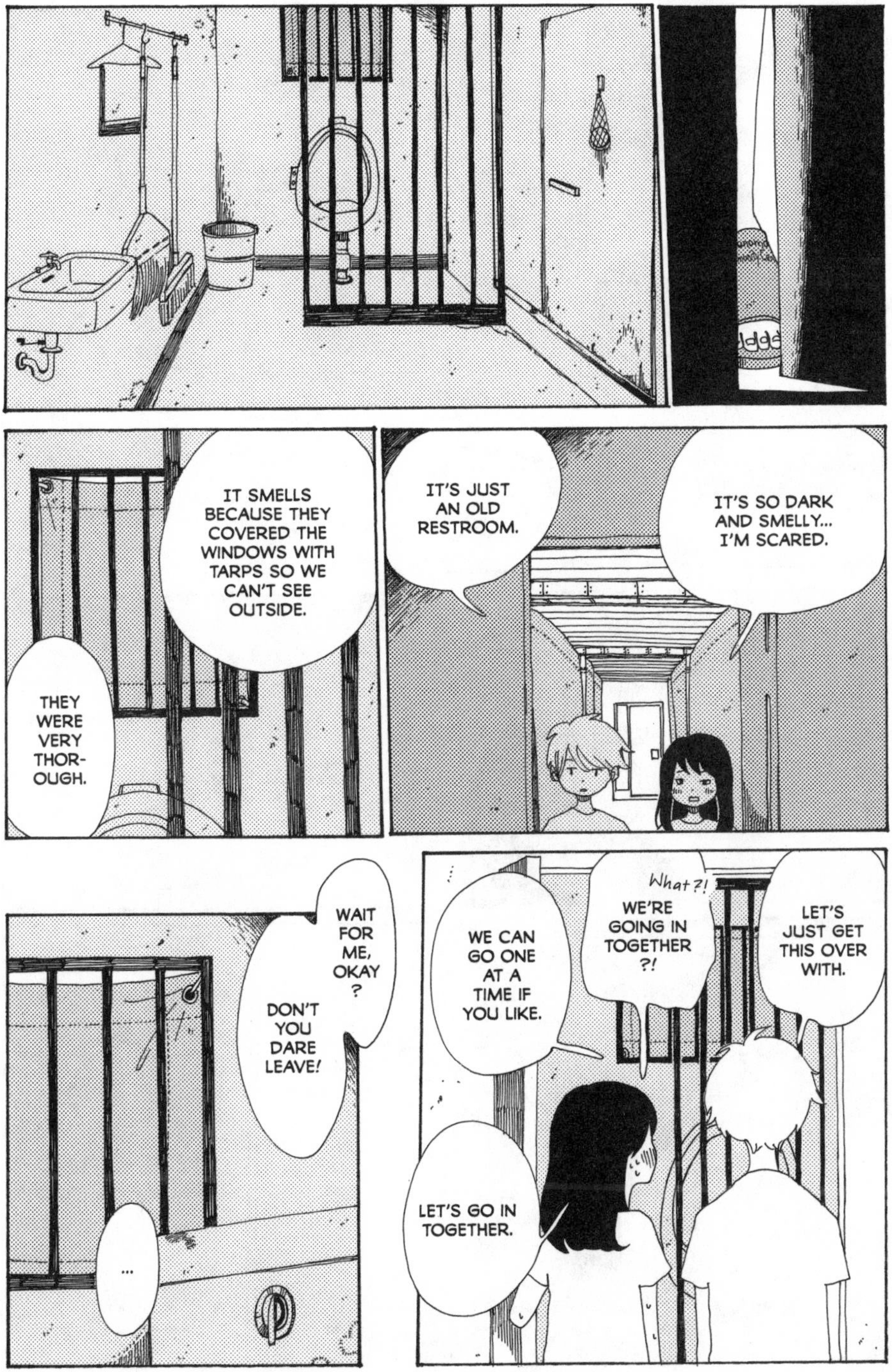
IT'S SO DARK AND SMELLY... I'M SCARED.
IT'S JUST AN OLD RESTROOM.
IT SMELLS BECAUSE THEY COVERED THE WINDOWS WITH TARPS SO WE CAN'T SEE OUTSIDE.
THEY WERE VERY THOR-OUGH.
LET'S JUST GET THIS OVER WITH.
What?!
WE'RE GOING IN TOGETHER?!
WE CAN GO ONE AT A TIME IF YOU LIKE.
LET'S GO IN TOGETHER.
WAIT FOR ME, OKAY?
DON'T YOU DARE LEAVE!
...

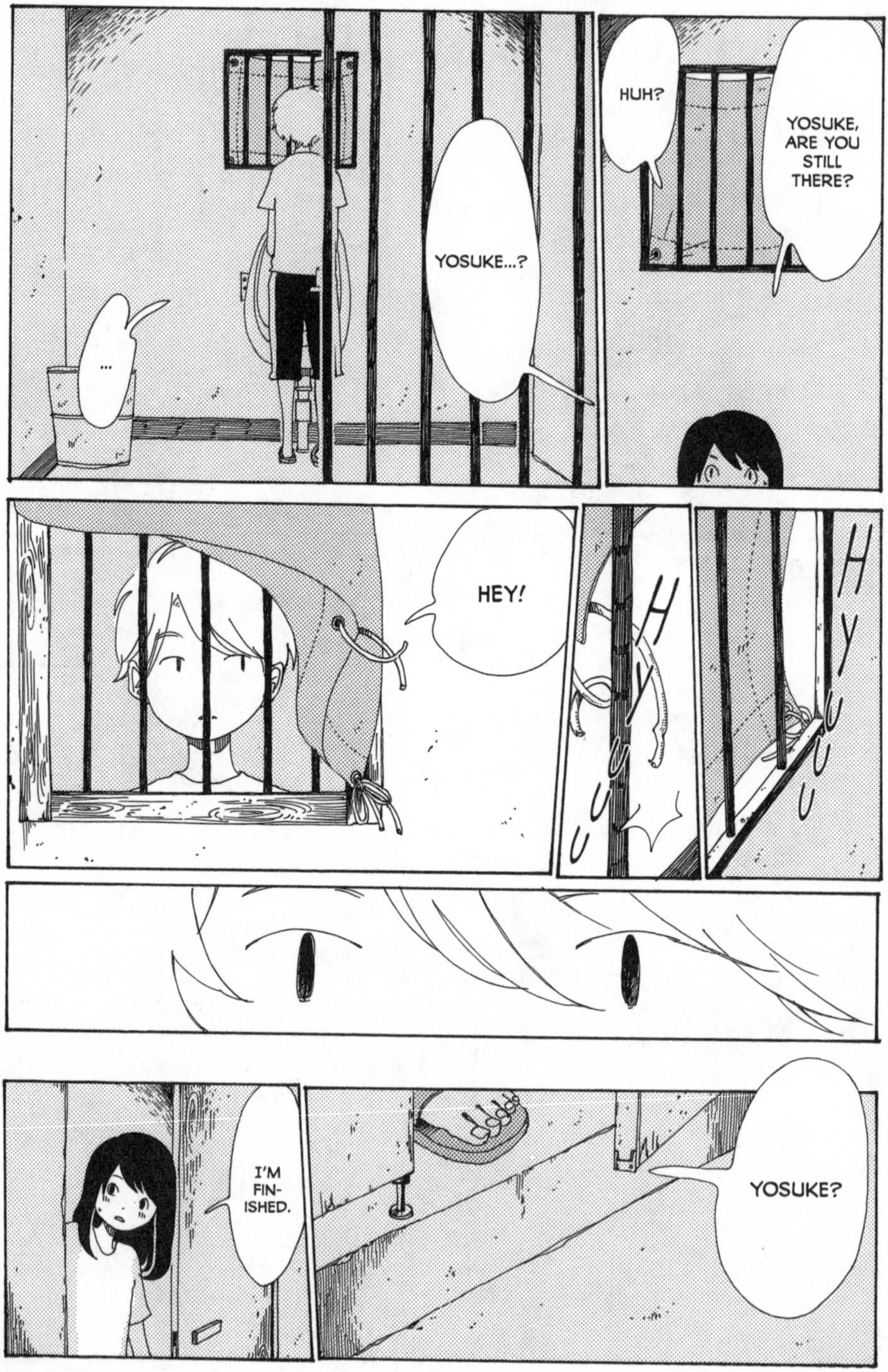
YOSUKE, ARE YOU STILL THERE?
HUH?
YOSUKE...?
...
Hyuuuu
Hyuuuu
HEY!
YOSUKE?
I'M FIN-ISHED.

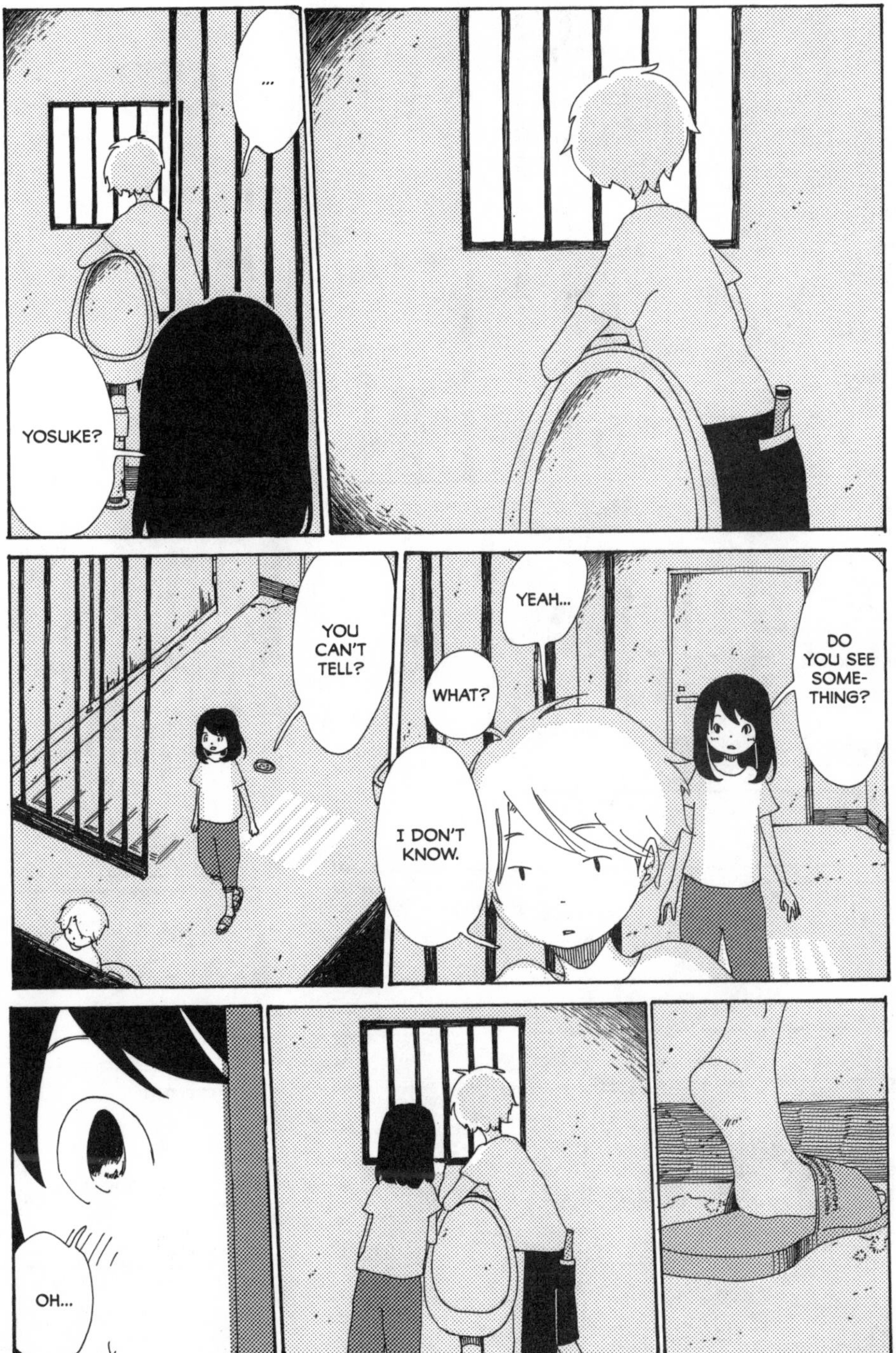
...
YOSUKE?
DO YOU SEE SOMETHING?
YEAH...
WHAT?
I DON'T KNOW.
YOU CAN'T TELL?
OH...

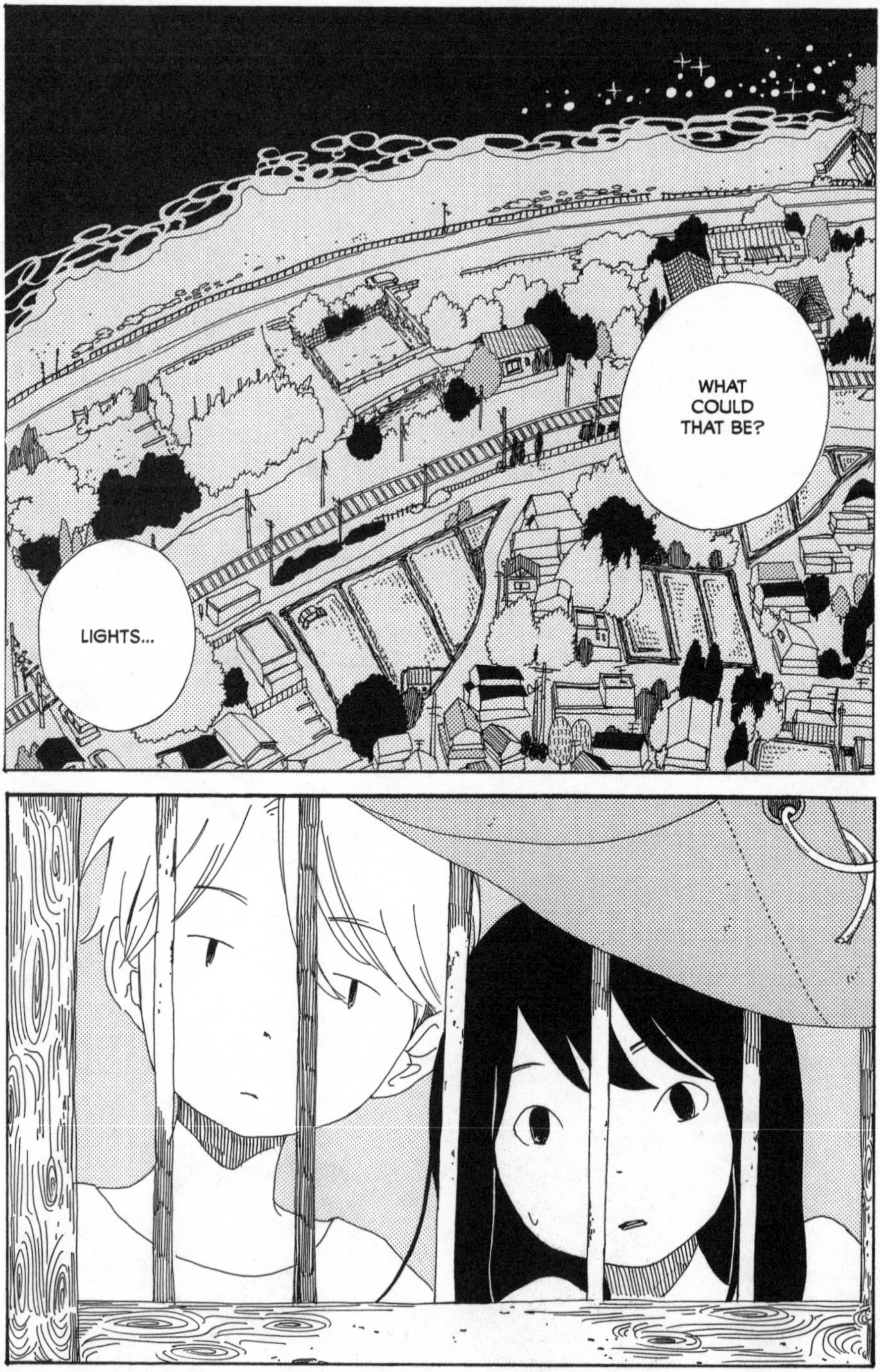
WHAT COULD THAT BE?
LIGHTS...

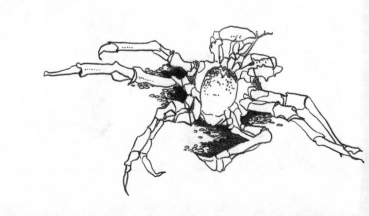

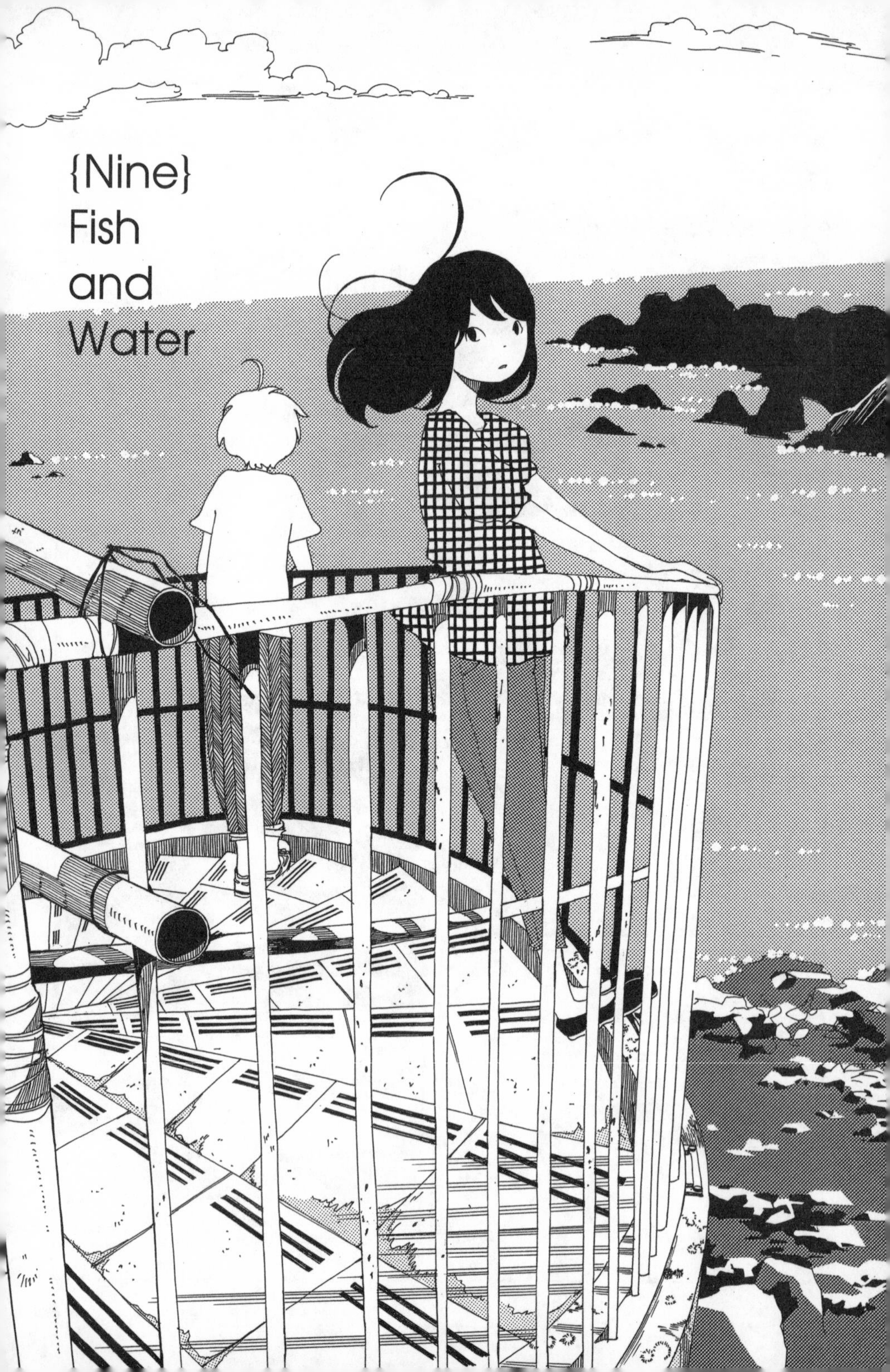
{Nine}
Fish
and
Water

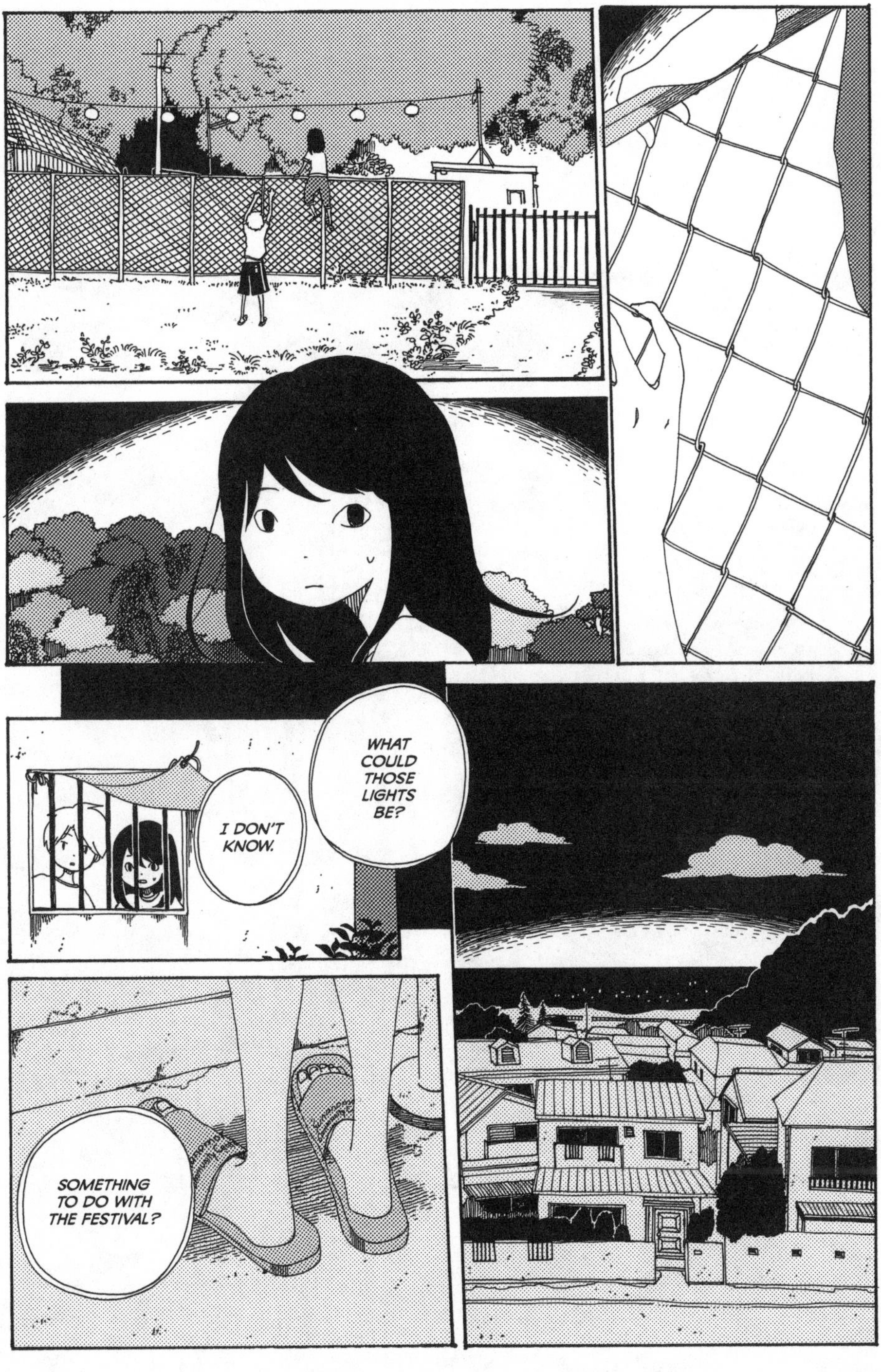
WHAT COULD THOSE LIGHTS BE?
I DON'T KNOW.
SOMETHING TO DO WITH THE FESTIVAL?

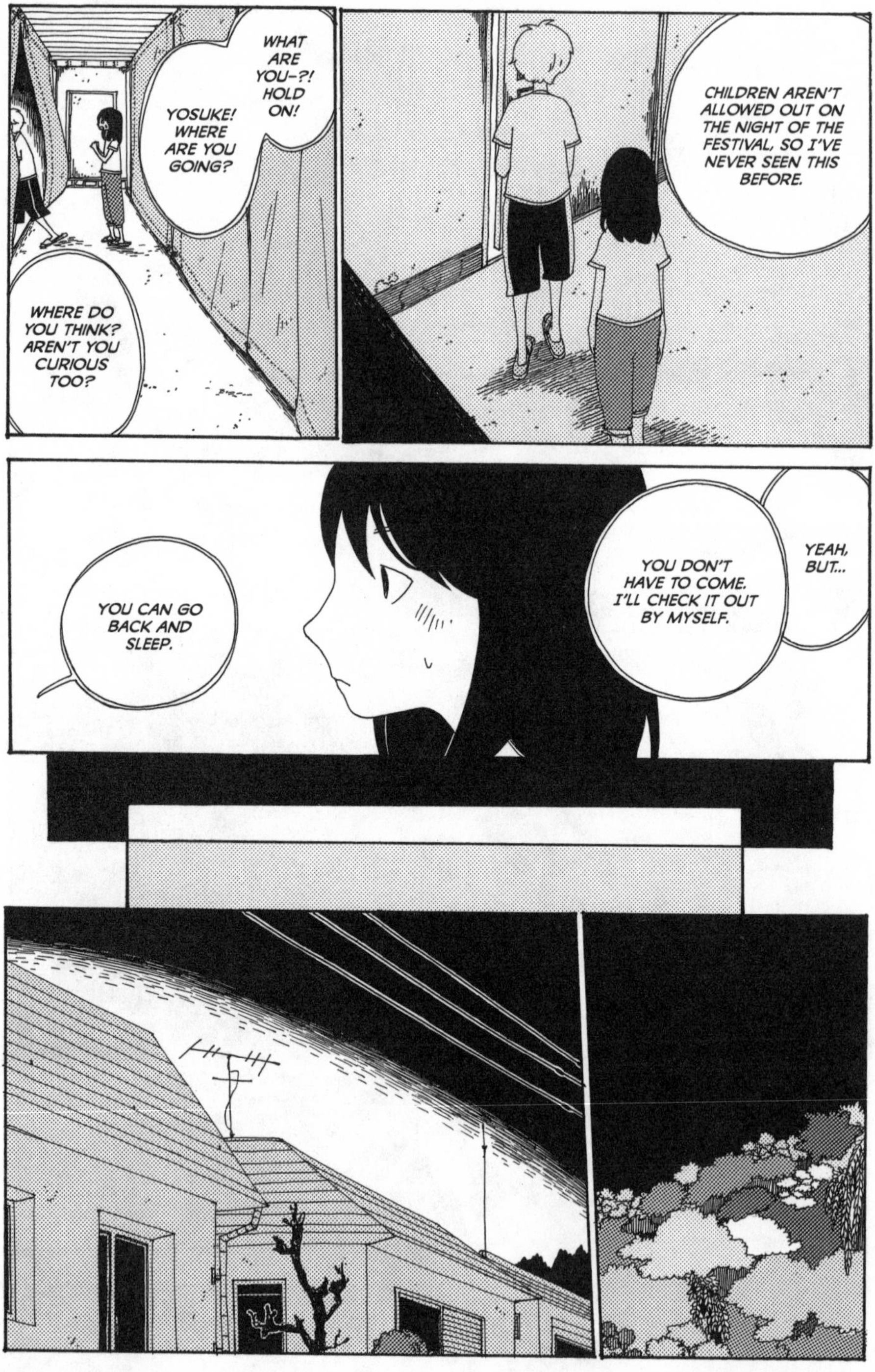
CHILDREN AREN'T ALLOWED OUT ON THE NIGHT OF THE FESTIVAL, SO I'VE NEVER SEEN THIS BEFORE.
WHAT ARE YOU–?! HOLD ON!
YOSUKE! WHERE ARE YOU GOING?
WHERE DO YOU THINK? AREN'T YOU CURIOUS TOO?
YEAH, BUT...
YOU DON'T HAVE TO COME. I'LL CHECK IT OUT BY MYSELF.
YOU CAN GO BACK AND SLEEP.

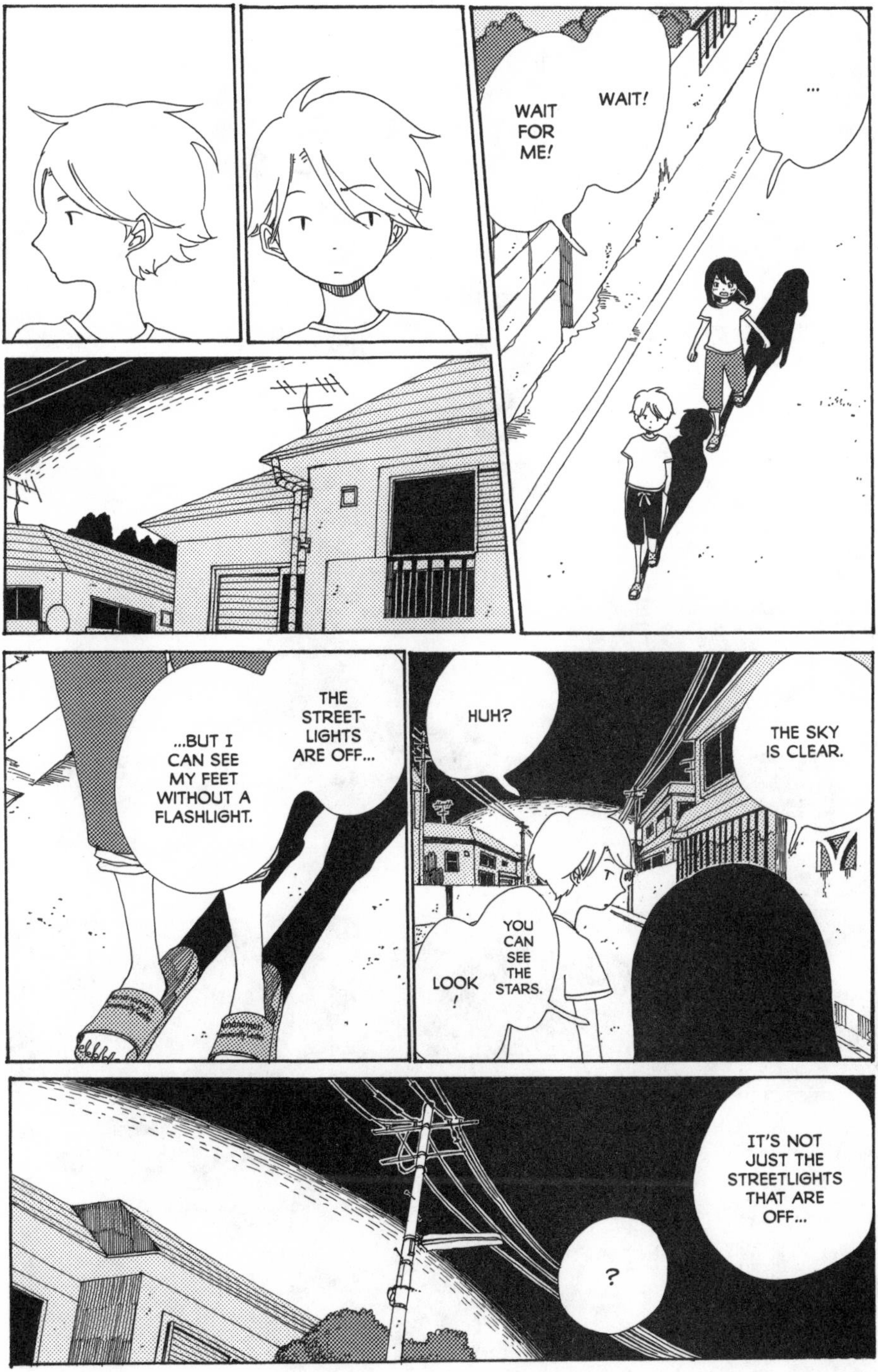
...
WAIT!
WAIT FOR ME!
THE SKY IS CLEAR.
HUH?
YOU CAN SEE THE STARS.
LOOK!
THE STREET-LIGHTS ARE OFF...
...BUT I CAN SEE MY FEET WITHOUT A FLASHLIGHT.
IT'S NOT JUST THE STREETLIGHTS THAT ARE OFF...
?

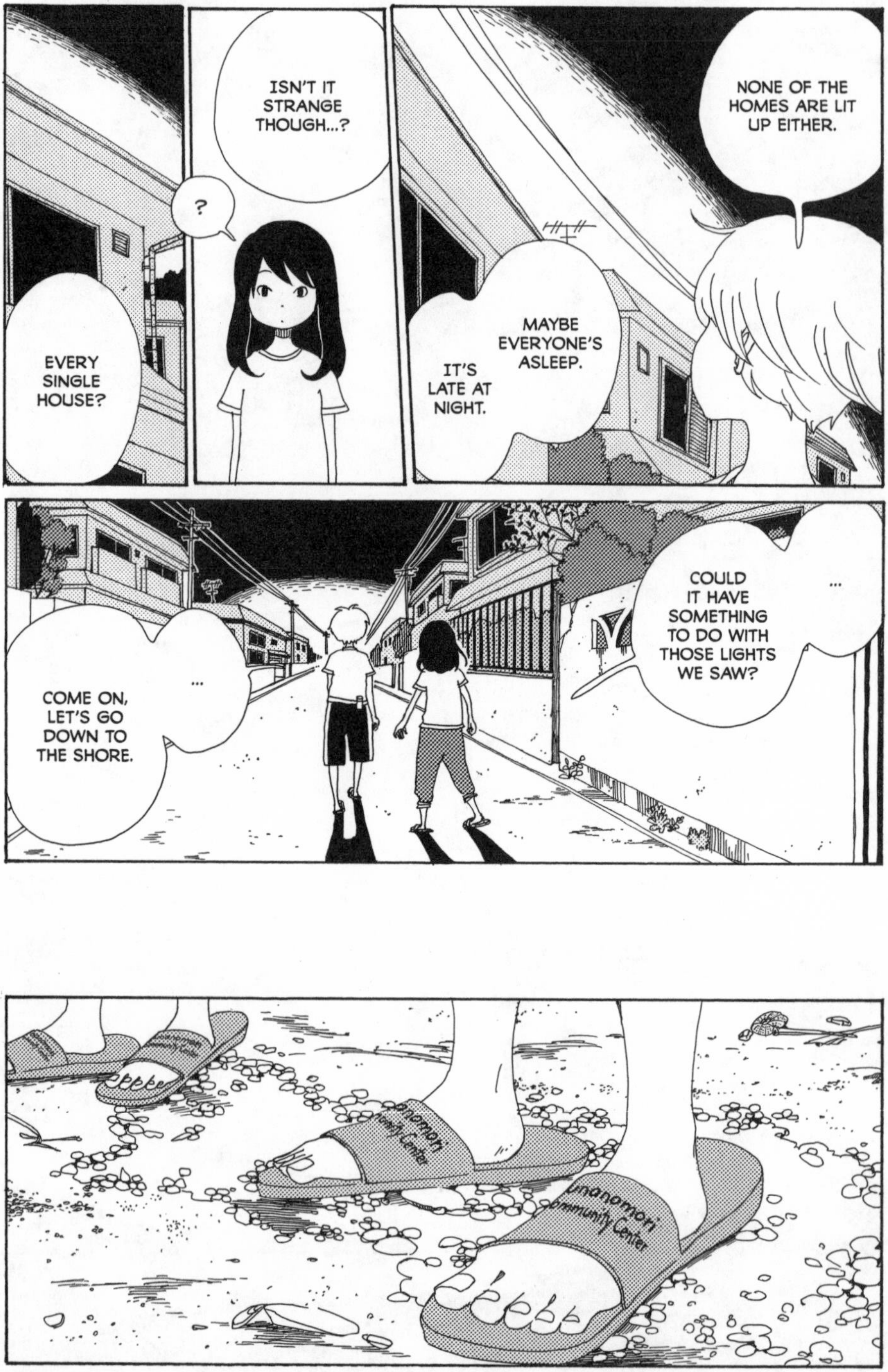
NONE OF THE HOMES ARE LIT UP EITHER.
MAYBE EVERYONE'S ASLEEP.
IT'S LATE AT NIGHT.
ISN'T IT STRANGE THOUGH...?
?
EVERY SINGLE HOUSE?
...
COULD IT HAVE SOMETHING TO DO WITH THOSE LIGHTS WE SAW?
...
COME ON, LET'S GO DOWN TO THE SHORE.

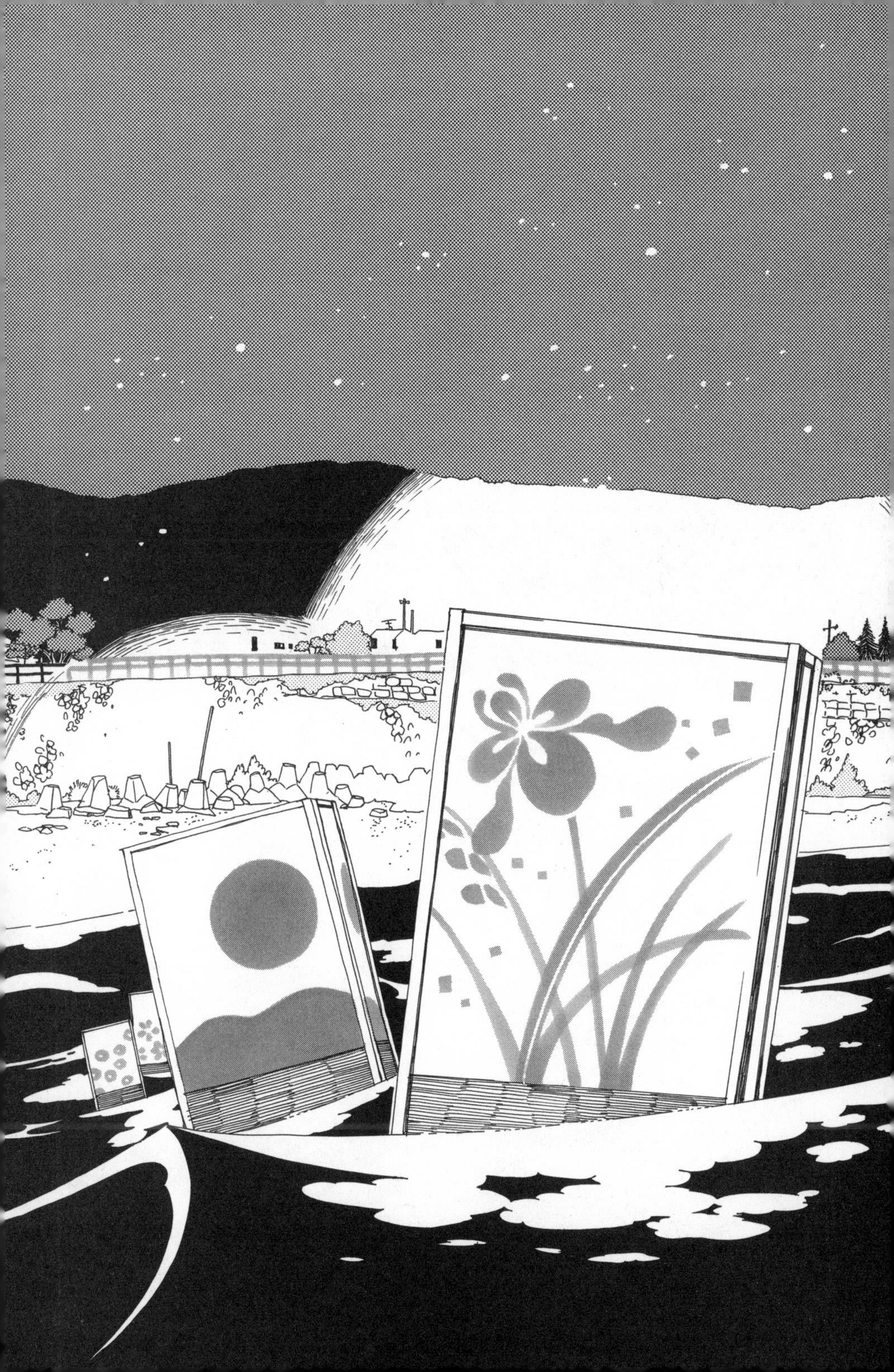

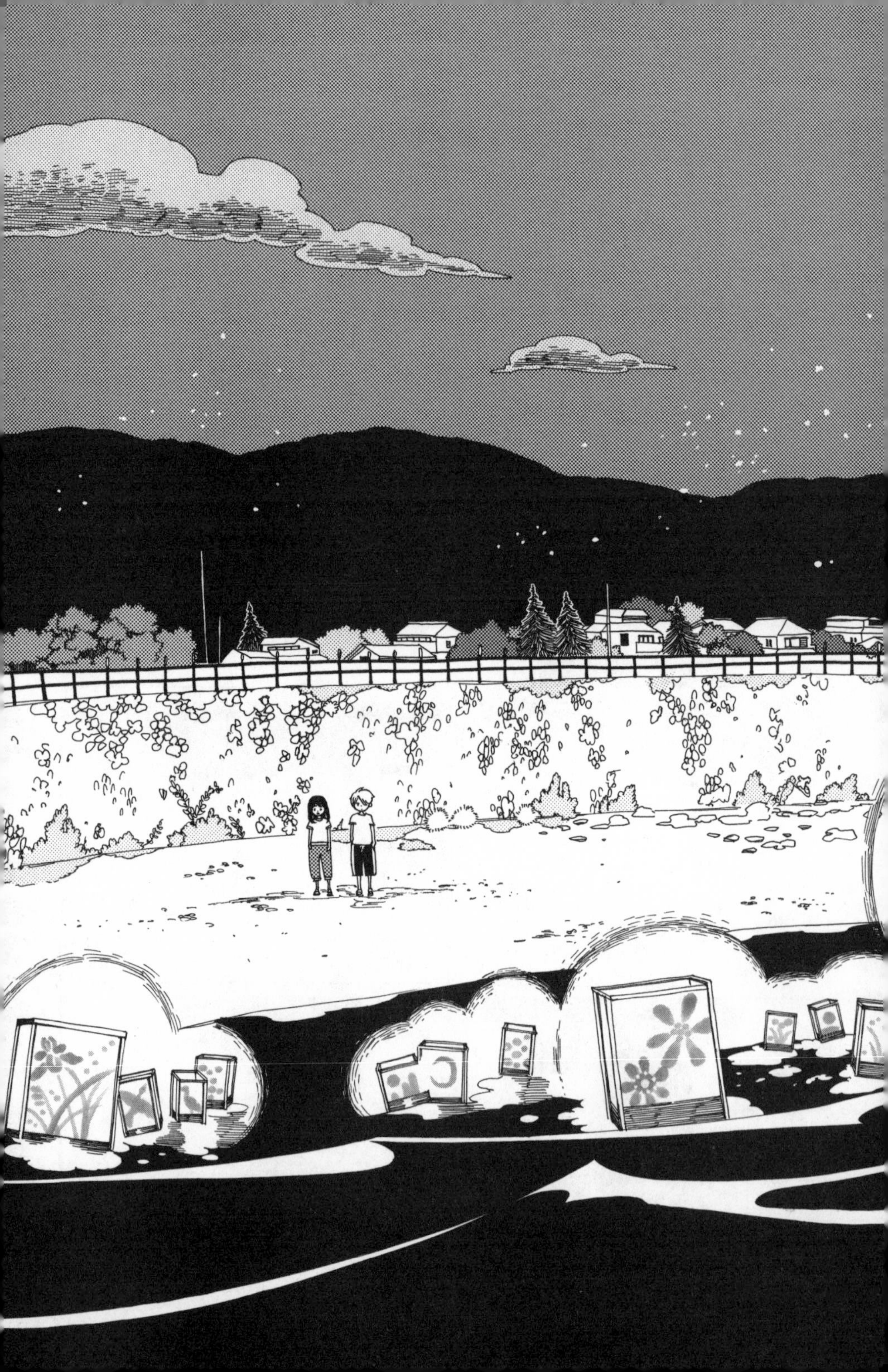

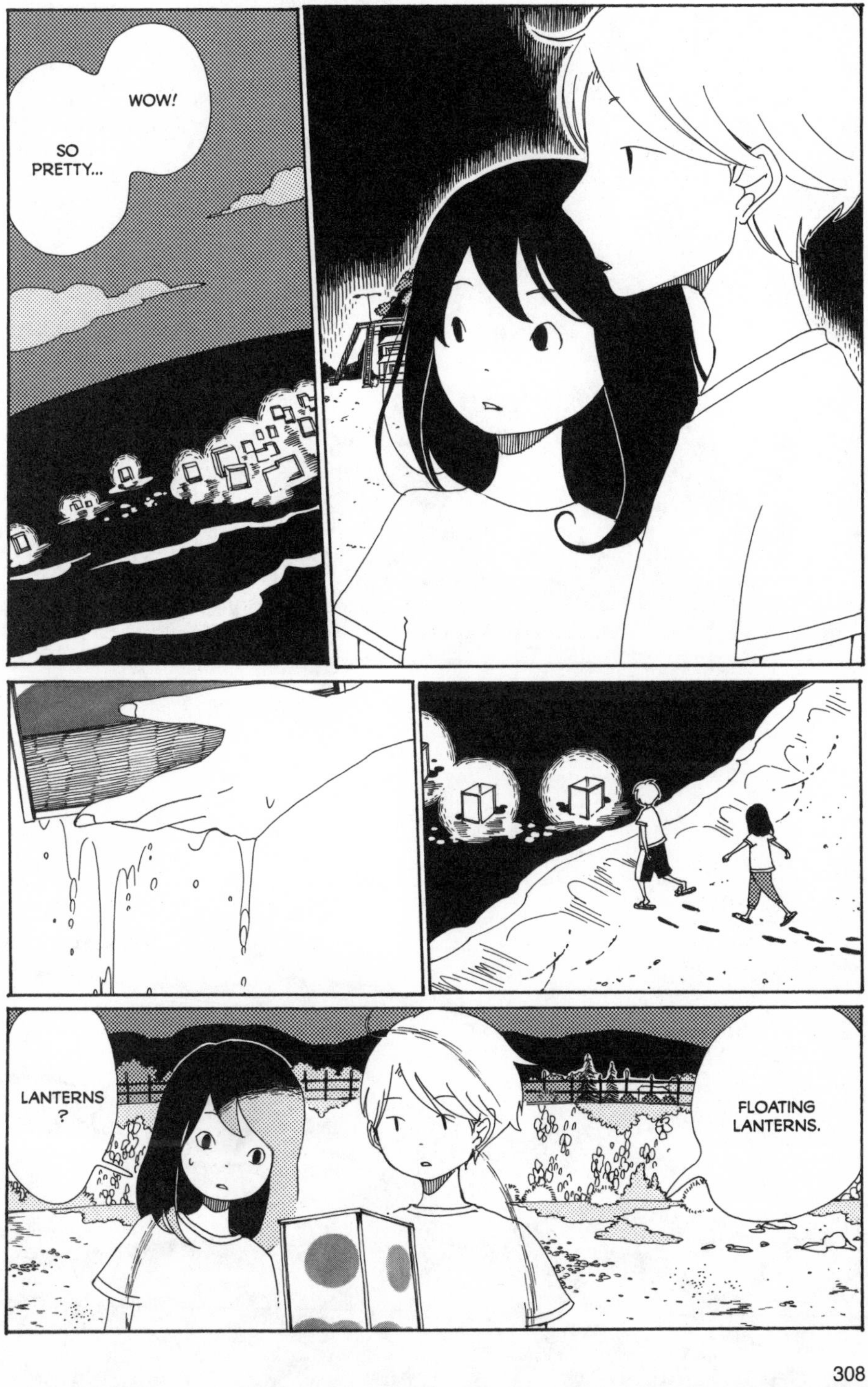
WOW!
SO PRETTY...
FLOATING LANTERNS.
LANTERNS?

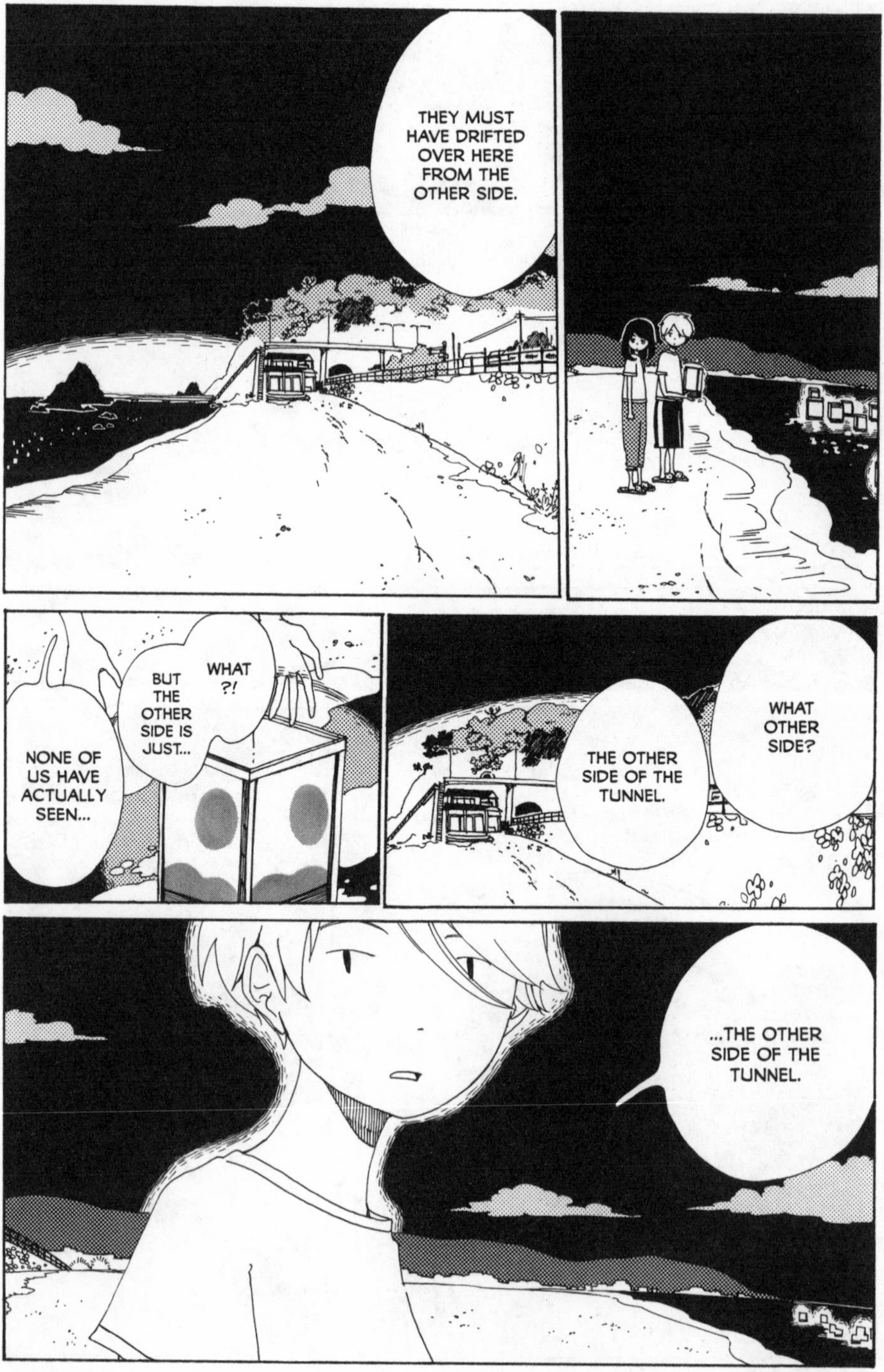
THEY MUST HAVE DRIFTED OVER HERE FROM THE OTHER SIDE.
WHAT OTHER SIDE?
THE OTHER SIDE OF THE TUNNEL.
WHAT ?!
BUT THE OTHER SIDE IS JUST...
NONE OF US HAVE ACTUALLY SEEN...
...THE OTHER SIDE OF THE TUNNEL.

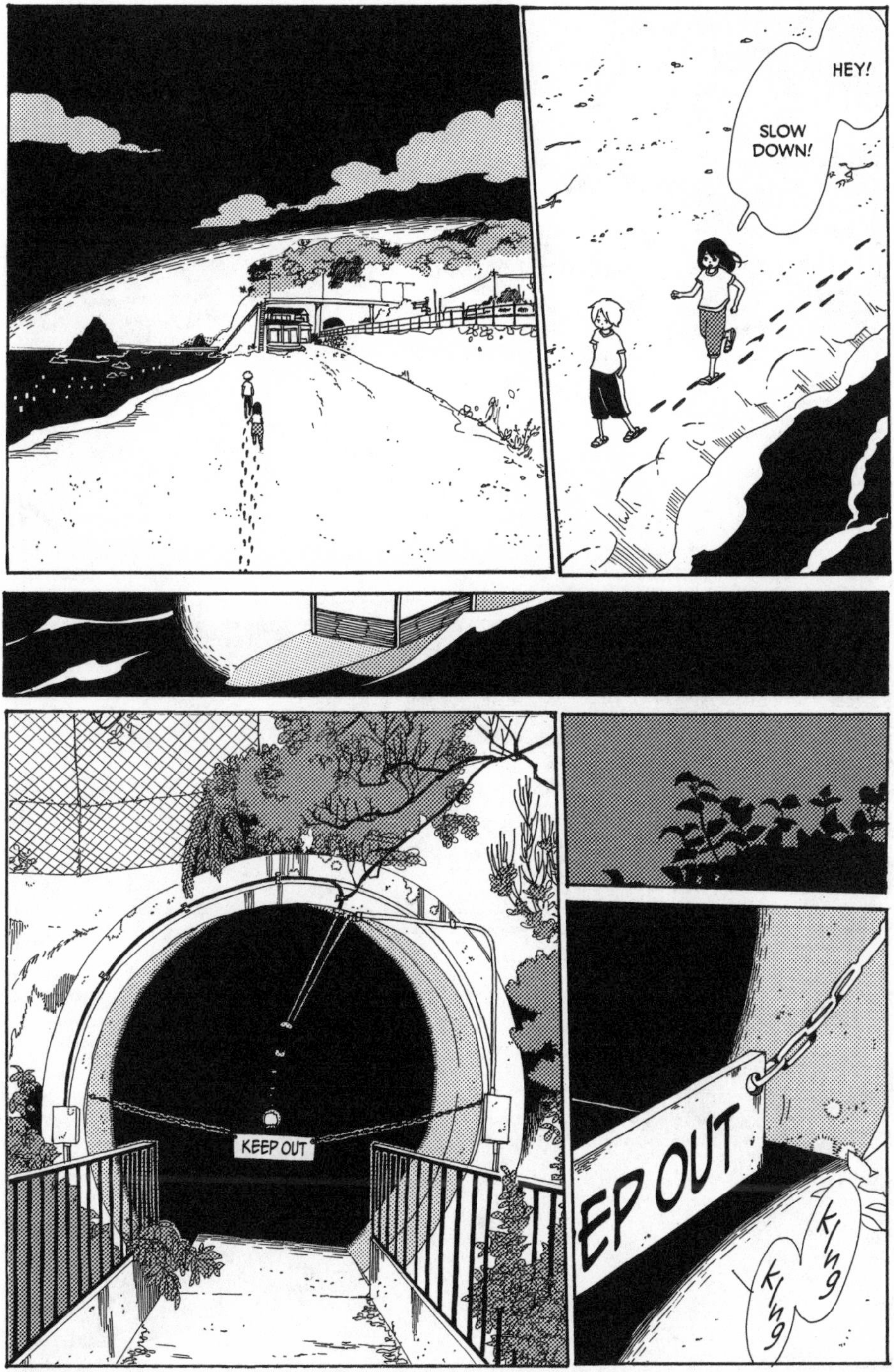
HEY!
SLOW DOWN!
EP OUT
Kling
Kling
KEEP OUT

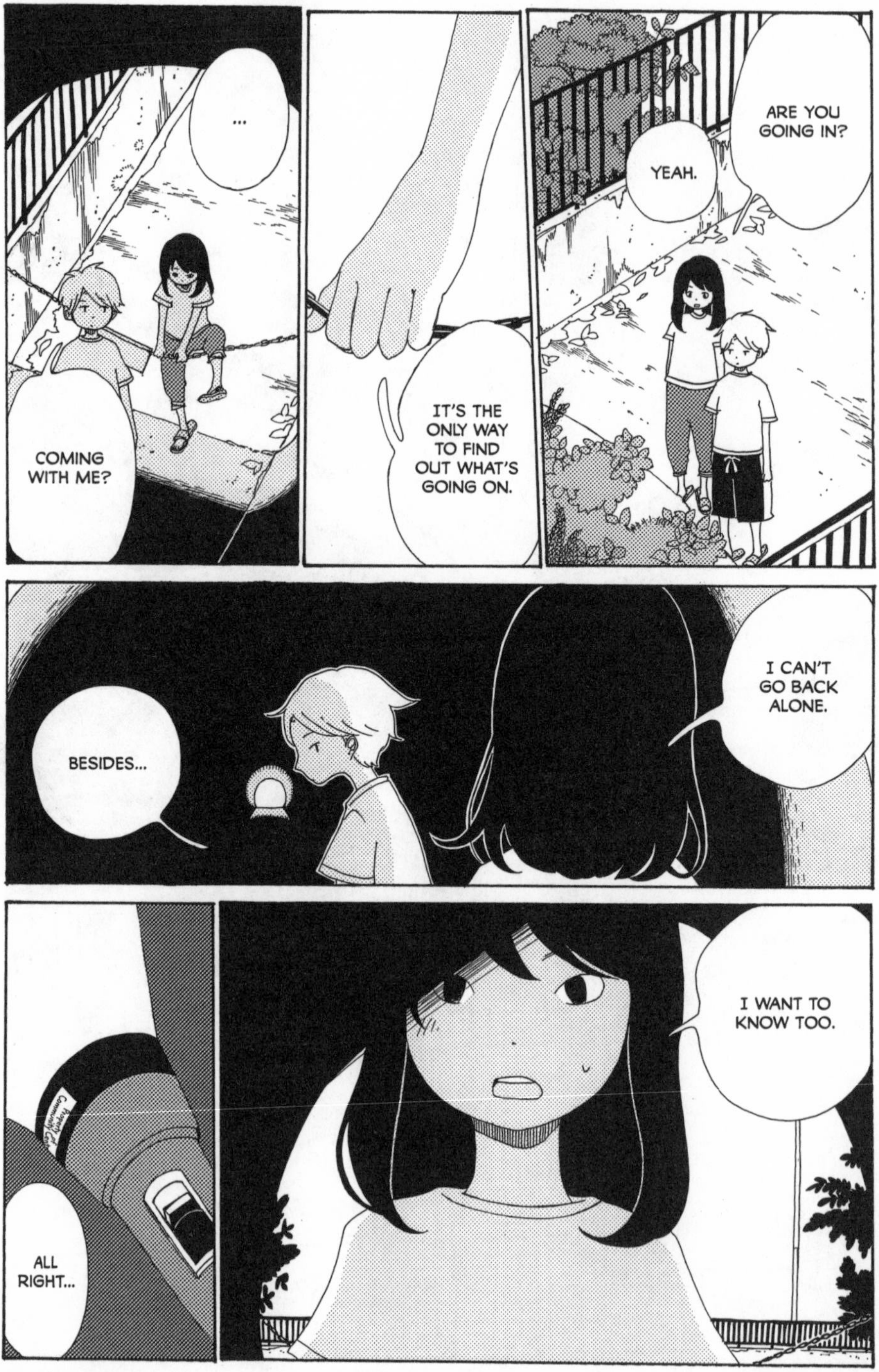
ARE YOU GOING IN?
YEAH.
IT'S THE ONLY WAY TO FIND OUT WHAT'S GOING ON.
...
COMING WITH ME?
I CAN'T GO BACK ALONE.
BESIDES...
I WANT TO KNOW TOO.
ALL RIGHT...

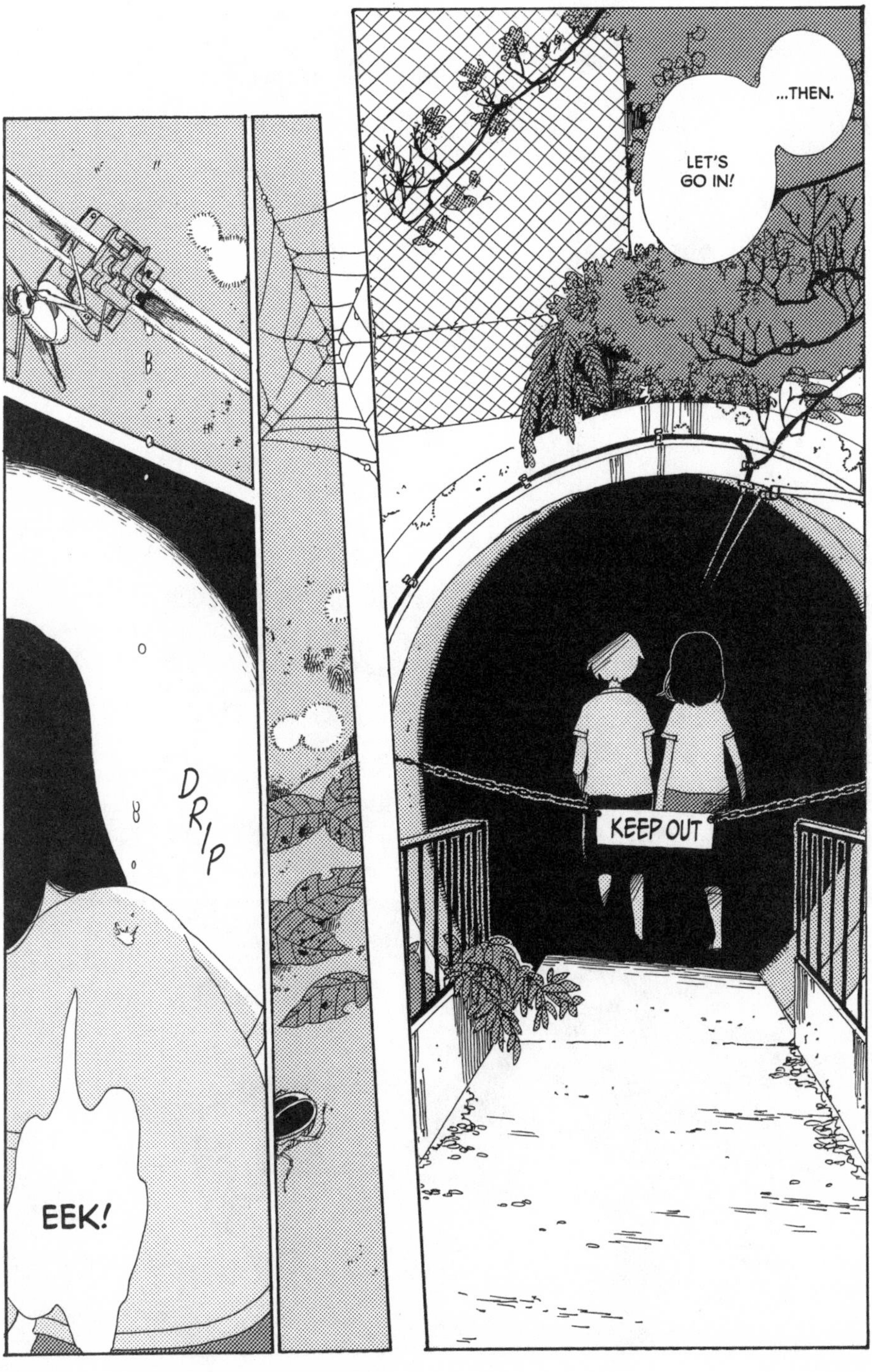
...THEN.
LET'S GO IN!
KEEP OUT
DRIP
EEK!

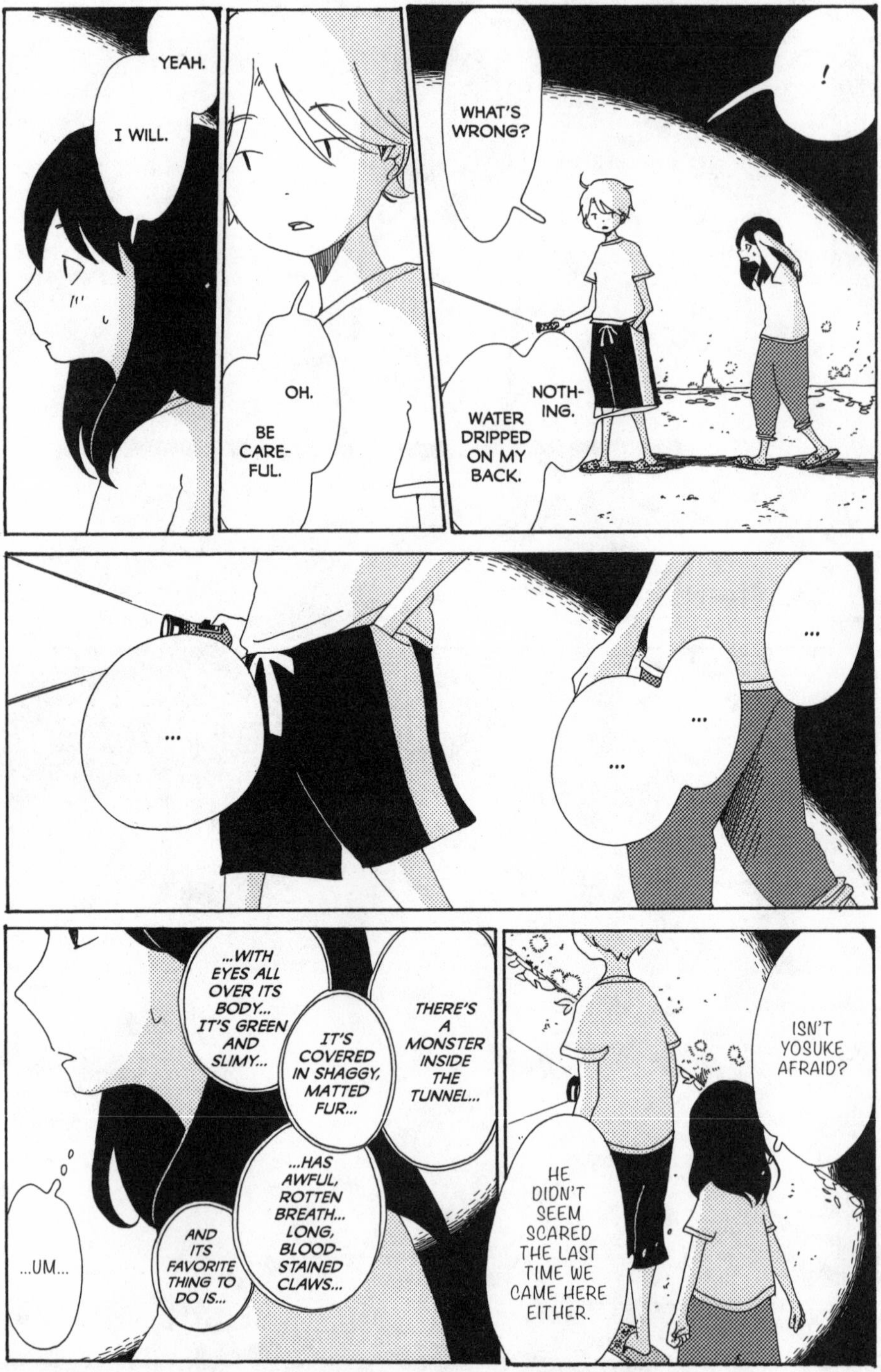
!
WHAT'S WRONG?
NOTHING.
WATER DRIPPED ON MY BACK.
OH.
BE CAREFUL.
YEAH.
I WILL.
...
...
...
...
ISN'T YOSUKE AFRAID?
HE DIDN'T SEEM SCARED THE LAST TIME WE CAME HERE EITHER.
THERE'S A MONSTER INSIDE THE TUNNEL...
IT'S COVERED IN SHAGGY, MATTED FUR...
...WITH EYES ALL OVER ITS BODY... IT'S GREEN AND SLIMY...
...HAS AWFUL, ROTTEN BREATH... LONG, BLOOD-STAINED CLAWS...
AND ITS FAVORITE THING TO DO IS...
...UM...

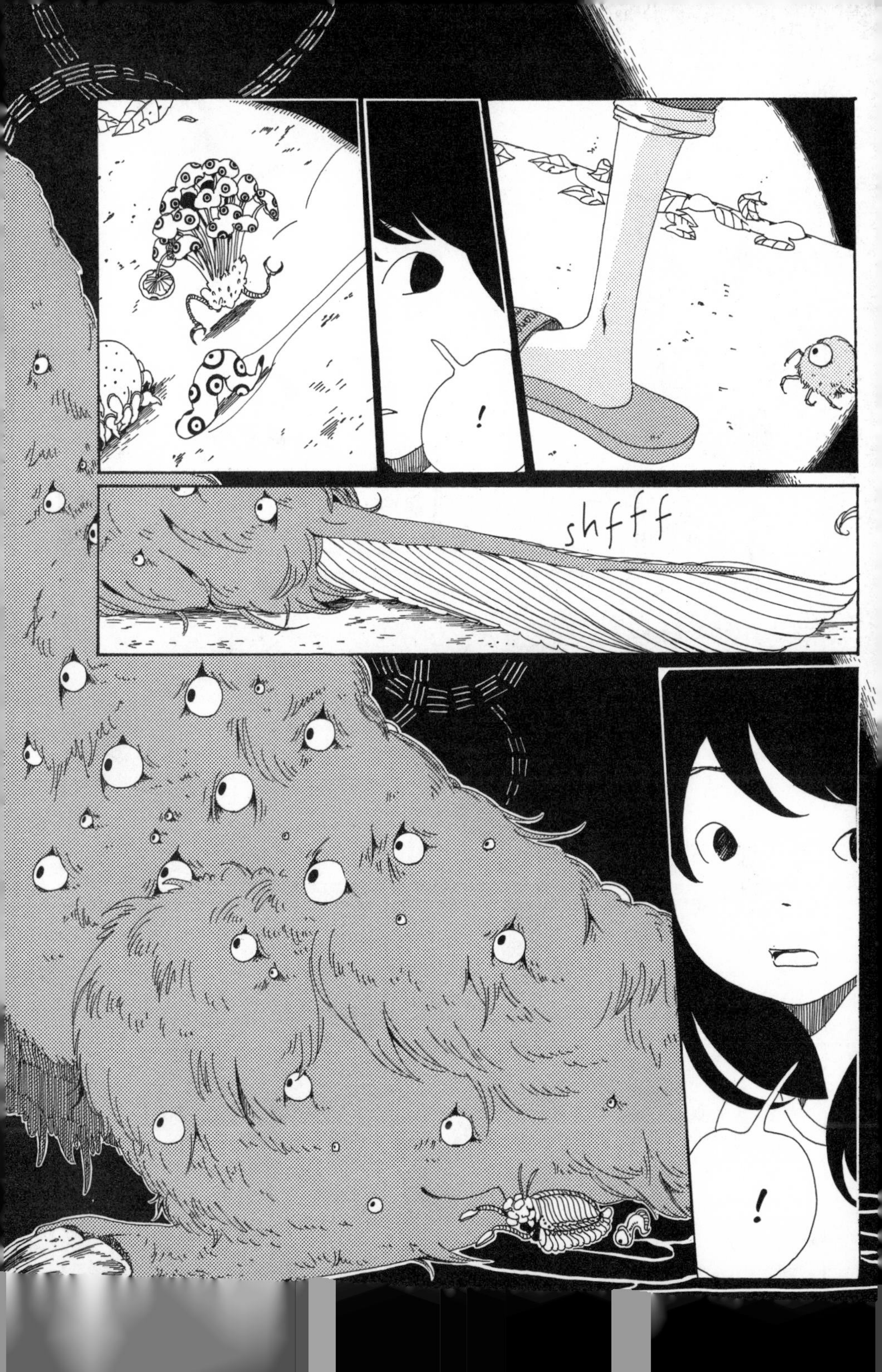
!
shfff
!

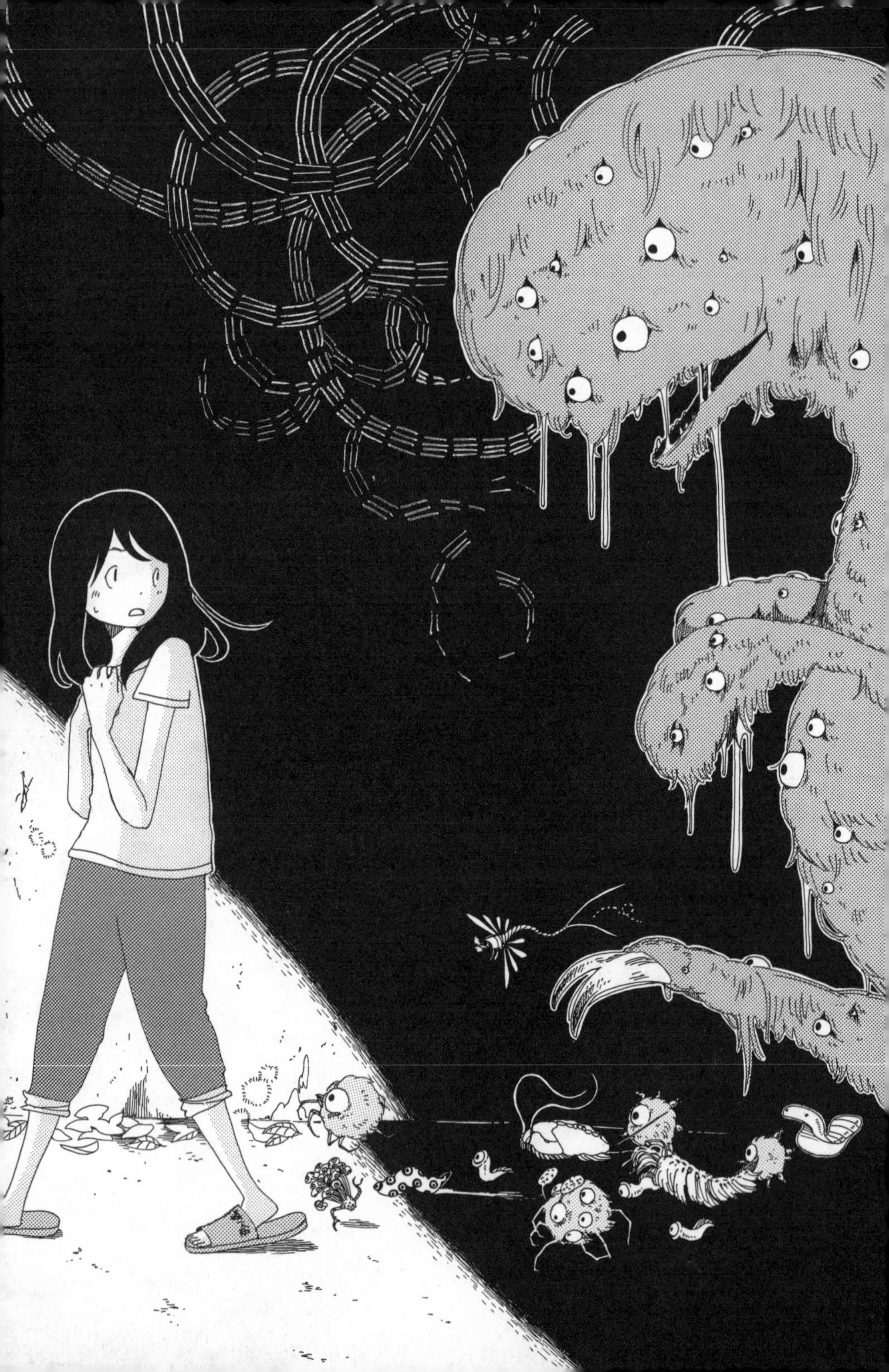

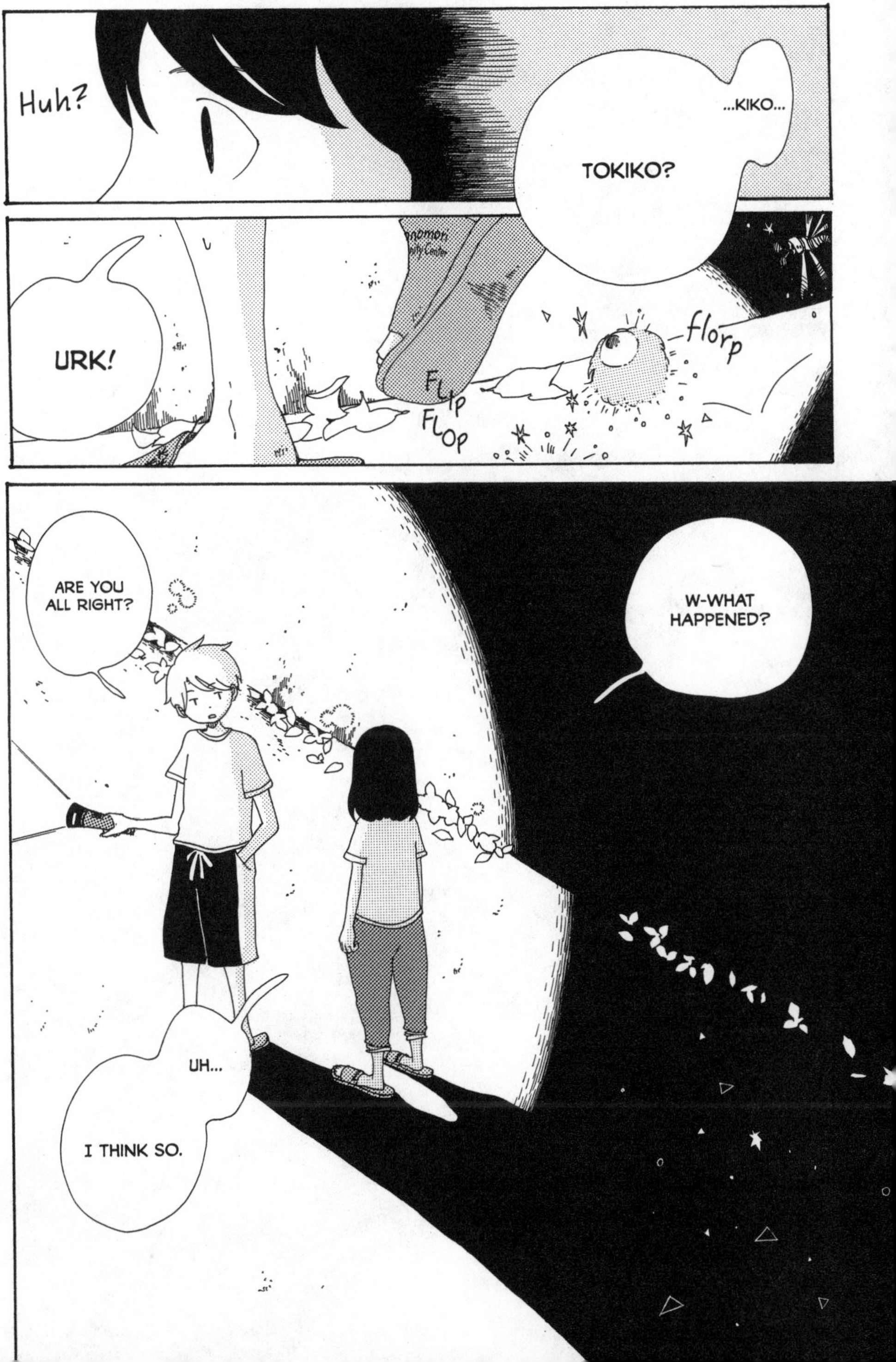
...KIKO...
TOKIKO?
Huh?
florp
FLIP FLOP
URK!
W-WHAT HAPPENED?
ARE YOU ALL RIGHT?
UH...
I THINK SO.

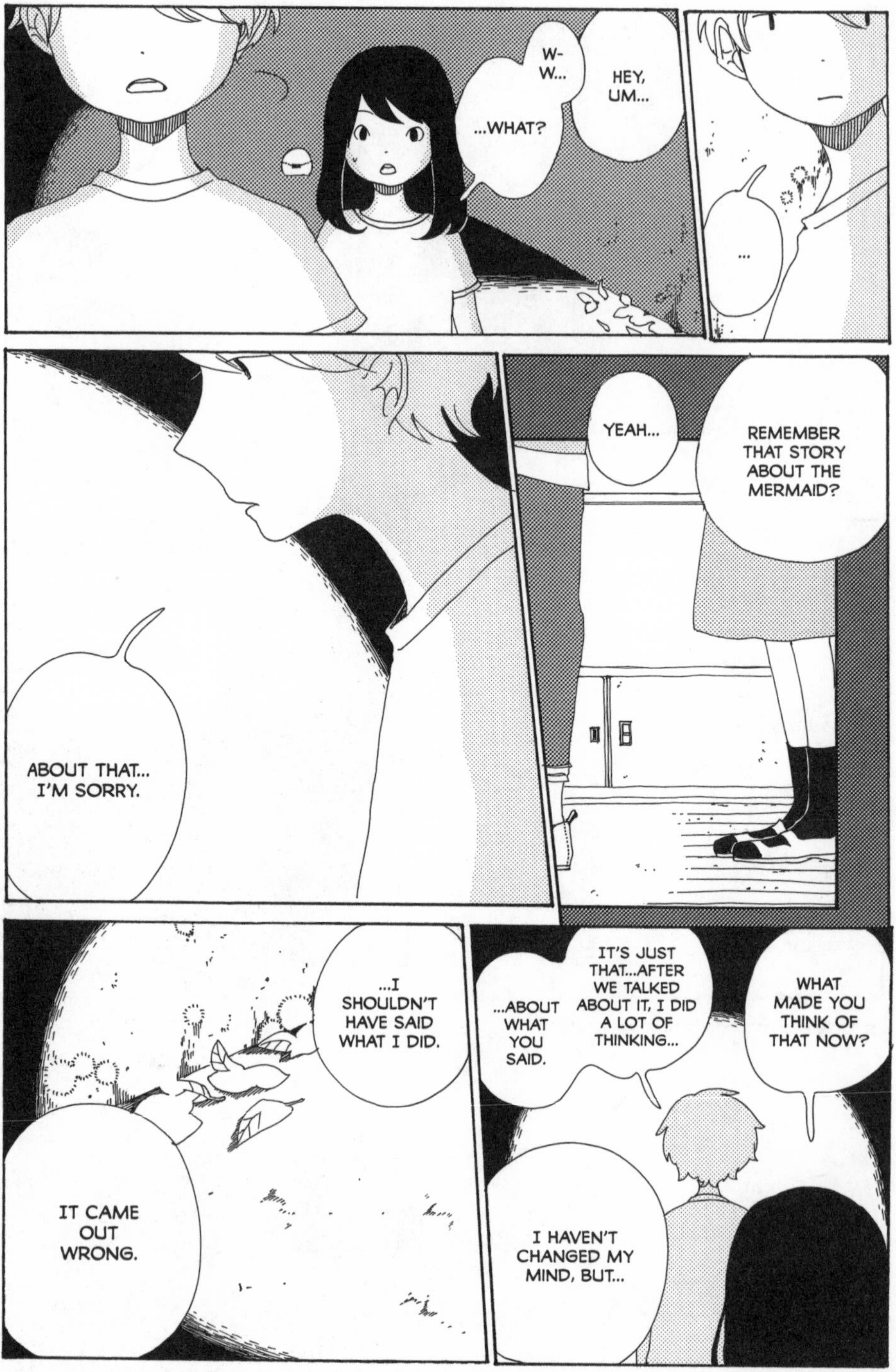
...
HEY, UM...
W- W...
...WHAT?
REMEMBER THAT STORY ABOUT THE MERMAID?
YEAH...
ABOUT THAT... I'M SORRY.
WHAT MADE YOU THINK OF THAT NOW?
IT'S JUST THAT...AFTER WE TALKED ABOUT IT, I DID A LOT OF THINKING...
...ABOUT WHAT YOU SAID.
I HAVEN'T CHANGED MY MIND, BUT...
...I SHOULDN'T HAVE SAID WHAT I DID.
IT CAME OUT WRONG.

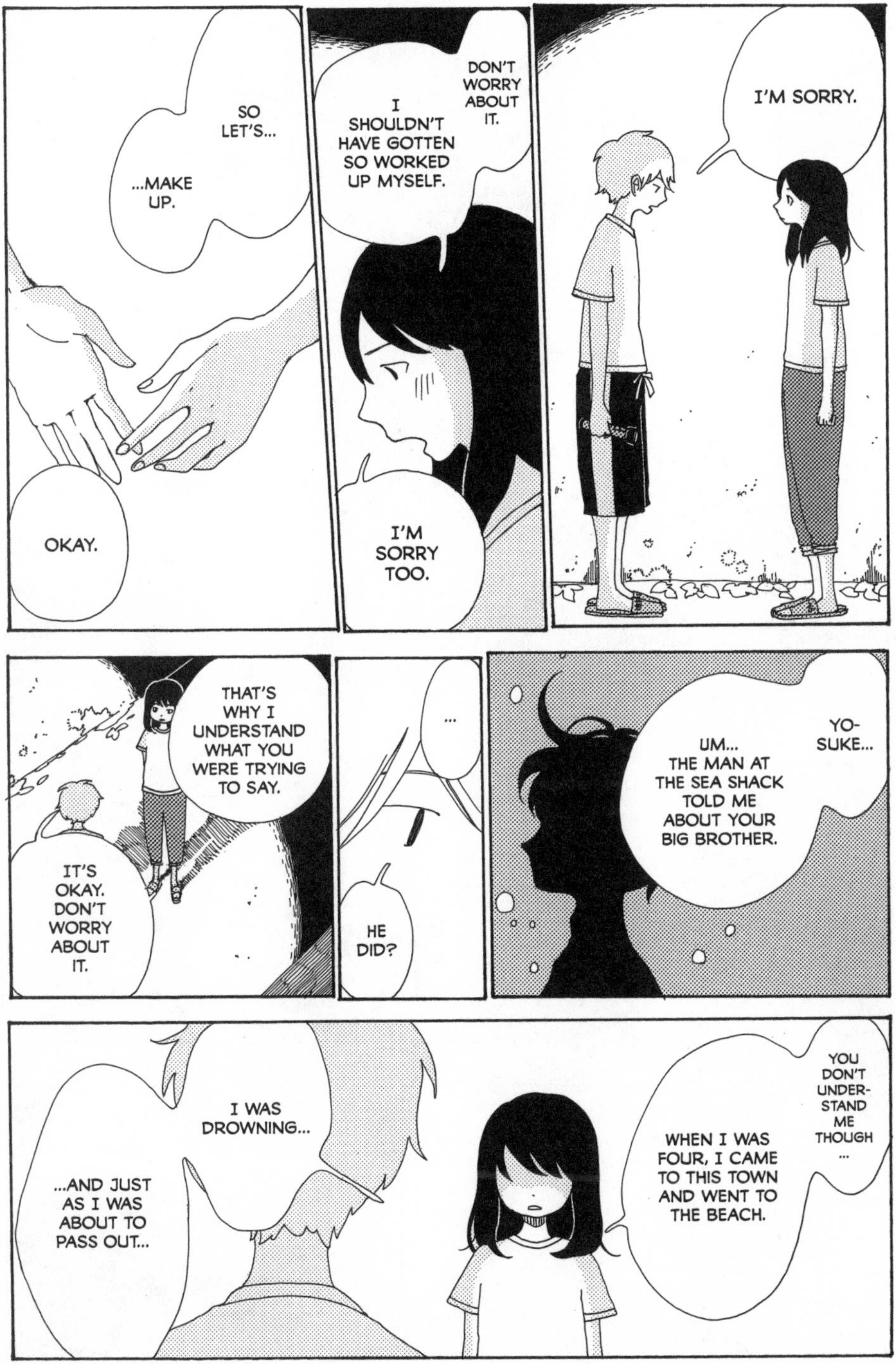
I'M SORRY.
DON'T WORRY ABOUT IT.
I SHOULDN'T HAVE GOTTEN SO WORKED UP MYSELF.
I'M SORRY TOO.
SO LET'S...
...MAKE UP.
OKAY.
YO-SUKE...
UM... THE MAN AT THE SEA SHACK TOLD ME ABOUT YOUR BIG BROTHER.
...
HE DID?
THAT'S WHY I UNDERSTAND WHAT YOU WERE TRYING TO SAY.
IT'S OKAY. DON'T WORRY ABOUT IT.
YOU DON'T UNDER-STAND ME THOUGH...
WHEN I WAS FOUR, I CAME TO THIS TOWN AND WENT TO THE BEACH.
I WAS DROWNING...
...AND JUST AS I WAS ABOUT TO PASS OUT...

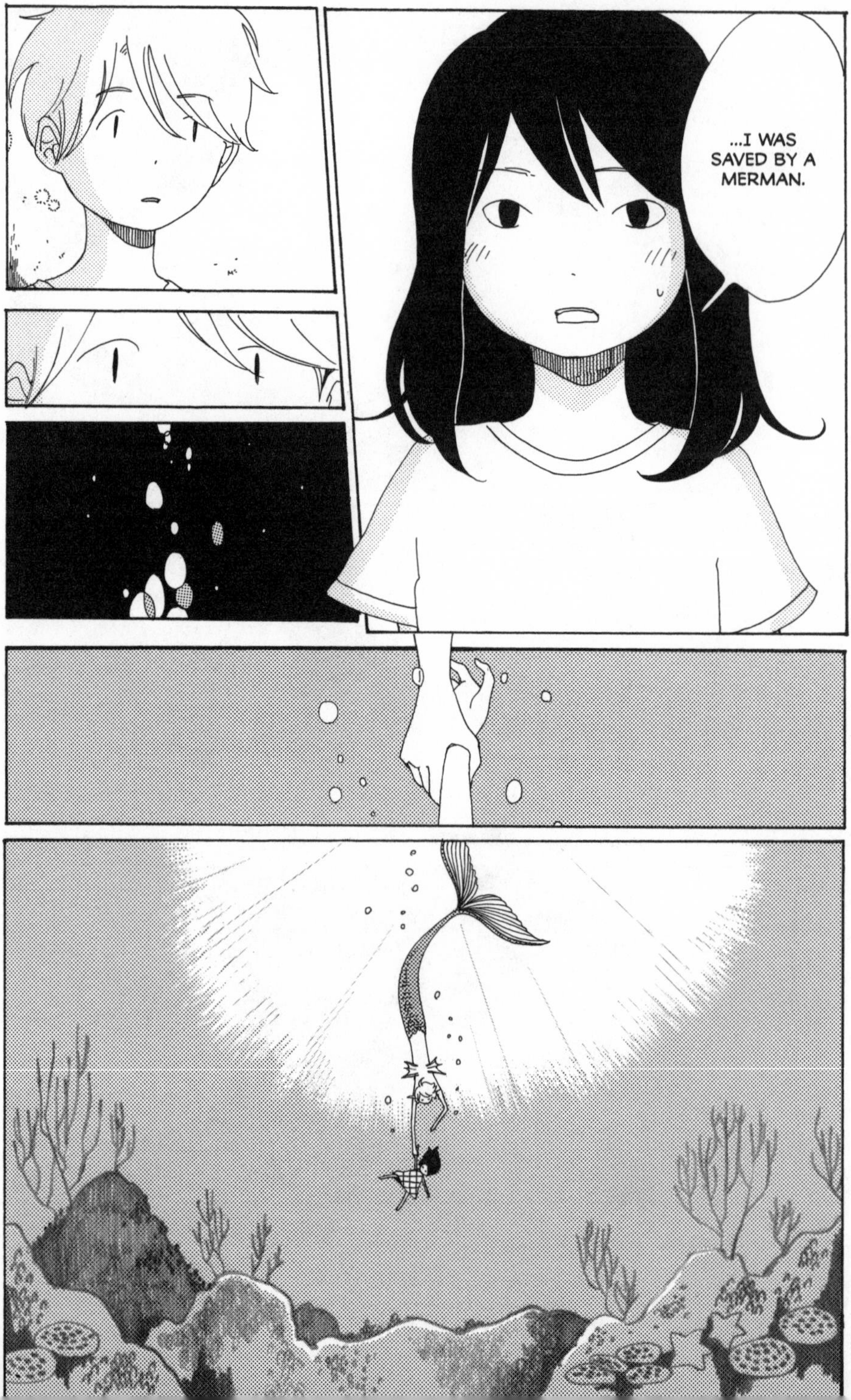
...I WAS SAVED BY A MERMAN.

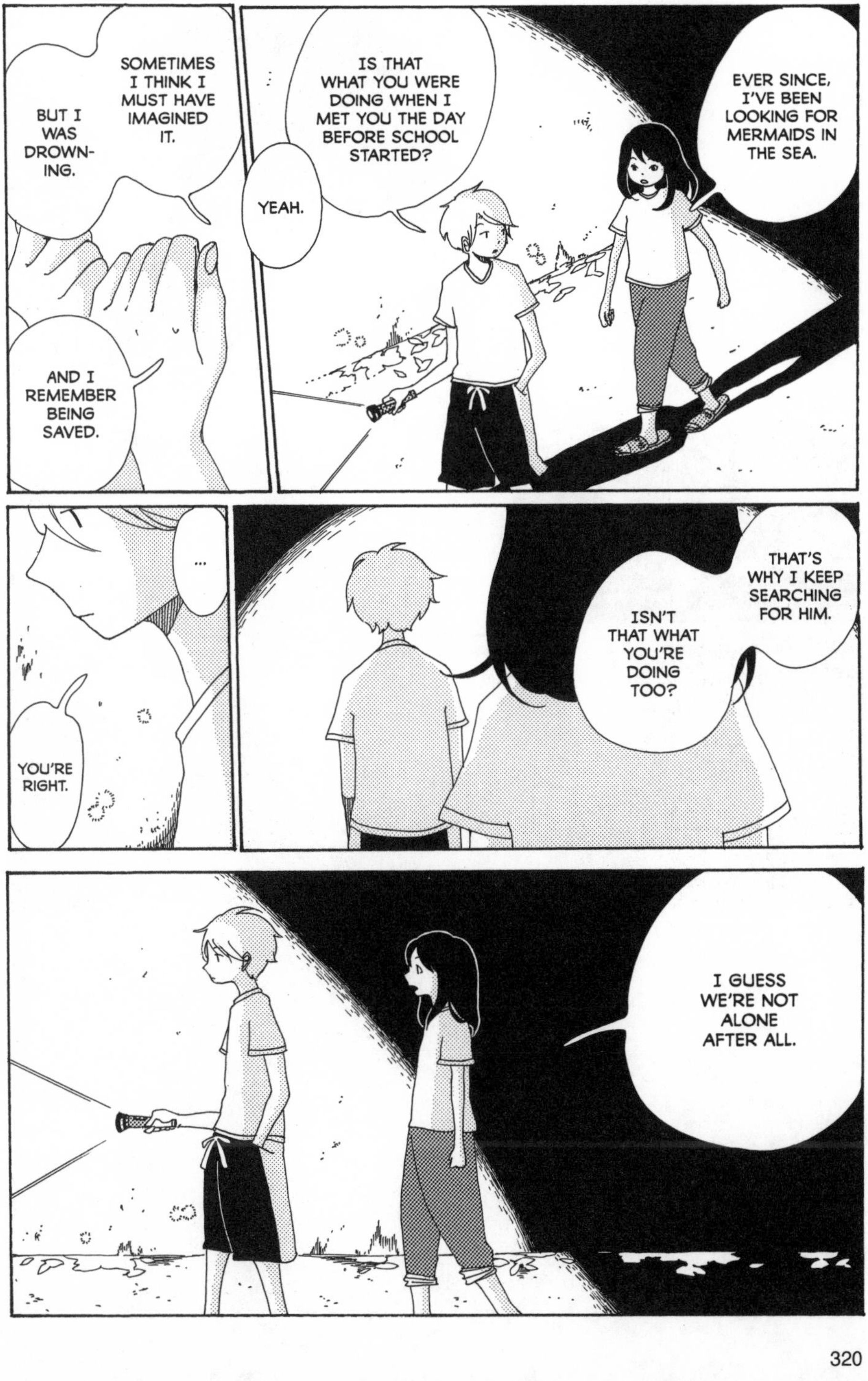
EVER SINCE, I'VE BEEN LOOKING FOR MERMAIDS IN THE SEA.
IS THAT WHAT YOU WERE DOING WHEN I MET YOU THE DAY BEFORE SCHOOL STARTED?
YEAH.
SOMETIMES I THINK I MUST HAVE IMAGINED IT.
BUT I WAS DROWNING-ING.
AND I REMEMBER BEING SAVED.
THAT'S WHY I KEEP SEARCHING FOR HIM.
ISN'T THAT WHAT YOU'RE DOING TOO?
...
YOU'RE RIGHT.
I GUESS WE'RE NOT ALONE AFTER ALL.

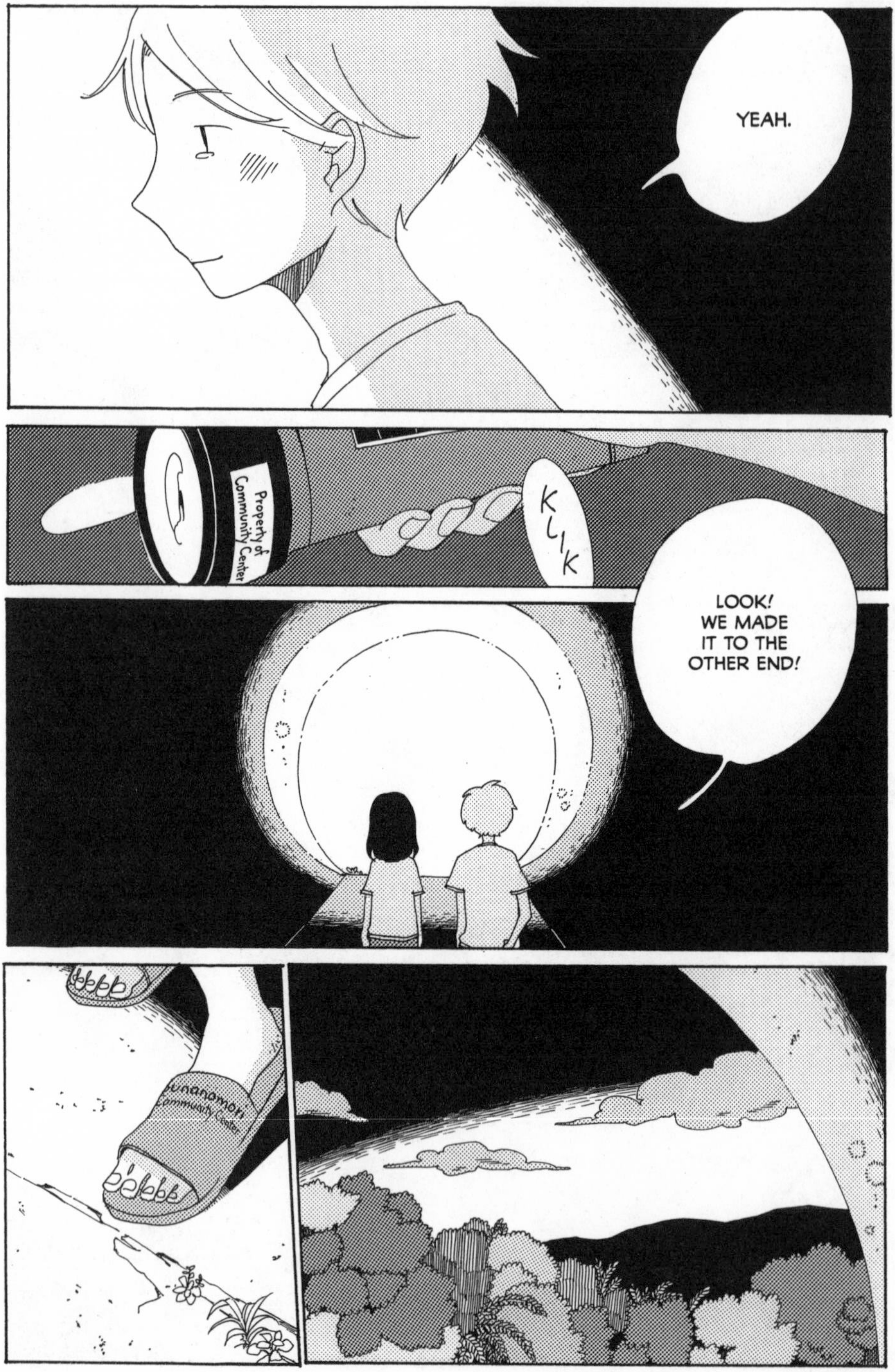
YEAH.
Property of
Community Center
KLIK
LOOK! WE MADE IT TO THE OTHER END!
Community Center

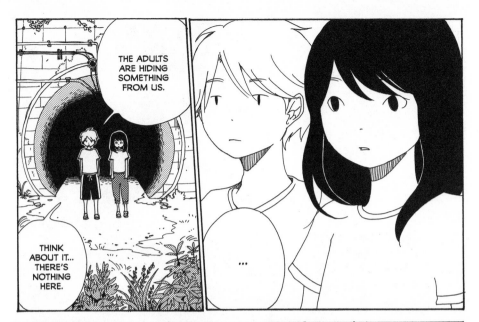

THE ADULTS ARE HIDING SOMETHING FROM US.

THINK ABOUT IT... THERE'S NOTHING HERE.

...

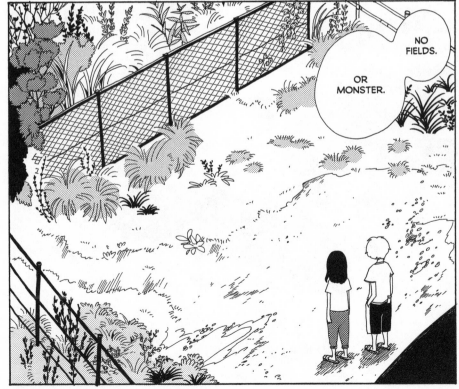

NO FIELDS.

OR MONSTER.

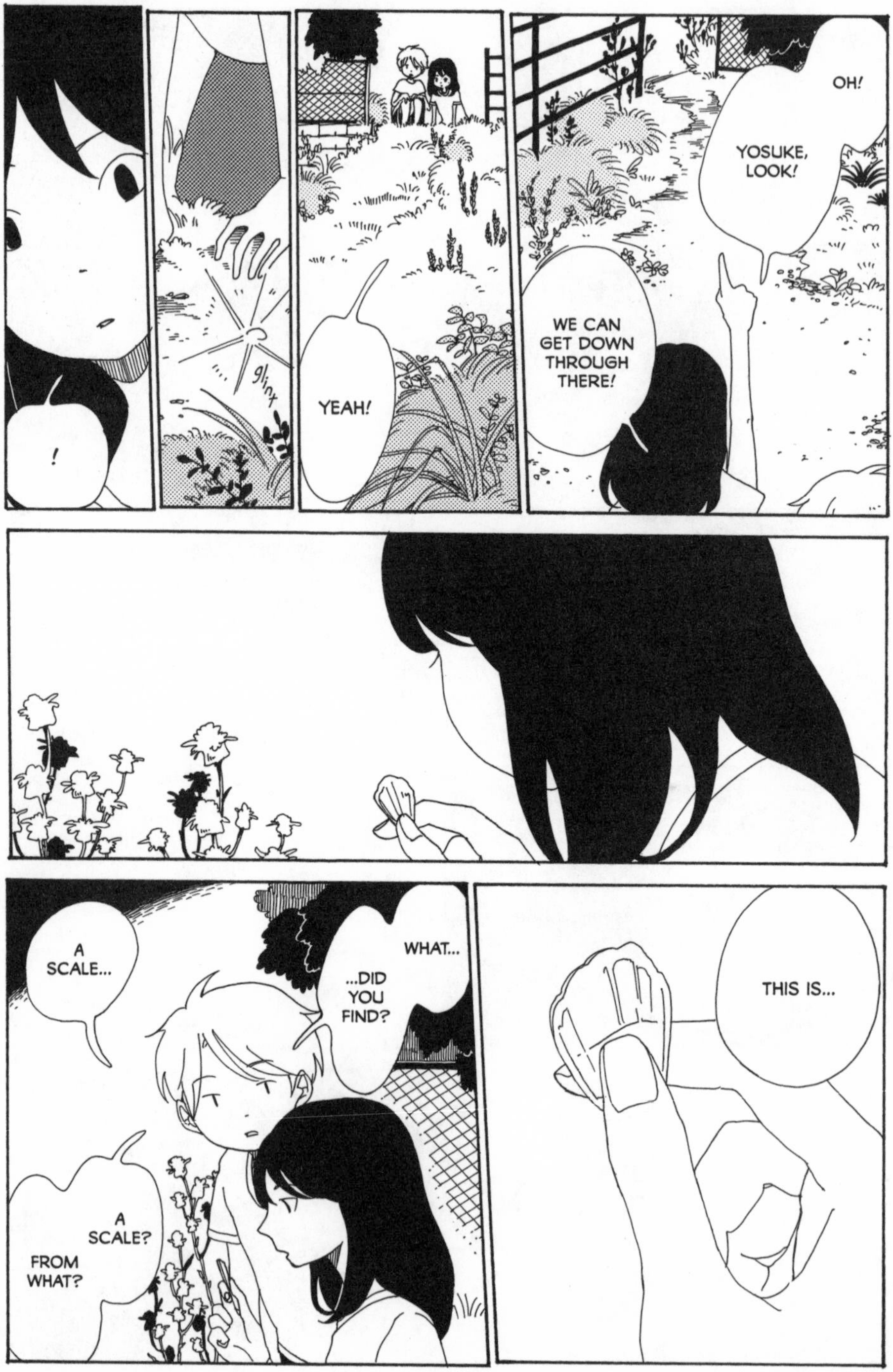

OH! YOSUKE, LOOK!
WE CAN GET DOWN THROUGH THERE!
YEAH!
glint
!
THIS IS...
WHAT... ...DID YOU FIND?
A SCALE...
A SCALE? FROM WHAT?

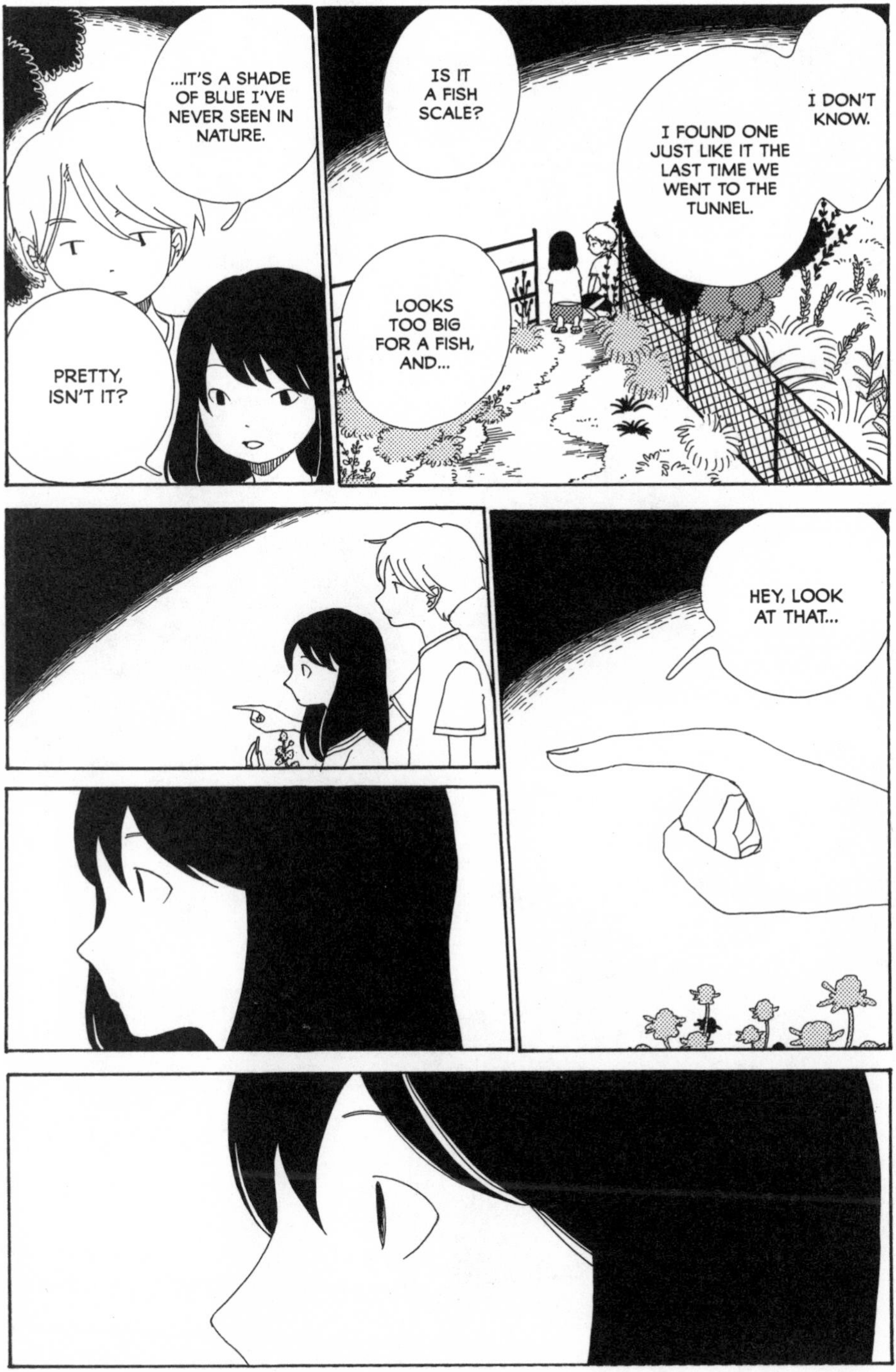
I DON'T KNOW.
I FOUND ONE JUST LIKE IT THE LAST TIME WE WENT TO THE TUNNEL.
IS IT A FISH SCALE?
LOOKS TOO BIG FOR A FISH, AND...
...IT'S A SHADE OF BLUE I'VE NEVER SEEN IN NATURE.
PRETTY, ISN'T IT?
HEY, LOOK AT THAT...

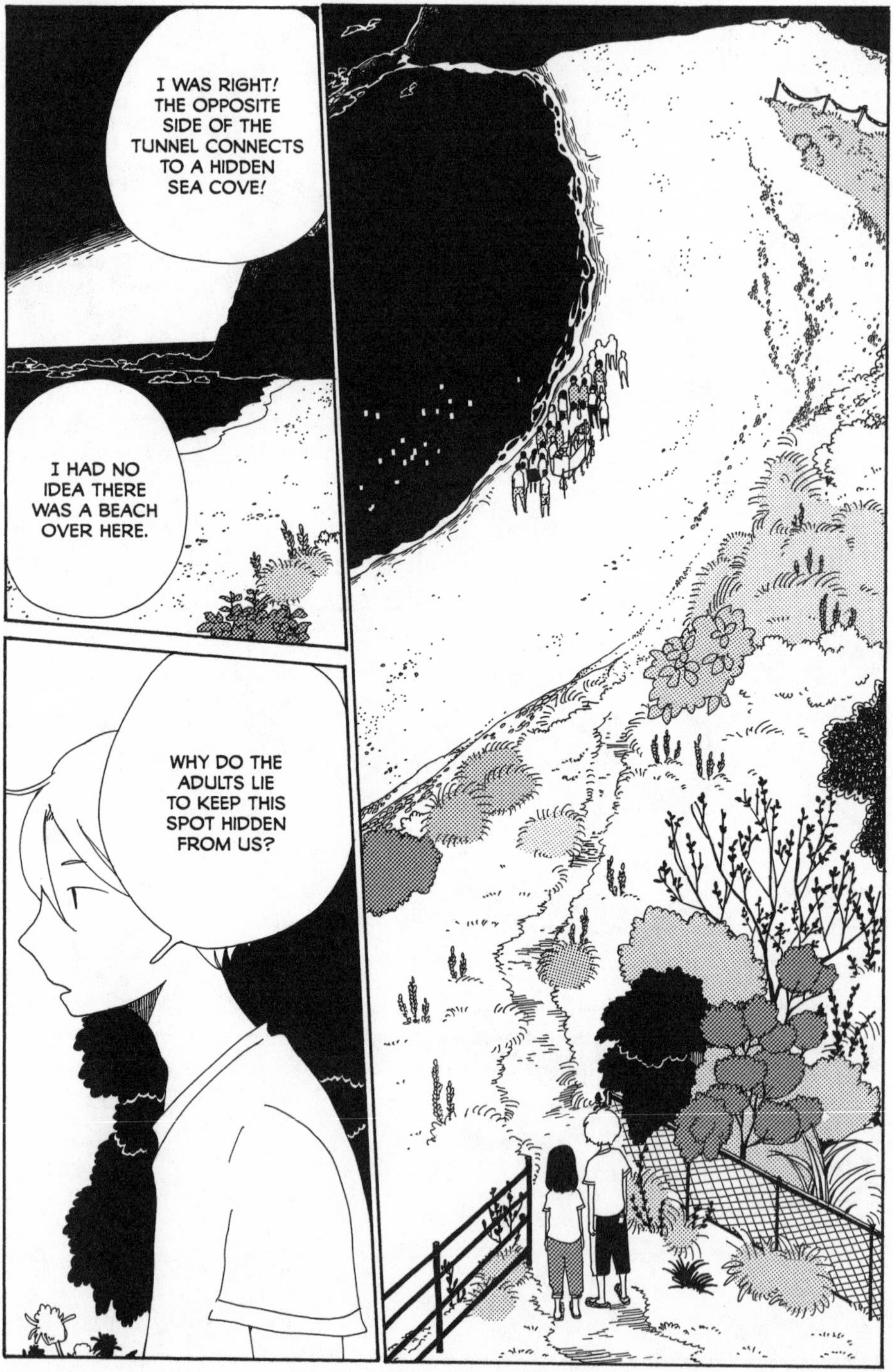
I WAS RIGHT! THE OPPOSITE SIDE OF THE TUNNEL CONNECTS TO A HIDDEN SEA COVE!
I HAD NO IDEA THERE WAS A BEACH OVER HERE.
WHY DO THE ADULTS LIE TO KEEP THIS SPOT HIDDEN FROM US?

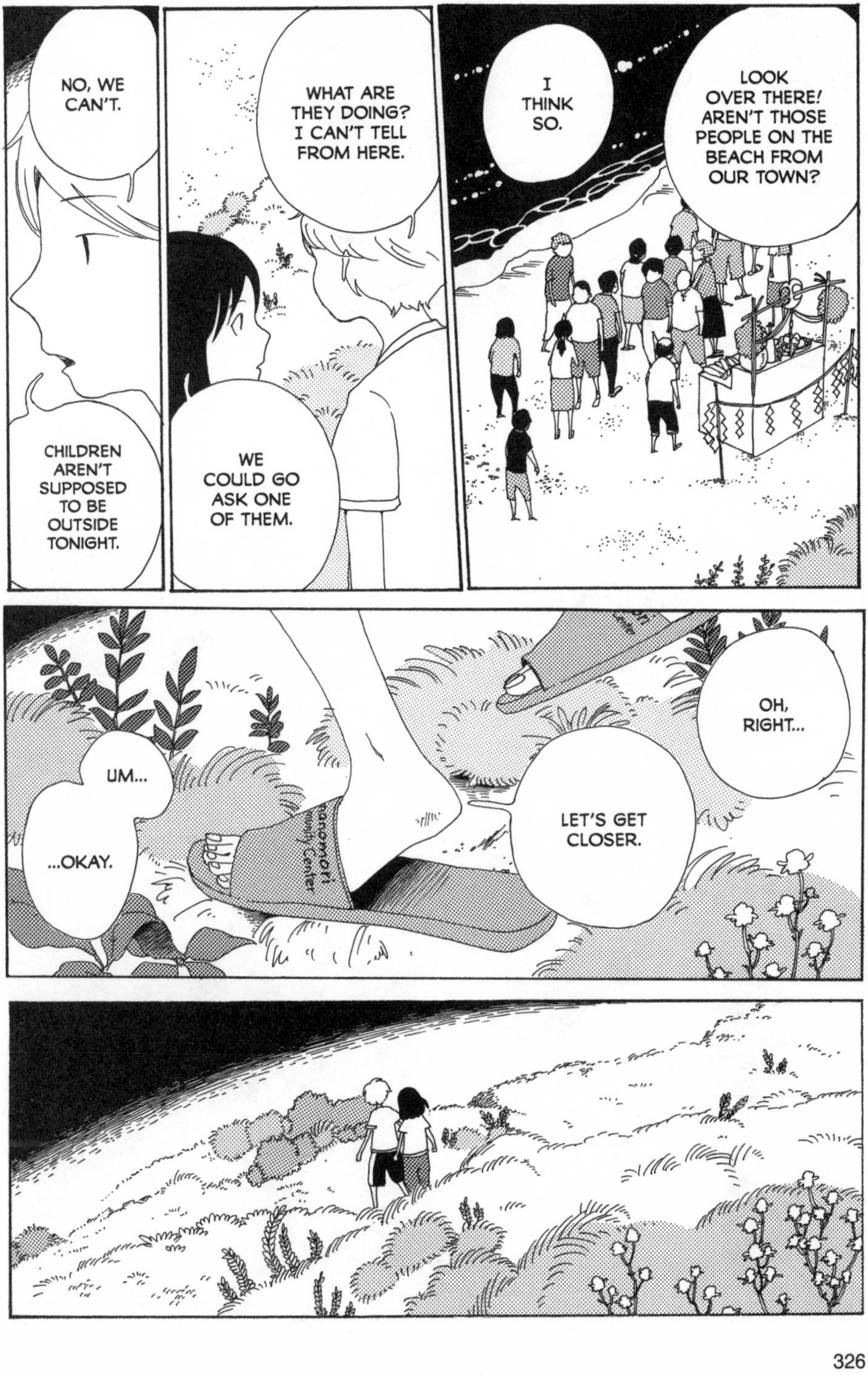
LOOK OVER THERE! AREN'T THOSE PEOPLE ON THE BEACH FROM OUR TOWN?
I THINK SO.
WHAT ARE THEY DOING? I CAN'T TELL FROM HERE.
WE COULD GO ASK ONE OF THEM.
NO, WE CAN'T.
CHILDREN AREN'T SUPPOSED TO BE OUTSIDE TONIGHT.
OH, RIGHT...
LET'S GET CLOSER.
UM...
...OKAY.

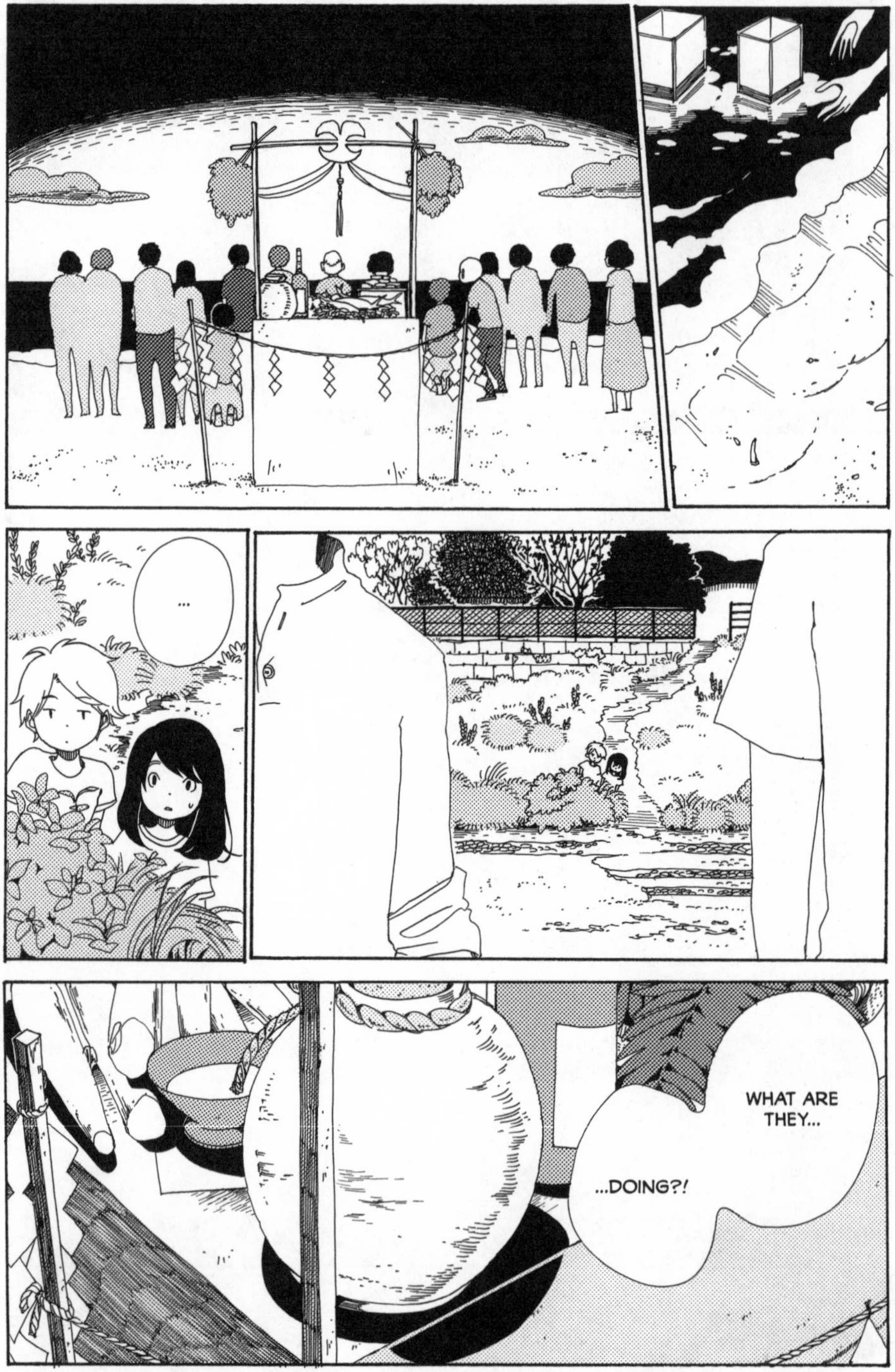
...
WHAT ARE THEY...
...DOING?!

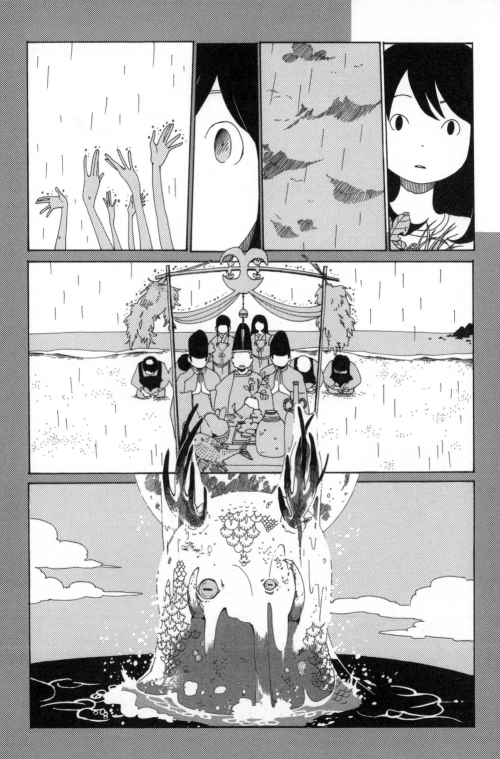

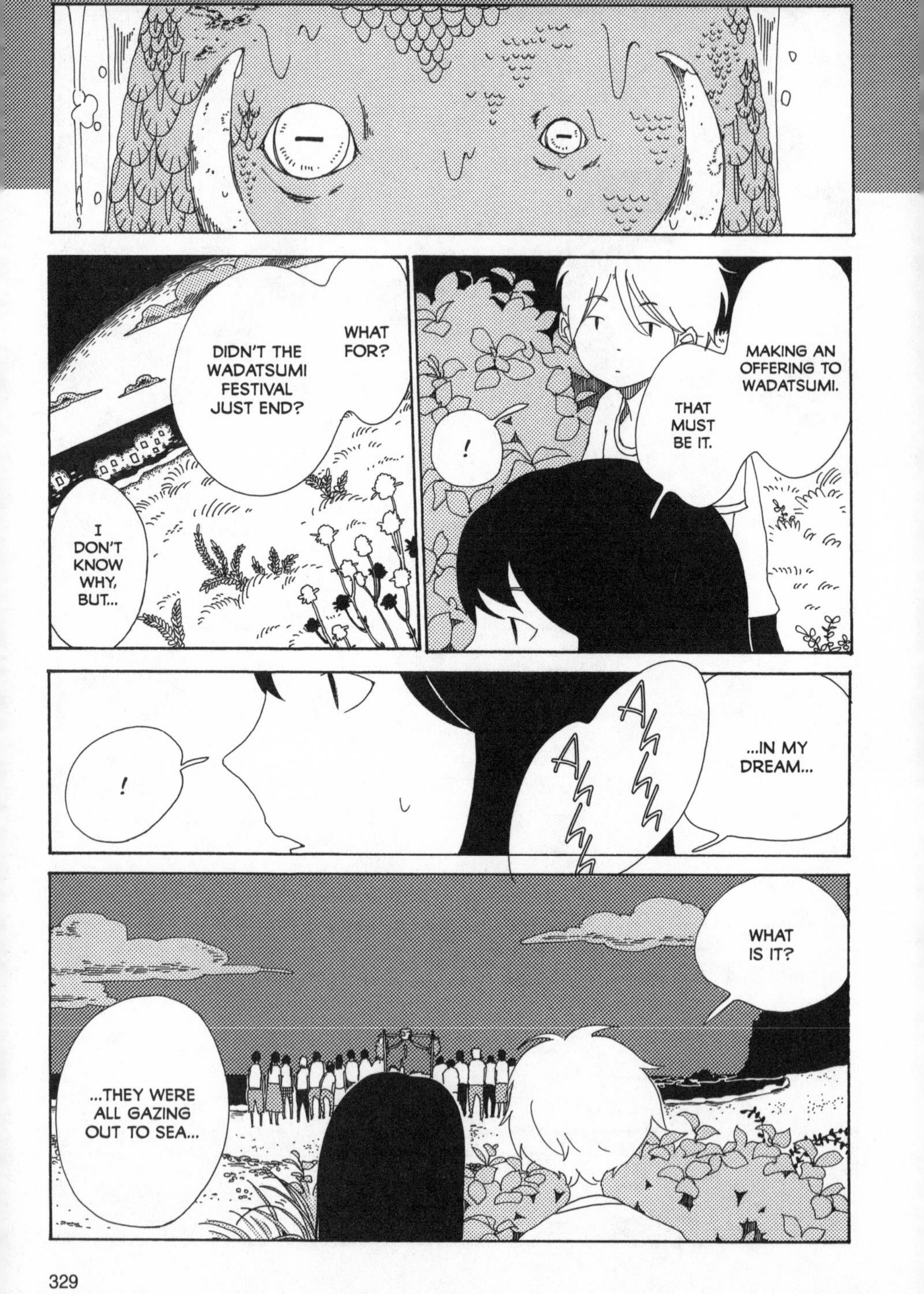
MAKING AN OFFERING TO WADATSUMI.
THAT MUST BE IT.
!
WHAT FOR?
DIDN'T THE WADATSUMI FESTIVAL JUST END?
I DON'T KNOW WHY, BUT...
...IN MY DREAM...
AHHH
AHHH
!
WHAT IS IT?
...THEY WERE ALL GAZING OUT TO SEA...

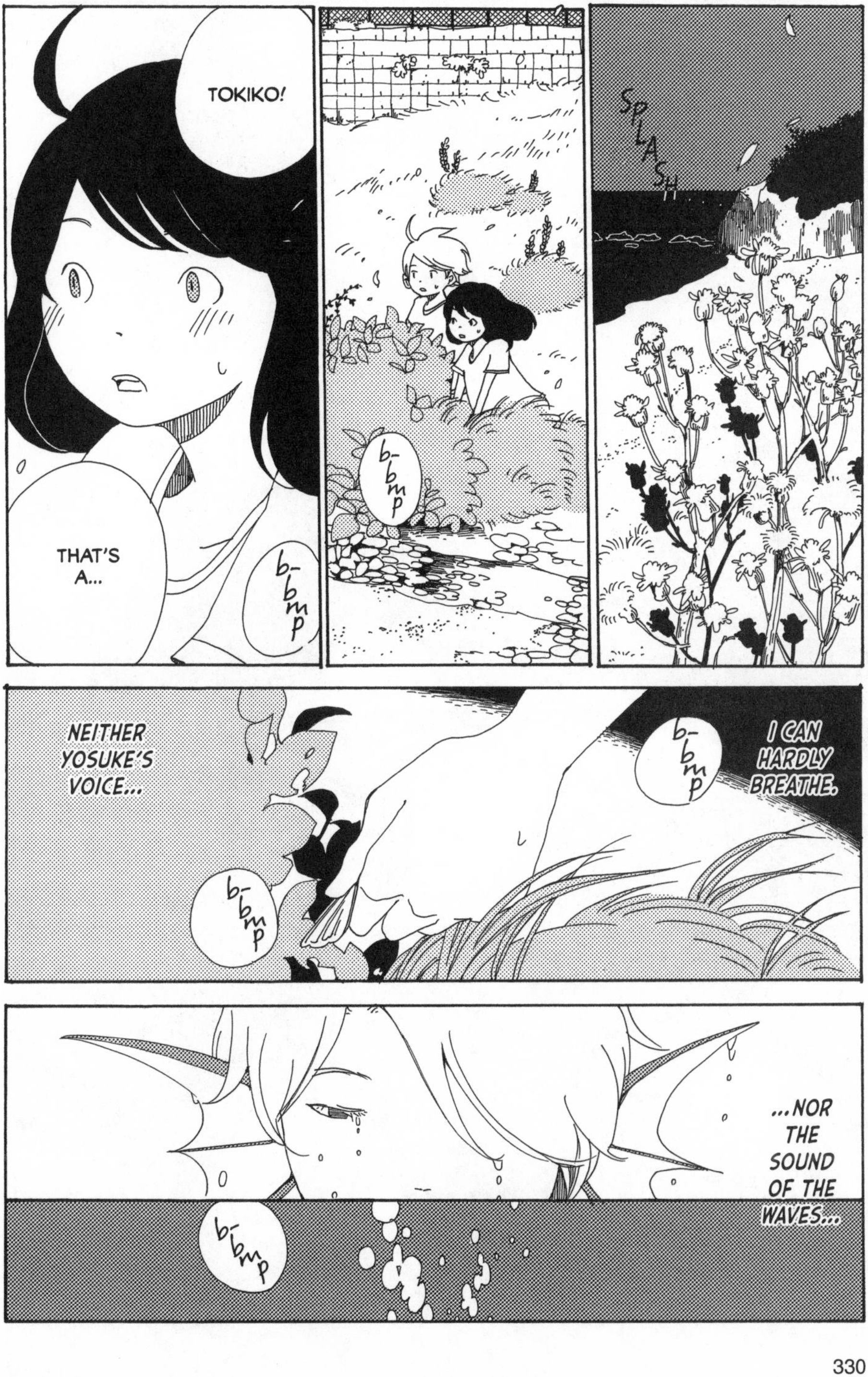
SPLASH
b-bmp
TOKIKO!
b-bmp
THAT'S A...
b-bmp
I CAN HARDLY BREATHE.
NEITHER YOSUKE'S VOICE...
b-bmp
...NOR THE SOUND OF THE WAVES...
b-bmp

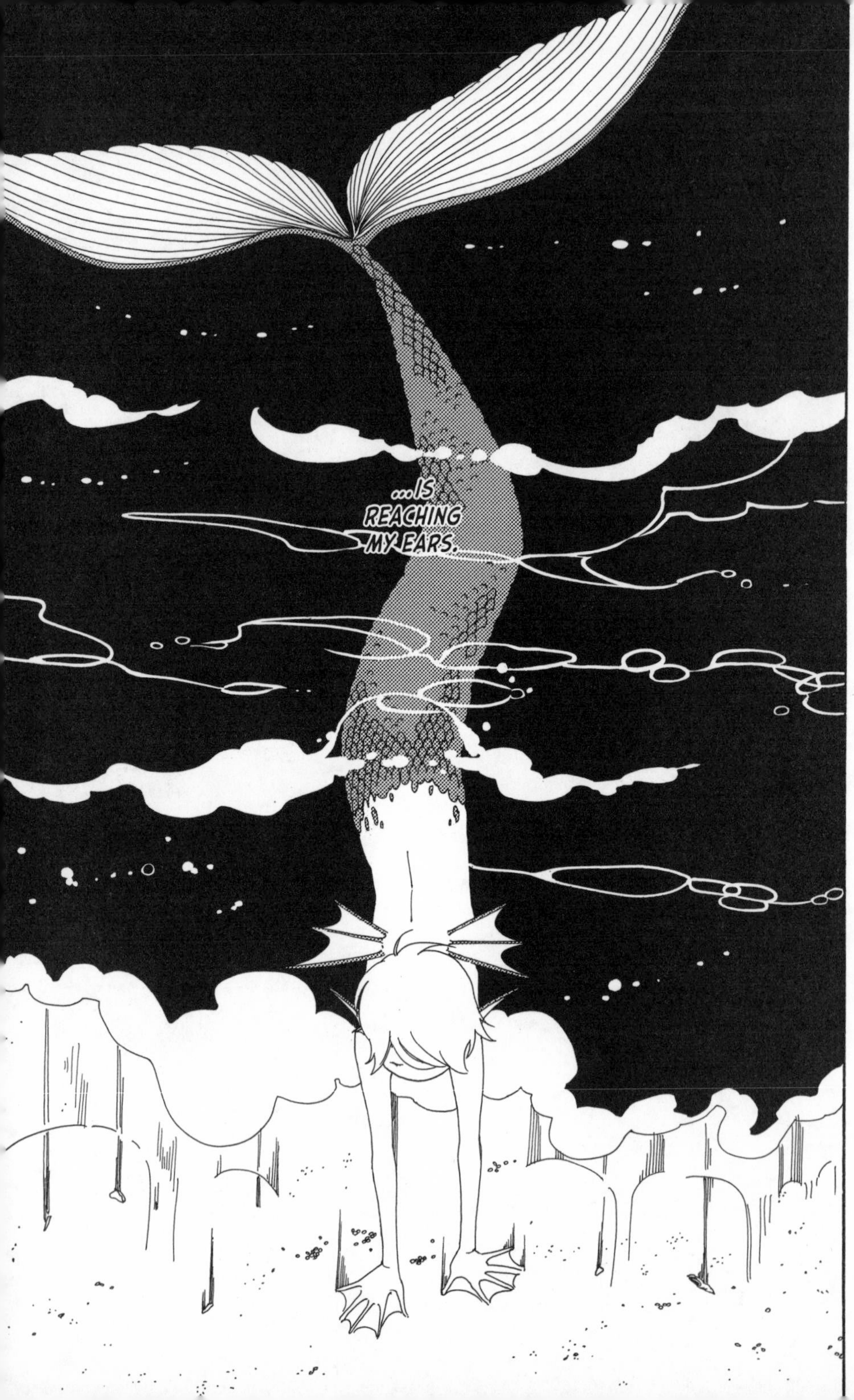
...IS REACHING MY EARS.

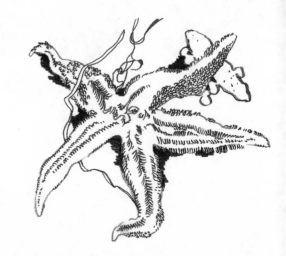

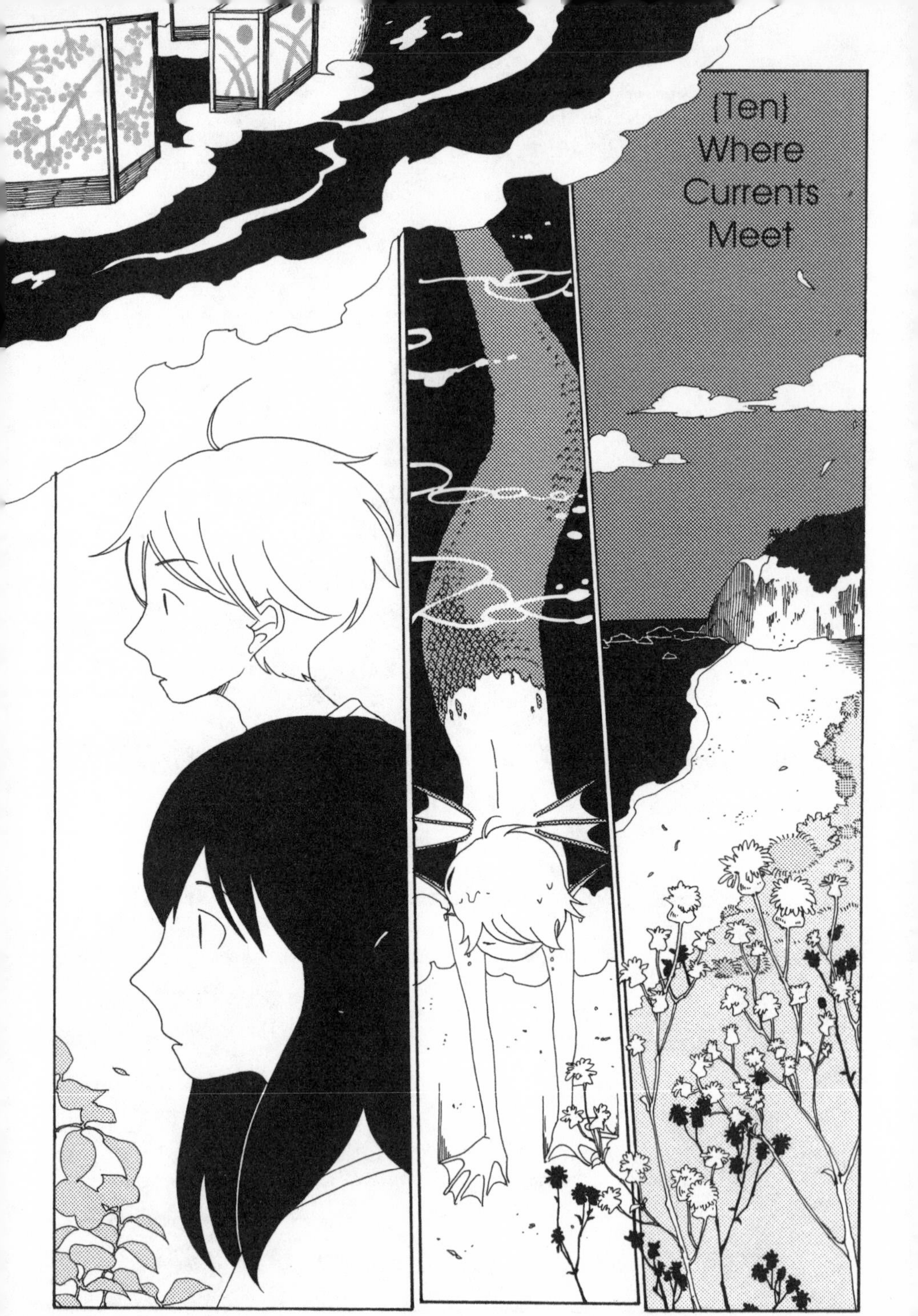
{Ten}
Where
Currents
Meet

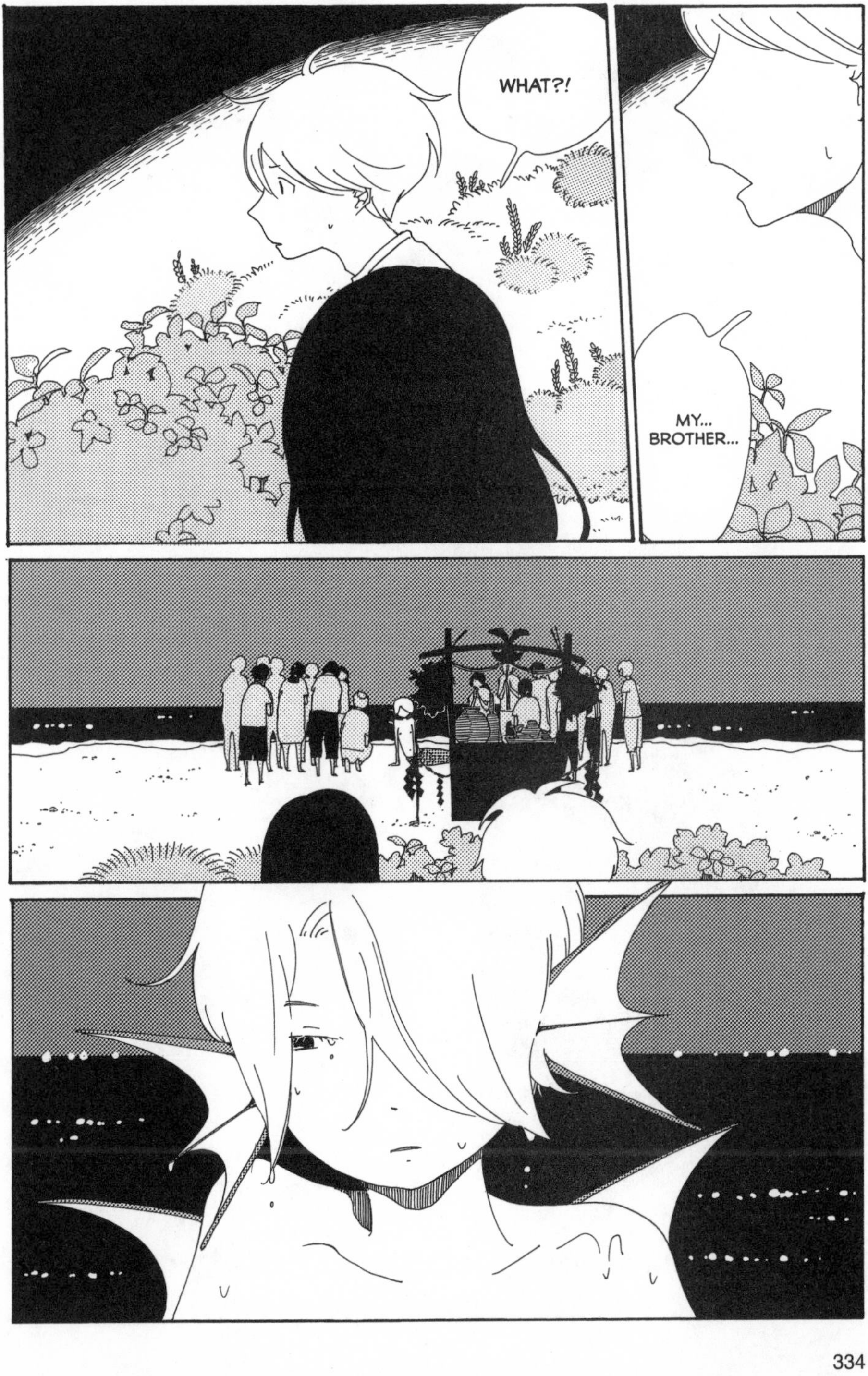
MY... BROTHER...
WHAT?!

{Ten} Where Currents Meet

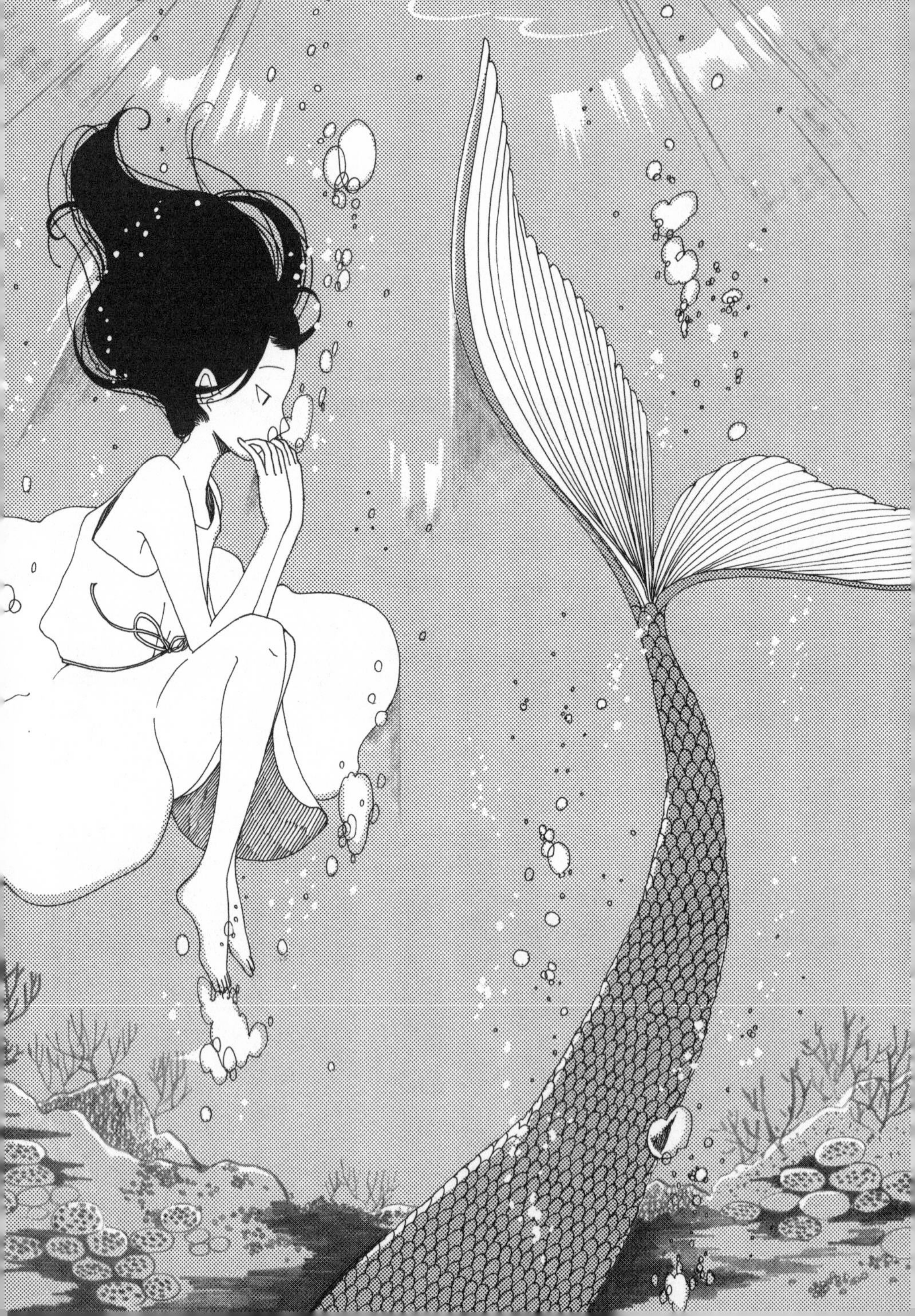

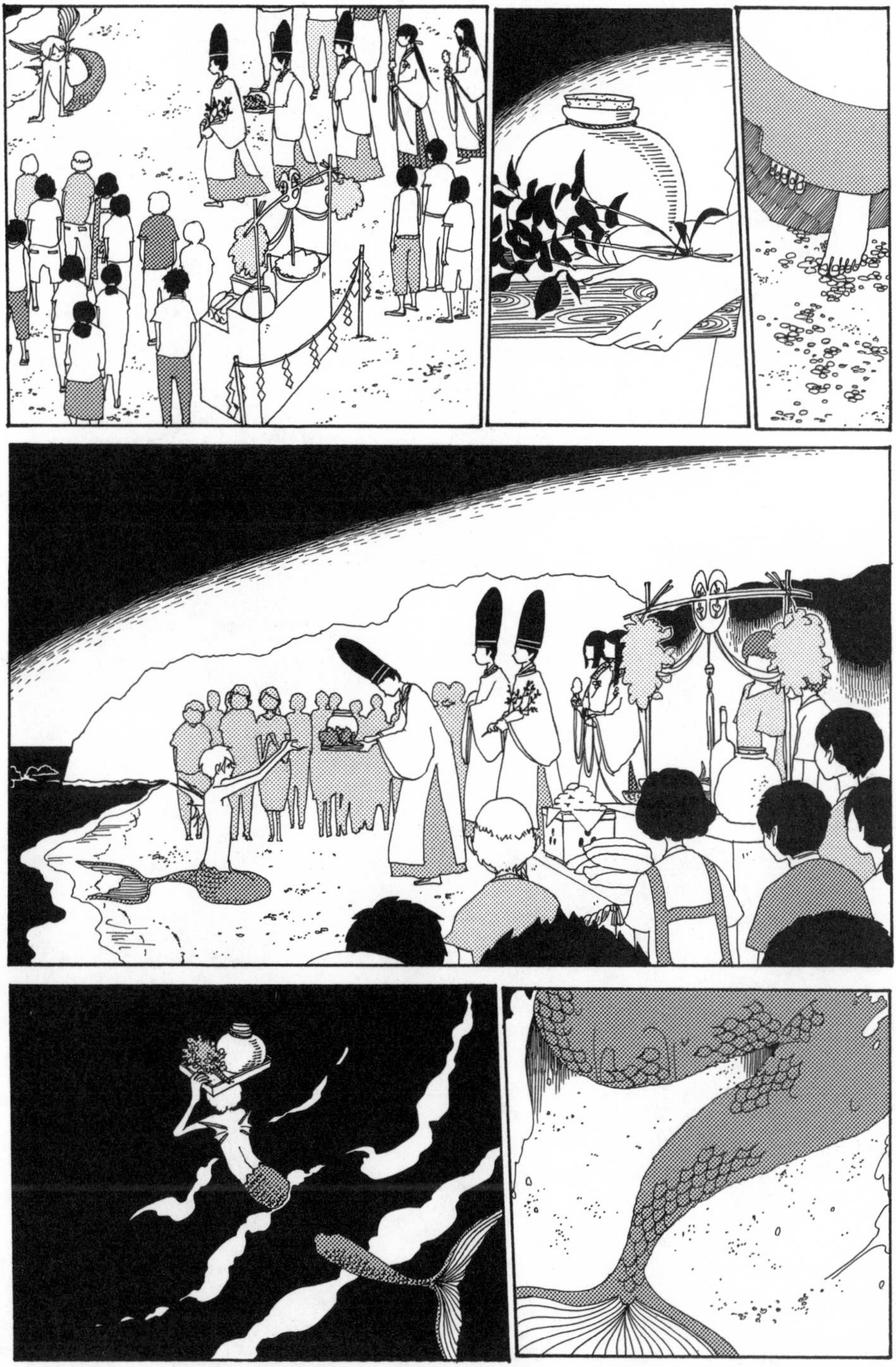

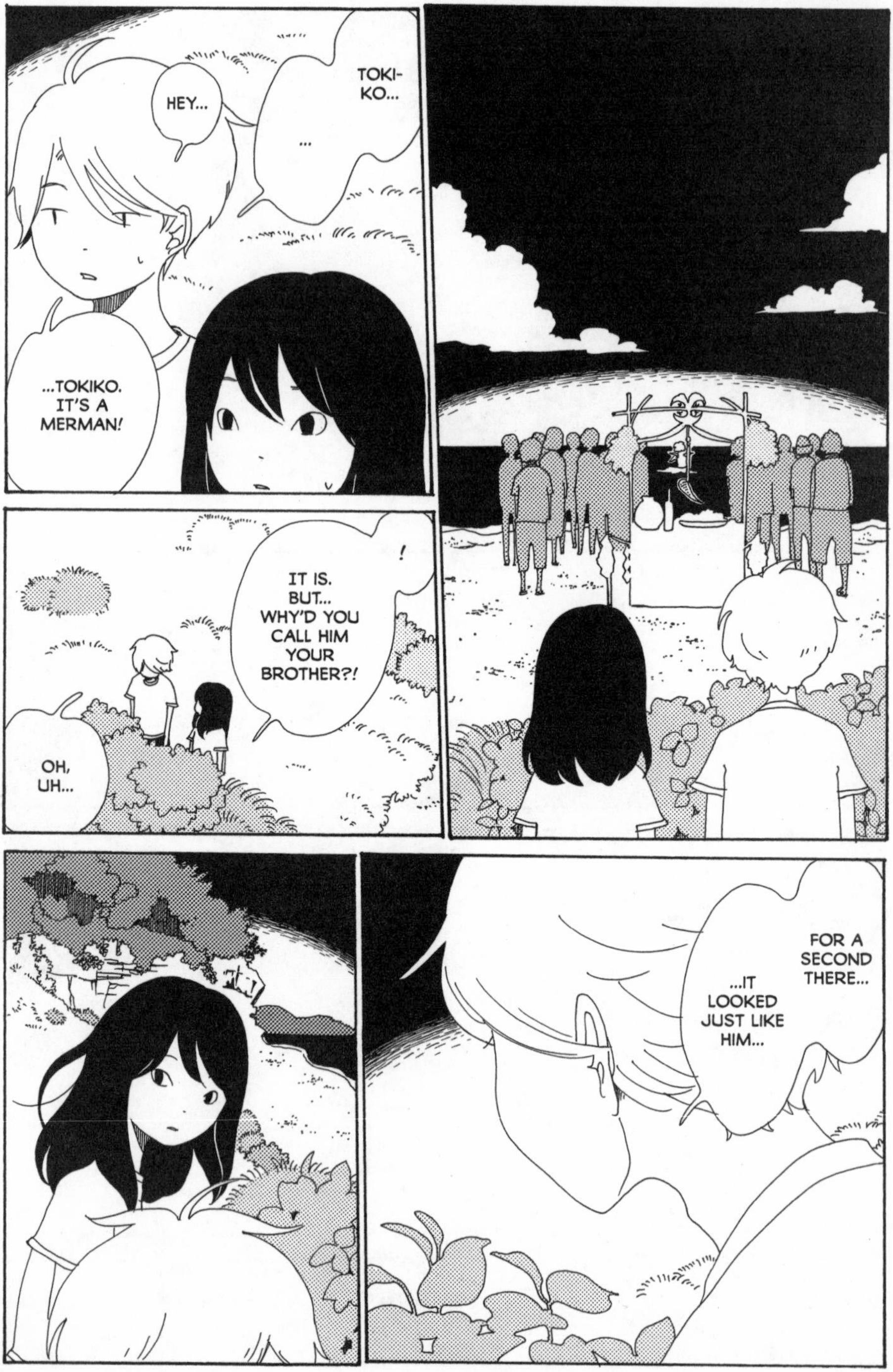
TOKI-KO...
...
HEY...
...TOKIKO. IT'S A MERMAN!
!
IT IS. BUT... WHY'D YOU CALL HIM YOUR BROTHER?!
OH, UH...
FOR A SECOND THERE...
...IT LOOKED JUST LIKE HIM...

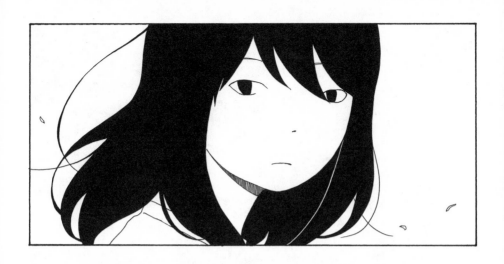

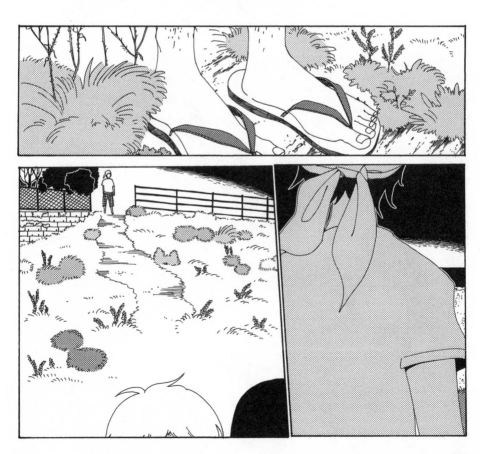

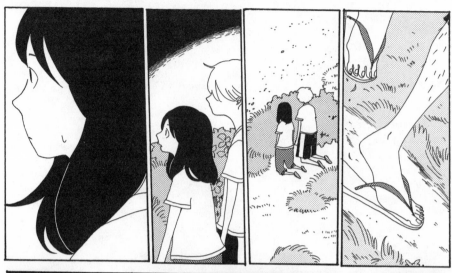

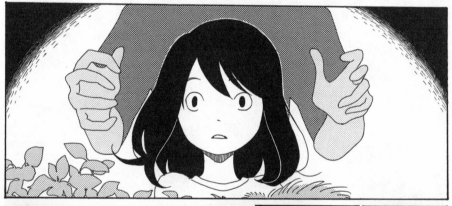

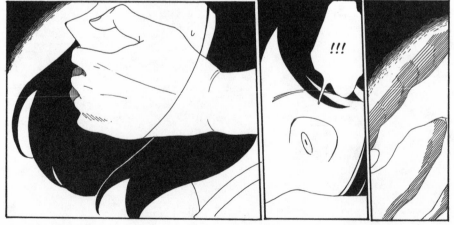

339

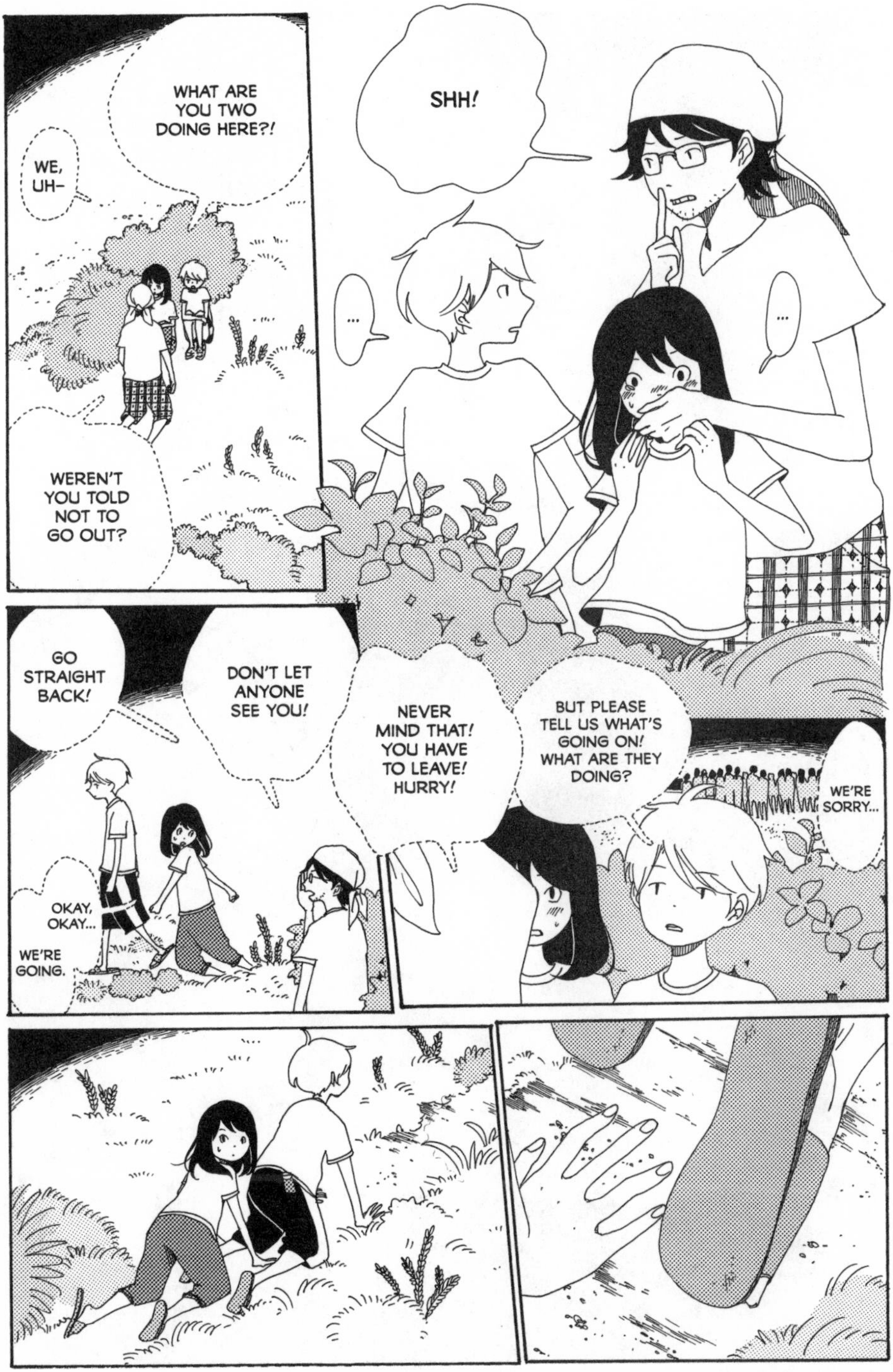
SHH!
...
...
WHAT ARE YOU TWO DOING HERE?!
WE, UH-
WEREN'T YOU TOLD NOT TO GO OUT?
WE'RE SORRY...
BUT PLEASE TELL US WHAT'S GOING ON! WHAT ARE THEY DOING?
NEVER MIND THAT! YOU HAVE TO LEAVE! HURRY!
DON'T LET ANYONE SEE YOU!
GO STRAIGHT BACK!
OKAY, OKAY...
WE'RE GOING.

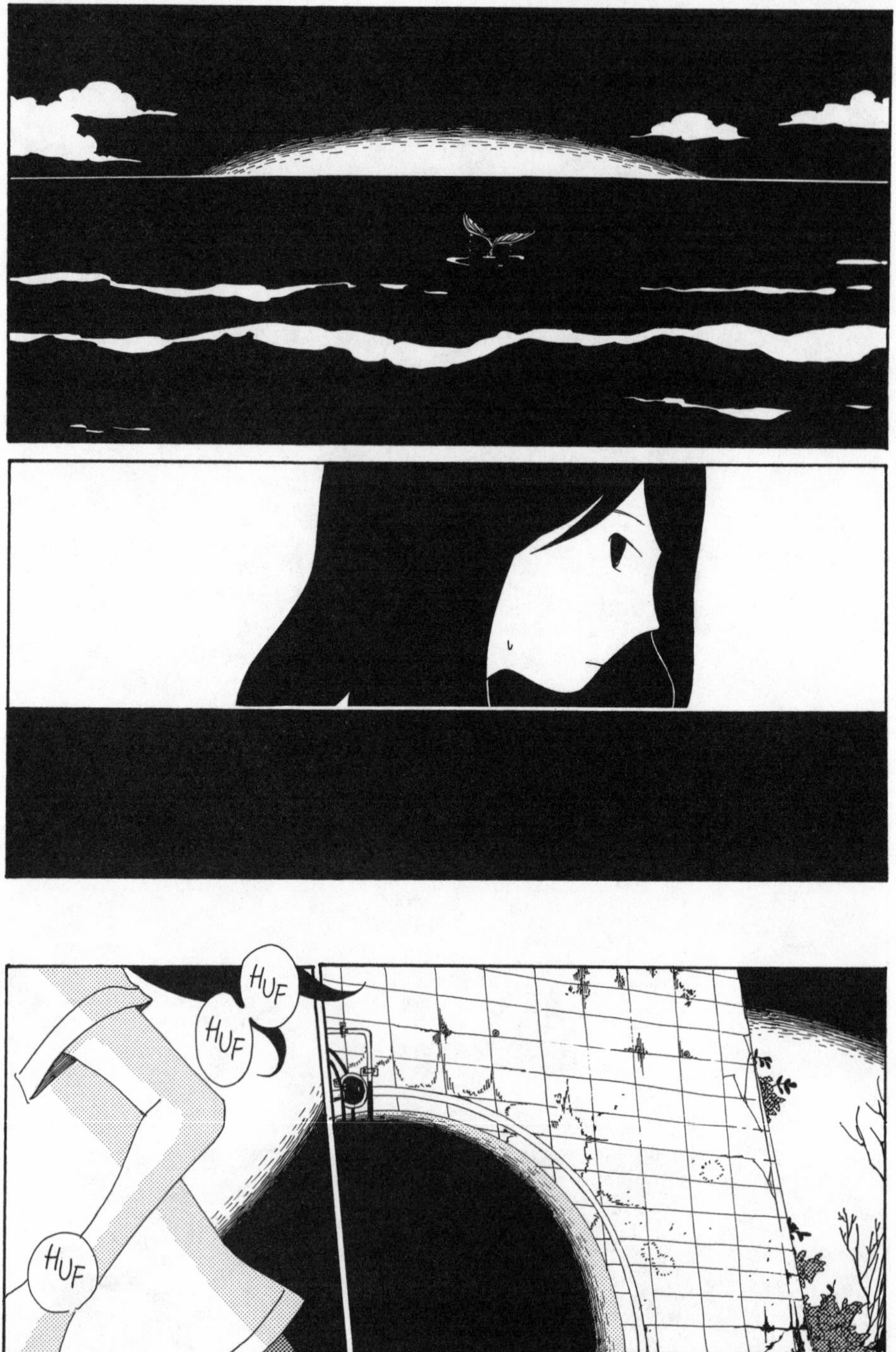
HUF
HUF
HUF

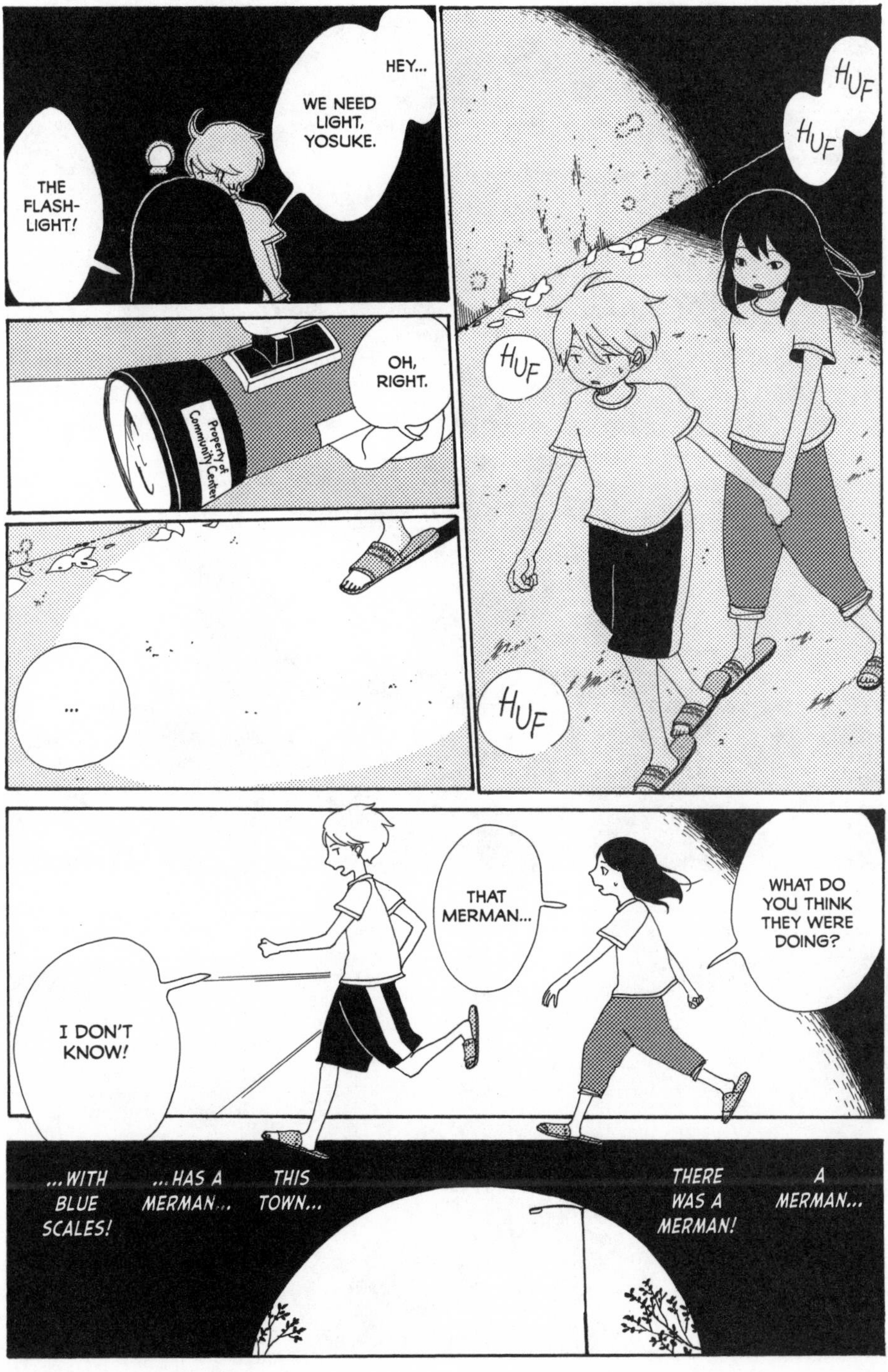
HUF
HUF
HUF
HUF
HEY...
WE NEED LIGHT, YOSUKE.
THE FLASH-LIGHT!
Property of Community Center
OH, RIGHT.
...
WHAT DO YOU THINK THEY WERE DOING?
THAT MERMAN...
I DON'T KNOW!
A MERMAN...
THERE WAS A MERMAN!
THIS TOWN...
...HAS A MERMAN...
...WITH BLUE SCALES!

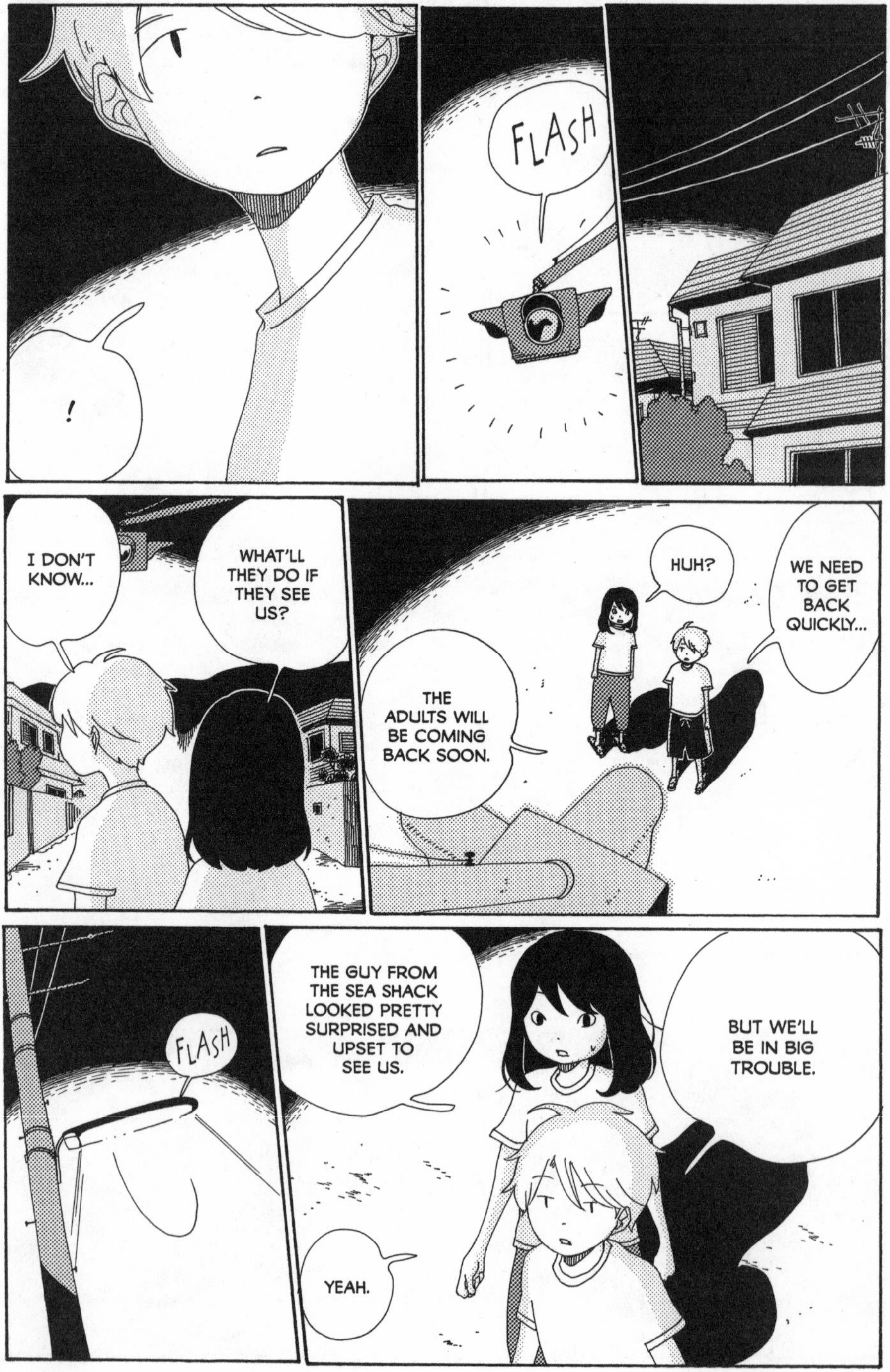
FLASH
!
WE NEED TO GET BACK QUICKLY...
HUH?
THE ADULTS WILL BE COMING BACK SOON.
WHAT'LL THEY DO IF THEY SEE US?
I DON'T KNOW...
BUT WE'LL BE IN BIG TROUBLE.
THE GUY FROM THE SEA SHACK LOOKED PRETTY SURPRISED AND UPSET TO SEE US.
YEAH.
FLASH

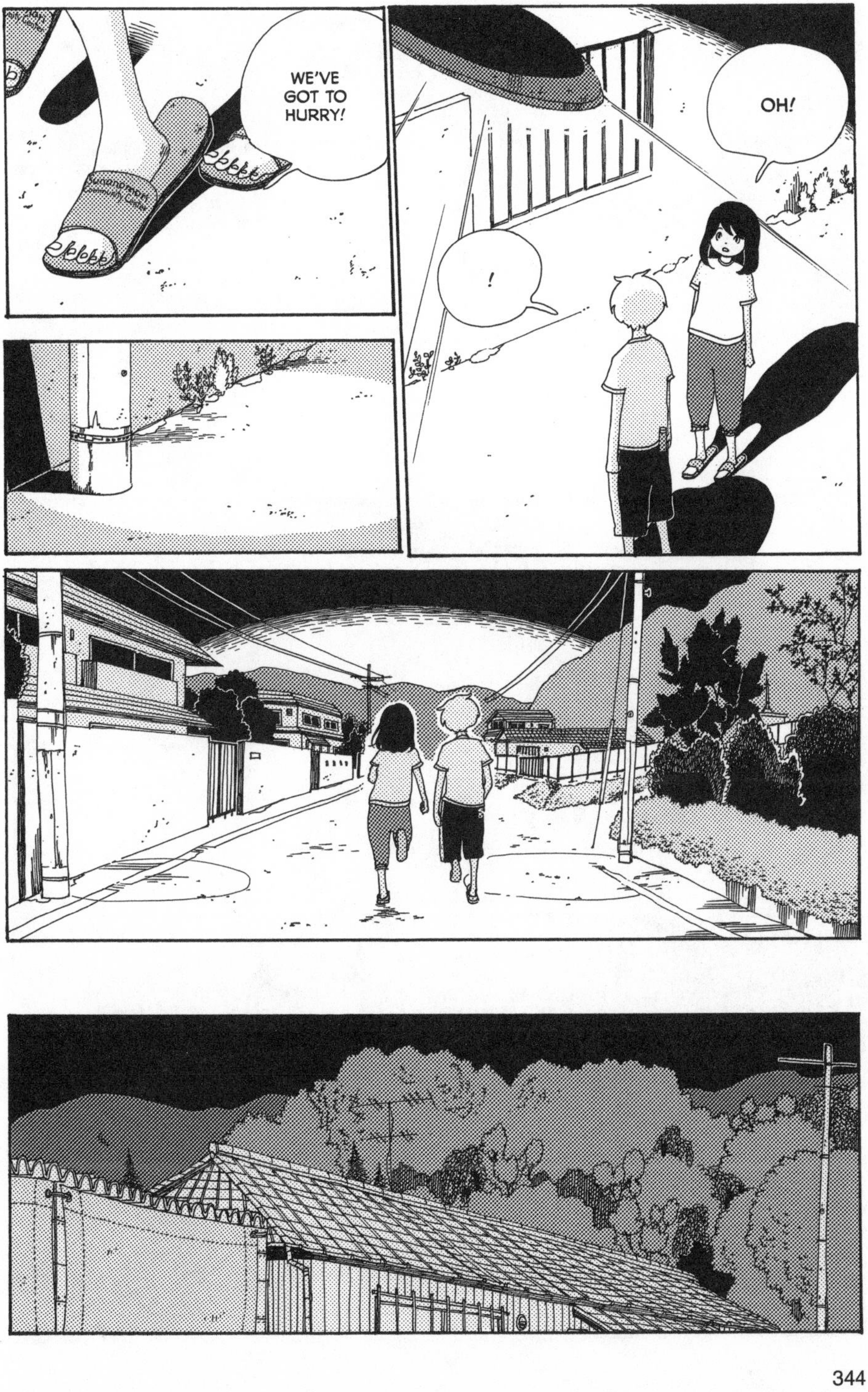
OH!
!
WE'VE GOT TO HURRY!

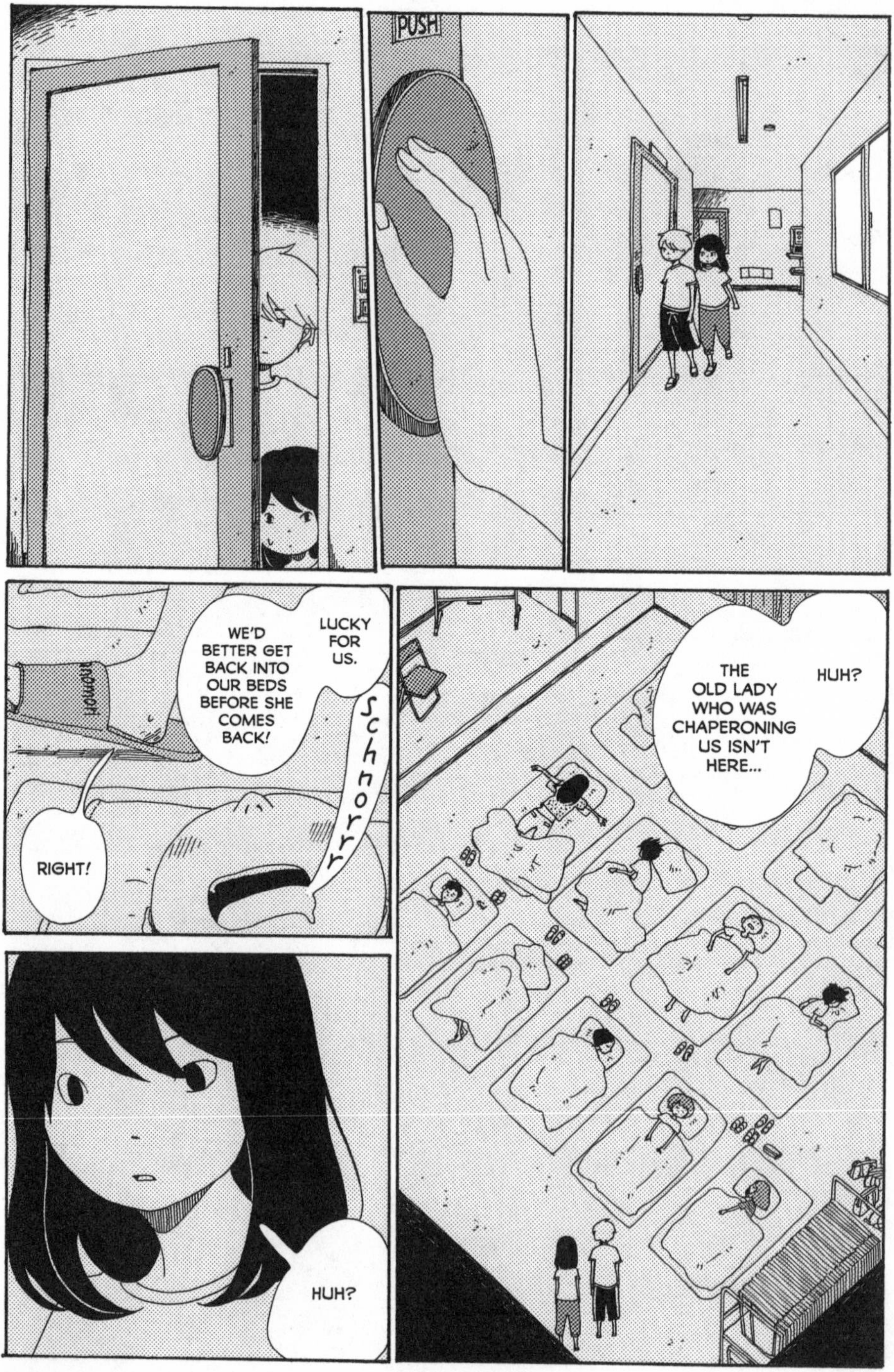
PUSH
HUH?
THE OLD LADY WHO WAS CHAPERONING US ISN'T HERE...
LUCKY FOR US.
WE'D BETTER GET BACK INTO OUR BEDS BEFORE SHE COMES BACK!
Schnorrry
RIGHT!
HUH?

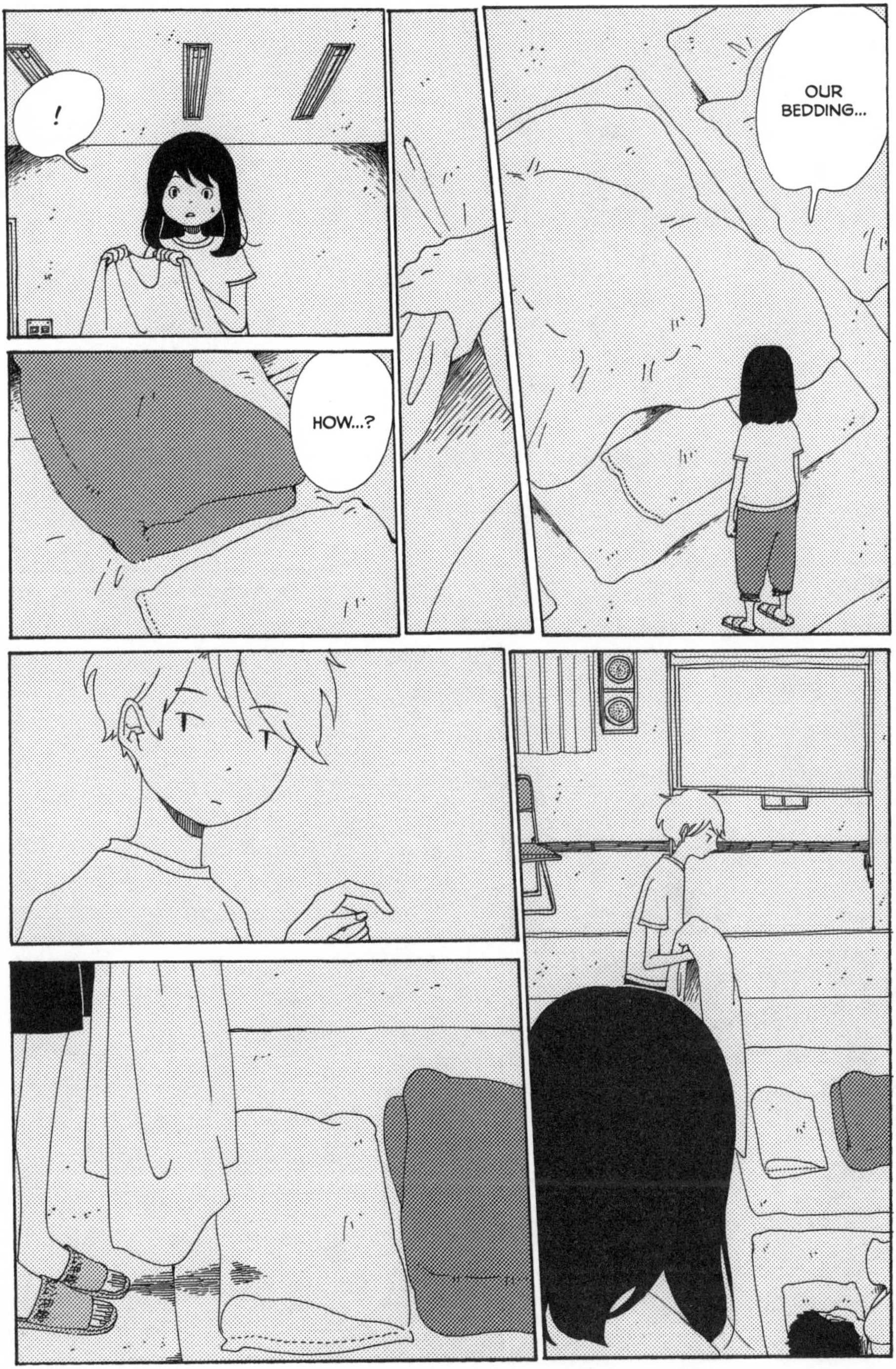
OUR BEDDING...
!
HOW...?

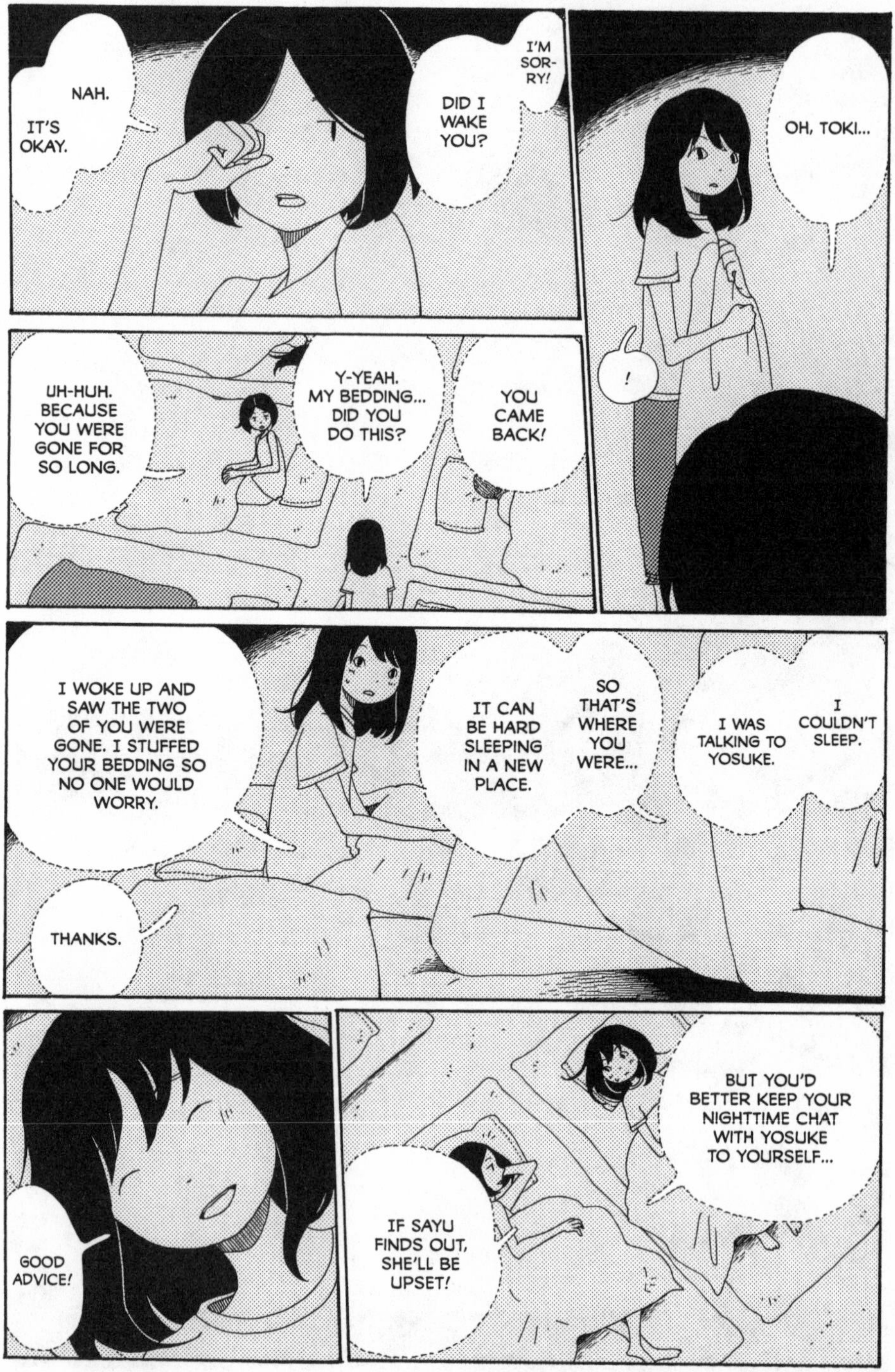
OH, TOKI...
!
I'M SORRY!
DID I WAKE YOU?
NAH. IT'S OKAY.
YOU CAME BACK!
Y-YEAH. MY BEDDING... DID YOU DO THIS?
UH-HUH. BECAUSE YOU WERE GONE FOR SO LONG.
I COULDN'T SLEEP.
I WAS TALKING TO YOSUKE.
SO THAT'S WHERE YOU WERE...
IT CAN BE HARD SLEEPING IN A NEW PLACE.
I WOKE UP AND SAW THE TWO OF YOU WERE GONE. I STUFFED YOUR BEDDING SO NO ONE WOULD WORRY.
THANKS.
BUT YOU'D BETTER KEEP YOUR NIGHTTIME CHAT WITH YOSUKE TO YOURSELF...
IF SAYU FINDS OUT, SHE'LL BE UPSET!
GOOD ADVICE!

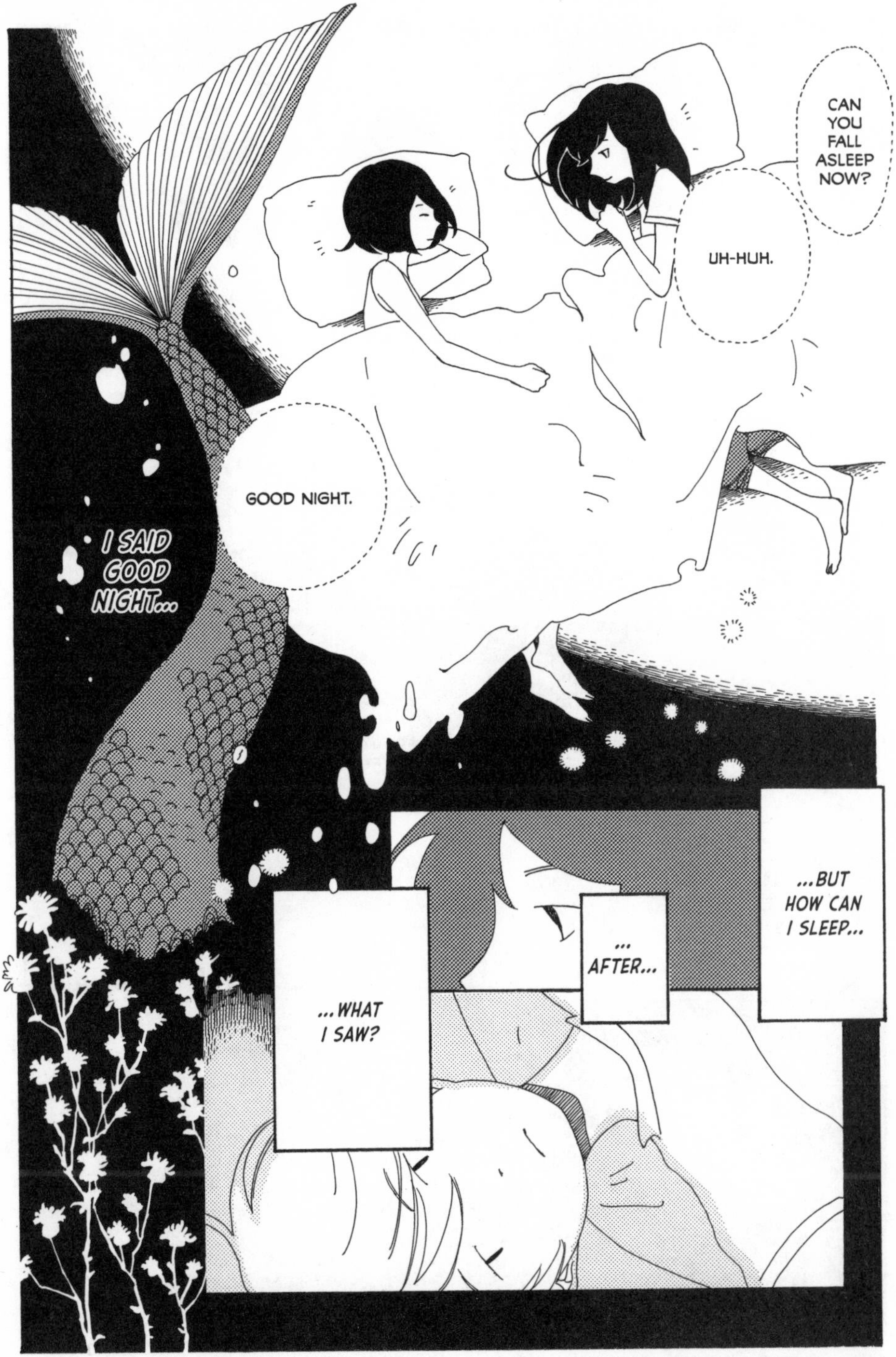
CAN YOU FALL ASLEEP NOW?
UH-HUH.
GOOD NIGHT.
I SAID GOOD NIGHT...
...BUT HOW CAN I SLEEP...
... AFTER...
...WHAT I SAW?

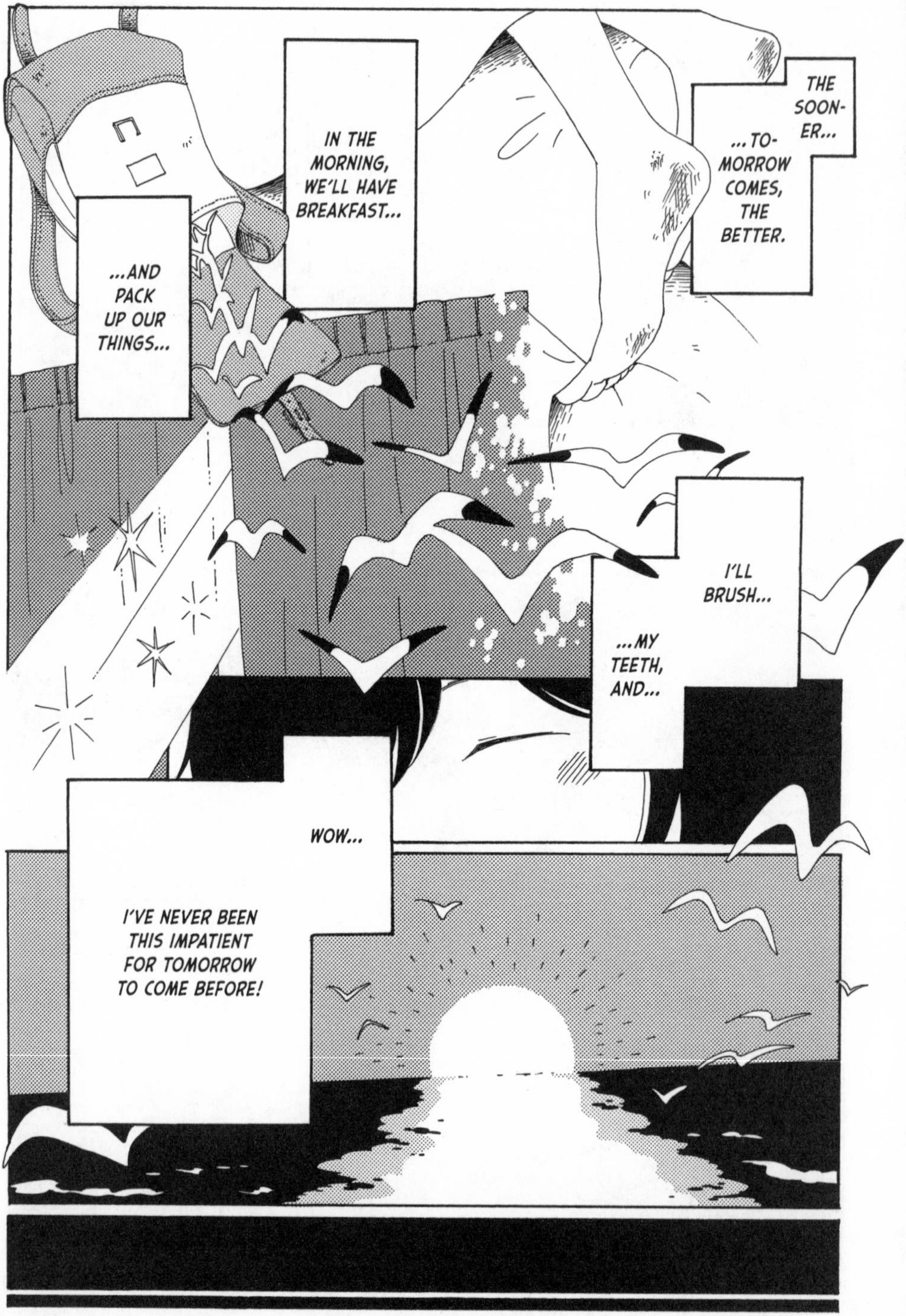
THE SOONER...
...TOMORROW COMES, THE BETTER.
IN THE MORNING, WE'LL HAVE BREAKFAST...
...AND PACK UP OUR THINGS...
I'LL BRUSH...
...MY TEETH, AND...
WOW...
I'VE NEVER BEEN THIS IMPATIENT FOR TOMORROW TO COME BEFORE!

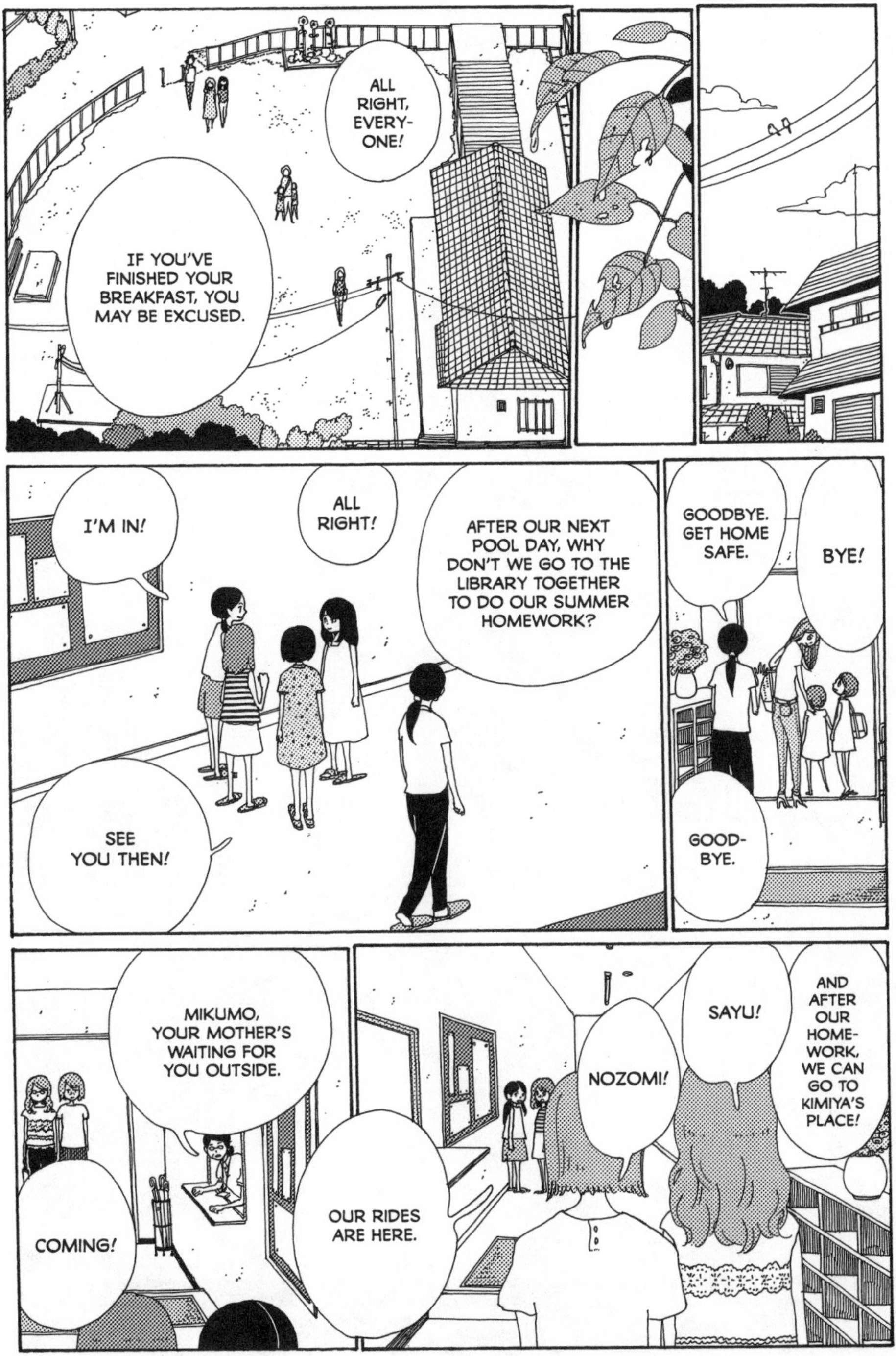
ALL RIGHT, EVERYONE!
IF YOU'VE FINISHED YOUR BREAKFAST, YOU MAY BE EXCUSED.
BYE!
GOODBYE. GET HOME SAFE.
GOOD-BYE.
AFTER OUR NEXT POOL DAY, WHY DON'T WE GO TO THE LIBRARY TOGETHER TO DO OUR SUMMER HOMEWORK?
ALL RIGHT!
I'M IN!
SEE YOU THEN!
AND AFTER OUR HOME-WORK, WE CAN GO TO KIMIYA'S PLACE!
SAYU!
NOZOMI!
OUR RIDES ARE HERE.
MIKUMO, YOUR MOTHER'S WAITING FOR YOU OUTSIDE.
COMING!

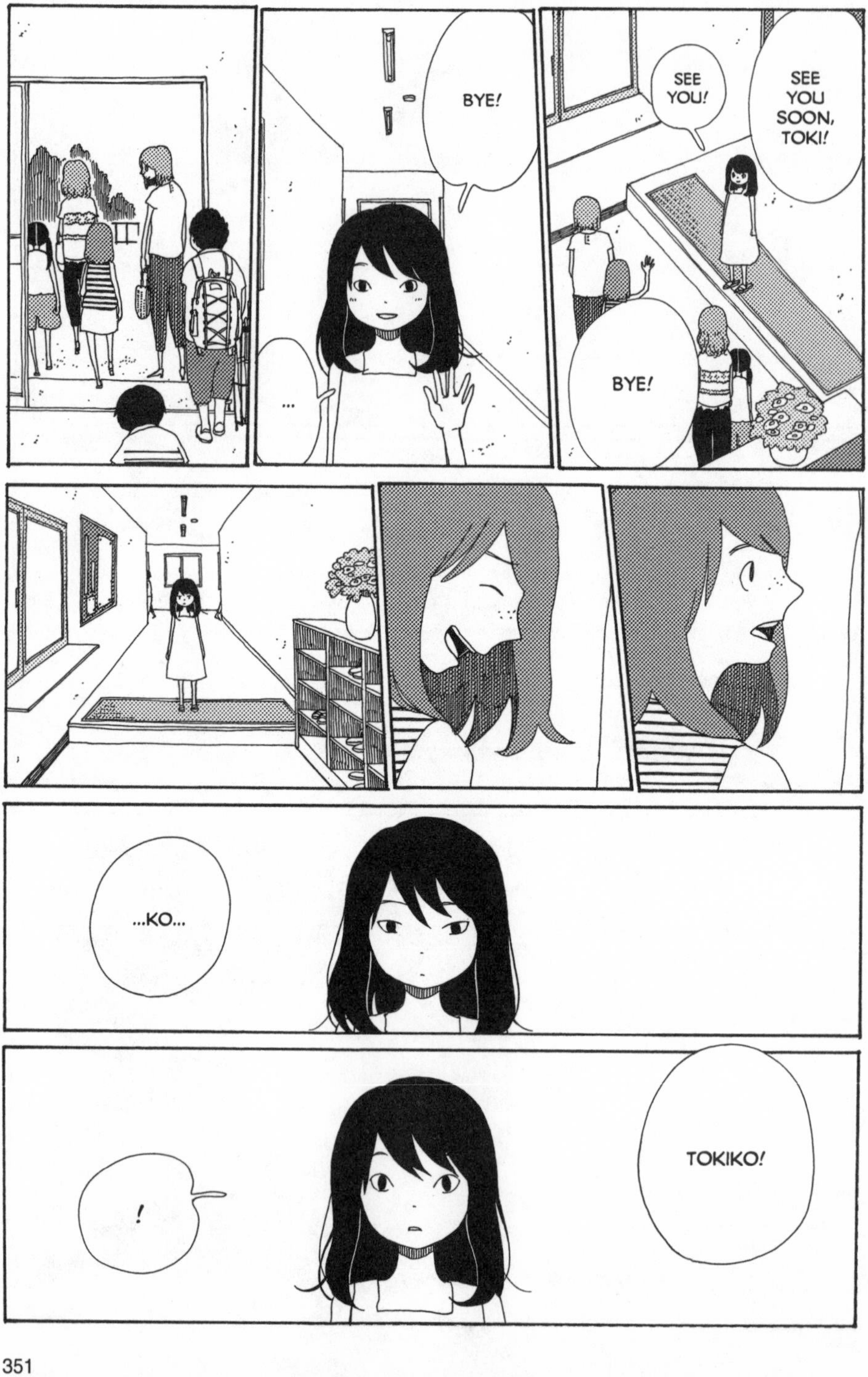
SEE YOU SOON, TOKI!
SEE YOU!
BYE!
BYE!
...
...KO...
TOKIKO!
!

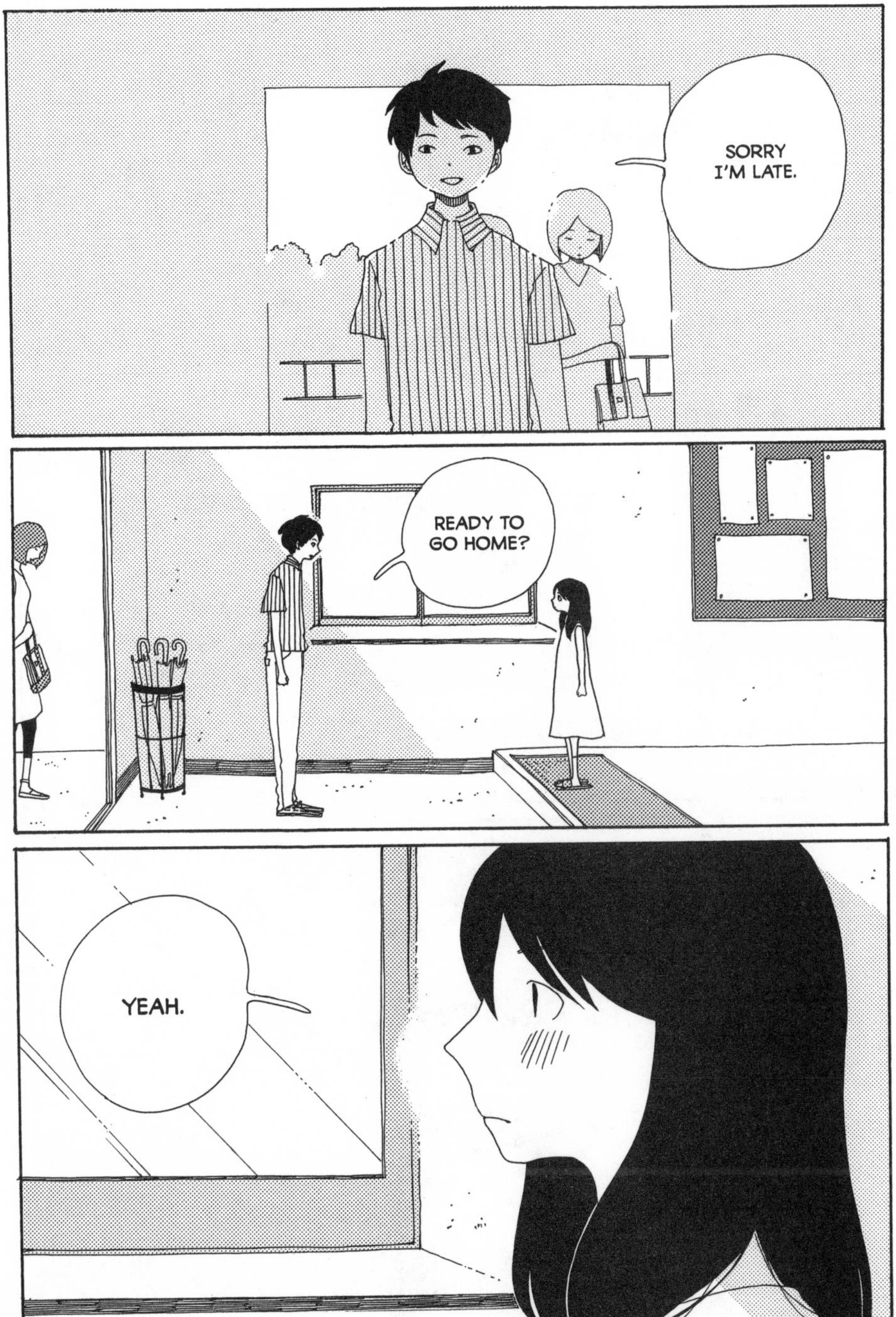
SORRY I'M LATE.
READY TO GO HOME?
YEAH.

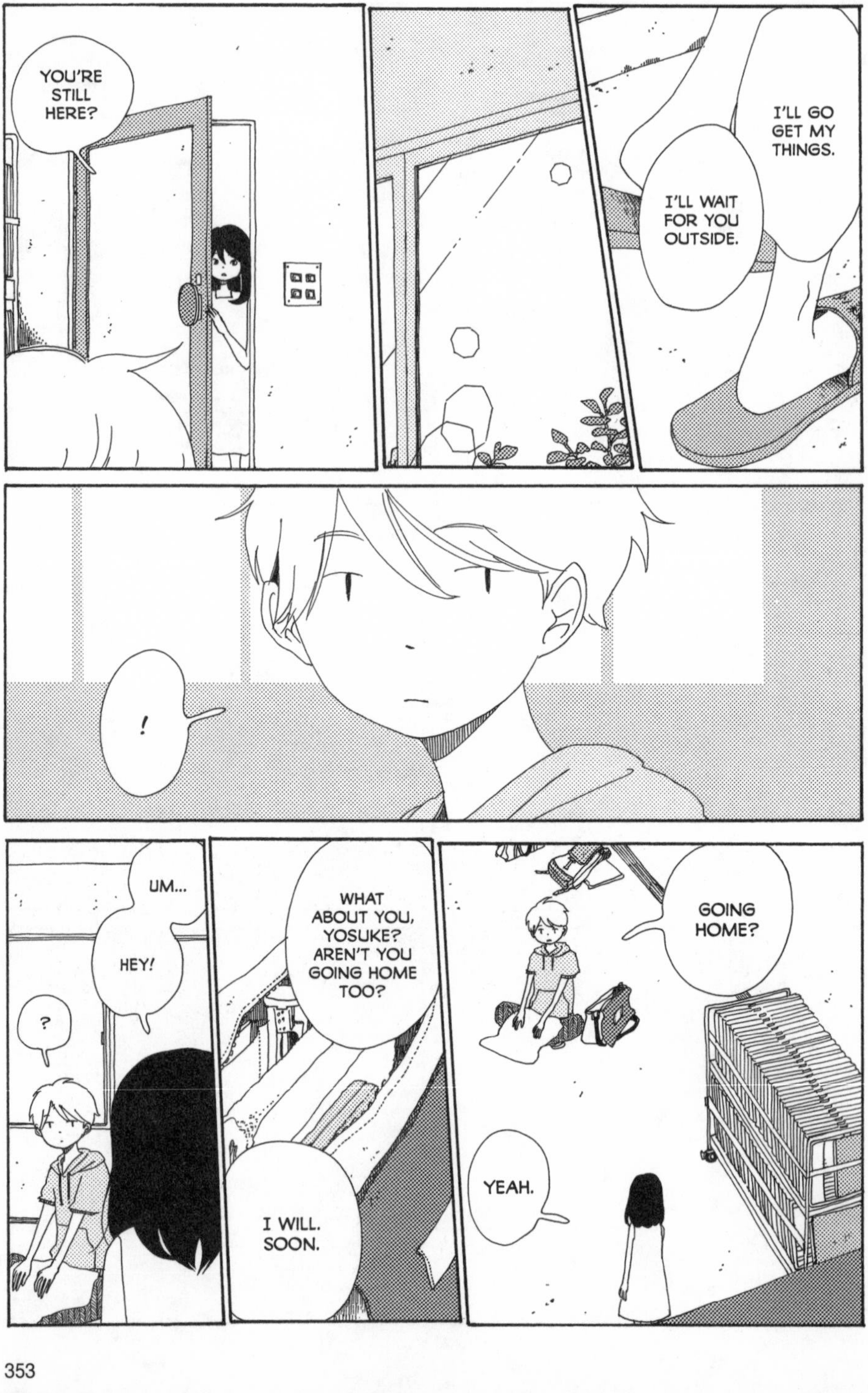
I'LL GO GET MY THINGS.
I'LL WAIT FOR YOU OUTSIDE.
YOU'RE STILL HERE?
!
GOING HOME?
YEAH.
WHAT ABOUT YOU, YOSUKE? AREN'T YOU GOING HOME TOO?
I WILL. SOON.
UM...
HEY!
?

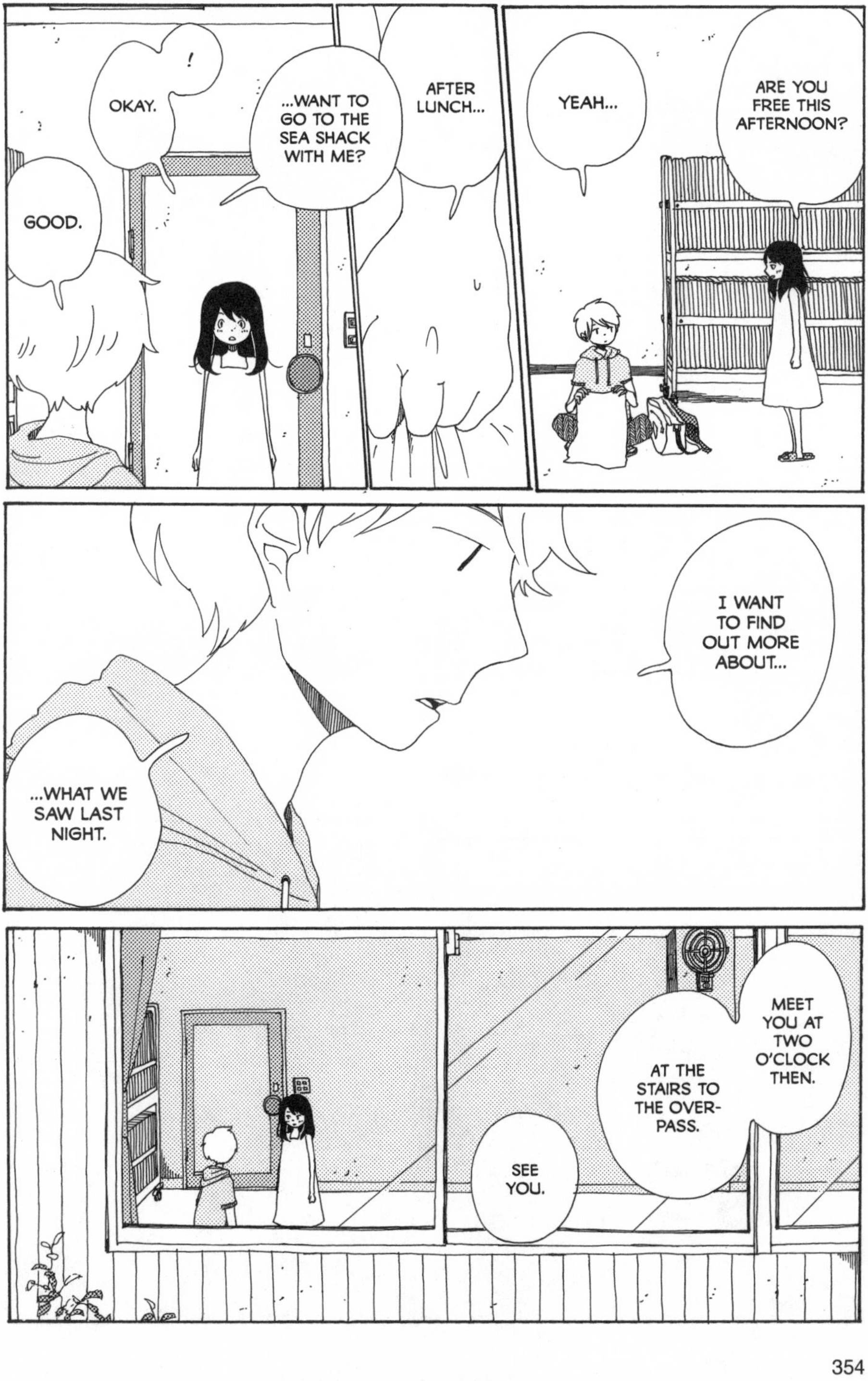
ARE YOU FREE THIS AFTERNOON?
YEAH...
AFTER LUNCH...
...WANT TO GO TO THE SEA SHACK WITH ME?
!
OKAY.
GOOD.
I WANT TO FIND OUT MORE ABOUT...
...WHAT WE SAW LAST NIGHT.
MEET YOU AT TWO O'CLOCK THEN.
AT THE STAIRS TO THE OVER-PASS.
SEE YOU.

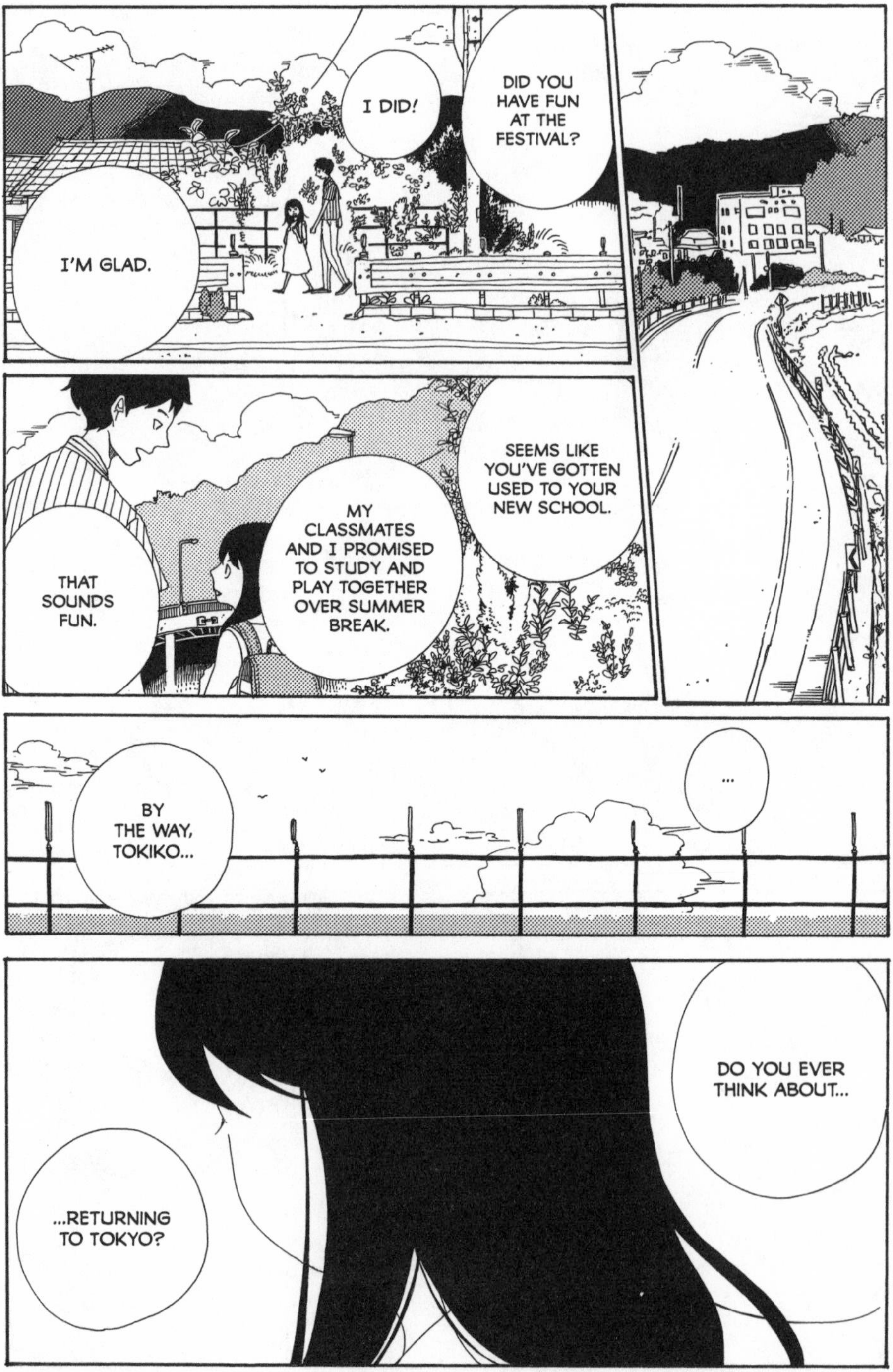
DID YOU HAVE FUN AT THE FESTIVAL?
I DID!
I'M GLAD.
SEEMS LIKE YOU'VE GOTTEN USED TO YOUR NEW SCHOOL.
MY CLASSMATES AND I PROMISED TO STUDY AND PLAY TOGETHER OVER SUMMER BREAK.
THAT SOUNDS FUN.
...
BY THE WAY, TOKIKO...
DO YOU EVER THINK ABOUT...
...RETURNING TO TOKYO?

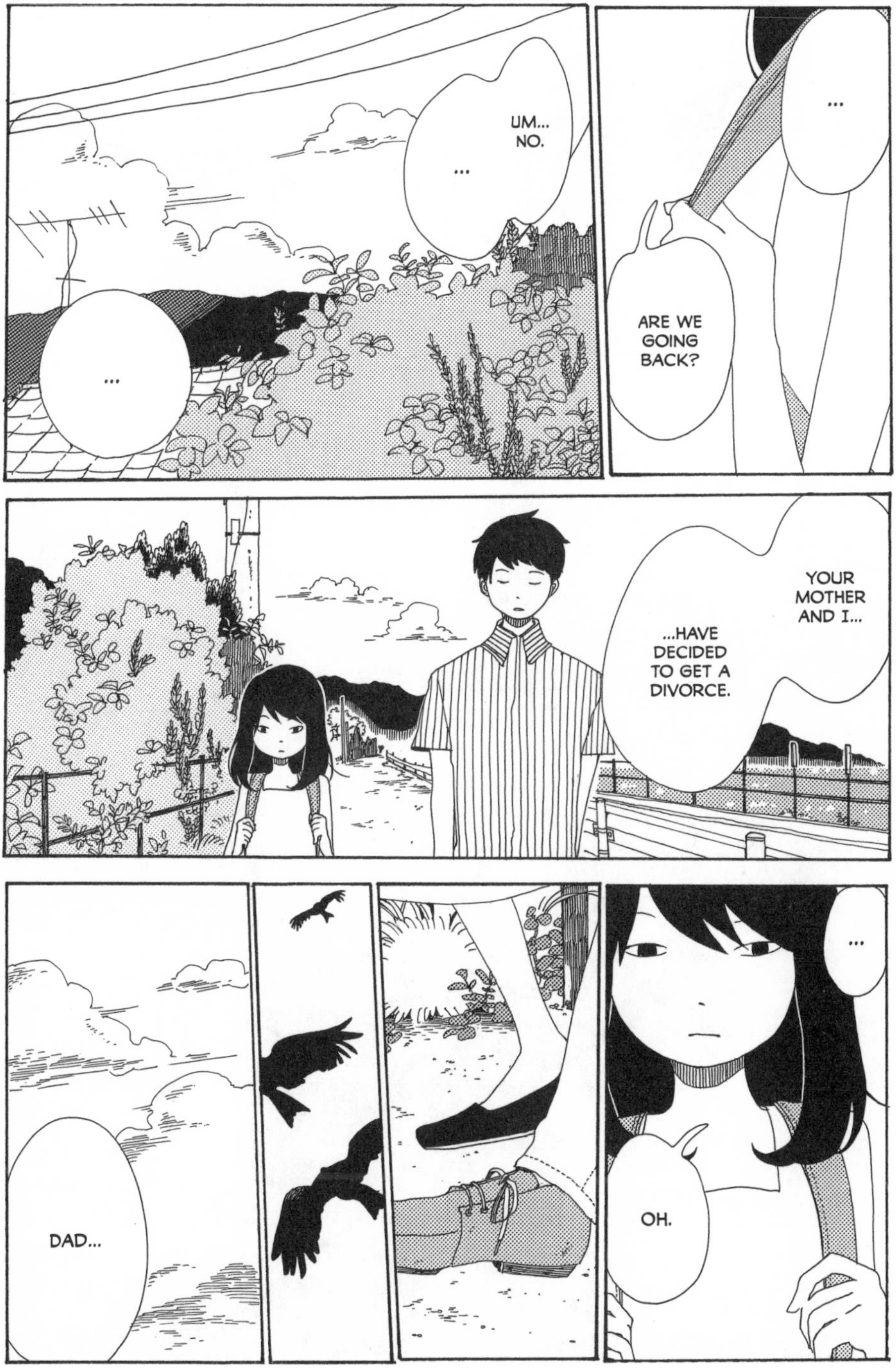
...
ARE WE GOING BACK?
UM... NO.
...
...
YOUR MOTHER AND I...
...HAVE DECIDED TO GET A DIVORCE.
...
OH.
DAD...

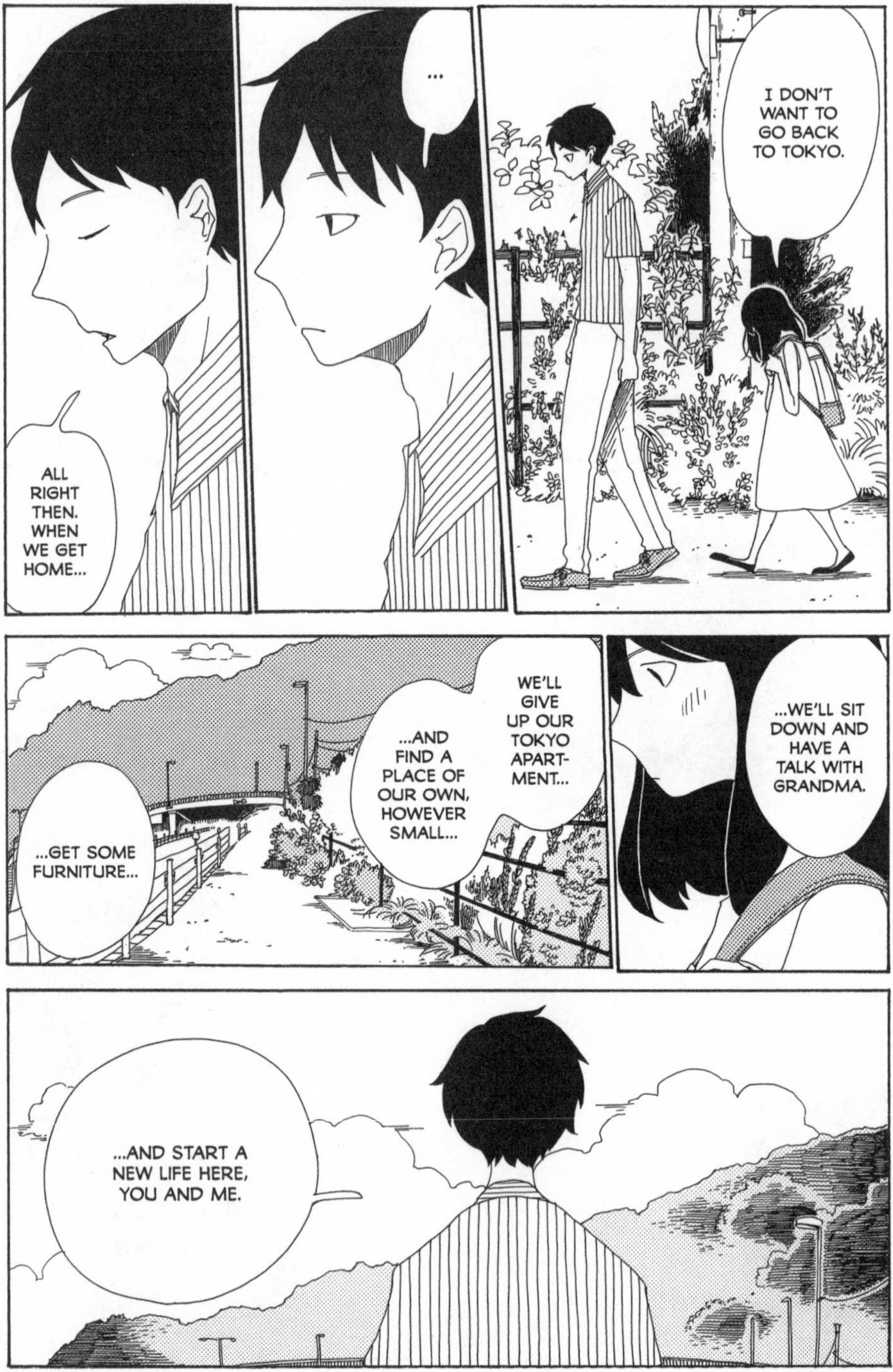
I DON'T WANT TO GO BACK TO TOKYO.
...
ALL RIGHT THEN. WHEN WE GET HOME...
...WE'LL SIT DOWN AND HAVE A TALK WITH GRANDMA.
WE'LL GIVE UP OUR TOKYO APARTMENT...
...AND FIND A PLACE OF OUR OWN, HOWEVER SMALL...
...GET SOME FURNITURE...
...AND START A NEW LIFE HERE, YOU AND ME.

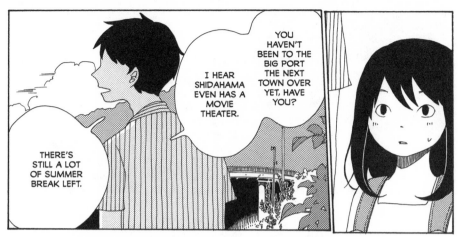

YOU HAVEN'T BEEN TO THE BIG PORT THE NEXT TOWN OVER YET, HAVE YOU?
I HEAR SHIDAHAMA EVEN HAS A MOVIE THEATER.
THERE'S STILL A LOT OF SUMMER BREAK LEFT.
YOU HAVE SO MUCH TO LOOK FORWARD TO!
THIS IS THE FIRST TIME I'VE SEEN DAD SHED A TEAR.
IT'S SHIMMERING IN THE MORNING SUNLIGHT.
YEAH. I DO.
IT'S LIKE...

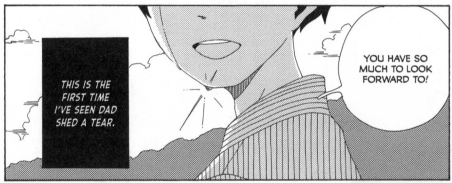

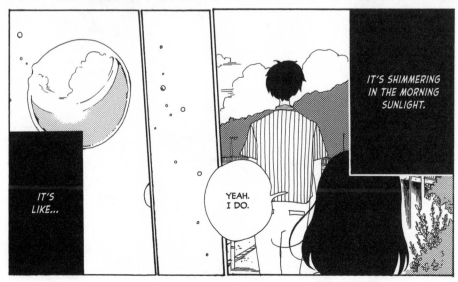

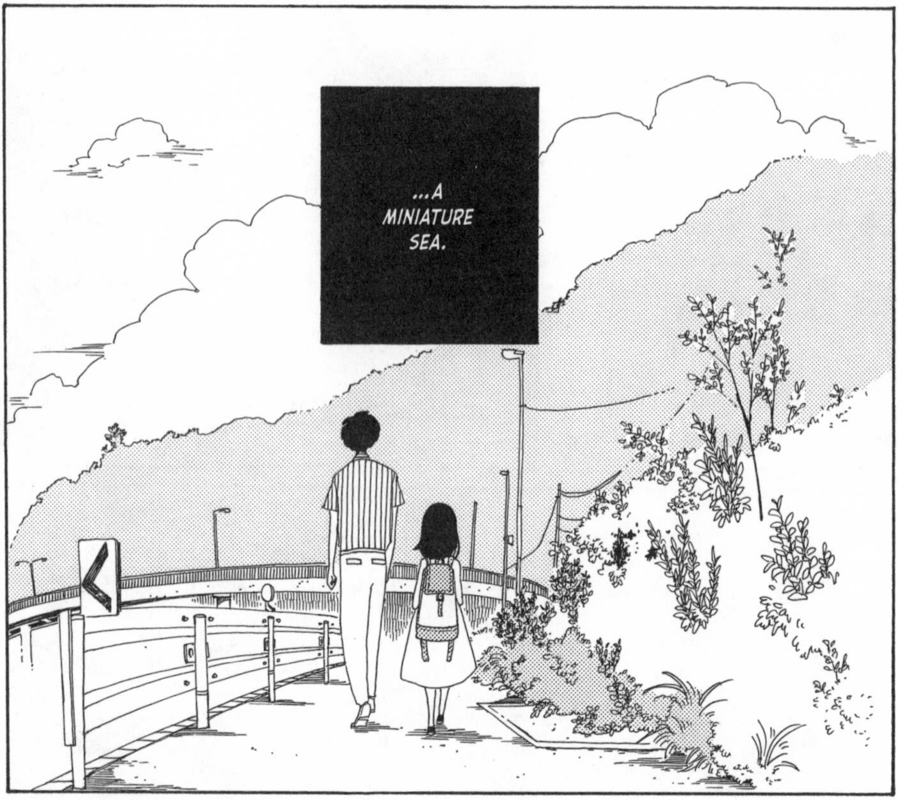
...A MINIATURE SEA.
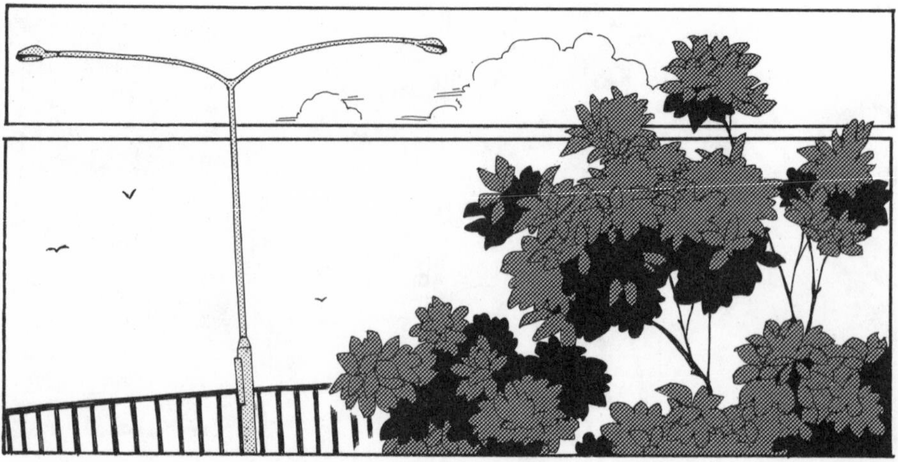

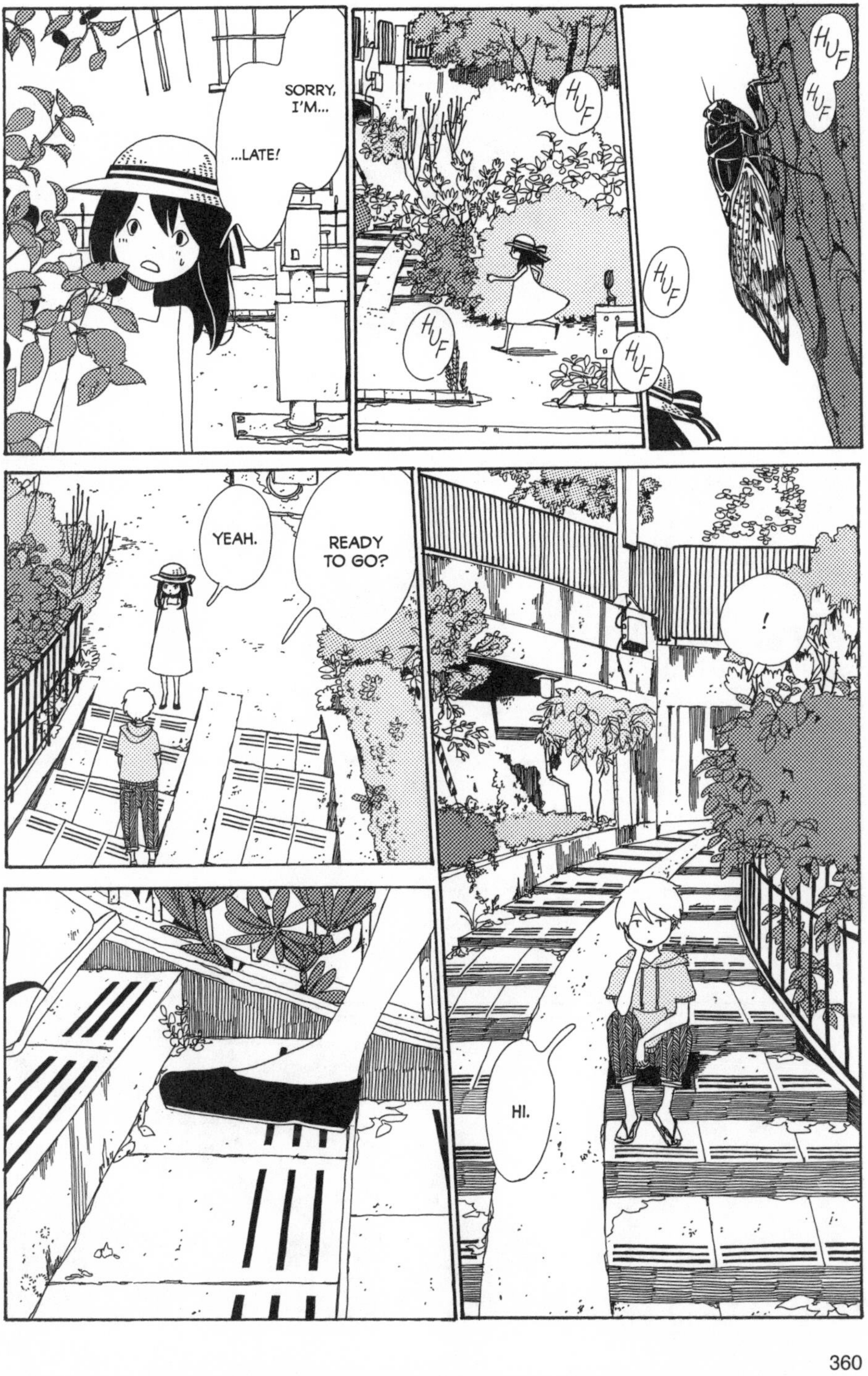
HUF HUF
HUF
HUF
HUF
HUF
SORRY, I'M...
...LATE!
!
HI.
READY TO GO?
YEAH.

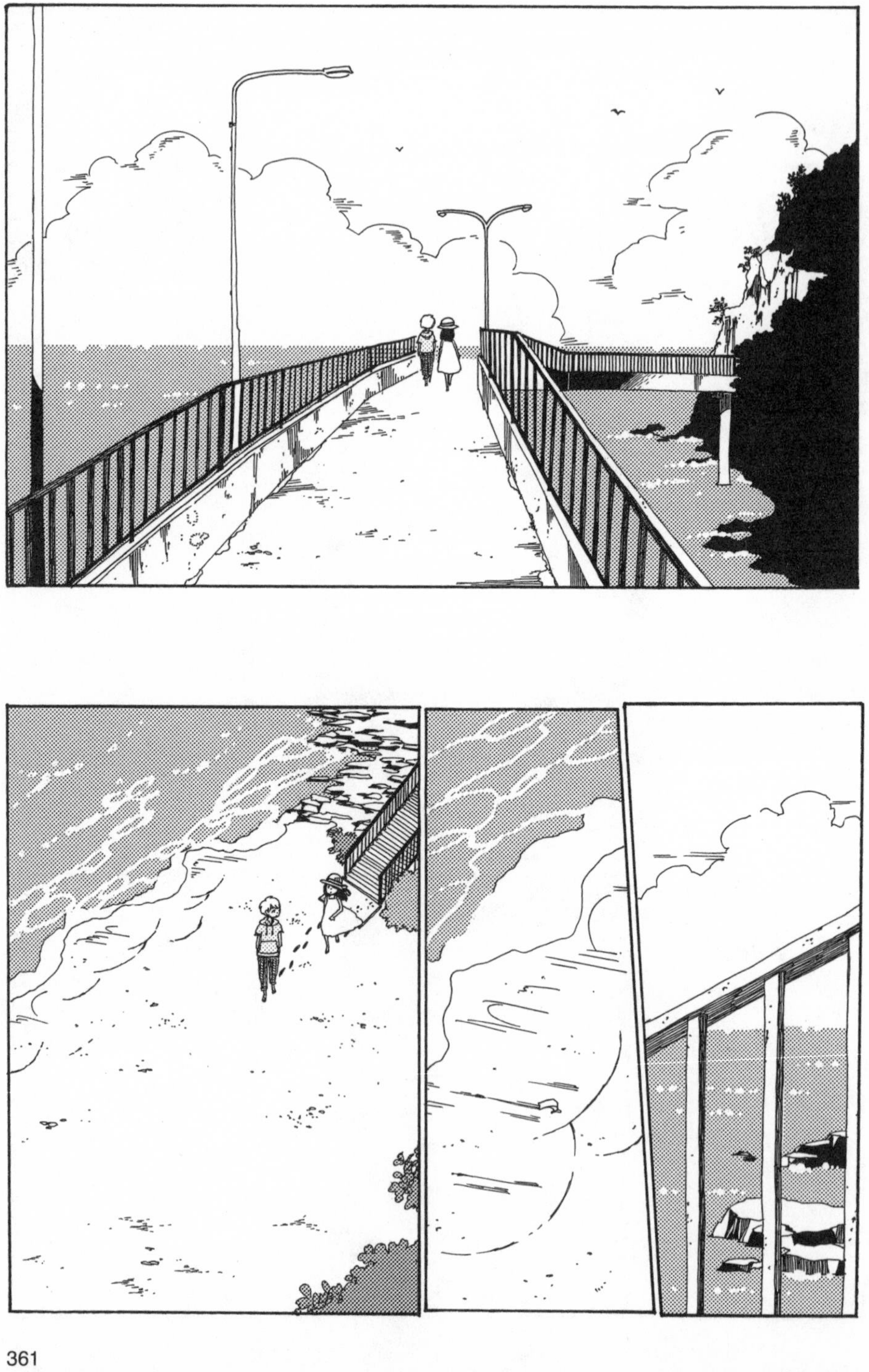

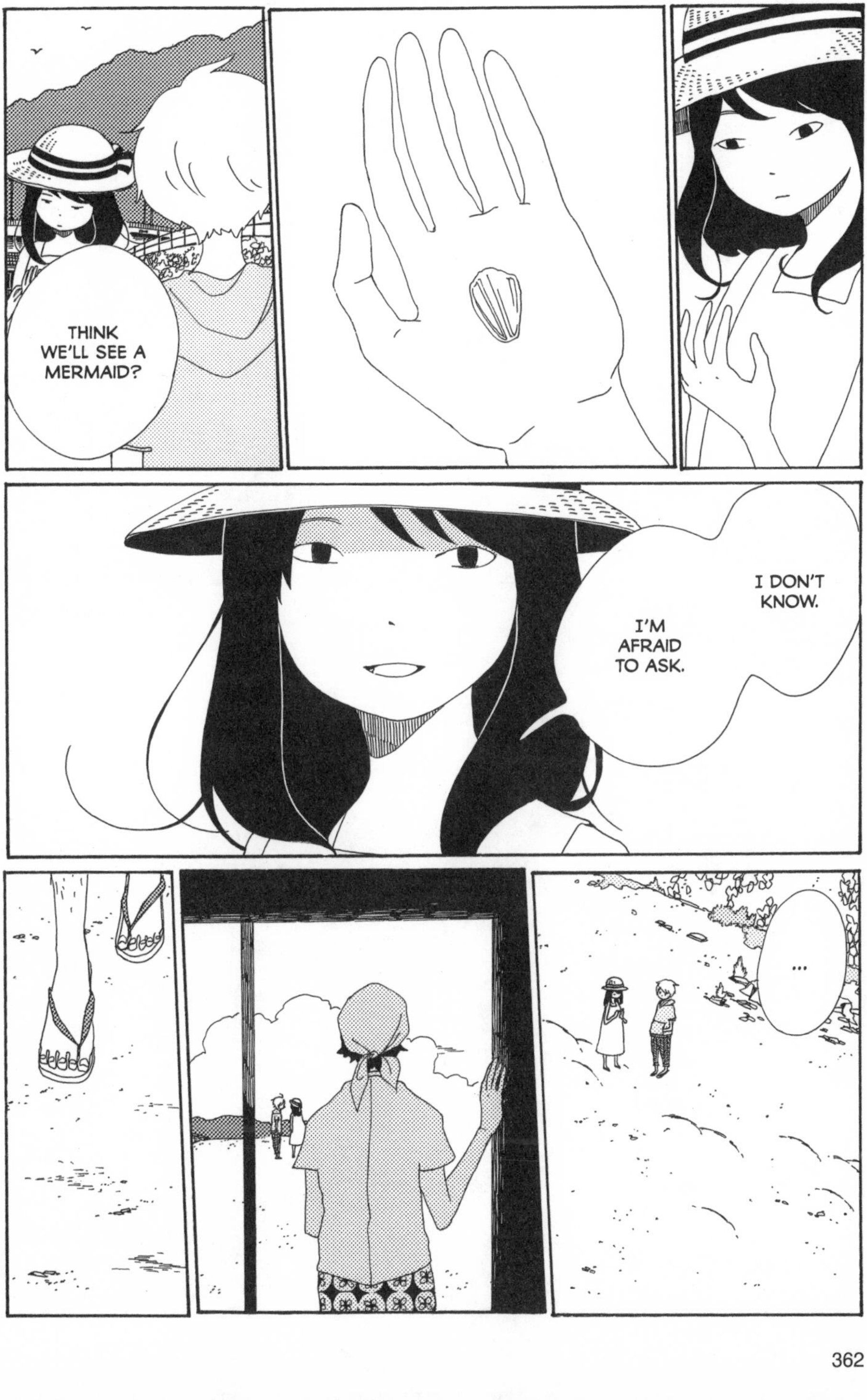
THINK WE'LL SEE A MERMAID?
I DON'T KNOW.
I'M AFRAID TO ASK.
...

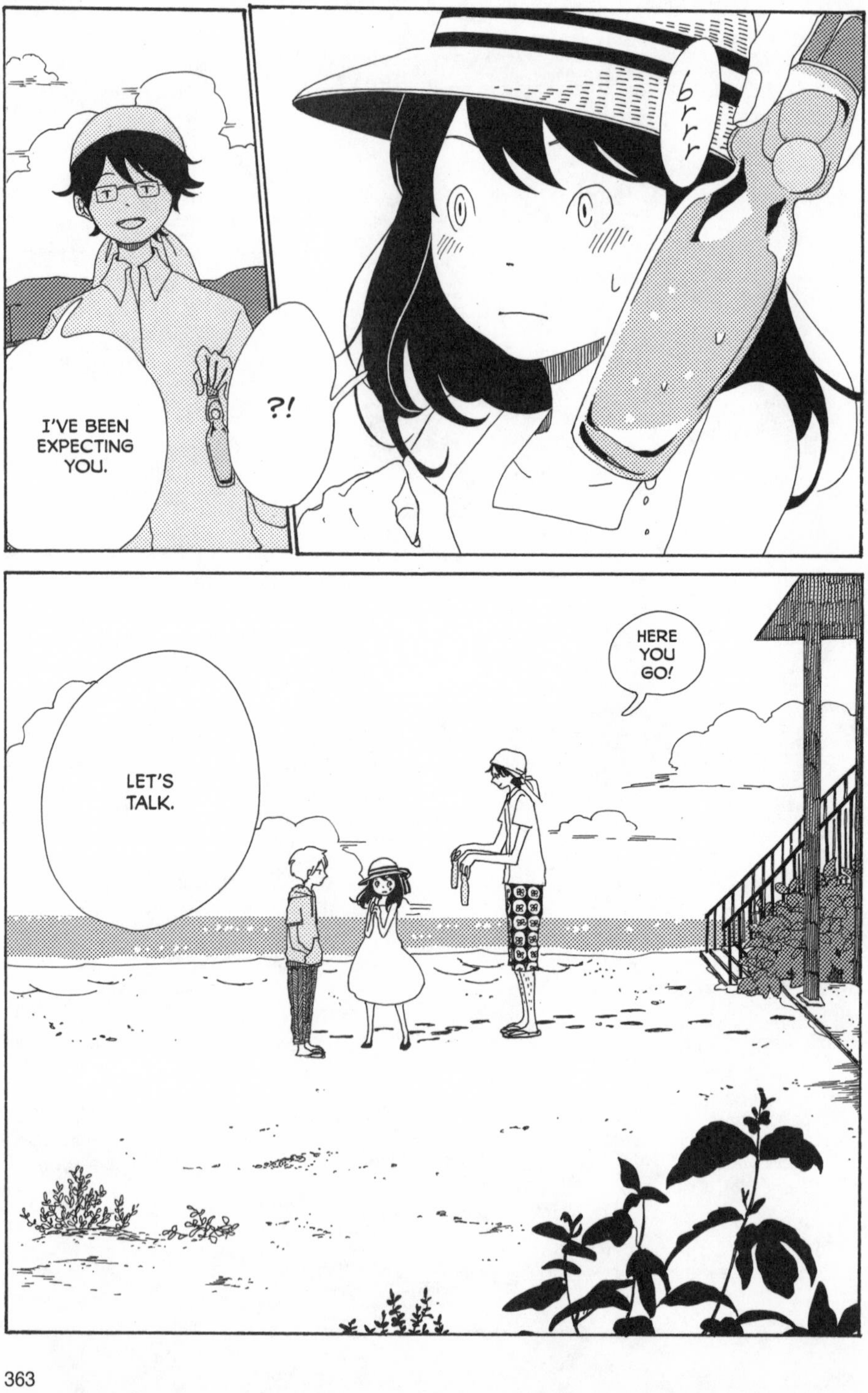
brrr
?!
I'VE BEEN EXPECTING YOU.
HERE YOU GO!
LET'S TALK.

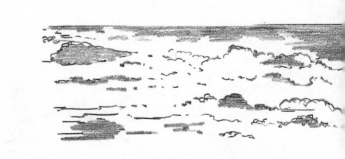

{Eleven} Tranquil Seas

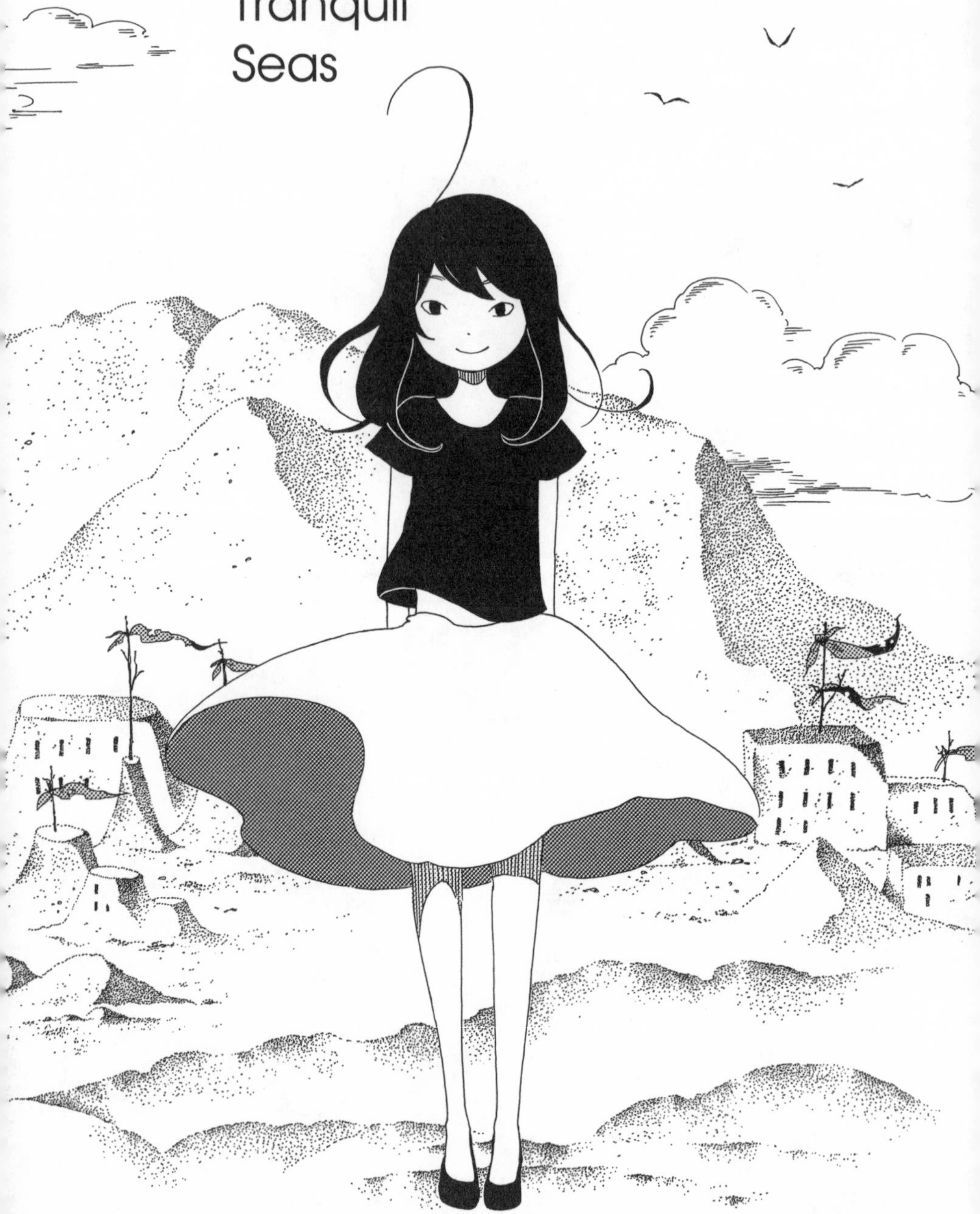

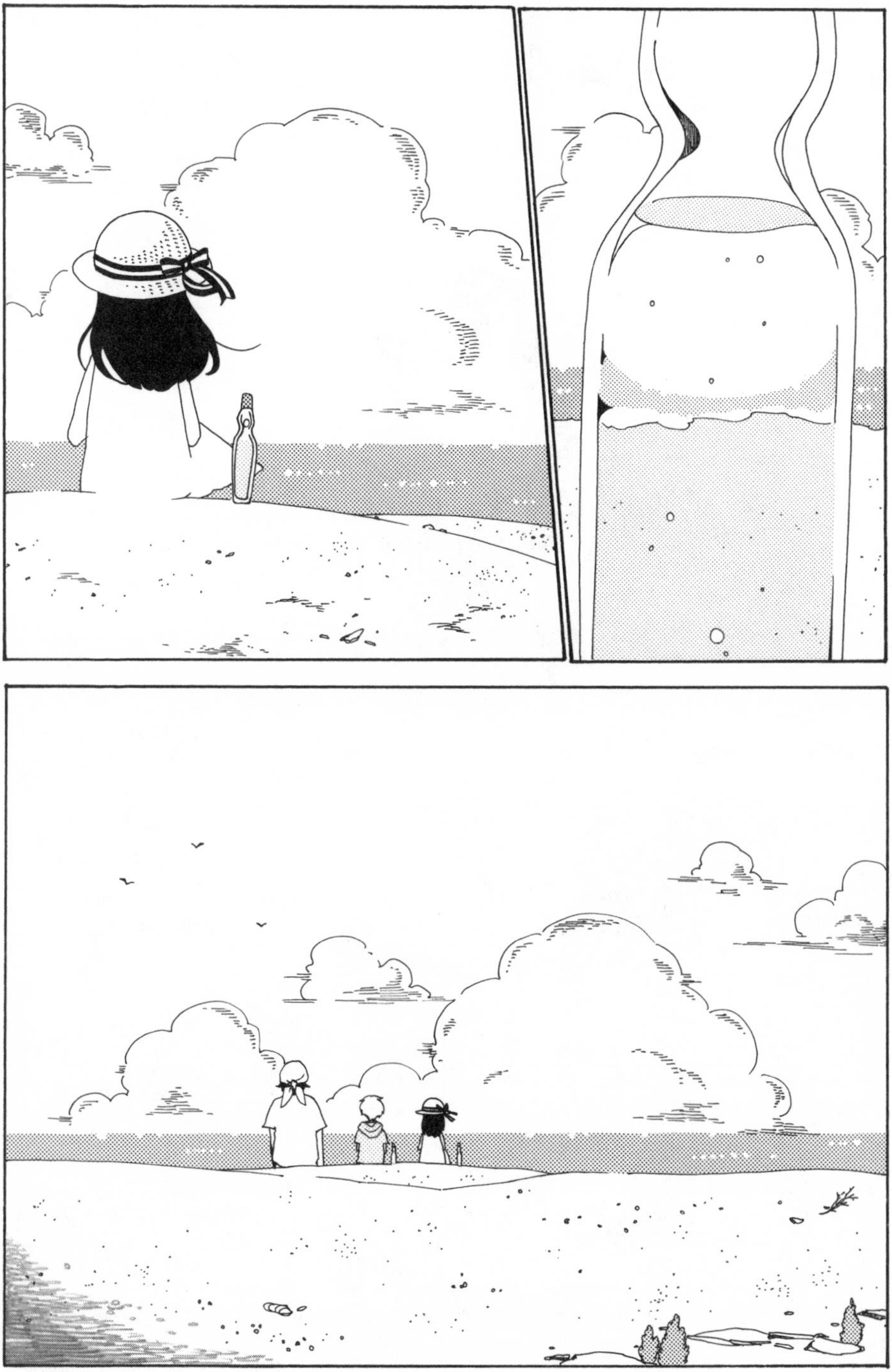

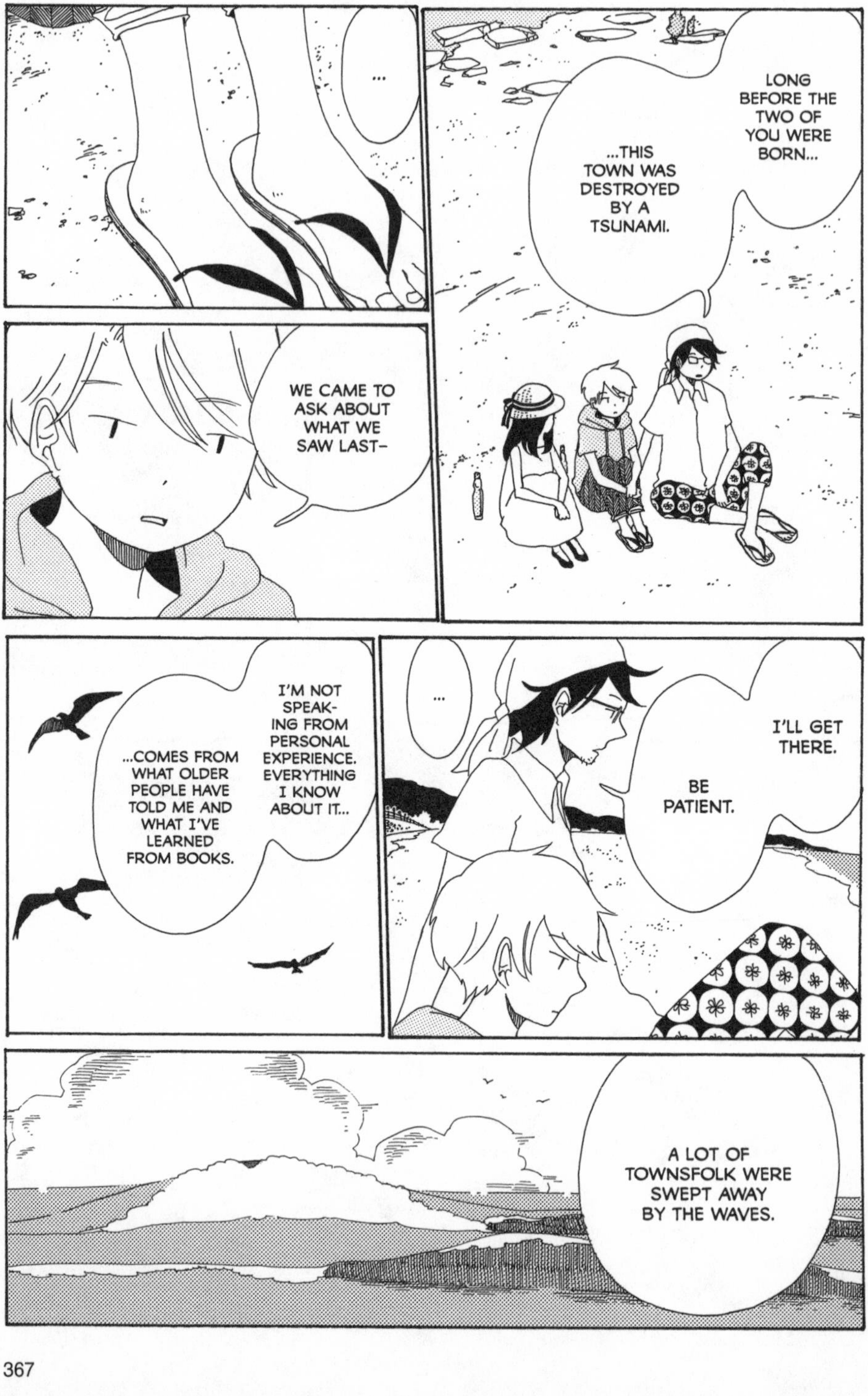
LONG BEFORE THE TWO OF YOU WERE BORN...
...THIS TOWN WAS DESTROYED BY A TSUNAMI.
...
WE CAME TO ASK ABOUT WHAT WE SAW LAST-
I'LL GET THERE.
...
BE PATIENT.
I'M NOT SPEAK-ING FROM PERSONAL EXPERIENCE. EVERYTHING I KNOW ABOUT IT...
...COMES FROM WHAT OLDER PEOPLE HAVE TOLD ME AND WHAT I'VE LEARNED FROM BOOKS.
A LOT OF TOWNSFOLK WERE SWEPT AWAY BY THE WAVES.

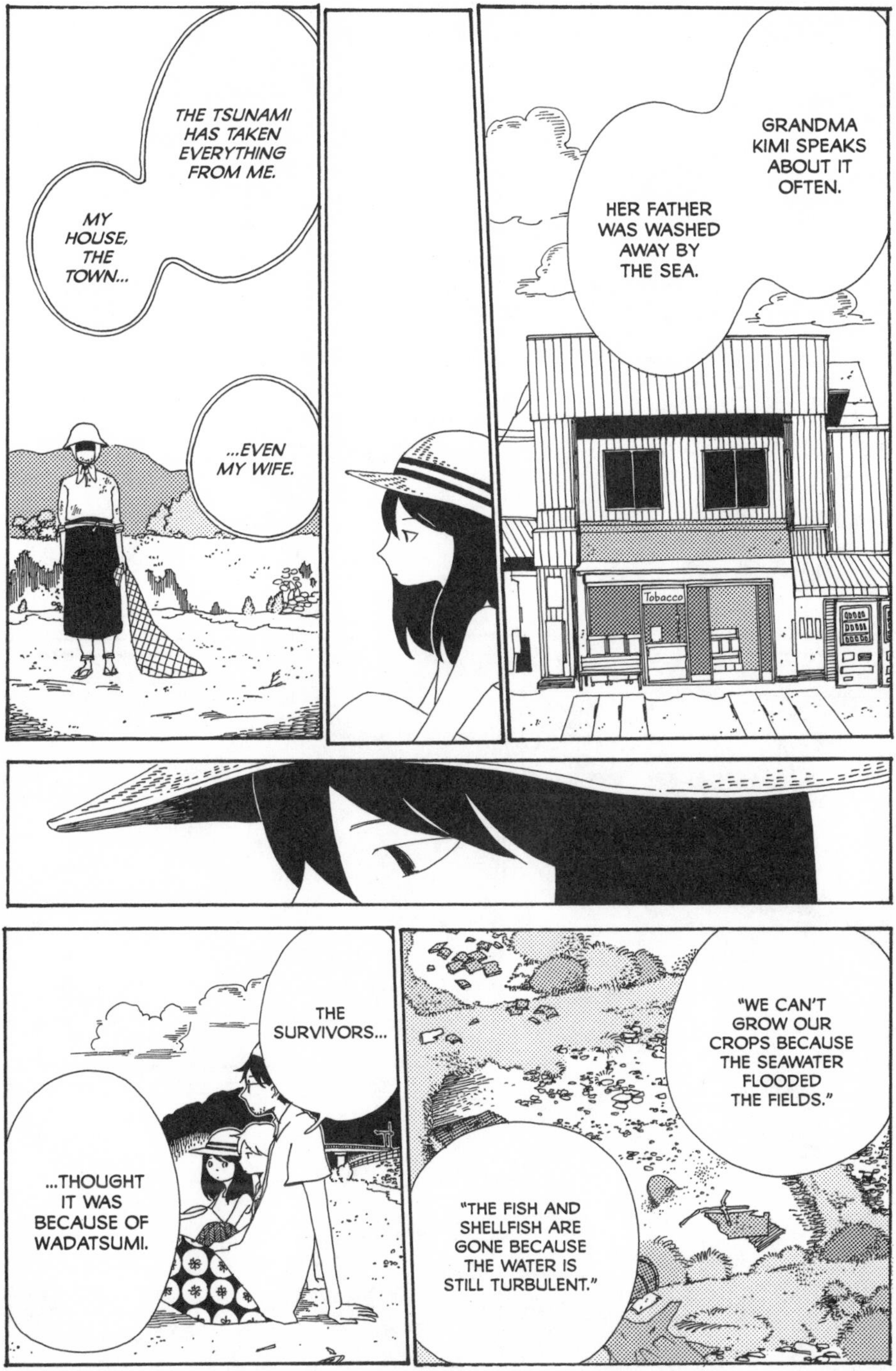
GRANDMA KIMI SPEAKS ABOUT IT OFTEN.
HER FATHER WAS WASHED AWAY BY THE SEA.
Tobacco
THE TSUNAMI HAS TAKEN EVERYTHING FROM ME.
MY HOUSE, THE TOWN...
...EVEN MY WIFE.
"WE CAN'T GROW OUR CROPS BECAUSE THE SEAWATER FLOODED THE FIELDS."
"THE FISH AND SHELLFISH ARE GONE BECAUSE THE WATER IS STILL TURBULENT."
THE SURVIVORS...
...THOUGHT IT WAS BECAUSE OF WADATSUMI.

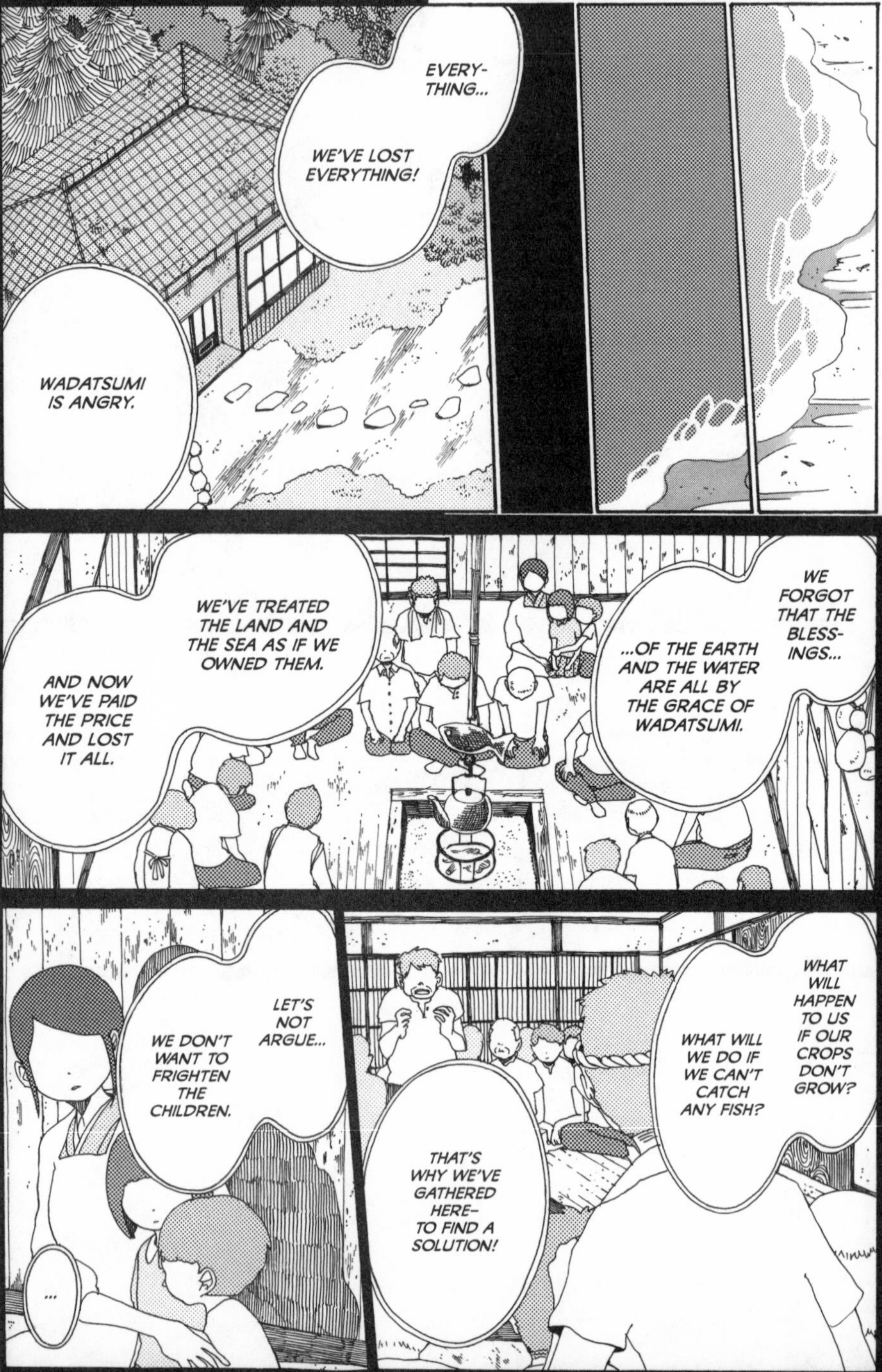
EVERYTHING...
WE'VE LOST EVERYTHING!
WADATSUMI IS ANGRY.
WE FORGOT THAT THE BLESSINGS...
...OF THE EARTH AND THE WATER ARE ALL BY THE GRACE OF WADATSUMI.
WE'VE TREATED THE LAND AND THE SEA AS IF WE OWNED THEM.
AND NOW WE'VE PAID THE PRICE AND LOST IT ALL.
WHAT WILL HAPPEN TO US IF OUR CROPS DON'T GROW?
WHAT WILL WE DO IF WE CAN'T CATCH ANY FISH?
THAT'S WHY WE'VE GATHERED HERE– TO FIND A SOLUTION!
LET'S NOT ARGUE...
WE DON'T WANT TO FRIGHTEN THE CHILDREN.
...

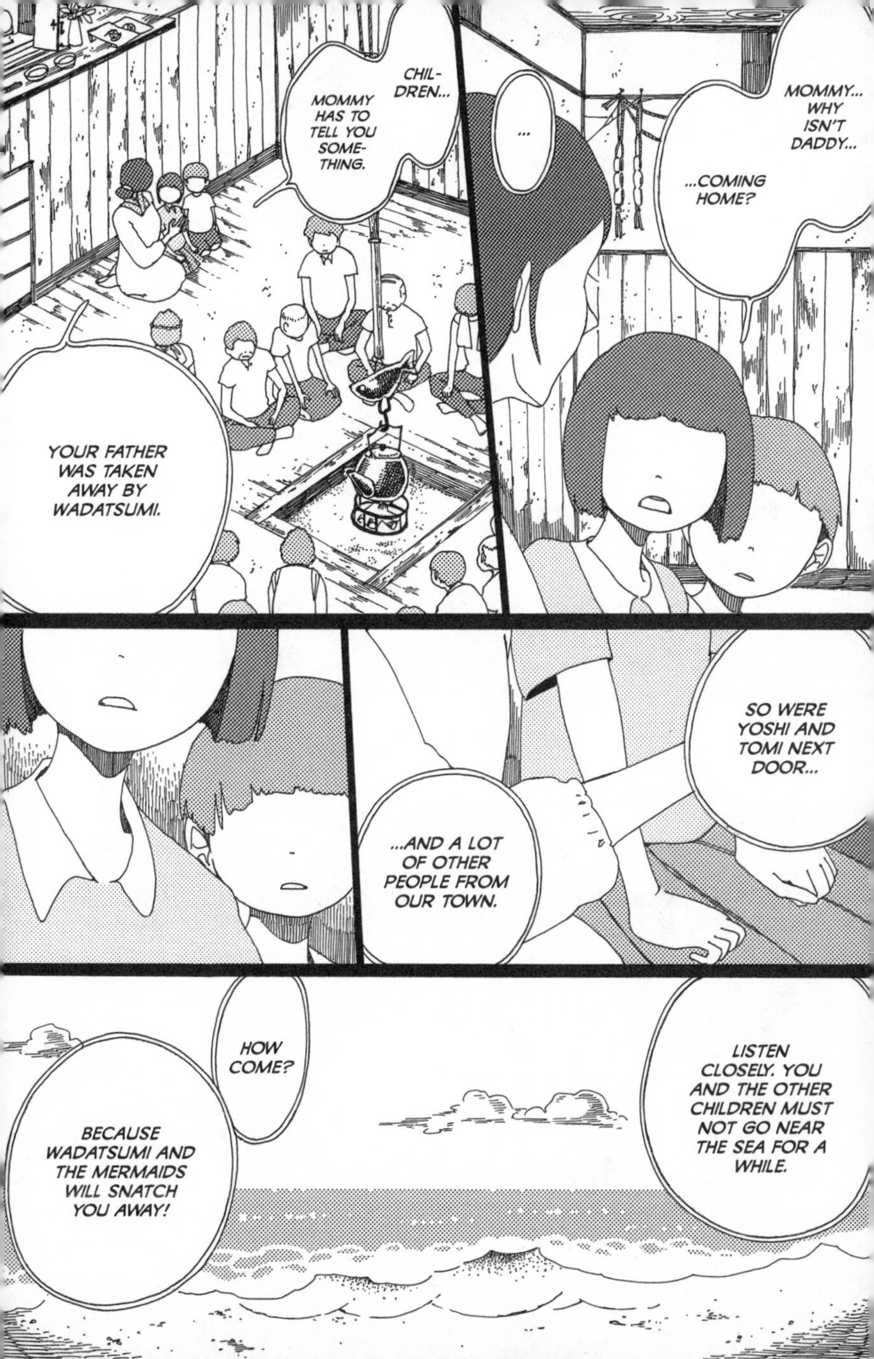
MOMMY... WHY ISN'T DADDY...
...COMING HOME?
...
CHIL-DREN... MOMMY HAS TO TELL YOU SOME-THING.
YOUR FATHER WAS TAKEN AWAY BY WADATSUMI.
SO WERE YOSHI AND TOMI NEXT DOOR...
...AND A LOT OF OTHER PEOPLE FROM OUR TOWN.
LISTEN CLOSELY. YOU AND THE OTHER CHILDREN MUST NOT GO NEAR THE SEA FOR A WHILE.
HOW COME?
BECAUSE WADATSUMI AND THE MERMAIDS WILL SNATCH YOU AWAY!

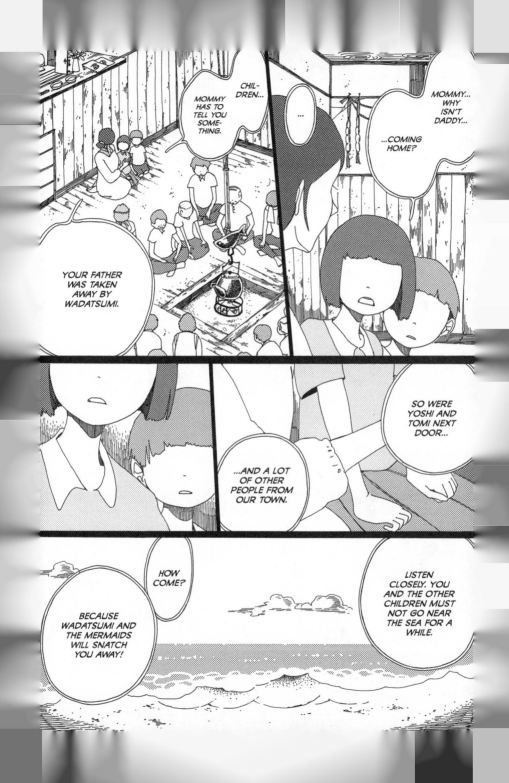

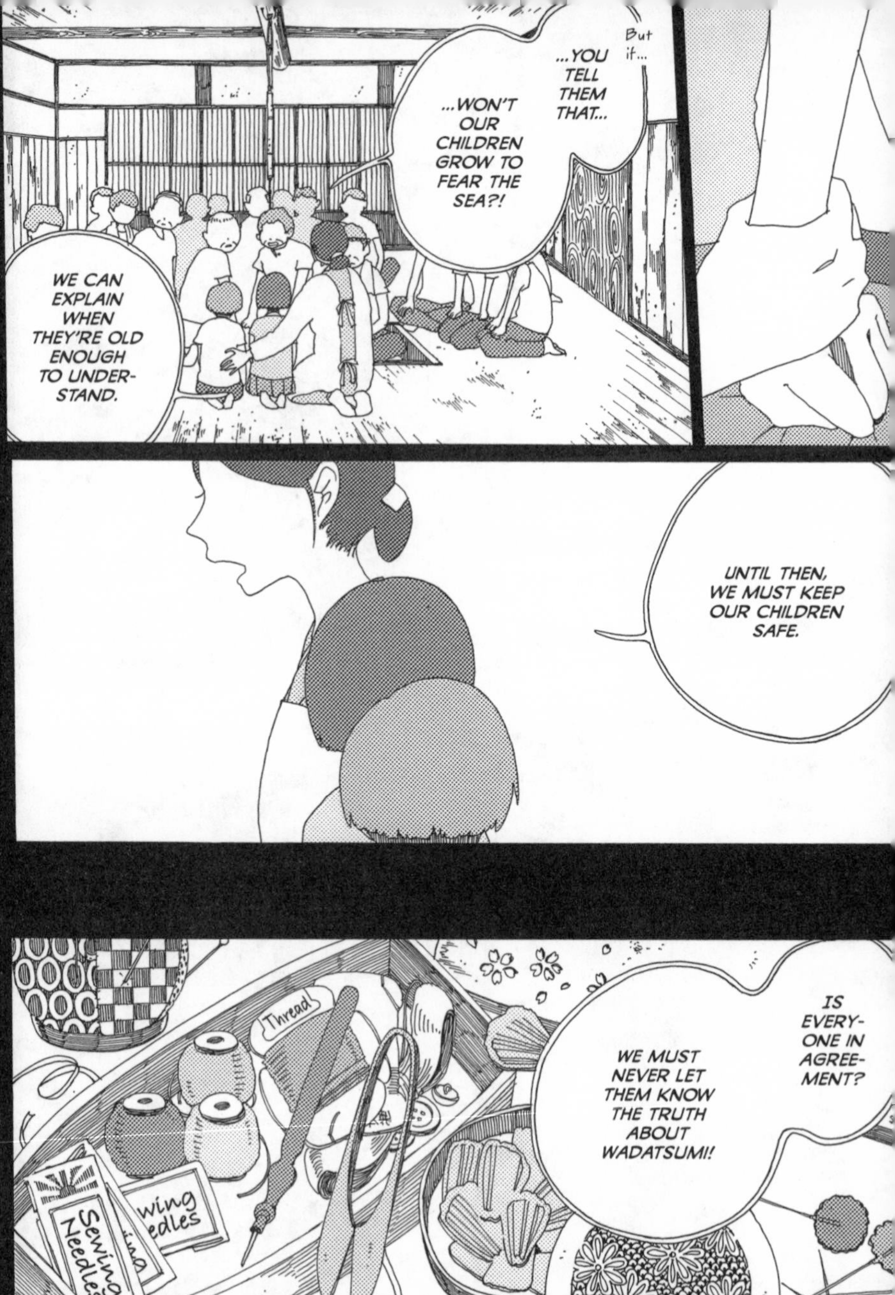
But if...
...YOU TELL THEM THAT...
...WON'T OUR CHILDREN GROW TO FEAR THE SEA?!
WE CAN EXPLAIN WHEN THEY'RE OLD ENOUGH TO UNDER-STAND.
UNTIL THEN, WE MUST KEEP OUR CHILDREN SAFE.
IS EVERY-ONE IN AGREE-MENT?
WE MUST NEVER LET THEM KNOW THE TRUTH ABOUT WADATSUMI!
Thread
Sewing Needles

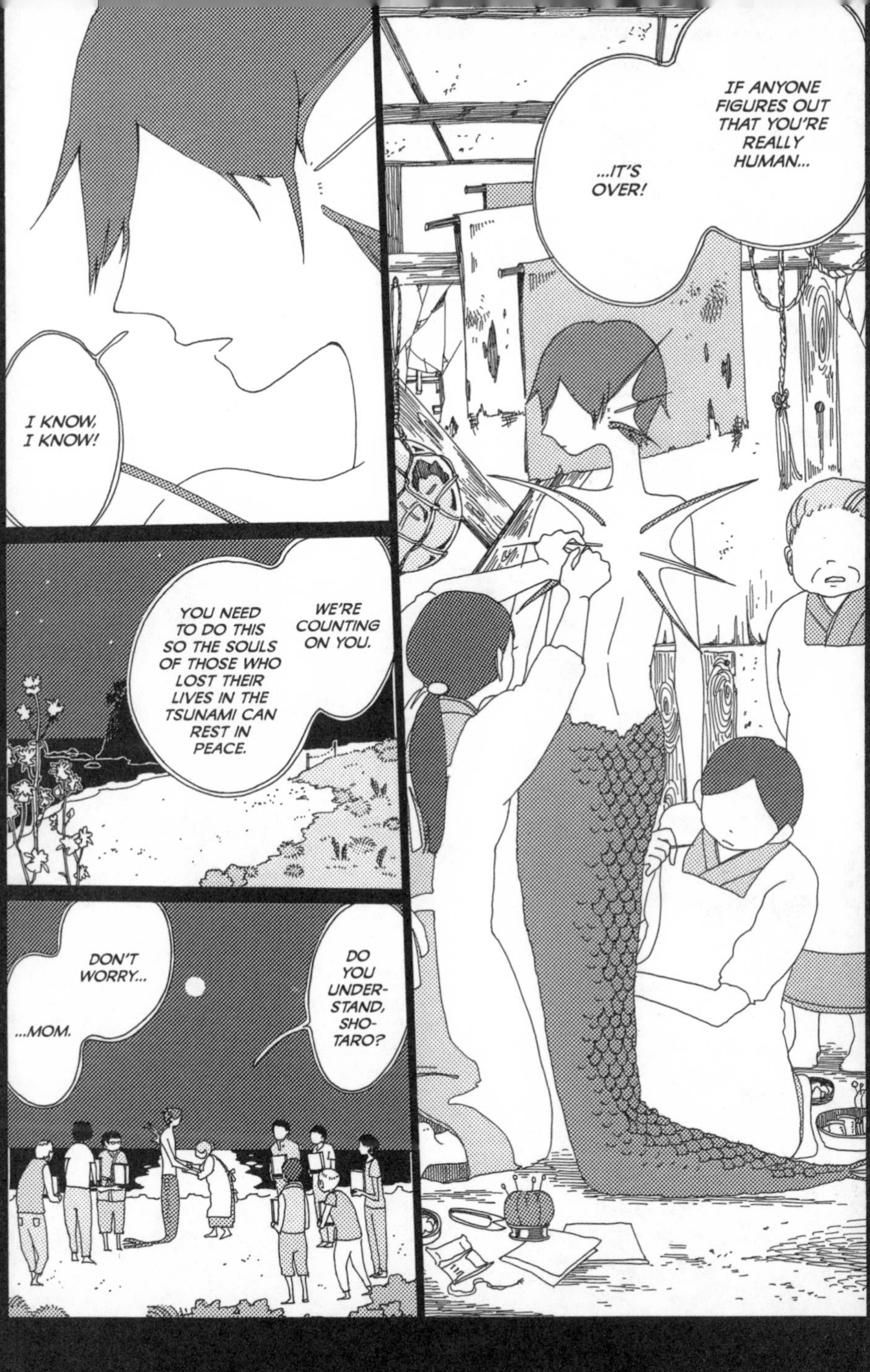
IF ANYONE FIGURES OUT THAT YOU'RE REALLY HUMAN...
...IT'S OVER!
I KNOW, I KNOW!
WE'RE COUNTING ON YOU.
YOU NEED TO DO THIS SO THE SOULS OF THOSE WHO LOST THEIR LIVES IN THE TSUNAMI CAN REST IN PEACE.
DO YOU UNDER-STAND, SHO-TARO?
DON'T WORRY...
...MOM.

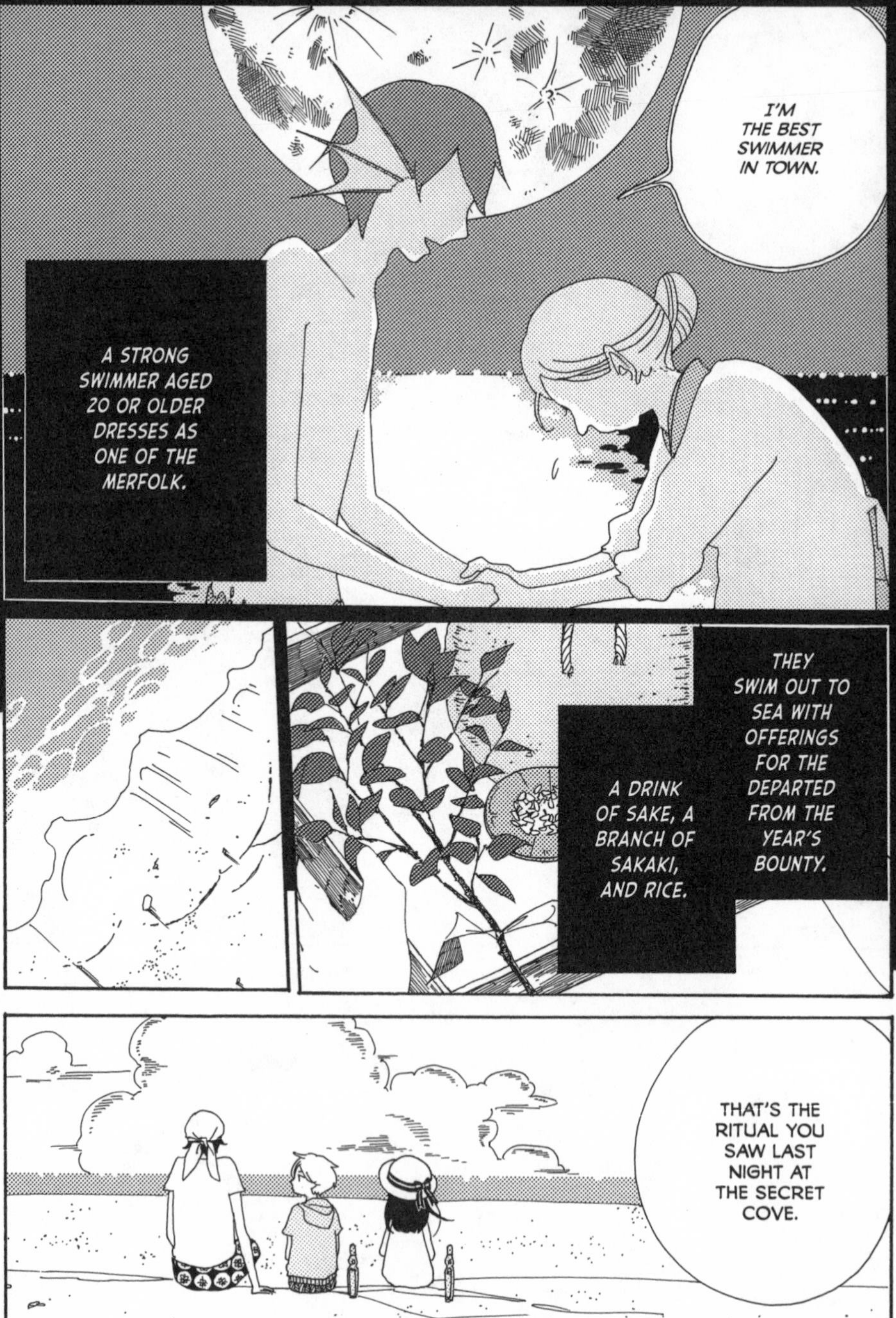
I'M THE BEST SWIMMER IN TOWN.
A STRONG SWIMMER AGED 20 OR OLDER DRESSES AS ONE OF THE MERFOLK.
THEY SWIM OUT TO SEA WITH OFFERINGS FOR THE DEPARTED FROM THE YEAR'S BOUNTY.
A DRINK OF SAKE, A BRANCH OF SAKAKI, AND RICE.
THAT'S THE RITUAL YOU SAW LAST NIGHT AT THE SECRET COVE.

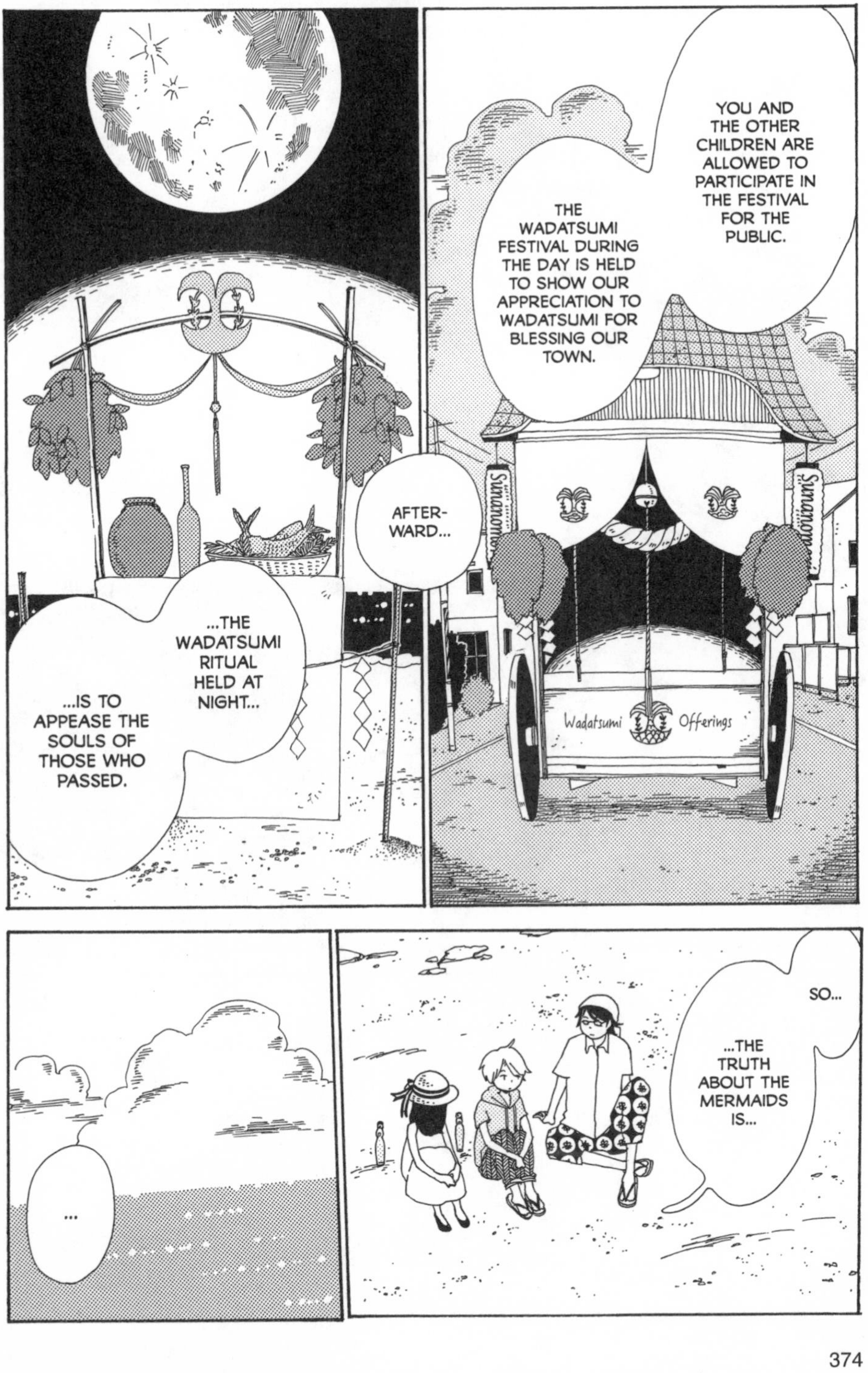
YOU AND THE OTHER CHILDREN ARE ALLOWED TO PARTICIPATE IN THE FESTIVAL FOR THE PUBLIC.
THE WADATSUMI FESTIVAL DURING THE DAY IS HELD TO SHOW OUR APPRECIATION TO WADATSUMI FOR BLESSING OUR TOWN.
Wadatsumi Offerings
AFTER-WARD...
...THE WADATSUMI RITUAL HELD AT NIGHT...
...IS TO APPEASE THE SOULS OF THOSE WHO PASSED.
SO...
...THE TRUTH ABOUT THE MERMAIDS IS...
...

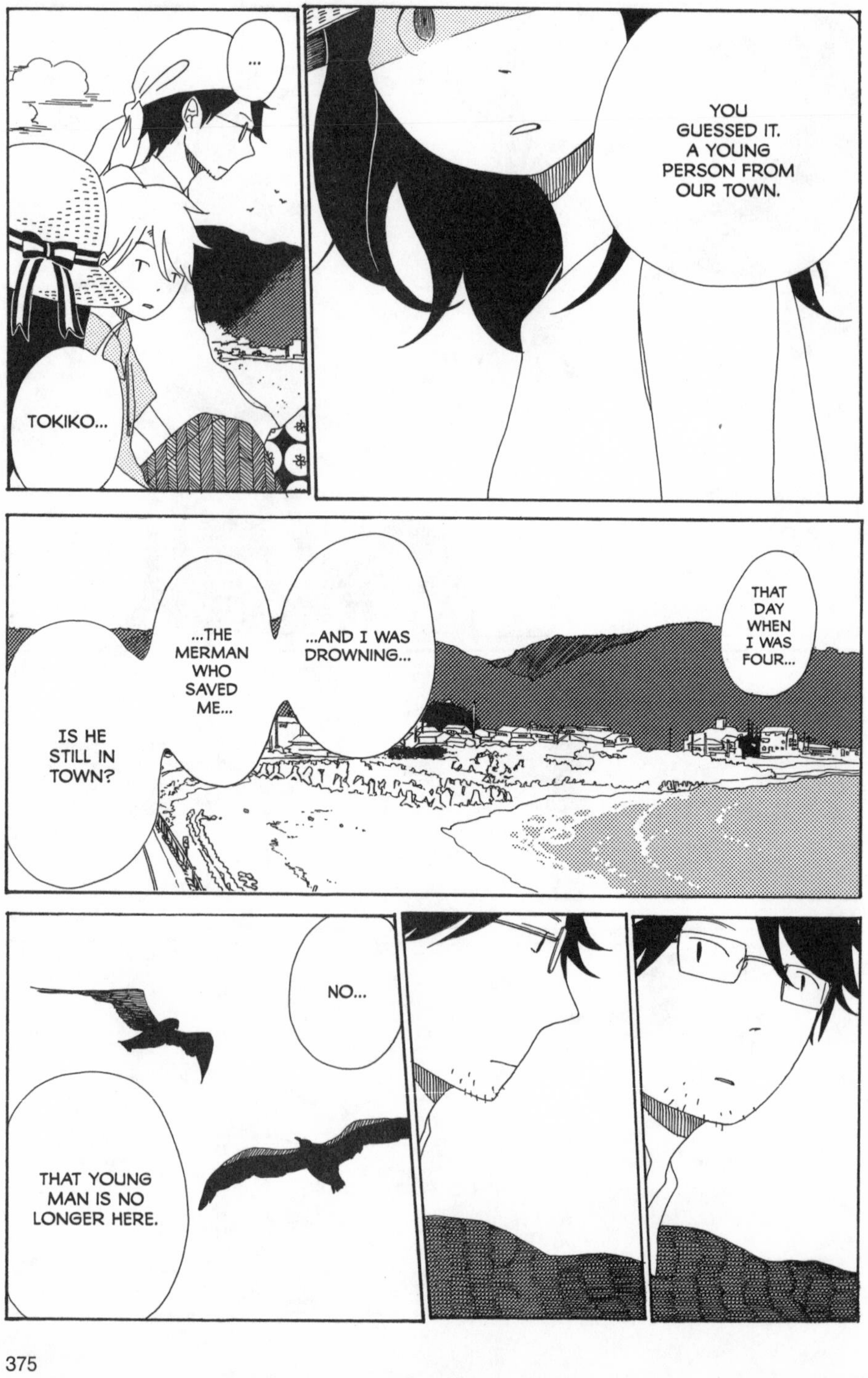
YOU GUESSED IT. A YOUNG PERSON FROM OUR TOWN.
...
TOKIKO...
THAT DAY WHEN I WAS FOUR...
...AND I WAS DROWNING...
...THE MERMAN WHO SAVED ME...
IS HE STILL IN TOWN?
NO...
THAT YOUNG MAN IS NO LONGER HERE.

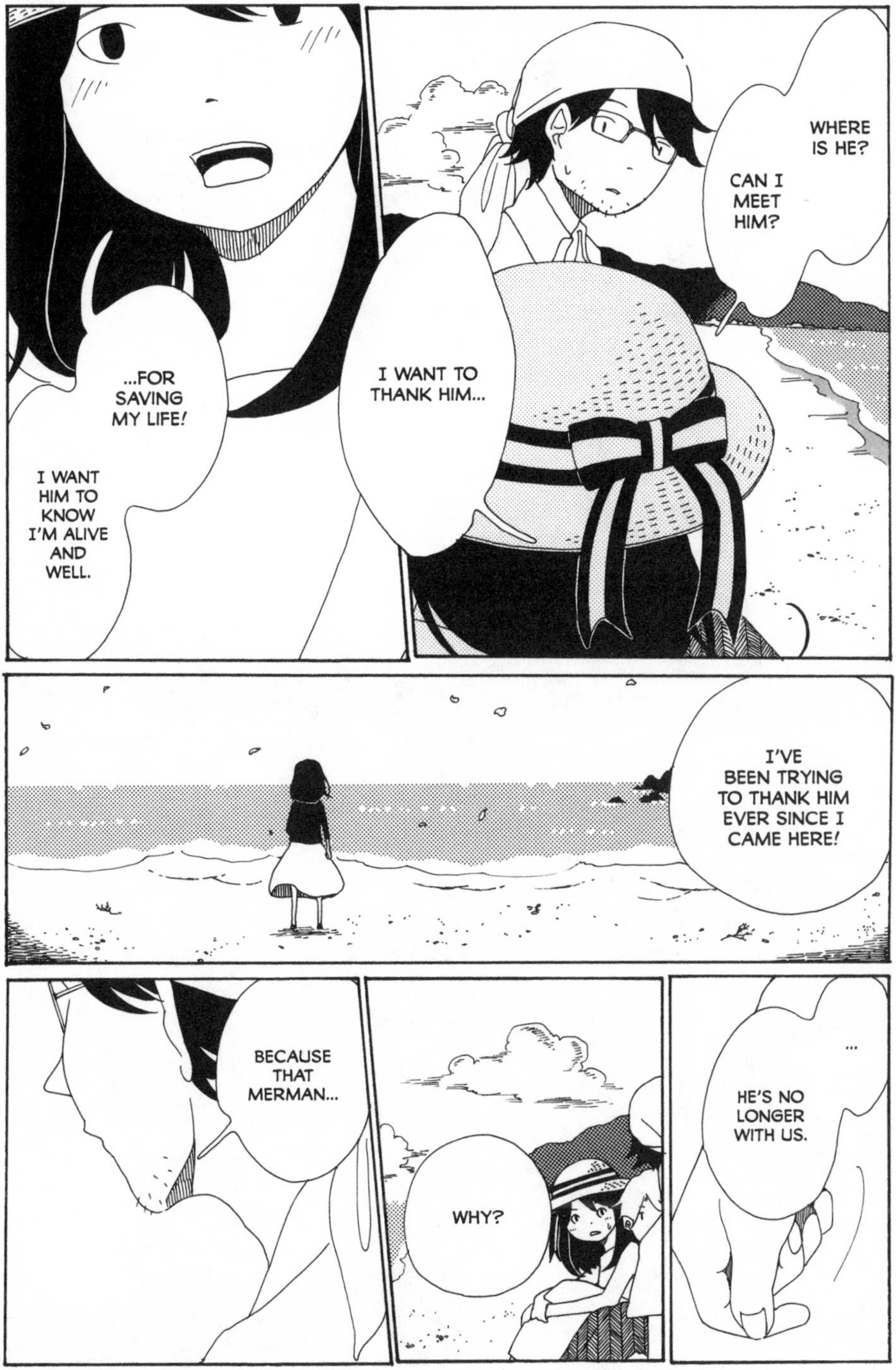
WHERE IS HE?
CAN I MEET HIM?
I WANT TO THANK HIM...
...FOR SAVING MY LIFE!
I WANT HIM TO KNOW I'M ALIVE AND WELL.
I'VE BEEN TRYING TO THANK HIM EVER SINCE I CAME HERE!
...
HE'S NO LONGER WITH US.
WHY?
BECAUSE THAT MERMAN...

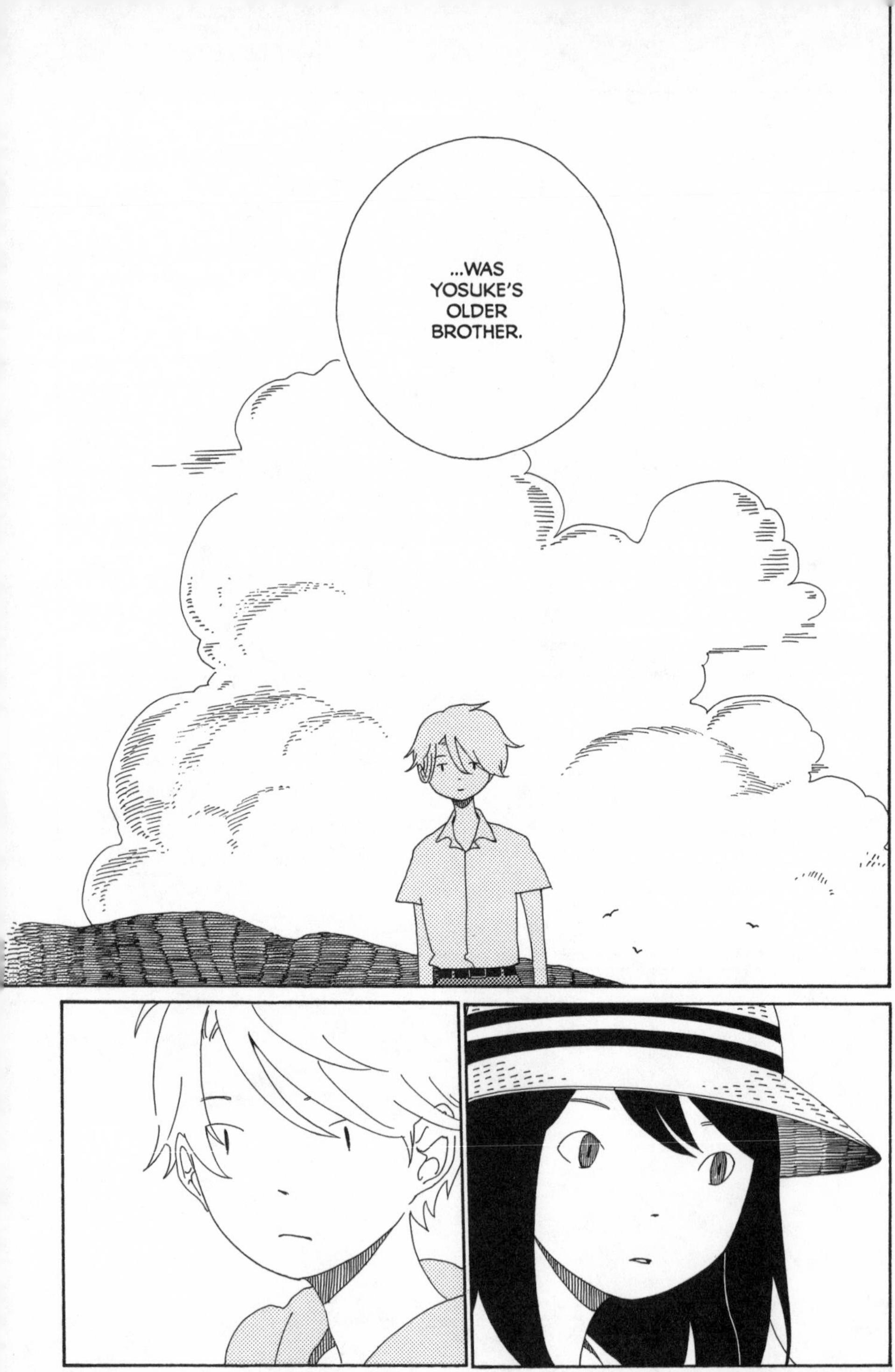
...WAS YOSUKE'S OLDER BROTHER.

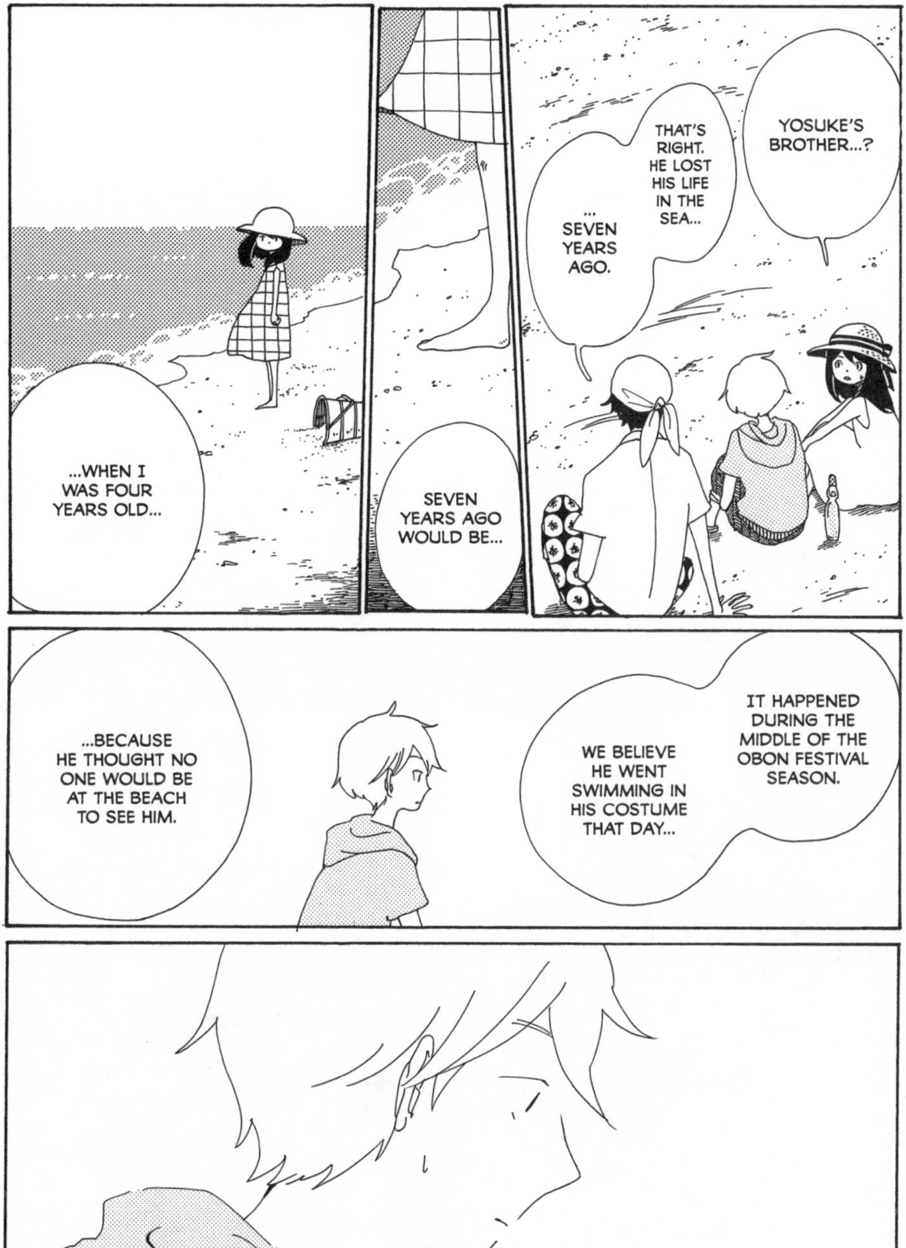
YOSUKE'S BROTHER...?
THAT'S RIGHT. HE LOST HIS LIFE IN THE SEA...
... SEVEN YEARS AGO.
SEVEN YEARS AGO WOULD BE...
...WHEN I WAS FOUR YEARS OLD...
IT HAPPENED DURING THE MIDDLE OF THE OBON FESTIVAL SEASON.
WE BELIEVE HE WENT SWIMMING IN HIS COSTUME THAT DAY...
...BECAUSE HE THOUGHT NO ONE WOULD BE AT THE BEACH TO SEE HIM.

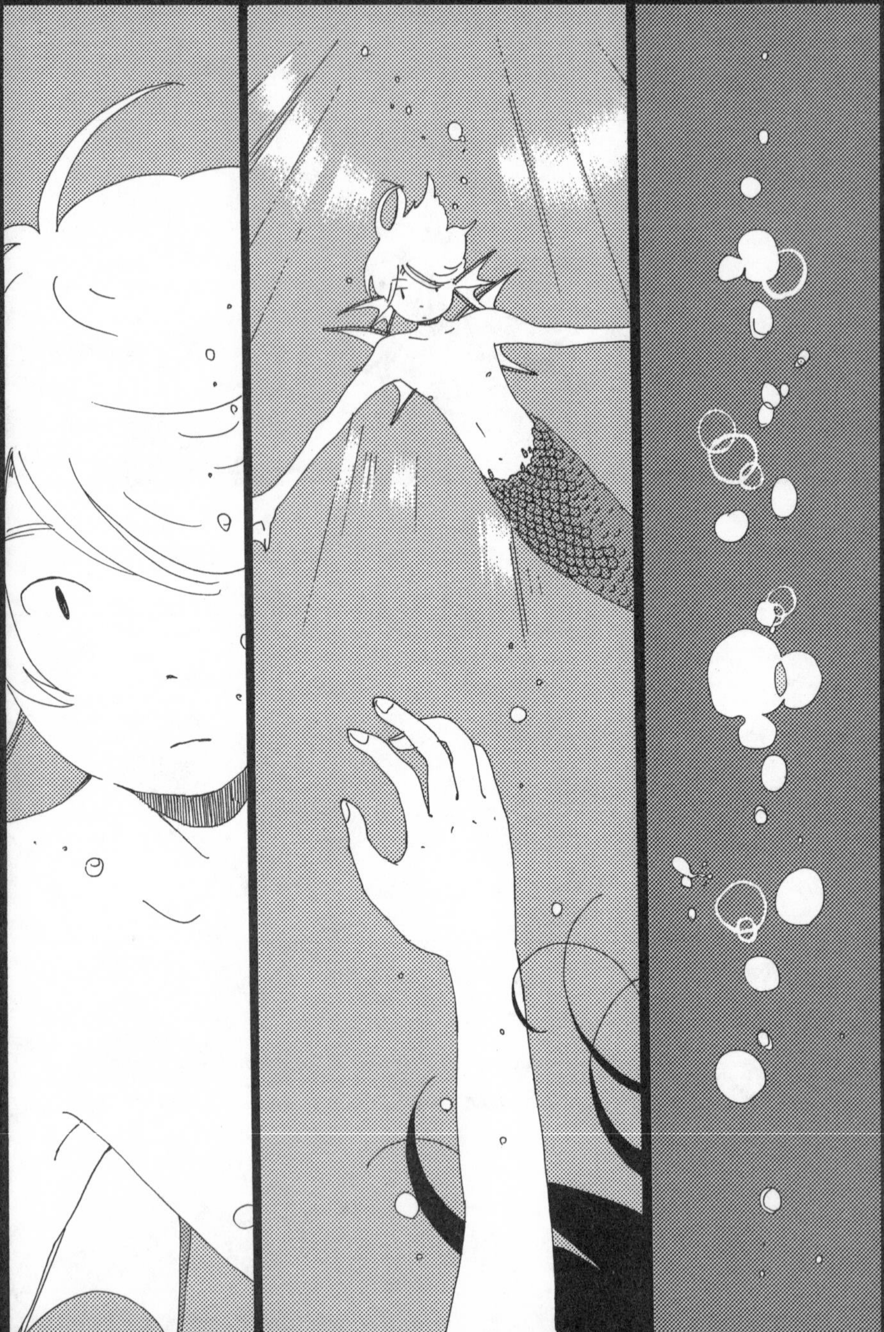

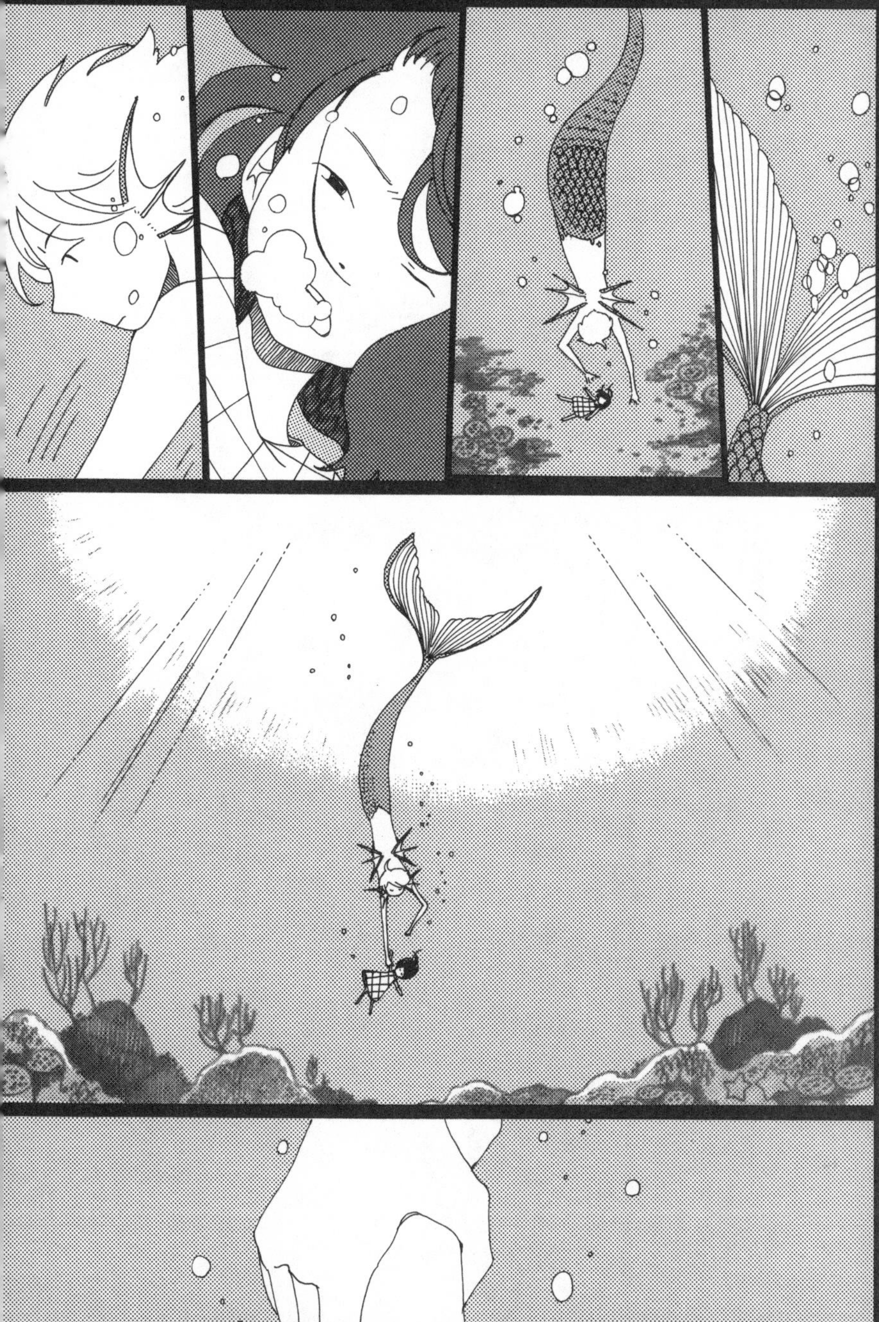

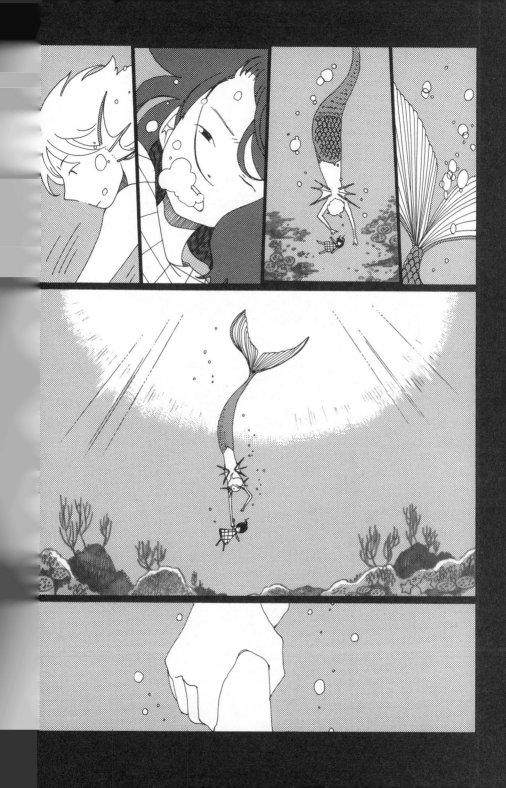

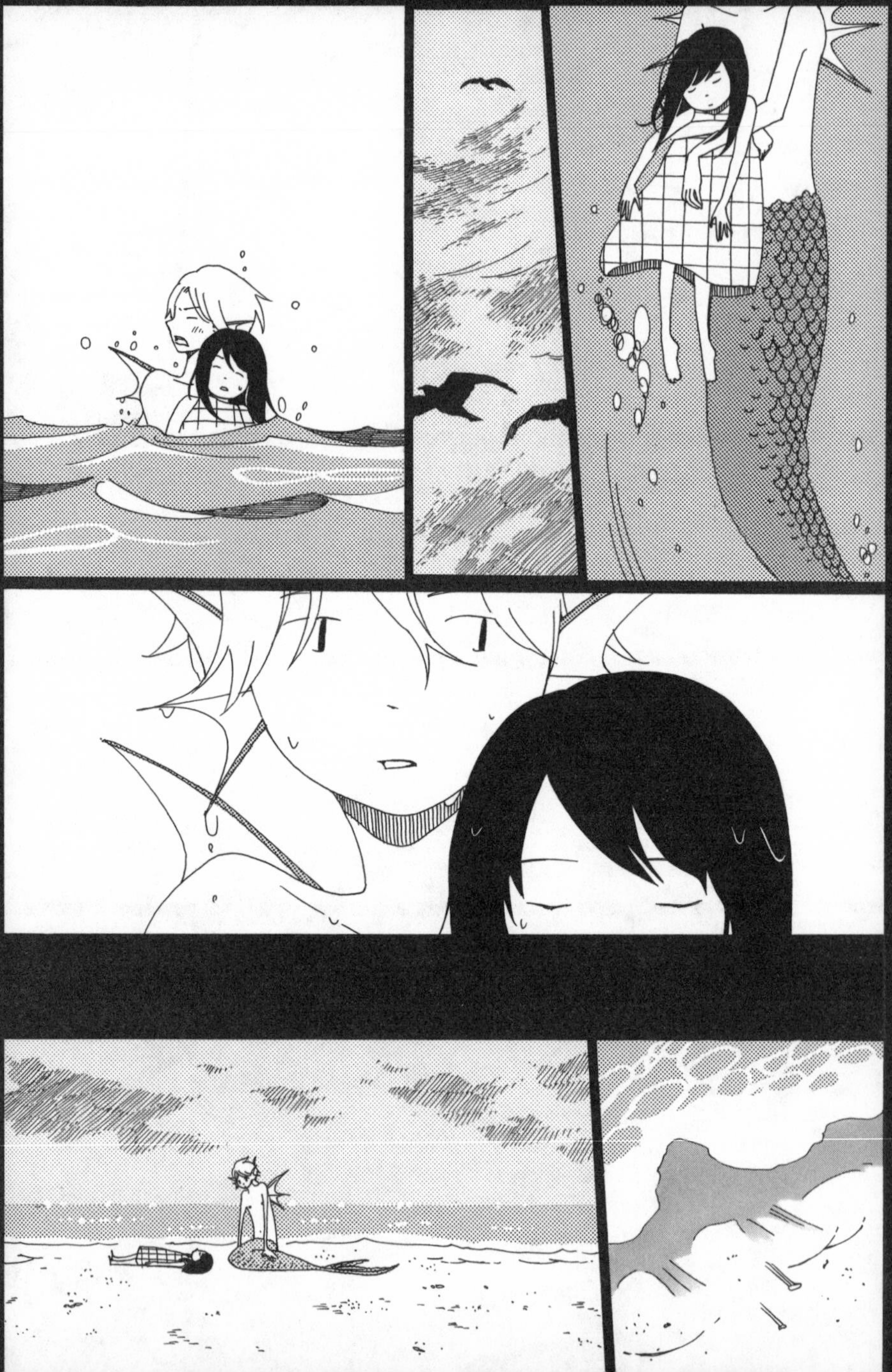

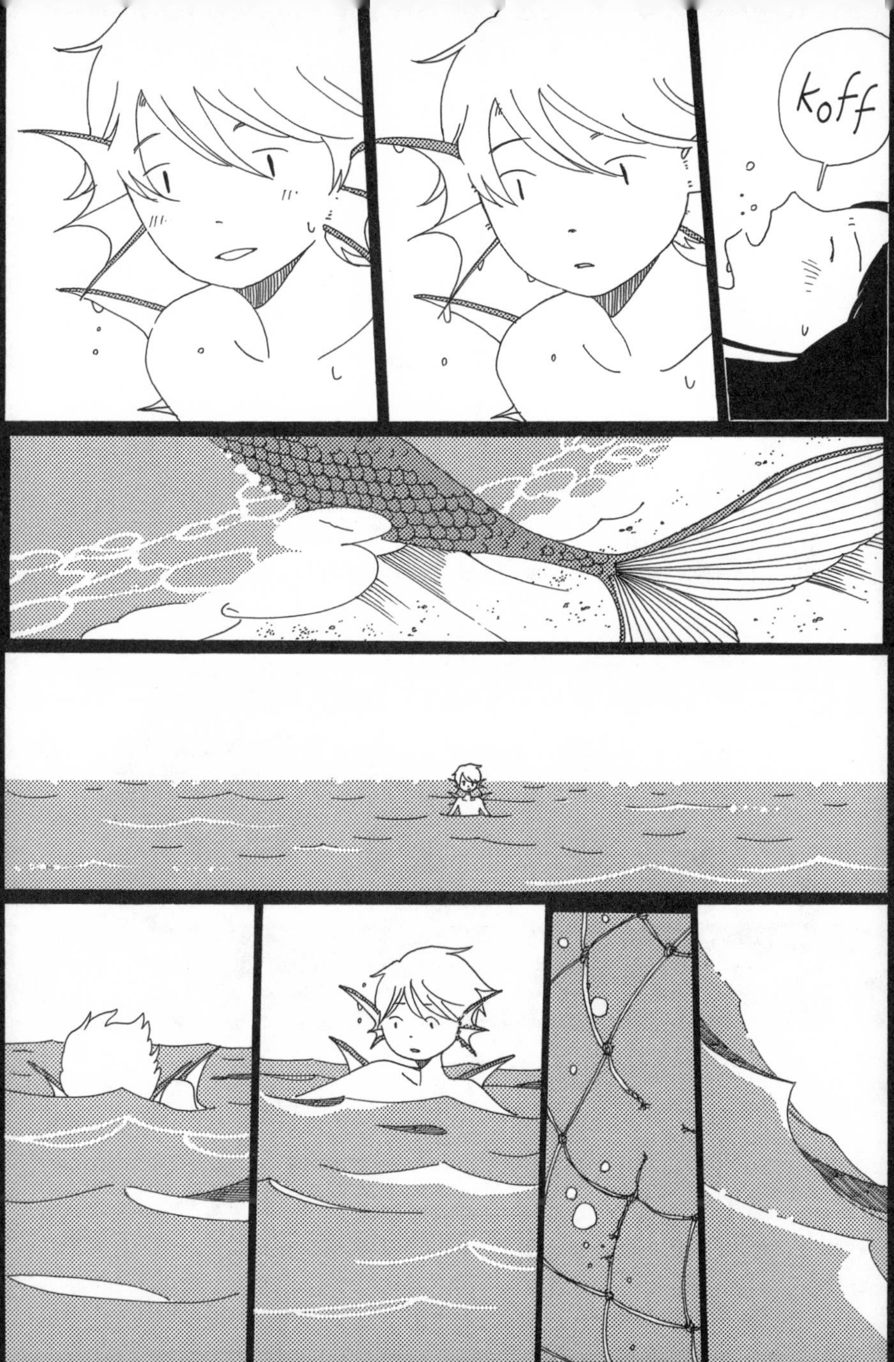
koff

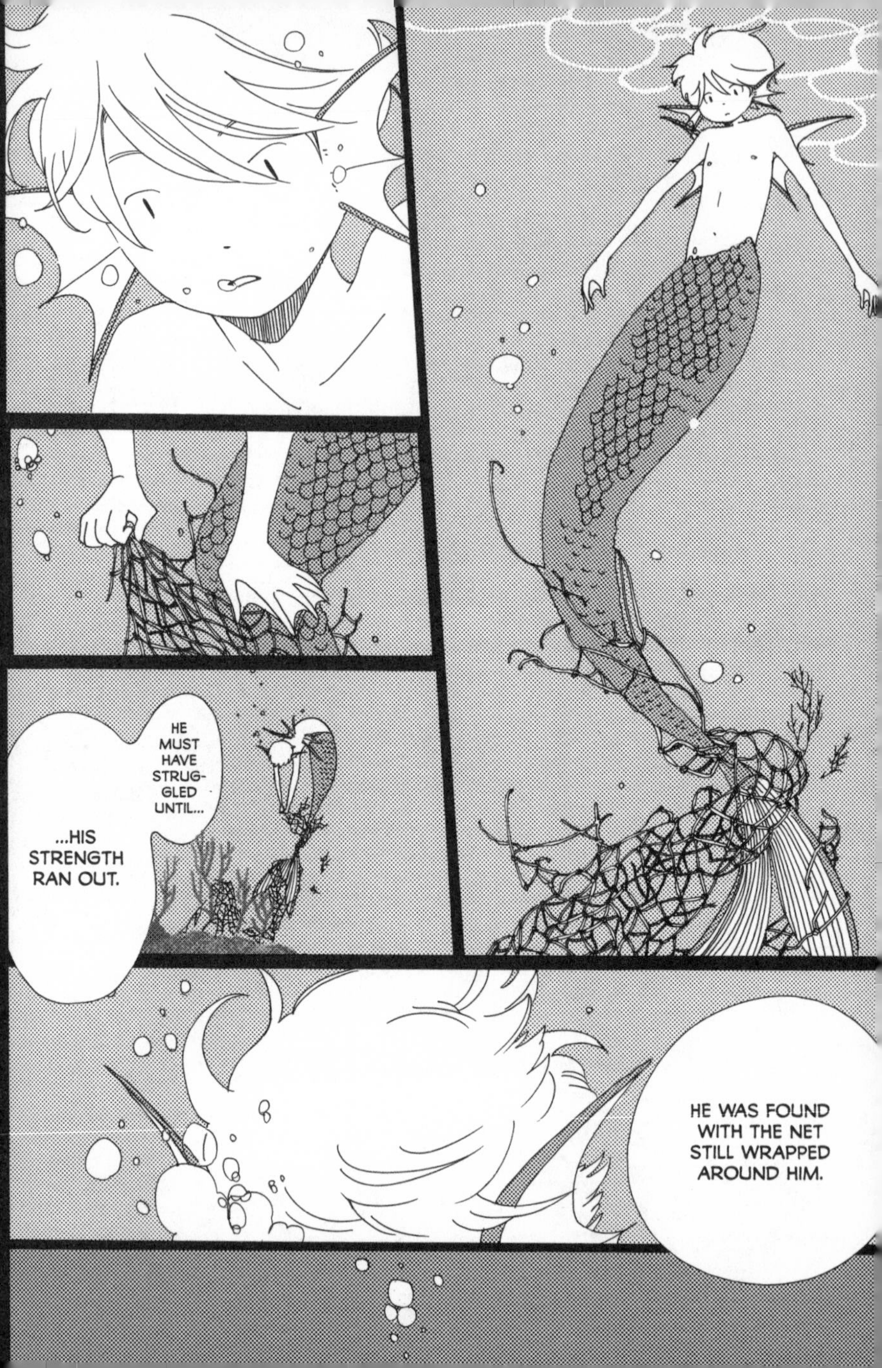
HE MUST HAVE STRUG-GLED UNTIL...
...HIS STRENGTH RAN OUT.
HE WAS FOUND WITH THE NET STILL WRAPPED AROUND HIM.

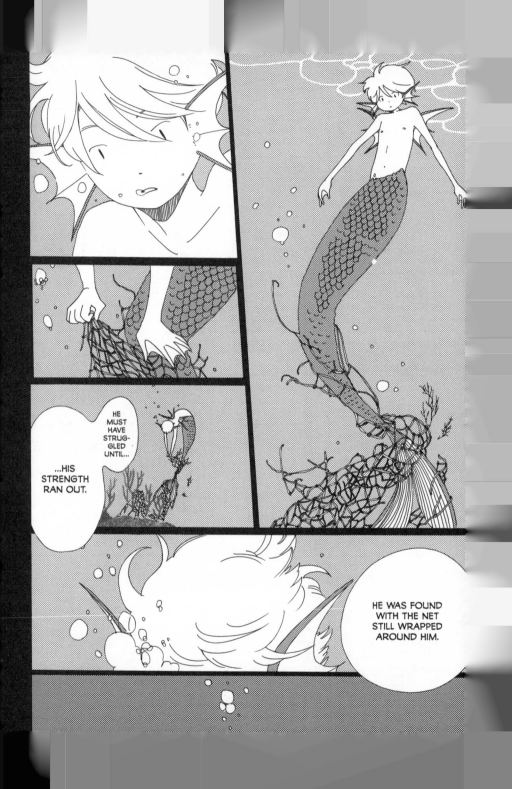

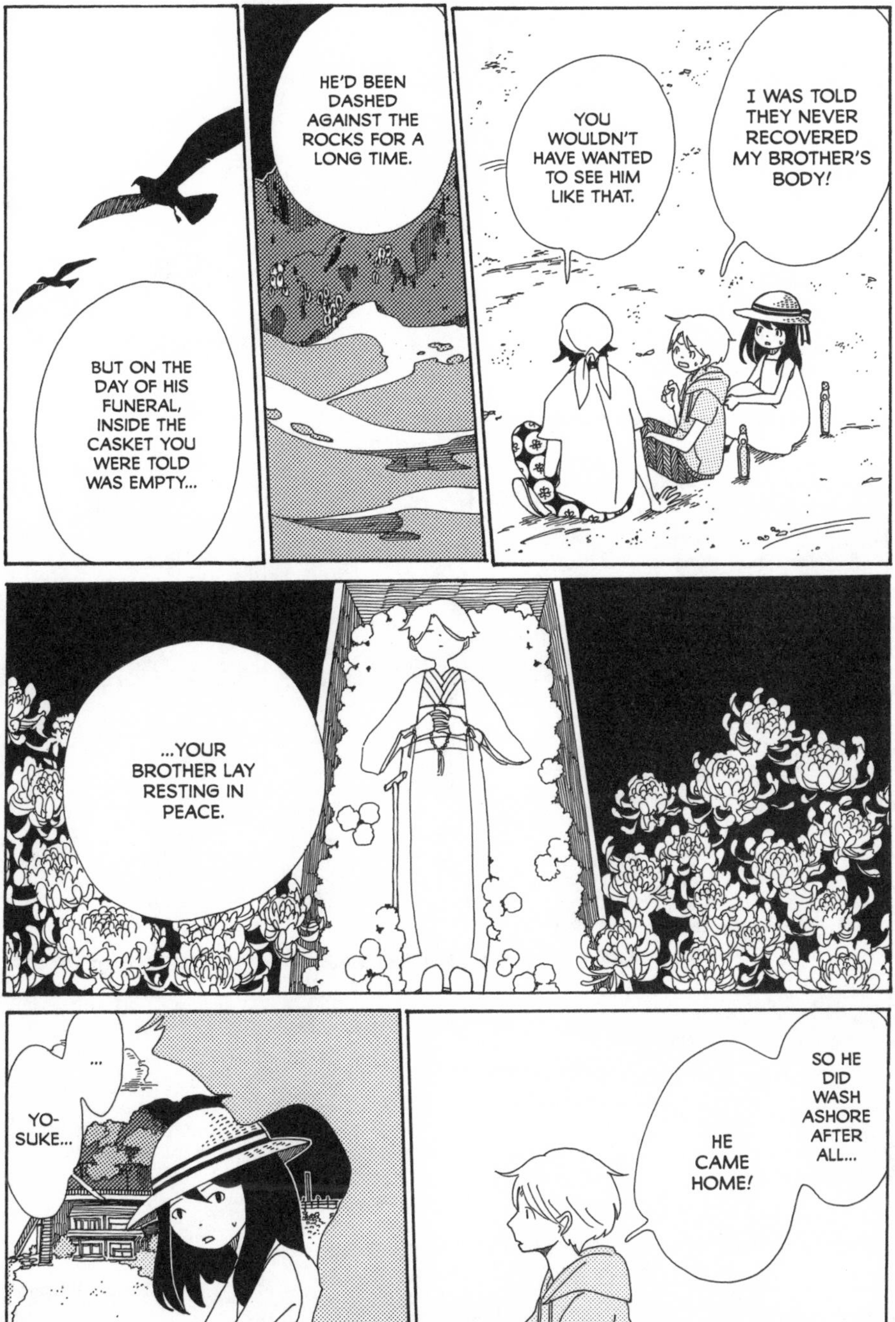
I WAS TOLD THEY NEVER RECOVERED MY BROTHER'S BODY!
YOU WOULDN'T HAVE WANTED TO SEE HIM LIKE THAT.
HE'D BEEN DASHED AGAINST THE ROCKS FOR A LONG TIME.
BUT ON THE DAY OF HIS FUNERAL, INSIDE THE CASKET YOU WERE TOLD WAS EMPTY...
...YOUR BROTHER LAY RESTING IN PEACE.
SO HE DID WASH ASHORE AFTER ALL...
HE CAME HOME!
...
YO-SUKE...

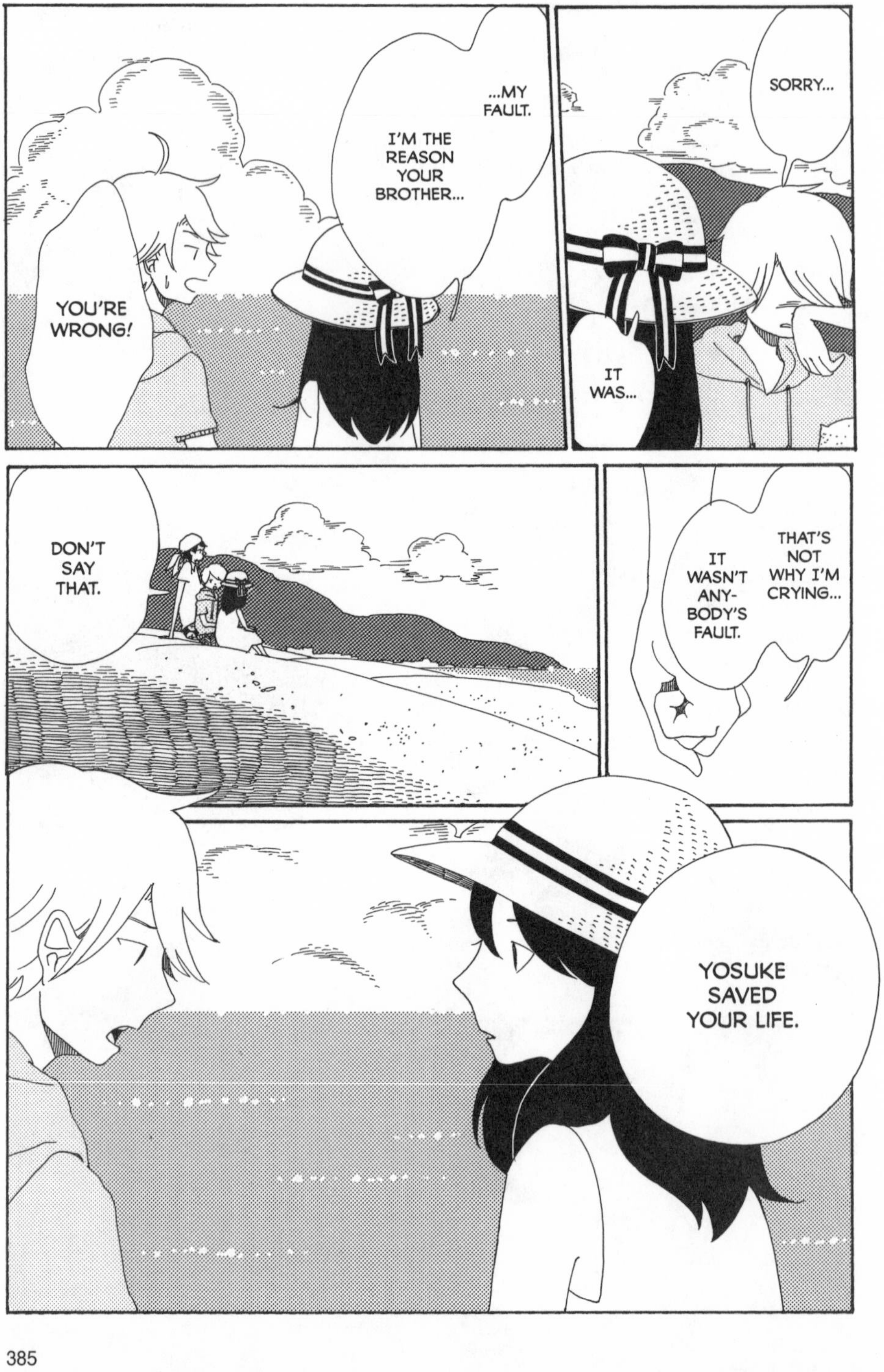
SORRY...
IT WAS...
...MY FAULT.
I'M THE REASON YOUR BROTHER...
YOU'RE WRONG!
THAT'S NOT WHY I'M CRYING...
IT WASN'T ANY-BODY'S FAULT.
DON'T SAY THAT.
YOSUKE SAVED YOUR LIFE.

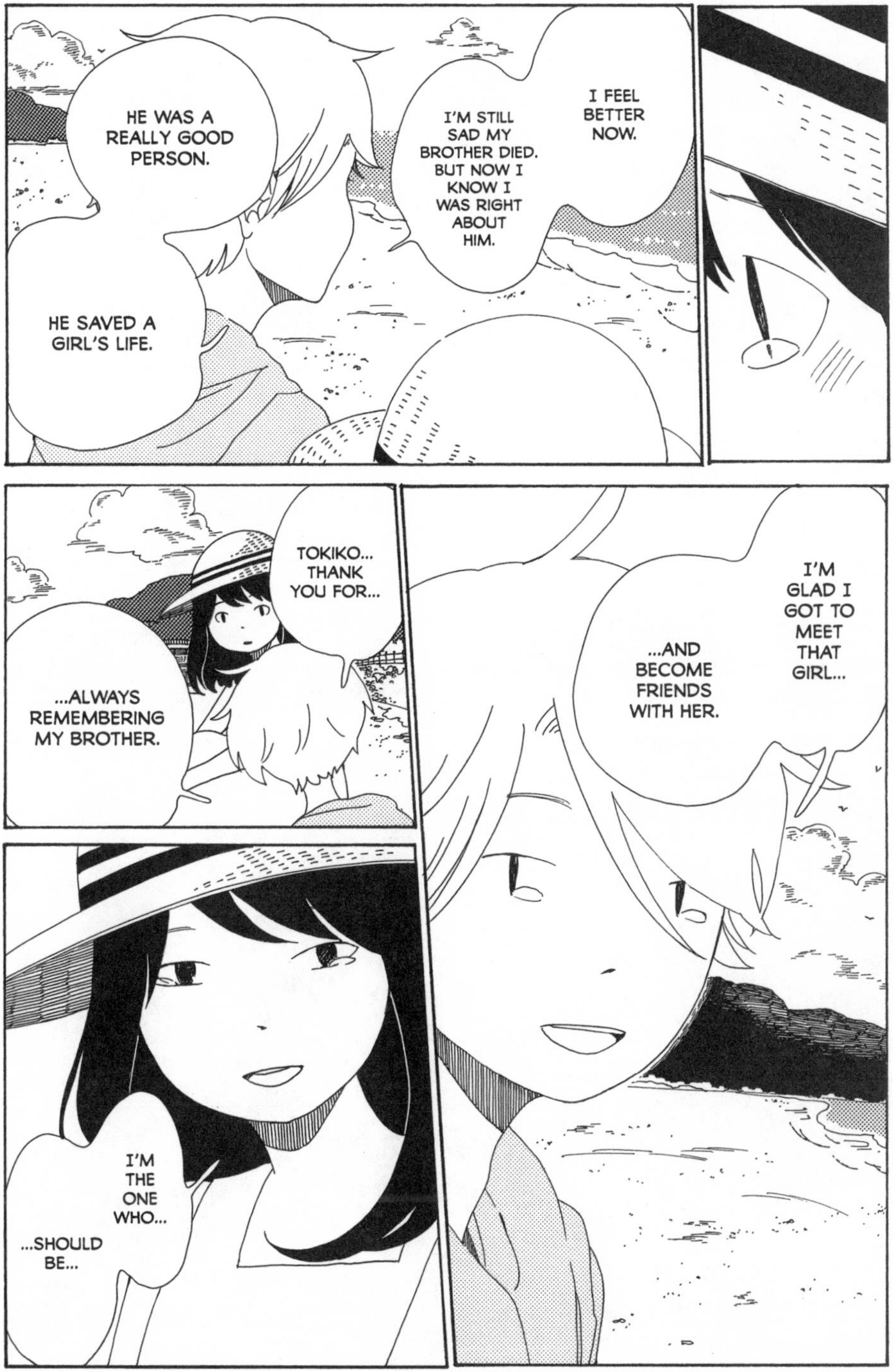
I FEEL BETTER NOW.
I'M STILL SAD MY BROTHER DIED. BUT NOW I KNOW I WAS RIGHT ABOUT HIM.
HE WAS A REALLY GOOD PERSON.
HE SAVED A GIRL'S LIFE.
I'M GLAD I GOT TO MEET THAT GIRL...
...AND BECOME FRIENDS WITH HER.
TOKIKO... THANK YOU FOR...
...ALWAYS REMEMBERING MY BROTHER.
I'M THE ONE WHO...
...SHOULD BE...

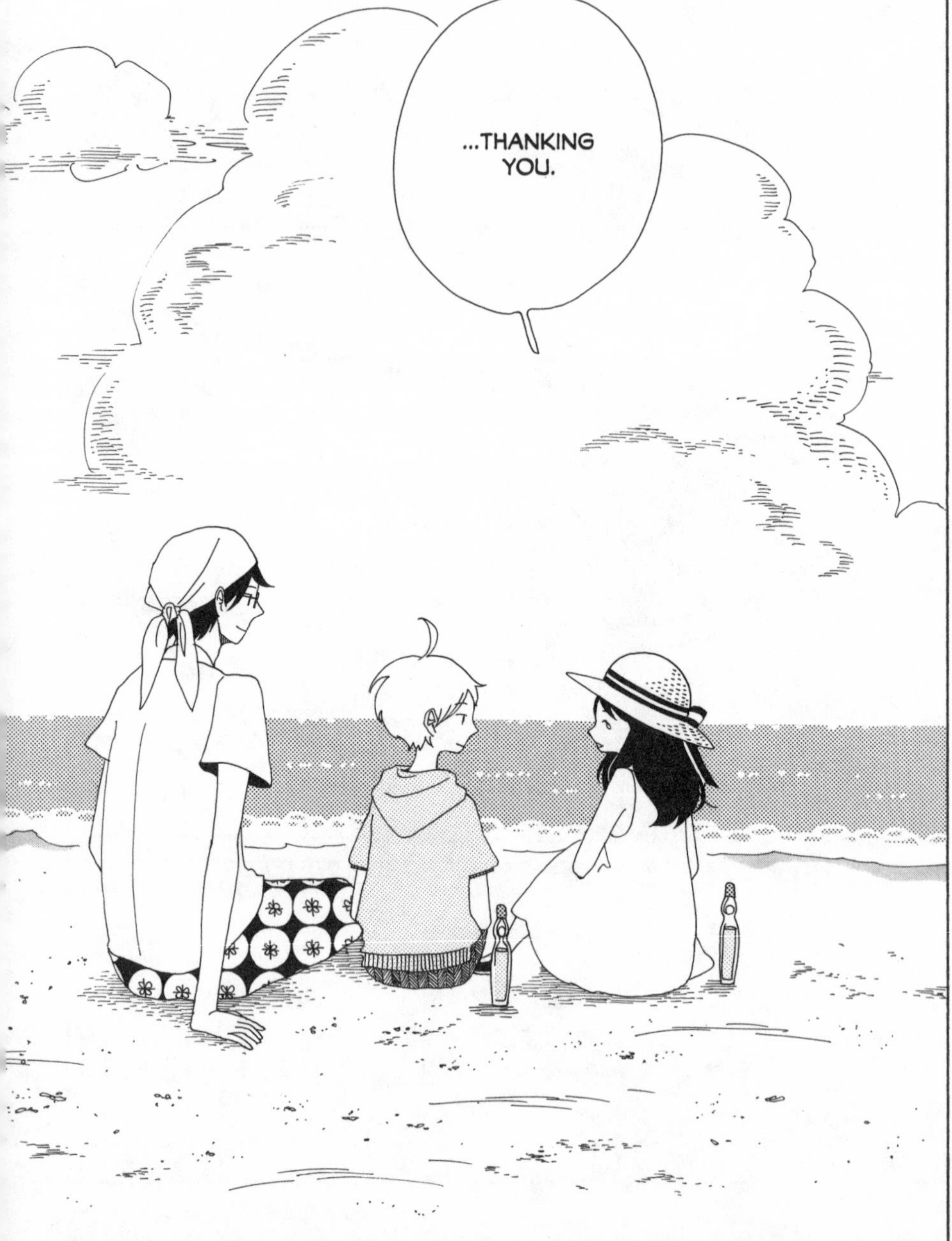
...THANKING YOU.

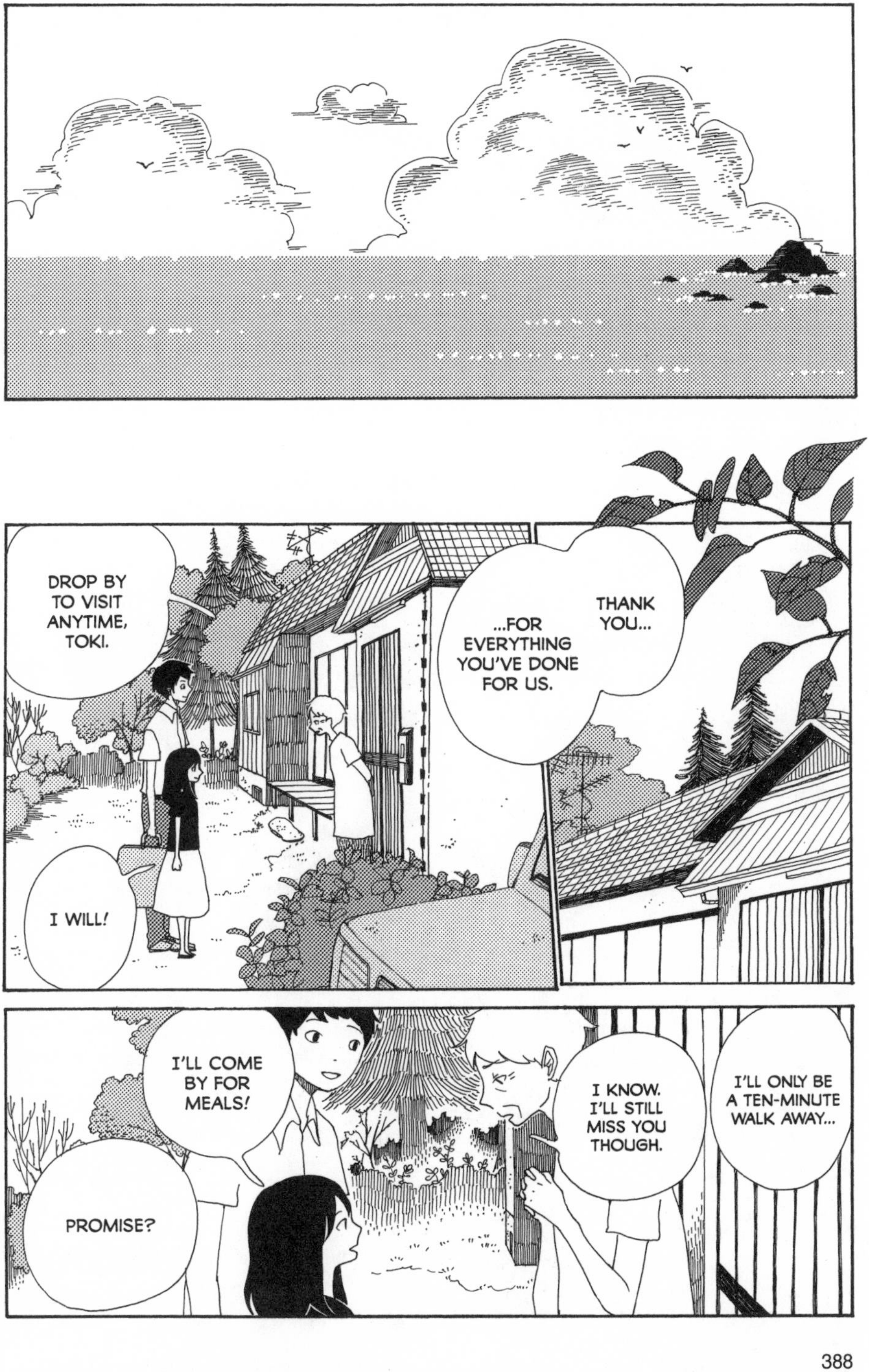
THANK YOU...
...FOR EVERYTHING YOU'VE DONE FOR US.
DROP BY TO VISIT ANYTIME, TOKI.
I WILL!
I'LL ONLY BE A TEN-MINUTE WALK AWAY...
I KNOW. I'LL STILL MISS YOU THOUGH.
I'LL COME BY FOR MEALS!
PROMISE?

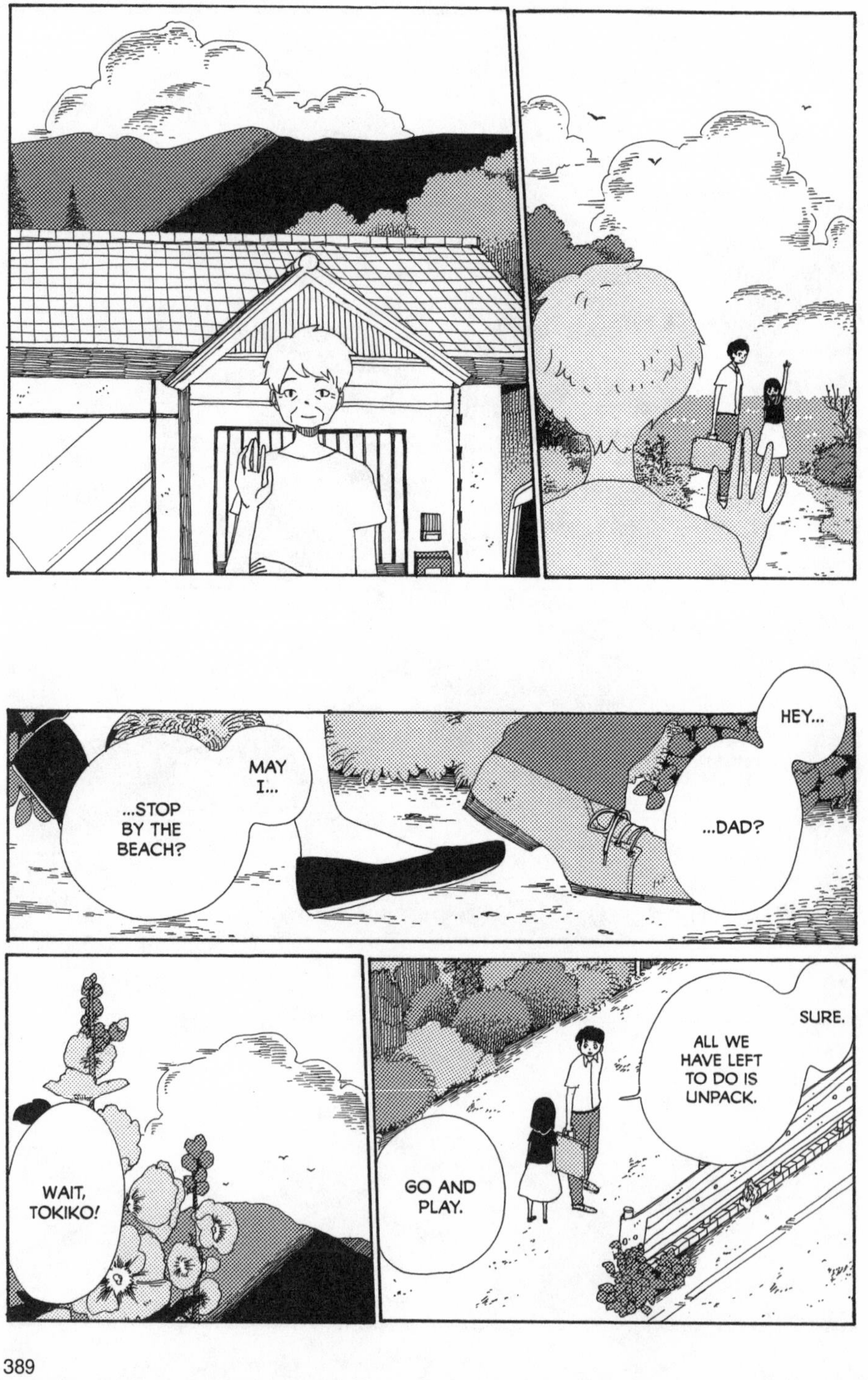
HEY... ...DAD?
MAY I... ...STOP BY THE BEACH?
SURE.
ALL WE HAVE LEFT TO DO IS UNPACK.
GO AND PLAY.
WAIT, TOKIKO!

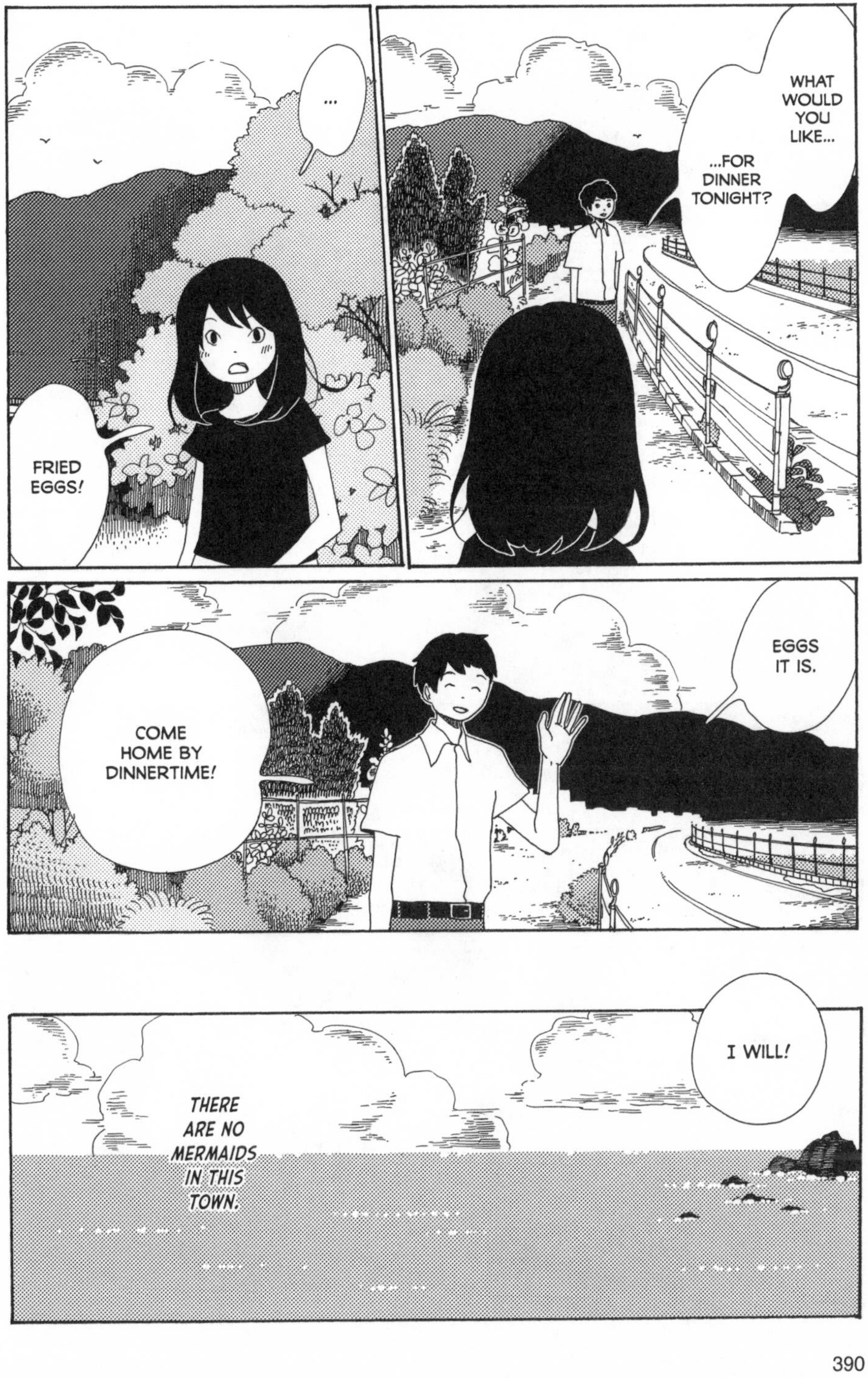
WHAT WOULD YOU LIKE...
...FOR DINNER TONIGHT?
...
FRIED EGGS!
EGGS IT IS.
COME HOME BY DINNERTIME!
I WILL!
THERE ARE NO MERMAIDS IN THIS TOWN.

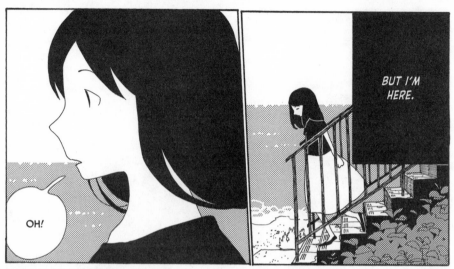

BUT I'M HERE.
OH!
YOU'RE ALL HERE!
ARE YOU DONE MOVING, TOKI?
YEAH.
WHAT ARE YOU DOING?
BUILDING A TOWN OF SAND.
I KNOW NOW THAT WITH THE PASSAGE OF TIME...
IF YOU BUILD IT HERE, THE WAVES WILL WASH IT AWAY.
HUH?
YOU THINK THEY'LL REACH THIS FAR?
AT HIGH TIDE THEY MIGHT.

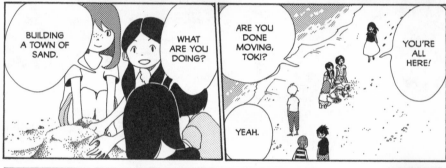

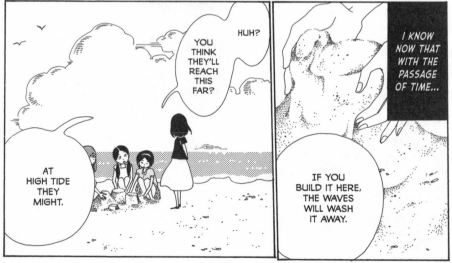

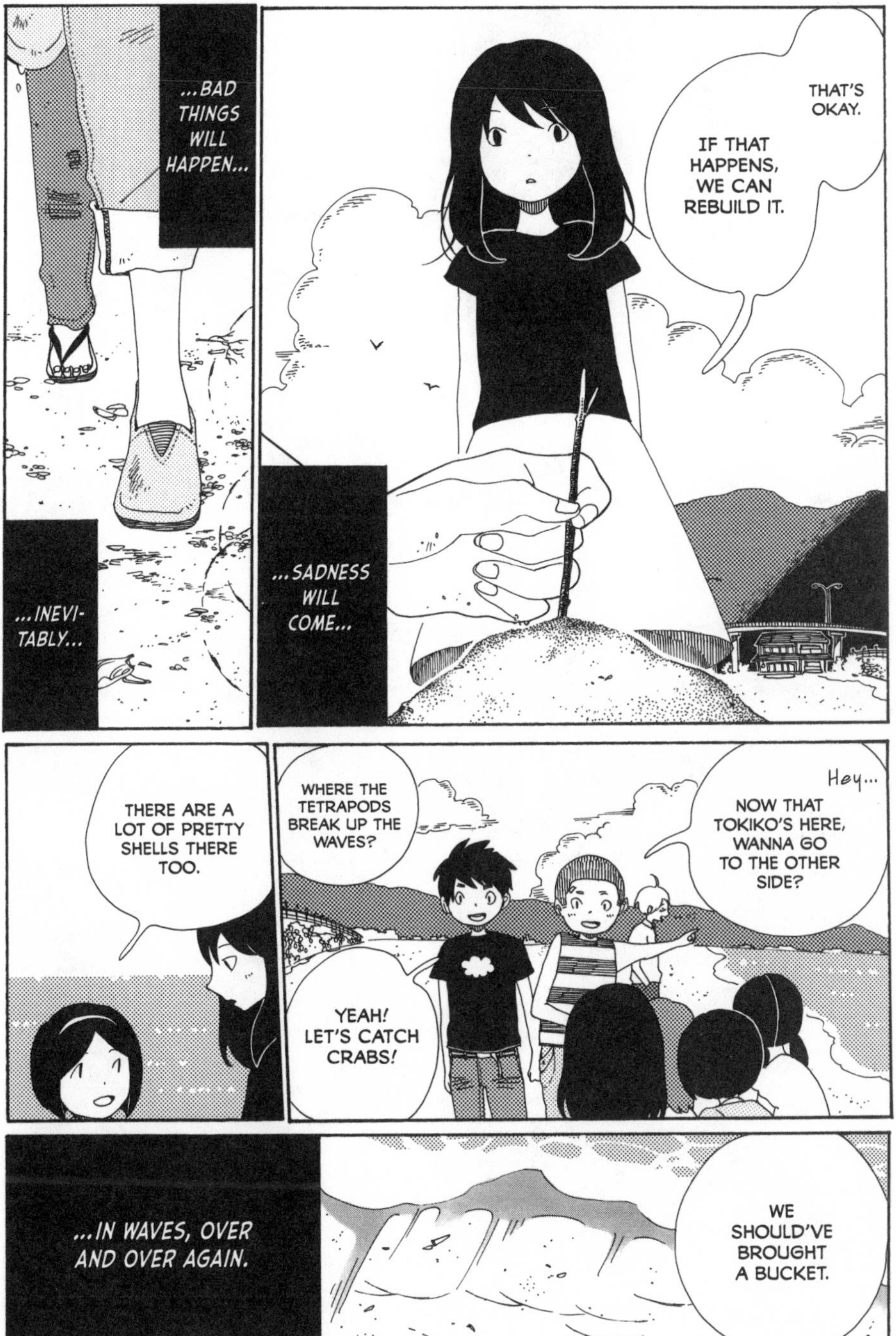
THAT'S OKAY.
IF THAT HAPPENS, WE CAN REBUILD IT.
...SADNESS WILL COME...
...BAD THINGS WILL HAPPEN...
...INEVI-TABLY...
Hey...
NOW THAT TOKIKO'S HERE, WANNA GO TO THE OTHER SIDE?
WHERE THE TETRAPODS BREAK UP THE WAVES?
YEAH! LET'S CATCH CRABS!
THERE ARE A LOT OF PRETTY SHELLS THERE TOO.
WE SHOULD'VE BROUGHT A BUCKET.
...IN WAVES, OVER AND OVER AGAIN.

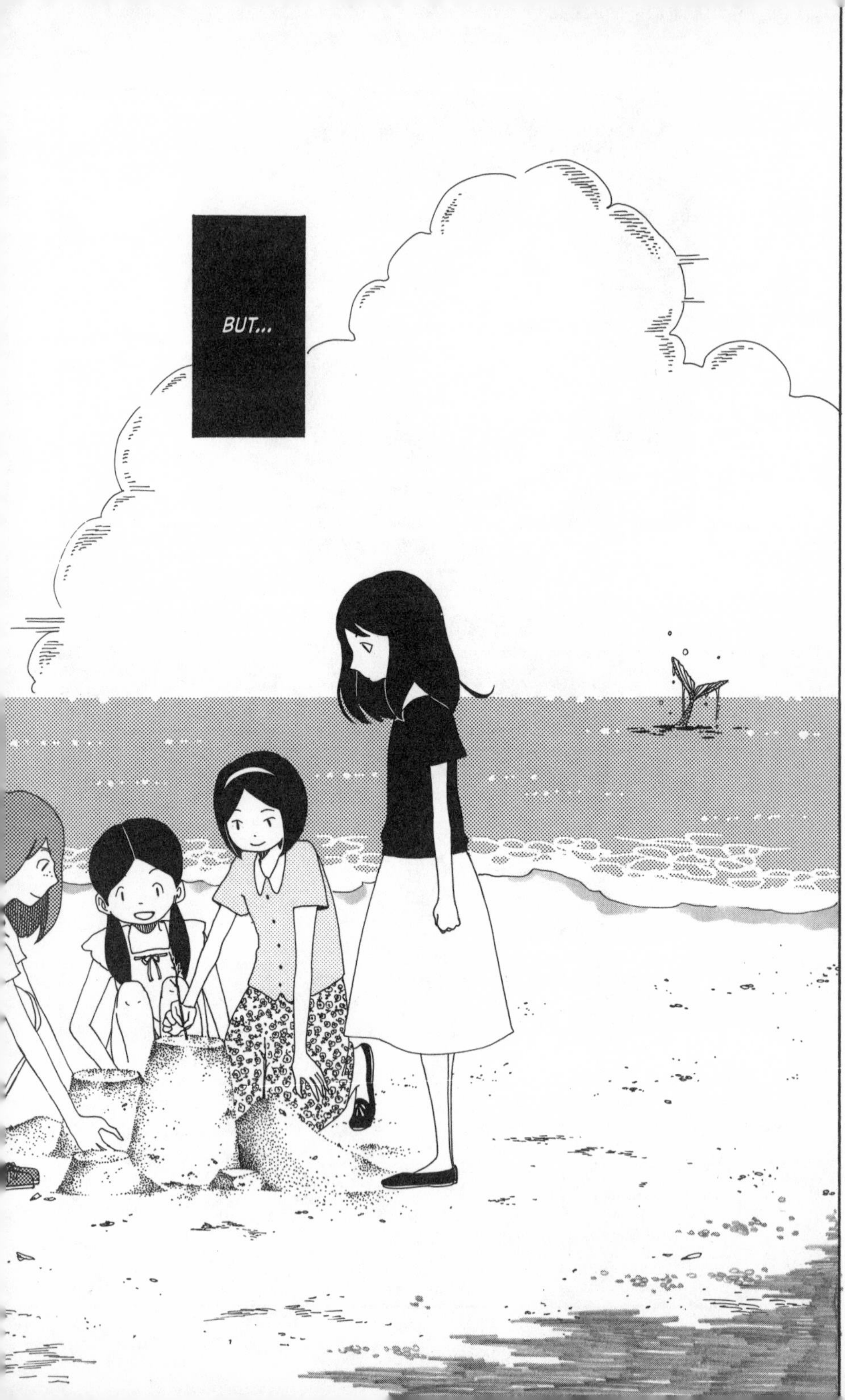
BUT...

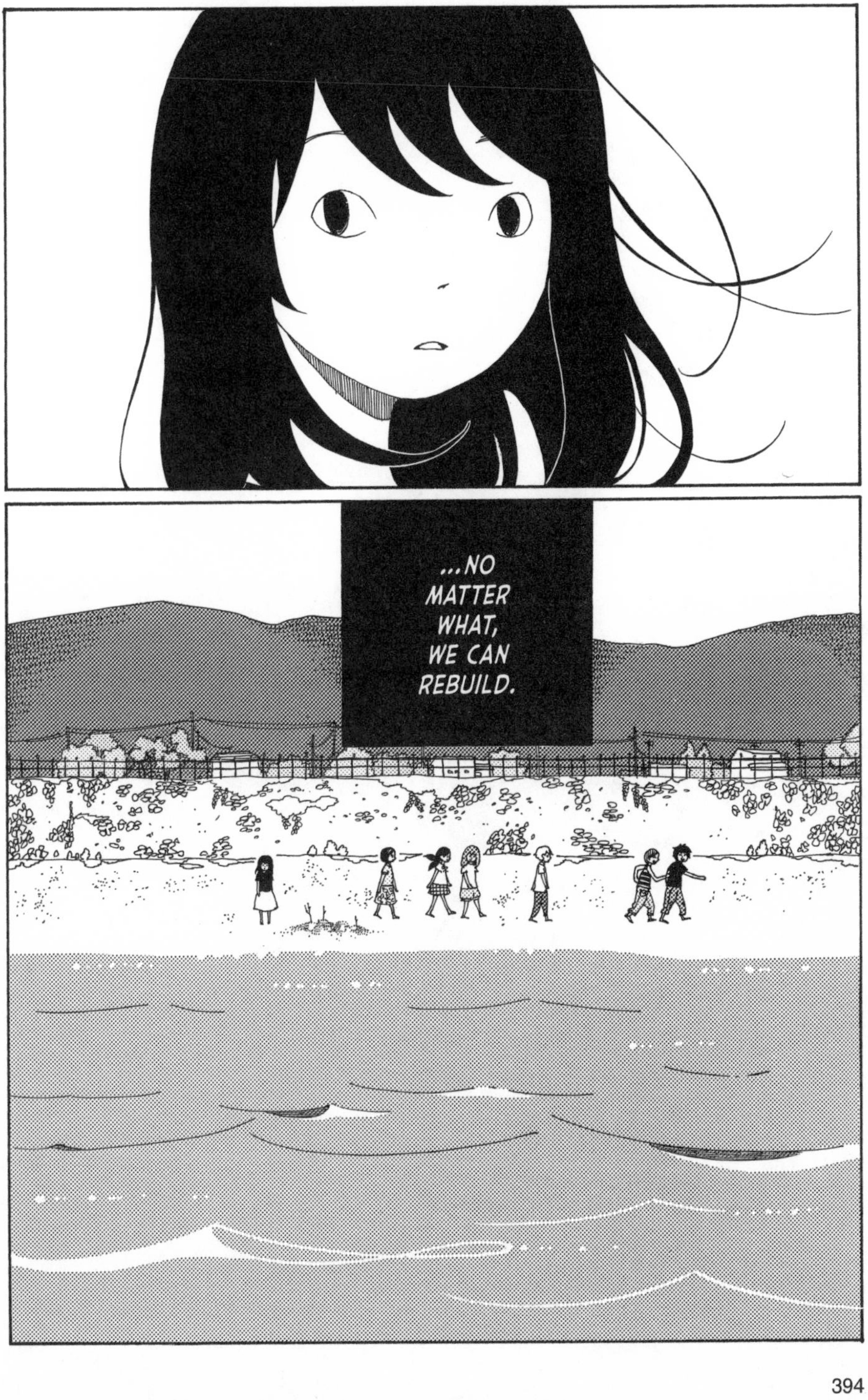
...NO MATTER WHAT, WE CAN REBUILD.

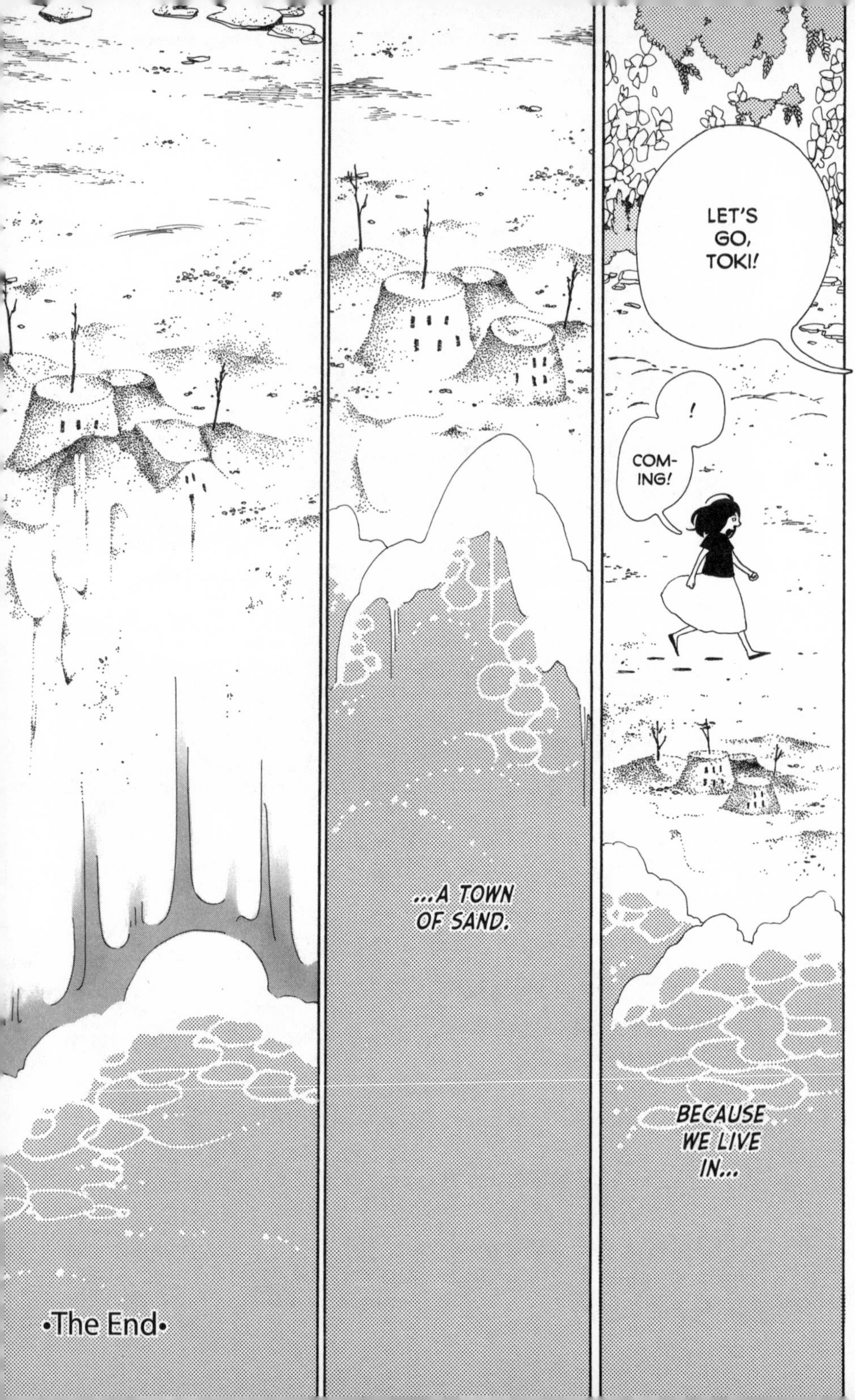
LET'S GO, TOKI!
!
COMING!
BECAUSE WE LIVE IN...
...A TOWN OF SAND.
•The End•

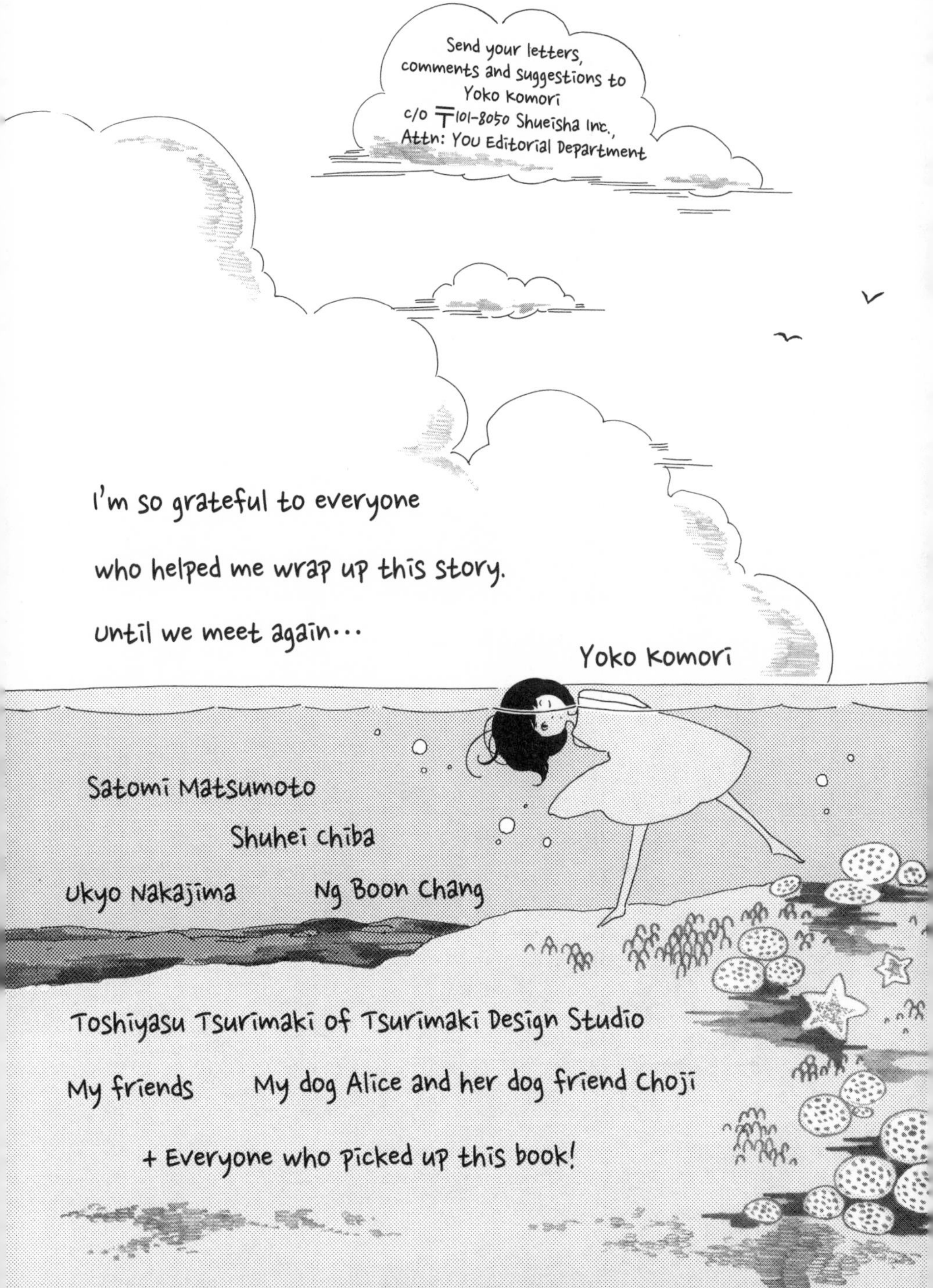
Send your letters,
comments and suggestions to
Yoko Komori
c/o 〒101-8050 Shueisha Inc.,
Attn: YOU Editorial Department
I'm so grateful to everyone
who helped me wrap up this story.
Until we meet again...
Yoko Komori
Satomi Matsumoto
Shuhei Chiba
Ukyo Nakajima
Ng Boon Chang
Toshiyasu Tsurimaki of Tsurimaki Design Studio
My friends
My dog Alice and her dog friend Choji
+ Everyone who picked up this book!

A Note from the Author

Hello. My name is Yoko Komori.

Thank you very much for picking up a copy of
Mermaid Scales and the Town of Sand.

I went to the seashore to do research,
but now I want to return just to collect
shells and gaze out into the distance.

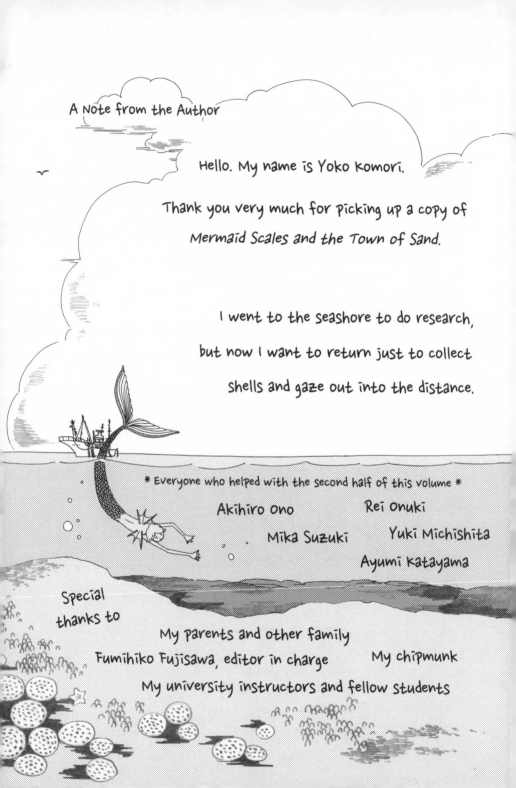

* Everyone who helped with the second half of this volume *

Akihiro Ono   Rei Onuki

Mika Suzuki   Yuki Michishita

Ayumi Katayama

Special
thanks to
My parents and other family
Fumihiko Fujisawa, editor in charge   My chipmunk
My university instructors and fellow students

Author's Notes

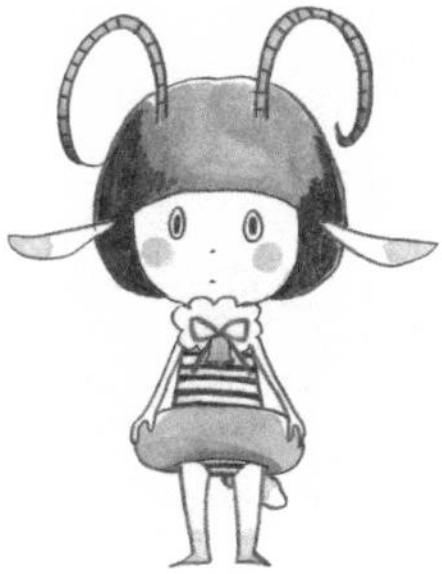

This is the quiet story of a little girl who moves to a small town. I hope you enjoyed it.

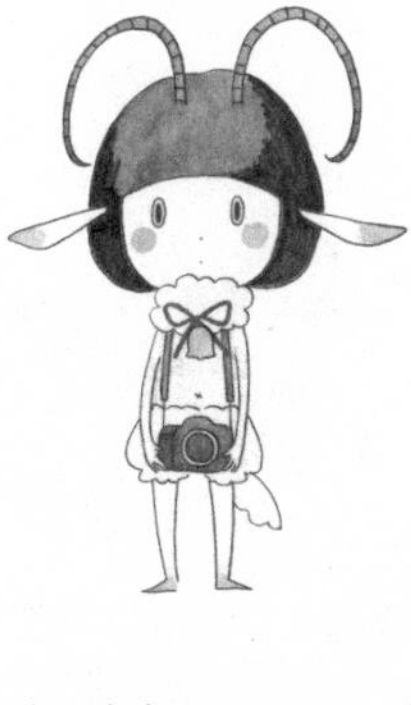

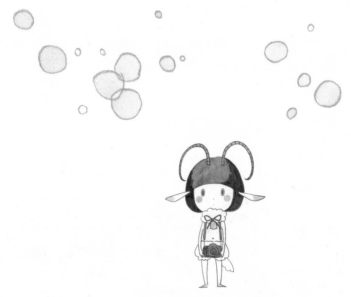

Trying to picture a map of the whole world as you look out to sea is a magical experience. I took just a tiny part of this world and put it in a frame.

MERMAID SCALES
AND THE TOWN OF SAND

VIZ Signature Edition

STORY AND ART BY
YOKO KOMORI

Translation/JN Productions
English Adaptation/Annette Roman
Touch-Up Art & Lettering/Susan Daigle-Leach
Cover & Interior Design/Yukiko Whitley
Editor/Annette Roman

AOI UROKO TO SUNA NO MACHI © 2013 by Yoko Komori
All rights reserved.
First published in Japan in 2013 by SHUEISHA Inc., Tokyo
English translation rights arranged by SHUEISHA Inc.

The stories, characters, and incidents mentioned in
this publication are entirely fictional.

Printed in Canada

Published by VIZ Media, LLC
P.O. Box 77010
San Francisco, CA 94107

10 9 8 7 6 5 4 3 2 1
First printing, February 2023

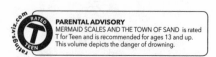

PARENTAL ADVISORY
MERMAID SCALES AND THE TOWN OF SAND is rated
T for Teen and is recommended for ages 13 and up.
This volume depicts the danger of drowning.

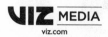 **MEDIA**
viz.com

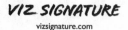 **VIZ SIGNATURE**
vizsignature.com

You may be reading the wrong way.

In keeping with the original Japanese comic format and to preserve the orientation of the original artwork, this book reads from right to left—so action, sound effects, and word balloons are completely reversed. Please turn to the other side of the book to get started!

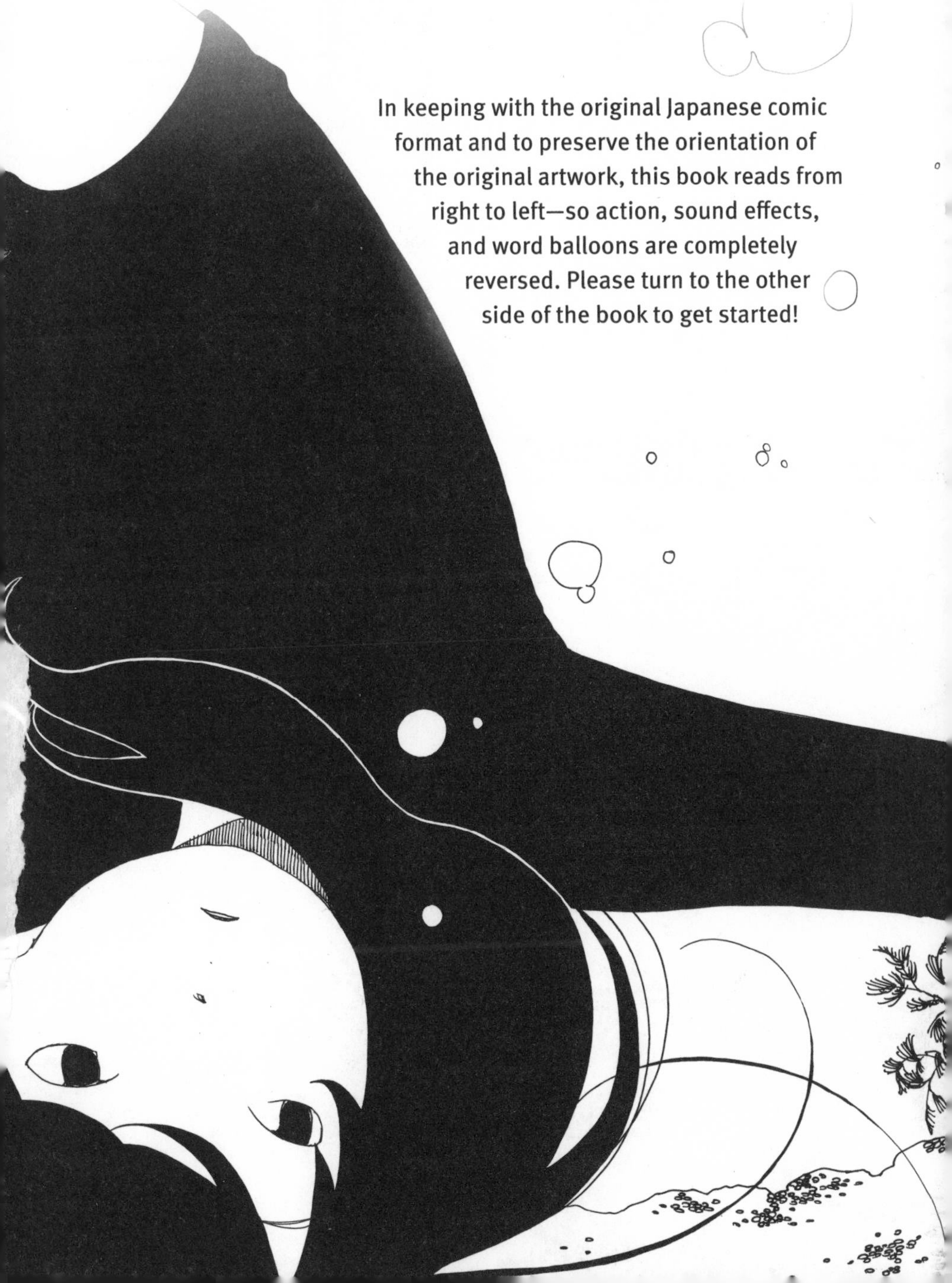